Building Inclusive Education in K-12 Classrooms and Higher Education:

Theories and Principles

Kiyoji Koreeda
Toyo University, Japan

Masayoshi Tsuge
University of Tsukuba, Japan

Shigeru Ikuta
Otsuma Women's University, Japan

Elizabeth Minchin Dalton
Dalton Education Services International, USA

Linda Plantin Ewe
Kristianstad University, Sweden

A volume in the Advances in Educational Technologies and Instructional Design (AETID) Book Series

Published in the United States of America by
    IGI Global
    Information Science Reference (an imprint of IGI Global)
    701 E. Chocolate Avenue
    Hershey PA, USA 17033
    Tel: 717-533-8845
    Fax: 717-533-8661
    E-mail: cust@igi-global.com
    Web site: http://www.igi-global.com

Copyright © 2023 by IGI Global. All rights reserved. No part of this publication may be reproduced, stored or distributed in any form or by any means, electronic or mechanical, including photocopying, without written permission from the publisher. Product or company names used in this set are for identification purposes only. Inclusion of the names of the products or companies does not indicate a claim of ownership by IGI Global of the trademark or registered trademark.

Library of Congress Cataloging-in-Publication Data

Names: Koreeda, Kiyoji, 1960- editor. | Tsuge, Masayoshi, 1958- editor. |
  Ikuta, Shigeru, 1949- editor. | Dalton, Elizabeth M., editor. | Ewe,
  Linda Plantin, 1974- editor.
Title: Building inclusive education in K-12 classrooms and higher education:
  theories and principles / Edited by Kiyoji Koreeda, Masayoshi Tsuge, Shigeru
  Ikuta, Elizabeth Minchin Dalton, and Linda Plantin Ewe.
Other titles: Research on global movements toward inclusive settings in
  K-12 classrooms and higher education settings
Description: Hershey, PA : Information Science Reference, [2023] | Includes
  bibliographical references and index. | Summary: "The Handbook of
  Research on Global Movements Toward Inclusive Settings in K-12
  Classrooms and Higher Education discusses various inclusive practices in
  K-12 classrooms and higher education all over the world and presents
  problems and challenges that educators are struggling to overcome.
  Covering key topics such as educational technology, global movement, and
  inclusive education, this major reference work is ideal for
  administrators, policymakers, industry professionals, researchers,
  academicians, scholars, practitioners, instructors, and students"--
  Provided by publisher.
Identifiers: LCCN 2023000683 (print) | LCCN 2023000684 (ebook) | ISBN
  9781668473702 (hardcover) | ISBN 9781668473740 (paperback) | ISBN
  9781668473719 (ebook)
Subjects: LCSH: Inclusive education--Cross-cultural studies. | Education
  and globalization--Cross-cultural studies. | Education--Effect of
  technological innovations on--Cross-cultural studies. | Education,
  Higher--Effect of technological innovations on--Cross-cultural studies.
Classification: LCC LC1200 .H32 2023 (print) | LCC LC1200 (ebook) | DDC
  371.9/046--dc23/eng/20230209
LC record available at https://lccn.loc.gov/2023000683
LC ebook record available at https://lccn.loc.gov/2023000684

This book is published in the IGI Global book series Advances in Educational Technologies and Instructional Design (AE-TID) (ISSN: 2326-8905; eISSN: 2326-8913)

British Cataloguing in Publication Data
A Cataloguing in Publication record for this book is available from the British Library.
All work contributed to this book is new, previously-unpublished material. The views expressed in this book are those of the authors, but not necessarily of the publisher.
For electronic access to this publication, please contact: eresources@igi-global.com.

Advances in Educational Technologies and Instructional Design (AETID) Book Series

Lawrence A. Tomei
Robert Morris University, USA

ISSN:2326-8905
EISSN:2326-8913

Mission

Education has undergone, and continues to undergo, immense changes in the way it is enacted and distributed to both child and adult learners. In modern education, the traditional classroom learning experience has evolved to include technological resources and to provide online classroom opportunities to students of all ages regardless of their geographical locations. From distance education, Massive-Open-Online-Courses (MOOCs), and electronic tablets in the classroom, technology is now an integral part of learning and is also affecting the way educators communicate information to students.

The **Advances in Educational Technologies & Instructional Design (AETID) Book Series** explores new research and theories for facilitating learning and improving educational performance utilizing technological processes and resources. The series examines technologies that can be integrated into K-12 classrooms to improve skills and learning abilities in all subjects including STEM education and language learning. Additionally, it studies the emergence of fully online classrooms for young and adult learners alike, and the communication and accountability challenges that can arise. Trending topics that are covered include adaptive learning, game-based learning, virtual school environments, and social media effects. School administrators, educators, academicians, researchers, and students will find this series to be an excellent resource for the effective design and implementation of learning technologies in their classes.

Coverage

- K-12 Educational Technologies
- Adaptive Learning
- Curriculum development
- Game-Based Learning
- Educational Telecommunications
- Instructional design
- Instructional Design Models
- Hybrid Learning
- Virtual School Environments
- Bring-Your-Own-Device

IGI Global is currently accepting manuscripts for publication within this series. To submit a proposal for a volume in this series, please contact our Acquisition Editors at Acquisitions@igi-global.com or visit: http://www.igi-global.com/publish/.

The Advances in Educational Technologies and Instructional Design (AETID) Book Series (ISSN 2326-8905) is published by IGI Global, 701 E. Chocolate Avenue, Hershey, PA 17033-1240, USA, www.igi-global.com. This series is composed of titles available for purchase individually; each title is edited to be contextually exclusive from any other title within the series. For pricing and ordering information please visit http://www.igi-global.com/book-series/advances-educational-technologies-instructional-design/73678. Postmaster: Send all address changes to above address. Copyright © 2023 IGI Global. All rights, including translation in other languages reserved by the publisher. No part of this series may be reproduced or used in any form or by any means – graphics, electronic, or mechanical, including photocopying, recording, taping, or information and retrieval systems – without written permission from the publisher, except for non commercial, educational use, including classroom teaching purposes. The views expressed in this series are those of the authors, but not necessarily of IGI Global.

Titles in this Series

For a list of additional titles in this series, please visit: http://www.igi-global.com/book-series/advances-educational-technologies-instructional-design/73678

Perspectives on Indigenous Pedagogy in Education Learning From One Another
Sheila Cote-Meek (York University, Canada) and Taima Moeke-Pickering (Laurentian University, Canada)
Information Science Reference • © 2023 • 310pp • H/C (ISBN: 9781668434253) • US $215.00

Strategies for Promoting Independence and Literacy for Deaf Learners With Disabilities
Nena Raschelle Neild (Gallaudet University, USA) and Patrick Joseph Graham (Rochester Institute of Technology, USA)
Information Science Reference • © 2023 • 354pp • H/C (ISBN: 9781668458396) • US $215.00

Perspectives of Cognitive, Psychosocial, and Learning Difficulties From Childhood to Adulthood Practical Counseling Strategies
Maria Sofologi (University of Ioannina, Greece) Georgios Kougioumtzis (National and Kapodistrian University of Athens, Greece) and Christiana Koundourou (University Neapolis, Cyprus)
Information Science Reference • © 2023 • 433pp • H/C (ISBN: 9781668482032) • US $215.00

Handbook of Research on Redesigning Teaching, Learning, and Assessment in the Digital Era
Eleni Meletiadou (London Metropolitan University, UK)
Information Science Reference • © 2023 • 498pp • H/C (ISBN: 9781668482926) • US $270.00

Establishing Digital Competencies in the Pursuit of Online Learning
Eva Podovšovnik (University of Primorska, Faculty for Tourism Studies, Slovenia) Tonia De Giuseppe (University of Benevento-Giustino Fortunato, Italy) and Felice Corona (University of Salerno, Italy)
Information Science Reference • © 2023 • 330pp • H/C (ISBN: 9781668470107) • US $215.00

Technology-Driven E-Learning Pedagogy Through Emotional Intelligence
Pooja Chaturvedi Sharma (Apeejay School of Management, India) Rohit Bansal (Vaish College of Engineering, India) and Ram Singh (Maharishi Markandeshwar University, Mullana-Ambala, India)
Information Science Reference • © 2023 • 296pp • H/C (ISBN: 9781668476390) • US $215.00

Fostering Science Teaching and Learning for the Fourth Industrial Revolution and Beyond
Garima Bansal (Australian Council for Educational Research, India) and Umesh Ramnarain (University of Johannesburg, South Africa)
Information Science Reference • © 2023 • 300pp • H/C (ISBN: 9781668469323) • US $215.00

701 East Chocolate Avenue, Hershey, PA 17033, USA
Tel: 717-533-8845 x100 • Fax: 717-533-8661
E-Mail: cust@igi-global.com • www.igi-global.com

EDITORIAL ADVISORY BOARD

Girma Berhanu, *University of Gothenburg, Sweden*
Sean Bracken, *University of Worcester, UK*
Koki Doi, *Doshisha Women's College of Liberal Arts, Japan*
Britt Tatman Ferguson, *National University, USA*
Jenn Gallup, *Idaho State University, USA*
Tracy Galvin, *Glasgow Caledonian University, UK*
Susie Gronseth, *University of Houston, USA*
Kazue Kanno, *Tokai University, Japan*
Mohamed Khalifa Ismail, *Early Childhood Education Foundation, Egypt*
Aashna Khurana, *Pratham Education Foundation, India*
Emma Leifler, *University of Gothenburg, Sweden*
Mette Molbæk, *VIA University College, Denmark*
Kimberely Fletcher Nettleton, *Morehead State University, USA*
Camilla Nilvius, *Linnaeus University, Sweden*
Pamela Trotman Reid, *Wayne State University, USA*
Christine Sollenberger, *National University, USA*
Jiaojiao Wu, *Guizhou University of Engineering Science, China*

Table of Contents

Preface xvi

Acknowledgment xxi

Section 1
Inclusive Education: Theory and Policy

Chapter 1
Creating an International Collaboratory for Leadership in Universally Designed Education:
INCLUDE as a Global Community of Practice 1
> *Elizabeth Dalton, Dalton Education Services International, USA*
> *Richard M. Jackson, Boston College, USA*
> *Sean Bracken, University of Worcester, UK*
> *Ashiya Abdool Satar, University of South Africa, South Africa*
> *Mustapha Aabi, University of Ibn Zohr, Morocco*
> *Aashna Khurana, ASER Centre, USA*
> *Luigia Nicholas, Stellenbosch University, South Africa*
> *Oressa K. Power, William James College, USA*
> *Linda Plantin Ewe, Kristianstad University, Sweden*

Chapter 2
Universal Design for Learning: Accessible Learning Environments and School Development 21
> *Mette Molbæk, VIA University College, Denmark*
> *Lotte Hedegaard-Sørensen, Aarhus University, Denmark*

Chapter 3
Implementing UDL in a University Setting: Overcoming Barriers One Checkpoint at a Time 39
> *Andy Smidt, The University of Sydney, Australia*
> *Tonnette Stanford, The University of Sydney, Australia*
> *Dagmar Kminiak, The University of Sydney, Australia*
> *Isobelle Montague, The University of Sydney, Australia*
> *Jessica Buhne, The University of Sydney, Australia*

Chapter 4
Towards Equity and Inclusion Excellence Using Diverse Interventions 59
 Emma Kristina Leifler, University of Gothenburg, Sweden & Karolinska Institutet, Sweden

Chapter 5
Universal Design for Learning as Support for the Inclusion of Deaf Student Teachers in Training 80
 Marcia Mirl Lyner-Cleophas, Stellenbosch University, South Africa
 Claudia Priscilla Saunderson, Stellenbosch University, South Africa
 Lizelle Josephine Apollis, Stellenbosch University, South Africa

Chapter 6
Evolution and Implementation of Inclusive Education in the Maldives: Hurdles and the Way
Forward 98
 Mariyam Shareefa, Islamic University of Maldives, Maldives
 Visal Moosa, Islamic University of Maldives, Maldives
 Adhila Rushdhee, Department of Inclusive Education, Maldives
 Shuhudha Rizwan, National Institute of Education, Maldives

Chapter 7
Inclusive Education Practices in Taiwan 119
 Hsuan-Ling Chen, University of Tsukuba, Japan
 Masayoshi Tsuge, University of Tsukuba, Japan

Chapter 8
Flexible, Relevant, and Accessible Curriculum: The Role of the Universal Design for Learning
Framework in Three Countries 131
 David G. Evans, The University of Sydney, Australia
 Rosmalily binti Salleh, Ministry of Education, Malaysia
 Abdul Basit, Department of Special Education, Government of the Punjab, Lahore, Pakistan
 Cathy Little, The University of Sydney, Australia

Section 2
Content-Specific Theory and Policy

Chapter 9
Co-Teaching Collaboration in K–12 Inclusive Classrooms: Relevance for Leadership 147
 Jennifer L. Fleming, Wise County Regional Learning Academy, USA
 Carol A. Mullen, Virginia Tech, USA

Chapter 10
Exploring Ways to Design Mathematics Education Promoting Inclusion and Equity for Every
Student 166
 Helena Roos, Malmö University, Sweden

Chapter 11
Critical Whiteness as a Professional Approach to Inclusive Teaching in Teacher Education 182
    Anne Schröter, Leibniz University, Hannover, Germany
    Britta Konz, Johannes Gutenberg University, Mainz, Germany

Chapter 12
Special Education Policy in the United States and Ireland: Comparisons and Analysis Through
the Lens of Universal Design for Learning 196
    Andrea R. Harkins-Brown, School of Education, Johns Hopkins University, USA
    Margaret Flood, Maynooth University, Ireland

Chapter 13
The Universal Design for Learning in the Context of Brazilian Education: Challenges and
Possibilities for Inclusive Education 226
    Elizabete Cristina Costa-Renders, University of São Caetano do Sul, Brazil

Chapter 14
The Professional Development Needs of Special Education Teachers Teaching Students With
Autism Spectrum Disorder in Western China 241
    Chen Han, University of New South Wales, Australia
    Therese M. Cumming, University of New South Wales, Australia
    Geraldine Townend, University of New South Wales, Australia

Chapter 15
Engaging on Common Ground: Inclusion of the Gifted Student in the Classroom 260
    Kimberely Fletcher Nettleton, Morehead State University, USA
    Michael W. Kessinger, Morehead State University, USA
    Lesia Lennex, Morehead State University, USA

Compilation of References 284

About the Contributors 326

Index 336

Detailed Table of Contents

Preface xvi

Acknowledgment xxi

Section 1
Inclusive Education: Theory and Policy

Chapter 1
Creating an International Collaboratory for Leadership in Universally Designed Education:
INCLUDE as a Global Community of Practice 1
    Elizabeth Dalton, Dalton Education Services International, USA
    Richard M. Jackson, Boston College, USA
    Sean Bracken, University of Worcester, UK
    Ashiya Abdool Satar, University of South Africa, South Africa
    Mustapha Aabi, University of Ibn Zohr, Morocco
    Aashna Khurana, ASER Centre, USA
    Luigia Nicholas, Stellenbosch University, South Africa
    Oressa K. Power, William James College, USA
    Linda Plantin Ewe, Kristianstad University, Sweden

To foster strong global movements toward more inclusive educational resources around the world, higher education serves a crucial role. Universities face numerous challenges in the development of inclusive services for those with differing needs. While global collaborative efforts often provide great inspiration for community and educational system change, professionals do not always know exactly what changes should be made or how to go about making these changes more inclusive. Resources and online professional learning networks that are open to all and readily available online are one way to address these challenges. The INCLUDE Collaboratory gathers and provides open opportunities for professionals around the world to connect, learn, discuss, and develop ongoing collaborative relationships. The authors present the background, history, structure, and work of the INCLUDE Collaboratory, highlighting the following: Concept, vision, and purpose; organizational timeline and evolution; organizational development; thematic priorities, and future planning.

Chapter 2
Universal Design for Learning: Accessible Learning Environments and School Development 21
    Mette Molbæk, VIA University College, Denmark
    Lotte Hedegaard-Sørensen, Aarhus University, Denmark

This chapter presents the use of universal design for learning as a means to understand and develop more accessible and inclusive practices in Danish schools. The chapter sets the scene by highlighting the influence of global and local policies on inclusive and exclusive practices in schools. From this point of departure, the chapter outlines the universal design for learning framework as an educational strategy for implementing inclusive education. Based on two research projects, it is shown how the framework can contribute to bringing a new direction to understanding and working with inclusion, while also developing a teaching practice that helps overcome some of the dilemmas that teachers experience in their daily practice in classrooms. The chapter also presents perspectives on how universal design for learning can be part of and support development in a whole-school approach.

Chapter 3
Implementing UDL in a University Setting: Overcoming Barriers One Checkpoint at a Time 39
    Andy Smidt, The University of Sydney, Australia
    Tonnette Stanford, The University of Sydney, Australia
    Dagmar Kminiak, The University of Sydney, Australia
    Isobelle Montague, The University of Sydney, Australia
    Jessica Buhne, The University of Sydney, Australia

UDL principles are not consistently applied in the tertiary sector in Australia and appear infrequently in government policies. There is limited research about UDL in Australia and few studies that describe the challenges in implementing UDL across a whole tertiary institution. In this chapter the authors present an approach taken at the University of Sydney, focusing on supporting academics to understand UDL, identify areas in their own teaching that already use UDL principles, and select one or two new strategies to add to their courses each year. This approach starts with an acknowledgement that change is challenging, and that change can be incremental rather than requiring a whole course review to embed UDL principles. The authors identified institution-specific levels to support academics to choose strategies that would be relatively easy to implement. To date, teaching staff who have used these resources have found them valuable.

Chapter 4
Towards Equity and Inclusion Excellence Using Diverse Interventions 59
    Emma Kristina Leifler, University of Gothenburg, Sweden & Karolinska Institutet, Sweden

Although inclusive education (i.e., education that does not include separate special education classes) is legislated and pervasive worldwide, the implementation of educational inclusion is poor. To create more inclusive school settings, we need to explore what constitutes good practice. Moreover, we need evidence of effective interventions that address student needs. This chapter provides evidence from two interventions aimed at improving inclusion (NDC AI and SKOLKONTAKT®). These mixed methods, which merge quantitative and qualitative data, show that professional development enhances the inclusive skills of teachers and group training of students improves social skills, school attendance, and participation, leading to less loneliness, making the whole school's social environment better. Unexpectedly, the teachers became more aware of social impairments and developed new concrete tools to handle conflicts and bullying.

Chapter 5
Universal Design for Learning as Support for the Inclusion of Deaf Student Teachers in Training 80
Marcia Mirl Lyner-Cleophas, Stellenbosch University, South Africa
Claudia Priscilla Saunderson, Stellenbosch University, South Africa
Lizelle Josephine Apollis, Stellenbosch University, South Africa

South Africa is a society historically marred by exclusion and discrimination based on inter alia race, gender, economic status, disability, and language. The restoration of dignity, diversity, equity, and inclusion is a high priority. At Stellenbosch University (SU), policies such as the Language Policy (2021), Disability Access Policy (2018) and Assessment Policy (2022) have fostered redress inclusive of students with disabilities. This chapter reviews how shifts were implemented using the above-mentioned policies by highlighting how flexibility was introduced in the education of Deaf students in the Faculty of Education at SU having UDL in mind. The chapter traces teaching, learning, and assessment support in Deaf student teacher training at SU. The conclusion is that policies assist in facilitating changing environments while promoting inclusivity in flexible curricula and support practices.

Chapter 6
Evolution and Implementation of Inclusive Education in the Maldives: Hurdles and the Way
Forward 98
Mariyam Shareefa, Islamic University of Maldives, Maldives
Visal Moosa, Islamic University of Maldives, Maldives
Adhila Rushdhee, Department of Inclusive Education, Maldives
Shuhudha Rizwan, National Institute of Education, Maldives

This chapter shares the journey of a developing island nation in their effort to implement a nation-wide inclusive education system. The chapter intends to bring to forefront key milestones, challenges faced, and the way forward in the expedition towards realizing full inclusion in schools. Towards this end, the authors engaged multiple sources of data including (i) legal, policy and other relevant documents from the local context, (ii) focus group discussions with experts, and (iii) interviews with practitioners. Insights from these multi-source explorations are triangulated and discussed in the light of local and international literature. Recommendations for moving towards enhancing and expanding inclusion in the education system are offered with specific focus on policy and practice, which can benefit the education system not only at the local level but also at the global level.

Chapter 7
Inclusive Education Practices in Taiwan 119
Hsuan-Ling Chen, University of Tsukuba, Japan
Masayoshi Tsuge, University of Tsukuba, Japan

With a view toward inclusion, Taiwan's special education law has undergone eight amendments since 1984. The learning environment for children with disabilities has also shifted from segregation to integration and inclusion. Currently, the learning environments for special needs education in Taiwan include regular classrooms, resource classrooms, special needs classes, itinerant visits, and special needs schools. To achieve "inclusive education," Taiwan's elementary and junior high schools are also implementing a variety of approaches. This chapter focuses on "the practice of inclusive education in

Taiwan" and discusses the contents of the current " Taiwanese-type" inclusive education practices and school cases from the development process and status of inclusive education in Taiwan.

Chapter 8
Flexible, Relevant, and Accessible Curriculum: The Role of the Universal Design for Learning
Framework in Three Countries 131
>   David G. Evans, The University of Sydney, Australia
>   Rosmalily binti Salleh, Ministry of Education, Malaysia
>   Abdul Basit, Department of Special Education, Government of the Punjab, Lahore, Pakistan
>   Cathy Little, The University of Sydney, Australia

Education is a right for all children and youth. It has been stated in international initiatives for over five decades. Curriculum frameworks across cultural contexts are interpreted in differing ways by class teachers (e.g., direct interpretation, materials developed by government or commercial bodies). Yet students with disabilities continue to be marginalised from a robust and meaningful curriculum on the basis that the curriculum is 'not for them,' or that teachers are not professionally equipped to make modifications to support access, participation, and learning. This chapter seeks to explore how the universal design for learning framework can be used to ensure all learners are contributing members within the regular classroom. This exploration will consider contexts from three countries to illustrate how the UDL framework can be used to develop flexible, meaningful, and accessible curriculum for all learners. This exploration will illustrate the barriers posed by school structures, mindsets of educators, and rigid interpretation and use of curriculum frameworks and materials.

Section 2
Content-Specific Theory and Policy

Chapter 9
Co-Teaching Collaboration in K–12 Inclusive Classrooms: Relevance for Leadership 147
>   Jennifer L. Fleming, Wise County Regional Learning Academy, USA
>   Carol A. Mullen, Virginia Tech, USA

Disseminating knowledge about instructional strategies in collaboratively taught K–12 classrooms can improve the learning environment for students with disabilities. This literature review identifies ways that co-teaching occurs in general education settings and is facilitated by stakeholders. Research questions were: What evidence-based strategies are utilized in cotaught K–12 inclusive classrooms? And how is the co-teaching initiative supported by the parties responsible for their development, implementation, and success? Evidence-based strategies for the general classroom are described along with stakeholder responsibilities. The comprehensive synthesis of salient sources is US based and limited in applicability. Practitioners might consider the solutions and recommendations presented when navigating co-teaching and inclusive practices. Trends favor the instructional co-teaching approach for infusing inclusive strategies, and support research and application. This analysis contributes to the growing body of research on effective collaborative teaching strategies.

Chapter 10
Exploring Ways to Design Mathematics Education Promoting Inclusion and Equity for Every Student 166
Helena Roos, Malmö University, Sweden

The aim of this chapter is to reflect on how inclusion and equity can be used when moving from defining them theoretically and identifying critical aspects, into using them practically in designing mathematics education. In this chapter inclusive and equitable education is understood as an education striving for every student's opportunity to take part in learning processes in mathematics. Theoretically Ainscows' framework for inclusion and equity is combined with Skovsmoses' notions regarding inclusive landscape of investigation. This combination is done to create a conceptual framework for promotion of inclusion and equity in mathematics education. The result of the meta-analysis displays seven interrelated critical aspects: see the students; develop and anchor inclusion and equity principles; supportive administration and organization; educational strategies; tasks; representations; collaborations and mathematical discussions. These aspects need to be considered in the implementation of inclusive and equitable mathematics.

Chapter 11
Critical Whiteness as a Professional Approach to Inclusive Teaching in Teacher Education 182
Anne Schröter, Leibniz University, Hannover, Germany
Britta Konz, Johannes Gutenberg University, Mainz, Germany

Teachers are in a powerful position in the context of education in schools. They produce and reproduce norms and expectations of normality in relation to their students and their diversity. This does not mean intentional exclusion, but processes that are subtle. However, these processes can have an immense impact on students' educational careers, achievement, well-being, and participation. Therefore, inclusive education in schools requires a professionalisation of teacher education at universities, where future teachers are sensitised in dealing with inequality dimensions. While dimensions such as gender and disability have received attention for a long time, the dimension race and the significance of racist structures and dynamics in education have only recently come into focus in the German discourse. In this chapter, Critical Whiteness will be discussed as a professional approach to inclusive teaching in higher education.

Chapter 12
Special Education Policy in the United States and Ireland: Comparisons and Analysis Through the Lens of Universal Design for Learning... 196
Andrea R. Harkins-Brown, School of Education, Johns Hopkins University, USA
Margaret Flood, Maynooth University, Ireland

A global human rights and social justice agenda has influenced governments to recognize their responsibility to achieve a system of inclusive education for students with disabilities. Inclusive education in the United States is defined by the premise that all eligible students be provided with a free appropriate public education, as outlined by the Individuals with Disabilities Education Act. In Ireland, though now in a period of review, the Education of Persons with Special Educational Needs Act is considered a coherent framework for inclusive education for students with special educational needs. Internationally, universal design for learning is recognized as an approach that supports the development of inclusivity in schools. This chapter outlines the national policies governing special education in American and Irish schools. Using a UDL lens, this chapter provides a synthesis of key principles of the IDEA and EPSEN; highlights alignments between these acts and the principles of UDL; and compares the policies to provide a critical analysis within an international context.

Chapter 13
The Universal Design for Learning in the Context of Brazilian Education: Challenges and
Possibilities for Inclusive Education 226
    Elizabete Cristina Costa-Renders, University of São Caetano do Sul, Brazil

The topic discussed in this chapter is teacher professional development committed to inclusive education. The text presents partial results of a research on the application of the principles of universal design for learning in school inclusion processes in Brazilian schools. It aims to present and reflect on the reports of the participating teachers about the challenges and possibilities of building inclusive education based on UDL. On the one hand, the challenges consist of difficulties in designing activities to include all students considering the class heterogeneity, the institutional bureaucratization that compromises the time to plan teaching, and the scarce means to overcome such difficulties. On the other hand, advances demand the democratic management of school, the ethical leap arising from inclusive education, and the epistemological supports of universal design for learning and pedagogy of seasons. The results of the introduction of UDL are promising and show improvements, but structures and skills need a more permanent pedagogical companionship.

Chapter 14
The Professional Development Needs of Special Education Teachers Teaching Students With
Autism Spectrum Disorder in Western China.. 241
    Chen Han, University of New South Wales, Australia
    Therese M. Cumming, University of New South Wales, Australia
    Geraldine Townend, University of New South Wales, Australia

Students with autism spectrum disorder (ASD) often require specialised support. This highlights the need for the provision of high-quality professional development to improve teachers' skills to support these students. There is a dearth of literature investigating the types, duration, and quality of professional development that influence teacher practices with students with ASD in the Chinese context. This chapter aims to fill the gap and explore the professional development needs of special education teachers teaching students with ASD in Western China. The results of the study conducted by the authors indicated that teachers in Western China had a strong desire to participate in autism-specific professional development, but it was rarely available and/or did not meet their needs. The chapter concludes with implications and directions for future teacher professional development in special education.

Chapter 15
Engaging on Common Ground: Inclusion of the Gifted Student in the Classroom 260
    Kimberely Fletcher Nettleton, Morehead State University, USA
    Michael W. Kessinger, Morehead State University, USA
    Lesia Lennex, Morehead State University, USA

Educational programs for gifted students are varied, with many schools in the United States using a pullout program to address the needs of students. In spite of these programs, unless gifted students are educated in a school dedicated to their educational needs, gifted students will spend the majority of their time in a mainstream classroom. In this environment, gifted students often languish, becoming bored or losing interest in learning. Classroom teachers and teacher preparation programs can address this waste by purposely creating a program to include gifted student.

Compilation of References 284

About the Contributors 326

Index 336

xvi

Preface

INTRODUCTION

For nearly 30 years now, since the Salamanca Statement and Framework for Action on Special Needs Education was developed at the World Conference on Special Needs Education (UNESCO, 1994), the inclusion of students with differing needs and disabilities in education systems around the world has been both a major focus of discussion within the education profession, and a major implementation challenge. Anyone who has spent time as an educator knows that there is a very long and bumpy road that separates inclusive education theory from actual practice. It is a road that can be navigated successfully, however, detailed "maps" and pathways must be provided, so that educators can obtain the knowledge, tools, and strategies they need in order to effectively diversify their instruction and their classrooms.

It is with this realization in mind that this team of editors, from three different countries, decided to collaborate and develop a book (or books) to document what is happening around the world regarding inclusive education, or the *Global Movements Toward Inclusive Settings in K-12 Classrooms and Higher Education*. Drs. Koreeda, Tsuge, and Ikuta are all professionally accomplished university educators in Japan, specializing in the education of special needs students and the teachers who work with them. Dr. Plantin Ewe lives and works in Sweden as a researcher and a special needs teacher educator. She is keenly interested in relational pedagogy. Dr. Dalton worked in K-12 and higher education for more that 35 years, and currently consults in curriculum development, assistive technology, and Universal Design for Learning. Together, these editors pooled their resources and international connections to gather 30 chapters from educators around the world who are working to elevate and expand inclusive education in their local communities, their own countries and across the globe.

While the original intention was to produce one globally-focused book, the response from colleagues, old and new, was impressive – producing so many valuable chapters that the originally conceived book has grown into two partner books; *Building Inclusive Education in K-12 Classrooms and Higher Education: Theories and Principles*, and *Developing Inclusive Environments in Education: Global Practices and Curricula*. Together, these books present a snapshot of current global perspectives and global initiatives to support the growth of inclusive education around the world. The books can also be used effectively as separate resources, depending upon the readers' needs and the type of content sought. Each book contains a wide diversity of perspectives from professionals around the world, who share their expertise and add to the available "maps" that can lead us closer to a fully inclusive world for all.

In this current, digitally-connected world, development of relationships and an understanding of different cultural contexts is not only possible – it is critical for us to continue to sustain our global society. This is emphasized in the 2030 Agenda for Sustainable Development and the 17 associated Sustainable

Preface

Development Goals of the member states of the United Nations – with Goal 4 focused on Quality Education, or more clearly stated "ensure inclusive and equitable quality education and promote lifelong learning opportunities for all" (United Nations, 2015). It is our hope that these partner books presenting a global picture of inclusive education efforts and perspectives in such diverse environments and different countries will help to move the world community a few steps closer to an inclusive society for all.

These two partner books include the following topics:

- Concept of Inclusive Education
- Concept of Universal Design for Learning
- Concept of Accessible learning
- Concept of Special Needs Education
- Government Policy for Inclusive Education Settings
- Universal Design Curricula in Inclusive Education - Global Examples
- Pre-service schoolteachers' curricula in teacher education - Global Examples
- In-service schoolteachers training-courses for inclusive settings - Global Examples
- Practices in Inclusive Settings at K-12 Classrooms and Higher Education - Global Examples
- Practices in Special Needs Education – Global Examples
- Educational Technologies to Help Make Learning Inclusive and Transformation - Global Examples

ORGANIZATION OF THE BOOK

Building Inclusive Education in K-12 Classrooms and Higher Education: Theories and Principles is organized into two sections, "Inclusive Education Theory and Policy" and "Content-Specific Theory and Policy." Each section presents the theory and policy of inclusive education in various countries and regions. A total of 15 chapters are included in this book. A brief description of each of the chapters follows:

Section 1, "Inclusive Education Theory and Policy" is focused on the Universal Design for Learning (UDL) and various ideas about inclusive education. This section begins with the chapter (Chapter 1) by Elizabeth Dalton, Richard Jackson, Sean Bracken, Ashiya Abdool Sata, Mustapha Aabi, Aashna Khurana, Luigia Nicholas, Linda Plantin Ewe, which present the background, history, structure, and work of the INCLUDE Collaboratory. The INCLUDE Collaboratory gathers and provides open opportunities for professionals around the world to connect, learn, discuss and develop ongoing collaborative relationships.

The next chapter (Chapter 2) by Mette Molbæk and Lotte Hedegaard-Sørensen, "Universal Design for Learning: Accessible Learning Environments and School Development," presents the use of Universal Design for Learning as a means to understand and develop more accessible and inclusive practices in Danish schools. The chapter also presents perspectives on how Universal Design for Learning can be part of and support development in a whole-school approach. Especially important are the author's findings about the importance of student input and voice to classroom engagement and inclusion.

The third chapter (Chapter 3) by Andy Smidt, Tonnette Stanford, Dagmar Kminiak, Isobelle Montague, Jessica Buhne, "Implementing UDL in a University Setting: Overcoming Barriers one Checkpoint at a Time," present an approach taken at the University of Sydney in Australia, focusing on supporting academics to understand UDL, identify areas in their own teaching that already use UDL principles and select one or two new strategies to add to their courses each year. They identified institution-specific levels to support academics to choose strategies that would be relatively easy to implement.

xvii

Preface

The fourth chapter (Chapter 4), "Towards Equity and Inclusion Excellence using Diverse Interventions," by Emma Leifler, provides evidence from two interventions aimed at improving inclusion (NDC AI and SKOLKONTAKT®). These mixed methods, which merge quantitative and qualitative data, show that professional development enhances the inclusive skills of teachers and group training of students improves social skills, school attendance, and participation, leading to less loneliness, making the whole school's social environment better.

The fifth chapter (Chapter 5), "The Universal Design for Learning in the Context of Brazilian Education: Challenges and Possibilities for Inclusive Education" by Elizabete Cristina Costa Renders, describes teacher professional development committed to inclusive education. This chapter presents some results of a research on the application of the principles of Universal Design for Learning in school inclusion processes in Brazilian schools. Will be very informative for readers.

The sixth chapter (Chapter 6) by Mariyam Shareefa, Visal Moosa, Adhila Rushdhee, Shuhudha Rizwan, "Evolution and Implementation of Inclusive Education in the Maldives. Hurdles and Way Forward," focuses on the journey of a developing island nation in their effort to implement a nation-wide inclusive education system. Recommendations for moving towards enhancing and expanding inclusion in the education system are offered with specific focus on policy and practice, which can benefit the education system not only at the local level but also at the global level.

The seventh chapter (Chapter 7) by Hsuan-Ling Chen and Masayoshi Tsuge, "Inclusive Education Practices in Taiwan," focuses on the positive role that peers can and should play as advocates and volunteer supporters of students with disabilities in an inclusive setting in Taiwan. And practical examples are offered in this chapter.

The eighth chapter (Chapter 8) by David G Evans, Rosmalily binti Salleh, Abdul Basit, Cathy Little, "Flexible, Relevant and Accessible Curriculum: The Role of the Universal Design for Learning Framework in Three Countries," seeks to explore how the Universal Design for Learning framework can be used to ensure all learners are contributing members of the regular classroom. This exploration will use three country contexts to illustrate how the Universal Design for Learning can be used to develop flexible, meaningful and accessible curriculum for all learners.

Section 2, "Content-Specific Theory and Policy," describes educational policies in various countries and regions, and frameworks for supporting k12 class students with various disabilities. This section begins with the chapter (Chapter 9) by Jennifer Fleming and Carol Mullen, "Coteaching Collaboration in K–12 Inclusive Classrooms: Relevance for Leadership." This chapter presenting a carefully designed literature review of research and practice in the coteaching model, as a means to support inclusive education. This chapter provides excellent content for our readers, with global potential for implementation.

The next chapter (Chapter 10) by Helena Roos, "Exploring ways to design mathematics education promoting inclusion and equity for every student," describes a meta-analysis of inclusive teaching and learning in relation to mathematics, along with two studies of teacher and student perspective. In this chapter inclusive and equitable education is understood as an education striving for every student's opportunity to take part in learning processes in mathematics.

The third chapter (Chapter 11) by Anne Schröter and Britta Konz, "Critical Whiteness as a Professional Approach to Inclusive Teaching in Teacher Education," describes Critical Whiteness as a professional approach to inclusive teaching in higher education. While dimensions such as gender and disability have received attention for a long time, the dimension race and the significance of racist structures and dynamics in education have only recently come into focus in the German discourse.

xviii

Preface

The fourth chapter (Chapter 12) by Andrea R. Harkins-Brown and Dr. Margaret Flood, "Special Education Policy in the United States and Ireland:Comparisons and Analysis Through the Lens of Universal Design for Learning," outlines the national policies governing special education in American and Irish schools. Using a UDL lens, this chapter provides a synthesis of key principles of the IDEA and EPSEN; highlights alignments between these acts and the principles of UDL; and compares the policies to provide a critical analysis within an international context.

The fifth chapter (Chapter 13) by Marcia Mirl Lyner-Cleophas, Claudia Priscilla Saunderson, Lizelle Josephine Apollis, "Universal Design for Learning as Support for the Inclusion of Deaf Student Teachers in Training," reviews how shifts were implemented using the above-mentioned policies by highlighting how flexibility was introduced in the education of Deaf students in the Faculty of Education at Stellenbosch University in South Africa having UDL in mind. The chapter traces teaching, learning and assessment support in Deaf student teacher training at SU.

The sixth chapter (Chapter 14) by Chen Han, Therese M Cumming, Geraldine Townend, "The Professional Development Needs of Special Education Teachers Teaching Students with Autism Spectrum Disorder in Western China," describes comprehensive support on including students with complex developmental needs and the professional development needed to support them. Focused in China, the paper highlights some of the unique challenges and also similar challenges that educators in China face.

The seventh chapter (Chapter 15) by Kimberely Nettleton, Michael Kessinger, Lesia Lennex, "Engaging on Common Ground: Inclusion of the Gifted Student in the Classroom," describes Educational programs for gifted students in the United States. In spite of these programs, unless gifted students are educated in a school dedicated to their educational needs, gifted students will spend the majority of their time in a mainstream classroom. In this environment, gifted students often languish, becoming bored or losing interest in learning. Classroom teachers and teacher preparation programs can address this waste by purposely creating a program to include gifted students.

Kiyoji Koreeda
Toyo University, Japan

Masayoshi Tsuge
University of Tsukuba, Japan

Shigeru Ikuta
Otsuma Women's University, Japan

Elizabeth Minchin Dalton
Dalton Education Services International, USA

Linda Plantin Ewe
Kristianstad University, Sweden

REFERENCES

UNESCO. (1994). *The Salamanca Statement and Framework for Action on Special Needs Education. World Conference on Special Needs Education: Access and Quality, Salamanca, Spain.* UNESCO. https://unesdoc.unesco.org/ark:/48223/pf0000098427

United Nations. (2015). *The 17 Sustainable Development Goals. UN Department of Economic and Social Affairs.* UN. https://sdgs.un.org/goals

Acknowledgment

The editors wish to express their gratitude to contributors, reviewers and all those who helped with this research. Special thanks to the Editorial Advisory Board members for their support, encouragement, and insightful comments.

Kiyoji Koreeda is grateful for the opportunity to publish this book together with the editors and colleagues around the world who are promoting inclusive education. He hopes that support for children with special educational needs will be further enhanced.

Masayoshi Tsuge hopes that this book will contribute to the further development of inclusive education around the world. And he would like to thank everyone involved for giving him the opportunity to contribute to the creation of this book.

Shigeru Ikuta wishes to acknowledge valuable contributions of all the students and more than 300 schoolteachers all over the world using a handy aid with multimedia-enabled dot-code technologies. He is also grateful to the support by "JSPS KAKENHI Grants" and by the "Otsuma Grants-in-Aid for Individual Exploratory Research." Shigeru Ikuta thanks to the encouragement given by his family, Atsuko, Nobuhiro, Sayaka, Isao, and Saki. He especially celebrates his mother's 100 years birthday from his heart in July 2023.

Elizabeth Dalton wishes to thank all of the talented, dedicated, and inspiring educators around the world who work tirelessly in their classrooms and beyond to support and challenge their students, all with their own diverse needs and abilities, to learn and thrive and reach for their own stars. Without such educators, the world would be at a terrible loss, and these books would not be possible.

Linda Plantin Ewe extends her sincere appreciation to Drs. Koreeda, Tsuge, Ikuta, and Dalton for graciously inviting her to serve as one of the editors for this book. Collaborating with these esteemed researchers has been an absolute delight, as their wealth of expertise and knowledge has greatly enriched the project.

The editors appreciate the hard work of everyone at IGI-Global, who worked to ensure the timely production of the present two books. Ms. Melissa Wagner and Ms. Jocelynn Hessler provided invaluable editorial assistance during the preparation process.

Kiyoji Koreeda
Toyo University, Japan

Masayoshi Tsuge
University of Tsukuba, Japan

Shigeru Ikuta
Otsuma Women's University, Japan

Elizabeth Dalton
Dalton Education Services International, USA

Linda Plantin Ewe
Kristianstad University, Sweden

Section 1
Inclusive Education: Theory and Policy

Chapter 1
Creating an International Collaboratory for Leadership in Universally Designed Education:
INCLUDE as a Global Community of Practice

Elizabeth Dalton
Dalton Education Services International, USA

Aashna Khurana
ASER Centre, USA

Richard M. Jackson
Boston College, USA

Luigia Nicholas
Stellenbosch University, South Africa

Sean Bracken
University of Worcester, UK

Oressa K. Power
William James College, USA

Ashiya Abdool Satar
University of South Africa, South Africa

Linda Plantin Ewe
Kristianstad University, Sweden

Mustapha Aabi
University of Ibn Zohr, Morocco

ABSTRACT

To foster strong global movements toward more inclusive educational resources around the world, higher education serves a crucial role. Universities face numerous challenges in the development of inclusive services for those with differing needs. While global collaborative efforts often provide great inspiration for community and educational system change, professionals do not always know exactly what changes should be made or how to go about making these changes more inclusive. Resources and online professional learning networks that are open to all and readily available online are one way to address these

DOI: 10.4018/978-1-6684-7370-2.ch001

challenges. The INCLUDE Collaboratory gathers and provides open opportunities for professionals around the world to connect, learn, discuss, and develop ongoing collaborative relationships. The authors present the background, history, structure, and work of the INCLUDE Collaboratory, highlighting the following: Concept, vision, and purpose; organizational timeline and evolution; organizational development; thematic priorities, and future planning.

INTRODUCTION

Higher education serves a crucial role in fostering strong global movements toward more inclusive educational resources around the world (Bracken & Novak, 2019). However, universities face numerous challenges in supporting the development of inclusive services for those with differing needs. Significant barriers, such as distance from service centers, funding for accessible technologies, knowledge regarding effective practices for design-based research and student-teacher relationships, and lack of available implementation models of evidence-based practices, continue to exist (Ewe, 2019; Messiou, 2017; Wilcox et al., 2021; Fovet, 2021). Many global factors have contributed to the developing worldwide awareness of and movement toward inclusive education. Historically, the United Nations Educational, Scientific and Cultural Organization (UNESCO) has played a major role in expanding awareness of and guidelines for global inclusive education. As a result of the World Conference on Education for All in Jomtien, Thailand, UNESCO published the World Declaration on Education for All and Framework for Action to meet Basic Learning Needs (UNESCO, 1990). This declaration started a series of worldwide collaborations on inclusive education, resulting in the Salamanca Statement and Framework for Action on Special Education Needs (UNESCO, 1994), the Dakar Framework for Action (UNESCO, 2000), and policy guidelines on inclusion in education (UNESCO, 2009). The world, through continued leadership from the United Nations, has continued to make positive strides in guiding disability rights (United Nations, 2006; 2016) and inclusive education (UNESCO, 2020).

While the many collaborative efforts listed above have provided great inspiration for community and educational system changes in countries around the world, educational professionals do not always know exactly what changes should be made or how to go about making these changes to make our systems of education more inclusive. Resources open to all and readily available online are one way to address these questions. Open Educational Resources (OER) can increase accessibility, but teachers need support and guidance to understand how to adjust these in order to guarantee accessibility for all students in their classroom (Tavares, Vieira & Pedro, 2021).

Additionally, online professional learning networks (PLNs) are widely sought as vehicles for connection, collaboration, and shared research toward mutual goals (Trust et al., 2016; Carpenter et al., 2022). In 2019, two education professors met at a conference and discovered that they had a shared interest and desire to establish a way for educators around the world who were interested in inclusive and universally designed education to connect with each other. Dr. Richard Jackson (Boston College, USA) and Dr. Sean Bracken (University of Worcester, UK) first conceptualized the International Collaboratory for Leadership in Universally Designed Education (INCLUDE). Drs. Jackson and Bracken are experts in Universal Design for Learning (UDL) and established INCLUDE as a means of sharing UDL and other evidence-based diverse learning approaches with professionals throughout the world by leveraging the power of digital technology and online communications (CAST, 2022). Karin Muff (2014) defined a Collaboratory as an open space for all stakeholders where action learning and action research join forces,

International Collaboratory for Leading Universally Designed Education

and students, educators and researchers work with members of all facets of society to address current dilemmas. This then was the objective for INCLUDE, to create a dynamic and innovative global space for educators, learners and practitioners to engage with a shared purpose of establishing a socially-just approach to advancing diversity, equality and inclusion within and beyond teacher education and higher education. To ground the efforts of INCLUDE and to establish clear targets for the work, several IN-CLUDE leaders and post-secondary educators researched and developed INCLUDE's Action-Oriented Values (INCLUDE, 2020). These values guide the work of the collaborative and maintain our focus on open, globally available inclusive education for all.

The remainder of this chapter provides an overview of INCLUDE's development to date. In the first section, a rationale is provided for the establishment of a dynamic network of like-minded learners and educators willing to respond to the global imperative for meeting the requirements of increasingly diverse students. Once the rationale has been explored, the nature of systems and processes developed to facilitate a global network for professional development and research is identified. This section illustrates how an effective Collaboratory requires a cadre of specialist volunteers to attend to the maintenance of its web and social media presence. The chapter concludes with an overview of where INCLUDE may best orient its focus and energies over the forthcoming years.

BACKGROUND

In its emergent and still nascent existence, the INCLUDE Collaboratory stands alone in its' bold mission and vision for educational opportunity worldwide. As governmental and non-governmental entities endeavor to expand and enrich educational opportunities for the common good, who will benefit? Will it be those who are already well on their way toward contributing to society, as in the "rich get richer", or could it be those who have been historically neglected, excluded, or otherwise marginalized? Great societies are judged based on how they care for and treat their young and most vulnerable. Even greater societies are praised for how they engage and include their most vulnerable. Such progress occurs over time, requiring a labor of love and taking on locally agreed-upon forms, for the world is still vast and complex and no single solution can work for all.

What it takes to engage and include traditionally marginalized individuals in the educational enterprise will necessarily take on many forms. This is especially the case because the nature of 'inclusion' has moved beyond a singular focus on disability rights and is increasingly cognisant of the diversity of identity markers, such as socio-linguistic and cultural background, race and ethnicity, sexuality and gender identities and the complex intersections between these markers that play out in diverse jurisdictions and geographic spaces (Crenshaw, 2017). This begs the question: can a single guiding framework or unifying theory inspire and support such efforts? Universal Design for Learning (UDL), at least for the present, appears to be doing that. UDL (Rose & Meyer, 2002; Meyer, Rose, & Gordon, 2014) shifts the blame for educational maladies from the learner to the learning environment. Based on accumulated evidence from the learning sciences, environments can now be designed to support a variety of ways to engage learners, identify multiple means for expressing what the learner knows and can do, and supply the learner with multiple varieties of media and materials. In contrast to frameworks that target deficits for differential treatment, UDL increases flexibility and choice to the curriculum, thus reducing barriers to access, participation, and progress (Hitchcock et al., 2002; Rose, Meyer & Hitchcock, 2005).

UDL's popularity in the United States owes much to the disability rights movement, progressive legislation, and life in the digital age. INCLUDE's meaning and purpose are best expressed in its name, which as an acronym, spells out elements critical to the Collaboratory's very existence. The "IN" in INCLUDE signifies international engagement as an intention or commitment of the organization. The "C" stands for a Collaboratory, a center without walls, independent of place, and just right for communication in the digital age. The "L" signifies leadership, not of a top-down or bottom-up sort, but leadership that is distributed and emergent from within the ongoing practices of the Collaboratory. The "U" stands for universal, not to be interpreted as a one-size-fits-all solution to global challenges, but instead as an attitude or disposition toward equity and equal opportunity for all through design thinking. The "D" signifies Design as a mindset for planning so that barriers to learning can be eliminated and affordances for improving the human condition can be discovered or invented. Finally, the "E" stands for Education, which must be extended to all to attain a productive and fulfilling life in society. Together, these constituent elements move the Collaboratory to action in service of equity and inclusion for all.

Each of these critical elements had its origin in the late 1990s when the U.S. Congress required separate states to provide access to the general education curriculum for students with disabilities. Previously, under U.S. Public Law 94-142 passed in 1975, students with a disability were only entitled to a special education, tailored to address their disability-specific needs. To support inclusion, the curriculum that was never intended for students with disabilities in the first place now had to be transformed to reach **all** students. In practice, accessible materials had to be in the hands of students just in time to participate in instruction. Classroom practices had to employ activities that would engage all learners equally, and assessment procedures had to fairly measure what students know and can do as a result of their learning.

A paradigm shift was required to accomplish what many policymakers in the U.S. believed to be illogical and impossible. Previously, lack of learning was attributed to the deficits of students with disabilities. This long-enduring deficit paradigm yielded practices intended to reduce the impact of disability. A new paradigm would shift blame away from deficits to the curriculum for limiting access. Following a set of design principles, the curriculum could be made accessible, usable, and measurable for the broadest possible range of learners.

At the Center for Applied Special Technology (CAST), such a paradigm or framework for the design of accessible learning environments was under development and ready for deployment to support the implementation of federally mandated curriculum access. This new paradigm, now widely known as Universal Design for Learning or UDL, asserted that the curriculum itself was disabled and composed of numerous unintended barriers that prevented learning by students with disabilities. In 2000, CAST, along with several partners, including Boston College, was awarded a multi-year federal grant to provide the nation with guidance on how to make curriculum access a reality for all U.S. students with disabilities. The work of the Center at CAST and partner affiliates over a five-year period led to many district and state-level implementations of UDL across the U.S.

As the adoption of the new paradigm spread across the states and into several Canadian provinces, educational leadership roles and functions remained divided between general and special education. If the inclusion of U.S. students with disabilities in the general education curriculum was to become a reality, there would be a great need for joint responsibility among leadership personnel. To address this need, Boston College and CAST were awarded federal funds to establish the first postdoctoral UDL Fellows program. Based on priorities identified by a national group of stakeholders meeting in Washington, D.C. in 2007, eight UDL Fellows were recruited between 2009 and 2014 to work toward those priorities.

International Collaboratory for Leading Universally Designed Education

By 2015, interest in Universal Design from around the world was apparent and this was identified in a growing body of literature exploring the applications of UDL from a more global and transnational perspective (Bracken & Novak, 2019; Ferguson et al, 2019; Fovet, 2021; Gronseth & Dalton, 2019). Further, in recognition that educationalists were extending the application of the UDL framework beyond its traditional domain within a disability rights context, movement grew to consider the representation, empowerment and learning requirements of more culturally diverse learners (Hanesworth, Bracken and Elkington, 2019), and to tackle significant societal barriers to learning such as racism (Fitzgerald, 2020). Thus, here was a need to extend the concept of UDL leadership developed at Boston College and CAST to a global scale. From the fortuitous encounter between Sean Bracken and Richard Jackson resulting in the founding of INCLUDE, the active participation of INCLUDE's Steering Group, and the wider participation of the Collaboratory's membership, this global and virtual community of practice will thrive for many years to come.

INCLUDE: ACCESSIBLE GLOBAL NETWORKING

The INCLUDE Collaboratory is a global network of accessibility and inclusion experts and learners that in and of itself is concerned with inclusion and accessibility through communication and digital community building. The network has purposefully created inroads and access to membership from multiple potential constituents such as entry-level educators as well as more established researchers and professionals. As further explored below, it also emphasizes the necessity for UDL application to draw upon the lived experiences of learners. In doing so, it increasingly aims to harness the potential for diverse constituents to learn from one another through dynamic and complementary research-informed initiatives that generate new insights and knowledge.

Accessibility and inclusion-focused global networking require strategic communication across cultures, countries, and regions. The use of social media, email, and search engines can vary in different contexts, and knowledge disseminators, therefore, need to be mindful of how digital poverty and inequities may create significant barriers to learning, especially in contexts of global inequities (Satar, 2019). Therefore, INCLUDE utilizes multiple media platforms to facilitate access to networking and resources across its international membership base. INCLUDE utilizes this structured approach to coordinate information and communicate key messages through the most suitable pathways to the designated audiences while assimilating accessible design theories into its strategic communications approach.

Strategic Communications

The strategic approach to communications provides a framework for sharing information and developing associations across diverse global settings and contexts to bring together like-minded individuals who can advance the global inclusive education agenda that underpins the UN Sustainable Development Goals (SDGs) with reference to goals 4 and 9 (United Nations, 2022; Peter, 2020). This endeavor is transnational in nature. A global strategic communications approach, hence, enables wide-ranging collaboration that brings together inclusion professionals from different walks of life to share their knowledge and experience through various media, platforms, and approaches (Tench, Meng, & Moreno, 2022; O'Connor & Shumate, 2018). This multidisciplinary approach draws on communication practices found in, inter alia, public relations, mass communication, social media marketing, advertising, and organizational strategy to facilitate global liaisons with the intention of long-term goal-attainment and sustainability of the core vision of the organization. INCLUDE's communication strategy consists of a social media presence, online professional development opportunities, a website, email listservs and strategic planning meetings that facilitate community networks.

Examples of social media applications for outreach purposes can be found in all phases of the communications management process. INCLUDE's presence can be felt on Twitter, Facebook, Instagram, YouTube, and LinkedIn, enabling the group to connect to and engage with people across borders.

The INCLUDE Website

The INCLUDE website is a vital center for information that is an environment for the INCLUDE community and provides access to professional development programming and resources. A regularly updated website of quality design is essential to maintaining the attributes of the community, providing clarity on INCLUDE's programming and goals, and encouraging repeated engagement (Zhou, Tao, et al., 2009). Attachment to a community is built through bonds with other group members, and through identity-based attachment felt as connections to the group holistically (Ren et al., 2012, p.843). INCLUDE seeks to enhance the group's identity by providing information about the group to its members and representing all members of the Collaboratory as potential collaborators to the resources and event programming. While group identity and interpersonal bond-based attachments enable participation in an online group, member retention is a challenge for online communities, possibly due to the presence of competing engagements for members (Ren et al., 2012).

Engagement Through Professional Development Opportunities

INCLUDE seeks to remain sustainable by having the Collaboratory determine the nature of engagement and content. The steering committee guides the collaborating network, ensures access to events and incorporates diverse voices in topical programming. Fostering participation through group identity-based attachments in an online community is comparably easier for leadership (Ren et al., 2012, p.859). INCLUDE further enhances the Collaboratory by supporting bond-based attachment between members in smaller communities at professional development events. Support from peers is particularly important while enabling educators to pursue professional development aiming to better support inclusion. Educators participating in such a community of learning, meaning, and knowing are relationally situated in social negotiations inside the community (Lave, 1991, p.67).

Fostering a sense of support and negotiating meaning through the varied social and cultural lenses of an international community of various training and levels of experience is particularly challenging but necessary and valuable. The effectiveness of online professional learning communities is shown to be more stable, enduring, and successful when a community has structured engagement (Gaible & Burns, 2007, p.64), such as within INCLUDE. Through digital communication opportunities, members exchange information and network for their own projects but also sustain INCLUDE by participating in community events. The Collaboratory is routed in the situated context and mutual expectations for professional development (Luo et al., 2020, p.19). Common understandings, goals, and the tensions between national voices are freely explored in the online professional learning space through a "flat world" where colleagues may be "next door or across oceans," (Lieberman & Mace, 2009, p.85). This environment seeks to nourish local communities and benefit the international learning community.

International Collaboratory for Leading Universally Designed Education

Social Media Outreach

Social media outreach is an integral element of 21st-century operations, and understanding its role in the context of outreach and marketing is critical for researchers and social media managers (e.g., Fong and Burton, 2008; Kumar et al., 2016; Schultz & Peltier, 2013). Most existing studies focus on organizational issues, such as customer relationship management (Trainor et al., 2014), brand management (Asmussen et al., 2013), innovation management (Gebauer et al., 2013), and employee recruitment (Sivertzen et al., 2013). These studies frame advancements in communication studies through boosting organizations' outreach, marketing, and management context. INCLUDE uses social media as a strategic communications tool to reach potential members and inform them about opportunities, such as upcoming webinars, blogs written by experts in the field of UDL, and the expansion of the repository of resources on our website.

As social media moves from "buzz word" status to strategic tool, more communications practitioners are developing their skills related to online communication technology. INCLUDE focuses on creating posts according to routines or guidelines already established by these platforms. Therefore, at INCLUDE, the communications team keeps up with trends in social media and is adept in creating creative and accessible content. INCLUDE applies different measures such as spreading videos via YouTube, posting blogs on the website, and sharing the links on social media. INCLUDE displays information in multiple ways, including creating graphics to show the timeline of our organization. Additionally, when posting content on social media, accessibility is considered, so each image is posted with accompanying alternative text and Camel Case for hashtags. All information is presented in the form of text as well as graphics at minimum.

With unparalleled access to information, audiences desire a sense of engagement, refined brand awareness, and accessibility (Postman, 2009), which has inspired INCLUDE to implement purposeful social media for community communications and outreach. A Google form that records interest is maintained and circulated before each webinar. This list is updated after every webinar, and contact information of new subscribers is collated in a master sheet that serves as a comprehensive mailing list of people who are interested in getting updates on INCLUDE's work.

Social Media Governance

INCLUDE also focuses on social media governance as a means to advance the establishment of social media in its communication practices. Here, governance refers to the logic of action and the causal relations between structures, interests, and interactions (Kooiman, 2007). Further, it involves the formal or informal frameworks that synchronize the actions of the members of an organization within the social web. At INCLUDE, before any information is posted on social media handles, all the relevant stakeholders come together to share what needs to be said and what the information would look like. For instance, when a webinar announcement must be made, the presenters provide their biographies and information about the webinar that they want people to know about, then the communications team and the professional development team that organize the webinar develop the social media content. After this, the communications team adjusts the information according to social media platforms' established guidelines and routines. The information is then shared using email listservs to those who have subscribed to INCLUDE's mailing list.

Additionally, INCLUDE has also developed its Social Media Governance Protocols, also known as blogging policies or social network guidelines. These guidelines mark out and recommend how social media communications shall be carried out by all the members of an organization to maintain consistency and how it can enable everyone to become communicators in participative online environments (Bell, 2010; Turner, 2010; Wright & Hinson, 2009). An example of this includes using hashtags like #INCLUDECollaboratory, #KeepINCLUDing, during the webinars to provide a live feed to people on social media or an anchor for those who wish to promote INCLUDE on social media platforms. This encourages INCLUDE members and subscribers to engage in conversation threads, share their work with one another and act as an INCLUDE participant. Even during webinars, INCLUDE reminds people of these protocols if they wish to tweet or post on LinkedIn.

Future Media Plans

INCLUDE's goal is to establish an accessible global network of inclusion scholars and practitioners in different global, regional, local, and transnational contexts through pragmatic communication methods that enhance collaboration and do not simply rely on passive message dissemination. Utilizing a strategic communication approach to engage with inclusion scholars and practitioners from various contexts enhances the engagement and collaboration between experts in the field.

INCLUDE: ELEVATING LEARNER VOICE

While policies and curricula can hypothesize about the student learning experience and devise ways and methods to remove barriers to their learning, in the flow of ongoing experience and dynamics of change, most commonly, student stories have not yet been told and properly incorporated to inform policy and curriculum growth and development. Teachers, policymakers, and curriculum designers will always have stories to uncover, understand and integrate. Student voice has recently gained significant interest among educators and scholars as a key element to the success of student learning, a welcomed shift in policy and pedagogy by educational institutions worldwide. Transformations by faculty leadership and in the classroom that proactively integrate the student voice are crucial to promote engagement, trust, democracy, and, ultimately, ensure learning outcomes (Morris, 2019). "Student Voice" is certainly a positive conceptual change that must not disappear as a simple fad. It must be given due support from the educational leadership, policymakers, and teachers so that it may be sustained and developed.

In the classroom context, the best teaching practices are those that are in tune with the student experience (Balou, 2011; Matthews & Dollinger, 2023). Teaching is not merely a set of operational procedures and techniques. Students are more likely to be engaged and learning outcomes met when students co-own knowledge and co-create change rather than just consuming and adapting to it. Teachers strive to focus their efforts on optimizing the relevance and usability of what is to be taught in the most pleasant and smoothest way possible. In the process, they tend to make decisions on the students' behalf, thinking that as teachers, they understand what students' concerns, needs and expectations are better than they do. This may, whether intentionally or unintentionally, lead to a belief that the student has weaker intellectual capacities than the teacher in making decisions that relate to students in the first place: in other words, a lesser mind.

While previous experiences with other students tend to help enhance current experiences, the problem is that students are never the same. Teaching commonly is a series of repetitive learning activities presented relatively in the same way in preparation for the same goals; however, students are not the same

International Collaboratory for Leading Universally Designed Education

and what they want is not the same (Cook-Sather, 2018). While students may often be seen through the lens of the teacher's own experiences and this may support teacher empathy and develop a foundation for some emotional rapport with students, teachers' assumptions, attitudes, and stereotypes serve here as a lens through which they judge what matters to students. However, from two different lenses - the teacher's and the student's - the same matters would probably be perceived very differently. Individuals' experiences are never the same, and even if they are, these experiences never influence people in the same way. Thus, making assumptions about students based on the teacher's experiences, which may turn out not to be true, is unlikely to help teachers systematically make accurate predictions about students' needs and expectations. The development of high-quality teacher-student relationships, where teachers can authentically understand and address students' needs instead of prioritizing their expert perspective on what they "think" students may need, would be an important step toward improving curricula and educational policies (Balou, 2011).

Understanding the student or learner's voice requires getting the learner's perspective first-hand by providing favorable platforms for them to tell stories about their experience and perspective. Learners' stories can certainly feed into teacher instruction, can influence the creation processes of course materials, and can transform students from passive consumers to co-creators of knowledge. As student voice is not congruous, it is not static either. It is contingent and fluid. It changes based on the student experience and social circumstances, but generally in predictable patterns. For first-year higher education students, it may be all about transitioning into university. University is a different environment than high school, complete with its own material demands and learning expectations, a transformative process with bumps in the road for many. For final-year graduating students, it is more likely about transitioning out of university. These students are largely concerned about job prospects and employability. Productive student-to-student relationships can significantly aid students in finding and sharing their voice with confidence.

Not all changes in a learner's experience are predictable. Non-linear changes are often abrupt, unexpected, and difficult to predict (Cook-Sather, 2018). An example of this is the recent global pandemic, which has understandably prompted a hastened transition to online education: a completely different experience triggering a shift in student voice. During the suspension of in-class, face-to-face learning, student voice has more than ever spoken out about accessibility and the assessment of learning. Despite the accompanying upset and concerns, the pandemic's digital transformation of learning provides favorable opportunities for the learner voice to flourish through changes in educational methodology and guidelines.

The INCLUDE Learner Voice Task Team is comprised of the voices of students, supported by educators. Students must play a pivotal role in the changes they want to see; therefore, the taskforce team highly values the voice of the learner in this regard, elevating and promoting perspectives that support diversity in instruction, UDL, equity, and accessibility. The team holds various roles and responsibilities relating to communications, INCLUDE content creation and organizational structures. The team organizes programs such as student blogs and conferences to widely share the student voice. Through an annual Learner Voice conference, the team supports learners with different backgrounds, cultures, abilities, and interests to engage with each other, which is a priority of the Collaboratory. Student voice differs from other strong voices in education and can be learned from. The relationship between teacher and learner perspective is important to both understand and recognize in the pursuit of inclusion in education and beyond. The pandemic has shown that flexibility is necessary and possible in education, however, further efforts will be needed for implementation to be intentional and student-centered.

INCLUDE: PROFESSIONAL DEVELOPMENT AND TRAINING

Starting Up

As the INCLUDE Collaboratory began to take shape, there was a shared vision among the original Steering Committee members to address the action-oriented values adopted by INCLUDE through a strong focus on professional development and training for educators around the world, which is a critical priority for the field (Feng, 2012; Holmqvist & Lelinge, 2021; Rose & Doveston, 2015). In order to reach a global community of educators, it was necessary to concentrate on developing an online presence and begin to frame out what would soon grow into the INCLUDE Collaboratory website. The website would serve as INCLUDE's primary outward-facing identity to motivate educators interested in inclusive education (Beach & Willows, 2014). A small team was assembled, and after several months, the INCLUDE website was launched in April 2020.

One of the many challenges faced by INCLUDE's website team was identifying, developing, and finalizing content for the website, as well as designing and launching the website itself. To do this, INCLUDE reached out through our varied professional networks and contacts to identify individuals who wanted to contribute either their time or content or both to help build INCLUDE's website. Approximately 20 individuals responded to our call for involvement and were divided into website development and website content teams. To organize the information, it was projected that to post to the website, thematic categories would be needed. Each theme was represented by a separate tab on the website. These early content tabs were Connect, Learn, Apply, Change, and Share. Content received through website team members and the INCLUDE Steering Committee was logically organized according to these five themes. Professional Development and Training grew to be responsible for what would take place through the Learn theme to provide the growing international community of members with relevant and high-quality professional development experiences.

The INCLUDE Collaboratory, through its Steering Committee, developed a set of twelve aims for the organizations, which are available on the INCLUDE website at https://include.wp.worc.ac.uk/

The Professional Development and Training Team actively works to address two of these specific aims:

- To seek out and promote opportunities for collaborative international pedagogy and research focused on the design, application, and impact of Universal Design throughout all sectors of formal and informal education.
- To enhance global collegiality in the field of inclusive education through the formation of a community of professional practitioners for the expression of ideas or innovation in the field of Universally Designed education.

In order to address the global interest and need for inclusive education development and training, INCLUDE has been committed to offering online professional development events free of charge. This is extremely important in order to expand the availability of such information and training for ALL educators (Dutta, 2016; Pawlowski & Hoel, 2012).

International Collaboratory for Leading Universally Designed Education

INCLUDE Webinars

As INCLUDE developed a network of global educators interested in inclusive education and UDL, the Professional Development & Training Team identified topical areas for potential webinars and invited various professionals in the field to share their work and knowledge as a webinar to the global community. Since 2020, free one-hour Professional Development Webinars have been offered by INCLUDE on a regular basis. Many of these live, online webinars have been recorded and are available on the INCLUDE website as professional development resources. The list of INCLUDE PD webinars available as of 2022 includes (INCLUDE, 2022):

- Access to Build to Internalize: A Model for International UDL Implementation through Online Professional Development for India and UAE;
- Rear-view mirror: reflecting about practice through the lens of Universal Design for Learning principles and practices to inform learning design;
- The impact of Universal Design for Learning in higher education, and the road we are on in Sweden;
- Brazil's UNIFESP Accessibility Portal: Inclusive and Open Design to Support Inclusion in Higher Education;
- Promoting UDL principles and strategies for inclusive learning: The Redesigning Blended Courses Project at the University of Cape Town;
- Delivering A Graduate Course in Universal Design for Learning: Reflecting on Eighteen Years of Experiences;
- Mission Accomplice: Practicing Antiracism with UDL; and
- Entrepreneurial Leadership Program Renewal: Centering Student Voice and Choice

INCLUDE Blog

For each of the INCLUDE webinars, presenters are asked to develop an accompanying blog to be made available on the INCLUDE website, to further the communities' professional opportunities to learn and understand many different sides of inclusive education and UDL. In addition, members of the INCLUDE Steering Committee and others, including student members, have written and shared their views as INCLUDE blog posts. Two areas of unique importance to the INCLUDE community highlighted in the blog are (a) promoting research efforts in inclusive education and UDL, and (b) emphasizing critical importance of learner voice in inclusive education system development. Whenever possible, INCLUDE seeks to elevate these two areas through blog posts, webinars, and other available means such as conference presentations, articles, and book chapters.

Conferences

The INCLUDE Collaboratory seeks to establish a regular conference on inclusive practices, inclusive education research, and UDL soon, but during the past several years, INCLUDE has partnered with the University of Ibn Zohr to offer the International Conference on Education Quality (ICEQ), held in Agadir, Morocco. INCLUDE has been directly involved in the planning and programming of this conference, now in its sixth year as of 2023. ICEQ presents papers on research and practice in areas relating to the improvement of educational quality around the world, with a strong focus on inclusive education. Each year, education professionals from Morocco, across Africa, and around the world participate in the conference program, collaborating and sharing their work and establishing connections with other researchers and practitioners. During ICEQ 2022, INCLUDE offered a half-day research symposium to shine a light on the importance of international research collaborations focusing on inclusive education and UDL. INCLUDE continues to partner with ICEQ to expand access to high-quality information and resources in support of inclusive education, the expansion of universal design, and UDL practices and research efforts.

Additionally, ICEQ shares INCLUDE's belief in the importance of elevating learner voice and holds a day-long student conference within the main ICEQ program, which is specifically designed, developed, and presented by and for students. During this time, students from around the world share their work, their views, and their priorities as students in higher education settings. Understanding the student perspective directly from students is critical for responsive and equitable education system development and is a shared goal of ICEQ and the INCLUDE Collaboratory. INCLUDE will continue, in collaboration with ICEQ and the University of Ibn Zohr for the foreseeable future, exploring the possible need for and interest in developing an INCLUDE-led conference on inclusive education, universal design, and UDL with global reach throughout the educational community.

Professional Resources

During INCLUDE's early development, significant energies were placed into gathering helpful resources in different areas of interest for educational professionals who wanted to learn more about inclusive education and UDL. As the resources were assembled, they were organized into logical categories and posted to the INCLUDE website. The identification and securing of resources will continue for INCLUDE, and will populate INCLUDE's website with up-to-date materials and information important to the field.

INCLUDE's resources are organized under the following titles: Accessibility guidelines; online courses (including MOOCs); tech tools; curriculum design; tool kits; materials; assessment; physical spaces; and legislation standards and guidelines. Each area is represented by a tab on the INCLUDE website that opens to a listing and links to resources on the topic.

Future Direction for Professional Development & Training

INCLUDE believes in the value and use of practical examples to expand the understanding of inclusive educational practices and research. Additionally, INCLUDE believes in the value of open educational resources to decrease barriers of access for those around the world. To these ends, INCLUDE will continue to provide webinars, informational blogs, and diverse resources that address the practical aspects of developing and implementing inclusive education and UDL. It will continue to offer information, professional support and professional development that is openly available to the worldwide educational community via the internet.

New initiatives for the future include exploring the establishment of an online professional peer-reviewed journal on inclusive education, universal design, and UDL, as well as continuing to work toward establishing an annual or biannual global online conference to highlight these same areas. Additionally, INCLUDE hopes to grow a global university network that will develop and offer Graduate-level training

International Collaboratory for Leading Universally Designed Education

in UDL. Strategic development and planning are taking place within the INCLUDE Collaboratory that will support and sustain current and future initiatives.

INCLUDE: EXPANDING RESEARCH IN INCLUSIVE EDUCATION AND UDL

While a significant amount of research on inclusive education and UDL has appeared in the lexicon since the publication of the Salamanca Statement in 1994, most tend to be focused on theory rather than practice, and there is a 'sense of lack of progress' in the field. Additionally, theories empirically showing success in the development of more inclusive school systems, schools and classrooms are lacking in the literature (Nilholm, 2020). In South Africa, lack of progress toward the implementation of inclusive education appears to be linked with a lack of clarity in the policy, such as the existing ambiguity about the goals for inclusion and the means through which they can be achieved (Donohue & Bornman, 2014). A review of Eastern European research on inclusion indicates strong political and social attitudinal barriers to the implementation of inclusive education (Stepaniuk, 2019). If global inclusive education is to live up to its promise of equity of educational opportunity and experience for all, the need for expanded research in this area is clear.

From the inception of the INCLUDE Collaboratory, a focus on helping to grow research opportunities and collaborations around the world has led to several specific actions. First, research was elevated to one of four thematic foci of the Collaboratory. These themes include research, learner voice, professional development, and communication. Secondly, several webinars highlighting existing research in the field have been offered through the INCLUDE webinar series. Recordings of most webinars are available on the INCLUDE website, providing a diverse representation of inclusive education and UDL applications in higher education and other settings. Finally, working to actively grow global research sharing and collaboration, INCLUDE developed, sponsored, and offered a half-day research symposium as part of the ICEQ2022 conference entitled "Researching to Include: An Interactive Seminar for Aspiring and Inspiring Researchers". This interactive session highlighted existing research in the areas of learner voice, technology, and intersectionality, and brought researchers together in active online discussions to focus on how they might work together in future research-focused collaborations. As INCLUDE continues to grow and expand its research focus, these and other research opportunities will be made available through the INCLUDE Collaboratory. There is an emerging body of research from across the INCLUDE network (see for example, Aabi & Bracken, 2023), and this will be further enhanced as greater opportunities arise for research groups to plug into a ready-made network of transnational colleagues eager to enhance a research-informed exploration of cross-cultural interpretations and implementations of UDL.

CONCLUSION: REFLECTIONS ON THE FUTURE OF INCLUDE

The potential applications for UDL are multifarious, cross-disciplinary, and geo-culturally unpredictable, so the nature of how INCLUDE charts its future must incorporate a level of creative flexibility to facilitate meaningful growth that is sustainable for all. INCLUDE's solid foundations have served colleagues well over the past several years. However, now INCLUDE needs to develop imaginative scenarios that will maximise the potential of collegiate learning that move beyond a classroom mindset and take learning into authentic or virtually simulated spaces.

Building on action-oriented values (INCLUDE, 2020), INCLUDE must develop ways to facilitate exchanges of ideas, insights and research that encourage shared learning activities as a community habit. INCLUDE's professional development sessions have gone a long way towards realising this goal, and the challenge is to grow the learning from these insightful learning sessions. Recent discussions among the Steering Group of INCLUDE identified that setting up an *International Journal for Universal Design and Universal Design for Learning* would provide a mechanism for a growing number of colleagues across the world to have a shared space where learning based on premises of equality, diversity and inclusion can be exchanged within and beyond disciplines and where researched insights can also be tested across borders and in a diversity of socio-cultural contexts.

To date, INCLUDE has featured in-depth insights from diverse settings, altering our learning focus from the internal to the external. It has prompted learning from those who may be perceived as different, and thereby addresses a tendency towards 'othering' in transnational learning where, as shared by Knight et al (2022), there may be a tendency to view difference as exotic or 'other' and this can lead to cultural judgements that contrast learner difference in terms of how inclusion may be practiced and perceived in differing contexts. INCLUDE shifts that power perspective enabling practitioners to take the next step of learning, away from one's own cultural context and to learn *with* and *from* 'the other.' A continued challenge for INCLUDE is to enable facilitative ways to connect networks of educators, students, and researchers within differing global contexts so that the potentials for universal design and universal design for learning can be more fully realised. To this end, INCLUDE supports having home-based productive networks that conjoin colleagues and learners together to create a virtual space where these networks can be linked together with like-minded research networks in other settings. Providing colleagues with a venue for disseminating their ideas, for example, through an international conference where ideas from differing cultural contexts can be shared and exchanged, would continue to move the critical inclusive educational agenda forward. The initial experiences of INCLUDE have been fruitful and emergent towards a more inclusive and dynamic, networked interaction of learners and educators, where learning from grappling with complex questions regarding accessibility for all can then be applied in a diversity of settings. This is not merely a theoretical conundrum but one with meaningful applications for learning across the globe.

To rise to this vision, an investment of time and energy by a more diffuse group of agents will be required. Over the forthcoming phases of the Collaboratory, if the true dynamic potential of the purposefully oriented network is to be realised, differing ways of governing and sustaining the network will need to be considered, growing from the insightful community ideas exploring how to best serve the needs of INCLUDE's global constituents. Creative and strategic development is needed for a more sustainable and meaningful INCLUDE Collaboratory to emerge, especially in contexts where the modes for creating, accessing, and diffusing accessible and inclusive pathways to learning continue to change apace. The challenges are great, but the potential outcomes for learners and education professionals around the world to establish equitable, sustainable, and inclusive education environments for ALL are too important not to continue with commitment and determination on our shared-values-based journey.

REFERENCES

Aabi, M., & Bracken, S. (2023). Drawing from the global to act local: How Universal Design for Learning lends itself to facilitating inclusion in Moroccan higher education. In, Kelly, A., Padden, L., Fleming, B (Eds) (2023) Making Inclusive Higher Education a Reality: Creating a University for All. London: Routledge. doi:10.4324/9781003253631-17

Asmussen, B., Harridge-March, S., Occhiocupo, N., & Farquhar, J. (2013). The multi-layered nature of the internet-based democratization of brand management. *Journal of Business Research*, 66(9), 1473–1483. doi:10.1016/j.jbusres.2012.09.010

Bahou, L. (2011, January). Rethinking the challenges and possibilities of student voice and agency. *Educate*, (Special Issue), 2–14.

Beach, P., & Willows, D. (2014). Investigating teachers' exploration of a professional development website: An innovative approach to understanding the factors that motivate teachers to use Internet-based resources. *Canadian Journal of Learning and Technology / La revue canadienne de l'apprentissage et de la technologie, 40*(3), Canadian Network for Innovation in Education. https://www.learntechlib.org/p/148504/

Bell, J. (2010). Clearing the AIR. *Communication World, 27*(1), 27–30.

Bracken, S., & Novak, K. (Eds.). (2019). *Transforming higher education through universal design for learning: An international perspective*. Routledge. doi:10.4324/9781351132077

Carpenter, J. P., Krutka, D. G., & Trust, T. (2022). Continuity and change in educators' professional learning networks. *Journal of Educational Change, 23*(1), 85–113. doi:10.100710833-020-09411-1

CAST. (2022). *About Universal Design for Learning*. CAST. https://www.cast.org/impact/universal-design-for-learning-udl

Clarke, P. (2020, June 17). What Is Strategic Communications? *Medium*. https://medium.com/@Peter_Clarke/what-is-strategic-communications-8738b713e77

Cook-Sather, A. (2018). Tracing the Evolution of Student Voice in Educational Research. In R. Bourke & J. Loveridge (Eds.), *Radical Collegiality through Student Voice*. Springer. doi:10.1007/978-981-13-1858-0_2

Crenshaw, K. W. (2017). *On intersectionality: Essential writings*. The New Press.

Donohue, D., & Bornman, J. (2014). The challenges of realising inclusive education in South Africa. *South African Journal of Education, 34*(2), 1–14. https://www.sajournalofeducation.co.za/index.php/saje/article/view/806/415. doi:10.15700/201412071114

Dutta, İ. (2016). Open educational resources (OER): Opportunities and challenges for Indian higher education. *Turkish Online Journal of Distance Education, 17*(2), 0-0. doi:10.17718/tojde.34669

Ewe, L. P. (2019). ADHD symptoms and the teacher-student relationship: A systematic literature review. *Emotional & Behavioural Difficulties, 24*(2), 136–155. doi:10.1080/13632752.2019.1597562

Feng, Y. (2012). Teacher career motivation and professional development in special and inclusive education: Perspectives from Chinese teachers. *International Journal of Inclusive Education*, *16*(3), 331–351. doi:10.1080/13603116.2010.489123

Ferguson, B. T., McKenzie, J., Dalton, E. M., & Lyner-Cleophas, M. (2019). Inclusion, universal design and universal design for learning in higher education: South Africa and the United States. *African Journal of Disability*, *8*(1), 1–7. PMID:31392169

Fong, J., & Burton, S. (2008). A cross-cultural comparison of electronic word-of-mouth and country-of-origin effects. *Journal of Business Research*, *61*(3), 233–242. doi:10.1016/j.jbusres.2007.06.015

Fovet, F. (2021). UDL in higher education: A global overview of the landscape and its changes. In F. Fovet (Ed.), *Applying Universal Design for Learning Across Disciplines*. IGI Global. doi:10.4018/978-1-7998-7106-4.ch001

Fritzgerald, A. (2020). *Antiracism and universal design for learning: Building expressways to success*. CAST Professional Publishing.

Gaible, E., & Burns, M. (2007). *Using Technology to Train Teachers: Appropriate Uses of ICT for Teacher Professional Development in Developing Countries*. World Bank. https://documents.worldbank.org/en/publication/documents-reports/documentdetail/900291468324835987/using-technology-to-train-teachers-appropriate-uses-of-ict-for-teacher-professional-development-in-developing-countires

Gebauer, J., Füller, J., & Pezzei, R. (2013). The dark and the bright side of co-creation: Triggers of member behavior in online innovation communities. *Journal of Business Research*, *66*(9), 1516–1527. doi:10.1016/j.jbusres.2012.09.013

Gronseth, S. L., & Dalton, E. M. (Eds.). (2019). *Universal access through inclusive instructional design: International perspectives on UDL*. Routledge. doi:10.4324/9780429435515

Hanesworth, P., Bracken, S., & Elkington, S. (2019). A typology for a social justice approach to assessment: Learning from universal design and culturally sustaining pedagogy. *Teaching in Higher Education*, *24*(1), 98–114. doi:10.1080/13562517.2018.1465405

Hitchcock, C., Meyer, A., Rose, D., & Jackson, R. (2002). Providing New Access to the General Curriculum: Universal Design for Learning. *Teaching Exceptional Children*, *35*(2), 8–17. doi:10.1177/004005990203500201

Holmqvist, M., & Lelinge, B. (2021). Teachers' collaborative professional development for inclusive education. *European Journal of Special Needs Education*, *36*(5), 819–833. doi:10.1080/08856257.2020.1842974

INCLUDE. (2020). *Action Oriented Values*. INCLUDE. https://include.wp.worc.ac.uk/action-oriented-values/

INCLUDE. (2022). *INCLUDE Webinars*. INCLUDE. https://include.wp.worc.ac.uk/webinars/

Knight, C., Clegg, Z., Conn, C., Hutt, M., & Crick, T. (2022). 'Aspiring to include versus implicit "othering": Teachers' perceptions of inclusive education in Wales'. *British Journal of Special Education*, *49*(1), 6–23. doi:10.1111/1467-8578.12394

Kooiman, J. (Ed.). (2007). *Governing as governance*. Sage.

Kumar, A., Bezawada, R., Rishika, R., Janakiraman, R., & Kannan, P. K. (2016). From social to sale: The effects of firm-generated content in social media on customer behavior. *Journal of Marketing, 80*(1), 7–25. doi:10.1509/jm.14.0249

Lave, J. (1991). Situating learning in communities of practice. In L. B. Resnick, J. M. Levine, & S. D. Teasley (Eds.), *Perspectives on socially shared cognition* (pp. 63–82). American Psychological Association. doi:10.1037/10096-003

Lieberman, A., & Pointer Mace, D. (2009). Making Practice Public: Teacher Learning in the 21st Century. *Journal of Teacher Education, 61*(1-2), 77–88. doi:10.1177/0022487109347319

Luo, T., Freeman, C., & Stefaniak, J. (2020). "Like, comment, and share"—professional development through social media in higher education: A systematic review. *Educational Technology Research and Development, 68*(4), 1659–1683. doi:10.100711423-020-09790-5

Matthews, K. E., & Dollinger, M. (2023). Student voice in higher education: The importance of distinguishing student representation and student partnership. *Higher Education, 85*(3), 555–570. doi:10.100710734-022-00851-7

Messiou, K. (2017). Research in the field of inclusive education: Time for a rethink? *International Journal of Inclusive Education, 21*(2), 146–159. doi:10.1080/13603116.2016.1223184

Meyer, A., Rose, D., & Gordon, D. (2014). *Universal design for learning: Theory and Practice*. CAST Professional Publishing.

Morris, M. (2019). *Student Voice and Teacher Professional Development: Knowledge Exchange and Transformational Learning*. Palgrave Macmillan. doi:10.1007/978-3-030-23467-6

Muff, K. (Ed.). (2017). *The collaboratory: a co-creative stakeholder engagement process for solving complex problems*. Routledge. doi:10.4324/9781351285681

Nilholm, C. (2021). Research about inclusive education in 2020 – How can we improve our theories in order to change practice? *European Journal of Special Needs Education, 36*(3), 358–370. doi:10.1080/08856257.2020.1754547

O'Connor, A., & Shumate, M. (2018). A Multidimensional Network Approach to Strategic Communication. *International Journal of Strategic Communication, 12*(4), 399–416. doi:10.1080/1553118X.2018.1452242

Pawlowski, J., & Hoel, T. (2012). *Towards a Global Policy for Open Educational Resources: The Paris OER Declaration and its Implications*. White Paper, Version 0.2, Jyväskylä, Finland.

Postman, J. (2009). *SocialCorp: Social media goes corporate*. New Riders.

Ren, Y., Harper, F. M., Drenner, S., Terveen, L., Kiesler, S., Riedl, J., & Kraut, R. E. (2012). Building member attachment in online communities: Applying theories of group identity and interpersonal bonds. *Management Information Systems Quarterly, 36*(3), 841–864. doi:10.2307/41703483

Rose, D., & Meyer, A. (2002). *Teaching Every Student in the Digital Age: Universal Design for Learning*. ASCD.

Rose, D., Meyer, A., & Hitchcock, C. (2005). *The Universally Designed Classroom: Accessible Curriculum and Digital Technologies*. Harvard Education Press.

Rose, R., & Doveston, M. (2015). Collaboration across cultures: Planning and delivering professional development for inclusive education in India. *Support for Learning. Special Issue: Themes and Perspectives from India, 30*(3), 177–191.

Satar, A. A. (2019). Innovative Strategies for Creating Inclusive Spaces for Hearing-Impaired and Visually Impaired Students in an Open Distance And e-Learning (ODeL) Environment: A Case Study of the University of South Africa (Unisa). In Strategies for Facilitating Inclusive Campuses in Higher Education: International Perspectives on Equity and Inclusion (Vol. 17, pp. 253-267). Emerald Publishing Limited.

Schultz, D. E., & Peltier, J. J. (2013). Social media's slippery slope: Challenges, opportunities and future research directions. *Journal of Research in Interactive Marketing, 7*(2), 86–99. doi:10.1108/JRIM-12-2012-0054

Sivertzen, A. M., Nilsen, E. R., & Olafsen, A. H. (2013). Employer branding: Employer attractiveness and the use of social media. *Journal of Product and Brand Management, 22*(7), 473–483. doi:10.1108/JPBM-09-2013-0393

Stepaniuk, I. (2019). Inclusive education in Eastern European countries: A current state and future directions. *International Journal of Inclusive Education, 23*(3), 328–352. doi:10.1080/13603116.2018.1430180

Tavares, R., Vieira, R., & Pedro, L. (2021). Mobile app for science education: Designing the learning approach. *Education Sciences, 11*(2), 79. doi:10.3390/educsci11020079

Tench, R., Meng, J., & Moreno, A. (Eds.). (2022). *Strategic communication in a global crisis: National and international responses to the covid-19 pandemic* (1st ed.). Routledge. doi:10.4324/9781003184669

Trainor, K. J., Andzulis, J. M., Rapp, A., & Agnihotri, R. (2014). Social media technology usage and customer relationship performance: A capabilities-based examination of social CRM. *Journal of Business Research, 67*(6), 1201–1208. doi:10.1016/j.jbusres.2013.05.002

Trust, T., Krutka, D. G., & Carpenter, J. P. (2016). "Together we are better": Professional learning networks for teachers. *Computers & Education, 102*, 15–34. doi:10.1016/j.compedu.2016.06.007

Turner, R. (2010). The dawn of a new approach to security. *Computer Fraud & Security, 15*(4), 15–17. doi:10.1016/S1361-3723(10)70040-3

UNESCO. (1990). World declaration on education for all and framework for action to meet basic learning needs. Adopted at *World Conference on Education for All: Meeting Basic Learning Needs*. UNESCO.

UNESCO. (1994). The Salamanca statement and framework for action on special education needs. Adopted at *World Conference on Special Education Needs: Access and Quality*. UNESCO.

UNESCO. (2000). Dakar framework for action. Adopted at *World Education Forum*, Dakar, Senegal. UNESCO.

International Collaboratory for Leading Universally Designed Education

UNESCO. (2009). *Policy guidelines on inclusion in education*. UNESCO.

UNESCO. (2020). *Global education monitoring report 2020: Inclusion and education: All means all*. UNESCO. https://unesdoc.unesco. org/ark:/48223/pf0000373718

United Nations. (2006). *Convention on the rights of persons with disabilities*. UN. https://www.un.org/disabilities/documents/convention/Convoptprot-e.pdf

United Nations. (2016). *General comment No. 4 on the right to inclusive education. Committee on the Rights of Persons with Disabilities*. United Nations.

United Nations. (2022). *United Nations Sustainable Goals*. UN. https://www.un.org/sustainabledevelopment/sustainable-development-goals/

Wilcox, G., Fernandez, C. C., & Kowbel, A. (2021). Using evidence-based practice and data-based decision making in inclusive education. *Education Sciences, 11*(129), 129. doi:10.3390/educsci11030129

Wright, D. K., & Hinson, M. (2009). Examining how public relations practitioners actually are using social media. *The Public Relations Journal, 3*(3). https://www.prsa.org/

Zhou, T., Lu, Y., & Wang, B. (2009). The Relative Importance of Website Design Quality and Service Quality in Determining Consumers' Online Repurchase Behavior. *Information Systems Management, 26*(4), 327–337. doi:10.1080/10580530903245663

KEY TERMS AND DEFINITIONS

Accessibility: The nature of being able to be reached or obtained or easily used; commonly associated with quality services for those with disabilities.

CAST: The educational organization responsible for the development of the Universal Design for Learning principles and framework, located in Wakefield, Massachusetts, USA.

Collaboratory: A professional learning center without walls; an organization of researchers connecting and interacting together digitally across location barriers in order to work, learn and grow together by sharing information, skills and resources.

Differentiated Instruction: The process by which the instruction is tailored to meet the needs of the learner in a variety of ways.

Diversity: Variety and/or variability; in relation to people, involving a variation and/or range of differing factors such a societal, economic, ethnicity, race, gender, ability, etc.

Equity: Involves achieving fairness and justice for all; equity is not the *same* for all, but recognizes the need for adjustments to reduce barriers and achieve balance.

Inclusion: The state of being part of a group with equal access to opportunities and resources.

Inclusive Education: When all students can access, participate in, and benefit from equal opportunities in general education classrooms, regardless of their varying needs and abilities.

Learner Voice: Including the learner's voice in the co-creation, development and implementation of learning plans, policies, and pathways.

Professional Development: Taking part in continuing education and career training after entering the workforce to develop new skills and keep up-to-date in a profession.

Social Media: a means by which people interact to create, share, and exchange information and ideas in virtual communities such as websites and other applications.

Universal Design for Learning (UDL): A framework of principles and guidelines that addresses varied learning needs and differences by increasing flexibility and choice, thereby reducing access and participation barriers through variable curriculum design.

Universal Design: A set of principles guiding the design of physical spaces, products, and environments to be accessible to all people, regardless of age, disability, or other factors.

Chapter 2
Universal Design for Learning:
Accessible Learning Environments and School Development

Mette Molbæk
VIA University College, Denmark

Lotte Hedegaard-Sørensen
Aarhus University, Denmark

ABSTRACT

This chapter presents the use of universal design for learning as a means to understand and develop more accessible and inclusive practices in Danish schools. The chapter sets the scene by highlighting the influence of global and local policies on inclusive and exclusive practices in schools. From this point of departure, the chapter outlines the universal design for learning framework as an educational strategy for implementing inclusive education. Based on two research projects, it is shown how the framework can contribute to bringing a new direction to understanding and working with inclusion, while also developing a teaching practice that helps overcome some of the dilemmas that teachers experience in their daily practice in classrooms. The chapter also presents perspectives on how universal design for learning can be part of and support development in a whole-school approach.

INTRODUCTION

This chapter presents two different research projects that illustrate how universal design for learning, as an overall framework, can contribute to the development of flexible and accessible learning environments.

The first project illustrates how the framework has been part of a municipality's approach to developing teachers' competence in relation to creating dyslexia-friendly learning environments.

The second project illustrates how working systematically with students to develop teaching practices can result in greater student engagement while also increasing teachers' knowledge about individual students' interests, prerequisites and potential.

DOI: 10.4018/978-1-6684-7370-2.ch002

Copyright © 2023, IGI Global. Copying or distributing in print or electronic forms without written permission of IGI Global is prohibited.

The two projects contribute to further understanding of the implementation in practice of 'the why,' 'the what,' and 'the how' of universal design for learning.

BACKGROUND

Roger Slee stated that *Inclusion isn't dead, it just smells* funny (Slee, 2019). Inclusion, as it is stated in the Salamanca Statements, implies that *government must give the highest policy and budgetary priority to improve education service so that all children could be included* (UNESCO, 1994). Inclusion points to the need for a reform (Ainscow, 2020) of the entire school system, and this involves changes in terms of organisation, culture and the level of teaching.

Magnússon et al. (2019) argues that inclusive education as a policy phenomenon contains a range of ideas about the purpose and content of education and, furthermore, that the agenda of inclusion is competing with other political ideals regarding education, such as the agendas of accountability, testing and learning outcomes. Nordic research on inclusive education (Ensig & Johnstone, 2015; Köpfer & Oskarsdottir, 2019; Magnusson et al., 2019; Molbaek, 2018) has found that the Nordic education model (as a part of the social democratic welfare state) is challenged by transnational education policy with a focus on accountability and competition. Ensig & Johnstone (2015) analysed the paradoxical inclusive policy in Denmark, which legislated for both inclusive education (2010 and 2012) and increased learning outcome (supported by national tests measuring the same subjects as PISA). Thus, Engsig and Johnstone (2015) argue that the inclusion discourse in Denmark lies 'on a continuum that ranges from Salamanca-inspired, equity-focused inclusion to a more US-inspired, accountability-focused inclusion' (Engsig & Johnstone, 2015). In Danish ethnographic classroom research, the consequences of this policy are in focus. It has been found that although achievement and inclusion should be equally prioritised, teachers are focusing on achievement as their primary professional goal, and by doing so, they are promoting exclusion, albeit maybe not intentionally. The consequences of the neoliberal discourse on competitive individualism and the implementation of performance testing are focuses of subject teaching, whole-class teaching and teacher-controlled teaching—in sum, a more traditional form of teaching. This kind of teaching, as has been found in ethnographic research, is leading to increased exclusion, unequal opportunities and less democratic participation (Hedegaard-Soerensen & Penthin Grumloese, 2018). Similar research results have been found in Iceland (Gunnþórsdóttir & Bjarnason, 2014; Gunnþórsdóttir & Jóhannesson, 2014).

Universal design for learning and its principles (Rose and Meyer, 2002), as is argued in this chapter, can support the development of student-centred and inclusive teaching by taking into account that students have different prerequisites, interests, areas of potential and backgrounds. Thus, universal design for learning can support the development of teaching practices in diverse classrooms, and this is what is understood as inclusive education. Thus, the universal design for learning framework created by CAST (2018) can support the development of a teaching practice that in turn supports the ambition of a learning outcome for all; at the same time, it addresses and contradicts the more exclusionary processes.

MAIN FOCUS OF THE CHAPTER

This chapter focuses on the level of teaching and thus suggests that if the political ambition of implementing and developing an inclusive learning environment is to smell better, a focus on the link between

Universal Design for Learning

teaching (subject teaching in practice) and inclusion is needed (Hedegaard-Sørensen, 2021, 2022; Molbaek, 2018). This focus on both inclusion and subject teaching in practice was included in two research reviews on inclusive education (Hedegaard-Sørensen, 2021, 2022). In the process of searching for studies it became clear, that studies with this combination of inclusion and subject teaching are infrequent – in a very comprehensive research field of inclusive education.

This can explain one aspect of the funny smell of inclusive education. If the didactic dimension is not a part of the discussion about inclusion (in theories, research and teacher education), the challenges that teachers are confronted with in the classroom will not be part of the discussion. Inclusive education takes place definitively in classrooms during subject teaching, and the challenge for teachers is to create access for all.

Universal design for learning can contribute to connecting subject teaching with inclusion, and it needs to be discussed at a definitive level so as not to leave the discussion on teaching/didactics and inclusion at the level of attitudes and ideologies (Avramidis & Norwich, 2010). Furthermore, universal design for learning can contribute to the development of schools and teaching practices that live up to the Salamanca Statement's vision of improving education services so that all children are included. Göransson and Nilholm (2014) identified the following four different understandings of inclusive education: (1) inclusion as the placement of pupils with disabilities in mainstream classrooms, (2) inclusion as meeting the social/academic needs of pupils with disabilities, (3) inclusion as meeting the social/academic needs of all pupils and (4) inclusion as the creation of communities (Göransson & Nilholm, 2014). Universal design for learning can support the development of schools and teaching practices so that they consider the differences between students (e.g. some have disabilities), and the goal for such development is that schools and teaching practices meet both the social and the academic needs of all.

WHY IS UNIVERSAL DESIGN FOR LEARNING NEEDED IN DENMARK?

A common and major international change that has affected the way teachers provide students with opportunities to participate in education is the policy of inclusion, which was clearly formulated in the Salamanca Declaration of 1994. Thus, for almost three decades, the right of all students to be taught together with their peers in general education classes in 'a school for all' has been the basic principle for all teachers in the 92 countries that signed the declaration. Several actions have been taken to support and develop more inclusive schools in Denmark. Through the Inclusion Law (2012), Special Education Law (2013), Reform of the Public School (2014) and the Day Care Law (2018), practice and legislation focusing on special education needs (SEN) and inclusion have been rethought over the last decade.

This implies that in Denmark, the development of inclusive environments has been highly prioritised at both higher government and lower municipal levels and in the field of pedagogical and didactic practices in day care, pre-school and primary schools. In practice, among its consequences has been a rise in the number of resource consultants supporting teachers with specialist educational knowledge and practices. This means that working with and knowledge about SEN are often delegated to other professions to support teachers in schools. This system of support is traditionally organised in the form of meetings with various kinds of professionals who analyse and decide adequate actions to support all students' participation. As a result of this practice, a division between teachers has emerged. Teachers primarily focus on students' learning outcome, and consultants/special education teachers focus primarily on students' overall well-being. This way of distributing different tasks when supporting student learning results in a lack of attention towards the dynamics and relations between students' learning outcome and opportunities to participate in the learning environment. Also, the division of tasks to support students' opportunities to participate has implied a rise in the number of professionals needed to see and understand the full picture of a student's needs.

Seen in this light, there is a need for a more common understanding of and focus on collaboration between professionals in schools if the ambition of having more inclusive schools is to be delivered. Here, the principles behind universal design for learning have something important to offer. Universal design for learning can offer an overall understanding of good and inclusive teaching at a more definitive level and as something that has close links to the practice of teaching. The framework can offer teachers and teams including other professionals (e.g. educational psychologists, pedagogues and special needs educators/inclusion counsellors) focused didactic points of attention that can support the development of teaching practices in classrooms—a development that focuses on accessibility to classroom activities for different students.

Danish research on collaboration has emphasised that teachers' practice produces processes of both inclusion and exclusion (Hansen et al., 2020). This underlines the need for a focus on and discussion of teachers' actual practice as well as choices in their daily classroom practice and in the processes of planning teaching. Thus, it becomes important in both the initial training and the further education of teachers to stress the crucial importance of planning for diversity by offering different ways to achieve engagement, perception and action. Here, universal design for learning supports an ongoing curiosity about how inclusion and teaching can be connected so that all children's access to learning is ensured. The research reviews on inclusion and exclusion processes in teaching mentioned earlier (Hedegaard-Sørensen, 2021, 2022) underpin this need for connecting professionals and professional perspectives, rather than there being division between those professionals working on learning outcomes and those on well-being and inclusion. Teachers and other professionals can collaborate on developing a practice of teaching that is student-centred and takes into account that different students require different learning and teaching arrangements. In addition, all students need common professional strategies for building classroom environments that support well-being and student engagement. Overall, the Danish field of schooling needs, as the reviews have supported, a break with the one-size-fits-all approach to teaching, as it is exclusionary.

Often, teachers experience dilemmas about how to support both individual students and groups of students as a whole. Here, universal design for learning offers a framework and a way of thinking that makes it possible to create teaching that is flexibly adapted and adjusted in relation to students' various prerequisites, interests, areas of potential and needs. This means that it is a way of teaching—and not least of preparing for teaching—that takes students' differences into account from the outset without the need to make individual teaching and action plans.

Thus, universal design for learning may provide answers to the following questions:

- How do we treat children differently without stigmatising some as unsuitable or for not participating?
- How do we plan without having to make individual plans for each student?
- How do we ensure different ways of learning and participating in education?
- How do we create learning environments that support students' own agency and motivation for learning and education?

Universal Design for Learning

Universal design for learning offers a framework for teaching and the development of teaching that both supports a learning environment that is good for all students and ensures that there is a focus on some of the didactic techniques that can be absolutely crucial for a few students (Hargreaves & Braun, 2021). As a set of basic principles, universal design for learning is not a specific method but a framework that supports the development of teaching that brings together inclusion, learning, learning environment and specialist pedagogy to a greater extent, thus supporting a social model of disability. In concrete terms, this means that teachers' professional attention to inclusion (ensuring all children's access and participation) and to children acquiring knowledge in different subjects at school are not seen as two different things.

All children have the right to participate and learn within the social and academic communities in local schools. This requires teaching based on children's various interests and potentials (personal preferences. talents and curiosities), backgrounds (culture and socio-economic position) and needs (functional impairments and learning difficulties).

UNIVERSAL DESIGN FOR LEARNING AS A LYNCHPIN IN THE DEVELOPMENT OF INCLUSIVE PRACTICE

In the following sections, two different projects are presented to show how the universal design for learning framework has been used to both understand and facilitate the development of school practices with the aim of achieving more inclusive and flexible learning environments.

Through the examples from two different research studies, it is shown how teachers and supervisors can use universal design for learning to break out of a one-size-fits-all approach to teaching. From them, it becomes clear how important it is to begin with teaching planning that takes children's differences into account as a starting point and which aims to make teaching so flexible that these differences are accommodated.

In the following two sections, the focus and framework of the different projects are presented, and it is then shown how universal design for learning can be used in very different ways to both identify and qualify teachers' work in creating more flexible, and thus inclusive, learning environments. The aim of the examples is both to specify how universal design for learning can be used to understand and develop more inclusive learning environments and to show the extent to which it can be used.

Universal Design for Learning as A Framework for The Development of Dyslexia-Friendly Learning Environments

In the first project, universal design for learning was part of the framework used by a municipality to develop teachers' competence in relation to creating a dyslexia-friendly learning environment. There was thus a focus on the challenges of a certain student group and the barriers that group faced in terms of participating. There was also a desire to identify how to create the best conditions for this group's participation in teaching, in terms of providing multiple ways of engagement, representation and action and expression.

Often, dyslexic students experience challenges in accessing information that other students easily gather. They face barriers to gaining access to knowledge, for example, if there is no opportunity to listen to a text instead of reading it. Similarly, it becomes difficult for dyslexic students to express themselves if they are part of a learning environment in which they are only meant to do so in writing. These barriers will of course also affect the students' engagement and motivation to participate in lessons and their own learning processes. In addition, working with students' motivation and commitment is also an important part of working in and for a dyslexia-friendly learning environment. Being dyslexic requires extra effort, and thus extra commitment. It is therefore particularly important that teachers are aware of how they can support students' engagement and motivation when compensatory IT equipment is to be used to enable work with impressions and expression.

Based on knowledge about dyslectic students' barriers to learning and participating, the teachers initially participated in a course focusing on both specific assistive technologies supporting dyslexic students' opportunities to participate and how the overall learning environment could be organised to support a dyslexic-friendly setting in the classroom. At the beginning of the course, the universal design for learning principles and guidelines were presented and used to zoom in on specific elements that would support multiple means of engagement, representation and expression regarding specifically the group of dyslexic students. Also, universal design for learning was presented as an overall didactic framework to discuss how all children in the classroom could be supported.

During the course, the teachers learned, discussed and tested how different assistive technologies could be a (more) natural and commonly practiced part of teaching and learning. Here, universal design for learning was used to frame the discussions and evaluations, and the educators asked the teachers to discuss specific questions related to dyslexic students' needs for them to participate.

Figure 1 shows selected examples of how the universal design for learning framework from CAST (2018) was used in the teachers and teams' work when they focused on dyslexic students.

Universal Design for Learning

Figure 1. Example of how the universal design for learning framework from CAST (2018) was used to develop more dyslexia-friendly learning environments

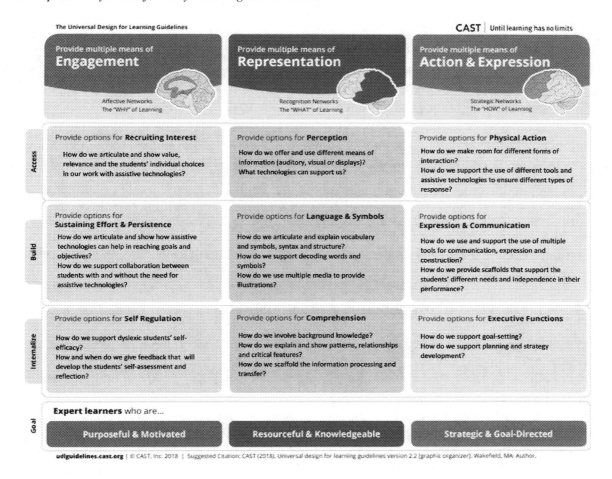

As shown in Figure 1, the universal design for learning template with the guidelines was used to select specific questions related to teaching dyslectic students. Also, it was decided to formulate specific questions to the teachers with the aim of facilitating discussions on the development of their daily practice in their classrooms. Finally, the notion of taking 'baby steps' was underpinned (Murawsky & Scott, 2019), as was the importance of focusing on one principle during a period at the beginning.

Later in the course, the researchers observed the teachers' practices in the classroom. Here, the above template was used to both structure the observations and analyse them. When using the universal design for learning framework as a way of mapping the teachers' work with dyslexic-friendly settings in the classroom, it became clear that the teachers had very different understandings and practices regarding supporting dyslectic students' opportunities to participate, even though they had all taken part in the course. As a teacher said in the evaluating interview *there are still some who have not fully understood the extent*. This led to a discussion on how to ensure that teacher training would actually result in new forms of practice in the classrooms.

In the evaluation interview, the teachers stated that the presented universal design for learning framework supported both their understanding of and practice in a dyslexic-friendly setting and that it also made it easier to create a setting taking all students needs into account. As a teacher said *we have all become more aware that it is not only the dyslexic who have to have it in a different way*

Also, the common framework facilitated dialogues with colleagues about teaching and learning students' opportunities. At the same time, they specified that these discussions and reflections about their didactic choices before, during and after their teaching should be prioritised and framed even more in an organisational setting. Also, it was a central point that the teachers would ask for more feedback on their own learning processes - feedback that should be very close to their daily practice.

When looking back at the project and how the teachers worked with the universal design for learning principles and developed dyslexia-friendly learning environments, it becomes clear that the overall school culture and the teachers' opportunities to attain support and guidance were crucial. At some schools, the teachers worked alone, which resulted in them becoming frustrated with both not getting sufficient help and there being uncertainty towards the expectations for their own and the students' results. At schools where the local reading and writing consultant took the role of the local project leader, the teachers met and both discussed and tried out different ways of supporting a more flexible and thus differentiated learning environment.

Student Engagement Through Increased Influence

The second project zooms in on 'the why' in the universal design for learning framework, and thus on the relation between students' engagement and their influence on teaching. From research on students' influence on teaching, working methods, for example, are closely linked to students' engagement and participation in classroom activities (Hedegaard-Sørensen & Penthin Grumloese, 2020; Tangen, 2009; Ulvseth et al., 2017). 'Being involved in' and 'being listened to' what is going on in school is crucial to students' feelings of belonging and engagement. The relation between influence and engagement was examined in the Erasmus+ 'Reaching the hard to reach' project (2017–2020) (Hedegaard-Sørensen & Penthin Grumloese, 2020), an EU-funded research and innovation project in which five countries established collaborations on education between children and teachers (Messiou & Ainscow, 2020). The overall aim was to improve the practice of teaching and to develop more inclusive learning environments in which every child could participate, develop and learn. The research project focused on children's involvement as researchers in the planning and adjustment of teaching practices. In each of the five countries, six schools participated using a new approach called 'inclusive inquiry', which drew on the 'organisational paradigm' (Clark et al. 1995) and focused on features within schools that facilitated responses to diversity or posed barriers to participation for some pupils. Furthermore, the methodology aimed to produce evidence that could create a space for rethinking by interrupting the existing discourses of teachers. The main question concerned whether children could be involved in teaching planning in such a way that the engagement of and participation by all students would be increased.

The overall finding from the study was that working with students' involvement and 'engagement' creates a desire to learn. In addition, it can help students to get to know themselves better as learners, while the teachers get to know the students better as learners. It is a crucial prerequisite for teachers to acquire the knowledge necessary to be able to adapt the what and the how of learning to different students.

In the Erasmus+ project, a group of children were selected (three from each class) to work closely with teachers to develop the teaching. The children taking part were between the ages of 9 and 11. Based

Universal Design for Learning

on all the students' statements about different dimensions of the teaching, the children were involved in collaborating with teachers to organise, observe and evaluate the teaching. This enabled an exploration of what happens when students have significant influence on the planning of teaching and when teachers are 'forced' to listen to the children's contributions. This placed the teacher's attention more on how children can contribute knowledge from the classroom in the planning of teaching. One teacher from the Erasmus+ project said: 'As a teacher, I have learned that the children's observations are razor sharp. They see much more than we ourselves do in the lesson.'

As an example of a collaboration on teaching development between students and teachers, the pupils and their teacher chose to focus on working together in pairs and on movement and variety in the teaching. In planning a lesson, the students and teacher discussed the advantages and disadvantages of working with best friends. The students put into words that not everyone works equally well in this way, and that a best friend is not necessarily the best partner. Another discussion focused on how important it is to be physically active during the day and in lessons and how teaching could include more outdoor and indoor activities, whereby the students could have multiple means of action when learning about a specific topic.

In the Erasmus+ project, the children pointed to the following needs:

- To be active.
- For variation in forms, methods and materials.
- For technology to be included in teaching.
- For the degree of difficulty of the teaching content to be appropriate (the students differed here).
- For working with the right people in group work (not with a best friend, but also not with someone who is very different).
- Not to sit in a chair for too long (movement).
- For the teacher not to talk too much.

In the work on supporting student engagement, universal design for learning invited teaching in all its phases (planning, implementation and evaluation) to be adapted and organised flexibly based on children's different backgrounds, assumptions and interests. In this project, the teachers' work to support 'the why' of learning was in focus. Giving students the opportunity to engage in the planning and evaluation of teaching – systematically – can increase their engagement and participation in classrooms. In addition, working with a broader, deeper knowledge of the children's backgrounds, interests and prerequisites can form an important starting point for each of 'the why' (engagement), 'the what' (representation) and 'the how' (action and expression) of learning. Thus, an initial comprehensive focus on 'the why' of learning could be a good starting point for working with and developing other sub-elements of the universal design for learning framework, since the individual elements of the framework are mutually dependent.

Data from the inclusive inquiries conducted in the six Danish schools indicated that collaborating with children on the practice of teaching could expand and support all pupils' participation (inclusion) and achievement (learning outcome) by having more children and teachers discover the diversity of children in new ways. The findings of previous research (Hedegaard-Soerensen & Penthin Grumloese, 2018) have indicated that Danish teachers are preoccupied with subject teaching and whole-class teaching, rather than with differentiated teaching. They endeavour to reach out to most of the children but not all of them. Differentiated and inclusive teaching is simply not part of their teaching practice. During inclusive inquiries, the teachers' professional perspective changed; they realised the diversity of the children (their different outsets for being engaged), and they obtained new perspectives on some of them (sometimes contradicting negative expectations).

The following is an empirical example from the hub school in the ReHaRe-project. It illustrates how engaging students in dialogues about teaching should look like, if the above-mentioned benefits is in focus:

Student 1: Maybe some of us will finish before time, and then it will be boring. Maybe we could get another assignment. It should not be a reward; if it's a reward, then we just choose to work with an easy animal, and then we don't really learn anything, since we don't work with it properly.

Teacher: What can we do about it?

Student 1: Perhaps we could have more tasks to choose from. For example, when you have finished your task, you must draw an animal.

Teacher: So, it would be nice to vary between investigating, drawing, writing and presenting knowledge?

Student 1: Yes.

Student 2: It would be like another lesson I remember. We worked together in pairs, and we had to draw animals and get information about the animals. Then we had to do a lot of fun things.

Student 1: If we had planned the lesson differently, no one would have been noisy or disruptive.

Teacher: How should the lesson be changed or improved? What do you suggest?

The students in the above dialogue were being listened to, and their suggestions for adjusting lessons were being taken seriously. This is how students' involvement should look like, since it would increase their engagement and participation. The message is not that the students must be responsible for the teaching and learning process but that they should be offered influence and given the opportunity and space to be active and self-organised within certain frameworks that teachers and other professionals have set. The project found that it actually makes teaching better when students and teachers collaborate on the teaching. Also, students get more out of the teaching when they help set the agenda, and it became clear that students can to a very large extent contribute with productive ideas on how lessons can be planned to meet their need for multiple means of engagement, representation and expression.

Furthermore, it was found that students who are otherwise labelled as 'hard to reach' will gain the courage to participate and believe in themselves when they are given influence and listened to. When children have influence on their teaching, they gain ownership and the desire and courage to participate in lessons. As a teacher pointed out after a joint reflection: *'It's fun to hear what the children think about the teaching, and what the children say is so meaningful. It's so cool to see what happens when children experience being taken seriously.'*

Universal Design for Learning

UNIVERSAL DESIGN FOR LEARNING AS PART OF DAILY PRACTICE AND SCHOOL CULTURE

Based on existing international research and the experiences with universal design for learning from the two research projects mentioned earlier, this section outlines some possible ways to work with the framework. The purpose of this section is partly to summarise some of the points about the applicability of universal design for learning at both the school and classroom level and partly to highlight how schools can support work with and collaboration on it.

Supporting Inclusion in Teachers' Daily Practice

From the work with and research on universal design for learning, it becomes clear that the framework supports the planning of more flexible and thus inclusive learning environments. In addition, the universal design for learning framework can builds bridges across the professional attention in classrooms toward inclusion and teaching and thus can form an outset for interdisciplinary collaboration. In other words, the framework can constitute the concrete and daily content of inclusive education and of collaboration about creating inclusive learning environments.

The universal design for learning principles and checkpoints support and supplement the traditional core concepts in relation to teaching and learning. In this way, universal design for learning both connects with teachers' daily practice in the classroom and expands their own and their students' opportunities to make a school for all by taking a dynamic view on how the subjects, objectives and methods are intertwined with the students' needs and interests. Thus, universal design for learning can teach us about the very important insight: Inclusive education is not about some students, it is about all students and their different engagements in classroom activities.

In one of the early books on universal design for learning, Meyer et al. (2014) showed how teachers can use the framework for understanding central didactic concepts, such as goals, evaluation, methods and materials, thereby connecting the universal design for learning approach with teachers' ongoing and daily reflections. The professional attention to all students in all the phases of teaching is what teachers are reflecting about – alone and together in professional learning environments.

When one looks at learning objectives through a universal design for learning optic, it is important, among other things, to formulating the goals for the subject in such a way that separates them from the means to support opportunities to solve tasks in different ways. Furthermore, one must consider each of the areas of engagement, representation and expression to ensure that students' both are motivated and acquire new knowledge through representation and expression. Finally, it becomes crucial to set goals so that every student is challenged optimally, which can be facilitated through student involvement and by talking to students about the goals and the way their learning outcomes are evaluated.

In relation to the choice of methods and materials, it is important to work with different methods that can support students' different ways of working with a subject. This can be done, among other things, through variations in teaching methods, giving students the opportunity to choose their own method and offering different materials for both representation and expression (e.g. printed texts, digital texts, film or sound).

When it comes to supporting students' engagement (cf. the universal design for learning framework), it becomes important to offer students choices of content and tools, different levels of difficulty and different places for learning.

To support students' learning through multiple means of representation (cf. the universal design for learning framework), it is important that students see different examples that incorporate various media (e.g. photos, sound or writing). Here, it also becomes central that the teacher should actively connect the content and the learning objectives to the surrounding society and context and thus emphasise what is most important.

In relation to supporting the students' expression (cf. the universal design for learning framework), it is key to give students the opportunity to work with materials in various ways to support different ways of expressing themselves. It is also important to work with ongoing and definitive feedback in relation to their learning outcomes and processes.

Rose and Meyer (2002) pointed out that the traditional way of evaluating students' outcomes can be both unfair and wrong. Thus, an assessment of a student's work and results can be misleading if only specific ways of approaching the material, working with it and expressing oneself are planned.

If the universal design for learning principles are used as a starting point for the way in which students' learning is evaluated, more ways will be created to assess the student's work, which can provide a more accurate and comprehensive picture of their competences. In continuation of the above, evaluation from a universal design for learning perspective must be understood as an ongoing process that focuses on the student's progress in relation to set goals, an assessment of both learning outcomes and the learning process and help for the teacher, who is given the opportunity to adjust the teaching based on new information.

There are several factors that justify the need to work with different ways of evaluation. Since all students are different, a standardised assessment is therefore not able to capture a student's knowledge and progression if it is not considered which forms of evaluation are most suitable when assessing students' ways of learning.

Universal Design for Learning as Part of Co-Teaching and Professional Learning Communities

Universal design for learning can be a central point of departure and a framework in both co-teaching and professional learning communities where teachers, students and other professionals plan, implement and evaluate teaching with a focus on how multiple means of engagement, representation and expression are developed. Here, the framework contributes to a common look at the didactics behind inclusive learning environments and supports the joint development of inclusive education. Universal design for learning can become a common starting point in collaboration between professionals. This can advantageously be organised with inspiration from action learning or professional learning communities, where professionals meet and work on a specific focus related to their teaching and the students' learning. In the selection and planning of actions that can support the work goals, the universal design for learning framework and its sub-elements can be used to help open up new possibilities for action for both students and teachers. When a team, for example, selects a sub-element from the framework for closer focus, the framework can be used in observations of whether the initiated changes lead to the desired result and/or whether other important conditions and changes are observed in other parts of the model that can contribute to the desired development.

Finally, the framework can be an important tool in the team's analyses and subsequent decisions on new actions, as it can both support a common didactic focus and at the same time offer a flexible view on relations and sub-elements in teaching that support students' participation and learning.

Universal Design for Learning

Teachers as Learners

When working with universal design for learning, it is important to stress that teachers themselves are in a process of learning when the framework is a natural part of their daily practice. Thus, working with universal design for learning can be seen by teachers as a journey across a spectrum ranging from universal design for learning explorer to universal design for learning expert (Novak & Rodriguez, 2018). Based on this continuum, either the individual teacher or the team can decide on and reflect upon the level of ambition and not least create a framework for goals and evaluating the work with and collaboration on the universal design for learning framework. The following rubric template (Figure 2) can provide a starting point and help clarify and instil the most important things in relation to the work with students' engagement, representation and actions/expression.

Figure 2. Universal design for learning implementation rubric
(Novak, 2019)

	UDL EXPLORER	UDL NOVICE	UDL INTERMEDIATE	UDL ADVANCED	UDL IDOL
Provide Multiple Means of Engagement	I am aware of the process of providing students with multiple means of engagement and am exploring ways to incorporate it into my practice either through professional development, research, or some classroom application.	My classroom is an environment in which students are directed to share their ideas on their interests as it relates to content, and set goals for their own learning, including reflecting on their progress and achievement of those goals in some lessons, on some days.	My classroom is an environment in which students are encouraged to share how content is relevant and valuable to their own interests, and set goals for their own learning, including reflecting on their progress and achievement of those goals in some lessons, on some days.	My classroom is an environment in which students are encouraged to share how content is relevant and valuable to their own interests, and set goals for their own learning, including reflecting on their progress and achievement of those goals in most lessons, on most days.	My classroom is an environment in which students are empowered to make connections between content and their own interests, and make choices that drive their learning experiences, including consistently setting goals, reflecting on their progress and achievement of those goals, in every lesson, every day.
Provide Multiple Means of Representation	I am aware of the process of providing students with multiple means of representation and am exploring ways to incorporate it into my practice either through professional development, research, or some classroom application.	My classroom is an environment in which students are provided multiple resources and materials to support their learning and build their understanding of concepts in order to achieve the goals of a lesson on some days.	My classroom is an environment in which students are provided multiple resources and materials to support their learning and build their understanding of concepts in order to achieve the goals of a lesson on most days.	My classroom is an environment in which students are encouraged to choose reputable resources and materials to personalize their learning and build their understanding of concepts in order to achieve the goals of a lesson on most days.	My classroom is an environment in which students are empowered to choose reputable resources and materials to personalize their learning and build their understanding of concepts in order to achieve the goals of a lesson every day.
Provide Multiple Means of Action & Expression	I am aware of the process of providing students with multiple means of action and expression and am exploring ways to incorporate it into my practice either through professional development, research, or some classroom application.	My classroom is an environment in which students are provided options that allow them to demonstrate mastery of standards in different ways, and select which devices/technologies they need to demonstrate their knowledge and skills, in some lessons, on some days.	My classroom is an environment in which students are provided options that allow them to demonstrate mastery of standards in different ways, and select which devices/technologies they need to demonstrate their knowledge and skills, in most lessons, on most days.	My classroom is an environment in which students are encouraged to independently create authentic products that allow them to demonstrate mastery of standards, and choose which devices/technologies they need to demonstrate their knowledge and skills, in most lessons, on most days	My classroom is an environment in which students are empowered to independently create authentic products that allow them to demonstrate mastery of the standard, and choose which devices/technologies they need to demonstrate their knowledge and skills, in every lesson, every day.

As mentioned in the project focusing on developing dyslexia-friendly learning environments, the universal design for learning framework can also be used as an observational tool to assess the extent to which teaching supports all students' means of engagement, representation and expression (Basham et al., 2020). For example, a manager, teacher or counsellor can use universal design for learning as a common observational framework that can subsequently form a starting point for analyses and discussions of the observed practice.

One can also use the framework together with students and look for new ways to achieve student engagement, representation and expression. As we see in the project focusing on the involvement of students' views and proposals, students often have very important contributions that can easily be included in daily teaching practice.

When the universal design for learning framework is used as an observation and/or evaluation tool, it can help bring insight into what is successful in terms of creating opportunities for participation for all children. It can also make the teacher more aware of where and how the next changes in teaching can be made, so that increased opportunities for participation are created for the students who still face barriers to participating and learning.

Sustainable Implementation

If universal design for learning is to be a part of teachers' daily practice, it becomes important to draw attention to several aspects surrounding teachers' practice and collaboration (Rose & Meyer, 2002). Thus, a sustainable implementation of the framework requires national and organisational prioritisation and connection to other initiatives.

Firstly, universal design for learning can advantageously be included in teacher training as an example of and a concretisation of how to work with educational differentiation and more flexible learning environments. Here, the framework offers a definitive and clear overview of the central elements related to teaching for diversity and inclusion.

Secondly, there are several attention points that need to be addressed at both the school and the municipality level if universal design for learning is to be a natural and daily practice. Thus, it becomes crucial to do the following:

- Prioritise and support technology and media that can create different paths to representation, expression and engagement.
- Focus on the organisation of teachers' work, which means that teachers also get the opportunity to learn and practice universal design for learning, such as through time for and opportunities to share knowledge and good practice and collaborate with others who are testing universal design for learning.
- Ensure support from managers and resource staff who ensure that universal design for learning is continuously featured in conversations about teaching and as a way of developing teachers' practice.
- Redefine teachers' and other professionals' roles so that teachers and other professionals in both special and general education meet to develop teaching that supports all children's participation.
- Increase cooperation between teachers and resource staff with the aim of creating better ways for representation, expression and engagement through joint planning, development and implementation of the teaching.
- Involve parents, pupils and the local environment using both information about and participation in the work to create more flexible learning environments.

Universal Design for Learning

- Search for alternative ways to create time and resources to work with universal design for learning, such as through foundations and/or opportunities for collaboration with external parties who can contribute to the work with UDL

WHAT IS NEXT IN DENMARK?

In Denmark, differentiated teaching has been a basic principle in all teaching for many years. Even though it is an obligation for all teachers in our schools to provide different opportunities for students to participate in academic activities, teachers are still challenged in relation to providing them with more and better opportunities to participate and learn. Here, universal design for learning offers a very clear and common frame for both reflection on and discussions of how to ensure all students' participation.

Thus, universal design for learning offers and invites the development of both a common language and practice regarding inclusion. Thus, the framework can become a natural next step in the nationwide task of developing more flexible and inclusive schools. Universal design for learning is very novel in Denmark, but based on both international and own research, it seems to be very useful for future work, as it offers a common and applicable focus on how to develop multiple means of engagement, representation and expression.

By letting teachers' actual didactic choices in teaching be the focal point for work with and collaboration on inclusion, the focus is expanded from the challenges and needs of individual students to the didactic actions of professionals. This supports a more contextual view of the potential barriers for inclusion that opens up both more options and a shared responsibility to support all students' ways of learning and participation in social and academic activities.

The potential realised by collaborating on universal design for learning is, among other things, that it will be the actual didactic choices of the professionals that will be the lynchpin for the development of teaching in which more children can participate. The framework offers a common language that can definitely guide teachers and educators in their work and collaboration and which can help keep the focus on changes in the way that teaching is practiced.

Therefore, universal design for learning can also contribute to work on inclusion, co-teaching and flexible forms of organising teaching by (re)thinking teachers' didactic work and collaboration with colleagues as essential to ensure the academic, personal and social development of all students.

However, if the framework is to become a real (collaborative) tool, it will require both teachers and internal and external resources to know about it and find it meaningful to work with the didactic framework as a starting point for the development of inclusive learning environments. Taking this into account, it becomes important to emphasise that the most important thing is not to follow the universal design for learning framework slavishly and to read about it in depth. The most important thing is to get started and try out individual changes and, together with colleagues, investigate and discuss whether these changes will contribute to developing teaching so that students thrive and learn.

In this work, universal design for learning is a framework that creates the development of and flexibility in teaching. As a starting point, focusing on engagement, representation and expression can frame development and collaboration. Here, the students' perspectives are very crucial.

REFERENCES

Ainscow, M. (2020). Promoting inclusion and equity in education: Lessons from international experiences. *Nordic Journal of Studies in Educational Policy*, 6(1), 7–16. doi:10.1080/20020317.2020.1729587

Avramidis, E., & Norwich, B. (2010). Teachers' attitudes towards integration/inclusion: A review of the literature. *European Journal of Special Needs Education*, 17(2), 129–147. doi:10.1080/08856250210129056

Basham, J. D., Gardner, J. E., & Smith, S. J. (2020). Measuring the implementation of UDL in classrooms and schools: Initial field test results. *Remedial and Special Education*, 41(4), 231–243. doi:10.1177/0741932520908015

CAST. (2018). *Universal Design for Learning Guidelines version 2.2*. CAST. http://udlguidelines.cast.org

Clark, C., Dyson, A., Milward, A., & Skidmore, D. (1995). Dialectical analysis, special needs and schools as organisations. In C. Clark, A. Dyson, & A. Milward (Eds.), *Towards inclusive schools*. Fulton.

Ensig, T. T., & Johnstone, C. J. (2014). Is there something rotten in the state of Denmark? The paradoxical policies of inclusive education – Lesson from Denmark. *International Journal of Inclusive Education*, 19(5), 469–486. doi:10.1080/13603116.2014.940068

Göransson, K., & Nilholm, C. (2014). Conceptual diversities and empirical shortcomings – A critical analysis of research on inclusive education. *European Journal of Special Needs Education*, 29(3), 265–280. doi:10.1080/08856257.2014.933545

Hargreaves, A., & Braun, H. (2012). *Leading for all: Final report of the review of the development of essential for some, good for all: Ontario's strategy for special education reform devised by the Council of Directors of Education*. Council of Directors of Education.

Hedegaard-Sørensen, L. (2021). *Inklusion og eksklusion i undervisningen [Inclusion and exclusion in teaching]*. Pædagogisk Indblik, Aarhus Universitet. https://dpu.au.dk/fileadmin/edu/Paedagogisk_Indblik/Inklusio n_og_eksklusion/14_-_Inklusion_og_eksklusion_i_undervisninge n_-_15-12-2021.pdf

Hedegaard-Sørensen, L. (2022). *Inklusion og fag [Inclusion and subjects]*. Pædagogisk Indblik, Aarhus Universitet. https://dpu.au.dk/viden/paedagogiskindblik/inklusion-og-eksk lusion-i-skolen

Hedegaard-Sorensen, L., & Grumløse, S. P. (2018). Exclusion: The downside of neoliberal education policy. *International Journal of Inclusive Education*, 24(6), 631–644. doi:10.1080/13603116.2018.1478002

Hedegaard-Sørensen, L., & Penthin Grumloese, S. (2020). Student-teacher-dialogue for lesson planning: Inclusion in the context of national policy and local culture. *Nordic Journal of Studies in Educational Policy.*, 6(1), 25–36. doi:10.1080/20020317.2020.1747376

Hedegaard-Sørensen, L., Riis-Jensen, C., & Tofteng, D. (2018). Interdisciplinary collaboration as a prerequisite for inclusive education. *European Journal of Special Needs Education*, 33(2), 382–395. do i:10.1080/08856257.2017.1314113

Universal Design for Learning

Köpfer, A., & Óskarsdóttir, E. (2019). Analysing support in inclusive education systems – A comparison of inclusive school development in Iceland and Canada since the 1980s focusing on policy and in-school support. *International Journal of Inclusive Education, 23*(7–8), 876–890. doi:10.1080/13603116.2019.1624844

Magnússon, G., Göransson, K., & Lindqvist, G. (2019). Contextualizing inclusive education in educational policy: The case of Sweden. *Nordic Journal of Studies in Educational Policies, 5*(2), 67–77. doi:10.1080/20020317.2019.1586512

Messiou, K., & Ainscow, M. (2020). Inclusive inquiry: Student-teacher dialogue as a means of promoting inclusion in schools. *British Educational Research Journal, 46*(3), 670–687. doi:10.1002/berj.3602

Meyer, A., Rose, D. H., & Gordon, D. (2014). *Universal Design for Learning: Theory and practice.* CAST.

Molbaek, M. (2018). Inclusive teaching strategies – Dimensions and agendas. *International Journal of Inclusive Education, 22*(10), 1048–1061. doi:10.1080/13603116.2017.1414578

Molbaek, M., & Hedegaard-Sørensen, L. (In press). *Universal Design for Learning – fleksible og tilgængelige læringsmiljøer for alle [Universal design for learning – flexible and accessible learning environments for all].*

Murawski, W., & Scott, K. L. (Eds.). (2019). *What really works with universal design for learning.* Corwin Press.

Novak, K. (2019). *UDL implementation rubric.* Novak Education. https://www.novakeducation.com/blog/udl-implementation-rubric

Novak, K., & Rodriguez, K (2018). *The UDL progression rubric.* CAST.

Rose, D. H., & Meyer, A. (2002). *Teaching every student in the digital age: Universal design for learning.* ASCD.

Slee, R. (2013). How do we make inclusive education happen when exclusion is a political predisposition? *International Journal of Inclusive Education, 17*(8), 895–907. doi:10.1080/13603116.2011.602534

Slee, R. (2019). *Inclusive education isn't dead, it just smells funny.* Routledge.

Slee, R., & Allen, J. (2001). Excluding the included: A reconsideration of inclusive education. *International Studies in Sociology of Education, 1*(2), 173–192. doi:10.1080/09620210100200073

Tangen, R. (2009). Conceptualising quality of school life from pupils' perspectives: A four-dimensional model. *International Journal of Inclusive Education, 13*(8), 829–844. doi:10.1080/13603110802155649

Ulvseth, H., Jørgensen, C., & Tetler, S. (2017). *Elevers engagement i undervisningen – om metoder til inddragelse af alle elevers stemmer* [Pupils' involvement in teaching – About methods for including the voices of all pupils]. Dafolo.

KEY TERMS AND DEFINITIONS

Collaboration: The action of working with someone to produce or do something.

Diversity: The state of being diverse and a practice or quality of including and involving people from a range of different backgrounds and with different needs and orientations.

Flexible learning environments: An approach to teaching in which students' different needs and ways of learning are addressed and taken in account.

Inclusion: The practice or policy of providing equal access to opportunities and resources for people who might otherwise be excluded or marginalised.

Policy: A course or principle of action adopted or proposed by an organisation or individual.

Professional learning communities: A method to foster collaborative learning among colleagues within a particular work environment or field. It is often used in schools as a way to organise teachers into working groups of practice-based professional learning.

School development: A way of strengthening the overall functionality of schools and improving the mechanisms for delivering education in the classroom as well as the broader school environment.

Teaching: Ideas or principles taught by an authority, imparting knowledge to or instructing (someone) as to how to do something.

Chapter 3
Implementing UDL in a University Setting:
Overcoming Barriers One Checkpoint at a Time

Andy Smidt
The University of Sydney, Australia

Isobelle Montague
The University of Sydney, Australia

Tonnette Stanford
The University of Sydney, Australia

Jessica Buhne
The University of Sydney, Australia

Dagmar Kminiak
The University of Sydney, Australia

ABSTRACT

UDL principles are not consistently applied in the tertiary sector in Australia and appear infrequently in government policies. There is limited research about UDL in Australia and few studies that describe the challenges in implementing UDL across a whole tertiary institution. In this chapter the authors present an approach taken at the University of Sydney, focusing on supporting academics to understand UDL, identify areas in their own teaching that already use UDL principles, and select one or two new strategies to add to their courses each year. This approach starts with an acknowledgement that change is challenging, and that change can be incremental rather than requiring a whole course review to embed UDL principles. The authors identified institution-specific levels to support academics to choose strategies that would be relatively easy to implement. To date, teaching staff who have used these resources have found them valuable.

DOI: 10.4018/978-1-6684-7370-2.ch003

Copyright © 2023, IGI Global. Copying or distributing in print or electronic forms without written permission of IGI Global is prohibited.

INTRODUCTION

Universal Design for Learning (UDL)is a framework for designing educational experiences that are accessible and effective for all students, including those with disabilities and diverse learning needs. It is, however relatively underused in the higher education sector (Fovet, 2020a). In the Australian context, a recent scoping review (Jwad et al., 2022) noted that UDL principles are not consistently applied in the tertiary sector. Jwad et al., reported that UDL appears infrequently in Government policies and few articles have been published. The articles that are available about UDL in the Australian Higher Education (HE) sector are from researchers about individual courses (For example Garrad & Nolan, 2022; Hitch et al., 2019; Pitman, 2022) and are not yet describing the process of implementing UDL at an institutional level. Jwad et al. (2022) recommended that, in Australian universities, training in UDL should be a requirement for instructors involved in course design tailored to the institution. They also recommend that educators and learning designers share and document learnings for continued improvement of the implementation of UDL.

In this chapter we will describe the approach taken at the University of Sydney to support educators to embed UDL in their teaching. The reader will learn about UDL in the higher education sector specifically in Australia and how we chose to create resources for educators at our university.

BACKGROUND

UDL in Higher Education

The Universal Design for Learning framework and Guidelines were developed by the Centre for Applied Special Technology, now named, and recognized globally as CAST (CAST, 2018). CAST was initially founded in 1984 to explore ways of using new technologies to enable students with disabilities access to better educational experiences (CAST, 2022). Over time, as CAST researchers tested and refined their principles, priorities, and vision, they came to a new understanding of how to improve education for all learners using flexible methods and materials, through the approach of Universal Design for Learning. This includes the current 9 guidelines and 31 checkpoints which can be used to improve teaching and learning for all people, and which is based on scientific insights into how humans learns (CAST, 2018) Whilst variations in the definition of UDL exists, it is clear. In higher education, UDL is used to create inclusive learning environments that support the success of all students, regardless of their background, learning style, or ability (Black et al., 2014; Cumming & Rose, 2022; Jwad et al., 2022).

Internationally, Universal Design for Learning has been specified in public policies, such as the Higher Education Opportunity Act of 2008, which was the first federal legislation to define and endorse UDL in the USA (Cast, 2018). Other examples of UDL in Higher Education includes the framework published by the Taylor Institute for Teaching and Learning at Calgary University Canada (Jwad et al., 2022).

Fovet (2020a) observed that in the last decade of UDL in higher education across North America, institutions tended to work in an insular fashion. He described how institutions were intent on 'reinventing the wheel' and demonstrated secrecy and lack of openness to share good UDL practices. It is uncertain as to whether this may be a similar practice in Australia, and hence also contributing to why only few examples of UDL practice at an institute level are published. To open cross institutional learning, Fovet

Implementing UDL in a University Setting

(2020a) recommended the need for rich and wide networks to remedy the hindrance to the overall development of UDL at national and international levels.

Although UDL is valuable to plan inclusive teaching, there will always be students who need individual adjustments for example students with hearing loss may need sign language interpreters. The modifications to include captions during lectures may not be sufficient for a student with a hearing loss to participate in live activities or presentations. UDL will bridge that gap to some extent but individual adjustments will still be required by some.

UDL in Higher Education in Australia

In Australia, the Department of Education releases student equity and other data relating to enrolments and completions of all approved Australian Higher Education Institutions (Australian Government, 2022). The number of students with self-reported disability has grown steadily over recent years (Kilpatrick et al., 2017). In 2019, students with disability represented 7.7% of enrolments, an increase in comparison to 5.8% in 2014 (Koshy, 2020). Students with disabilities are recorded to have the fastest rate of growth amongst the six recognized equity groups in Australian higher education (non-English speaking backgrounds, women in non- traditional areas, indigenous, low socio-economic status, regional and remote locations, and disability). However, despite the growing numbers of students with a disability accessing higher education, meeting the needs of learner diversity is not yet fully articulated at a national level in Australian Government policy. The Scoping Review (Jwad et al., 2022) identified that references to UDL appeared in only a small number of policies and tertiary (both higher education and vocational education and training) institute websites. This was likely attributed to lack of Government reinforcement and the manner in which UDL in the tertiary sector has been slowly implemented. Whilst some examples of the UDL approach in higher education in Australia have been published, only few examples of applying UDL at an institute level were located through the Scoping Review.

To increase UDL application in Australia, work was undertaken through the Australian Disability Clearinghouse Education and Training (ADCET)(n.d.) and the National Disability Coordination Officer Program (Australian Government, 2020) to increase tertiary sector knowledge of UDL and enhance cross institutional learnings of UDL implementation. Since 2022, Australian tertiary teaching staff can access a freely available Universal Design for Learning in Tertiary Education eLearning resource which provides an overview of the principles and practices of UDL in tertiary settings and aims to support understanding of designing, developing, and implementing UDL into teaching practice (*Disability Awareness*, 2020). In addition, 2022 saw the emergence of a national UDL Community of Practice facilitated by the Australian Disability Clearinghouse on Education and Training. The Community of Practice (Australian Disability Clearinghouse on Education and Training, n.d.) connects tertiary educators, learning designers and practitioners together, with the aim of sharing good practice to inform and improve UDL implementation across the Australian tertiary education sector.

A recent study (O'Donovan et al., in press) examined the perceptions and experiences of higher education teaching staff across Australia to understand participants' previous experiences of UDL and their perceived barriers and facilitators for UDL implementation. The study included both survey and focus group participant feedback with several participants sharing that their institutions have inclusion and equity policies embedded in their values, and that the institutions conceptually endorsed UDL, however UDL was not necessarily mentioned in policy. In addition, participants did not know if institutional policy included UDL goals and that a lack of institutional leadership, and commitment to access and inclusion in the university strategy and policy was considered a barrier to the implementation of UDL. Participants in the study also substantiated the value of using Communities of Practice to create a space where UDL experiences can be shared, and where they can receive pedagogical support to apply a UDL lens to course materials, particularly for certain course elements.

In Australia, there have been Disability Standards for Education since 2005 (Ruddock, 2005). These were revised in 2020 and included submissions from the tertiary sector which called for UDL to be reinforced in the Standards to reduce the need for individual adjustments for people with disability and to minimize the need to retrofit accessibility to existing curricula (Jwad et al., 2022). In Australia, there is both growing interest about UDL, as well as increasing opportunities to connect with like-minded individuals to navigate the challenges of UDL implementation, share good practice and learn from colleagues. This is indicated by the engagement of academics and disability practitioners in the national community of practice, as well as availability of resources such as the UDL in Tertiary Education eLearning resource, of which there were 917 course registrations in 2022 (ADCET, 2022). The term academic is used in Australia to describe teaching staff (including professors, lecturers, and tutors). We use this term throughout the rest of the chapter.

UDL as Social Justice

Fovet (2020b) argues that UDL is an approach that focuses on a progressive reform of pedagogical practice. UDL involves designing curricula from the outset that will meet the needs of all learners rather than the costly practices of retrofitting material and providing students with accomodations. However, truly inclusive education can be viewed with a social justice lens as including all students including those from a range of socio-economic backgrounds, cultural groups, age groups and genders (Hockings, 2010). Implementing a curriculum that is designed to be inclusive for all has the potential to impact more than those with a disability and has the potential to impact social justice.

UDL AT THE UNIVERSITY OF [DE-IDENTIFIED]

The University of Sydney

The University of Sydney is a sandstone institution founded in 1850. It is Australia's first university and was founded on two 2 core principles, religious tolerance, and academic merit. The University of Sydney has been regularly ranked in the top 50 Universities, currently sitting at 41st in the world. Based on 2019 enrolments the university has 73,000 students and 8,100 staff from 2018 statistics. There are 380,000 alumni in more than 170 countries.

Disability Services

The University of Sydney is committed to becoming a world-class leader in social and economic participation of people with disability in the life of the University. This is being achieved through a variety of different measures. The principal support for students with a disability is Inclusion and Disability Services (IDS). Registration with IDS provides students with access to academic adjustments designed to offset impacts their registered condition/s may have on their studies.

Implementing UDL in a University Setting

As of 2021 there were 2,249 enrolled domestic students who identified as having a disability but were not utilizing available support. There were 1184 students identified as having a disability and were engaged with support. There are 2367 students registered with IDS at the University of Sydney.

Process of Receiving Disability Supports

Students register with IDS by having their health practitioner complete a form which contains a diagnosis and impact of condition section, followed by sections pertaining to each area of study for students and the health practitioners to detail specific impacts and or difficulties. The student then has a 1:1 consultation in which the impacts of the student's condition on their studies will be discussed in detail and appropriate adjustments will be determined.

After the registration appointment and adjustments have been determined, IDS develops the student's academic plan. This informs teaching staff that the student is registered with IDS and explains what adjustments the student requires and why. The academic plan does not include a diagnosis or other details which are considered private but instead lists the impacts of the condition and the reasonable adjustments required to allow the student to complete the specific course at a similar level to their peers who do not have a disability. A new academic plan is required for every semester. There were 3,853 academic plans in 2022.

The academic plan is sent to our Academic Plan champions. Each faculty has either an individual or a team assigned to this role who are the first point of contact for distributing and implementing the plans amongst relevant teaching staff each semester.

Many adjustments are straightforward for academics to implement, and the academic plan will be the only resource needed. In cases where the recommended adjustment does not easily apply to an assessment task, other support can be provided. IDS staff will regularly liaise with academic staff to work together to find solutions that aim to uphold the academic integrity of the task and allow the student an equitable assessment task option. Each faculty also has a disability liaison officer (DLO) who is an academic. This person typically understands the needs of the academic as well as the student.

Applying adjustments to assessment tasks that are not designed to be altered is not always seamless and does not always result in an ideal outcome for the student or the academic. IDS are therefore involved in championing the implementation of Universal Design for Learning across the University by holding key stakeholder forums every semester. Multiple stakeholder forums have centered around the topic of Universal Design for learning. The most recent forum held during the Universities Disability Inclusion Week was open to all University staff. The forum involved a keynote presentation designed to inform academic staff about UDL and give them the tools to start implementing it in their teaching and course design.

A key component of the University of Sydney's commitment to ensuring the inclusion of people with a disability is the Disability Inclusion Action plan (DIAP). The Disability Inclusion Action Plan 2019-2024 is based on six key objectives that all have specific actions and measurable outcomes. The DIAP is overseen by a consultative group that meets twice every semester to monitor performance and outcomes.

There are UDL specific objectives being:

- 2.2.5 The University Curriculum will demonstrate application of the principles of Universal Design for Learning.

- 2.2.6 The University of Sydney is recognised as a national leader in UDL and well-designed and delivered curriculum.

The university has made a commitment to implementing Universal Design for Learning (UDL) through implementation of the Disability Inclusion Action Plan which aims to embed universal design thinking into daily practice. However, despite this commitment, changing practice is a slow process that involves buy-in from all staff and at all levels.

Despite the commitment of the Disability Inclusion Action Plan and various projects supporting UDL within the university, there remains limited implementation of UDL by academics. Students who register with inclusion and disability services report that in some courses they need to argue for their reasonable adjustments to be implemented and some who prefer not to register to avoid stigma.

Theoretical Framework

We used the Stages-of-Change Model by James Prochaska and Carlo DiClemente (Figure 1)(1986) as our theoretical framework. This model was developed to understand addiction but has been widely used to explain why systemic change is complex. The Stages-of-Change model posits that individuals move through six stages of change: precontemplation, contemplation, preparation, action, maintenance, and termination. The model illustrates that change is difficult and requires planning, action and maintenance. It also illustrates the circular nature of change; whereby small changes can be built on from one year to the next.

Figure 1. Stages of change model from Prochaska and DiClemente

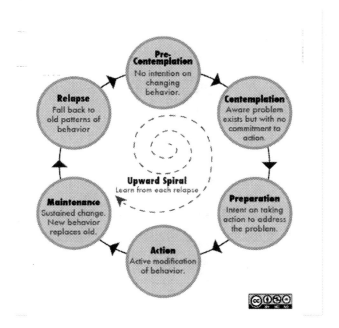

Implementing UDL in a University Setting

In the context of UDL implementation, applying the stages of change model can be used to emphasize the circular nature of educational design. The concept of a cycle of planning in UDL is not new as illustrated by Rao & Meo (2016). These authors described the cycle of instructional planning including first planning goals, then assessments, methods and materials, the lesson itself and finally a reflection by the teacher. Our approach takes this further than just a cyclical individual lesson but a circular approach to a whole course. It also includes the important aspects of contemplating change, planning for change, and reflecting on that change.

The classical description of UDL includes a significant investment at the design stage; however, in our institution it was not clear that faculty were ready for that kind of change One of the barriers in UDL implementation is the sense that this is an overwhelming task with multiple factors. In a busy university where teachers must integrate a range of requirements into their units, it is easy for UDL to be relegated to the "too hard" box. Our aim was to remove that barrier by providing well curated resources to facilitate every teacher starting off the process focusing on one small change at a time.

Our personal experience of implementing UDL into individual units of study was that making modifications to activities to make them more engaging, and into assignments to allow students choice in the modality of their assignments was relatively easy. Student feedback indicated that they valued the changes *"One of the best aspects of this unit was that despite not being content heavy, I still have learnt so much more than other units" ...." I really enjoyed .... how supportive the learning environment was where I felt that I was able to express my opinions or ask questions without judgement or hesitation"*.

Following implementation at a single course level, we wanted to create resources for other staff. We identified that some changes were easier than others and so we divided the UDL diagram from CAST into three levels based on ease of implementation. Level one includes aspects that already exist in our system that instructors can implement immediately. Level two identifies features that are relatively easy to implement with a small amount of planning and level three includes more complex ideas that might significantly move towards UDL but require more planning and support than the earlier levels.

From this we created a suite of resources to support faculty to determine which of the checkpoints they were already using successfully. This involved analyzing the available tools for staff within the university and creating resources to demonstrate how to use each one. Our resources included a self-assessment tool, a Canvas site explaining UDL, an interactive version of the UDL diagram and a set of workshops delivered widely throughout the university.

In this section, we will explain our process (figure 2) and how we used an incremental approach starting from changing one checkpoint to support staff to implement UDL in their courses.

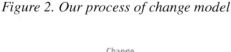

Figure 2. Our process of change model

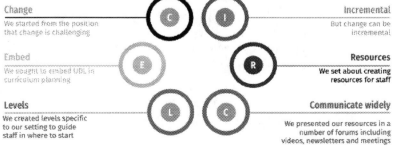

Step 1: Change Our approach started by acknowledging that change is challenging.

Step 2: Embed We focused on times of year when curricula planning was taking place and focused on building UDL into the process of curriculum planning.

Step 3: Levels We identified 3 levels of complexity from the CAST diagram and provided supports to teachers to identify easy aspects to change in their specific course.

Step 4: Incremental We emphasized that change is incremental and encourage teachers to focus on one or two things to change each time the course is delivered.

Step 5: Resources We created a suite of resources that were accessible to staff in order to communicate that implementing change was a relatively easy process. We did this by explicitly demonstrating how to incorporate UDL changes, by providing links and instructional resources for numerous tools whilst giving concrete examples of how the UDL updates may look in their educational context.

Step 6: Communicate Widely Next, we sought to communicate about our resources widely. This included several presentations throughout the university.

Timeframe

Our project included work from two educational designers and one academic knowledgeable in building the Canvas site. We then included a range of other educational designers and academics to bring together the UDL forum. The whole project took around 6 months. Other institutions considering this approach would need to look at resourcing and expertise within their own higher educational setting to determine whether this can be achieved in a similar timeframe.

Our Project

In mid-2021, in collaboration between academics and educational designers, we formed a project with the goal of informing educators within our faculty of the benefits of incorporating UDL principles into their teaching. Our plan was to remove perceived barriers by providing a well curated suite of resources and to break down the guidelines into accessible chunks, focusing on one small change at a time.

We understood the importance of getting 'buy-in' from our academics, and the need to communicate widely that implementing UDL does not need to be difficult. In fact, many teachers were already incorporating these principles without being aware of it (Black et al., 2014). Therefore, we aimed to advocate the use of UDL in a way that was relevant for each individual educator in a simplified, agile, and ongoing process where they could build on the great things they were already integrating into their teaching.

To appeal to time poor academics (Bennett et al., 2017), our message was that UDL implementation is a worthy investment. In designing assessments and learning activities for all students that are barrier free, UDL can remove the need for some academic plans (Draffan et al., 2017; Fidelak & van Tol, 2021), which can be time consuming, complex to implement and involves students often having to overcome anxiety in disclosing their learning needs. In addition, engaging students in their learning, delivering choice, promoting collaboration, and providing authentic assessments can improve the learning outcomes for all students, not just those with academic plans (Ralabate, 2011). These changes can also lead to an improvement in student feedback scores at the end of semester (Beck Wells, 2022; Kortering et al., 2008), which we knew was an important factor for most unit coordinators.

Our aims were therefore to create a suite of resources that would:

Implementing UDL in a University Setting

a. Allow academics to identify UDL features of their own teaching.
b. Break UDL down into manageable chunks with clear links to resources at our university.
c. Divide UDL into levels to guide novice UDL users where to start.
d. Provide clear exemplars of UDL practices within the university.

Creating the LMS

Our first step in addressing the feedback that Universal Design for Learning seemed complex and overwhelming was to design and create a new UDL Learning Management System (LMS) (Canvas site) specifically for academics, with resources to help simplify the ideas and principles. An LMS that has been designed well can play an important role in facilitating and streamlining learning (Lee & Lee, 2014). As such, our team planned a coherent organization and layout with simple navigational options in accessing the materials. This involved breaking up the complex three-network UDL model into smaller sections whilst illustrating the ideas through multiple media (CAST, 2018). We displayed our content in flexible formats including text, graphics, and videos (UDL checkpoint 2.5) because we knew that providing multiple options for connecting with our materials would enable our academic learners to absorb the content in a way that suited them. We also ensured that each page met accessibility standards and could be read by screen-reader technology.

1. Created a welcome video

Online videos can be effective in reducing barriers, creating social presence, and fostering the human connection between instructors and learners (Hibbert et al., 2016). Therefore, we decided to create a welcome video on the home page of our LMS site featuring our Associate Dean of Education and the leading academic in our team. In this short video (3mins), we explained the goals of our project, how to navigate the Canvas site, introduced the accompanying resources, whilst explaining the benefits of UDL.

In this video, the Associate Dean of Education welcomed staff and noted that *"we are very lucky to have an extremely diverse cohort of students who learn and express themselves in many different ways. It's so important, therefore, that we as academics and educators adapt our teaching, learning and assessment to match the way our students now learn."*

2. Created levels of increasing complexity

Alongside providing information about the three pillars of UDL (Multiple Means of Engagement, Multiple Means of Action and Expression and Multiple Means of Representation) we further divided our material into three levels of increasing complexity. We analyzed the resources available within our organization and identified available resources so that we could specify the checkpoints that would be easiest for academics to implement.

a. Level 1

The level 1 ideas identified resources that our institution already has or actions that teachers may already do. For example, for checkpoint 7.2 (Optimizing relevance, value, and authenticity) one of our suggestions was embedding videos in LMS sites that allow interactions and comments from students (figure 3). This was an example of a tool that is readily available within our systems that many teachers are already utilizing. For those who were not, it is a simple and effective suggestion that can be applied with little effort. The tool we used belongs to the Canvas suite of resources and allows students to comment or answer questions during video playback. In the image below you can see how students are commenting about the video during playback and engaging with each other via this media.

Figure 3. Example of comments on video weekly task

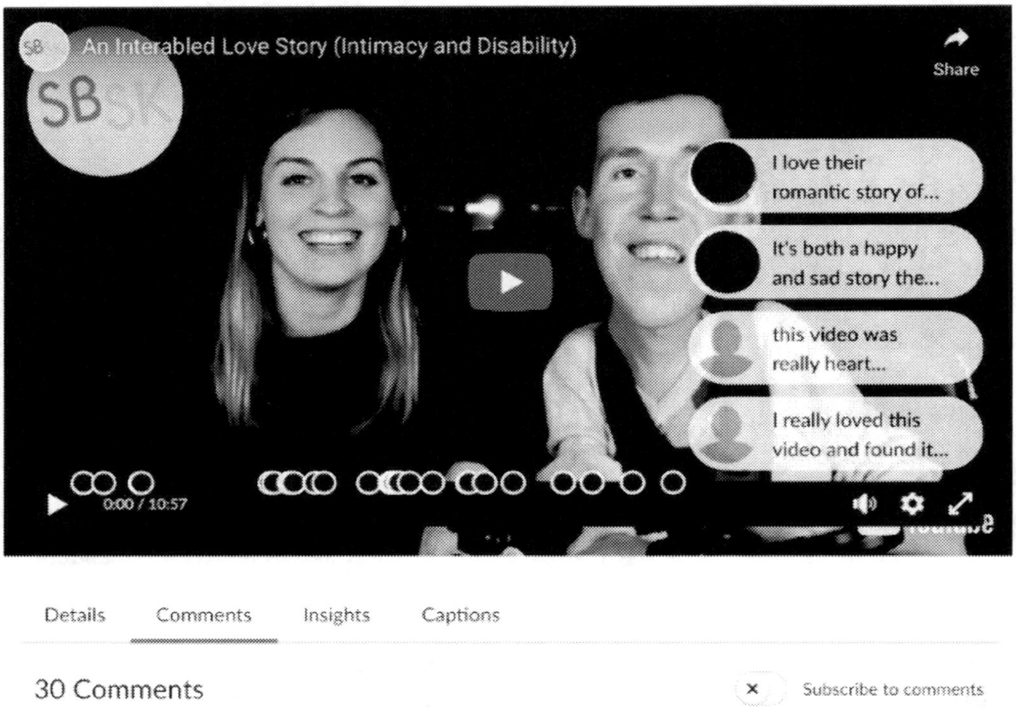

b.   Level 2

Level 2 identified ideas that are easily implemented with limited small changes to teaching. For example, for checkpoint 5.3 (build fluencies with graduated levels of support for practice and performance) one of our suggestions was to create a trial exam or quiz that is identical in format to a highly weighted final exam/quiz. This would allow students to familiarize themselves with the format and process and therefore, not lose valuable time in working out how the exam is presented during the high-stakes version. Another suggestion was creating a low weighted version of an assignment earlier in the semester, prior to a higher weighted version of a similar assignment later in the unit.

Our LMS (Canvas) does not allow you to do this with just one or two steps (hence it is not a level 1 suggestion), but this is something that most academics would find relatively easy to do and is therefore rated as level 2.

Implementing UDL in a University Setting

c. Level 3

Level 3 identified ideas that take more planning and support. For example, for checkpoint 7.3 (minimizing threats and distractions) one of our suggestions was to create an accepting and supportive classroom environment by utilizing interactive presentation tools (such as Mentimeter). These tools can enhance interactivity, create a sense of fun, promote engagement and positive classroom dynamics (Vallely & Gibson, 2018). Additionally, these tools can be used to support an inclusive and safe space for students to share thoughts and opinions because they allow participants to contribute anonymously. This can empower students who lack confidence in speaking up or those who are fearful of answering questions incorrectly in a classroom environment (Mayhew et al., 2020)

3. Self-Assessment Tool

To assist academics to identify their own use and understanding of UDL level, we created an interactive self-assessment tool that is accessible on the home page of our LMS (figure 4). Users are asked a series of questions related to their experience in implementing UDL. Based on the results, the self-assessment tool can identify the UDL concepts that they are already incorporating into their teaching. Additionally, the results direct the academic to the appropriate resources on the UDL Canvas site based on our leveling system (level 1, 2 or 3). From there, they can explore additional tasks that we recommended, based on their experience levels.

Figure 4. Slide from UDL workshop explaining the self-assessment tool

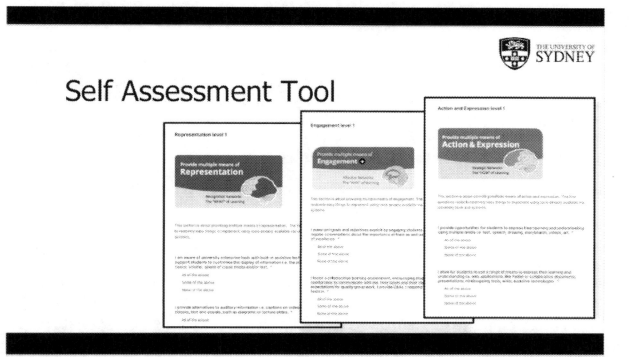

4. Case Study / Exemplar site

To model the UDL practices demonstrated in our UDL Canvas resource site, we provided access to an exemplar Canvas site that academics could navigate and explore as students typically would. The exemplar site is a copy of a real LMS for an elective course (REHB2026) that was designed to be completed entirely online.

Supporting this resource, was a two-part video series where the course coordinator provided a tour explaining how various aspects of the site adhered to UDL guidelines. For example, as the course coordinator navigated through the site from week-to-week, the design choice to use consistent colors, symbols and page layouts was pointed out whilst also directing the viewer to the relevant UDL checkpoint (7.3 - minimize threats and distractions).

Within this case study, the course coordinator explained how she consciously adopted numerous UDL principles within the learning activities and assessments.

a. Guidelines 7-9: Provide multiple means of engagement.

The coordinator of REHB2026 was aware of the importance of providing choice and autonomy (UDL 7.1) for her learners. In the video, she explained that in the first week of the course *"students were offered choice in the delivery style of the unit including 2-hour lectures on zoom, brief lectures alongside self-directed material or an entirely self-directed model. Students were offered the chance to consider the impact of each of these on their learning. They chose to meet weekly on zoom for a short session (30 mins) during which time the key concepts for the week were explained and they were provided with a tour of the Canvas material for that week and any questions they had were answered. Students commented that they valued being offered a choice. They felt respected as learners, and they liked that only two weeks of the semester required attendance."*

The coordinator of REBH2026 specifically focused on building a community of learners (UDL 8.3) within this course. *"This is particularly important and challenging, particularly during COVID where all teaching was online"*. In REHB2026, several assignment tasks involved peer feedback which was set up in a way that resulted in the students feeling supported. One student commented that feedback from *"peers who are doing the exact same assignment"* who provide feedback, allows the student to *"really ... understand what they are saying, and you can implement it a bit better because they know what you are going through and they know the expectations"*.

b. Guidelines 1-3: Provide multiple means of representation.

Providing material in different ways for all students to be able to access and understand the content seems obvious for students with vision or hearing loss (UDL 1.2 and UDL 1.3). However, it is also relevant for all learners, as individuals may simply grasp information more quickly or efficiently through visual or auditory means than they do through printed text. In REHB2026, the material was offered through a range of sources including video recordings of mini-lectures, YouTube and other publicly available videos, and both formal and informal written text (UDL 3.4). Offering multiple formats allows students the opportunity to explore the content repeatedly which supports students to make connections with and between concepts and their background knowledge (UDL 3.1).

Implementing UDL in a University Setting

One of the key guidelines in UDL relates to providing options for language and symbols (UDL 2.1). In REHB2026, one activity early in the semester involved students watching Youtube videos about disability and creating group definitions of key vocabulary.

Students were given the following instructions.

- Find a partner (or small group) to work with (for those of you who are doing this asynchronously, sign up for a partner)
- Spin the wheel on the Padlet (see figure 5)
- Watch/read the resource based on your wheel spin.
- Discuss the different resources you investigated with at least one other classmate and come to a consensus definition of "what is disability".
- Type your definition into a slide that includes your name!
- Add more slides if you need to at the end.

Figure 5. Padlet containing wheel spin and YouTube videos

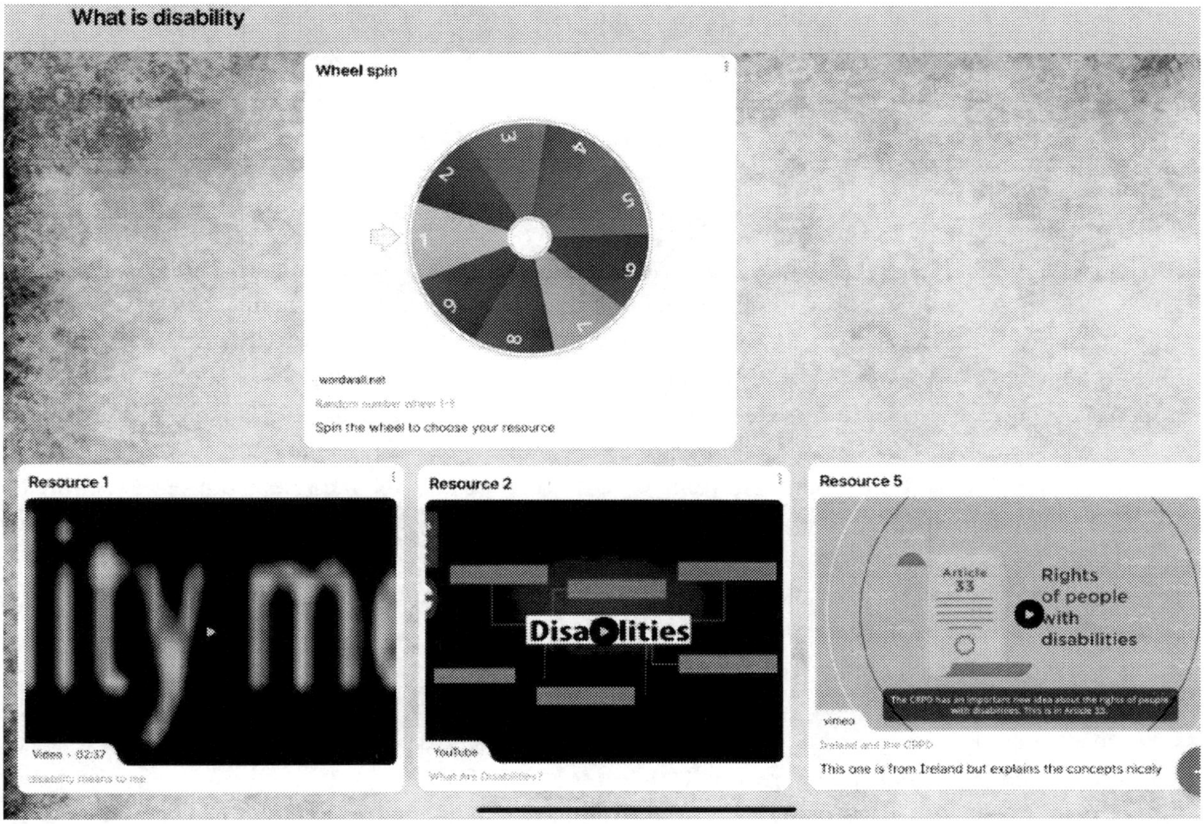

This activity included a number of UDL principles including:

- engaging students (UDL 8.2)

- being interactive and facilitating group collaboration (UDL 8.3).
- clarifying vocabulary (UDL 2.1).
- By using Google Slides collaboratively allowed students to work together in problem solving and allowed the teacher to keep an eye on group progress without intruding into discussions taking place in breakout rooms (UDL 7.3).
  c. Guidelines 4-6: Provide multiple means of action and expression

Providing multiple means of action and expression is vital for students with a disability to allow them to demonstrate their learning. Some academics feel that essay writing is an essential feature of university, however, it is important to determine whether or not the learning objective relates to writing in a formal academic style. If it does, then an essay is appropriate. If, however, that is not a learning objective, then it is appropriate to create assessments that allow students to demonstrate learning in a range of different media (UDL 5.1). Assessments that are authentic, such as writing reports in the style that would be appropriate in the workplace, allow students to communicate their learning and maintain their motivation through the use of authentic activities (UDL 7.2).

In REHB2026, one of the key learning objectives is for students to become advocates for people with a disability. The final assignment involves students participating in a debate where they need to effectively argue their side in a live debate. Students create short videos arguing their side of the debate which directly links to the learning objective of advocacy.

5. Student and teacher interviews

Included within our UDL LMS site and accompanying the exemplar site was a bank of short, chunked videos that included interviews. In these videos the students and teacher discussed the REHB2026 Canvas site and two assessments within this unit that incorporated the UDL principles discussed above.

Our team made the decision to not only interview the course coordinator of REBH2026, but also two of her students. We did this because we understood the power of the student perspective; without their feedback, we could not accurately determine which learning activities and assessments were working and/or if any were misfiring (Brookfield, 2017).

Firstly, we interviewed the course coordinator and the students live via three zoom sessions (due to COVID-19 we could not film in person). We then asked each subject to record themselves answering the same questions on their smartphones so that we had access to a second higher resolution version of each interview. We did this to ensure, as much as possible, that we had reasonably high-quality audio and visuals. This was pivotal because extraneous distractions, such as poor framing, unnecessary visual elements and/or low-quality audio, can disturb cognitive processing and remove the focus from the essential content for the viewer (Mayer, 2014).

When editing these interviews, we linked each aspect of the learning activity or assessment that the interviewees were describing to the relevant UDL principles through clear and bold graphics. We did this to simplify the concepts and to highlight concrete examples of their applicability. We also kept each video short, under 5-minutes, in line with recommendations in maximizing viewer engagement (Brame, 2016).

These interviews proved incredibly insightful and the student's reported valuing three specific areas that related to UDL.

a. Easy to navigate, organized LMS sites

Implementing UDL in a University Setting

The students we interviewed specifically mentioned the importance of having an LMS site that was organized and easy to navigate. They also liked that the lecturer would dedicate a few minutes at the start of each week showing the students how to find all the relevant learning resources for the week ahead.

"We were given a tour of canvas each week... I found this helpful as a first-year student who was somewhat new to Canvas because the activities varied from week to week and so it was really helpful to clarify what it was we needed to do" [Scarlett]

b.   Choice

Students reported enjoying the activities and assessments that provided individual choice (UDL 7.1). This gave them a greater sense of ownership, value, and creative autonomy (UDL 7.2)

"what I really enjoyed.... was the creative outlets that we were allowed to use throughout the whole semester" [Sophie]

c.   A low weighted assessment task prior to a high weighted final assessment task

The students' appreciated having a low weighted assessment task prior to a higher weighted final assessment. In REBH2026, the final week 13 assignment was a highly weighted debate activity. Inspired by UDL principles, he course coordinator designed a similar task (worth fewer marks) which the students completed in week 7. The students appreciated the opportunity to practice and gather feed-forward feedback (Meer & Chapman, 2014) on the low stakes task that they could then apply to their high stakes assessment in Week 13 (UDL 8.4).

"I really think that being able to have some prep to the final assignment was key in helping me understanding what was required and settling my nerves" [Sophie]

6.   Communicated widely

Once we had completed our suite of resources which included the UDL LMS site, the self-assessment tool, the exemplar site, and the bank of chunked videos, we provided a series of workshops for staff across the faculty (Carballo et al., 2019).

We advertised our workshops as widely as possible by writing a series of articles, blogs, Yammer posts, and newsletter pieces where we reflected on our approaches and invited staff to register. We also spread the word within the various schools in the faculty by presenting in several forums, meetings and contributing to school-level newsletters and announcements.

We ran the faculty-wide workshops in late 2021 and they proved so successful that we were invited to expand and run university-wide workshops. This included running a full day symposium with the goal of bridging the gap between UDL ideas and action. Here academics across the University of [de-identified] were invited to attend a variety of workshops in a flexible manner, whether that be for an hour-long session or the full day.

Following this, our academic lead on this project was invited to present at a workshop within the Modular Professional Learning Framework (MPLF) (Pattison et al., 2022), a professional development workshop that promotes inclusive teaching practices.

In early 2022, the project expanded beyond the University of Sydney when we presented our project at a TED-style talk at the UDL IRN (Implementation and Research Network) summit (https://summitondemand.udl-irn.org/udl-within-the-framework-of-a-model-of-change/). This summit aims to advance understanding and share knowledge and best practice implementation of UDL across educational institutions around the world.

OUR IMPACT SO FAR

Since launching our UDL project in September 2021, we have been pleasantly surprised by the level of interest and engagement from staff in this short space of time. Our project quickly evolved and grew from a contained faculty-specific endeavor to a university-wide educational project and beyond. We believe this is because UDL is a framework that is being embraced and adopted by educational institutions across the globe due to its proven effectiveness in optimizing teaching and learning for students of all abilities.

Since launching our project, including our suite of resources, in September 2021, there have been 226 voluntary staff enrolments into our UDL LMS site and over 61,000 page views.

After running our numerous workshops within our faculty and then University-wide, we received unsolicited verbal and written feedback from staff across the university that has been enthusiastic and positive. These include:

"I appreciated the insights of the participants…about different approaches and considerations of UDL" (UDL symposium participant 2021)

"I will incorporate strategies for multiple means of engagement into my classes next semester" (workshop attendee, 2022)

"The short videos and explanations are practical and concrete, and really reduce the barrier to entry for staff. The constant references back to UDL principles and guidelines, [and] the expertly curated resources …are really helpful to connect the rather overwhelming UDL framework with tangible things that educators can do in their day-to-day practice" (workshop attendee, 2021)

FUTURE AIMS

In alignment with the University of Sydney's 2032 strategy, we ultimately want to empower all our students, so they are confident in their abilities, feel challenged, rewarded, and have a sense of belonging in their studies.

If UDL principles were to be successfully adopted across the University, we will see a wide-scale inclusion of constructively aligned units of study (Biggs, 1996). These courses will move away from tra-

Implementing UDL in a University Setting

ditionally restrictive tasks and provide students with more choice and authentic activities that are relevant to real-world contexts. Students will increasingly be provided learning activities and assessments that are scaffolded with feedforward feedback, allowing them to continuously develop their understanding of complex ideas and concepts (Beaumont et al., 2011)

In the long term, we hope to see a significant decrease in academic plans (Layer, 2017) because courses across the university will be designed to accommodate students of all abilities, including those on the margins, not just the 70 per cent of students in the middle (Meyer & Rose, 2005). Learning materials for students will be varied, accessible and engaging. Assessment tasks will evolve to allow students greater choice and creativity, allowing learners to demonstrate their understanding in a way that suits them.

There may be a pivot away from traditional unidirectional lectures and move towards interactive, inclusive classroom environments where students are actively engaged in their learning. In these spaces, students will not only grasp ideas through acquisition, but also through practice, allowing a deeper level of connection to their learning (Laurillard, 2013).

Finally, we anticipate improved feedback scores from students across the University. As UDL is increasingly incorporated into the curriculum, greater equity, diversity, and inclusion will be experienced in our classrooms. More students from diverse backgrounds and abilities will excel in their studies, and these factors will flow into increased satisfaction for course coordinators and their learners.

REFERENCES

Australian Disability Clearinghouse on Education and Training. (n.d.). *Communities of practice*. ADCET. https://www.adcet.edu.au/resources/communities-of-practice

Australian Disability Clearinghouse on Education and Training (ADCET). (n.d.). ADCET. https://www.adcet.edu.au/

Australian Government. (2020, November 27). *National Disability Coordination Officer Program*. Department of Education. https://www.education.gov.au/access-and-participation/ndco

Australian Government. (2022, October 10). *Higher Education Statistics*. Department of Education. https://www.education.gov.au/higher-education-statistics

Beaumont, C., O'Doherty, M., & Shannon, L. (2011). Reconceptualising assessment feedback: A key to improving student learning? *Studies in Higher Education, 36*(6), 671–687. doi:10.1080/03075071003731135

Beck Wells, M. (2022). Student perspectives on the use of universal design for learning in virtual formats in higher education. *Smart Learning Environments, 9*(1), 1–12. doi:10.118640561-022-00218-6

Bennett, S., Dawson, P., Bearman, M., Molloy, E., & Boud, D. (2017). How technology shapes assessment design: Findings from a study of university teachers. *British Journal of Educational Technology, 48*(2), 672–682. doi:10.1111/bjet.12439

Biggs, J. (1996). Enhancing teaching through constructive alignment. *Higher Education, 32*(3), 347–364. doi:10.1007/BF00138871

Black, R. D., Weinberg, L. A., & Brodwin, M. G. (2014). Universal Design for instruction and learning: A pilot study of faculty instructional methods and attitudes related to students with disabilities in higher education. *Exceptionality Education International*, *24*(1). doi:10.5206/eei.v24i1.7710

Brame, C. J. (2016). Effective Educational Videos: Principles and Guidelines for Maximizing Student Learning from Video Content. *CBE Life Sciences Education*, *15*(4), es6. doi:10.1187/cbe.16-03-0125 PMID:27789532

Brookfield, S. (2017). *Becoming a critically reflective teacher*. Jossey-Bass, A Wiley Brand.

Carballo, R., Morgado, B., & Cortés-Vega, M. D. (2019). Transforming faculty conceptions of disability and inclusive education through a training programme. *International Journal of Inclusive Education*, 1–17. doi:10.1080/13603116.2019.1579874

CAST. (2018). *Universal Design for Learning Guidelines version 2.2*. CAST. http://udlguidelines.cast.org

CAST. (2022, May 16). *Timeline of innovation*. CAST. https://www.cast.org/impact/timeline-innovation

Cumming, T. M., & Rose, M. C. (2022). Exploring universal design for learning as an accessibility tool in higher education: A review of the current literature. *Australian Educational Researcher*, *49*(5), 1025–1043. doi:10.100713384-021-00471-7

Disability Awareness. (2020, March 10). Disability Awareness. https://disabilityawareness.com.au/elearning/disability-awareness/

Draffan, E. A., James, A., & Martin, N. (2017). Inclusive teaching and learning: What's next? *The Journal of Inclusive Practice in Further and Higher Education*, *9*(1). https://eprints.soton.ac.uk/415140/

Fidelak, D., & van Tol, K. (2021). Reducing accommodation requests in post-secondary education by implementing practical UDL strategies. In *Handbook of Research on Applying Universal Design for Learning Across Disciplines* (pp. 48–71). IGI Global. doi:10.4018/978-1-7998-7106-4.ch003

Fovet, F. (2020a). Universal design for learning as a tool for inclusion in the higher education classroom: Tips for the next decade of implementation. *Education Journal*, *9*(6), 163–172. doi:10.11648/j.edu.20200906.13

Fovet, F. (2020b). Beyond novelty: "Innovative" accessible teaching as a return to fundamental questions around social justice and reflective pedagogy. In Enhancing Learning Design for Innovative Teaching in Higher Education (pp. 22-42). IGI Global.

Garrad, T.-A., & Nolan, H. (2022). Rethinking higher education unit design: Embedding Universal Design for learning in online studies. *Student Success*, *13*(2). doi:10.5204sj.2300

Hibbert, M., Kerr, K. R., Garber, A. A., & Marquart, M. (2016). The human element. In *Creating Teacher Immediacy in Online Learning Environments* (pp. 91–112). IGI Global. doi:10.4018/978-1-4666-9995-3.ch006

Hitch, D., Brown, P., Macfarlane, S., & Watson, J. (2019). The transition to higher education: Applying Universal Design for Learning to support student success. In *Transforming Higher Education Through Universal Design for Learning*. Routledge., doi:10.4324/9781351132077-6

Hockings, C. (2010). *Inclusive learning and teaching in higher education: A synthesis of research.* Higher Education Academy.

Jwad, N., O'Donovan, M.-A., Leif, E., Knight, E., Ford, E., & Buhne, J. (2022). *Universal Design for Learning in Tertiary Education: A Scoping Review and Recommendations for Implementation in Australia.* Monash. https://research.monash.edu/en/publications/universal-design-for-learning-in-tertiary-education-a-scoping-rev

Kilpatrick, S., Johns, S., Barnes, R., Fischer, S., McLennan, D., & Magnussen, K. (2017). Exploring the retention and success of students with disability in Australian higher education. *International Journal of Inclusive Education*, *21*(7), 747–762. doi:10.1080/13603116.2016.1251980

Kortering, L. J., McClannon, T. W., & Braziel, P. M. (2008). Universal Design for Learning: A Look at What Algebra and Biology Students With and Without High Incidence Conditions Are Saying. *Remedial and Special Education*, *29*(6), 352–363. doi:10.1177/0741932507314020

Koshy, P. (2020). *Equity student participation in Australian higher education: 2014--2019.* National Centre for Student Equity in Higher Education. https://www.voced.edu.au/content/ngv:88552

Laurillard, D. (2013). *Teaching as a design science: Building pedagogical patterns for learning and technology.* Routledge. doi:10.4324/9780203125083

Layer, G. (2017). *Disabled students sector leadership group (DSSLG) inclusive teaching and learning in higher education as a route to excellence.* Department for Education.

Lee, S.-Y., & Lee, H.-S. (2014). Analysis of the Influence of Factors Related to Student Satisfaction with Web-based University Courses: Comparison between 2005 and 2014. In Advanced Science and Technology Letters. doi:10.14257/astl.2014.59.17

Mayer, R. E. (2014). Incorporating motivation into multimedia learning. *Learning and Instruction*, *29*, 171–173. doi:10.1016/j.learninstruc.2013.04.003

Mayhew, E., Davies, M., Millmore, A., Thompson, L., & Bizama, A. P. (2020). The impact of audience response platform Mentimeter on the student and staff learning experience. *Research in Learning Technology*, *28*(0). doi:10.25304/rlt.v28.2397

Meer, N. M., & Chapman, A. (2014). Assessment for confidence: Exploring the impact that low-stakes assessment design has on student retention. *International Journal of Management Education*, *12*(2), 186–192. doi:10.1016/j.ijme.2014.01.003

Meyer, A., & Rose, D. H. (2005). The future is in the margins: The role of technology and disability in educational reform. In D. H. Rose & A. &. H. Meyer (Eds.), The universally designed classroom: Accessible curriculum and digital technologies (pp. 13–35). Harvard Education Press.

Pattison, P., Bridgeman, A., Bulmer, A., McCallum, P., & Miles, R. (2022). Renewing the Sydney undergraduate curriculum. *Higher Education*, 1–18. doi:10.100710734-022-00982-x PMID:36536882

Pitman, T. (2022). *Supporting persons with disabilities to succeed in higher education: Final Report.* Curtin University. https://www.ncsehe.edu.au/wp-content/uploads/2022/03/Pitman_Curtin_EquityFellowship_FINAL.pdf

Prochaska, J. O., & Diclemente, C. C. (1986). Toward a Comprehensive Model of Change. In W. R. Miller & N. Heather (Eds.), *Treating Addictive Behaviors: Processes of Change* (pp. 3–27). Springer US. doi:10.1007/978-1-4613-2191-0_1

Ralabate, P. K. (2011). Universal Design for Learning: Meeting the Needs of All Students. *ASHA Leader*, *16*(10), 14–17. Advance online publication. doi:10.1044/leader.FTR2.16102011.14

Rao, K., & Meo, G. (2016). Using Universal Design for Learning to Design Standards-Based Lessons. *SAGE Open*, *6*(4), 2158244016680688. doi:10.1177/2158244016680688

Ruddock, P. (2005). *Disability standards for education 2005*. Commonwealth of Australia. Federal Register of Legislative Instruments F2005L007672006

Vallely, K. S. A., & Gibson, P. (2018). Engaging students on their devices with Mentimeter. *Compass (Eltham)*, *11*(2). doi:10.21100/compass.v11i2.843

KEY TERMS AND DEFINITIONS

Academic Plan: A document that specifies the adjustments needed for a student with a disability for each course they take.

Course Coordinator: The course coordinator is responsible for all aspects of a specific course (unit of study). They will often teach in the course but also set up the LMS, coordinate external lecturers, tutors, and markers. They will arrange for modification in the academic plan to be implemented and ensure that all students can access the learning material.

Cycle of Planning: This refers to the concept of planning taking place either year by year or semester by semester. Teachers plan content with reference to various policies and learning objectives. They then reflect on the success of the semester and modify the content for the next time the course is taught.

Elective course: Elective courses are courses students can choose, allowing them to study topics of interest. Electives, when added to the core courses, make up the total number of units needed to complete the degree.

Inclusion and Disability Services (IDS): IDS provides support to students who have a disability to ensure that they can gain access to the adjustments and services they need to succeed in their studies. They meet with the student, review medical documentation, and create an academic plan.

Learning Management System (LMS): A Learning Management System is software that helps teachers create, manage, organize, and deliver online learning materials to learners. It is also known as a Virtual Learning Environment (VLE).

Tertiary: Formal post-secondary education, including public and private universities, colleges, technical training institutes, and vocational schools.

Chapter 4
Towards Equity and Inclusion Excellence Using Diverse Interventions

Emma Kristina Leifler

University of Gothenburg, Sweden & Karolinska Institutet, Sweden

ABSTRACT

Although inclusive education (i.e., education that does not include separate special education classes) is legislated and pervasive worldwide, the implementation of educational inclusion is poor. To create more inclusive school settings, we need to explore what constitutes good practice. Moreover, we need evidence of effective interventions that address student needs. This chapter provides evidence from two interventions aimed at improving inclusion (NDC AI and SKOLKONTAKT®). These mixed methods, which merge quantitative and qualitative data, show that professional development enhances the inclusive skills of teachers and group training of students improves social skills, school attendance, and participation, leading to less loneliness, making the whole school's social environment better. Unexpectedly, the teachers became more aware of social impairments and developed new concrete tools to handle conflicts and bullying.

INTRODUCTION

Inclusive education has become internationally pervasive (Norwich, 2013; UN, 1994) and is based on the social model of disability where democracy and human rights are fundamental (Thomas & Loxely, 2001). There is still a discrepancy between policy and practice for inclusive education without clear guidance for professionals (Leifler, Borg, Bölte, 2022b), even in high socio-economic countries.

Inclusive education is complex and difficult to define as it varies according to different historical, geographical, and theoretical contexts (Florian, Black-Hawkins & Rouse, 2017). UNESCO (2015: 101) provides a distinct definition of inclusive education: "Ambitious approaches to inclusion are commonly grounded in a rights-based approach that aims to empower learners, celebrate diversity, and combat dis-

DOI: 10.4018/978-1-6684-7370-2.ch004

Copyright © 2023, IGI Global. Copying or distributing in print or electronic forms without written permission of IGI Global is prohibited.

crimination. It suggests that, **with adequate support**, all children, irrespective of their different needs, should be able to learn together."

Inclusion in education addresses how school systems deal with inequality and injustice such as fewer opportunities for students with individual needs or disabilities that affect their ability to participate in learning. Nevertheless, a narrow perspective of inclusion that focuses on learner characteristics or disabilities may not shed enough light on the complexity of the learning environment and the reciprocal relationships between children and their environment. Theorists and practitioners of inclusion do not always agree. For example, some see the medical or deficit model as the reason for the increase in students who need special education, including the rise of the influence of the "SEND industry" (i.e., Students with Special Educational Needs and Disabilities) to serve students with disabilities and learning difficulties (Tomlinson, 2012). If the learning environment is inclusive enough, there is less need for additional support; however, what is generally provided must be grounded in and with a broad competence of what each child in a classroom might need for learning and academic achievement, feelings of belonging and inclusion, as well as well-being and mental health.

There is a gap between ideals and practices where practical experiences of inclusion involve many practical challenges. The common concept a "school for all" used in several countries (Norwich, 2013) is in line with inclusive language, yet conceptual ambiguity without clear guidance for practice of what is really meant can lead to professionals struggling to understand and create educational inclusion. Some frameworks can be used as tools for analysis of inclusion in practice (Florian & Spratt, 2013). Other researchers have developed guidelines such as Index of Inclusion (Booth & Ainscow, 2011) or an instrument for measuring inclusion (Leifler et al., 2022b). Worldwide, schools have yet to determine the best way to enhance inclusion for students with special educational needs and disabilities and their peers. Facilitating the participation of students with SEND–e.g., neurodevelopmental conditions (NDCs)–in regular schools is complex and needs further exploration.

In recent years, educators have promoted teaching all students, irrespective of special needs, in mainstream school settings. We cannot ensure advantageous inclusion for all individuals without several approaches and interventions targeting the learning environment and explicit impairments. Educational inclusion for students with NDCs requires implementing innovative interventions as well as evidence-based methods and strategies. Therefore, this chapter addresses two key areas for improved educational inclusion: the competence and practice-based interventions conducted in naturalistic settings such as the school environment.

Specifically, this chapter discusses two research projects aimed at enhancing inclusion: Neurodevelopmental Condition Awareness Intervention, NDC AI (Leifler, 2020) and Social Skills Group Training in Naturalistic Settings (SKOLKONTAKT®) (Leifler et al., 2022). The exploratory studies examine teachers' self-efficacy, inclusion capacity, and readiness to meet diversity in the classroom and social validity from an intervention for increased social skills and participation among adolescents with social impairments. This chapter explores and presents socially valid interventions close to practice that contribute to inclusion actions.

Towards Equity and Inclusion Excellence Using Diverse Interventions

BACKGROUND

Inclusive Education

Traditions of inclusive education and special education are often seen as contrasting philosophies. Special education derives from the medical or deficit approach, which assumes some learners require additional or different approaches to learning due to disabilities or learning difficulties. Inclusive education, however, does not highlight disabilities or the concept *special* as it emphasizes these differences as a reflection of a natural diversity among a population, shifting the emphasis from some students to all students (Leifler, 2022). Inclusive education focuses on the learning environment and how to provide learning for all, whereas special education focuses on the individual's needs and/or disabilities. Some theorists believe that the integration model is impossible and ignores the reality of the situation, but some theorists believe new ways of inclusive education need more exploration (Hornby, 2015, 2021; Ravet 2011).

In Hornby's *inclusive special education* approach, the core components and values from inclusive education are combined with extended knowledge of special needs and marginalized learners. Although these traditions might be different, both align with the rights-based perspective and the right of the child. In this inclusive special education approach (i.e., the integrative model), all children belong, and diversity is celebrated although students' needs and disabilities are not over-looked. Moreover, general teacher competences are broadened, and knowledge of explicit needs and disabilities serves inclusion values. The author believes that interventions and strategies originally derived from special education can be implemented and integrated into the inclusive environment as a natural part of the pedagogy and didactics.

Inclusion, according to the author, is how we interpret, talk about, interact, and act around inclusion–i.e., inclusion is an act more than a statement. According to this view, inclusion is a process that includes analysing and measuring inclusion in practice and includes the individuals themselves whose environments we aim to improve. Educational inclusion for students with special educational needs and disabilities starts with the right to belong and participate. All students should be provided adequate support and adjustments in the learning environment, and the support and adjustments should be developed and designed in dialogue with the child and youth as much as possible. In this project, the focus is on children and youth with NDC, although what serves these children might also benefit other children in the classroom.

Inclusive Education in Policy

The Salamanca declaration was one of the first historic event that formed the development of inclusive education (UN, 1994). The values were raised from the human rights-based perspective, as indicated from the United Nations Declaration of Human Rights (UN, 1948). Several international legal acts and frameworks for inclusive education have been derived from the Salamanca declaration. The acts and documents state that the education system must be designed to meet the needs of all children. The objectives are to prevent and hinder discrimination of students with disabilities.

According to policy and democracy, regular school settings should offer high-quality education to all children. UNESCO (2005) concludes that truly inclusive education has two perspectives on a learning-friendly environment: the child-friendly and the teacher-friendly perspectives. This view is in line with the objectives with this research presentation, which focuses on the development of the students as well as teachers.

61

"Inclusive education is about equity, participation, compassion, sustainability, respect for diversity, and seeing the potential in all individuals."

Inclusive Education for Students with Disabilities

Neurodevelopmental disorders (NDD's) is an umbrella term for different types of conditions that cause social and adaptive impairment (APA, 2013). Autism spectrum disorder (ASD) and attention deficit hyperactivity disorder (ADHD) are conditions or disorders linked to NDD's. In the terminology, the abbreviation NDC's (neurodevelopmental conditions) highlight the natural neurodiversity among individuals and the aim is to avoid the deficit perspective.

Although many high- and middle-income countries require inclusive education for autistic and other students with NDC, implementing such a mandate has been difficult (Pellicano, Bölte & Stahmer, 2018). Inclusive education consists of a broad repertoire of activities aimed at helping, developing, and transforming people to live in a community of equals. Required skills for taking part in a community include being able to communicate, interact, and take part in the work or school environment. Social communication challenges are defining features of autism and are associated with other NDCs. Children and youth with NDCs have deficits in several cognitive and social domains (e.g., executive functions, language, memory, theory of mind, and generalizing knowledge), which can affect their functioning in the school context (Bölte, 2014; Lord et al., 2021; Thorell, 2007). Deficits in social skills affect the child's ability to cooperate with peers, make friends, understand the teacher's non-verbal communication, and comprehend written texts that demand social knowledge (APA, 2013). For these students and their teachers, the teacher-student relationship does not work well, resulting in students experiencing low self-esteem and school failure (Plantin, Ewe & Aspelin, 2021). Furthermore, research indicates that students with NDCs experience less school participation, more bullying and social exclusion, and insufficient social support (Hodges et al., 2021; Leifler et al., 2022b). Students with autism and/or ADHD have complex needs that require urgent action to ensure better school outcomes and healthy lives (Lord et al., 2021).

Students with autism and other neurodevelopmental conditions have similar needs, and the support given might also benefit other SEND students. However, this diversity must be met appropriately, which requires broad competence, empathy, and understanding of the variation in functioning. Although interventions and treatment programs for individuals with NDCs exist, the empirical support for their effectiveness is limited (Bölte, 2014), especially in naturalistic settings (Lord et al., 2021). Moreover, these programs are often implemented unevenly, and generalizing a program's usefulness in different contexts is limited (Parsons et al., 2011). Therefore, the research-based support and educational strategies for students with NDCs vary and interventions are rare in some settings (Leifler, Carpelan, Zakrevska, Bölte, & Jonsson, 2020), although efforts to enhance inclusion and improve school outcomes for students with SEND have not been completely successful (Florian et al., 2017).

Challenges for Student with Disabilities in Inclusive Settings

Inclusion of students with disabilities such as autism and ADHD is not trivial and requires extensive knowledge and sensitivity by all professionals that meet and teach the students. Lack of teacher awareness of the condition is a threat to inclusion. There is a broad consensus that inclusion is more than physically integration in school (Ainscow, Booth & Dyson, 2006).

Inclusive education in a holistic view means the student can access and develop within the school environment, which can be divided into the physical environment, the psychosocial and the pedagogical/didactical (Leifler, 2022). In teachers' inclusive skills there is a need of a broad competence where the knowledge of inclusion should be holistic. In this teacher competence and awareness, the whole learning environment should be accommodated adequate and sufficient for student diversity and different needs. Teachers need to be aware of disabilities and obstacles to learning while maintaining high expectations for all children.

If schools are not well-equipped, adequate, and appropriate and professionals are not prepared to teach all students, students with NDCs and other conditions and disabilities are at risk for poor health, social exclusion, and low quality of life (Jonsson et al., 2019; Parsons et al., 2011). For a student with a NDC, a regular classroom can be challenging, including changes and transitions, peer and group work, instructions and tasks, assessments, non-literal or ambiguous meaning of language, social participation, and rules for conversation, and play and interaction. Education and learning have multi-faceted perspectives where learning takes place in social environments and making meaning is a process. Learning also takes places in a student's mind, so difficulties in cognitive functioning make it difficult for a student to understand and organize experiences in school and other contexts.

Inclusive Pedagogy to Support Inclusion

Multileveled and multidimensional inclusive pedagogy is complex and the uncertainty about its meaning can lead to tensions or less actions. For example, the view that SEND students belong to a special category could inhibit general teachers from developing the necessary skills that would ensure an inclusive learning environment. Inclusive pedagogy focuses on two questions: Who am I teaching and what are the obstacles or barriers to learning? However, focusing on the who does not mean categorizing children but on identifying the needs that exist and extending what is available in the general classroom to enhance and improve learning for all children. In these inclusive special didactics (Leifler, 2022), understanding, empathy, and the belief that all children can learn and have the capacity to develop are emphasized as the learning environment is only adjusted to address the explicit diversity of the students. The knowledge needed is broad and a continuous process for professionals, seeing difficulties in learning not deficits in learners while maintaining an awareness of the impairment associated with, for example neurodevelopmental disorders.

Odom, Cox, and Brock (2013) underscore the need for more implementation science where a model or program is evaluated in real-world settings. Odom et al. describe five important phases for high-quality implementation science: initial professional development, implementation, evaluation, program quality check, and development of evidence-based practice. This is in line with Bond et al. (2016), who discuss the evidence for a framework for ASD professional development at different levels, for practitioners in general settings, as well as for specialist practitioners. Watkins et al. (2019) recommend further guidance is needed for researchers and practitioners about how to train teachers to deliver and prioritize interventions with fidelity, although they do not describe how this should be done. There is a dilemma between what we know we need to do and who is responsible for doing it, as inclusion is an act. Nevertheless, researchers must share the evidence with policy and decision makers. One approach to avoid poor implementation is to add aspects of social validity to research studies. Social validity refers to an assessment of consumer acceptability and satisfaction of an intervention.

The inclusion of children and youth with more complex needs and behavioral difficulties in educational setting is an ongoing issue and a challenge for politicians and policy shapers. The debate is sometimes unhelpful for teachers and the students who are affected, as these debates often raise unsettling questions. Worldwide, there is a desire for inclusion and equity in school. For example, the United Nation's 2030 Agenda for Sustainability Development highlights equity in schools (UN, 2022). To fulfil this goal will require more knowledge and evidence of what works and for whom and in which settings. Furthermore, the knowledge of what best serves the needs of the child must come from several perspectives and research fields, including education, psychology, and sociology. In this chapter, the author discusses two inclusion interdisciplinary projects and how the explored interventions consider the whole child and the relationship between the individual and the environment.

Interventions for Reducing the Knowledge Gap Among Students

The central objective of inclusive education is to support every student's academic learning, and social and emotional development. Therefore, it is important to identify individual needs and eventual learning difficulties to design optimal and effective interventions. There are interventions and accommodations designed to reduce barriers to learning. To support and reduce the knowledge gap among students the support should depend on the individual needs of the child or youth, to avoid *one-size fits all*. Students with special educational needs and disabilities are a heterogeneous group and there is a need for a broad repertoire of knowledge and evidence-based practice to support diversity in the classroom.

Research evidence of high-quality interventions valuable for students with e.g., NDCs include behavioral approaches, skills-based interventions, and environmental interventions (Leifler, 2022). There is a great body of social skills training for students with NDCs; some interventions target the individual and some target the environment (Watkins et al., 2019), but individual training is most common. Long-term training is most beneficial (Jonsson et al., 2019), although shorter training has also produced positive effects and improved participants' satisfaction (Afsharnejad et al., 2019; Leifler et al., 2022a).

"Social skills training can be designed in a variety of ways; however, most programs include social interactions, instruction of basic social skills, role-play, feedback, and play."

Teacher Training for Inclusive Purposes

One form of environmental intervention is teacher training. In the inclusive classroom, teachers have the right competence to meet classroom diversity. Teachers are supposed to design learning for a broad range of individuals, including students with NDCs. As student diversity places considerable demands on teachers, general teachers need professional development. The teacher is an important factor for students' learning, and support from teachers is essential for accommodating students with special needs in general classrooms (Leifler, 2020). Professional development comes in many forms and varies over time and content (Leifler, 2020). Professional development is preferable when it is framed around practice and grounded in teachers' problems and interests. One method for teachers' learning and development is lesson study, including a cyclic process and collaboration (Norwich, 2020).

Professional development is a major trajectory for inclusion, as all staff should take part in the training (Petersson-Bloom, 2022; Ravet, 2011). Teachers who are prepared and offered experiences with and strategies for teaching SEND students have more positive attitudes about inclusion and teaching in a diverse classroom of learners (de Boer, Pijl, & Minnaert, 2011). In the education system, the move

Towards Equity and Inclusion Excellence Using Diverse Interventions

towards inclusive education is a changing process, where enhanced knowledge about explicit diagnoses and specific learning difficulties is essential for avoiding risks of marginalization and poor academic achievement.

Recent research and studies conducted in Swedish school settings have shown how inclusive classrooms with interventions derived from special education can improve learning for students with NDCs (Leifler, 2020; Petersson-Bloom, 2022; Klefbeck, 2021). To be effective, teachers need to understand the cognitive profile of students with NDCs, so professional development of teachers can improve students' outcomes as well as prevent teacher burnout (Petersson-Bloom, 2022). Promising professional development includes courses in collaboration, interdisciplinary work, and iterative processes (Hodges, Cordier, Joosten & Bourke-Taylor, 2021; Rajotte et al., 2022).

Previous research shows that teachers' self-efficacy is associated with teacher readiness to teach for student diversity (Leifler, 2020; Tschannen-Moran & Woolfolk Hoy, 2001). Teachers are more willing to persist and preserve when they believe in their own capability (Bandura, 1997). Teacher self-efficacy is defined as a judgement of one's own capabilities to meet and teach all children and youth, even when students have disabilities or lack of motivation (Tschannen-Moran & Woolfolk Hoy, 2001).

A growing body of research has identified that teachers need more training about how to establish inclusive learning environments and how to teach students with a wide range of SEND (Bölte, Leifler, Berggren & Borg; 2021; Florian & Linklater, 2010; Forlin, 2010; Petersson-Bloom, 2022). Pellicano et al. (2018) shed light on how to clarify the goal for inclusion and what it takes to implement inclusive practices, which is currently poorly understood except for a vague understanding of what inclusion means. That is, the current recommendations, regulations, and guidelines are not aligned with reality. The authors show how most countries are failing to include autistic children and youth. A serious problem for the education system is despite attempts of students with disabilities achieving educational goals and participating equally in the learning environment, inclusive education is not met in a satisfactory manner.

Social Skills Group Training for Social Inclusion

Students with NDCs have impairments that may hinder their success in inclusive settings. Regulations for inclusive education for students with NDCs include the right of these students to be educated alongside typically developed peers. However, students with NDCs still receive special education and are educated in segregated settings. If we strive for improved inclusive education, interventions derived from special education should be implemented in regular school settings (Watkins et al., 2019). The social impairments associated with NDCs can be mitigated if students with NDCs are provided with support in social activities or given explicit social skills training. Learners with NDCs are more likely to experience social, emotional, or behavior difficulties and therefore also sometimes have severe difficulties forming relationships. Interaction and communication with teachers and classmates can be difficult because social communication deficits and the interventions should be implemented in the student's natural environment to ensure sustainability and generalization. For students with NDCs, opportunities to interact with their typically developed peers have increased as more children with SEND are educated in regular school settings. However, without appropriate support, these students are at risk for social exclusion.

Social skills training is a behavioral approach where the individual is given training and/or therapy to develop social skills. The training can be conducted individually or in a group and can take place in a clinical setting or a naturalistic setting such as school. Despite large effects, teachers seldom implement social skills interventions (Watkins et al., 2017). Social skills training has been shown to be effective

(Leifler et al., 2022a; Watkins et al., 2019) and is a promising approach to enhance social inclusion. Multiple strategies have been proposed to promote social interaction and communication for children and youth with social difficulties, and interventions targeting social skills have attracted the most attention (Watkins et al., 2017).

Social skills training encompasses many educational methods–e.g., social stories, video modeling, social problem solving, pivotal response training, scripting procedures, computer-based teaching, prompting procedures, and self-monitoring (Coco, Fridell, Borg & Bölte, 2023). As school is a social arena, the training can preferably take place where students naturally interact with peers and teachers. The naturalistic setting is valuable for several reasons–e.g., the setting is close to the students, the setting generally promotes trust and safety, and the setting allows for collecting generalized knowledge (Leifler et al., 2022a).

INTERVENTIONS FOR INCLUSION

Materials and Methods

Study 1

The first study in this synthesis is an intervention for teachers' learning, designed after the lesson-study methodology (Leifler, 2020). The study is an interventional study with the purpose of investigating how and what teachers learn in a designed lesson study model of professional development. The objectives were to explore teacher readiness to teach for student diversity and teacher self-efficacy.

Theoretical Framework

The theoretical framework in this study is grounded in the Human Environment Interaction Model (Küller, 1991) and the theory of self-efficacy (Bandura, 1997).

Evidence-based strategies and methods known as effective and valuable for students with NDC's were divided into three domains of the learning environment, the physical, the psychosocial and the pedagogical/didactical. The domains are described in the Human Environment Interaction Model (Küller, 1991), and how different factors interrelate and influence students' learning.

Participants and Setting

Teachers (n = 26) from three mainstream schools participated. There were 20 female professionals and 5 male professionals. The mean level of years of experience was between 11 and 15 years. The teachers participated in three cycles of professional development with a balance between theory and practice with explicit focus on evidence-based methods and strategies known for improving the development and well-being of students with NDCs. The professional development lasted over five months and was conducted in the school setting. The content and aim of the program are shown in Table 1, adapted from Rajotte et al. (2022).

Intervention

The intervention for teachers' learning took part in the school environment and were three times with two hours each time. The time between sessions was about two weeks. The intervention consisted of a four-step process; study, plan, do and reflect (Norwich, 2020). The researcher showed and modelled evidence-based strategies and how to adjust and accommodate the learning environment, the pedagogical/didactical, the physical and the psychosocial. The explicit evidence-based artefacts modelled for teachers are described in the appendices 1-3 in Teachers' capacity to create inclusive learning environments (Leifler, 2020). The intervention is described in detail in table 1 and the theoretical framework is presented in table 2.

Table 1. NDC awareness intervention

Cycle 1	Cycle 2	Cycle 3
Pre-test Theory – presented in an iterative lesson Evidence-based practice for students with NDCs	Evaluation of the accommodations implemented in the learning environment Feedback from researcher Theory – presented in an iterative lesson Evidence-based practice – deepened approach	Evaluation of the accommodations implemented in the learning environment Feedback from researcher Theory – presented in an iterative lesson
Discussions Diagnosis of the learning environment Areas of improvement Plans for accommodations Homework – theoretical text	Discussions of the texts (homework) Diagnosis of the learning environment Areas of improvement Plans for accommodations Homework – theoretical text	Discussion – consensus of inclusive values Discussions of the texts (homework) Post- test Social validity questions

In total, the intervention was 6 hours with the content divided into three cycles (see table 1). In between the three cycles, teachers read assignments about the theory of inclusion education and reflected over the abilities, disabilities, and functioning of students with NDCs. Teachers inventoried needs and obstacles for learning in their classroom and implemented special support for students between session one and two and two and three. The implementation was further discussed and evaluated in collaboration with colleagues and the researcher.

Table 2. Theoretical framework and overall content of the professional development program

Core features of the professional development	Change in knowledge, self-efficacy, and inclusion skills	Change in inclusive practice	Improved inclusion and participation
Content focus evidence-based methods and strategies for students with NDC. Theory of executive functions and impairments. **Special didactics** The art of teaching. The material, scaffolding structures, tasks, and activities for learning. **Active learning and collaboration** Discussions and reflections with colleagues and researchers. Feedback from researchers regarding the implementation of support. **Cyclic and iterative process** Lesson study cycles.	Knowledge of disabilities and difficulties with learning. Analysing the learning environment to support students more effectively. Development of self-efficacy and beliefs about own skills and the right for the child to belong in the general classroom.	More knowledge of concrete accommodations and adjustments targeting students with NDC. Staff create more inclusive activities and environments.	Better prerequisites for all students including those who are autistic or with ADHD or other disabilities.

Data Analysis

The measurements in the study were self-efficacy and inclusion skills of the teachers, which were measured before and after the intervention using a survey. In addition, a case student, additional fieldnotes, and a follow-up interview were used for social validity. The following statements comprised the survey: I have enough competence to teach children with NDC; I have enough competence to adjust the learning context for children with NDCs; I know many concrete and valuable accommodations for students with NDCs; and I need professional development to meet and teach children with NDCs. The items were indexed for the concept teachers' self-efficacy and scored on a four-point Likert scale. The reliability analysis with Cronbach's alpha was $a = 0.80$. The significance was measured by Wilcoxon signed ranks test as well as with paired-samples t-test.

The survey had open-ended questions that asked the teachers to describe how they adjust the learning environment in three domains: the physical, the psychosocial, and the pedagogical/didactical. Pre-intervention examples were thematically coded and compared with post-intervention outcomes. The variables were quantified at pre- and post-test.

Finally, the teachers were asked to describe how they would prepare and provide support for a case student with NDC. The answers were quantified and thematically grouped into the three domains of the learning environment (Küller, 1991). Comparisons were made pre- and post-intervention.

Social validity was measured by questions to the participants regarding the length of the program, the relevance of the subject content and follow-up material and wishes for more professional development and to school management regarding the effects on changing teacher attitudes and actual changes of practice.

Results

The intervention for teachers' learning demonstrated significant changes in teachers' self-efficacy as well as inclusive teaching skills. Scores on the self-efficacy were significantly higher following the

Towards Equity and Inclusion Excellence Using Diverse Interventions

training in all items and in the indexed concept. The learning environment was divided and categorized into three domains: the pedagogical/didactical, the physical, and the psychosocial. These data were analyzed and quantified. The largest change was seen in the psychosocial environment (from 42 to 84 accommodations in teachers' quantified answers). In this area, teachers developed skills for building positive relationships with students, preventing challenging behavior and breakouts, raising students' social position in the class, and support in and before social interactions such as peer and group work. The change in accommodations from pre- to post-test in the physical environment was from 46 to 70 and in the pedagogical/didactical from 110 to 159. In these two areas, teachers developed skills associated with scaffolding to tasks and assessment, understanding the need of breaks, clear instructions, stimuli sanitizing areas for students with sensory issues, and repetition for working memory. To conclude, the accommodations teachers knew based on evidence-based methods rose from their initial values in all areas. In 23 of the 26 teachers' responses, there were increases in accommodations described for the case students. After the intervention, the teachers believed an enhanced learning environment was provided. Teachers described the NDC AI intervention as valuable and felt they were seldom provided with professional development for better inclusive skills. The results show that teachers were more capable and prepared to teach students with NDCs after the intervention. Although not long-term, the intervention enhanced the school's readiness for meeting classroom diversity.

Study 2

The second study in this synthesis is the evaluation of social skills group training using SKOLKON-TAKT®. This program is derived from the clinical version, KONTAKT®, a manualized, structured social skills group training for children and adolescents with high-functioning autism. This study examined the social validity of social skills group training in a naturalistic setting.

Theoretical Framework

The content in the social skills group training program is derived from cognitive therapy theories, psychoeducation, cognitive training, and behavior activation principles.

Social validity refers to perceived feasibility and acceptability with intervention procedures. In order to maximize and evaluate intervention success we must determine if the intervention has significant importance to the individuals whose environment we are aiming to improve. In this study, social validity was categorized using the work by Wolf (1978) and thematically divided into satisfaction, acceptability, and feasibility.

Participants and Setting

The training was conducted in school and the intervention was implemented by school professionals. Participants in the second study were recruited from an on-going RCT of social skills group training at a school in Stockholm, Sweden. Before the training, teachers identified students who would benefit from the intervention and the teachers asked these adolescents to participate. Informed consent was addressed to both adolescents and their parents. The study is a multi-responder study where participants are the students, the facilitating teachers, and the school management (principals). This triangulation increases the validity through the convergence of information from different participants. A qualitative approach using in-depth interviews with students, teachers, and school leaders was applied. Data were collected using semi-structured interviews. Participants were from both SKOLKONTAKT® (the training group) and the active control group. The control group received other forms of structured social activities that fit mainstream education plans. Social validity was measured using interviews with the students, the facilitating teachers, and the school management. Both the control group and active group were interviewed. The sample included 13 students, 5 teachers, and 2 school managers (N = 20). The students, aged between 17 and 20 years (M = 18), had a primary diagnoses of ADHD and autism with comorbidity in some cases. The program was transformed into digital, where the training was on-line due to Covid-19 and the two formats were compared. An overview of the content of the training is presented in Table 3.

Intervention

The participants received social skills training in their natural daily educational environment. The training was delivered in sessions and aligned with social events and skills needed in the school's social environment and in overall society. The training formats in SKOLKONTAKT® are presented in table 3.

Table 3. Characteristics of SKOLKONTAKT®

Target areas	Techniques	Training elements	Principles	Setting and content
Social rules initiating social overtures, social cognition, interaction, perception of verbal and non-verbal signals.	Cognitive behavior therapy, psychoeducation, observable learning, cognitive training, behavior, and activation principles.	Activities, opening formats, discussion, computer-based training, tasks, social activities, homework assignments, themes and issues aligned with social impairments, understanding self and conflict training.	Regular feedback, progress in training, teacher and parents provided with information for support.	Groups of 4–7 members, meeting three times a week, 1.5 hour in 12 weeks. School staff as group leaders, individual student goals.

Data Analysis

Results were analyzed according to social validity as described by Wolf (1978) and categorized into satisfaction, acceptability, and feasibility. The interview guide was developed for the different groups of informants and based on the work by Wolf (1978). Interview guide can be found in Leifler et al., 2022a. Interviews were audio recorded and transcribed verbatim. Data was first analyzed for each group of participants separately and linked to the social validity categories. Thereafter the synthesized results were pooled into the thematic landscape: facilitators, barriers, social behavioral change, and implementation.

Results

The results from the social skills group training were thematically organized according to social validity following Wolf's guidelines (1978). The head themes were categorized into the following headings: positive indicators, behavior change, implementation, and barriers. The social skills group training was described as possible to implement in the school setting. In the responses from the adolescents, positive

Towards Equity and Inclusion Excellence Using Diverse Interventions

indicators were reduced speech anxiety, safe environment, improved well-being, better school attendance, less loneliness, better self-awareness, and new relationships at school. The adolescents made the following observations: "The discussions were good"; "I found the themes very valuable for discussion since the themes were about a lot of things youth worry about"; "When you discuss it in a group, you feel less alone with your thoughts"; "It creates calmness and life is less awkward"; and "For the first time in my life, I actually have some friends". For this last statement, the adolescent showed the author a photograph in her phone as evidence of her new friendships as she had friends attend her birthday party for the first time in her life. It was her 18th birthday.

The teachers observed positive indicators such as more interactions in school, more tools to handle social difficulties and bullying at school, and large individual changes. Teachers believed training in this format is important and should be part of their teacher education as the intervention resulted in enhanced participation and well-being. They discussed the role of school and education and what skills are important for the future. They felt students with social impairments seldom have a chance to participate in the same way as their peers. One unexpected result, which was not the primary aim of the training, was improved school attendance as the students felt more socially included. The teachers made the following observations: "The training aimed to improve social skills, but also affected academic skills as we saw enhanced motivation among the adolescents and therefore more participation" and "The social environment in the whole school was improved since the group and activities were contagious and led to a positive feeling and group community all over the school".

The principals found that the new relations at the school enhanced the social environment and encouraged the students to come to school and participate in activities, increased awareness among the teachers, including participating teachers and the rest of the staff, and resulted in fewer conflicts at school. School management described generalized knowledge among staff since the training was discussed among school staff. The principals made the following observations: "It takes time and competes with other content that has to take place in school; however, we believe it is worth it"; "The collaboration with researchers worked fine, and it was valuable with feedback"; "The teachers found it hard in the beginning to be the implementers, but were given support by the researchers"; "We cannot believe how effective [the intervention] was on the adolescents' social skills"; "We saw former quiet students develop and bloom and were talking to teachers in the corridors"; "We also had students initiate social activities which has never happened before". The principals also believed that the students' new friends motivated them to come to school.

During the Covid-19 pandemic, the training was conducted via digital platforms and was described as developing. Hence face-to-face (i.e., IRL) training were perceived as more valuable. For some students with more severe social difficulties, the on-line training was described as an option, but IRL training was preferred overall. The teachers saw changes in students' social behavior during digital training too, although some students developed more relationships and friends to talk to at school during the physical training (IRL). All children and youth want to belong to a peer group based on their own personalities. Social skills group training is one approach towards improving social environments, and targeting the surroundings and peers is another. In this study, the individual training was central; peer interventions use trained peers to support students with, for example, autism. These peers are trained to interact with children with autism and social impairments, which was not a part of this training. Unexpectedly, the adolescents in the training group interacted more frequently with peers outside the training group, therefore peers developed enhanced awareness as well. Apparently, social skills group training is advantageous in naturalistic settings, but such training comes with challenges such as being resource and time demanding.

MERGED RESULTS FROM THE INTERVENTIONS

This section discusses the results from the teacher training and the social validity of social skills group training. In Table 4 (adapted from Leifler, 2022), the results from the two studies are merged.

Table 4. Key findings from the two studies, actions, and challenges

Key elements	Actions	Challenges
Support for students with NDC must be holistic, where the pedagogical/didactical, physical, and psychosocial environment is adjusted according to individual needs.	Implement and evaluate comprehensive models and interventions especially formed and designed for improved learning for students with NDC.	The need for broad knowledge and competence among all school professionals. Resource demanding and time issues.
Students with social difficulties are not given adequate support in the social environment. The holistic view of inclusion and inclusive values built in the organization.	Social skills training, group or individual. Professional development for all professionals. Inter-disciplinary collaboration, structures for professionals within and outside school to collaborate. Funding for schools.	Finding time and the right resources in school. Prioritization by principals. The shared responsibility–who takes the lead. Equity in funding opportunities.
School is a naturalistic setting for students and there is a need for more interventions implemented on different levels aiming to improve inclusive education.	Further develop evidence-based methods and interventions. Evaluating social validity. Practice-based action research.	The right competence among researchers and practitioners. Time and fundings. Highly valuing practice-based research.

DISCUSSION

This chapter presents two exploratory studies aimed at strengthening inclusive education. The studies describe interventions that use different approaches and content. The chapter can provide avenues for educators or policy makers to explore possibilities for school settings or actions for inclusion. There are many ways to offer interventions for students as well as professional development for teachers; however, the choice and implementation must be carefully considered and planned. Professional development is not without barriers. One barrier is the lack of evidence that the program makes teachers change their practice. Despite barriers, we need to start somewhere and professional development often comes with better understanding, which is in line with the findings from Rajotte et al. (2022) and Hodges et al. (2021). Furthermore, interventions provide professionals with the same knowledge base, an issue that Petersson-Bloom (2022) promote. Therefore, it is important that all professionals have the chance to participate.

We have students with NDCs and other SEND in regular classrooms and to meet their needs a holistic view of inclusion must be promoted, where being included means more than physically being placed in the classroom. All areas of the learning environment should be available. For example, the psychosocial includes student-student relations, teacher-student relations, social activities, and interactions in school activities and in the time between classes. This area needs further adjustments. The literature has identified a lack of sufficient support for students with NDCs and social impairments (Hodges et al., 2021; Leifler, 2022; Plantin-Ewe & Aspelin, 2021). In addition to a lack of focus on the psychosocial environment, recent literature has found that there is a lack of inclusive pedagogy, where learning is in focus with knowledge of what might cause difficulties for individual student (Leifler, 2022; Petersson-Bloom, 2022).

Towards Equity and Inclusion Excellence Using Diverse Interventions

Inclusion Excellence

The inclusion of students with NDCs in mainstream schools presents both challenges and opportunities for the various stakeholders, including students, peers, and teachers. Our studies have added evidence about what strategies are available to improve educational inclusion. Students with NDCs can and should be able to cope in inclusive settings if provided with sufficient and adequate support, although this goal remains unfulfilled (Leifler et al., 2022b). The author presents two approaches to this challenge that target teachers and students. These approaches, following UNESCO's recommendations (2005), provide a truly inclusive friendly environment for children and teachers who need support. The results illuminate the need of interventions and evidence-based methods in general school settings. When these methods are combined with an integrative model, special education is merged with values from inclusive education (Hornby, 2015; Ravet, 2011). All children and youth want to belong, participate, and value themselves as worthy and welcomed. Educational achievement is more than just academic skills–it is social, emotional, creative, and physical skills as well. To meet multi-faceted needs and to create truly inclusive environments, we need to broaden our views and be more flexible, understanding, creative, and especially brave and empathetic.

Although lacking a long-term perspective, the intervention for teachers improved their teaching of children with special needs. Thus, initiatives must start somewhere, and the intervention was a catalyst for the schools to continuously improve the learning environment. Teachers need opportunities for professional development regarding how to teach for classroom diversity to develop and strengthening their self-efficacy. Self-efficacy can be a motivation for action (Bandura, 1997). Teachers' acts, beliefs, and positive attitudes towards students with special educational needs and disabilities are crucial for inclusion in schools.

Social Inclusion

The second study showed large satisfaction from all participating groups, and the school environment was described as safe, practical, and a suitable environment to practice their newly developed skills. Furthermore, school attendance and students' well-being were enhanced, which had the added benefit of improved academic achievement, all urgent areas for youth in today's schools and society in general. Moreover, the intervention helped close the achievement gap while achieving inclusion. Despite the recognition of the challenges faced by students with NDCs in inclusive education, there is limited understanding of the role of the learning environment.

The school is the institution that fosters and educates young people and is a place where they live and learn together. The inclusive classroom is a milieu where diversity is the norm and those who struggle with learning should be given adequate support, a goal emphasized by UNESCO (2015). Business as usual will not improve inclusion and the responsibility is and should be shared among researchers, teachers, school leaders, and policy makers, from the micro perspective to the macro perspective. Students who fail in school present an economic cost for the global community and an emotional loss for the individual and the caregivers. According to Pellicano et al. (2018), inclusion is still an illusion, especially for the most vulnerable students.

As more students with NDCs attend regular education settings, the environment must be inclusive, especially the social environment. Children and youth want to belong and feel safe in the school environment. When they do not, students will continue to stay home, which is a natural defense. To improve, we must start with deep understanding, respect, and truly celebrate diversity. Therefore, future recommendations for research and practice include enhanced NDC awareness, where individuals' differences are met with empathy and love. Social skills group training might take time, effort, and resources, but the efforts will improve adolescents' well-being and help mitigate anxiety, self-harming behavior, and depression.

We, the author, and the collaborating research team, believe that it is important that social skills training programs, which do not impose a disproportionate burden on the individuals themselves and conducted in real world settings, need to be given more attention in both research and practice. We also believe in professional development in inclusive practices for all staff. This is in line with recommendations described in the Salamanca Declaration (UN, 1994). The second research project aimed to provide a measure of social and ecological validity from three perspectives: the student, the implementing teachers, and the school management. The emphasis was on students' voices. In the future, shaping socially valid interventions for inclusion should be done together with the implementers and individuals as meaningful participation is made together (Fletcher-Watson et al., 2019).

FUTURE RESEARCH DIRECTIONS

Inclusive education has several aspects and still needs further exploration. The questions that need further exploration address achievement, inclusion, evidence, and what counts as evidence of educational achievement (Florian et al., 2017). The questions are both conceptual and practical and address the gap in understanding of what creates an inclusive environment. Research of elements in inclusive pedagogy is needed where teachers and students are central. Moreover, explicit studies over how students are scaffolded and their individual development towards enhanced autonomy and agency are needed. The two studies in this chapter have brought attention to some areas for future research: how teachers can develop special didactics skills and how that is implemented in general as well as segregated school setting; how social skills group training can develop further and take place in schools' natural curricula; how schools can develop and organize inclusive education; and how inter-disciplinary collaboration among professionals can contribute to inclusive education.

CONCLUSION

Continual exploration of the effect of different interventions is important in reducing the achievement gap between students. Continual professional development is crucial for ensuring educators have knowledge that can improve their inclusive skills, self-efficacy, and abilities to meet all learners' needs. Inclusive pedagogy can combine traditions from special education with philosophies and values from inclusive education. It is all about the child and the right to belong, grow, and learn. Schools as educational instruction still need to find optimal adjustments in the learning environment and should serve as hubs for all children's learning, development, socializing, and enrichment. We cannot ensure inclusive education without continuously measuring and evaluating how it works in practice–i.e., it is an ongoing process. Inclusion excellence can be achieved with hard work and many actions. This chapter ends with a reflection for about the future from UNESCO: "Children who learn together, learn to live together" (2015, p. 1).

Towards Equity and Inclusion Excellence Using Diverse Interventions

ACKNOWLEDGEMENT

The studies were funded by the Swedish Research Council, [grant no 2017-06039]; for this, the author is thankful. The author would also like to thank all participants for their time, especially the adolescents for contributing with their views, which further helps in understanding how to create more inclusive communities.

REFERENCES

Afsharnejad, B., Falkmer, M., Picen, T., Black, M. H., Alach, T., Fridell, A., Coco, C., Milne, K., Perry, J., Bölte, S., & Girdler, S. (2022). "I met someone like me!": Autistic adolescents and their parents' experience of the KONTAKT social skills group training. *Journal of Autism and Developmental Disorders*, *52*(4), 1458–1477. doi:10.100710803-021-05045-1 PMID:33942186

Ainscow, M., Booth, T., & Dyson, A. (2006). Improving schools, developing inclusion. Routledge.

American Psychiatric Association (APA). (2013). *Diagnostic and Statistical Manual of Mental Disorders: DSM-5* (5th ed.). American Psychiatric Publishing.

Bandura, A. (1997). Self-efficacy. The exercise of control. *The Freeman.*

Bölte, S. (2014). Is autism curable? *Developmental Medicine and Child Neurology*, *56*(10), 927–931. doi:10.1111/dmcn.12495 PMID:24840630

Bölte, S., Leifler, E., Berggren, S., & Borg, A. (2021). Inclusive practice for students with neurodevelopmental disorders in Sweden. *Scandinavian Journal of Child and Adolescent Psychiatry and Psychology*, *9*(1), 9–15. doi:10.21307jcapp-2021-002 PMID:33928049

Bond, C., Symes, W., Hebron, J., Humphrey, N., & Morewood, G. (2016). Educating persons with autistic spectrum disorder – A systematic literature review. NCSE Research Reports No: 20. University of Manchester.

Coco, C., Fridell, A., Borg, A., & Bölte, S. (2023). *SKOLKONTAKT®, Manual. Social färdighetsträning i grupp* [Social skills group training, the manual]. Hogrefe.

De Boer, A., Pijl, S. J., & Minnaert, A. (2011). Regular primary schoolteachers' attitudes towards inclusive education: A review of the literature. *International Journal of Inclusive Education*, *15*(3), 331–353. doi:10.1080/13603110903030089

Fletcher-Watson, S., Adams, J., Brook, K., Charman, T., Crane, L., Cusack, J., Leekam, S., Milton, D., Parr, J. R., & Pellicano, E. (2019). Making the future together: Shaping autism research through meaningful participation. *Autism*, *23*(4), 943–953. doi:10.1177/1362361318786721 PMID:30095277

Florian, L., Black-Hawkins, K., & Rouse, M. (2017). *Achievement and Inclusion in Schools*. Routledge.

Florian, L., & Linklater, H. (2010). Preparing teachers for inclusive education: Using inclusive pedagogy to enhance teaching and learning for all. *Cambridge Journal of Education*, *40*(4), 369–386. doi:10.108 0/0305764X.2010.526588

Florian, L., & Spratt, J. (2013). Enacting inclusion: A framework for interrogating inclusive practice. *European Journal of Special Needs Education*, *28*(2), 119–135. doi:10.1080/08856257.2013.778111

Forlin, C. (2010). *Teacher education for inclusion. Changing paradigms and innovative approaches.* Routledge. doi:10.4324/9780203850879

Hodges, A., Cordier, R., Joosten, A., & Bourke-Taylor, H. (2021). Closing the gap between theory and practice: Conceptualisation of a school-based intervention to improve the school participation of primary school students on the autism spectrum and their typically developing peers. *Journal of Autism and Developmental Disorders*, *52*(7), 3230–3245. doi:10.100710803-021-05362-5 PMID:34862953

Hornby, G. (2015). Inclusive Special Education: Development of a new theory for the education of children with special educational needs and disabilities. *British Journal of Special Education*, *42*(3), 234–256. doi:10.1111/1467-8578.12101

Hornby, G. (2021). Are inclusive education or special education programs more likely to result in inclusion post-school? *Education Sciences*, *11*(304), 304. doi:10.3390/educsci11060304

Jonsson, U., Choque Olsson, N., Coco, C., Görling, A., Flygare, O., Råde, A., & Bölte, S. (2019). Long-term social skills group training for children and adolescents with autism spectrum disorder: A randomized controlled trial. *European Child & Adolescent Psychiatry*, *28*(2), 189–201. doi:10.100700787-018-1161-9 PMID:29748736

Klefbeck, K. (2021). Lesson Study as a Way of Improving School-Day Navigation for Pupils with Severe Intellectual Disability and Autism. *International Journal for Lesson and Learning Studies*, *10*(4), 348–361. doi:10.1108/IJLLS-03-2021-0024

Küller, R. (1991). Environmental assessment from a neuropsychological perspective. In T. Gärling & G. W. Evans (Eds.), *Environment; Cognition and Action: An integrated approach.* Oxford University Press.

Leifler, E. (2020). Teachers' capacity to create inclusive learning environments. *International Journal for Lesson and Learning Studies*, *9*(3), 221–244. doi:10.1108/IJLLS-01-2020-0003

Leifler, E. (2022). *Educational inclusion for students with neurodevelopmental conditions.* [PhD Thesis. Dep. of Women's and Children's Health. Karolinska Institute].

Leifler, E., Borg, A., & Bölte, S. (2022b). A multi-perspective study of perceived inclusive education for students with neurodevelopmental disorders. *Journal of Autism and Developmental Disorders*, *2022*(Jul), 4. doi:10.100710803-022-05643-7 PMID:35781856

Leifler, E., Carpelan, G., Zakrevska, A., Bölte, S., & Jonsson, U. (2020). Does the learning environment make the grade? A systematic literature review of accommodations for children on the autism spectrum in mainstream school. *Scandinavian Journal of Occupational Therapy*, *28*(8), 582–597. doi:10.1080/11038128.2020.1832145 PMID:33078981

Leifler, E., Coco, C., Fridell, A., Borg, A., & Bölte, S. (2022a). Social skills group training for students with neurodevelopmental disorders in senior high school: A qualitative multi-perspective study of social validity. *International Journal of Environmental Research and Public Health*, *19*(1487). PMID:35162512

Lord, C., Charman, T., Havdahl, A., Carbone, P., Anagnostou, E., Boyd, B., Carr, T., de Vries, P. J., Dissanayake, C., Divan, G., Freitag, C. M., Gotelli, M. M., Kasari, C., Knapp, M., Mundy, P., Plank, A., Scahill, L., Servili, C., Shattuck, P., & McCauley, J. B. (2021). The Lancet Commission on the future of care and clinical research in autism. *Lancet*, *399*(10321), 271–334. doi:10.1016/S0140-6736(21)01541-5 PMID:34883054

Norwich, B. (2020). *Lesson study for special needs and inclusive education*. Lesson Study Send. https://www.lessonstudysend.co.uk/

Odom, S., Cox, A., & Brock, M. (2013). Implementation science, professional development, and autism spectrum disorders. *Exceptional Children*, *79*(2), 233–251. doi:10.1177/0014402913079002081

Parsons, S., Guldberg, A., MacLeod, A., Jones, G., Punty, A., & Balfe, T. (2011). International review of the evidence on best practice in educational provision for children on the autism spectrum. *European Journal of Special Needs Education*, *26*(1), 47–63. doi:10.1080/08856257.2011.543532

Pellicano, E., Bölte, S., & Stahmer, A. (2018). The current illusion of educational inclusion. *Autism*, *22*(4), 386–387. doi:10.1177/1362361318766166 PMID:29600722

Petersson -Bloom. L. (2022). *Equity in education for autistic students. Professional learning to accommodate inclusive education.* [Doctoral Dissertation in Education, Malmö University].

Plantin Ewe, L., & Aspelin, J. (2021). Relational competence regarding students with ADHD– An intervention study with in-service teachers. *European Journal of Special Needs Education*, *37*(2), 293–308.

Rajotte, E., Grandisson, M., Hamel, C., Couture, M., Desmarais, C., Gravel, M., & Chrétien-Vincent, M. (2022). Inclusion of autistic students: Promising modalities for supporting a school team. *Disability and Rehabilitation*. doi:10.1080/09638288.2022.2057598 PMID:35389757

Ravet, J. (2011). Inclusive/exclusive? Contradictory perspectives on autism and inclusion: The case for and integrative position. *International Journal of Inclusive Education*, *15*(6), 667–682. doi:10.1080/13603110903294347

Thomas, G., & Loxley, A. (2001). *Deconstructing Special Education and Constructing Inclusion*. Open University Press.

Thorell, L. B. (2007). Do delay aversion and executive function deficits make distinct contributions to the functional impact of ADHD symptoms? A study of early academic skill deficits. *Journal of Child Psychology and Psychiatry, and Allied Disciplines*, *48*(11), 1061–1070. doi:10.1111/j.1469-7610.2007.01777.x PMID:17995481

Tomlinson, S. (2012). The irresistible rise of the SEND industry. *Oxford Review of Education*, *38*(3), 267–286. doi:10.1080/03054985.2012.692055

Tschannen-Moran, M., & Woolfolk Hoy, A. (2001). Teacher efficacy: Capturing an elusive construct. *Teaching and Teacher Education*, *17*(7), 783–805. doi:10.1016/S0742-051X(01)00036-1

United Nations Educational, Scientific and Cultural Organization (UNESCO). (1994). *The Salamanca Statement and framework for action on special needs education*. UNESCO.

United Nations Educational, Scientific and Cultural Organization (UNESCO). (2005). *Guidelines for inclusion: Ensuring Access to Education for All*. UNESCO.

United Nations Educational, Scientific and Cultural Organization (UNESCO). (2015). *Sub-Education Policy Review Report: Inclusive Education*. UNESCO.

United Nations (UN). *Sustainable Development Goals. Agenda 2030*. UN. https://www.un.org/sustainabledevelopment/sustainable-development-goals/

Watkins, L., Ledbetter-Cho, K., O'Reilly, M., Barnard-Brak, L., & Garcia-Grau, P. (2019). Interventions for students with autism in inclusive settings: A best-evidence synthesis and meta-analysis. *Psychological Bulletin*, *145*(5), 490–507. doi:10.1037/bul0000190 PMID:30869925

Watkins, L., O'Reilly, M., Ledbetter-Cho, K., Lang, R., Sigafoos, J., Kuhn, M., Lim, N., Gevarter, C., & Caldwell, N. (2017). A meta-analysis of school-based social interaction interventions for adolescents with autism spectrum disorder. *Review Journal of Autism and Developmental Disorders*, *4*(4), 277–293. doi:10.100740489-017-0113-5

Wolf, M. M. (1978). Social validity: The case for subjective measurement or how applied behavior analysis is finding its heart1. *Journal of Applied Behavior Analysis*, *1978*(11), 203–214. doi:10.1901/jaba.1978.11-203 PMID:16795590

KEY TERMS AND DEFINITIONS

Inclusive Special Education: This new focus and concept, presented by Hornby (2015), combines traditions from special education and inclusive education. According to Hornby, we need to go beyond the tension and dilemmas with the two traditions and start with the core ideas of inclusive education based on human-rights and democracy and create settings where all children can be taught together as far as possible. However, adequate support based on evidence from methods and strategies developed and derived from special education, explicitly for SEND children, is still needed. This integrative approach has been adapted by other researchers such as Ravet (2011).

Interventions: Interventions are common in medical settings as a specific strategy to address a problem or specific behavior. It is an act or something you provide to individuals aiming to have effects such as improving or changing a behavior. The intervention provides education in different ways. In educational settings, it can be different strategies for developing academic skills, and it can be professional development for teachers' learning. That is, such an approach must add something in a certain context with a specific content and measure the outcomes. Measurements are made before and after an intervention.

IRL *vs* Digital Training: In real life (IRL) training is a program or training that takes place face-to-face, for example, in a room or a classroom. The digital training is conducted virtually (i.e., on-line) with participants at home or elsewhere. Each training platform has both pros and cons and can affect how individuals respond to the training.

Learning Environment: The learning environment, sometimes referred to as the learning context, is the whole environment and context that surrounds the students during the school day. It is where all learning happens. It is the physical, psychosocial, and pedagogic/didactical environment. The physical environment includes the rooms, indoor and outdoor, where education activities take place. It is how

Towards Equity and Inclusion Excellence Using Diverse Interventions

rooms are organized and includes the acoustics and lighting in the rooms. The learning environment also includes school and class size and the resources that are available. The psychosocial environment is about trust, relationships, and mental health. It is participation, interaction, attitudes, culture, and communication. The pedagogical/didactical environment is the art of teaching, the didactics, and concrete phenomena such as instructions, materials, tasks, and learning activities, also known as artefacts.

Lesson Study: Lesson and learning studies are forms of professional development for teachers, which was developed in Japan and spread worldwide. It includes a cyclic process and starts with a problem or an area for development identified in teachers' actual practices. It aligns with the bottom-up perspective, and the topic teachers choose aims to improve learning for their students. Students' learning and progress are measured and evaluated in collaboration. Measuring teachers' learning, as done in this study (i.e., NDC AI), is less common, however.

Naturalistic Settings: Real-world settings are places where individuals naturally spend their time such as the home, the school, and the playground. Interventions implemented in naturalistic setting have less issues with generalization.

Neurodevelopmental Conditions: Neurodevelopmental conditions, also called neurodevelopmental disorders, highlight the natural variation in populations and puts less focus on disabilities. It is an umbrella term for conditions and diagnoses such as autism, ADHD, intellectual disability, and motor disorders. Dyslexia and dyscalculia are within NDCs. NDCs often have co-morbidities–i.e., these individuals could have more than one diagnosis. NDCs include various conditions that emerge in early childhood and can cause persistent impairments in cognitive, social, academic, or occupational functioning.

RCTs, Random Controlled Trials: Quantitative methods such RCTs are research designs where participants are randomly allocated to an intervention or control group (no intervention). The intervention aims to make a difference, for example, in social skills group training. The same measures are taken at the same time for both the intervention and control groups. In the study presented in this chapter, the control group were active–i.e., they were also doing something although with the same content as the training group. The control group only took part in social activities.

Social Skills Group Training: Social skills training is an umbrella term comprising different methods and training for individuals to train and develop social skills. It can be conducted individually or in a group. Some evidence suggests that social skills group training can improve social skills in individuals. Most social skills training is conducted in a clinical setting; however, this study was conducted in the school setting, also known as a naturalistic setting.

Special Didactics: The art of teaching includes how teaching is designed and prepared to meet classroom diversity. The general didactics are included as well as the "what", "why", and "how". However, in special didactics, the focus is on the "who"–i.e., who are we teaching and their characteristics. It is how learning is available for more students, and the adjustments needed when what works for most people does not work for everybody. Special didactics is grounded in cognition and children's learning. In special didactics, teachers are more flexible, creative, and have a broad knowledge of what different students might need. This partly aligns with universal design for learning, where the environment and content are carefully prepared and all barriers are analyzed and anticipated. That is, it is not an add-on; it is fundamental in the variation of teaching methods and materials.

Chapter 5

Universal Design for Learning as Support for the Inclusion of Deaf Student Teachers in Training

Marcia Mirl Lyner-Cleophas
Stellenbosch University, South Africa

Claudia Priscilla Saunderson
Stellenbosch University, South Africa

Lizelle Josephine Apollis
Stellenbosch University, South Africa

ABSTRACT

South Africa is a society historically marred by exclusion and discrimination based on inter alia race, gender, economic status, disability, and language. The restoration of dignity, diversity, equity, and inclusion is a high priority. At Stellenbosch University (SU), policies such as the Language Policy (2021), Disability Access Policy (2018) and Assessment Policy (2022) have fostered redress inclusive of students with disabilities. This chapter reviews how shifts were implemented using the above-mentioned policies by highlighting how flexibility was introduced in the education of Deaf students in the Faculty of Education at SU having UDL in mind. The chapter traces teaching, learning, and assessment support in Deaf student teacher training at SU. The conclusion is that policies assist in facilitating changing environments while promoting inclusivity in flexible curricula and support practices.

DOI: 10.4018/978-1-6684-7370-2.ch005

Copyright © 2023, IGI Global. Copying or distributing in print or electronic forms without written permission of IGI Global is prohibited.

UDL as Support for the Inclusion of Deaf Student Teachers in Training

INTRODUCTION

This chapter endeavours to explore the education of Deaf student teachers who primarily use South African Sign Language (SASL) as a means of communication, teaching, learning and assessment in South Africa. The specific context is higher education and Deaf student teacher training in the Foundation Phase (grades R – 3). The chapter goes about this exploration by highlighting the South African socio-political, economic, and educational landscape, foregrounding selected existing policies in the post-apartheid context and showing how these are being implemented. It furthermore fosters transformative practices and proposes flexible ways of responding to student diversity with specific reference to Deaf students. The universal design for learning (UDL) framework is highlighted as a means that enabled the success of Deaf students at Stellenbosch University (SU). In this chapter, Deaf students as a linguistic and cultural group that uses SASL as a means of communication is the reference group.

BACKGROUND

Fabric of Exclusion

South Africa emerged from hundreds of years of colonisation and discrimination that impacted its society on a large scale. The Dutch, Portuguese and English were the main colonisers, and South African indigenous people were deprived and lost much in land and economic growth through the periods of rule by these foreign nations. Apartheid was abolished in 1994 (Republic of South Africa [RSA], 1996), and South Africa had to slowly start to repair hundreds of years of damage left in its wake. This legacy is one of division and huge inequities in the country from a societal, economic, language, educational, health, wealth, and psychological perspective.

SU presents a microcosm of the South African legacy of inequity. It is still battling with redressing the pervasive inequalities in the broader society. On the one hand, the University has rich resources and a cohort of students with a legacy of affluence and privilege. On the other hand, it has a large contingent of students who struggle financially, socially and psychologically. Much attention has been paid to the racially unequal past and its transformation. However, students with disabilities also reflect these societal inequities and have also been left behind. With the advent of democracy, inclusive education became part of education policy (RSA, 2001), 22 years ago. This makes inclusive education very recent in its formation, and it is still in the process of development as we strive towards social justice in all its facets in South Africa and SU.

Creating Equitable Experiences in Education

Given the inclusive education policies that have taken root in South Africa and the education system and the incorporation of global policies, the country is clearly committed to creating inclusive experiences in schools and universities. The framework for inclusive education is captured in the country's education policy as contained in the Education White Paper 6: Special Needs Education: Building an Inclusive Education and Training System (RSA, 2001). This policy attempts to address the diverse needs of all learners who might experience barriers to learning. It also calls for a conceptual shift that is based on the premise that all learners and adults have the potential to learn, given the necessary support. The policy furthermore asserts that to make inclusive education a reality, there needs to be a conceptual shift regarding the provision of support for students who experience barriers to learning. Thus, the implementation of inclusive education serves as a means for augmenting equity and educational outcomes, and therefore higher education institutions are required to promote inclusion within the teaching and learning context in its broader sense (McKenzie & Dalton, 2020).

The Strategic Policy Framework on Disability for the Post-School Education and Training (PSET) System (RSA, 2018) provides a framework for inclusive education in the post school sector. It is one of the most recent education policy frameworks that is specifically dedicated to the PSET sector. This framework notes UDL and universal design (UD) as a means of support towards inclusion and proposes the incorporation of UD into faculty instruction and curricula, which can be of benefit to all students in the learning process. Providing institutionally accessible environments, using flexible classroom materials, applying a variety of technological tools, varying the delivery of information and instructions, and generally infusing universal design techniques are hallmarks of this PSET policy. This policy further notes that the PSET sector should focus on people's attitudes towards disability, social support and services, suitable formats of information, simplicity of language use, physical access, and flexibility of time.

The framework also regards the PSET sector as the cornerstone of an integrated and caring society of the 21st century. Student nurturing should be key, and an inclusive society acknowledging racial diversity, ethnic diversity, gender equity, disability and religious difference should be driven by the quest for human dignity. Key principles are equal rights, self-respect, self-sufficiency, social inclusion, mainstreaming and the right to self-representation. The rights to support systems, equitable resource allocation, accessibility and collaboration are all encouraged in this policy.

SU's history of embracing diversity started in the 1970s when the first blind students in law and music were enrolled. The Disability Unit (DU) was founded in 2007 at SU, and almost 100 students were enrolled. In 2022, SU had 573 enrolled students with disclosed disabilities and 824 students who were actively receiving support, according to the SU report on concessions (SU, 2022). In 2023, SU had 662 students with disclosed disabilities (SU, 2023). The need for a support service arose as an increasing number of students with disabilities entered university given the policy of inclusive education that took root in the school system from 2001. Students were increasingly empowered to attend schools, not only special schools, continue to postschool education, and gain higher qualifications to ensure their rightful place in society.

Support services for all students, including students with disabilities, exist to ensure equitable experiences for students. Students who are accepted to universities have proven a high level of cognitive functioning and success in school. Students are diverse in their ways of thinking and the speed at which they process information. Their vision, hearing, mobility, and creativity differ. Students have various talents and strengths. Embracing the richness of this diversity is invaluable as we increasingly realise that in any society, we must work together and support each other in our uniqueness to enable a variegated and enriched world. The Disability Access Policy (2018) at SU has its chief aim to become a universally accessible campus to provide equitable experiences. This is laid down in policy to address the diversity on its campus. Key concepts in this policy are universal access, universal design and universal design for learning which has relevance to this chapter. It states that its objectives include the provision of inclusive and universally accessible living, learning, and teaching environments. Both curricular and co-curricular spaces are relevant to inclusion. The SU Assessment Policy (2021) advocates for an assessment approach that is flexible. Faculties are encouraged to do various assessments throughout the module that would contribute to the final mark. Even though the traditional test-type assessments are used, the policy allows for an assessment strategy that considers a range of assessment forms.

At SU, there are several ways to ensure that all students can optimise their potential by creating equitable opportunities for this to happen. A range of resources and flexible thinking is needed to enable equitability. Students could need help with finances, assistance from support services to engage with their lecturers or the physical environment, support with their social integration, boosting of their psychological wellbeing and academic guidance such as proactive workshops regarding study skills or time management, to name but a few. Students are multifaceted and therefore could need support in numerous ways. It is vital that collaboration takes place alongside faculty to enable success. This is the best way to achieve the desired results as working in isolation is counterproductive. A triad of support services, the student and the faculty exist to optimise academic potential. These three elements need to work in unison to produce positive outcomes. To maintain the balance between the three, however, remains a challenge.

It is obligatory to empower students with the requisite skills in higher education to ensure sustainability. This means that students must also learn skills that will enable them to adjust to the broader society without the support provided at university. If a student uses certain assistive technologies and masters these thoroughly, these skills should be employed subsequently to support them and their livelihoods. Alternative modes of support in the world of work must be explored, and students should be empowered to be open to these possibilities as the resources available at university might not exist in the workplace.

Purpose of the Chapter

In this chapter, we take a glimpse at how a UDL approach can be employed to enable the successful study of Deaf student teachers in higher education, hereby raising the standard of the education of Deaf learners and adding to equitable redress in South Africa. Reflections on teaching and learning practices for Deaf student teachers are highlighted.

Deaf people that identify with a specific value system and beliefs form part of Deaf culture (therefore D is capitalised). People who do not identify their deafness with a particular value system use lower case "d" in deaf. These are other ways of identifying the spectrum of hearing (Brown, 2021). In the context of this chapter, we refer to Deaf people who use SASL as a means of communication, teaching and learning.

With SASL still on the cusp of being an official language in South Africa, the inclusion of SASL in schools has necessitated the higher education landscape to be more proactive about the inclusion of SASL in this sector. Pockets of expertise already exist in the school and post school sector, but the school sector in particular needs more teachers (including Deaf teachers) trained in SASL to improve the educational standards of Deaf learners in the entire educational system. Much more effort needs to go into ensuring practices that follow policies created for Deaf learners, such as teaching in their first language, which is SASL.

Although SASL is not an official 12th language yet, its use in schools for Deaf learners has taken root. Certain universities in South Africa also have SASL interpreters. At SU, SASL has been included in the Language Policy (2021). This has enabled us to have SASL interpreters as part of the Language Centre's interpretation services together with English, Afrikaans and Xhosa interpretation. This policy has also enabled the training of Deaf students at university.

Focus on Deaf Education in South Africa

Multilingualism Within the South African Context

According to Thomas (2022), South Africa has 11 official languages with SASL poised to become the 12th. Despite the official status of these languages, the language of instruction at most schools is English with Afrikaans and other indigenous languages offered as second or third languages. Variations also occur in the various provinces. At university, given the range of languages that students use as their home language, the most common language of instruction is English. This is based on its international and local language of common usage. South Africa grapples with finding a means to not exclude anyone and to proffer at least one common language understood by all, bearing in mind the histories and legacies of the many languages used in the country. SASL has not yet been officially recognised as an official language in South Africa. It is in the final throes of its promulgation, even though it is now recognised as a language that students can offer as their home language (first language or mother tongue) in schools.

South African Sign Language: Efforts to Include in Curricula

SASL is officially recognised by the Department of Basic Education in South Africa. This is the department in charge of the phase of education prior to entering a university, which includes schooling from Grade R to Grade 12 (matric). SASL has been offered as a home language at schools since 2015. The shift was part of the democratic inclusion of Deaf students in the school system as up till then, SASL was not officially recognised in schools. The first group of Grade 12 students who used SASL as a first language finished their schooling in 2018 (Bell, 2021). A few students have entered university since then and a few before 2018, despite the official recognition of SASL in schools in 2015 only. Higher education and the postschool environment thus had to prepare for these students.

The higher education landscape contains a few pockets of expertise where SASL is taught as an academic discipline through which university students can gain credits. Additionally, a limited number of universities employ SASL as a medium of instruction, sometimes in certain faculties only. These universities include the University of Cape Town, the University of the Witwatersrand, the University of the Free State and Stellenbosch University. Given the inclusion of SASL at schools, the number of Deaf students who graduate from universities will increase and the inclusion of Deaf people in society will improve.

Challenges Within the Educational Context of the Deaf Learner

The educational outcomes of persons with disabilities, including persons who are Deaf, are among the worst in South Africa. Some of the contributing factors to this sad reality are the lack of knowledge and training on how to address the educational and learning needs of Deaf learners. Another factor that impacts Deaf learners' educational journey negatively is the fact that Deaf teacher training at particularly the lower grades of education (such as primary school) is lacking and not properly understood. In 2015 and 2016, only five and four Deaf matriculants respectively achieved a pass that qualified them to apply to higher education institutions (Deaf Federation of South Africa, 2018). In this regard, Kelly et al. (2020) concurs that Deaf learners in South Africa have significant difficulty communicating with their

UDL as Support for the Inclusion of Deaf Student Teachers in Training

teachers and that teachers of Deaf learners are not sufficiently trained to understand the educational and support needs of their learners.

On a positive note, Parkin (2010) believes that for the most part, Deaf learners are fully capable of reaching the same educational goals that are expected of any other learner. The author furthermore states that this is not surprising because Deaf learners mostly must operate within learning environments of low expectations and are perceived by the system and most role-players as not being able to achieve success.

Even within an inclusive framework and despite various pro-disability policies, Deaf learners still experience numerous barriers, including psychosocial, economic, and financial challenges. Other challenges involve policy implementation, teacher training, flexible assessment, curriculum adaptations, and flexibility and attitude regarding disability and inclusion.

Within the Department of Basic Education, there are insufficient specialist skills and knowledge regarding Deaf learners and their needs, which makes it particularly challenging to advise on appropriate Deaf education practices and support (Parkin, 2010). Furthermore, although SASL is recognised in most education policy documents in South Africa, challenges arise when these policies need to be implemented (Parkin, 2010). Another aspect that is concerning is the lack of inspection and control of teachers of Deaf learners regarding curriculum implementation, teaching methodology and qualification requirements (Parkin, 2010). Parkin states that many teachers enter the classroom with little or no experience with Deafness, nor are they required to have any qualifications. This leads to an inability of teachers to communicate with learners, which often creates situations where the responsibility to teach the respective teacher about communicating effectively in the classroom falls on the learner. This slows the pace at which teaching and learning take place. Parkin (2010, p. 491) makes the assertion that "learners are only taught up to the level at which their teacher can communicate with them". This demonstrates why teacher training of Deaf teachers is so vital and why the educational levels of Deaf learners are so low.

A further challenge that Deaf learners face is transitioning from school to post-school education. Transitioning involves a process of planning that considers a learner's interests, preferences and level of functioning. Often, discussions with higher education institutions do not occur early enough and learners are not accepted to study or are accepted into courses that university staff deem suitable without considering the individual ideals of Deaf learners. Once Deaf students are admitted, they may experience a variety of challenges. Bell and Swart (2018), assert that there could be many reasons why these barriers exist. The authors offer the following reasons: lack of support; lack of awareness of the accommodation needs of these students; the 'invisibility' and uniqueness of their hearing loss and thus complex support needs; teaching staff ignoring calls to attend disability-related, professional development courses; attitudinal barriers of faculty members; and lack of financial and human resources.

Howell (2006) reports that these barriers have profound and sustained effects on students' psychological and social functioning. While inclusive education is a global imperative (United Nations, 2006) and a national priority in South Africa, students with disabilities, especially in higher education, continue to face a variety of barriers – physical, social, and attitudinal (Foundation of Tertiary Institutes of the Northern Metropolis, 2011; Ndlovu & Walton, 2016). Given this, the quality of these students' educational experience is affected. It has also been suggested by Reindal (1995) that students with sensory disabilities encounter so many practical difficulties that their ability to study can be compromised, which results in attrition and failure to persist in higher education.

A variety of support mechanisms are available to Deaf students in South African universities, but these vary from university to university. The types of support available include academic tutors, manual notetaking, instructional and curricula adaptations, language modification, extra time for tests and examinations, induction loop systems, real-time captioning, and assistive devices (Bell & Swart, 2018). Although these supportive practices are available at some institutions of higher education, it remains a challenge to ensure that all Deaf students in higher education can participate equally in all academic-related activities.

Students With Disabilities and the Teaching, Learning and Assessment Context in Higher Education

People with disabilities have made remarkable strides regarding integration into domains that they were excluded from for years. Among those achievements is increased access to higher education. Yet, despite this shift to wider participation, students with disabilities remain significantly underrepresented and sometimes under-supported. In this regard, the literature suggests that higher education institutions are still lagging in terms of improving the academic success of students with disabilities by allowing them to access the general curriculum as well as alternative and flexible assessment opportunities. This has become a serious concern, with numerous academics and researchers directing attention to the need for adequate strategies and approaches that address issues such as curriculum and assessment adaptations, accessibility and support services provision to be developed and put in place in higher education institutions (Chiwandire & Vincent, 2019).

This calls for a global shift within the teaching and learning context toward effective and flexible teaching and assessment practices, such as the creation of stimulating learning environments, respect and recognition of student diversity, and awareness of the diverse learning needs that students might bring into learning spaces. It is imperative that all role players in higher education spaces, especially faculty members, make every reasonable effort to provide all students, especially students with disabilities, with opportunities to succeed. Furthermore, faculty are positioned at a pivotal point in the academic experience of all students, and they can positively impact student outcomes and engagement while mitigating feelings of isolation, discouragement, and insecurity, which are commonly experienced by especially students with disabilities in higher education (Francis et al., 2019). Therefore, to ensure that all students, especially students with disabilities, persist and graduate, it is crucial for all role-players in the higher education domain to reimagine, redesign and align the policies, teaching approaches, support models, attitudes, structures, and technologies that they provide within the teaching and learning context (Pitman et al., 2021).

Universal Design for Learning Framework Within the Teaching and Learning Context

With this in mind, Brand et al. (2012) propose UDL as a framework that addresses and conceptualises the need for a more pliable and flexible curriculum designed to address barriers and enable students with diverse needs to be included in the learning process. Moreover, regarding eliminating potential barriers to learning in higher education spaces, UDL is widely hailed as a best and appropriate practice, according to Mitchell (2010). The author furthermore defines UDL as the "planning and delivering of programs with the needs of all students in mind, from the outset and it applies to all facets of education, from curriculum, assessment, and pedagogy to classroom and institution design" (ibid, p13).

The proposal of UDL is in line with the social model of disability as opposed to the medical model of disability. The medical model views disability as an 'individualised problem' and focuses on what is 'wrong' with the individual as opposed to what is wrong with the environment or context or what the individual needs. The social model, in contrast, does not perceive disability as inherent to the individual or as a deficit that needs to be cured. This model rather focuses on identifying and addressing the barriers and deficits within the environment that hinder individuals with disabilities so that they can have equal access to learning and other opportunities. The social model, therefore, emphasises the importance of the redesigning, rearranging, and restructuring of academic or educational environments to enable all students to flourish and have access to teaching and assessment approaches that address the learning and support needs of all students (Pitman et al., 2021). This model links with the tenets of inclusive education.

Faculty members are positioned fundamentally as active champions for UDL. Approaches and strategies that aim to reduce learning barriers in the classroom for all students and to advocate for the advancement of inclusive learning cultures should start here (Mitchell, 2010; Hills et al., 2022). Due to its provision of multiple means of representation, engagement, action and expression, the UDL framework offers a promising model to facilitate curriculum access and flexible assessment opportunities for all students in higher education settings. This flexibility and diverse strategies and approaches facilitate access to learning for all students by taking their diverse learning needs and abilities into consideration. Important to note is that the application of UDL principles and strategies is not limited to the teaching of content and how to engage students, but rather extends to flexible assessment opportunities as well. Although this will not be without challenges, with the right mindset, attitude, and knowledge of UDL as well as a well-defined purpose of assessment that aligns with the objectives of the course, it is possible to overcome most challenges (Alsalamah, 2020).

Three Principles of Universal Design for Learning and how This can Manifest in Deaf Students' Teacher Training

We trace the journey of Deaf students doing teacher training for Deaf learners in the Foundation Phase (early grades) during their studies at SU. Their journeys are weaved into the three principles of UDL below. Their successful study encompassed a measure of flexibility and an openness to engaging more closely with the students' and their specific needs. Motivation, flexibility, collaboration lecturer encouragement, mentoring and coaching went a long way in ensuring the students' success (Lamprecht, 2022; Segars, 2021).

Principle 1: Multiple Means of Engagement—The 'Why' of Learning

The 'why' of learning impacts our affective networks and stimulates interest and motivation for learning. This looks at how interest is piqued and sustained. The propensity to persevere and self-regulate come into play here. The affective network is therefore required to interpret the world in terms of emotional significance and impact and, therefore, acts as an emotional filter as we view everyday actions and make decisions based on emotion and motivation. It furthermore assists in influencing the decision to either persist or shut down when confronted with challenging issues. Within the educational context, emotional challenges have a tremendous impact on a student's academic performance and engagement (Rose & Strangman, 2007).

When reflecting on the Deaf student teacher experience, it became clear that most of the challenges experienced with academics emanated from being a Deaf student. The recent impact of the COVID-19 pandemic also had a significant impact on the experience of Deaf students. Especially the shift between face-to-face and online learning created an uncertain, unstable, and unpredictable context. The emotional and academic struggle became real. Student teachers were fearful and uncertain. It was challenging to understand what was being said in the news on television networks during these uncertain times and not being able to hear updated information on COVID. Being a Deaf student teacher in a predominantly hearing community in both a class and an out-of-class context contributed to experiencing feelings of loneliness and isolation. Furthermore, being forced to abruptly leave campus because of COVID-19 sparked panic and anxiety. The main medium through which Deaf students were taught and communicated was via SASL. This presented a challenge in the off-campus environment coupled with feelings of vulnerability, low resilience levels and personal difficulties.

It was challenging to navigate academics from home, and it was easy for Deaf students to fall behind and feel a sense of an inability to cope and come up with effective strategies that would mitigate the sudden pivot to off-campus teaching and learning. The lack of confidence to reach out to lecturers and to ask for help impeded academic focus, resulting in underachievement and disconnection from academics. Feelings of alienation and being misunderstood crept in. There was a sense that other students and certain lecturers were not sympathetic to and understanding of the learning needs of Deaf students which impacted their mental health as well as their academic progress negatively. When a student, especially one with a disability, must contend with domestic strife, mental health challenges and relationship difficulties, it can lead to a downward spiral of deteriorating academic performance.

At this point, Deaf students became disengaged and considered quitting their studies. This situation then called for an urgent need to step in and think about alternative modalities given the changed context. Creativity and reviewing other ways of reaching the academic outcomes took root. Anchored within a UDL support framework, a support approach and plan were established to pique and regain interest and to assist with self-regulation, becoming motivated and purposeful. Two weekly coaching and mentoring sessions were scheduled. Getting other stakeholders such as the family involved to ascertain what was happening in the background was useful. A family member would sometimes join the coaching sessions as an additional support. During these sessions and through the provision of multiple means of engagement, the students could share learning needs, feelings, and experiences. This was done through, for example, self-reflective writing and online coaching sessions during which support was provided by a SASL interpreter. This helped to foster engagement in the academic work given the sudden shifts amidst the pandemic.

Choices in explicit learning goals were also addressed and facilitated during these sessions. Realistic goals were set with appropriate challenges. After a few weeks, feelings of positivity and re-energising took place. This was evident in students starting to engage and communicate once they started to feel a bit better. Once students showed this interest again, reaching out to lecturers was evident. Spontaneity set in as students awoke from their state of being disengaged. A co-creation of the academic tasks could be put in place as ways were sought to reach the specific outcomes of the academic work that needed to be completed. The response from certain lecturers was positive. Plans to complete outstanding activities, assignments and missed tests took place. Based on the principles of UDL and in the spirit of fairness and multiple opportunities for learning and assessment, the academic outcomes could be reached successfully.

Principle 2: Multiple Means of Representation—The 'What' of Learning

This principle focuses on how information or learning content was customised or how alternative ways of teaching were explored. Deaf students differ in the ways that they perceive and comprehend information.

UDL as Support for the Inclusion of Deaf Student Teachers in Training

It is therefore important to think about diverse ways of accessing content. Some may simply understand information quicker or more efficiently through other means than printed text. The second principle of UDL, providing multiple means of representation, ensures that learning and transfer of learning occur through a variety of representations that can improve learning opportunities (National Center on Universal Design for Learning, 2012).

On reflecting on the work with Deaf student teachers, various stakeholders facilitated the teaching and learning journey. A range of support modalities and alternative teaching strategies to access module content were needed. It was important to establish clear boundaries regarding the responsibilities of the lecturers and the interpreters as the interpreters were the conduits through which educational material and all other information was conveyed. It was important for students to take ownership and be responsible for their academic journey. Learning material was presented in multiple forms. Alternatives for auditory information was offered by sharing information in more ways other than sound and voice alone. For example, all audio material was supported with subtitles and/or text descriptions as well as full transcriptions. The auditory description of content was also available in Word format.

Other means of representation of academic material included access to SASL interpreters with whom the Deaf students had an established relationship. The interpreters could interpret the content uploaded on SUNLearn (the online learning management system), video record these and then send these video recordings to the students.

SASL is a visual language. This makes it challenging for students to watch interpreted videos, follow a sign language interpreter while simultaneously taking notes. In some of the lectures, note takers were appointed to take notes and share these with Deaf students. However, Deaf student teachers were encouraged to take notes where possible.

To encourage independence, all email correspondence was sent directly to the students. The SASL interpreters were very involved in the educational process and was copied in all communication. If any clarification was needed by the students, they could engage with the interpreters. Additionally, they could include whoever else they were comfortable with as part of the communication process, such as other support staff in the team.

A biweekly fixed time to meet was arranged. These sessions allowed the opportunity for questions regarding the learning content, assignments, tests and so forth. Close monitoring took place where Deaf students had to confirm attendance or non-attendance a day in advance and had to come prepared with specific questions. Preferences for who should join the sessions was discussed.

Extensions on teaching and learning activities, communicated in advance, were allowed because sometimes the students had to wait for interpreted recordings of content which also took longer to work through. It was also important to break down large assignments into components to provide frequent opportunities for assessment and feedback to minimise or correct errors.

These presented flexible and creative ways in which content was represented and helped the students make sense of the content. A guided process to ensure understanding was possible within this UDL framework.

Principle 3: Multiple Means of Action and Expression—The 'How' of Learning

Multiple means of action and expression provide options for how students express what they have learned and how they respond to learning (CAST, 2018). Students differ in the ways that they can navigate a learning environment and express what they know. For example, some may be able to express themselves well in writing but not speech. It should also be recognised that a great deal of strategy, practice and organisation is required to provide multiple and flexible means of expression and to provide students with alternatives for demonstrating what they have learned. Therefore, allowing students to choose and indicate preferences can be an effective method for students to demonstrate their learning and will allow them to take responsibility and ownership of their choices and their teaching and learning journey.

In the process of incorporating some of the UDL principles into the assessment process for Deaf students, several strategies and methods were applied. Assessment concessions are a norm, and any student can apply for this based on a difficulty that impacts their academic work. The difficulties could be of a medical, psychological, or learning nature. Currently, this is applied as a concession or accommodation in our context, so strictly speaking it is not free for any student to get or apply for. There must be a specific need. This is not in keeping with UDL.

However, with Deaf students, such concessions can be applied for. Deaf student teachers were allowed extra time for tests and examinations because extra processes were needed. Much flexibility had to take place. A 60-mark assessment paper took about four hours to complete, excluding breaks. Deaf students had no control over this. Allowing extra time is, however, not always sufficient to make assessments more accommodating for Deaf students. Exhaustion sets in with lengthy assessments, therefore granting more rest breaks became necessary. Considerations were given to doing the exam in two parts over two days, but logistically this was not possible at the time. Assessments had to be arranged in a different location which required travel and various people's schedules. Flexibility was practised by incorporating more breaks.

Furthermore, it should not be assumed that Deaf student teachers cannot experience reading challenges. Given the deficits in language acquisition at a young age due to the lack of hearing, the compounded effects of language development can impact reading ability in later years. The principles of reading aloud to support Deaf student teachers during assessments were applied. This improved the flow of the assessment and thus indirectly supported the focus of the students. This is how the reading-out-load process was implemented: The student, the interpreter and the lecturer each had a printout of the assessment paper (text modality) at hand. The lecturer read the questions aloud while the interpreter listened and signed the questions (sign language as modality) to the student while the lecturer was reading (real-time interpretation). Under normal circumstances, the interpreter usually first reads the text and then communicates the content to the student, but it was not necessary in this situation.

The rephrasing of complex words is another UDL-based strategy that was integrated into the assessment process. Academic language is used in higher education settings to formulate assessment questions. The questions therefore may include the use of complex grammatical language structures and high-order low-frequency words. The use of language should therefore also be considered so that it does not create an assessment barrier. During the assessment session, it was necessary at times to rephrase some of the questions. Though the questions were simplified in terms of words and formulation, it was important not to change the difficulty level of the questions to maintain the standard of the assessment.

It is easy to assume that students with hearing impairments can express themselves comfortably in writing. Given that the language structure of SASL is different to English or Afrikaans, Deaf students were granted the use of a scribe. This meant that the interpreter also acted as the students' scribe and would write down verbatim answers. The administration of transcription involved additional actions that further extended the time of the assessment session. During the examination sessions, both audio recordings and video recordings were used. Video recordings furthermore served as verification of the validity of the assessment processes and supported the quality control processes between the interpreter, the lecturer and the heads of the programme and faculty. This secured the integrity of the assessment process.

CONCLUDING THOUGHTS

It is important to note that this process did not present a watered-down teaching, learning and assessment opportunity for the Deaf student teachers in training. Rather, it illuminates the potential that UDL strategies could offer in terms of teaching, learning and assessment opportunities. Furthermore, these strategies and approaches can target learning barriers effectively based on the principles of UDL. This approach proposes that barriers exist in the learning environment of the learner, not within the individual learner. Therefore, it is of the essence to find multiple methods of helping all students, including those with disabilities, to access the curriculum, access flexible and multiple assessment opportunities, and achieve success. This is exactly what UDL can offer (Hills et al., 2022).

Lyner-Cleophas (2019) concurs by arguing that students with disabilities are legally entitled to participate fully in the curriculum once they are enrolled at a higher education institution. The author furthermore notes that one of the ways that faculty can promote the inclusion of students with disabilities in teaching and learning spaces is through the provision of accessible and flexible curricular and assessment practices supported by established and appropriate policies and legislation.

SOLUTIONS AND RECOMMENDATIONS

Thinking about Universal Design for Learning

UDL is a framework that considers the diverse and wide range of variations in abilities and skills with which various students present. It offers a set of guidelines and principles for the development and delivery of an inclusive curriculum and is based on comprehensive and thorough research. Within the South African context, the main goal is to position UDL at the core of the inclusive education policy domain and to contemplate and explore how this approach can support the reimagining and redesign of policies and their implementation.

Furthermore, at the core of UDL is the creation and development of resources, goals, strategies, and flexible assessment options to make the teaching and learning experience as accessible as possible for all students, including students with disabilities. In this sense, within the context of classroom practices, UDL draws its essence from the social model of disability. This model indeed argues that disability is not an inherent label or a deficit of individuals but is rather anchored in the interaction between people's personal personifications and expectations of the environment (Berghs et al., 2019).

Dalton et al. (2012) emphasises the increased responsibility of higher education institutions to effectively support and teach students with diverse learning styles and needs through inclusive education models. Students have the right and the need to be taught and learn in ways that are flexible and accessible to them. Additionally, they need to have access to diverse options for demonstrating what they have learned. This demonstrates the urgent need for faculty members and teachers to acknowledge and recognise that students with diverse learning needs do have the right to equal access to the curriculum and to equal opportunities to learn.

In South Africa, an inclusive education policy has been adopted to support inclusive education and address barriers to learning in the education system. These include (i) the provision of reasonable accommodation, where needed, to meet individual student needs; and (ii) the provision of support within the general education system to facilitate education. Adaptability also requires responsiveness to the changing nature of education.

UDL has been in existence since the 1990s, yet it is not always the first method of teaching and learning that is chosen when materials for curricula are developed. For too long, teaching and learning methods were tailored with the average person in mind, without considering students diversity including students with disabilities. As the study population is growing in diversity, higher education institutions should consider adapting their curricula, teaching strategies and assessment methods to meet the needs of their entire student population (Dalton et al., 2019; Fovet, 2021; Lyner-Cleophas, 2020).

The PSET sector finds itself in a space where there is an opportunity to reimage what support to students in higher education could look like, and it is not realistic or desirable to return to a pre-pandemic world without any reflection or change. While universities are committed to learning from the pandemic and embracing change where it has the potential to enhance the quality of academia and transform the student experience, it is nevertheless clear that returning to how support was offered to students before the pandemic seems more convenient than continuing with the measures that were put in place in higher education during the pandemic. We need to make the most of the benefits that came with a virtual method of collaboration while at the same time bringing back the advantages of in-person experiences (Lyner-Cleophas et al., 2021). UDL is based on the premise that some students have difficulty accessing traditional curricula due to their learning preferences and needs being different from those of the traditional student (Meyer et al., 2014).

Future Research Directions

More research about transformative training that is based on the values and guidelines of inclusive education and UDL to generate positive attitudes toward inclusive education is necessary. This might enable faculty members to respond positively to the individual needs of students through curriculum adjustments and the design of flexible resources and assessment opportunities.

Reflexivity must be examined as teacher trainers reflect on and think about their teaching practices, with specific reference to Deaf teachers in training. This in turn can inform new policies and practices in the ever-changing educational setting. How these can inform policy are important markers for policy and practice improvement. As some staff embark on UDL practices, it is important to introduce these practices to the broader education environment. In this way, other faculties can read about how UDL can be practised, serving as an impetus for them to embark on the same strategies to promote inclusion of all students.

Deaf students who become Deaf teachers of Deaf students can become exemplars of what can be achieved. To this end, it is important for qualified Deaf teachers to do research about their experiences at universities and in the world of work, with specific reference to teaching Deaf students.

Deaf teachers at universities who do research should focus on educational aspects such as UDL. Flexibility is one way to do teaching, learning and assessments, keeping the outcomes in mind. Universities should also encourage more prospective Deaf students to become teachers of Deaf students.

Lecturers of Deaf students can add value to this body of work. In this way, they can assist lecturers in all faculties in higher education and form a community of practice that fosters UDL in its multiple applications.

CONCLUSION

Having policies in place enables enhanced, relevant and ever-changing practices. Therefore, policies in higher education should be revisited and reviewed constantly to ensure that they remain abreast of the latest developments in this landscape. There is a specific need to review and renew teaching, learning and assessment models, policies, and practices as a response to the diversity of students. Greater interaction should occur between faculty and support services to inform each other's policies and work.

Inclusive education and UDL are increasingly recognised as fundamental models for supporting all students, especially students with disabilities. Inclusive education enables all students to thrive academically and emotionally and to graduate successfully. The success of students with disabilities is important not only for the students' individual benefit but also for their successful integration into the broader society. The emerging shifts in the 21st century necessitate transforming educational practices in the way that teachers teach, and students learn. These shifts provide evidence for a need to examine and explore the changes necessary in transforming professional development experiences. Therefore, it is crucial that all role-players, especially faculty members in the higher education domain, are challenged to collectively reimagine and redesign teaching, learning and assessment strategies. Policy can be informed better and vice versa.

REFERENCES

Alsalamah, A. (2020). Assessing students in higher education in light of UDL principles. *American Research Journal of Humanities & Social Science*, *3*(1), 24–27.

Bell, D. (2021). South Africa has advanced the use of sign language. But there are still gaps. *The Conversation.* https://theconversation.com/south-africa-has-advanced-the-use-of-sign-language-but-there-are-still-gaps-168424https://theconversation.com/south-africa-has-advanced-the-use-of-sign-language-but-there-are-still-gaps-168424

Bell, D., & Swart, E. (2018). Learning experiences of students who are hard of hearing in higher education: Case study of a South African university. *Social Inclusion (Lisboa)*, *6*(4), 137–148. doi:10.17645i. v6i4.1643

Berghs, M., Atkin, K., Hatton, C., & Thomas, C. (2019). Do disabled people need a stronger social model: A social model of human rights? *Disability & Society*, *34*(7-8), 1034–1039. doi:10.1080/0968 7599.2019.1619239

Brand, S., Favazza, A. E., & Dalton, E. M. (2012). Universal design for learning: A blueprint for success for all learners. *Kappa Delta Pi Record*, *48*(3), 134–113. doi:10.1080/00228958.2012.707506

Brown, N. (2021). Deafness and hearing loss in higher education. In N. Brown (Ed.), *Lived experiences of ableism in academia. Strategies for inclusion in higher education* (pp. 141–158). Bristol University Press. doi:10.2307/j.ctv1nh3m5m.17

CAST. (2018). *Universal Design for Learning Guidelines version 2.2.* CAST. http://udlguidelines.cast.org

Chiwandire, D., & Vincent, L. (2019). Funding Mechanisms to Foster Inclusion in Higher Education Institutions for Students with Disabilities. *African Journal of Disability*, *8*, 1–12. doi:10.4102/ajod. v8i0.503 PMID:30899686

Dalton, E., Lyner-Cleophas, M. M., Ferguson, B., & Mckenzie, J. (2019). Inclusion, universal design and universal design for learning in higher education: South Africa and the United States. *African Journal on Disability.* https://journals.co.za/doi/abs/10.4102/ajod.v8i0.519

Dalton, E. M., Mckenzie, J. A., & Kahonde, C. (2012). The implementation of inclusive education in South Africa: Reflections arising from a workshop for teachers and therapists to introduce universal design for learning. *African Journal of Disability*, *1*(1), 1–7. http://dx.doi.rg/10.4102/ajod.v1i1.13. doi:10.4102/ajod.v1i1.13 PMID:28729974

Deaf Federation of South Africa. (2018). *Report on performance of deaf learners in schools for the deaf in South Africa in 2017.* DFSA. http://www.included.org.za/wp-content/uploads/2017/03/Grade1 2Report_2016_DeafSA_final.2.pdf

Foundation of Tertiary Institutes of the Northern Metropolis. (2011). *Disability in higher education project report.* UCT. www.uct.ac.za/usr/ disability/reports/annual_report_10_11.pdf

Fovet, F. (2021). *Reshaping graduate education through innovation and experiential learning. Using universal design for learning as a lens to rethink graduate education pedagogical practices.* Royal Roads University.

Francis, G. L., Duke, J. M., Fukita, M., & Sutton, J. C. (2019). "It's a constant fight:" Experiences of college students with disabilities. *Journal of Postsecondary Education and Disability*, *32*(2), 247–261. https://files.eric.ed.gov/fulltext/EJ1236871.pdf

Hills, M., Overend, A., & Hildebrandt, S. (2022). Faculty perspectives on UDL: Exploring bridges and barriers for broader adoption in higher education. *The Canadian Journal for the Scholarship of Teaching and Learning*, *13*(1). doi:10.5206/cjsotlrcacea.2022.1.13588

Howell, C. (2006). Disabled students and higher education in South Africa. In B. Watermeyer, L. Swartz, T. Lorenzo, M. Schneider, & M. Priestley (Eds.), *Disability and social change: A South African agenda* (pp. 164–178). HSRC Press.

Kelly, J. F., McKinney, E. L., & Swift, O. (2020). Strengthening teacher education to support deaf learners. *International Journal of Inclusive Education*, *26*(13), 2289–1307. doi:10.1080/13603116.2020.1806366

Lamprecht, S. (2022). *Commitment and resilience enable deaf teacher to realise his dream.* Stellenbosch University. https://www.sun.ac.za/english/Lists/news/DispForm.aspx? ID=9651

Lyner-Cleophas, M. (2019). Assistive technology enables inclusion in higher education: The role of Higher and Further Education Disability Services Association. *African Journal of Disability*, 8(6), 1–6. doi:10.4102/ajod.v8i0.558 PMID:31534917

Lyner-Cleophas, M. M. (2020). The prospects of universal design for learning in South Africa to facilitate the inclusion of all learners. In S. L. Gronseth & E. M. Dalton (Eds.), *Universal access through inclusive instructional design: International perspectives on UDL* (pp. 35–45). Routledge.

Lyner-Cleophas, M. M., Apollis, L., Erasmus, I., Willems, M., Poole, L., Minnaar, M., & Louw, P. (2021). Disability Unit practitioners at Stellenbosch University: COVID-19 pandemic reflections. *Journal of Student Affairs in Africa*, 9(1), 223–234. doi:10.24085/jsaa.v9i1.1440

McKenzie, J. A., & Dalton, E. M. (2020). Universal design for learning in inclusive education policy in South Africa. *African Journal of Disability*, 9, a776. doi:10.4102/ajod.v9i0.776 PMID:33392062

Meyer, A., Rose, D. H., & Gordon, D. (2014). *Universal design for learning: Theory and practice.* CAST Professional Publishing.

Mitchell, D. (2010). *Education that fits: Review of international trends in the education of students with special educational needs. Final report.* University of Canterbury.

National Center on Universal Design for Learning. (2012). *UDL Guidelines - Version 2.0.* NCUDL. http://www.udlcenter.org/aboutudl/udlguidelines/principle3

Ndlovu, S., & Walton, E. (2016). Preparation of students with disabilities to graduate into professions in the South African context of higher learning: Obstacles and opportunities. *African Journal of Disability*, 5(1), 1–8. doi:10.4102/ajod.v5i1.150 PMID:28730040

Parkin, I. (2010). Factors affecting deaf education in South Africa. *American Annals of the Deaf, 155*(4), 490-493. https://www.jstor.org/stable/26235088seq=1#metadata_info_tab_contents

Pitman, T., Brett, M., & Ellis, K. (2021). Three decades of misrecognition: Defining people with disability in Australian higher education policy. *Disability & Society*, 38(25), 1–19. doi:1 doi:0.1080/09687599.2021.1937061

Reindal, S. M. (1995). Some problems encountered by disabled students at the University of Oslo: Whose responsibility? *European Journal of Special Needs Education*, 10(3), 227–241. doi:10.1080/0885625950100304

Republic of South Africa. (1996). *Constitution of the Republic of South Africa, Act No. 2 of 1996.* Government Printer.

Republic of South Africa. (2018). *Strategic Policy Framework on Disability for the Post-School Education and Training System.* Republic of South Africa. https://www.dhet.gov.za/SiteAssets/Gazettes/Approved%20Strategic%20Disability%20Policy%20Framework%20Layout220518.pdf

Republic of South Africa, Department of Education. (2001). *Education White Paper 6: Special Needs Education: Building an Inclusive Education and Training System.* Republic of South Africa DoE. https://www.education.gov.za/Portals/0/Documents/Legislation/White%20paper/Education%20%20White%20Paper%206.pdf?ver=2008-03-05-104651-000

Rose, D. H., & Strangman, N. (2007). Universal design for learning: Meeting the challenge of individual learning differences through a neurocognitive perspective. *Universal Access in the Information Society, 5*(4), 381–391. doi:10.100710209-006-0062-8

Segars, S. (2021). *Deaf student's accomplishment a first for SU.* Stellenbosch University. https://www.sun.ac.za/english/Lists/news/DispForm.aspx?ID=8824

Stellenbosch University. (2018). *Disability Access Policy.* Stellenbosch University. http://www.sun.ac.za/english/policy

Stellenbosch University. (2021). *Assessment Policy.* Stellenbosch University. http://sunrecords.sun.ac.za/controlled/C4%20Policies%20and%20Regulations/SU%20Assessment%20Policy_FINAL.pdf

Stellenbosch University. (2021). *Language Policy.* Stellenbosch University. http://sunrecords.sun.ac.za/controlled/C4%20Policies%20and%20Regulations/English%20Language%20Policy_final_2Dec2021.pdf

Stellenbosch University. (2022). *Report: Centre for Student Counselling and Development (CSCD): Reasonable accommodation for exams and tests.* Stellenbosch University.

Stellenbosch University. (2023). *Student Information System Support. Students with disabilities statistics.* Stellenbosch University.

Thomas, D. (2022). *South African Sign Language Approved as South Africa's 12th Official Language.* EWN. https://ewn.co.za/2022/05/28/south-african-sign-language-approved-as-sa-s-12th-official-language

United Nations. (2006). *Convention on the rights of persons with disabilities.* UN. www.un.org/disabilities/documents/convention/convoptprote.pdf

KEY TERMS AND DEFINITIONS:

Deaf student teachers: These are students that are Deaf and subscribe to Deaf culture and learn by means of sign language interpreters that interpret academic material. They are also in the process of becoming teachers to Deaf students.

Department of Basic Education: This department oversees education in South Africa from Grade R (pre-school) to Grade 12 (school leaving certificate).

Foundation Phase: In South Africa this is the phase of education from Grade R to Grade 3. Learning areas covered are Literacy, Numeracy and Life Skills.

Higher education (HE): In the South African context, higher education refers to universities and universities of technology.

Post school education and training (PSET): In the South African context, the PSET sector refers to universities, technical and vocational education and training institutions, community education and training colleges as well as skills providers.

South African Sign Language (SASL): SASL is a sign language used in South Africa by Deaf people. It is promising to become the official twelfth language of the country.

Student success: These are students who achieve successful study in any given year and degree.

Students with disabilities: In the Stellenbosch University context, students with disabilities refer to any student that has disclosed a disability and can provide collateral documents about this, when accepted to the university or when seeking support for a diagnosed disability.

Universal Access (UA): This is an overarching term to describe accessibility and inclusion for all from a range of perspectives to avoid exclusion. This term includes accessibility of people according to transportation, physical buildings, information, websites, gender and disability.

Universal design for learning (UDL): UDL is an approach to teaching, learning and assessment that acknowledges student diversity and is flexible in reaching teaching and learning outcomes.

98

Chapter 6
Evolution and Implementation of Inclusive Education in the Maldives:
Hurdles and the Way Forward

Mariyam Shareefa
Islamic University of Maldives, Maldives

Visal Moosa
Islamic University of Maldives, Maldives

Adhila Rushdhee
Department of Inclusive Education, Maldives

Shuhudha Rizwan
National Institute of Education, Maldives

ABSTRACT

This chapter shares the journey of a developing island nation in their effort to implement a nation-wide inclusive education system. The chapter intends to bring to forefront key milestones, challenges faced, and the way forward in the expedition towards realizing full inclusion in schools. Towards this end, the authors engaged multiple sources of data including (i) legal, policy and other relevant documents from the local context, (ii) focus group discussions with experts, and (iii) interviews with practitioners. Insights from these multi-source explorations are triangulated and discussed in the light of local and international literature. Recommendations for moving towards enhancing and expanding inclusion in the education system are offered with specific focus on policy and practice, which can benefit the education system not only at the local level but also at the global level.

DOI: 10.4018/978-1-6684-7370-2.ch006

Copyright © 2023, IGI Global. Copying or distributing in print or electronic forms without written permission of IGI Global is prohibited.

BACKGROUND

Inclusive Education: A Contextual Definition

Inclusive education is generally considered as a multi-dimensional concept that celebrates and values individual differences and diversity (Hornby, 2015). The term 'inclusion' is defined as ensuring all people have the opportunities and the assistance necessary to fully participate in their community, their education, and their workplace (UNESCO, 2004, 2005, 2020a). This notion is well regarded across the globe as it promotes access to the general educational curriculum and opportunities for friendship and social connections (Miyauchi, 2020). In fact, many countries have developed policies for including students with complex learning profiles (SCLP) in mainstream classes (Leung & Mak, 2010; Mangope & Mukhopadhyay, 2015).

In the context of Maldives, the term 'inclusive education' is defined as providing education to students of all categories who require special assistance in education in the mainstream setting, as far as possible, or by means of alternative educational pathways (Ministry of Education - MoE, 2021). The categories of students recognized in the inclusive education policy are (i) students with disabilities, (ii) students who require special learning assistance including those with learning disabilities and the gifted, and (iii) students under special circumstances such as those who have experienced tragedies, trauma, disasters, etc.

The Country Context

The Republic of Maldives is an archipelago comprising 1192 small coral islands of which 187 are inhabited. These islands are scattered across 26 natural atolls which are grouped into 20 clusters (atolls) for administrative purposes. The population of the country as of 2019 is 372,739 (Maldives Bureau of Statistics - MBS, 2020) while about a quarter of which are students (MoE, 2019).

Until 2014, the Maldives followed a 5-2-3-2 education system reflecting the primary, middle school, lower secondary, and higher secondary levels of schooling. This has changed since the transition to the new national curriculum framework (NCF) in 2015 whereby (i) the kindergarten is recognized as part of formal schooling, (ii) key stages are introduced to refer to more precise levels of education within the prevailing level of pre, primary, and secondary level.

The Maldives has made impressive achievements on access to K-12 public free education. The country has achieved significant milestones in terms of providing universal primary education for all way back in 2002 (UNDP, 2014). Additionally, the net enrolment rate (NER) of early childhood education has made remarkable progress from 51.2% in 2001 to 99.6% in 2017 (MoE, 2016). Furthermore, while the NER of primary and lower secondary are 95.9% and 90.5% respectively in 2018, the NER reached 100% for both the levels in 2019 (MoE, 2019).

Inclusive education has become a topic of utmost attention in the Maldives. Since the first inclusive education policy in 2013, a number of revisions have been brought to the policy - the most recent revision was made in 2021. The inclusive education policy is the key document which lays out the specifics and the key responsibilities of the implementing agencies towards realizing full inclusion in education. These standards range from making policies and guidelines to provision of resources and trained staff (MoE, 2021).

Rationale for this Chapter

Unlike the homogeneity of the past years, students in today's classrooms represent a plethora of cultural, ethnic, linguistic, academic, socioeconomic, and cognitive backgrounds (Ricketts, 2014). It extends not only to race, economic, cultural, and language barriers, but also to a wide-ranging spectrum of learning needs. Regardless of this diversity, in many schools, it is still common to observe the whole class sitting at a desk, listening to the teacher, and taking notes to prepare for an exam. However, educators believe such an approach is faulty, because learning is not a one-size-fit-all process (Nedellec, 2015). Hence, it is mandatory for schools to adopt a truly inclusive approach that gives learners equitable access to the curriculum and instruction (Nel et al., 2011).

The purpose of this chapter is to share the journey of a developing island nation in their effort to implement a nationwide inclusive education system. The chapter intends to bring into spotlight key milestones, challenges encountered, and the way forward in the expedition towards realizing full inclusion in schools as anticipated in the inclusive education policy. Towards this end, we engaged multiple sources of data including (i) legal, policy and other relevant documents from the local context, (ii) focus group discussions with experts, and (iii) interviews with practitioners. Insights from these multi-source and multi-method explorations are triangulated and discussed in the light of local and international literature. Recommendations for moving towards enhancing and expanding inclusion in the education system are offered with specific focus on policy and practice which can benefit the education system not only at the local level but also at the global level.

LITERATURE REVIEW

Inclusive education is a concept that has evolved over time, from the integration of children with disabilities into mainstream classrooms to the inclusion of all students regardless of their differences. This section reviews research studies and literature relevant to the journey of evolution and implementation of inclusive education under three major themes.

Driving Forces for Inclusive Education

There are several driving forces behind the push for inclusive education around the world. One of the main drivers is the increasing awareness of the need for inclusive education as a human rights issue. International agreements and conventions, such as the Convention on the Rights of Persons with Disabilities (CRPD) and the Education for All (EFA) framework, have emphasized the importance of inclusive education for children with disabilities and other marginalized groups (United Nations, 2006).

Legislative frameworks and policies play a crucial role in driving inclusive education (Carrington et al., 2022). These frameworks and policies establish the legal and organizational framework for inclusive education, provide guidelines for implementing inclusive practices, and ensure that schools and other educational institutions are held accountable for providing inclusive education to all students. Without these frameworks and policies, inclusive education would not be effectively implemented and sustained in schools and other educational institutions.

According to Balli (2016), inclusivity is very much dependent on society's efforts to integrate individuals with disabilities, particularly through the actions of parents advocating for their children's inclusion in society. The author argues that without the advocacy and push from parents, there would be no progress in the development of educational policies or improvements to legal frameworks related to inclusive education. Therefore, it is apparent that parents play a vital role in fostering the implementation of inclusive education in schools by advocating for their child's rights, collaborating with educators, and actively participating in the education of their children. In fact, parents can be powerful partners in the inclusive education movement (Ainscow, 2019).

In the Maldives, the government has been actively pushing for inclusive education as a way to ensure that all children are included in the mainstream education system. The Maldives Education Act 2021, the Inclusive Education Policy 2013, and the new Inclusive Education Policy 2021, set the legal framework for inclusive education in the country, while the Maldives Education Sector Plan 2019-2023 highlights inclusive education as a priority (Ministry of Education & Ministry of Higher Education, 2019). The government has also established an inclusive education department in 2018, to oversee the implementation of inclusive practices in schools and provide support to students and teachers for proper implementation of inclusive education. Furthermore, the Maldives has ratified the CRPD, which includes provisions for the right to inclusive education for persons with disabilities (UNICEF, 2021c).

Inclusive Education Journey in Other Developing Countries

Bangladesh was one of the first countries in South Asia to ratify the Convention on the Rights of the Child (CRC) and CRPD in 1990 and 2007 respectively (UNICEF, 2021a). According to UNICEF (2021a), unlike other countries, Bangladesh adopted the principles of CRPD to amend the constitution in 2011, mandating universal, free, and compulsory education for all children, and prohibiting discrimination in education based on religion, race, caste, sex or place of birth. However, progress in implementing CRPD has been slow, with barriers such as limited facilities and inaccessible infrastructure, lack of accessible transportation, and negative attitudes of families, teachers and communities hindering the provision of quality inclusive education for all, especially those with disabilities.

In Sri Lanka, with the introduction of the Compulsory Education Policy in 1998, efforts have been made to increase access to education for marginalized groups such as girls and children with disabilities (UNESCO, 2021b). In 2003, the National Policy on Disability was launched, which shifted from 'special education' to 'inclusive education' recognizing that special education can cause further marginalization. Several other initiatives were followed, including the ratification of CRPD in 2016 and the development of the Inclusive Education Plan 2019–2030. However, the process of providing inclusive education has been slow and faced challenges such as the Civil War and negative attitudes of some members of the community towards inclusive education (UNICEF, 2021e). Despite the policy frameworks, the practice of educating children with disabilities in the country is still geared towards special education in segregated settings.

In Bhutan, the journey towards inclusive education began with the establishment of the first special school for children with visual impairments in 1973. After several policy initiatives, the country adopted the National Policy on Special Educational Needs in 2012, advocating the right of children with disabilities to education on an equal basis with others, without discrimination, from early childhood to vocational or technical and tertiary education. Another major policy initiative was the Bhutan Education Blueprint 2014-2024 (UNESCO, 2021b). Despite government commitment to resource allocation and funding for education of children with disabilities, the commitment to inclusive education where all children have access to quality education in mainstream classrooms is insignificant.

In Nepal, the journey towards inclusive education began with the adoption of the Special Education Policy in 1996, which ensured that all children with various disabilities had the right to education. However, it wasn't until the ratification of CRPD in 2010 and the adoption of the Consolidated Equity Strategy 2014, that guarantees an inclusive education system, that Nepal began to prioritize the inclusion of children with disabilities in mainstream schools (UNICEF, 2021d). This commitment was further strengthened by Article 31 of the 2015 Constitution, which ensures compulsory and free education for all children up to the secondary level. However, Nepal has faced several challenges in implementing inclusive education. One major challenge has been the lack of trained teachers and resources to support children with disabilities in mainstream schools (Regmi, 2017).

Global Challenges for Implementing Inclusive Education

Misalignment Between Policies and Practices

One major global challenge for providing inclusive education is the misalignment between policies and practices. In a study that explored the inclusive education practices in the Philippines, Muega (2016) discovered that outdated policies and centralized regulations impede understanding on how to incorporate students with diverse learning needs in general education settings. In the same research, Muega (2016) also found that policy guidelines that promote inclusive education puts a heavy burden on unequipped and underprepared school systems. As argued by the author, without providing resources and opportunities for teacher capacity building, legislated directives and inclusive education policies would be ineffective. This argument is supported by Subba et al. (2019), stating that despite being well-accepted by teachers, the policies often lack the necessary resources, support services, facilities, and expertise to effectively serve students with diverse learning needs in general education settings.

Lack of Adequately Trained Teachers

In many countries, teachers are not adequately prepared to teach students with disabilities, and lack the skills and knowledge needed to create inclusive classrooms (UNESCO, 2020b). According to UNESCO (2020b), schools should be reformed to better support teachers in embracing student diversity and viewing individual differences as opportunities for learning. Many studies conducted worldwide including Parveen and Qounsar (2018) argue that lack of necessary training and continuous professional development support for teachers lead to difficulties in identifying and addressing the needs of students with disabilities. It is also common that limited training and professional development lead teachers to have negative attitudes towards inclusive education (Carrington, 1999). In the Maldives too, general education teachers are reluctant to accept students with disabilities in their classrooms with the belief that the children should be taught better by teachers who are specially trained to teach them in special settings (Rizwan, 2017).

Pressures of Performativity

Another key challenge to effective inclusive education is the increasing pressures that some education systems have to improve the rankings at global, national and school levels (UNESCO, 2020a). Valle and Connor (2019) argue that the pressure on teachers to account for student progress by examination results marginalizes students with diverse learning needs, who are often excluded to ensure that schools can maintain high performance scores. According to Valle and Connor (2019), inner workings of school systems are driven by academic achievement, performance, and related funding formulas.

Awareness, Attitudes, and Practices

In many cultures, individuals with disabilities are stigmatized and may be seen as less valuable members of society. According to the United Nations (2016), despite global advancements, 40% of the world's population still does not have access to education. The report also emphasizes that it is not enough to just eliminate discriminatory policies; the subtler forms of discrimination, such as attitudes and deeply embedded practices, must be addressed and eliminated. UNICEF (2021f) report on the mapping disability-inclusive practices in South Asia states that discrimination and negative attitudes towards people with disabilities are a widespread issue in the region. The report also affirms that while education and disability policies aim to increase awareness and change attitudes, the level of implementation varies among countries, which are very much dependent on the unique country contexts.

Lack of Disaggregated Data

Availability of reliable, comprehensive, and disaggregated data on children with disabilities is a constant challenge all across the world. According to Ainscow (2020), it is important to know who is included, segregated, and excluded from schooling to address access and equity issues. Engaging with evidence, including views of children and families, and data on contextual factors such as resources and attitudes can help promote inclusion and equity in education (Ainscow, 2020). According to UNICEF (2021f), lack of disaggregated education data is a significant challenge for policy and programme development and implementation in the South Asia region. One of the main recommendations for governments by UNICEF (2021f) in the report on the mapping disability-inclusive practices in South Asia is to improve data on children with disabilities as accountability is inextricably linked with the availability of reliable and robust data. Similarly, this is one of the recommendations given to specific to Maldivian government too.

METHODOLOGY

Research Design

This investigation adopted case study approach to showcase the journey of a developing island nation in their effort to implement a nationwide inclusive education system. The case study technique enabled to obtain rich data and in-depth comprehension from a range of sources eliciting multiple experiences and perspectives (Tracy, 2013).

Participants

In this study, important data were collected from key stakeholders who have first-hand experience of the inclusive education journey of the country. Thus, we selected two types of participants for the study:

experts (n=4) and practitioners (n=7). These informants were selected via purposive sampling method, and they comprised 11 female participants in total.

Amongst the aforementioned 11 members, four experts participated in the focus group discussion (FGD). These specialists were selected based on their depth of expertise in the field as they are regarded among the forerunners who made significant contributions to the national milestones. Table 1. presents demographic details of the FGD participants while Table 2 shows details of the practitioners.

Table 1. Participant demographics of the FGD

	P1	P2	P3	P4
Gender	Female	Female	Female	Female
Experience in the field of inclusive education	25yrs	19yrs	21yrs	16yrs
Highest qualification	MEd	MEd	BEd	DipEd
Work experience at the MoE	Yes	Yes	No	No

Along with these specialists, three experienced teachers, two leading teachers (LTs), and two principals were purposively selected from different regions of the country. All these practitioners come from schools that have continued to practice inclusive education since the beginning of the policy implementation.

Table 2. Participant demographics of the practitioners

	P1	P2	P3	P4	P5	P26	P7
Gender	Female	Female	Female	Female	Female	Female	Female
Experience in teaching	10yrs	17yrs	10yrs	13yrs	25yrs	18yrs	10yrs
Experience in SEN	8yrs	7yrs	7yrs	7yrs	10yrs	8yrs	10yrs
Highest qualification	MEd	MEd	MEd	MEd	MEd	MEd	BA
Designation	Teacher	Principal	SEN Tr	SEN Tr	Principal	LT	LT

Data Collection

We engaged multiple sources of data including (i) legal, policy, and other relevant documents from the local context, (ii) focus group discussions (FGD) with experts, and (iii) interviews with practitioners. Following are some details about these data collection methods.

Document Analysis

In this study, a total of 24 formal documents were collected and analysed. These documents belong to four major categories (1) legislative documents (e.g., laws, regulations, policies, circulars), (2) statistics, (3) educational tools (e.g., teacher development packages, handbooks, guidelines), and (4) information from institutional websites (MoE and DoIE).

Evolution and Implementation of Inclusive Education in the Maldives

FGD With Key Experts

The FGD was held with four influential figures from Maldives who have been working in the inclusive education sector since the very beginning of its journey. During the FGD, after describing the study, participants' consent was sought. The group discussion was led by the primary researcher who encouraged participants to respond to the discussion openly in order to elicit a variety of accurate viewpoints on each of the discussion topics.

Interview With Practitioners

An interview schedule was developed well in advance of the practitioners' interviews. The schedule provided specific questions to be asked during the interview in their preferred order. The eight-item schedule was created with the intention of acquiring a greater understanding of inclusive education implementation and the challenges practitioners encounter in their efforts to implement the policy of inclusive education.

Data Analysis

Data obtained from the above sources were analyzed using the process of thematic analysis (Braun & Clarke, 2006). Accordingly, the below-mentioned steps were followed in the analysis process.

1. Data preparation: First, the data collected through legal, policy, and other relevant documents, FGDs, and interviews were organized and prepared for analysis. This involved transcribing interviews and FGDs, creating summaries or annotations of key points, and extracting relevant information from legal and policy documents.
2. Data coding: Next, a coding scheme was developed, and the data were coded by assigning relevant codes to each piece of information in the dataset.
3. Data analysis: With the coded data, the analysis began. This involved identifying patterns or trends in the data, comparing and contrasting information across different sources, and exploring relationships between different themes or concepts.
4. Synthesising findings: Finally, the findings were synthesized into a coherent narrative that addressed the research objectives. This involved summarizing key findings, highlighting similarities and differences across different sources of data.

To strengthen rigour and trustworthiness of the findings, the themes that came out of all the sources were cross-checked and triangulated with each other. Figure 1 illustrates data triangulation procedure, and how final themes were determined from the data sources.

Figure 1. Process of data analysis

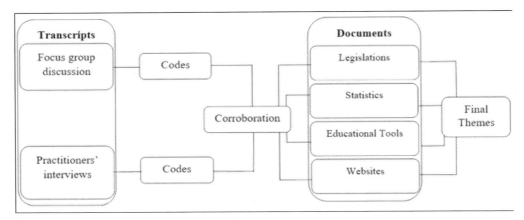

FINDINGS

Evolution of Inclusive Education in Maldives

The findings of the current study reveal that the evolution of inclusive education in the Maldives could be described under two phases. The first phase witnessed certain developments subject to moral obligations whereas, the second phase is accompanied by several legal obligations. In a report published by UNICEF (2021), the year 2010 is identified as the cornerstone for the legal framework for disability-inclusion in education in the Maldives. Hence, in describing the evolution of inclusive education in the country, the year 2010 is considered the point of separation. Apparently, the historical roots of inclusive education in the Maldives are believed to be grounded in the provision of education for students with special needs or, more specifically, those with special education needs (SEN) (Pinnock & Athif, 2015). Figure 2 depicts how inclusive education started and evolved over time highlighting the major milestones throughout.

According to Figure 2, the first phase of inclusive education in the Maldives runs from 1985 until 2010. There is not much documented evidence available to showcase the series of developments that took place during this phase. Hence, data from the FGD was used to learn development of activities during this time. Accordingly, the journey of inclusive education in the Maldives began at Jamaluddin School located at the capital city of Male'. The entire focus at that time was to cater for basic educational needs of deaf children in the locality.

In 2002, there was a circular from the Ministry of Education (MoE) mandating schools nationwide to make special arrangements such as building ramps and establishing facilities such as libraries and laboratories on the ground floor of the school buildings to cater for the needs of students as well as staff and parents who may require special accommodations (Ministry of Education, 2002). This is the first identified evidence of the desire to cater for the needs of SEN students across the country.

In 2003, SEN education was started in two other schools in the capital city namely, Imaduddin School and Ghiyasuddin School, the former currently serving as one of the three SEN (inclusion) hub schools (UNICEF, 2021c). Until this time, the focus was on children with special needs, such as the case of Jamaluddin School, which catered for the deaf. In contrast, the inception of SEN education in the two new

Evolution and Implementation of Inclusive Education in the Maldives

schools (especially Imaduddin School) is considered the beginning of scaling up the focus of educating students with SEN as emphasized by members of the FGD.

As indicated in Figure 2, data from the FGD revealed that a number of significant activities in promoting education of SEN students were carried out in 2007. Among these is the expansion of SEN education, which was confined to the capital city until then, to four atolls (Hdh., Sh., Gdh., and Addu) across the country.

Further, in 2007, a tool kit to identify SEN students was developed with technical expertise from overseas. As highlighted by members of the FGD, this was the time when the community started realizing the need for and right to education of students with SEN, which until then, people believed it was 'normal' for those special kids to be deprived of education. From 2007, SEN education was slowly expanded to a few selected atolls each year. In 2009, Inclusive Education Advisory Committee was established, despite the focus at that time was still more on education for children with SEN.

Figure 2. Historical trajectory of developing inclusive in the Maldives

- 1985 Began in JS as special education
- 2003 Start of SEN at Immaduddin (at a significant scale) and Ghiyasunddin is marked as the scaling up
- 2007 Expanded to one island iin four selected atolls (Hdh. Sh. Gdh. Addu)
- 2007 Secured overseas expertise to develop survey tool to collect data on SEN needs country wide. This was the time when community started realising the need and right to education of the SEN students. The focus was to bring SEN students who are deprived of education to schools.
- Expansion to few selected atolls each year.
- 2009 Inclusive education advisory committee established (focused on SEN)
- 2010 Adoption of UNCRPD
- 2010 ratification of disability act
- 2012 national inquiry on education for SEN conducted
- 2013 inclusive education policy (still more focused on SEN)
- 2014 policy to expand SEN at least one school in each atoll
- 2015 new curriculum started rolling out with incorporation of inclusion principles in it (changes to assessment and pedagogy)
- 2016 policy to train at least one SEN teacher in every school
- 2017 national symposium to train inclusive education ambassadors
- 2018 inclusive education coaches from Australia - Transition from SEN to inclusion
- 2018 from a SEN unit to a department
- 2019 strategic plan made
- 2020 first ever education act - chapter 8 of education act is dedicated for inclusive education
- 2021 revised IE policy in accordance with the education act
- 2022 Inclusive pedagogy (UDL, DI, Co-teaching, Assistive technology, Response to intervention) and teacher training for it on-going in pilot schools

The year 2010 is marked as a significant year, and as the beginning of the second phase of evolution of inclusive education in the Maldives as it marks the inception of legal support for the provision of education to SEN students. As indicated in Figure 2, in 2010, the law on 'protection of the rights of persons with disabilities and provision of financial support' (also known as the Disability Act) was ratified (Protection of the Rights of Persons with Disabilities and Provision of Financial Support, Law No. 8/2010, 2010). Moreover, in the same year, the UNCRPD was adopted (UNICEF, 2021c).

A key milestone in the journey towards inclusive education in the Maldives is the enactment of the inclusive education policy in 2013. Subsequently, a designated unit was established within the National

Institute of Education (NIE) to facilitate execution on the policy (di Biase & Maniku, 2021). The policy acknowledged a broader definition of students who need special attention incorporating three broad categories of such students: these are children who need additional learning support, children with special needs, and children under special circumstances.

As per the FGD, in 2014, a policy was enacted to expand education of students with SEN to at least one school in each atoll. In 2015, the new national curriculum began to be implemented. As emphasized in the FGD, the new curriculum is a significant contribution to inclusion since it incorporates inclusive pedagogy and assessment. In the same year, a national policy on disability was formulated (UNICEF, 2021c).

From 2016 onwards, there seems to be a stronger focus on developing human resources as depicted in Figure 2. This includes (i) policy on training a SEN teacher in every school across the country, (ii) conducting a national symposium to train inclusive education ambassadors, and (iii) training inclusive education coaches from overseas. By the year 2017, 185 out of 212 government schools had some form of education for students with SEN which was only 52 in 2014 (di Biase & Maniku, 2021). In 2018, the SEN unit was transformed into the Department of Inclusive Education (DoIE). A five-year strategic plan (2020-2025) for inclusive education was made in 2019 (UNICEF, 2021c).

The strongest legal support for the provision of inclusive education is the ratification of the first ever Education Act of Maldives in 2020 (Education Act, Law No. 24/2020, 2020). Subsequently, significant changes were made to the Inclusive Education Policy of 2013 first in 2020 (MoE, 2020) to align with UNCRPD, and next in 2021 (MoE, 2021b) to align with the new Education Act.

The Current State of Implementing Inclusive Education

Findings of this study reveal that the progress of inclusive education and its implementation throughout the country has been steady over the years. Findings from the document analysis indicate that momentum towards inclusion in schools is striving as a nationwide educational effort. Updates of activities available from websites of relevant authorities show that all the schools are provided with trained SEN teachers, school-based in-service trainings are enhanced, and modules of teachers' pre-service training courses have mandatory components related to inclusive education in their curriculum.

Further, findings reveal that with the help of MoE, most schools have a systematic referral system in place now. As revealed from the FGD, regarding the referral system, a toolkit development is underway at DoIE. Additionally, it was discovered that schools have committed leaders to improve practice of inclusivity as it was a requirement of the Inclusive Education Policy. Practitioners' interview data also confirms these facts. During the Interview, one of the principals confirmed her contributions in the development of individual curriculum plans (ICP) and teaching of SCLP in her respective school.

In addition to the above, findings show that major inclusive teaching strategies are incorporated into the teaching and learning process. The inclusive education policy also states that such strategies have to be adopted in the teaching and learning process. Members of DoIE in FGD explained that attempts to train teachers for these areas are currently underway. So far, teachers of two selected schools in the islands have completed formal trainings on these strategies. Likewise, there are hub schools who implement vocational trainings as a policy driven effort.

Furthermore, as confirmed from the data, there were numerous and frequent in-service training provided in view of facilitating inclusive education. In this regard, in 2022, workshops on inclusive pedagogy were conducted for teachers from all schools across the country. Additionally, training was conducted

Evolution and Implementation of Inclusive Education in the Maldives

for representatives from higher education institutions on the newly formulated teacher training standards for inclusive education, and sample teacher training modules were developed. Moreover, teachers from schools in Shaamiluveshi (inclusive school environment) pilot islands were given hands-on training on inclusive pedagogy and assistive technology. Teachers were also trained on braille and sign language under the same project. Apart from these, numerous short term in-service trainings, workshops, and seminars were conducted in recent years.

Challenges That Hamper Implementation of Inclusive Education

Data obtained from the sources reveal two major categories of specific challenges: (1) teacher-centered challenges, and (2) management-centered challenges. The subsequent sections explicate details of these challenges.

Teacher-Centered Challenges

The three main types of challenges that are closely related to teachers are (i) the number of trained teachers, (ii) attitudinal barriers, and (iii) expertise of existing teachers.

In relation to the first barrier, the 2020 statistics of students with CLP reveal that there is a total of 368 teachers teaching students with CLP of which 291 are trained to the minimum requirement. As for the requirement of the Inclusive Education Policy (MoE, 2013, 2020, 2021b), the most lenient calculation would yield 708 teachers indicating a huge deficiency of at least 471 qualified trained teachers. Hence, lack of trained teachers in the field is a major concern that needs to be addressed by the concerned agencies.

The second barrier that is centred on teachers, as noticed from the FGD and interviews, is about attitudinal barriers. Changing the mindset of teachers and the management members is highlighted by several participants. According to the experts as well as practitioners, teachers need to have positive thinking towards promoting inclusivity, and training principals and leading teachers (LTs) on this aspect should be emphasized. "The principals and LTs are the most important people to be trained in order to implement inclusivity in schools. Without changing their mindset, it's very difficult", an experienced LT articulated her concerns on the matter.

In relation to the third barrier, lack of curriculum awareness is highlighted by many interviewees. Teachers need to have thorough knowledge about adopting and adapting curriculum components to cater to the needs of SCLP in the mainstream classes. Many interviewed practitioners admit that despite all the efforts, mainstream teachers do not have adequate knowledge of developing ICP based on the curriculum outcomes and indicators. As reported by the participants, a significant number of mainstream teachers demonstrate low levels of content and pedagogical knowledge in a general teaching setting. Moreover, the members of FGD highlighted that although existing SEN teachers are trained for teaching in segregated settings, there still needs stronger integration of inclusive education training in general teacher training programs. Further, although inclusion related modules are integrated into teacher training programmes to some extent, graduates of teacher training courses do not possess the required competency of knowledge and skills.

School Management and MOE-Centered Challenges

Findings reveal four major challenges that are closely related to the school management or the MoE. They are (i) management and monitoring of statistics related to SEN students, (ii) collaboration between stakeholders, (iii) human resources development, and (iv) school management members' lack of commitment.

As confirmed by the participants, there lacks adequate consistency in collecting data about SEN students in the country. Likewise, information about these children needs to be securely saved and managed so that appropriate decisions can be taken by the concerned authorities. There has to be a streamlined effort in doing these tasks. Currently, according to the government policies, Gender Ministry is supposed to maintain a database about people with disabilities. At the same time, MoE is also trying to establish a database named "Fahivashi portal" at DoIE for every child with ICP. As explicated by the members of the FGD, the databases are not managed appropriately at the time of this study.

In addition to the above, collaboration between the stakeholders in the school community is identified as a major drawback that hampers inclusive practices. This includes school management members, parents as well teachers. As identified from the interviews, lack of collegiality and collaboration between mainstream teachers and SEN teachers is a major concern to everybody.

Moreover, human resources development is also a major challenge for successful implementation of inclusive education. "If we are giving the service, we need human resources. At least we need speech therapists. We need those facilities in the school", one of the participants elaborated. Teachers were eagerly waiting for a day when such professional assistance is available in schools so that full-fledged services are provided to the needed ones in their schools. Similarly, in order to be fully inclusive, schools need to have more teaching assistants to work as co-teachers so that effective implementation takes place.

The final challenge in this category is about school management members' lack of commitment. Even though some have leaders who show their full support and guidance to promote inclusive education, it is not the same in all the schools across the country. "Members of the school senior management need to properly understand the significance of inclusive education and its implementation phases", asserted a SEN teacher. It was also inferred from the analysis, that there exists some ambivalence about the roles of school management members in the provision of inclusivity for all students enrolled in their respective schools.

DISCUSSION

The foregoing findings illustrated that formally the inclusive education journey began in the Maldives in 1985 at a school in Male' with a special education focus. Major milestones achieved and transitions took place over the three and half decades in the inclusive education journey of Maldives include, ratifying UNCRPD and Disability Act in 2010, enrolling Inclusive Education Policy in 2013, enacting Education Act in 2020, revising the Inclusive Education Policy in 2021 with a huge focus on inclusive pedagogy, and other crucial milestones. In addition, the result also exposed that there are obstacles to be resolved for making the inclusion process smooth. The major obstacles portrayed from the result of the study include teacher-centered challenges such as (i) number of teachers trained, (ii) attitudinal barriers, (iii) teacher expertise; and management-centered challenges such as (i) management and monitoring of statistics related to SCLP, (ii) collaboration between stakeholders, (iii) human resources development, and (iv) lack of commitment from school management members.

Evolution and Implementation of Inclusive Education in the Maldives

Presented ahead is a critical analysis of the journey as well as the key challenges in the light of local and international literature.

The Journey Compared

Maldives, being a developing country and an island nation has achieved high milestones in the South Asia region with regard to inclusive education practices after the ratification of UNCRPD in 2010 onwards. In contrast, in Bangladesh, being the very first country in South Asia that ratified UNCRPD in 2007, there is a wide gap between students with and without disabilities who complete primary school education in the country, and the implementation of UNCRPD is slow (UNICEF, 2021a). On the other hand, ratification of UNCRPD in Sri Lanka and Bhutan are far behind when compared to Maldives and other countries in the South Asia region though Sri Lanka introduced Universal Free Education Policy in 1945 and Bhutan commenced inclusive journey in 1974 (UNICEF, 2021b). Likewise, Nepal ratified UNCRPD in the same year as Maldives, however, there are several challenges faced in the country to make students with disabilities fully participate in mainstream classes (Regmi, 2017). In contrast, Kiribati, an island nation in the Pacific region has achieved remarkable milestones by having a short history of inclusive education (UNESCO, 2021a). In this regard, an Education Act was enacted in 2013, and several milestones achieved via government initiatives and collaboration done between civil organisations (UNESCO, 2021a) by laying local legislations and policies similar to those in the Maldives.

In fact, the milestones achieved so far in the Maldives within the two eras of inclusive education practices emerged so far implies that most of the driving forces for pushing towards inclusive education mentioned in the international literature are apparent in the Maldivian context. For instance, increasing awareness of the need for inclusive education as a human right via international legislations such as UNCRPD and the EFA framework (United Nations, 2006), recognising that inclusive education is essential for promoting social and economic development (UNESCO, 2018), legislative frameworks and policies in place (Carrington et al., 2022), and parent advocacy are considered as the driving forces for inclusive education, and most of these driving forces lead Maldives to move towards inclusive education.

A Gradual but Continuous Journey

The findings of the current study revealed that a gradual transition process is taking place in the Maldives from segregated special education practices to fully inclusive practices. The distinct efforts in this transition process have been revitalized in the past few years by entrusting a broad mandate to DoIE for implementing the Strategic Action Plan 2019-2024, and by drawing necessary nationwide legislations to ensure equitable quality education for all. For instance, the results of the study showed that as per the policy and other planning documents of MoE and DoIE, momentum of inclusion in school is striving as a nationwide education practice. All the schools are provided with a minimum of one special education teacher. Pre-service training courses have incorporated mandatory components related to inclusive education (DoIE, 2022a). To speed up the transition process, inclusive pedagogy training and implementation are initiated in the schools such as training and implementation of universal design for learning, co-teaching models, differentiated instruction, assistive technology, response to intervention, and many more. Subsequently, teachers' willingness to implement inclusive education has increased (Rushdhee, 2021).

The literature on inclusive education practices in the South Asian countries do not show this kind of systematic transition taking place to achieve a full inclusion model in those countries (see for example, (UNICEF, 2021a; UNICEF, 2021b). Nevertheless, Kiribati took relevant practices such as using assistive technology to give access to the students with disabilities to take part in the learning process (UNESCO, 2021a). In the Maldivian context, it is in the very infant stage for applying assistive technology though teacher training on assistive technology commenced in the year 2022. In fact, with the provision of more adequate support and resources, the transition of segregation to inclusion can be made more effective and rapid.

Lack of Human Resource: A Major Challenge

Expediting teacher training for inclusive education is one of the key themes that emerged while analyzing policy documents, available statistics, and extracts of experts in the field of inclusive education in Maldives. The result portrayed that there is a huge deficiency of human resource availability to cater all the SCLP, with regard to the total number of trained special education teachers needed for supporting SCLP, teacher motivation and confidence in teaching SCLP, and adequate level of both content and pedagogical knowledge required in general teaching settings. The depicted results urged for enhancing both pre-service and in-service teacher training on inclusive education.

Nevertheless, the recent training statistics available at the DoIE showed numerous trainings and projects focused on enhancing the capacity of both pre-service and in-service teachers are on-going. DoIE has been continuing these efforts in the past four years (DoIE, 2021, 2022a). Further, inclusive pedagogy training and implementation are taking place in the selected schools of Maldives (DoIE, 2022a). While the current efforts of DoIE in providing in-service training is commendable, the need for exposure to more authentic learning experiences was echoed from the findings.

Additionally, although developing teacher training standards for inclusive education (TTSIE) that mandates higher education Institutions in the Maldives to revise existing inclusive education modules by June 2023 is in place, the actual implementation of these are yet to happen. While this initiative would cater for training general education teachers for inclusion, the number of trained special education teachers are much less than the policy requirements. Countries such as Sri Lanka have introduced introductory training to all teachers and principals back in 2009 (UNICEF, 2021e). Therefore, a system level noteworthy actions are apparent to enhance both pre-service and in-service teacher training to create a capable human resource force that is required for enhancing inclusive education in the Maldives.

RECOMMENDATIONS: THE WAY FORWARD

The results of the study illustrated that there are two broad categories of challenges faced by schools while working on implementing inclusive education namely (i) teacher-challenges and (ii) management-centered challenges.

While some of the recent initiatives designed by DoIE is noteworthy in addressing some of the identified challenges, it is observed that establishing a successful set up for implementation of inclusive education is not an easy feat. Educators need to acknowledge and address the drawbacks to ensure quality of children's experiences and outcomes in inclusive classrooms. The following six recommendations are therefore offered in light of the findings of this investigation.

Establish a Monitoring Mechanism of Pre-Service Teacher Training Programs

To make teachers capable of delivering high-quality inclusive education, concerned authorities need to ensure that pre-service teacher training programs conducted at universities and colleges expedite future teachers' acquisition of inclusive pedagogical knowledge and skills. It is crucial to strengthen and closely monitor how the knowledge and skills delivery within the modules of teacher preparation programmes take place. Teacher trainees need to be exposed to model teaching so they can observe and learn techniques from more experienced educators. Likewise, it is crucial for teacher candidates to practice inclusive pedagogies that facilitate them with first-hand experiences of using the techniques.

Scale Up Training of Specialized Education Teachers

Additional SEN teachers are required to teach children with severe complex learning profiles. Concerned authorities need to scale up training of specialized teachers who are well-prepared to work with severe cases of students with CLP. Evidently, there are several students attending schools who require close monitoring and guidance of not only mainstream teachers, but exclusively trained SEN teachers too. Hence, the 'one SEN teacher for each school' policy does not make it adequate to cater the needs of these students as some schools have a higher number of students with such severity.

Need-Based Provision of Specialized Professionals

For successful implementation of inclusive education, specialized professionals (such as speech therapists and physiotherapists) are required to be available in schools. If not in every school, this provision could be made available in the nearest localities within the islands or the atolls. Some of these facilities can be made accessible through the regional hospitals situated in the islands/atolls.

Provision of Authentic Experience to Strengthen Practice of Quality Teaching

Teacher exchange programs can be enhanced to provide more exposure to skilled teachers using effective instructional strategies in inclusive classrooms. Practising teachers can have peer observations within the school or can visit model schools where these strategies are implemented successfully. These exchange programs can be implemented consistently and have to be conducted under the supervision of DoIE/MoE, and records of the teachers who undergo these programmes have to be well maintained.

Enhance Inclusive Leadership

School leaders are required to become more knowledgeable about inclusive education and its implementation. Members of the school management can participate in professional development programs to update and extend their knowledge base and improve their performance of inclusion in their respective schools. Becoming an inclusive leader would enable them to facilitate different sources of expertise and perspectives to improve teacher collaboration within the school community.

Availability of Up-to-Date Data

It is necessary to make data gathered from concerned authorities made available to the public or at least for the purpose of research. Data maintenance and availability are important as they can assist in planning and setting of future goals. Additionally, the availability of data is crucial for academics and researchers who conduct investigations about the provision of inclusive education in the country.

CONCLUSION

This chapter showcased the journey towards inclusive education in Maldives, and elicited the challenges that were encountered over this journey from the perspectives of key experts and practitioners. These challenges were then carefully examined in terms of their relevance towards achieving broader standards of inclusion set forth in the related policy documents. Accordingly, several recommendations were made which could possibly be incorporated into a strategic plan for executing full inclusion in the education system of the country.

REFERENCES

Ainscow, M. (2019). *Ensuring inclusive education for all*. Routledge.

Ainscow, M. (2020). Inclusion and equity in education: Making sense of global challenges. *Prospects*, *49*(3-4), 123–134. doi:10.100711125-020-09506-w

Austin, V. L. (2016). Introduction to the special issue pedagogies and behaviors that benefit students with exceptional learning needs. *Insights into Learning Disabilities*, *13*(1), 1–6.

Balli, D. (2016). Importance of Parental Involvement to Meet the Special Needs of their Children with Disabilities in Regular Schools. *Academic Journal of Interdisciplinary Studies*, *5*(1), 147–152. doi:10.5901/ajis.2016.v5n1p147

Braun, V., & Clarke, V. (2006). Using thematic analysis in psychology. *Qualitative Research in Psychology*, *3*(2), 77–101. doi:10.1191/1478088706qp063oa

Carrington, S. (1999). Inclusion needs a different school culture. *International Journal of Inclusive Education*, *3*(3), 257–268. doi:10.1080/136031199285039

Carrington, S., Lassig, C., Maia-Pike, L., Mann, G., Mavropoulou, S., & Saggers, B. (2022). Societal, systemic, school and family drivers for and barriers to inclusive education. *Australian Journal of Education*, *66*(3), 251–264. doi:10.1177/00049441221125282

Department of Inclusive Education. (2020). *Students with complex learning profile: statistics 2020*. Department of Inclusive Education.

Department of Inclusive Education. (2021). *Annual Report 2021*. Department of Education.

Department of Inclusive Education. (2022a). *Annual Report 2022*. Department of Inclusive Education.

Evolution and Implementation of Inclusive Education in the Maldives

Department of Inclusive Education. (2022b). *Shaamiluveshi project activity report on ICT, monitoring and PD (unpublished report).* Department of Inclusive Education.

Department of Inclusive Education. (2022c). *Transforming inclusive pedagogy: inclusive teachers for inclusive schools (unpublished report).* Department of Inclusive Education.

Department of Inclusive Education. (2022d). *Transforming inclusive pedagogy: training of in-service teachers (unpublished report).* Department of Inclusive Education.

di Biase, R., & Maniku, A. A. (2021). Transforming Education in the Maldives. In P. M. Sarangapani & R. Pappu (Eds.), *Handbook of Education Systems in South Asia. Global Education Systems* (pp. 545–573). Springer. doi:10.1007/978-981-15-0032-9_14

Education act, Maldives (Law no. 24/2020), (2020).

Hameed, A., & Manzoor, A. (2019). Similar Agenda, Diverse Strategies: A Review of Inclusive Education Reforms in the Subcontinent. *Bulletin of Education and Research, 41*(2), 53–66.

Hornby, G. (2015). Inclusive special education: Development of a new theory for the education of children with special educational needs and disabilities. *British Journal of Special Education, 42*(3), 234–256. doi:10.1111/1467-8578.12101

International Disability Alliance. (2020). *What an inclusive, equitable, quality education means to us: report of the international disability alliance.* International Disability Alliance.

Leung, C. H., & Mak, K. Y. (2010). Training, understanding, and the attitudes of primary school teachers regarding inclusive education in Hong Kong. *International Journal of Inclusive Education, 14*(8), 829–842. doi:10.1080/13603110902748947

Maldives Bureau of Statistics. (2020). *Statistical Year Book 2020.* Ministry of Education.

Mangope, B., & Mukhopadhyay, S. (2015). Preparing teachers for inclusive education in Botswana: The role of professional development. *Journal of International Special Needs Education, 18*(2), 60–72. doi:10.9782/2159-4341-18.2.60

Ministry of Education. (2002). *Making special arrangements in schools for people with special needs (Circular no 02/2002)* [Khaassa ehee ah beynunvaa dharivarunna, muvazzafunnai, beleniverinnah khiyaalufulhu bahattavaigen schoolthakuge inthizaamuthah kurevvun]. Ministry of Education.

Ministry of Education. (2013). *Inclusive education policy (Circular no 02/2013).* Ministry of Education.

Ministry of Education. (2016). *School statistics.* Ministry of Education.

Ministry of Education. (2019). *School Statistics 2019.* Ministry of Education.

Ministry of Education. (2020). *Inclusive education policy (Circular no 22-E/CIR/2020/ 58)* [Hurihaa dharivarun shaamilukoggen thau'leemu dhinumuge usoolu]. Ministry of Education.

Ministry of Education. (2021a). Inclusive Educational Policy. Ministry of Education.

Ministry of Education. (2021b). *Inclusive education policy* [Hurihaa dharivarun shaamilukoggen thau'leemu dhinumuge siyaasathu]. Ministry of Education.

Ministry of Education. (2021c). *School statistics 2021/2022*. Ministry of Education.

Ministry of Education & Ministry of higher education. (2019). *Maldives education sector plan 2019-2023*.Ministry of Education.

Miyauchi, H. (2020). A systematic review on inclusive education of students with visual impairment. *Education Sciences*, *10*(11), 346. doi:10.3390/educsci10110346

Muega, M. A. (2016). Inclusive education in the Philippines: Through the eyes of teachers, administrators, and parents of children with special needs. *Social Science Diliman*, *12*(2), 5–28.

Nedellec, C. M. (2015). *Teachers' understanding of differentiated instruction in Swiss elementary schools. (Doctoral Dissertation). Available from ProQuest Dissertations & Theses. (Order No. 3718012).*

Nel, N., Kempen, M., & Ruscheinski, A. (2011). Differentiated pedagogy as inclusive practice: The "learn not to burn" curriculum for learners with severe intellectual disabilities. *Education as Change*, *15*(2), 191–208. doi:10.1080/16823206.2011.619145

Parveen, A., & Qounsar, T. (2018). Inclusive education and the challenges. *National Journal of Multidisciplinary Research and Development*, *3*(2), 64–68.

Pinnock, H., & Athif, A. (2015). Using special educational needs as an entry point for inclusive education in the Maldives. *Enabling Education Review*, *4*, 16–17.

Regmi, N. P. (2017). *Inclusive Education in Nepal - From Theory to Practice*. [Dissertation, Ludwig-Maximilians-University].

Ricketts, M. A. (2014). *The lived experiences of teachers in implementing differentiated instruction in the inclusive classroom*. [Dissertation, Walden University]. *ProQuest Dissertations & Theses*. (Order No. 3645551).

Rizwan, S. (2017). Mainstreaming students with disabilities: a survey of teachers' attitudes towards inclusion. In *Proceedings of International Teachers' Conference 4, Curriculum, Pedagogy & Assessment: Innovative Visions to Foster Effective Learning*. National Institute of Education.

Rushdhee, A. (2021). In-service teachers' perceptions on implementing universal design for learning in the republic of Maldives. *SAARC Journal of Educational Research*, *14*, 1–34.

Rushdhee, A. (2022). In-service teachers' sentiments, attitudes, and concerns on implementing inclusive education in the Republic of Maldives. *International Research Symposium on Education, IRSE, 2022*.

Subba, A. B., Yangzom, C., Dorji, K., Choden, S., Namgay, U., Carrington, S., & Nickerson, J. (2019). Supporting students with disability in schools in Bhutan: Perspectives from school principals. *International Journal of Inclusive Education*, *23*(1), 42–64. doi:10.1080/13603116.2018.1514744

Timberlake, M. T. (2018). Nice, but we can't afford it: Challenging austerity and finding abundance in inclusive education. *International Journal of Inclusive Education*, *22*(9), 954–968. doi:10.1080/13603116.2017.1412518

Tracy, S. J. (2013). *Qualitative Research Methods: Collecting Evidence, Crafting Analysis, Communicating Impact*. Blacwell Publishing., doi:10.5613/rzs.43.1.6

UNDP. (2014). *Maldives human development report 2014*. UNDP.

UNESCO. (2004). *Education for all: the quality imperative*. UNESCO.

UNESCO. (2005). *Guidelines for inclusion: ensuring access to education for all*. UNESCO.

UNESCO. (2018). *Inclusive education*. UNESCO.

UNESCO. (2020a). *Global education monitoring report 2020: inclusion and education: all means all*. UNESCO.

UNESCO. (2020b). *Towards inclusion in education: status, trends and challenges*. UnESCO.

UNESCO. (2021a). *Kiribati - inclusion*. UNESCO. https://education-profiles.org/oceania/kiribati/~inclusion

UNESCO. (2021b). *Sri Lanka - Inclusion*. UNESCO.

UNICEF. (2021a). *Disability-inclusive education practices in Bangladesh*. UNICEF.

UNICEF. (2021b). *Disability-inclusive education practices in Bhutan*. UNICEF.

UNICEF. (2021c). *Disability-Inclusive Education Practices in Maldives*. UNICEF.

UNICEF. (2021d). *Disability-inclusive education practices in Nepal*. UNICEF.

UNICEF. (2021e). *Disability-inclusive education practices in Sri Lanka*. UNICEF.

UNICEF. (2021f). *Mapping of disability-inclusive education practices in South Asia*. UNICEF.

United Nations. (2006). *Convention on the rights of persons with disabilities*. UN.

United Nations. (2016). *Disability and development report*. UN.

Valle, J. W., & Connor, D. J. (2019). *Rethinking disability: a disability studies approach to inclusive practices*. Routledge. doi:10.4324/9781315111209

KEY TERMS AND DEFINITIONS

Challenges: Difficulties and obstacles that can arise in the process of providing equal educational opportunities for all students, regardless of their individual characteristics and needs.

Evolution: It refers to the process of how inclusive education has changed and developed over time.

Implementation: It refers to the process of putting into practice the principles and policies of inclusive education in schools and other educational settings.

Inclusive Education: Inclusive education is an approach to education that aims to ensure that all students, regardless of their individual needs and characteristics, have equal access to high-quality education, and are able to participate fully in the learning process.

Key Milestones: It refers to a significant event or development that marks a major step forward in the progress of implementing inclusive education.

Teacher Development: It refers to the process of preparing and supporting teachers to work effectively with students of diverse needs and abilities, in order to promote inclusive education.

Way Forward: It refers to the path or strategy that can be taken to further advance and implement the principles and practices of inclusive education.

Chapter 7
Inclusive Education Practices in Taiwan

Hsuan-Ling Chen
University of Tsukuba, Japan

Masayoshi Tsuge
University of Tsukuba, Japan

ABSTRACT

With a view toward inclusion, Taiwan's special education law has undergone eight amendments since 1984. The learning environment for children with disabilities has also shifted from segregation to integration and inclusion. Currently, the learning environments for special needs education in Taiwan include regular classrooms, resource classrooms, special needs classes, itinerant visits, and special needs schools. To achieve "inclusive education," Taiwan's elementary and junior high schools are also implementing a variety of approaches. This chapter focuses on "the practice of inclusive education in Taiwan" and discusses the contents of the current " Taiwanese-type" inclusive education practices and school cases from the development process and status of inclusive education in Taiwan.

INTRODUCTION

With a view toward inclusion, Taiwan's special education law has undergone eight amendments since 1984. The learning environment for children with disabilities has also shifted from segregation to integration and inclusion. Currently, the learning environments for special needs education in Taiwan include regular classrooms, resource classrooms, special needs classes, itinerant visits, and special needs schools. To achieve "inclusive education," Taiwan's elementary and junior high schools are also implementing a variety of approaches. This chapter focuses on "the practice of inclusive education in Taiwan" and discusses the contents of the current ""Taiwanese-type"" inclusive education practices and school cases from the development process and status of inclusive education in Taiwan.

DOI: 10.4018/978-1-6684-7370-2.ch007

BACKGROUND

As for the current situation of special needs education in Taiwan, the number of students who attend resource classrooms while enrolled in regular classes in regular schools is about 56,235 (accounting for 76% of all students with disabilities), while the number of students enrolled in special needs classes in regular schools is reported to be 6597 (accounting for about 9% of all children with disabilities) (Ministry of Education, 2021). In other words, the condition of students with disabilities in Taiwan is that they attend resource classes while enrolled in regular schools.

With the publication of the Convention on the Rights of Persons with Disabilities (CRPD) (UN,2006), the Special Education Law in Taiwan has been amended accordingly. With the worldwide boom of "inclusive education," the implementation of "inclusive education" is also on the rise. The school evaluation criteria have also added the category of "inclusive education".

Searching with the keyword" inclusive education" in Airiti Library(Reference Search Engine), the number of search results for the 10 years before the revision of the Special Education Law in 2009 (2000-2009) was 93. In contrast, the number of documents in the 10 years after the amendment of the Special Education Law (2010-2019) increased to 221. The authors can see that the research on the practice of inclusive education in Taiwan is also growing in momentum.

This chapter will indicate the practice of inclusive education in Taiwan that include special education advocacy activities and volunteer programs for students in regular classes, interaction and joint learning by subjects for children with disabilities, and inclusive education activities in the classroom field curriculum for all students.

MAIN FOCUS OF THE CHAPTER

The Development of Inclusive Education and the Current State of Special Needs Education in Taiwan

Laws and Policies on Inclusive Education in Taiwan

The Constitution of Taiwan shall clearly state that "all citizens have the right and duty to receive education and have equal opportunity to receive education." The Constitution, the Convention on the Rights of Persons with Disabilities (CRPD), and the Regulations for the Implementation of Nine-Year National Education all state that students must be given appropriate access to school and cannot be denied access. The laws mentioned above do not use the terms "inclusive education" and "inclusion". But they do contain a principle on inclusion that ensures the right to education regardless of disability.

The Convention on the Rights of Persons with Disabilities was adopted by the United Nations General Assembly in 2006 and has been in force since 2008. In Taiwan, the Convention entered into force in 2014, and the Law implementing the Convention was published in the same year. Article 24 of the Convention on the Rights of Persons with Disabilities details the implementation of an integrated education system, including the provision of individualized support and reasonable adjustments to meet the individual needs of students. The focus of the Convention on the Rights of Persons with Disabilities is to guarantee the fundamental rights and freedoms of persons with disabilities and to promote their equal and full participation in the society and mentioned the principle of inclusive education.

Inclusive Education Practices in Taiwan

Before the Convention on the Rights of Persons with Disabilities was published, the Ministry of Education (1995) published the Report on Education for the People with Disabilities of the ROC, in which the term "inclusion" was mentioned. According to The Report on Education for the People with Disabilities of the ROC, "inclusion" refers to the transition of students with disabilities from specific institutions to the general community, or from special schools to regular schools.

In 2009, The Special Education Law has been substantially amended, and Article 18 clearly states that "the provision of special education and related services and facilities should be in line with the spirit of adaptation, individualization, community, availability and inclusion." Therefore, the idea of "inclusion" has been emphasized from The Report on Education for the People with Disabilities of the ROC in 1995. It is believed that the concept of inclusion will surely move forward in inclusive education practices as the Special Education Law is being revised and the Convention on the Rights of People with Disabilities.

The latest amendment to the Special Education Law is in 2019. However, the Ministry of Education intends to issue a draft amendment to the Special Education Law in 2023, which will overhaul 34 articles, with the main points of the amendment including emphasizing equality and non-discrimination, universal design, and promoting the concept of integrated education.

Process of Development of Inclusive Education in Taiwan

In the United States, the 94-142 Act of 1975 emphasized "principles related to inclusive education, including the educational rights of children with disabilities, equal assessment, least restrictive environment, and IEPs." The development of inclusive education in Taiwan has also been in part influenced by the U.S., and the field of learning for children with disabilities has shifted from isolation to integration and inclusion. Taiwan has also followed the global trend of promoting inclusive education, and the attitude to children with disabilities has changed from rejection and indifference to compassion, sympathy, and active support. The policy has changed from segregation to zero rejection (Wu, 2013).

The Law on Special Education of Taiwan has been published since 1984, and after eight modifications and revisions, the current Special Education Law was published in 2019. As the Law on Special Education is amended, it is moving toward the principle of inclusion, as Article 13, modified in 1997, clearly states that " Education should instruct children with disabilities to enroll in an environment appropriate to their needs and based on the principle of fulfilling the learning needs of students in the least restrictive environment (LRE). Since that time, the place of learning for students with disabilities has been shifted from special schools or classes to regular classes. In 2009, the Law on Special Education was substantially revised, and the term "inclusion" appears for the first time in the law, which the authors believe is a step for promoting and practicing inclusive education up to now.

Since that time, Taiwan has also enacted policies and laws related to the placement of children with disabilities, class sizes, and teacher training and curriculum development, and the school field will also work to promote inclusive education from now on.

The Current State of Inclusive Education in Taiwan

Due to the promotion of inclusive education, the number of children with disabilities enrolled in regular schools has increased from 51,089 in 1999 (85.98% of all children with disabilities) through 86,810 in 2009 (92.99% of all children with disabilities) and 111,033 in 2019 (95.67% of all children with disabilities).The percentage of students attending resource rooms, especially in elementary schools, also increased from 29.32% in 1999 to 56.90% in 2009 and 76.08% in 2019 (Ministry of Education, 1999; 2009; 2019). In terms of the enrollment of students with disabilities, it was observed that the number of students who the enrolled in regular schools and regular classes increased, with students with disabilities being able to learn in an environment of inclusion.

In addition, as the number of students enrolled in regular classes increased, the percentage of teachers who received at least 3 hours of training on special needs education increased to 76% in 2019 in order to expand the expertise of regular class teachers on special needs education (Ministry of Education, 2019). However, prior research surveying teachers reported that regular classroom teachers are less confident in their ability to work with children with disabilities and seek ways to help them solve their learning and behavioral problems (Hong, Xu, Wang, & Chan, 2018; Chiu, 2001; Xu & Chan, 2008).

While the above-mentioned, the teacher training program also includes a 3-credit special education-related course as an elective, and students are encouraged to take it. The in-service teachers who have received at least 3 hours of training on special needs education are more than 70%, but they are still slightly lacking in the ability to deal with and support students with disabilities enrolled in regular classrooms. Therefore, it is necessary to consider expanding the content of training and teacher training not only for teachers of special needs education but also for the regular class teachers.

Formerly, special education teachers and regular classes' teachers taught separately in those classes, but nowadays, with the promotion of inclusive education, most of special education students are attended resource classes while enrolled in regular schools. The role of the special education teacher has changed to a more diverse service provider, providing the necessary support to both the general education teacher and the student with special needs. The most common models of collaboration in Taiwan are Consulting Teacher Model, Cooperative Teaching Model, Supportive Resource Programs, and Instructional Assistants (Huang,2010). All of the above-mentioned methods of collaboration require the cooperation and communication between the regular classroom teachers and the special education classroom teachers. Therefore, collaboration between special education teachers and general education teachers has become increasingly important.

On the other hand, the results of the review to the Convention on the Rights of Persons with Disabilities in Taiwan in 2017 pointed out that although the percentage of students with disabilities enrolled in regular schools is very high, students with disabilities are still "placed" in the regular education system, which means that students with disabilities frequently experience difficulties about meeting behavioral expectations in regular education classrooms. Cheng (2012) analyzed a study on children with disabilities who were enrolled in regular classes and found that teachers had difficulties with children with developmental disabilities, such as children with ADHD who had trouble due to behavioral problems, children with ASD who had problems in controlling emotions and interpersonal relationships. As for peer relationships in the classroom, children with intellectual disabilities lack social skills, have poor adaptation skills, and have behavioral problems that prevent them from making friends or being rejected by peers (Xu, Wang, 2014). Wu (2005) stated that true inclusion is not only physical inclusion, but also mental barrier-free. Mental barrier-free means that accessibility of the psychological environment in society or school. It is including attitudes towards special education students or people with disabilities. Therefore, creating an environment of mental barrier-free for inclusion, is one of the challenges for inclusive education in Taiwan.

Inclusive Education Practices in Taiwan

Special Education Advocacy

According to Taiwan's Support Services for Students with Disabilities Measures, special education advocacy activities are activities that promote understanding, care, acceptance, and assistance for people with disabilities through learning, experiences, lectures, competitions, performances, visits and other related activities. Chiu (2021) and Ko, Chen (2009) indicated that special education advocacy activities including expert lectures, reading materials, video materials, disability simulation experiences, connecting with other subjects, school events, lectures on people with disabilities, and institutional exchanges.

As an example of a specific case study, Jian (2014) conducted a special education advocacy activity for fourth grade elementary school students called the Attitude Improvement Program for Children with Cognitive Disabilities. This advocacy activity used picture book reading, hands-on activities, and group activities, and children in the same class were able to learn about the characteristics of children with cognitive disabilities and become more compassionate and supportive as a result. Xu (2017) conducted special education advocacy activities for first-year middle school students through videos, reading materials and simulated experiences, and as a result, students can be more aware of special needs education.

In addition to special education programs for students, there are also programs for teachers. Lin (2021) conducted special education advocacy activities for teachers through a board game designed with the theme of understanding disabilities. This board game uses the concept of "discovering students' special needs" as a way for teachers to learn about "students' needs" and "ways to discover students' needs" during the game. According to the interview results of the board game, the participants were able to have a preliminary understanding of the terminology of special education during the game, and further discussions were held to gain a deeper understanding of the ways to identify the special needs of the students. The participants who experienced the game generally agreed that the game was able to convey the concept of "identifying students' special needs" to teachers in regular classes.

As mentioned above, the state of practice of special education advocacy activities in Taiwan is diverse, using multiple formats, and it is likely that many studies are conducted as programs when the teaching target is students in regular classrooms. Huang (2017) also pointed out that the more diverse the forms of special education advocacy activities are better. There are various ways to conduct special education activities, but each way has its limitations. For example, in the physical disability experience, the characteristics of non-physical disabilities are relatively difficult for students to understand or may cause misunderstanding. Moreover, since special education students are already diverse, the authors believe that the effectiveness of special education advocacy activities can be enhanced if the development of the variety of special education advocacy activities or use different methods of special education advocacy activities interchangeably.

Although prior research in Taiwan has shown that students' perceptions and attitudes can be changed, the main form of implementation was seen to be as programs, using multiple teaching materials and methods. Unfortunately, special education advocacy activities implemented as a program are not always implemented on an ongoing basis, even though they are effective, and it would be better if effective programs could be developed on an ongoing basis.

Implementing Inclusion Activities in Class-Field Courses

Implementing Inclusion Activities in Class-Field Courses means inclusive educational activities that are designed to engage the children with disabilities and normal children who participate in the classes through a variety of course topics and teaching methods (Hayashi, 2008). The curriculum allows children with disabilities to understand each other's features and interact with each other in a way that deepens their understanding of each other as human beings.

According to C Elementary School (2010), the participants of our school's Implementing Inclusion Activities in Class-Field Courses are all children in special needs classes and children in regular classes, and there are opportunities for children with disabilities to build relationships and understand communication. On the other hand, the purpose of this course is to foster the ability of children in regular classes to respect and work in groups, and to understand support methods (the ability of problem solving) for children with disabilities. As a flow of implementation, children in regular classes teach basic awareness of disabilities in advance, and while considering the needs of children with disabilities, appropriate inclusive educational activities (soccer, self-portrait, game of tag, etc.) are conducted, and then regular classes of children to conduct post-event discussions. In addition, the contents of classroom field curriculum inclusive education activities are individual, and according to the report of C Elementary School (2010), interaction and cooperation between children of disabilities and the children in regular class can be achieved through embodiments such as art, physical education, and games. It also reported that children with disabilities develop their own self-determination ability, and that healthy children also deepen their understanding of and support methods for children with disabilities from their experience of interacting with children with disabilities. Zhou and Chen (2019) observed Implementing Inclusion Activities in Class-Field Courses and found that pre- and post-learning and in-activity teaching methods the involved in the achievement of inclusion. They stated that it would be desirable to promote from the special-class teacher. Implementing Inclusion Activities in Class-Field Courses can relate to subjects that are interesting to students, and genuine exchanges between children with disabilities and healthy children can occur and they can grow together. Teachers who teach inclusive education activities feel that it is important not only to have expertise in special needs education, but also to understand the education system in general. Since the practical effect of the activity is related to the teacher's professional ability, we think that the Implementing Inclusion Activities in Class-Field Courses should incorporate the contents of teacher training and instructor development.

Volunteer Systems

Interaction between children with disabilities and regular students is not always limited to lessons. A common scene in the schools in Taiwan is that students in regular classes volunteer to assist special-needs children in their special education classes. Volunteer activities are regarded as activities for the "benefit of others," and Ito (2011) described the potential of volunteer activities to achieve self-realization, not only for the benefit of others but also for the benefit of oneself.

In a practical report on inclusive education activities at C Elementary School (2010), this school's special-needs class has a system of recruiting volunteers to assist in reading books and self-care with special-needs students during morning, break, and lunch breaks. Zhu (2019) also performed a two-month volunteer program for sixth-grade students with moderate to severe disabilities to exercise with them every morning. And during the service, volunteers would directly accompany and coach the special education

Inclusive Education Practices in Taiwan

class one-by-one in simple exercises and write a service log at the end of the service. The teachers will also provide advice to the volunteers. As a result, about half of the children reported a more positive change in their attitudes toward children with disabilities because they were volunteers.

Kung (2008) findings showed that the average student with personal experience had more positive attitudes toward peers with intellectual and physical disabilities than those who had no personal experience with peers with disabilities. The authors believe that volunteering in special education classes not only increases the communication experience with special education students, but also allows us to better understand the needs and difficulties of special education students through the service process. This indicates that through the experience of interacting with and supporting children with disabilities by volunteering, attitudes toward children with disabilities can be improved.

If schools establish a volunteer system, it will reduce the burden on special-needs teachers by ensuring that they have enough resources to support children with disabilities. In addition, students will gain a deeper awareness of children with disabilities and self-realization through their volunteer experience.

Interaction and Joint Learning by Subjects

The developmental unbalance is often said to be a feature of children with special needs education, but they are not behind in all subjects, so this means they are likely to be in the same class as the regular class. Children with cognitive disabilities may have the same level of language ability as children of the same age. The children with autism may also be able to concentrate in a class because they are interested in a subject. For inclusive education, students with and without disabilities should be able to learn and take classes together. Due to the limitations of their abilities, children with disabilities may not reach the academic level of their classmates, but they may still be able to attend classes with other children in lower grade classes, For example, Mr. R is a child with intellectual disabilities in the 5th grade of elementary school enrolled in a special-needs class, and due to his limited intelligence, his math level is lower than that of children of the same age. However, his emotions are stable, he can understand most of his teacher's instructions, and he has achieved the math level of a second grader, so he is able to take math classes with second graders. In addition, Hwang, Lee (2021) described a three-step process for the implementation of interaction and cooperative learning through subjects. During the preparation stage, the collaborators (teachers in charge and other subject teachers) should prepare lessons on this interaction and joint learning in advance, considering the learning atmosphere of the regular class, the teaching style of the teachers, and other factors. In the next tentative implementation stage, education on understanding disabilities should be taught to the students in the regular classes before conducting the interaction and joint learning. Also, during the implementation, while observing the learning and adaptation status of the children with disabilities, the authors will modify it gradually. Finally, the achievement of the goals for children with disabilities will be evaluated, and the effects of interaction and cooperative learning will be discussed.

Through interaction and joint learning by subjects, the authors believe that it is possible to promote interaction between children in the support class and children in the regular class. The benefits for children with disabilities will be to participate in society through learning in an environment of inclusion, and to improve their communication and social skills. On the other hand, the authors expect that children in regular classes will gain a better understanding of disabilities through their experiences in contact with children with disabilities.

Inclusive Education Practice at C Elementary School: School Festival About Inclusive Education

Since 1995, C Elementary School has been holding an annual school event called the " Sparkle of Life School Festival". The school festival is one of the most important school events, and according to the National Curriculum Guidelines, "the goal of school events is to form desirable human relationships, deepen a sense of group belonging and solidarity, cultivate a public spirit, and foster an independent and practical attitude to cooperate with others to build a better school life. Lin, Lee (2011) mentioned that school events deepen sentiments toward the school, while in addition, through the participation of the whole school, the sense of belonging to the school can be strengthened.

The "Sparkle of Life School Festival" of C Elementary School is a school festival with the concept of inclusive education. Posters about special needs education are displayed in the school's hallways, and all students go to the special needs class to interact with the children in the special needs class through games and simulated experiences to understand children with disabilities. Students can not only see the scenery of playing games in the special-needs class, but also see children from the special-needs class selling their own products and food as shopkeepers. Since a school event such as a festival is an event in which everyone in the school participates, it would be a good time to provide inclusive education while reinforcing a stronger sense of belonging to the school.

SOLUTIONS AND RECOMMENDATIONS

Inclusive education in Taiwan has the challenges of diversity of special education advocacy activities and ensuring the cooperation of all parties involved with students with disabilities (regular classroom teachers, special needs education teachers, and administrative personnel within schools) and the expertise of teachers.

Regarding the diversity of special education advocacy activities, Huang (2012) investigated the types and percentages of special education advocacy activities for elementary schools in Taitung, Taiwan, and the most frequently used methods were experiential activities for the physically challenged and video viewing. However, the communication activities and school activities mentioned in this paper were not frequently used. Nevertheless, the authors believe that different special education advocacy activities not only allow students to learn about special education according to their learning habits, but also allow for the interactive use of these methods to allow for more possibilities for the advancement of integrated education.

Regarding the collaboration of stakeholders of students with disabilities, activities related to inclusive education, such as classroom field curriculum inclusive education activities, interaction and joint learning, volunteer work, and school events, observed to increase opportunities for interaction with regular and special needs classrooms. When conducting classroom field curriculum inclusive education activities, interaction and joint learning, and volunteer activities, cooperation and communication between regular classroom teachers, other subject teachers, and teachers of special needs classes are expected to be essential because of the different groups of children participating in these activities. Therefore, teamwork among teachers is important.

In addition to in-school personnel, collaboration with other parties is also important. Su & Wang (2003) through the results of interviews with in-service teachers, found that " parents of children with disabilities, children in regular classes, parents of children in regular classes, school administrative personnel, and professional related organization personnel (Speech Therapist, Physical Therapist, Occupational Therapist, etc.) are powerful resources for the implementation of inclusive education. Inclusion includes the meaning of inclusiveness and oneness, which means that all people are involved. Therefore, collaboration and teamwork with all relevant parties is one of the keys to achieving inclusive education.

Regarding ensuring the professionalism of teachers, the results of a 2017 review of the implementation of the Convention on the Rights of Persons with Disabilities in Taiwan indicated that "some teachers have not received appropriate courses to support children with disabilities enrolled in regular classrooms." Also, a study by Su et al. (2003) stated that teachers are resistant to taking charge of classes with children with disabilities because they do not have a background in special needs education. Although the percentage of teachers in Taiwan who have received at least 3 hours of training on special education was 76% in 2019, he found that there are still a sizable number of teachers who lack confidence. The question of how to ensure the professionalism of teachers through training and teacher development will be a challenge for the realization of inclusive education in Taiwan.

FUTURE RESEARCH DIRECTIONS

Although there is an increasing trend of research on inclusive education, the number of practical studies related to inclusive education is relatively insufficient. This article indicated classroom field curriculum inclusive education activities, interaction and joint learning, volunteer work, and school events are the way to implement inclusive education, but the effect may vary depending on the target and the location. Therefore, it is important to verify the validity of these methods or to develop scales or scales to measure special education advocacy activities.

Advancing the concept of "inclusion" is important for inclusive education, Su et al. (2003) in their study pointed out that when promoting inclusive education, there are difficulties in questioning from parents of children in regular classes and that the interaction effect with children in regular classes is poor. The authors recognize that the attitudes and ideas on the part of the parents as the well as the students will always affect the students. It is believed that the one-sided efforts of schoolteachers cannot maximize the effectiveness of classes and activities related to inclusive education. The authors believe that students' values are difficult to change easily, but they will always change gradually as they become accustomed to an environment of inclusion. Therefore, the authors hope that the promotion of the concept of "inclusion" will not only take place within schools, but also be promoted across society.

CONCLUSION

Based on the above, inclusive education in Taiwan is diverse and includes not only common formats such as classroom field curriculum inclusive education activities, interaction and cooperative learning, and volunteer programs, but also school events and activities that are characterized by each school. It is more important for teachers to consider how they can take advantage of the ways mentioned above. Therefore, it is essential to ensure the expertise of teachers and their teamwork with other collaborators. In Taiwan, a high percentage of children with disabilities are enrolled in regular classes. From the viewpoint of learning place, they have time to learn together with children in regular classes, but the quality of learning and the effectiveness of the exchange must be emphasized from now on.

REFERENCES

Chang, Bey-Lih (2009) Inclusive Education in Taiwan. *National Taiwan Normal University Division of Educational Practicum and Professional Development Secondary Education*, *60*(4), 8-18.

Chen, H.-C. (2019) *Implementation of Inclusive Education of the Convention on the Rights of Persons with Disabilities in the Taiwanese Laws* [Unpublished master's thesis, National Cheng-chi University, Taipei, Taiwan].

Cheng, C.-F. (2012). The Growth out of Nothing in Special Education: Discussion on the Phenomenon of Marginalization of Students with Disabilities in Regular Class. *Special Education Quarterly*, *122*, 45–52.

Chiu, Y.-C. (2021). Inclusive Education and The Promotion Program of Special Education. *Student Affairs and Guidance Counseling*, *59*(4), 63–67.

Chu, S.-M., & Chen, S.-Y. (2019). Study on the Process of Implementing Inclusion Activities in Class-Field Courses-A Special Education Class of a Taipei Municipal Elementary School as a Case. *The Development of Special Education*, *68*, 43–56.

Chu, Y.-C., & Chang, S.-H. (2019). Service-Learning Program to Improve Elementary School Students' Peer Acceptance Attitude towards Students with Disabilities. *Special Education Forum*, *27*, 17-34.

Hsiu-li, K. (2008). *A study on peer acceptance towards mentally and physically challenged students in elementary school* [Unpublished master's thesis, National Pingtung University of Education, Pingtung, Taiwan].

Huang, H.-Y. (2017). *The Study of Special-Education Propaganda Executed by the Primary Schools in Taitung County* [Unpublished master's thesis, National Taitung University, Taitung, Taiwan].

Huang, Y.-F. (2010). A cooperative relationship and model between general teachers and special education teachers under integrated education. *Tung Wah Special Education*, *44*, 14–19.

Ito, T. (2011). An examination of motives for voluntary activities. Gakushuin University, The annual collection of essays and studies. *Faculty of Letters*, *27*, 35–55.

Jian, X.-H. (2014). *A study of peer acceptance program to improve peer acceptance of students with intellectual disabilities in elementary school* [Unpublished master's thesis, National Kaohsiung Normal University, Kaohsiung, Taiwan].

Ko, M. W., & Chen, M. H. (2009). Finding a stage for students with special needs - Promoting integrated education in Dunhua Junior High School. *National Taiwan Normal University Division of Educational Practicum and Professional Development Secondary Education*, *60*(4), 168–179.

Lai, M. J. (2012). *A study of the political effects of integrated education policies* [Unpublished master's thesis, National Taiwan Normal University, Taipei, Taiwan].

Lin, H.-C. (2021). *Identifying the Special Needs of Students: A Study of Board Game Design for Special Education Advocacy Activities* [Unpublished master's thesis, National Taipei University of Education, Taipei, Taiwan].

Lin, J. J. (2008). *A study of the integration of curriculum programs on the acceptance of special education students' attitudes by students in elementary school regular classes* [Unpublished master's thesis, National Taiwan University, Taitung].

Ministry of Education. (1995). Report on Education for the Physically and Mentally Handicapped in the Republic of China. Ministry of Education.

Ministry of Education. (1999). Report on Special Education Statistics in 1999. Ministry of Education.

Ministry of Education. (2009). Report on Special Education Statistics in 2009. Ministry of Education..

Ministry of Education. (2019). Report on Special Education Statistics in 2019. Ministry of Education.

Ministry of Education. (2021). Report on Special Education Statistics in 2021. Ministry of Education.

Su, Y.-H., & Wang, T.-M. (2003). Ideals and challenges of integrated education: The experience of teachers in elementary school regular classes. *Journal of Special Education Research, 24*, 39–62.

Sunny, X. (2017). *A Multicultural Curriculum Research of In-class Publicity Programs with Special Education Issue.* [Unpublished master's thesis, National Taiwan Normal University, Taipei, Taiwan].

Taipei City C Elementary School. (2010). *The authors are all good friends ~ Multi-Modal Area Curriculum Integration Activities in Zhongshan.* CIRN-Exemplar of Standards. https://cirn.moe.edu.tw/userfiles/file/benchmark/99/team/B39.pdf

Wong, H.-B., & Lee, K.-C. (2021). Implementation of a regular classroom curriculum for students with intellectual disabilities in a centralized special education class in elementary schools. *Taiwan Education Review Monthly, 10*(5), 147–152.

Xu, C.-F., & Wang, M.-C. (2014). Exploring the teaching of social skills for children with intellectual disabilities. *Yunjia Journal of Special Education, 20*, 28–36.

KEY TERMS AND DEFINITIONS

Implementing Inclusion Activities in Class-Field Courses: The children with disabilities and normal children who participate in the classes through a variety of course topics (sports, painting et.).

Interaction and Joint Learning by Subjects: The children with disabilities enrolled in special education classes who participate in the regular class's lesson. The determination of lesson participation is based on the children with disabilities' ability and individualized education plan (IEP).

Mental barrier-free: It also meant as a psychological accessibility. People treat others (like the people with special needs) without prejudice, and with a positive attitude. Let the people in need live, with or without foresight.

National Curriculum Guidelines: It is a basis for standardizing the curriculum of school teaching in Taiwan. It was announced for implementation after being reviewed and approved by the Ministry of Education of ROC.

Professional related organization personnel: In order to provide better support services for students with disabilities. In addition to special education teachers, health and medical, social work, independent living, and vocational rehabilitation professionals work together to help in learning, living, psychological, rehabilitation training, vocational counseling assessment, and transition counseling and services. For example: speech therapist, psychological counselor, physical therapist.

Special education advocacy activities: Approaches to Disabilities Awareness Education. Through experience and cooperation, participants can better understand or increase awareness of disabilities.

Support Services for Students with Disabilities Measures: The measures are formulated based on Article 33 of The Special Education Law in Taiwan. The purpose of this measure is to ensure that the needs of students with disabilities in school can be protected.

The Special Education Law: The purpose of this Law is to protect the right of the disabilities and the gifted. It is also the mother law related to special education in Taiwan.

Chapter 8

Flexible, Relevant, and Accessible Curriculum:
The Role of the Universal Design for Learning Framework in Three Countries

David G. Evans
The University of Sydney, Australia

Rosmalily binti Salleh
Ministry of Education, Malaysia

Abdul Basit
Department of Special Education, Government of the Punjab, Lahore, Pakistan

Cathy Little
The University of Sydney, Australia

ABSTRACT

Education is a right for all children and youth. It has been stated in international initiatives for over five decades. Curriculum frameworks across cultural contexts are interpreted in differing ways by class teachers (e.g., direct interpretation, materials developed by government or commercial bodies). Yet students with disabilities continue to be marginalised from a robust and meaningful curriculum on the basis that the curriculum is 'not for them,' or that teachers are not professionally equipped to make modifications to support access, participation, and learning. This chapter seeks to explore how the universal design for learning framework can be used to ensure all learners are contributing members within the regular classroom. This exploration will consider contexts from three countries to illustrate how the UDL framework can be used to develop flexible, meaningful, and accessible curriculum for all learners. This exploration will illustrate the barriers posed by school structures, mindsets of educators, and rigid interpretation and use of curriculum frameworks and materials.

DOI: 10.4018/978-1-6684-7370-2.ch008

INTRODUCTION

Education is a right of all children and youth. It has been stated in international initiatives for over five decades, and yet globally we seem to be running just as fast to ensure this important right is attained by all young people. The Global Education Mentoring Report *Inclusion and Education: All Means All* (UNESCO, 2020) reported on the progress of members' states towards meeting the intentions of Goal 4 of the Sustainability Development Goal 2030: "Ensure inclusive and equitable quality education and promote lifelong learning opportunities for all" (United Nations, 2015). It reiterated the complexities of addressing the needs of all students, in particular marginalised groups (e.g., students with disability).

BACKGROUND

Since the commencement of the COVID19 pandemic, educational opportunity has been adversely impacted for most learners (World Bank, 2020). This impact knew no economic or cultural bounds, and learners around the world have been adversely impacted in their ability to access a quality inclusive education. Countries have moved very quickly to address the learning loss that has occurred where the impact has been most severe on learners with disabilities. While prior to the pandemic these learners were at a high chance of not receiving a quality inclusive education, or attending school at all, these chances became much less. COVID19 education times have tested our professional capacities as educators to uphold the fundamental right of education.

The COVID19 disruptions have in many ways highlighted the tension educators have been facing over the past decades. The challenges of providing a quality inclusive education for all were brought to the fore in 1994 through the Salamanca Statement. The United Nations Convention on the Rights of Persons with Disabilities (CRPD, 2006) has been another significant international milestone. Article 24 on education requires member parties to provide education to persons without disabilities without discrimination and on the same basis as persons without disabilities. Yet, on the ten-year anniversary of the CRPD, General Comment No 4 reminded state parties of the challenges that learners with disabilities continue to face in obtaining their right to education on the same basis as persons without disabilities. The challenges can be conceptualised as exclusions or barriers that exist throughout education environments.

The persistence of exclusionary practices has been attributed to attitudes of educators and school communities towards persons with disabilities, limited flexibility within education systems, and the persistence in using a language of inclusion while maintaining traditional exclusionary practices (e.g., maintaining segregated education facilities that exclude students with disabilities from informal learning opportunities). Andriana (2018) reported the voice of primary school students with disabilities about their experiences in three 'inclusive' schools in Yogyakarta, Indonesia. While the language of inclusion was used (e.g., inclusion students, inclusion classrooms, inclusion teachers), there was little evidence of upholding the intent of quality inclusive education (e.g., educating students alongside their neighbourhood peers, accessing and sharing the same learning experiences).

This rhetoric of 'doing inclusion' or implementing a policy of inclusion, but upholding traditional exclusionary practices is described by Slee at al. (2021) as "mixaphobic" (p. 6). These gestures of inclusion contribute to the "profound challenges" (United Nations, 2006, p. 2) faced in upholding the intentions of global commitments (e.g., Convention on the Rights of Persons with Disabilities). However, classroom teachers who are key to meeting our obligations to ensure the right to education for students

Flexible, Relevant, and Accessible Curriculum

with disabilities work hard to uphold this right. They work within schooling contexts, and state systems of education.

A key concern teachers report about meeting the intent of quality inclusive education is that they do not have the professional skills and knowledge (Andriana, 2018; Sharma et al., 2015). Teachers offer watered-down and less robust learning experiences (Zhang & Zhao, 2019), require students with disabilities to be accompanied by a shadow teacher or teaching assistant, or refer students to a segregated 'inclusion' classroom (Andriana, 2018). The use of segregated classrooms, and development of more special schools for students with disabilities, is also found in developed countries. The Australian Institute of Health and Welfare (2017) reported that between 2003 and 2015 there had been a move towards students with more complex educational needs attending special schools. One reason given for this move was that special schools could provide more tailored support than the mainstream classrooms. Teachers are also concerned about the value and relevance of the curriculum offered in regular education settings.

CURRICULUM FRAMEWORKS

Quality inclusive education is the right of all learners no matter their ability, background, or identity. "All children should learn from the same flexible, relevant and accessible curriculum, one that recognizes diversity and responds to various learners' needs." (UNESCO, 2020, p. 21). A curriculum framework provides a set of "parameters, directions and standards for curriculum policy and practice" (IBE-UNESCO, 2017a, p. 6). Melvin et al. (2020), using the work of Bredekamp (2011), defined curriculum framework in the early childhood context:

(1)   Beliefs and goals about learning and development;
(2)   Learning experiences, including what and how children learn
(3)   Teaching strategies, including teachers approaches to providing learning experiences; and sometimes
(4)   Specific materials and resources that help teachers and children achieve those goals, including lesson plans, schedules, or classroom arrangements. (p. 11)

In viewing these two definitions of curriculum frameworks, it is evident that interpretations may be different across contexts (e.g., level of education, education jurisdictions, countries). How curriculum is defined, and designed, can impact how teachers go about providing quality education for all. These differences can be found across international borders.

In many countries curriculum frameworks are used by government departments of education to design materials, resources, and assessments that teachers will use and implement in their classrooms (e.g., Pakistan, Indonesia). In other parts of the globe (e.g., United States of America), commercial groups may work to interpret the standards and curriculum framework, design learning experiences, resources, and assessments for schools to adopt. Teachers in these instances often require strong pedagogical knowledge to implement and achieve the intentions of the curricula designed.

In other countries (e.g., Australia) teachers use the national curriculum framework to design classroom learning programs and experiences to meet the education needs of all students in their respective schools. In these instances, teachers require strong content knowledge in addition to pedagogical knowledge. Despite the differing approaches to enacting the intentions of curriculum frameworks, there are ongoing difficulties experienced by teachers in developing quality inclusive educational experiences. That is, educational experiences that evolve from:

... a process of systemic reform embodying changes and modifications in content, teaching methods, approaches, structures and strategies in education to overcome barriers with a vision serving to provide all students of the relevant age range with an equitable and participatory learning experience and environment that best corresponds to their requirements and preferences. (United Nations, 2006, p. 4)

In achieving these educational experiences, curriculum frameworks and standards need to be flexible from the beginning so they can be interpreted to design and provide learning experiences to the margins of student' strengths, interests, and motivations. Professional knowledge of teachers and educators can be enhanced and supported in ways that ensures ongoing refinement of the inclusive nature of school learning programs (e.g., collaborative planning, co-teaching).

For all students to learn from the same relevant and flexible curriculum, curriculum frameworks, standards and materials need to be interpreted by teachers in ways that allow for all students to participate and learn. This professional independence can be a blessing, and at the same time a scourge. On one side it allows for teachers to design and implement programs of work that address individual and personal needs of students. On the other, curricula used in a one-size-fits-all approach can exclude students – especially students from diverse and marginalised groups.

The universal design for learning framework provides opportunities for the goals of inclusive education to be met, and in doing so support the achievement of Sustainability Development Goal 4. The universal design for learning framework provides flexibility for interpreting curriculum frameworks and curriculum materials to meet the diverse educational needs of students (Meyer et al., 2014). It aims to support teachers in designing rich learning environments free of barriers (Nelson, 2014). It provides an opportunity for educators to consider how learning can be designed in a way that removes the need to provide separate curriculum options for students at the margins, to remove students with disabilities from education alongside neighbourhood peers, or exclude students from education all together (IBE-UNESCO, 2017).

PURPOSE

The aim of this chapter is to explore how the universal design for learning framework could be used to support access to general curriculum for all students from three countries, specifically Australia, Malaysia, and Pakistan. While each country has differing curriculum models, they are working towards creating inclusive education contexts. In each country, however, there is evidence that students with disability are excluded from access to the regular curriculum (e.g., separate curriculum frameworks, curriculum materials, or exclusion from education). As a result, they fall short of providing access to the same flexible curriculum (UNESCO, 2020) that is personalised to the needs of each student (IBE-UNESCO, 2017).

Australia

Background

Flexible, Relevant, and Accessible Curriculum

Australia is a multicultural country of 26 million people. While education is funded by the federal government and influenced by national agenda and policies, education is the responsibility of each of the six states and two territories. Within each state, education sectors (i.e., public, Catholic, independent) give direction to how schools uphold government mandates. Non-public sectors receive federal government funding in addition to fees they may charge families.

As part of a national agenda, states and territories offer 13 years of schooling: seven years at the primary level and six years at secondary level. These 13 years of schooling are underpinned by a strong early childhood curriculum framework entitled Early Years Learning Framework (DEEWR, 2009). Curriculum, assessment, and reporting in schools are addressed through the Australia Curriculum, Reporting and Assessment Authority (ACARA). Each state and territory are required to uphold the curriculum framework establish by ACARA, now in its 9th version (ACARA, 2023). The national curriculum is designed to ensure all young Australians "become confident and creative individuals, successful lifelong learners, and active and informed members of the community" (Council of Australian Governments - Education Council, 2019, p. 6).

Australia adopted a national, three-dimensional curriculum framework consisting of learning areas, general capabilities, and cross curriculum priorities in 2012. This framework provides flexibility in how teachers and education sectors can meet the individual needs of all young Australians including students with disabilities. At least two states chose to interpret the curriculum for their own state (e.g., New South Wales Education Standards Authority produces a set of syllabus documents based on the national curriculum).

Teachers use the Australian Curriculum framework to design the classroom curriculum. This expectation requires teachers to have strong content and pedagogical knowledge. In designing the classroom curriculum, teachers can create their own materials, assessments, and resources, or they can draw on a range of materials to which they have access. Teachers can focus on topics and areas that will relate to local and relevant experiences, providing relevance and currency to learners within the local community. Access to education for students with disabilities is fundamental to the Australian Curriculum, however, is often found difficult to achieve, or not relevant to this group of students.

In a review of the Australian Curriculum in 2014 (Australian Government, 2014), special education teachers claimed that the curriculum did not "cater for all students" (p. 5). While calls for an alternate curriculum to be designed for the Australian Curriculum were not followed, differing states and territories designed their own curriculum statements for students with disabilities (Humphreys & Jimenez, 2018). Hence, students with disabilities may not access and participate in education on the same basis as students without disabilities.

Malaysia

Background

Malaysia is a multiethnic and multicultural country in south-east Asia, which achieved its independence from British rule on 31 August 1957. The education system is heavily impacted by this colonisation. Changes and development can be seen pre-independence and post-independence, now with a national curriculum that represents Malaysian values and beliefs. The national curriculum is a set of subjects and standards used by pre, primary and secondary schools that all children access and learn. It covers what subjects are taught and the standards children should reach in each subject area.

Malaysia endorses a system of 6+5+2 of formal education. The national curriculum is offered in both public and private schools. Children receive education as early as the age of four, although this schooling is not compulsory. Many children attend preschool at the age of six years old, the precursor to formal schooling in Malaysia from seven years old. Formal schooling is provided for children and adolescents to the age of 17 years.

Pupils advance to secondary education despite their grades/results of their primary education. The Ujian Pencapaian Sekolah Rendah, UPSR (The Primary School Assessment Test) taken at the end of primary education was abolished in 2021. In transforming the assessment program in Malaysia, the Ujian Pentaksiran Tingkatan Tiga (PT3) for Form 3 pupils was also cancelled in 2022 after two years of postponement because of the COVID-19 pandemic. With the abolishment, school-based assessment was emphasised at all levels.

National Curriculum

The National Curriculum is interpreted in section 2 Act 550 as the prescribed curriculum. While the Education (National Curriculum) Regulations 1997 [P.U.(A)531/97] clarified the meaning of the National Curriculum, according to sub-regulations 3(1) as follows:

An educational programme that includes curriculum and co-curricular activities which encompasses all the knowledge, skills, norms, values, cultural elements and beliefs to help develop a pupil fully with respect to the physical, spiritual, mental and emotional aspects as well as to inculcate and develop desirable moral values and to transmit knowledge.

The Primary School Standard Curriculum (KSSR) was implemented in stages from 2011. It has been revised to meet the new policy under the Malaysian Education Development Plan (PPPM) 2013-2025, so that the quality of the curriculum implemented in primary schools is comparable to international standards. A standard-based curriculum representing international practice has been embodied in KSSR through the development of the Standard Curriculum and Assessment Document (DSKP) for all subjects containing Content Standards, Learning Standards and Performance Standards. This level of education is about building the skills, knowledge and values that can be enhanced and enriched in secondary school.

The Standards-Based Curriculum for Primary Schools (KSSR) and the Standards-Based Curriculum for Secondary Schools (KSSM) are based on six fundamentals strands: communication; spiritual, attitude and values; humanities; personal competence; physical development and aesthetics; and science and technology. These six strands support one another and are integrated with critical and creative thinking, and innovative skills. The integration aims to produce a balanced individual who appreciates and embodies each one of the stated strands and readies each student to pursue individual interests and motivations while also contributing the building of Malaysia's cultural capacities.

The curriculum framework that teachers work with in Malaysia provides opportunities to create a rich learning context for students. Teachers are supported through the provision of curriculum materials that are prepared for them centrally, for implementation across differing cultural groups. Use of these curricula for providing access to education for students with disabilities is less well developed. Clarity on how the curriculum framework can be applied to education for students with disabilities on the same basis as student without disabilities is unclear.

Flexible, Relevant, and Accessible Curriculum

Pakistan

Background

Pakistan is a country rich in history, wide variations in geography and with a strong religious background. A country of more than 230 million people, the task of providing education for all is a substantial undertaking. As a result, there is considerable variation in the approaches taken.

Education is a shared responsibility between the federal and provincial governments, as recognised by the Constitution of Pakistan 1973. Education is part of the concurrent Legislative List, representing its importance to the country and its people. Policy, planning, curriculum, syllabus, standards, and Islamic education are key topics on the concurrent Legislative list (Majeed, 2009).

National Curriculum

Pakistan has historically lacked a National Curriculum Framework (NCF). Public schools, private schools, the Deeni Madaris (i.e., religious education institute), and informal education prevail in Pakistan, with each of these education sectors having their own curriculum, assessment, and management processes. This situation provided a variety of inequalities and disparities, hence, uniformity in curricula and standards became an important issue in Pakistan.

As a result of these issues, the need for curriculum and consistency of implementation at the national level were part of national developments in education. As a result, in 2016 a National Curriculum framework was developed. Despite a call for public school, private institutions and Deeni Madaris to adopt the new curriculum, only public schools and a few low-income private schools adopted this national curriculum that comprised content, resources and materials, and assessments. The way the curriculum was implemented is the responsibility of class teachers, placing an emphasis on teacher professional knowledge to maximise the intentions of the curriculum.

The education of students with disabilities in Pakistan is most often the responsibility of the provincial, district or tehsil (i.e., village) level. Special education institutes provide guidance to teachers and schools on how to use the national curriculum to support students. These institutes are limited in number, and the support they provide classrooms is stretched beyond its current capacities. In many instances, students with disabilities access and participation in a curriculum is removed from that accessed by students without disabilities, or they are excluded from education.

CROSS CONTEXT DISCUSSION

Across each context common issues or barriers to designing curriculum inclusive of students with disabilities are present. In each context teachers report that the general curriculum is not appropriate for students with disabilities, resulting in 'special education' curriculum being developed or highly sought after. In each context, students with disabilities are excluded at a micro level (e.g., receive education from an unqualified teacher or member of the family in the classroom) or the macro level (e.g., receive an education in another classroom) (Cologon, 2019). In some instances, students with disabilities are excluded altogether from education.

Designing classroom curriculum using a national curriculum framework and/or materials developed commercially or by government that provides quality and dignified access and participation for all students is challenging for most teachers. Viewing this challenge through an inclusive educational lens where students are given their right to a quality inclusive education is one key to this challenge

(UNESCO, 2020). The universal design for learning framework is one lens that provides this opportunity. This framework will be used to address some of the challenges found with each of the contexts outlined, along with recommendation of how the knowledge of teachers and educators can be enhanced as part of everyday professional operation.

Inclusive Curriculum: Operationalising Principles

Designing the learning environment

Curriculum frameworks differ across international boundaries, yet in each of the three contexts discussed they can enable or disable participation by all students and learners. In the case of students with disabilities, each context sought to establish a national curriculum and these curricula were interpreted differently across jurisdictions and education sectors (e.g., Australia, Pakistan). The design of these national curricula did not strive from the beginning to be inclusive of all learners; in the case of Australia, retrofitting of the national framework was required (Australian Government, 2014). This oversight builds in inefficiencies from the beginning, and some students will be excluded.

In each context, there is evidence that educators were of the view that a common curriculum for all was not preferrable or possible. Yet the universal design for learning framework (CAST, 2023; Meyer et al., 2014) provides opportunities for educators at all levels of education to consider options for providing access, participation and learning in robust, meaningful, and personalised ways for all learners. Providing educators support is key to achieving education for all.

Structural barriers

The universal design for learning framework encourages educators to consider the barriers that learners face. In the first instance, it may be well worth considering the barriers that educators themselves pose to ensuring that all learners access and participate in educational learning. The attitudes of education communities have been found to be a persistent barrier (Boyle et al., 2020; Page et al., 2020; Sharma et al., 2015), and raising attitudes of teachers towards inclusive education beyond mildly positive has been difficult. While attitudes have been researched extensively over the past three decades, their importance is key to achieving quality inclusive practices in education (Avramidis, 2000).

Linked with attitudes are educator's self-efficacy (Kurniawati et al., 2014). Kitt et al. (2019), in discussing teacher preparation for inclusive education in Africa and Asia, make claim to the limited understanding of teachers across cultural contexts. Teacher's belief that they can enact inclusive practices in their classroom plays an important part in meeting the needs of all learners. Building this capacity using the universal design for learning framework, for example, to design barrier free learning environment using local curriculum is key to meeting the needs of all learners.

A third barrier that education settings pose centres around the ethos within a setting towards providing education for all. Hoppey and McLeskey (2014) posed that cultural and organisation qualities (e.g., a unified ethos of inclusive education) were central to building a school's capacity to be inclusive and the capacity of its members. In each of the contexts discussed, attitudes towards educating students with disabilities within the common curriculum framework was challenged. It was accompanied by limited evidence of leadership within schools about the core principles of inclusion and quality inclusive education pedagogies. Yet attitudes could be enhanced through strong leadership and personalised professional learning (Hoppey & McLeskey, 2014).

Curriculum design barriers

Flexible, Relevant, and Accessible Curriculum

In enacting the universal design for learning framework, educators need to know their learners (Kanter, 2019) and how they can design a learning environment to be barrier free. A key feature of the educational context is the physical environment. Providing physical access to a learning environment was a high priority of the three contexts examined, and governments and sectors have worked hard to remove obstacles. While more can be done, education communities working together can ensure everyday barriers can be removed. Planning classes to be at ground level for a student with cerebral palsy with mobility impairment was a regular consideration by school leaders in schools in Lahore, Pakistan (Basit & Evans, in preparation).

In discussing the education of students with disabilities across each of the three contexts, the issue of resources was raised (i.e., sufficient resources). The provision of sufficient funding for resources to support quality inclusive education is key, yet one must question how many resources are enough, and the nature of these resources and their benefits to educators and students. Provision of sufficient resources was an issue in all three contexts. Yet there are qualitatively differing ideas of sufficiency. In the Australian context, the Nationally Consistent Collection of Data provides the basis for ensuring resource provision to support students with disabilities well beyond that found in Pakistan and Malaysia. Further, these provisions of additional support often transpire in the form of a teaching assistant. In other contexts, the failure of families to provide a teaching assistant or support can result in a student being excluded from education alongside their neighbourhood peers (Kanter, 2019).

When working with teachers catering for students with complex education needs, each of the three universal design for learning principles provide opportunities for addressing the unique needs of students. Using multiple means of representation opens many options for teachers to consider (e.g., concrete, personalised images, technology) beyond those that may be mandated or required by curriculum designers. Evans et al. (2018) found that teachers in rural parts of Indonesia drew on existing community resources to heighten relevance and personalised examples for students with a diverse range of backgrounds. They did not require costly materials, or advanced electronic technologies to provide access and participation for all students. Further, teachers in heightening the relevance for students were able to draw on the principles of multiple means of engagement within the universal design for learning framework.

In classrooms where all learners are expected to demonstrate learning in the same manner poses another barrier. Giving students choice in how they represent their learning gives ownership to them, and it again does not mean having an assortment of expensive resources and options (e.g., advanced electronic technologies or assistive devices). Technology does not make a learning environment a universally designed learning environment. The design of an environment that provides "sufficient options – in both challenges and supports – so that all of its learners will be successful" is key to ensuring all learners can represent their learning (Rose et al., 2010, p. 7). A student with cerebral palsy in Pakistan, for example, working alongside a peer to co-construct a response in mathematics could be sufficient to ensure all learners can respond (Basit & Evans, in preparation).

At the more refined levels of the universal design for learning framework (i.e., guidelines, checkpoints), further examples can be found on how an existing curriculum framework can be used to design learning for all. Teachers will often express concern about the behaviour of students (e.g., do not complete tasks or attend, exhibit unwanted or aggressive behaviour towards other students). Developing strategies of self-regulation (Guideline 9) are skills required by all learners, and have been shown to enhance learning for students from a range of backgrounds across learning domains (Rogers et al., 2020). While this may not be clearly stated in a national curriculum (e.g., Pakistan) it is in other national curricula (e.g.,

Malaysia, Australia). In either case, teaching skills of self-regulation can be integrated across differing formal and informal curriculum areas without the need for specific curriculum statements.

Acquiring knowledge of concepts, procedures or learning strategies at grade level is a difficulty teachers view about students with disabilities educational experience. This difficulty is often perceived as a student centred 'problem' or deficit on the part of students. When viewed as an inadequacy of the learning environment (Kame'enui & Simmons, 1990), or barriers in the environment, however, allows for teachers to examine differing ways to build stronger learning environments. In the context of structured curriculum materials (e.g., textbooks, worksheets), teachers may need to break skills down further to provide guidance of information processing via means of representation, or provide greater levels of practice (e.g., schedule regular practice across a day; Checkpoint 5.3).

Mastering complex or large content domains can pose difficulties for students. In interpreting curriculum framework statements (e.g., Australia, Malaysia) supporting student comprehension can be achieved through careful sequencing of content, and making the big ideas of content conspicuous to students (Checkpoint 3.2). The level of support in identifying and mastering the big ideas within content can be graduated between students, with some receiving little guidance while others it may be quite explicit. In prepared curriculum resources these big ideas may not be apparent, and teachers will need to make them visible to students.

Developing strong literacy and numeracy skills is important for all learners and needs to be promoted at all stages of learning. They are key skills for life beyond school, and to becoming independent members of a community. In the Australian Curriculum these skills are outlined within the general capabilities dimension (ACARA, 2023), while in other curriculum resources they can be less evident. While the universal design for learning framework does not stipulate curriculum content, ensuring these skills are made visible in multiple ways is the responsibility of the teacher. It may require teachers to use alternate means of communication to support development of literacy skills; it may require secondary teachers to use relevant concrete resources to support the development of mathematical content in use in everyday situations.

Assisting students to be strategic learners involves supporting the development of goals. Goals could be for academic work, social behaviour, or life beyond school. All students benefit from this across all year levels. Teaching goal setting (Checkpoint 6.1) can be part of developing skills in self-determination and is linked to the skills of self- regulation. Promoting self-determination for students with disability is impactful on quality of life (Wehmeyer, 2020); self-regulated strategy development has been shown to be highly beneficial for all learners in developing writing skills (Rogers et al., 2020; Sanders et al., 2021). However, self-determination often does not appear in curriculum materials yet can be included within all areas of the curriculum by teachers.

Building Capacity: Teacher Preparation

A theme across each context was the creation of a teaching workforce that was prepared to enact inclusive education. In countries like Australia where there have been considerable resources given by national and state and territory governments to promote the education of students with disabilities, there appears to be little shift in teacher attitudes and self-efficiency. In Pakistan there is a desire for greater enhancement of teacher capacity from not-for-profit groups and community organisations, while in Malaysia work at the nation level (e.g., inclusive approaches to interpreting the curriculum) is promising. Yet there is ongoing reluctance by regular education schools and their teachers.

Flexible, Relevant, and Accessible Curriculum

Shifting teacher attitudes and self-efficacy in inclusive education will require focused and sustained professional learning for both pre-service and in-service teachers. While in Australia pre-service teachers will often complete a unit of study in special and inclusive education, the recent *Quality Initial Teacher Education* report (Australian Government, 2022) highlighted that graduating teachers did not feel prepared to provide education for students with disabilities in the regular classroom. Both Pakistan and Malaysia do not have such provisions, and there is evidence that pre-service teachers do not feel prepared (Sharma et al., 2015). There is evidence that indicates pre-service teachers feel they benefited from a unit of study in special and inclusive education as part of their teacher education course (Spandagou et al., 2009).

The impact of fostering pre-service teacher education knowledge, skills and understanding of universal design for learning during their training has received little attention. While studies on pre-service courses (e.g., Sharma et al., 2015; Spandagou et al., 2009) report on the impact of pre-service courses, they do not address impact of training in universal design for learning. Further research in this area could provide further insight into how pre-service teachers can be supported in their professional responsibility to be inclusive of all learners.

In-service teachers report mild to neutral attitudes towards inclusive education, with similar outcomes for self-efficacy (Avramidis et al., 2019). Yet building teacher self-efficacy in inclusive practice, and the use of inclusive framework such as the universal design for learning, is key to meeting national goals in Malaysia, Pakistan, and Australia. Australian and Chinese secondary school teacher attitudes towards universal design for learning was reported to be mildly positive (Chen & Evans, accepted).

Hoppey and McLeskey (2014) in outlining key themes in promoting quality inclusive schools highlight the benefits of "learner-centered professional learning" (p. 20). This approach seeks to personalise professional learning for teachers at the point of time knowledge and skills are needed. In the case of building capacity in teachers to use the universal design for learning framework, teachers can tailor professional learning to those elements of the framework that will assist them break down barriers and enhance the level of quality inclusive practice by using team-based approaches where teachers can problem-solve specific challenges they are facing in their classroom (e.g., using alternate communication to promote key literacy skills). This learning can be ongoing, facilitated through a specialist teacher, and linked directly to the learning and benefits for students.

CONCLUSION

The place of quality inclusive education is firmly stated within multiple international documents (e.g., CRPD, United Nations, 2006; General Comment No. 4, United Nations, Global Education Monitoring Report, UNESCO, 2020) and national statements, legislation, and policy. The intention of inclusive education becomes confused between the conceptualisation and the reality. In Pakistan, Malaysia, and Australia there was clear evidence that governments were pushing towards meeting their commitment under the Convention of the Rights of Persons with Disability (United Nations, 2006). Yet evidence about accessing the regular curriculum on the same basis as students without disabilities is troubled. Students across each context are mainstreamed or placed in the neighbourhood school yet are often excluded from access and participation in regular education provisions (e.g., the regular curriculum; Kanter, 2019).

In making the case that applying the universal design for learning framework can breakdown potential barriers teachers perceive in achieving the goals of inclusive education, this paper aimed to put forward suggestions to support in-service and pre-service teachers in becoming more confident in developing inclusive learning experiences. Yet teacher knowledge about differing features of curriculum needs to be supported, requires 'permission' to be pursued by education leaders and the professional wisdom of teachers to implement. Designing flexible, relevant and accessible curriculum that overcome the "persistent challenges" facing educators can move us forward in achieving the goals of inclusive education (United Nations, 2016, p. 2).

REFERENCES

Andriana, E. (2018). *Engaging with student voice through arts-informed methods: Exploring inclusion in three schools Providing Inclusive Education in Yogyakarta, Indonesia.* [Doctoral Thesis, University of Sydney].

Australia Government. (2022). Quality initial teacher education report. Australian Government.

Australian Curriculum, Assessment, Reporting Authority. (2023). *Australian curriculum* (9th version). Australian Curriculum. https://v9.australiancurriculum.edu.au

Australian Government. (2014). *Review of the Australian Curriculum: Final report.* Australian Government. https://www.education.gov.au/australian-curriculum/resources /review-australian-curriculum-final-report-2014

Australian Institute of Housing and Welfare. (2017). *Disability in Australia: changes over time in inclusion and participation in education.* AIHW. https://www.aihw.gov.au/getmedia/34f09557-0acf-4adf-837d-ead a7b74d466/Education-20905.pdf.aspx

Avramidis, E., Bayliss, P., & Burden, R. (2000). Student teachers' attitudes towards the inclusion of children with special educational needs in the ordinary school. *Teaching and Teacher Education, 16*(3), 277–293. doi:10.1016/S0742-051X(99)00062-1

Avramidis, E., Toulia, A., Tsihouridis, C., & Strogilos, V. (2019). Teacher's attitudes towards inclusion and their self-efficacy for inclusive practices as predictors of willingness to implement peer tutoring. *Journal of Research in Special Educational Needs, 19*(S1, s1), 49–59. doi:10.1111/1471-3802.12477

Basit, A., & Evans, D. (n.d.). Including all students in education: students with cerebral palsy in Pakistan.

Boyle, C., & Anderson, J. (2020). The justification for inclusive education in Australia. *Prospects, 49*(3-4), 203–217. doi:10.100711125-020-09494-x

Chen, H., & Evans, D. (2023). Moving towards inclusive education: Secondary school teacher attitudes towards universal design for learning in Australia. *Australasian Journal of Special and Inclusive Education.*

Cologon, K. (2019) *Towards inclusive education: A necessary process of transformation.* Report for Children and Young People with Disability Australia (CYDA).

Council of Australian Governments - Education Council. (2019). *Alice Springs (Mparntwe) education declaration.* Council of Australian Governments. https://uploadstorage.blob.core.windows.net/public-assets/ed ucation-au/melbdec/ED19-0230%20-%20SCH%20-%20Alice%20Springs %20(Mparntwe)%20Education%20Declaration_ACC.pdf

Flexible, Relevant, and Accessible Curriculum

Department of Education, Employment, and Workplace Relations (DEEWR). (2009). *The early years learning framework for Australia, belonging, being, becoming.* Department of Education, Employment and Workplace Relations (DEEWR). https://www.education.gov.au/child-care-package/national-quality-framework/approved-learning-frameworks

Evans, D., Andriana, E., Setiani, P., & Kumara, A. (2018). Building teachers' capacity to support all children in Pesisir Gunung Kidul. In M. Best, T. Corcoran, & R. Slee (Eds.), *Who's in? Who's out? What to do about inclusive education.* Sense.

Hoppey, D., & McLeaskey, J. (2014). What are qualities of effective inclusive schools? In J. McLeskey, N. Waldron, F. Spooner, & B. Algozzine (Eds.), *Handbook of effective inclusive schools: Research and practice* (pp. 17–29). Routledge. doi:10.4324/9780203102930.ch2

Humphreys, S., & Jimenez, B. (2018). The evolution of personalised learning: From different, to differentiated and now to universally designed. *Global Journal of Intellectual & Developmental Disabilities, 5*(4), 1–2. doi:10.19080/GJDD.2018.05.555666

IBE-UNESCO. (2017). *Training tools for curriculum development: Developing and implementing curriculum frameworks.* IBE-UNESCO.

Jimenez, B., & Hudson, M. (2019). Including students with severe disabilities in general education and the potential of universal design for learning for all children. In M. Schuelka, C. Johnstone, G. Thomas, & A. Artiles (Eds.), *SAGE Handbook of inclusion and diversity in education.* SAGE. doi:10.4135/9781526470430.n25

Kanter, A. (2019). The right to inclusive education for students with disabilities under international human rights law. In G. De Beco, S. Quinlivan, & J. Lord (Eds.), *The right to inclusive education under international human rights law* (pp. 15–57). Cambridge University Press. doi:10.1017/9781316392881.003

Kett, M., Deluca, M., & Carew, M. (2019). How prepared are teachers to deliver inclusive education: Evidence from Kenya, Zimbabwe and Sierra Leone. In N. Singal, P. Lynch, & S. Johansson (Eds.), *Education and disability in the global south: New perspectives from Africa and Asia* (pp. 203–222). Bloomsbury Academic. doi:10.5040/9781474291231.ch-011

Kurniawati, F., de Boer, A., Minnaert, A., & Mangunsong, F. (2014). Characteristics of primary teacher programmes on inclusion: A literature focus. *Educational Research, 56*(3), 310–326. doi:10.1080/00131881.2014.934555

Majeed, A. (2009). *Key reforms for quality improvement in education: New interventions in curricula and textbooks.* Ministry of Education, Government of Pakistan.

Melvin, S., Landsberg, E., & Kagan, S. (2020). International curriculum frameworks: Increasing equity and driving systemic change. *Young Children, 75*(1), 10–21. doi:10.2307/26906570

Meyer, A., Rose, D., & Gordon, D. (2014). *Universal design for learning: Theory and practice.* CAST Professional Publishing.

Nelson, A. (2014). *Design and deliver: Planning and teaching using universal design for learning.* Paul H Brookes.

Page, A., Mavropoulou, S., & Harrington, I. (2020). Culturally responsive inclusive education: The value of the local context. *International Journal of Disability Development and Education*, 1–14. doi:10.1080/1034912X.2020.1757627

Price & Slee, R. (2021). An Australian Curriculum that includes diverse learners: The case of students with disability. *Curriculum Perspectives, 41*(1), 71–81 doi:10.1007/s41297-021-00134-8

Rogers, M., Hodge, J., & Counts, J. (2020). Self-regulated strategy development in writing and mathematics for students with specific learning disabilities. *Teaching Exceptional Children, 53*(2), 104–112. doi:10.1177/0040059920946780

Rose, D., Gravel, J., & Domings, Y. (2012). UDL unplugged: The role of technology in UDL. In T. Hall, A. Meyer, & D. Rose (Eds.), *Universal design for learning in the classroom: Practical applications* (pp. 120–134). Guilford Press.

Sanders, S., Rollins, L., Mason, L., Shaw, A., & Jolivette, K. (2021). Intensification and individualization of self-regulation components within self-regulated strategy development. *Intervention in School and Clinic, 56*(3), 131–140. doi:10.1177/1053451220941414

Sharma, U., Shaukat, S., & Furlonger, B. (2015). Attitudes and self-efficacy of pre-service teachers towards inclusion in Pakistan. *Journal of Research in Special Educational Needs, 15*(2), 97–105. doi:10.1111/1471-3802.12071

Slee, R., Corcoran, T., & Best, M. (2021). Disability studies in education – Building platforms to reclaim disability and recognise disablement. *Journal of Disability Studies in Education, 1*(1-2), 3–13. doi:10.1163/25888803-00101002

Spandagou, I., Evans, D., & Little, C. (2008). *Primary education pre-service teachers' attitudes on inclusion and perceptions on preparedness to respond to classroom diversity.* Paper presented at the Australia Association for Research in Education National Conference, Brisbane.

UNESCO. (2020). *Global Education Monitoring Report 2020: Inclusion and education: All means all.* UNESCO.

United Nations. (2006). Convention on the rights of persons with disabilities and optional protocol. UN. https://www.un.org/development/desa/disabilities/convention-on-the-rights-of-persons-with-disabilities.html

United Nations. (2015). Transforming our world: The 2030 agenda for sustainability development. UN. https://sdgs.un.org/2030agenda

United Nations. (2016). *Convention on the rights of persons with disability: General comment No. 4.* UN. https://www.refworld.org/docid/57c977e34.html

Wehmeyer, M. (2020). The importance of self-determination to the quality of life of people with intellectual disability: A perspective. *International Journal of Environmental Research and Public Health, 17*(19), 7121. doi:10.3390/ijerph17197121 PMID:33003321

Flexible, Relevant, and Accessible Curriculum

World Bank. (2020). *Pivoting to inclusion: Leveraging lessons from the COVID-19 crisis for learners with disabilities*. World Bank. https://policycommons.net/artifacts/1248231/pivoting-to-inclusion/1805965/

Zhang, H., & Zhao, G. (2019). Universal design for learning in China. In S. Groseth & E. Dalton (Eds.), *Universal access through inclusive instructional design* (pp. 68–75). Routledge. https://www.taylorfrancis.com/chapters/edit/10.4324/9780429435515-8/universal-design-learning-china-haoyue-zhang-george-zhao doi:10.4324/9780429435515-8

Section 2
Content–Specific Theory and Policy

Chapter 9
Co–Teaching Collaboration in K–12 Inclusive Classrooms:
Relevance for Leadership

Jennifer L. Fleming
Wise County Regional Learning Academy, USA

Carol A. Mullen
Virginia Tech, USA

ABSTRACT

Disseminating knowledge about instructional strategies in collaboratively taught K–12 classrooms can improve the learning environment for students with disabilities. This literature review identifies ways that co-teaching occurs in general education settings and is facilitated by stakeholders. Research questions were: What evidence-based strategies are utilized in cotaught K–12 inclusive classrooms? And how is the co-teaching initiative supported by the parties responsible for their development, implementation, and success? Evidence-based strategies for the general classroom are described along with stakeholder responsibilities. The comprehensive synthesis of salient sources is US based and limited in applicability. Practitioners might consider the solutions and recommendations presented when navigating co-teaching and inclusive practices. Trends favor the instructional co-teaching approach for infusing inclusive strategies, and support research and application. This analysis contributes to the growing body of research on effective collaborative teaching strategies.

INTRODUCTION

The American special education system has long been governed by laws and policies that shape accommodations for special needs students. In a recent survey study of 300 school districts by the RAND Corporation, Diliberti and Schwartz (2023) found that teacher turnover has increased in the United States and is highest in urban and high-poverty areas, typically with the most vulnerable student populations. Staffing shortages were deemed acute for special education teachers. While teaching learners with spe-

DOI: 10.4018/978-1-6684-7370-2.ch009

cial needs was posited as a top priority, personnel vacancies prevent K–12 schools from meeting student needs and maintaining teacher quality. Nationally, as of 2022, 15% of public school students (7.2 million) received special education services (National Center for Education Statistics, 2022) in pandemic environments affected by unprecedented turnover in special educators and principals (Diliberti & Schwartz, 2023). Students with disabilities (SWD) cannot be adequately served in light of the diminishing number of special educators, service personnel, and principals (Mason-Williams et al., 2020).

To preserve the educational rights and dignity of SWD, it is expected that they should be in the general classroom to the maximum extent possible. Being schooled in the least restrictive environment (LRE) is a guiding principle in American public education, in accordance with the Individuals with Disabilities Education Improvement Act (IDEIA, 2004) and other federal legislation (see Beninghof, 2020; Friend, 2014). The cotaught model has gained popularity over the past 30 years in light of this requirement.

The purpose of this chapter is to identify ways that co-teaching occurs in general education settings and is facilitated by stakeholders. Accordingly, research questions guiding the synthesis of sources were,

1. What evidence-based strategies are utilized in cotaught K–12 inclusive classrooms?
2. How is the co-teaching initiative supported by the parties responsible for their development, implementation, and success?

The opportunity to analyze current research on teaching partnerships and effective practices in the in K–12 general education classroom motivated this work. By examining collaborative practices and crucial supports for this important instructional endeavor, the authors provide information about inclusive settings in K–12 classrooms. This chapter was penned by researchers of inclusion and disability in public education who work in a US state as a veteran special educator and educational leadership professor.

BACKGROUND

An overview of special education laws in the United States is warranted to bridge understanding of the national legal context with co-teaching inclusionary practices. During the 1950s and 1960s, the federal government began developing and validating practices for SWD and their families (US Department of Education [USDOE, 2010]). In 1965, the Elementary and Secondary Education Act of 1965 (ESEA)—the first federal program to fund the education of SWD in public schools and institutions—was approved. Later, the Education for All Handicapped Children Act of 1975 (EHA) guaranteed a free and appropriate education to SWD. Before EHA, "only one in five SWD" in American public schools was educated (Dudley-Marling & Burns, 2014, p. 14).

In 2004, the Individuals with Disabilities Education Act (IDEA) was reauthorized and named IDEIA. Changes included placement for SWD, familiarity with their data, and practitioner knowledge about current regulations and legal requirements (Bateman & Yell, 2019). These decisions must uphold the LRE delegated in the law. Per IDEIA (2004), "maintaining high expectations" for SWD and "ensuring their access to the general education curriculum" have improved the quality of schooling. Even when school personnel comply with their legal responsibilities, it can be challenging to satisfy exceptional learners' needs, especially in poorly staffed and low-resourced divisions (Diliberti & Schwartz, 2023; Mason-Williams et al., 2020; Mullen & Hunt, 2022).

Co-Teaching Collaboration in K–12 Inclusive Classrooms

Before EHA (1975), educators were left alone to address SWD's educational needs. From 1975 to 2001, the federal education and civil rights laws through IDEIA (2004) and Section 504 of the Rehabilitation Act of 1973 regulated educational practices on behalf of SWD. However, with the authorization of statutes (e.g., the Every Student Succeeds Act [ESSA, 2015]), special education departments were forced to reevaluate service delivery models for public school students. Consequently, more districts adopted co-teaching models in response to validated teaching methods. Nearly all students participated in state-mandated testing, and districts were held accountable for the results (Friend, 2014). In 2015, ESSA intensified legislative attention on rigorous standards for all students (Beninghof, 2020), and policy decisions have profoundly impacted instructional practices, according to Friend (2014).

Due to its complexity, *inclusion* is not "clearly defined or universally understood" (e.g., Krischler et al., 2019, p. 633). Friend and Cook (2004) did describe it as "a broad belief system or philosophy embracing the notion that all students should be welcomed members of a learning community [and] part of their classrooms even if their abilities differ" (p. 6). Without using the term inclusion, the IDEA addresses LRE and providing "educational services to SWD" in general education classrooms (p. 1). Inclusion is not merely a matter of physical placement in this setting; rather, SWD are expected to fully participate in their learning community and gain from such enrichment (Austin, 2001; Bateman & Yell, 2019; Beninghof, 2020; Friend et al., 2010, Hentz, 2018; Klimaitis & Mullen, 2021a, 2021b; Mullen & Hunt, 2022; Patrick, 2022).

Co-teaching is a collaborative teaching approach to inclusion from which all other inclusive strategies derive (Friend & Cook, 2004; Friend, 2021). Co-teachers are certified professionals, equal in status, who share their expertise, strengths, experiences, and perspectives, in addition to the responsibility for instructing in a coordinated fashion to benefit all students (Beninghof, 2020; Cook & Friend, 1995; Friend, 2014; Hentz, 2018). As partners, general and special educators use collaborative instructional strategies in the general classroom to deliver instruction to a diverse population to meet all "learning needs" (Friend et al., 2010, p. 11; Cook & Friend, 1995). In fact, "co-teaching is considered essential to the process of including SWD [in this setting]"; hence, making inclusion work with co-teaching is expected of parties accountable for its success (Scruggs & Mastropieri, 2017, p. 284).

In the American educational system, *SWD* is used to specify individuals with a physical or mental impairment who qualify for special education in the LRE and services based on federal legislation (IDEA, 1990, etc.). The research (e.g., Koh & Shin, 2017) reflects this terminology. Social emotional mental health needs increasingly attract attention from practitioners and researchers (e.g., Mullen & Hunt, 2022).

Regarding this chapter's first research question, strategies of collaborative teaching within the K–12 setting overlap and vary in the literature. Inclusion-conscious co-teaching practices center on large- and small-group instruction and substantially influence student learning (Cook & Friend, 1995; Friend, 2021; Hentz, 2018). For large-group instruction and team teaching, strategies are one teach, one observe/assist/ support, and small-group instruction utilizes support, parallel teaching, alternative teaching, and station teaching. Each practice is meant to be flexible and used interchangeably while personalizing learning and maximizing engagement. Teacher expertise is to be optimized for meeting individual needs. All strategies described here fall within the scope of the co-teaching model and are elucidated.

149

MAIN FOCUS OF THE CHAPTER

Issues, Controversies, and Problems

One issue in the world of co-teaching is that instructional responsibilities are legal, not only pedagogical. Federal and state regulations require access to quality instruction for all students. Another issue is that partners need leadership support and guidance to support student success (Beninghof, 2020; Cook & Friend, 1995; Friend et al., 2010; Friend, 2014; Smith, 2012). However, in the present-day culture of schooling in the United States and some other countries, highly qualified educators are not being attracted or retained in many divisions, which has exacerbated the need for teachers and support services on behalf of SWD (Al-Hendawi et al., 2023; Mason-Williams et al., 2020).

Even though co-teaching is a common approach to inclusion that gives SWD access to the general education curriculum, barriers remain (Strogilos et al., 2017). The research on co-teaching and the instruction of exceptional learners is somewhat under-explored, which is another problem. Educating SWD in inclusive classrooms is encouraged per legislative regulations, yet research on co-teaching is sparse (for examples, see Beninghof, 2020; Cook & Friend, 1995; Friend et al., 2010; Friend, 2014; Ford, 2013; Koh & Shin, 2017; Smith, 2012; Strogilos et al., 2017). Because the skills required to implement inclusive practices take time to develop (Ford, 2013)—and because special education's "infrastructure" varies considerably from established to emergent across countries (Al-Hendawi et al., 2023)—the collaborative model may not be readily available for study or observation. While these emerging studies in special education research contribute to global movements to educate SWD populations, more needs to be known about how co-teachers instruct and empower all learners.

Methods

To find applicable sources for this literature review, academic databases (EBSCOhost, etc.) and Google Scholar were searched at the home university's remote library. Research on inclusion in the United States was located using search terms (*co-teaching*, *differentiated instruction*, *evidence-based strategies*, *inclusion*, *inclusive setting*, *SWD*, *Universal Design for Learning*, and so forth). Out of 180 abstracts, 80 scholarly peer-reviewed sources (articles and books) were analyzed in their entirety, extending to legislation, governmental reports, and other public documents.

The articles reviewed, screened, and eventually selected for data analysis were in keeping with the premise that all strategies covered in this chapter are part of the co-teaching model. These published sources were situated in the US context, albeit not exclusively. All selected works used some of the search terms. Peer-reviewed journal articles were targeted, with citations spanning 2004 to 2023. The earliest academic source selected was a groundbreaking report by recognized leaders in the co-teaching movement (i.e., Friend & Cook, 2004). Statutes and other documents spanned 1965 to 2023. Predetermined codes (COT = co-teaching, STR = strategies, etc.) were generated from the research questions, search terms, and literature results. Coding processes followed qualitative research procedures (Miles et al., 2020) and addressed evidence-based, inclusive strategies and stakeholder responsibility for co-teaching (i.e., the two research questions). Sources were searched for particular terms (e.g., *co-teaching*), and a frequency count was made and the context/meaning recorded; in this manner, salient articles were identified and coded by both researchers. The results were organized in a data summary matrix, created with Microsoft Excel, that logged author/year, purpose/goals, methods/data sources, themes/findings, and

Co-Teaching Collaboration in K–12 Inclusive Classrooms

implications. In this 17-page table, color coding was used to track methods, findings, and implications. Categorically aggregating the data led to findings and implications. Sources were also cross-referenced with the research questions.

Limitations of this review are that it is not international or comprehensive in scope, and because the results are not generalizable, they may only apply to co-teaching in specific contexts. The implications are limited due to the inevitable shortcomings of using references mainly from a single country.

Results from this comprehensive synthesis follow to address the research questions. For the integrated analysis and both questions, six thematic areas are presented: differentiated instruction and universal design for learning (UDL), co-teaching education in K–12 schools, collaborative teaching strategies in the classroom, facilitators of inclusion-conscious co-teaching, barriers to inclusion-conscious co-teaching, and the role of leadership in inclusive schools, in addition to solutions and recommendations.

Differentiated Instruction and Universal Design for Learning

Teachers respond to all students' needs through differentiation, which is "guided by a growth mindset and general principles" (supportive learning environment, quality curriculum, etc.). Differentiation occurs through "content, process, product, affect, and learning environment." In accord with learners' "readiness, interest, and learning profile," "a variety of instructional approaches" (graphic organizers, learning/interest centers, etc.) are used (Lombardi, 2018, p. 145). To this end, *UDL* is an approach that supports teacher use of evidence-based strategies in cotaught inclusive classrooms and student demonstration of competency and understanding of concepts (Sukhai & Mohler, 2016). As Lombardi (2018) explained, principles of UDL foster students' interest "on authentic problems," and their capacity to make connections by being exposed to various forms of representation, information, and expression, and choice over topics/projects and ways of displaying their work (p. 76).

UDL-aligned strategies are instructional methods that educators utilize to ensure equal educational opportunity for all students. One strategy of UDL is frontloading vocabulary before undertaking a project. The quick write (whereby learners write what they know about a topic) surfaces prior knowledge. Another strategy, the think-aloud, involves teacher modeling of how to comprehend a text or task, and student practice through reading from a text or interacting with content (Johnson et al., 2021). Other strategies for engaging students with cognitive difficulties include examining text features, paraphrasing, and making predictions. Digital models, simulations, and software can help SWD understand abstract concepts; for example, if a science topic is the planets, a simulation can enable travel through space (Israel et al., 2013). Technology can also help reduce barriers to learning (Sukhai & Mohler, 2016), such as by using an iPad to enlarge text. Lessons are planned in advance with SWD so every learner can access the task. UDL targets obstacles and spurs deeper learning. From the perspective of deeper learning and 21st-century skills development, UDL can increase SWD's capacity for problem solving, critical thinking, creativity, communication, and collaboration (Klimaitis & Mullen, 2021b).

Co-teaching Education in K–12 Schools

SWD need access to general education curriculum in tandem with a special educator trained in "specially designed instruction" (Hentz, 2018). Special educators "look at specific tasks, break them down into their smallest components, diagnose difficulties, and brainstorm unique instructional solutions" (Beninghof, 2020, p. 177). As experts, they develop strategies for general education content so all learners gain.

151

To increase effectiveness, co-teachers must have a structure and format for planning lessons. Hentz's (2018) six-step BASICS strategy supports evidence-based strategies, and assists with creating lessons that enrich the co-teaching learning environment and meet diverse needs:

1. **B**ig ideas (critical questions, learning objectives, etc.) are aligned with standards.
2. **A**nalyze student data (e.g., Individualized Education Plan [IEP], accommodations, and targeted instruction) and identify what is needed to guide instructional planning.
3. **S**trategies are determined based on big ideas and analysis of student data.
4. **I**ntegrate co-teaching strategies required for lessons and monitor developments.
5. **C**ollaboratively reflect on lessons, student learning, and partners' roles.
6. **S**trategize to plan lessons using strategies, teacher expertise, and data.

The BASICS strategy, combined with coplanning, assists teaching partners with creating and participating in learning environments. Pairs need to determine what co-teaching models work best for each lesson and grouping (Hentz, 2018).

Consistent with the notion that all the strategies identified herein belong to the co-teaching model, Beninghof (2020) explained that strong partnerships thoughtfully blend models of co-teaching in the classroom (see Table 1 for a synopsis). Two co-teaching models, (1) Duet and (2) Map and Navigate, use adding, transforming, and complementing as approaches, as well as two types of groupings: readiness and mixed readiness. The Map and Navigate model is considered realistic and practical, given that many special educators do not have the luxury of collaborating with only one teacher. As specialists who work with numerous faculty, they may find it difficult to manage the demands of co-planning that the Duet model requires. With the Map and Navigate model, the general educator does most of the lesson planning (mapping), and the special educator decides how to approach/focus/personalize the delivery (navigating). Table 1 lists the two co-teaching models, three approaches, and two groupings. Each co-teaching arrangement would satisfy one from each area. For example, a co-teaching classroom may be a mixed-readiness group where partners use the Duet model while implementing the transforming approach. The model, approach, and grouping may change as needed to accommodate SWD in the general education classroom. As such, the co-teaching initiative is supported by pedagogues and other stakeholders that thoughtfully use, guide, or oversee co-teaching (models, approaches, and groupings) in harmony with their expertise and responsibility for successful implementation.

Co-Teaching Collaboration in K–12 Inclusive Classrooms

Table 1. Synopsis of co-teaching models, approaches, and groupings from Beninghof (2020)

Co-teaching Model	Description	Pros	Cons
Duet	Both teachers share the entire instructional process.	Most integrated for students; fully utilizes all expertise.	Most time intensive.
Map and Navigate	General educators manage the upfront planning. Special educators plan, deliver, and assess.	Both teachers engage in most phases of instruction.	Less input in planning for differentiation and instruction.
Co-teaching Approach	**Description**	**Pros**	**Cons**
Adding	One teacher leads while the other adds visually, verbally, or in other ways to enhance instruction.	No coplanning times; easier to implement.	Can overstep and does not fully utilize expertise.
Transforming	Teachers address readiness levels, learning preferences, and student interests.	Ensures that all levels and preferences are incorporated into instruction.	Assumes that variation in lessons will be tolerated.
Complementing	General educators attend to the curriculum. Specialists focus on access or complementary skills and special education strategies (mini-lessons, small groups, etc.).	Facilitates co-teaching and allocating tasks according to expertise. Sets an expectation that special education takes place in general education settings.	May slow down pacing.
Grouping Type	**Description**	**Pros**	**Cons**
Readiness Groups	Grouping occurs in accordance with readiness for learning skills; instruction is at members' level.	Allows for intentional enrichment and support.	Poor exposure to role models or diversity.
Mixed-Readiness Groups	Students work at different levels and paces.	Peers model language, etc., and students teach and learn from one another.	Learning levels may be too high or low.

Inclusive practices within K–12 schools differ and can be satisfying or disappointing for those involved. In four cotaught elementary classrooms in Greece, researchers explored how partners understood differentiated instruction and the "factors they perceived as crucial in determining the way differentiation is implemented in cotaught classrooms" (Strogilos et al., 2017, p. 1). Through 60 interviews and 57 observations with 34 pairs of general and special education co-teachers, it was apparent that differentiated instruction was used for "remedial" purposes, rooted in a deficit view of SWD, not as a context-oriented practice for an entire class. Factors determined to influence differentiation in the general education setting were training, collaboration, a reasonable number of students, and flexibility with covering the curriculum, all of which were obstacles in the teachers' classrooms. As expressed by the research team, hindrances to "the development of differentiated instruction" were "lack of training [and] collaboration," too many students in a class, and curricular rigidity (p. 1). Recommendations for instructional collaborators were to engage in deep learning by becoming "flexible," interrogate their own assumptions/belief structures (e.g., SWD learn better from individualized instruction), and deconstruct institutional–societal thinking and biases.

In inclusionary settings in the US, SWD spend more than 80% of their school day in the general education classroom (Baglieri et al., 2011), but "despite legislation and the best efforts of special educators, SWD continue to be segregated . . . for a majority or part of the school day" (Orr, 2009, p. 228). While there is progress, SWD have yet to be fully integrated into learning environments with other peers.

Many agree that the general education classroom is the appropriate placement for SWD if the learner can function without considerably altering the curriculum or expectations. Objections center on whether the general classroom is the best place to meet special education needs (Dudley-Marling & Burns, 2014; Murray, 2009). Tracing arguments against including SWD in general education environments, Dudley-Marling and Burns (2014) identified as common challenges: (a) general educators' lack of training and "specialized knowledge" for meeting the unique needs, (b) "large class sizes and inflexible curricula" that make accommodations trying, and (c) teachers' "disproportionate attention" on SWD as negatively affecting the rest of the class (p. 20). The need for buy-in from all involved and trusting each party's expertise were messages.

About the second research question guiding this chapter, steps for achieving desirable outcomes by the responsible parties include: (1) The IEP team builds relationships, and members have clearly defined roles and responsibilities to guide their work. (2) The team collects data and assesses each student's abilities. (3) Goals and strategies are established to assist learners' progress. (4) The strategies are applied while student progress is monitored. As such, educators must use research-supported practices directed at designing, implementing, and adjusting specialized curricula, and measuring student outcomes (Anastasiou & Kaffman, 2011; Dudley-Marling & Burns, 2014).

Collaborative Teaching Strategies in the Classroom

Considering evidence-based strategies in cotaught inclusive classrooms, in 1993, Friend and Cook introduced the six most "common co-teaching approaches" (e.g., Cook & Friend, 1995; Friend et al., 2010). Further development of the "collaboration framework" and its components—"personal commitment; communication skills; interaction processes; programs, applications, or services; and context"—later appeared (Friend, 2021, p. vi). In Hentz's (2018) reiteration of this model, the two approaches—"one teach, one observe" and "one teach, one assist"—were merged into "one teach, one observe/assist/support." When looking at further defining co-teaching approaches, Hentz noted that large- and small-group instruction can substantially influence student outcomes. Each of the approaches outlined by Hentz were considered effective in different classroom situations, while retaining flexibility for interchangeability in order to maximize student learning and engagement. Optimizing each teacher's expertise to meet individual student needs was also underscored. Table 2 delineates these approaches, specifying benefits and tips associated with each one.

Co-Teaching Collaboration in K–12 Inclusive Classrooms

Table 2. Co-teaching strategies, benefits, and tips (Hentz, 2018)

Strategy	Benefit	Tip
One Teach, One Observe/ Assist/ Support	Learners have a professional to support them during the instructional process.	• This approach is best used when one professional's expertise aligns with the lesson or when students' work requires monitoring. • Communicate roles with, and responsibilities for, each teacher to ensure parity. • Supportive co-teachers may collect data and provide individual guided practice as needed for student success. • Switch from "sage on the stage" to "guide on the side" during lessons. • If this approach is used daily, consider if two professionals are required to accomplish the instructional goals of the class.
Team Teaching	Working as a team allows both professionals to share their instructional strategies and techniques during a lesson.	• This approach is used on a limited basis and is best for debating topics, modeling collaboration, and sharing enthusiasm for the lesson. • Practice vigilance around teacher talk versus student talk. • Co-teachers feel comfortable sharing their expertise and speaking freely during large-group instruction. • Integrating appropriate humor and modeling collaborative dialogue and think-aloud can enhance instruction. • Co-teachers may switch to another approach based on students' needs.
Parallel Teaching	The reduction in the student-to-teacher ratio increases opportunities for discussion.	• Both professionals must have content or skill knowledge and comfort with the instructional content and process. • Strategically position groups so co-teachers can use nonverbal cues for time and noise-level monitoring for instruction to occur simultaneously. • Instructional content and strategies must be planned to address access points to the curriculum for all students. • Use flexible grouping to avoid creating a class within a class. • This approach allows for learners' varying views on a topic or skill.
Alternative Teaching	Co-teachers can conference with students and collect data on progress toward specific skill proficiency.	• Avoid using this approach during core instruction of content. • Students may take longer to learn tasks. • Small-group instruction can be for preteaching, reteaching, reviewing, extending, interviewing, or nurturing social skills. • Both educators occupy the alternative role during instruction based on expertise. • All students experience small-group instruction within a lesson.
Station Teaching	Each professional has equal status and is given the opportunity to provide students with individualized instruction.	• Physical arrangements account for movements and noise associated with each activity. • Stations can be completed in any order. • Special educators integrate specially designed instruction, accommodations, and modifications into content taught at the station. • This approach allows for differentiation and tiered learning. • Timing and voice volume are considered during planning.

In addition to these collaborative strategies, Mullen and Hunt (2022) discerned 13 instructional strategies that supported outcomes for students with an emotional disability. Based on feedback from nine special educators in two school districts in Virginia, they grouped these practices into social, academic, and behavioral domains. "Building relationships" and "creating a positive learning environment/healthy culture" spanned all domains, whereas the other strategies were more domain specific; for example, "fostering communication and listening" was categorized as social and behavioral (p. 465). As reported by the teacher interviewees, these instructional strategies supported the academic needs and growth of high-needs populations. But with the effects of COVID-19 on systems, they were apprehensive about the "quality of attention and care for this vulnerable population" in schools "reduced to crisis-induced online delivery systems that may be leaving SWD even further behind" (p. 22).

Teachers are urged to use evidence-based strategies to address social emotional mental health needs. Mullen and Hunt (2022) identified 40 of these strategies from research for disrupting student "complications," which "range from mental health issues to social skill deficits, removal from classrooms, and academic difficulties" (p. 457). Support strategies applied for cultivating affirming, healthy classroom cultures and positive relationships include "teacher praise," "clear instructional methods," "positive behavior support," and "valuing assessment and data-based decision-making" (p. 458).

Facilitators of Inclusion-Conscious Co-teaching

Facilitators of co-teaching environments range from relationship formation and planning to strategy identification, implementation, and assessment. Taking ownership of their co-teaching arrangement and outcomes, partners "develop a collaborative relationship," share "information about expertise, teaching philosophy, roles, and responsibilities," establish instructional procedures, and deliver instruction using specially designed practices; additionally, while building a classroom community that fosters student–teacher and student–student relationships, they use data to inform instruction (Hentz, 2018, p. 5; Mullen & Hunt, 2022).

Productive teaming in classrooms promotes professional development (PD) and strengthens inclusion-conscious co-teaching. This outcome emerged from Austin's (2001) study of partners' perceptions of co-teaching involving 139 collaborative K–12 educators from 9 school districts in New Jersey. (Each district had assigned a minimum of six teaching pairs to inclusive classrooms.) Respondents to the Perceptions of Co-teaching Survey and the 12 interviewed collaborators reported that their collaborative instructional experiences enhanced their PD. While the special education co-teachers experienced professional growth in content knowledge, the general education co-teachers affirmed special educators' skillfulness with classroom management and curriculum adaptation. As reported, these collaborative strategies resulted in "reduced student–teacher ratio, the benefit of another teacher's expertise and viewpoint, remedial strategies and review for all students, and the opportunity for the students without disabilities to gain [understanding]" (p. 251). Interviewees valued scheduled co-planning time (including during the summer), administrative support, adequate supplies, in-service training, and modified classrooms.

Because challenges to accessing science, technology, engineering, and mathematics (STEM) curriculum are pronounced for special education students, approaches for co-teaching STEM in inclusive settings also require consideration. To this end, Klimaitis and Mullen (2021b) identified seven strategies that enable SWD to experience STEM content: IEP review, student interest, relationship building, support staff, hands-on learning, intentional grouping, and classroom accommodation.

Barriers to Inclusion-Conscious Co-teaching

Barriers to co-teaching in general education settings reflect the macro picture. Regulations for state and educational leadership preparation programs typically require only minimal training in special education, yet these skills must be developed before entering the teaching profession (Da Fonte & Barton-Arwood, 2017; Koh & Shin, 2017; Strogilos et al., 2017). According to the Joint Legislative Audit and Review Commission (JLARC, 2020), the preparation of aspiring and novice teachers requires improvement. The USDOE's offices assist state and local special education personnel with educating SWD (Bateman & Yell, 2019), but skills preparation should occur in the credentialling and degree stages.

Even though inclusion is commonplace in education, impediments extend to inclusive settings (Orr, 2009), including school personnel with negative attitudes or who self-isolate, inadequate knowledge and skills, lack of preparedness for instructing collaboratively, insufficient administrative support, mandated

Co-Teaching Collaboration in K–12 Inclusive Classrooms

collaborative teaching assignments, schedules that do not favor the co-teaching initiative, utilizing inclusion as a way to explicitly socialize SWD, resistance to integrating SWD in general classrooms and trying new ways to serve them, a paucity of PD/training on inclusive practices, an absence of meaningful accommodations, and low expectations for SWD (Austin, 2001; Klimaitis & Mullen, 2021a, 2021b; Mullen & Hunt, 2022; Orr, 2009, Patrick, 2022).

As found, some teachers lack strategies for supporting SWD and are unaware of laws pertaining to special education, student classifications, and individual needs and accommodations (Casale-Giannola, 2012; Ford, 2013). However, this dire situation can be counteracted by nurturing inclusionary practices, claimed Orr (2009). An implication is that parties must assume responsibility for co-teaching assignments, and the legal and pedagogical dimensions of this work. A schoolwide pro-inclusion philosophy enables teachers to feel supported "when seeking inclusive learning environments" (Orr, 2009, p. 235). General education teachers who are welcoming of both special educators and students contribute to a positive climate and promotion of "co-teaching [that advances] equitable learning opportunities for all students" (Graziano & Navarrete, 2012, p. 109). Because these collaborative partnerships can now be seen in public schools, with advantages for students, some university programs are keeping pace with expectations (Graziano & Navarrete, 2012).

Regarding SWD's engagement in STEM lessons, common obstructions are adult support, time limitations, and student ability. These outcomes emerged from Klimaitis and Mullen's (2021a, 2021b) literature review and interviewing of 13 experienced special and general educators at 12 K–12 schools in Virginia. Orr (2009) found that the most frequently identified obstacle was general educators' negative attitudes from interviews with 15 novice special educators about their co-teaching experiences. Individuals not feeling ready to perform as a teaching team in inclusive settings was another major issue, which was mainly attributed to weak preparedness in their preservice programs. Twelve of the new special educators were co-teaching in general education classes for most or part of the day. Admitting to not knowing any inclusionary practices, they questioned their ability to implement inclusion. The duty to perform effectively as an instructional partner in special education is an expected competency.

Teacher buy-in was noted by Austin (2001) as a problem when co-teaching assignments are mandated. In this study, only 28% of general and special educators agreed with their inclusive classroom assignments. Patrick (2022) raised another organizational issue—school schedules that are not conducive to the co-teaching initiative make it difficult for partners to plan and make decisions.

Willingness to educate SWD inclusively is an obstacle, but the education of teaching staff can open minds. Rural general educators' responses to Murray's (2009) survey shed light on "how teachers' background, training, and support shape their views of teaching SWD" (pp. 14–15). While the district was inclusive and most SWD were mainstreamed in general education classes with support from the special education department, all respondents (N = 10) reported hardly any PD/training from their district, and 6 had little/no exposure to inclusive education in their preservice programs. But eight respondents felt positive about instructing all children, and three thought that having SWD in general education classes was reasonable with the support of a special educator. Objections to teaching SWD in this setting from two teachers were the time it takes and "classroom numbers [that] make it extremely difficult to give individual attention" (p. 16).

Role of Leadership in Inclusive Schools

Administrators have a legal and leadership responsibility for co-teaching relative to its development, implementation, and success. Teacher perceptions about the role of leadership in inclusive education are vital clues for administrations (Mullen & Hunt, 2022; Murray, 2009). As reported, leaders must support co-teachers' inclusive roles and consider "legal duties" and shared accountability "for protecting the welfare of vulnerable populations and working with their families"; administrators need to work with teachers to meet SWD needs and requirements and to get to know these students (Mullen & Hunt, 2022, p. 466). Based on Mullen and Hunt's findings, leaders and teachers' should "implement effective strategies that facilitate access to the curriculum; resolve barriers that prevent special needs populations from engaging in lessons; support PD that shares the latest information about disabilities and strategies; and promote equitable access to teachers and lessons" (p. 466).

Administrative support and commitment are foundational to the success of co-teaching and special needs populations (Austin, 2001) in and beyond the areas of PD/training, dedicated time, schedules, teacher–student ratios, student ability, and adult support. Districts and school administrators "are expected to disrupt inequities" that block opportunities for SWD to fully participate in inclusive settings and benefit from 21st-century learning (Klimaitis & Mullen, 2021b, p. 40). Building administrators are advised to guide teaching staff about enriching practices for SWD and co-teaching initiatives, so they should be familiar with evidence-based strategies that promote teaching and learning in inclusive settings (Austin, 2001; Bateman & Yell, 2019; Mullen & Hunt, 2022; Patrick, 2022).

Collaborative learning opportunities (workgroups, etc.), found Patrick (2022), can help teachers learn and improve. Such opportunities are shaped by organizational factors "influencing whether and how teachers engage in meaningful collaboration" (p. 4). With the shift of teaching norms from a culture of individualism to professional collaboration, teacher expertise is only part of the collaborative learning equation. Another part involves administrators' shaping of "organizational conditions of schools that facilitate collaborative learning opportunities" (p. 4). For example, Patrick (2022) found that the time allocated for "collaborative planning" greatly varied across contexts.

An issue for leadership is that not all US states prepare administrators and general educators with special education skills (JLARC, 2020). While SWD do spend more time in the general education classroom, many general educators admitted that "[they do not know] how to effectively teach and support SWD, including how to collaborate with special education teachers" (p. iv). Almost one-half of the special education directors responding to JLARC's survey in Virginia "indicated that they felt half or fewer of the general education teachers in their division have the skills necessary to support SWD," and about one-third reported that only "half or fewer of the building-level administrators . . . have the knowledge or skills to support SWD or their teachers" (p. iv).

Thrusting students, teachers, or administrators into learning environments where they are unprepared or lacking support is to be avoided (Anastasiou & Kauffman, 2011; Dudley-Marling & Burns, 2014). Thus, public schools and divisions should keep key factors for successful inclusion at the forefront. As examples, SWD need individualized and relevant learning objectives that are aligned to state standards. Even when provided specially designed instruction that nurtures successful academic and social progression, they should still be able to participate in routines, programs, and activities with classmates.

Co-Teaching Collaboration in K–12 Inclusive Classrooms

SOLUTIONS AND RECOMMENDATIONS

When determining and overseeing co-teaching implementation practices for inclusive classrooms, principals and other instructional leaders will want to consider research-informed solutions and recommendations. Similarly, in dealing with the issues, controversies, or problems presented in the literature, division leaders are advised to consult sources that describe situations, dilemmas, solutions, and so forth. Pertinent reference materials range from current regulations to studies for supporting or developing policies and procedures pertaining to cotaught content. Universities and colleges may utilize the findings for reviewing and improving preservice teacher and principal preparation programs. The following seven solutions and recommendations can assist co-teachers and leaders with their respective stakeholder roles, responsibilities, work, and effectiveness.

Time, Scheduling, and Support

To support co-teaching arrangements, leaders would ensure that the partners have reasonable school schedules and adequate time to develop their relationship, plan, instruct, and assess. Administrators' expectations for these teaching partnerships should be clear from the outset. They need to provide guidance and the necessary resources (policies, facilities, materials, tools, etc.) for safeguarding the co-teaching initiative and its effectiveness. In the spirit of being helpful and invested, and intervening as needed, administrators would monitor these partnerships on an ongoing basis so all involved are held accountable. In turn, district leaders would monitor the work of building leaders and provide guidance and resources for co-teaching SWD and all students in general classrooms.

Openness, Partnering, and Self-Assessment

Partners share their assessments of self (strengths and weaknesses) ranging from professional to social skills as a tactic for becoming interpersonally aware and meeting student needs. By getting to know each other, they can figure out how best to plan and approach their lessons. Having the same strengths (e.g., ability to connect with SWD on a personal level) and weaknesses (e.g., overplanning, etc.) allows the teachers to relate to one another. But differences promote balance, so they can learn from and complement each other. These discussions, including feedback on performance, help them to plan more effectively and efficiently, such as by identifying who will handle planning, lesson implementation, and assessment and which instructional strategies to adopt for a lesson. Administrations should encourage creating and reflecting on these critically important partnerships.

PD, Practices, and Co-teaching

Collaborators should receive PD on evidence-based effective practices for cotaught environments. Thus, administrators must provide job-embedded, evidence-based PD on effective practices through such means as trainings, demonstrations/modeling, conferences, coaching, and observations. Schoolwide PD and learning can benefit all teaching staff and their professional growth. Topical PD would include analysis of views on the integration of SWD in general education classrooms, reasons behind objections and concerns, and solution generation, all in the spirit of creating a healthy professional learning community.

Communication, Expectations, and Responsibilities

Partners need to have strong communication skills, set expectations, and share teaching responsibilities equally. Communication skills would be examined and modeled, and expectations, responsibilities, and roles for all stakeholders involved (general educator, special educator, principal, parent, etc.) would be established. Administration's vital role in the success of co-teaching includes communicating expectations for instructional partnerships, such as equally shared teaching responsibilities.

Needs, Accommodations, and Services

Instructional collaborators review and discuss all SWD's IEP documents as parties responsible for meeting their needs. Co-teachers need to know each learner's IEP needs and accommodations (accessibility, presentation of information, etc.) and provide the requisite services (adaptive devices, designated readers for the classroom, etc.). Administrators should monitor the services provided to SWD and their IEPs and LREs while overseeing the co-teaching partnership.

Monitoring, Facilitating, and Acting

Active leaders of inclusion monitor and support co-teaching partnerships, especially during their formation. Rather than leaving partners on their own, administrators are advised to provide oversight, be encouraging, and facilitate these partnerships. School schedules would be arranged so co-teachers can plan together. Administrators would seek openings to dialogue with a team about its growth, needs, and issues. They would listen to preferences and desires, which may include functioning as a two-person partnership for consecutive years. As an informed party, administrators would decide which supports best fit certain situations and what actions to take.

Compensation, Policy, and Protections

To support the intense work involved in co-teaching, maintain high morale, and increase the chance of success for every child, leaders would provide monetary compensation. Such arrangements may be more familiar in the context of teacher mentoring and induction programs. Additionally, school district policies must align with current federal and state regulations that govern instructional co-teaching as a recommended intervention for meeting targeted goals and promoting student learning. Provisions for these teaching partnerships that are codified in school policy (allocated time for planning, etc.) would help ensure that pairs' needs are met, their work and well-being are protected, and their endeavor is supported. Co-teaching practices in the context of special and general education that are missing in preservice teacher programs can be remedied by policy and curricular adjustments.

FUTURE RESEARCH DIRECTIONS

Future and emerging trends favor the instructional co-teaching approach for infusing inclusive strategies into K–12 general education settings. "Evidence-based instructional practices" are key to providing adequate instruction to SWD, and to maintaining quality of special education pedagogy and services

Co-Teaching Collaboration in K–12 Inclusive Classrooms

(Al-Hendawi et al., 2023, p. 7). Such practices are becoming more available in the literature, which may lead to expanded research and application. With the support of job-embedded, relevant PD and strong administrative support, the collaborative model can spread to more schools and general classrooms. Due to its increasing popularity, the cotaught inclusive approach is poised to contribute to global inclusion movements. More schools around the world can model strategies in instructional collaboration wherein SWD are skillfully and meaningfully integrated into the general education classroom. Educationally transformative education for all students, teachers, leaders, and parents involved could spur equity-geared schooling. Children and youth who are served by co-teaching initiatives in inclusive settings ideally become contributing global citizens. Research directions may reflect quality education and promising practices in globally localized contexts that shape citizens of the future.

However, havoc from the coronavirus is likely having an unwanted impact on the frequency or quality of strategies used. Opportunities for conducting site-based research could be impacted and obstacles to inclusive education pronounced within high-poverty and other struggling schools. To this end, special educators who had navigated the pandemic thought that "personalized contact [and] hands-on learning" were greatly restricted in online environments (Mullen & Hunt, 2022, p. 465). While veteran teachers did find ways to modify the curriculum for SWD, novice teachers were not able to accomplish this and also lacked a professional network. The new technologies (management systems, online platforms, etc.) for teaching virtually proved stifling, and everyone preferred a physical classroom.

Expanding the scope of this review could lead to studies of more schools, cultures, and countries. With increased sample sizes and culturally varying circumstances, research participants can offer more information and richer insights into pedagogical practices. The analysis of sources provided here can assist practitioners, researchers, and policymakers with supporting the co-teaching initiative on behalf of vulnerable students. Additional research on co-teaching models and strategies could paint a more comprehensive picture of what co-teachers think and do to create impactful inclusive environments. It would be good to know more about how leaders contribute to the complex world of co-teaching and care of special education students. More research is warranted on facilitators of, and barriers, to instructional partnering in schools, co-teaching models and evidence-based strategies, implementation and assessment in real-world settings, types of administrative support, and solutions to problems.

CONCLUSION

This review contributes to the growing body of research on effective collaborative teaching practices. Readers have been presented with evidence-based strategies used in cotaught inclusive classrooms, along with descriptions of collaboration and leadership. Information has also been provided on how co-teaching initiatives are supported by the parties responsible for their development, implementation, and success. The practices covered in this writing can assist teachers and leaders with enabling SWD's access to the general education curriculum and success in general classrooms. It is hoped that this review encourages the use of co-teaching arrangements to improve the learning environment for SWD and all learners, as well as clarify teachers' and leaders' crucial roles. In the United States, it is incumbent upon federal and state departments of education, in partnership with local school districts, to ascertain that co-teaching pairs are set up to provide specialized services (small-group settings, readalouds, etc.) in inclusive classrooms. Further, district and building leaders are accountable for ensuring that implemented practices foster student learning and outcomes. Positive organizational cultures and strong support infrastructures are essential for aiding students' growth and teachers' effectiveness. Supporting special education students inclusively, particularly in these times of crisis, presents both a challenge and an opportunity for schools.

AUTHORS' NOTE

This research received no specific grant from any funding agency in the public, commercial, or not-for-profit sectors. The two authors contributed equally to the manuscript, and are grateful for the editorial guidance and reviewers' constructive comments.

REFERENCES

Al-Hendawi, M., Keller, C., & Muhammad, S. K. (2023). Special education in the Arab Gulf countries: An analysis of ideals and realities. *International Journal of Educational Research Open*, *4*, 100217. doi:10.1016/j.ijedro.2022.100217

Anastasiou, D., & Kauffman, J. M. (2011). A social constructionist approach to disability: Implications for special education. *Exceptional Children*, *77*(3), 367–384. doi:10.1177/001440291107700307

Austin, V. L. (2001). Teachers' beliefs about co-teaching. *Remedial and Special Education*, *22*(4), 245–255. doi:10.1177/074193250102200408

Baglieri, S., Bejoian, L. M., Broderick, A. A., Connor, D. J., & Valle, J. (2011). [Re]claiming "inclusive education" towards cohesion in educational reform: Disability studies unravels the myth of the normal child. *Teachers College Record*, *113*(10), 2122–2154. doi:10.1177/016146811111301001

Bateman, D. F., & Yell, M. L. (2019). *Current trends and legal issues in special education*. Corwin. doi:10.4135/9781071800539

Beninghof, A. M. (2020). *Co-teaching that works structures and strategies for maximizing student learning* (2nd ed.). Jossey-Bass.

Casale-Giannola, D. (2012). Comparing inclusion in the secondary vocational and academic classrooms: Strengths, needs, and recommendations. *American Secondary Education*, *40*(2), 26–42.

Cook, L., & Friend, M. (1995). Co-teaching: Guidelines for creating effective practices. *Focus on Exceptional Children*, *28*(3), 1–16.

DaFonte, M. A., & Baron-Arwood, S. M. (2017). Collaboration of general and special education teachers: Perspectives and strategies. *Intervention in School and Clinic*, *53*(2), 99–106. doi:10.1177/1053451217693370

Diliberti, M. K., & Schwartz, H. L. (2023). *Educator turnover has markedly increased, but districts have taken actions to boost teacher ranks*. Rand Corporation. https://www.rand.org/pubs/research_reports/RRA956-14.html

Dudley-Marling, C., & Burns, M. B. (2014). Two perspectives on inclusion in the United States. *Global Education Review*, *1*(1), 14–31.

Education for All Handicapped Children Act. Pub. L. No. 94-142 (1975). https://www.govinfo.gov/content/pkg/STATUTE-89/pdf/STATUTE-89-Pg773.pdf

Elementary and Secondary Education Act, Pub. L. No. 89-10 (1965). https://www2.ed.gov/documents/essa-act-of-1965.pdf

Ford, J. (2013). Educating students with learning disabilities in inclusive classrooms. *Electronic Journal for Inclusive Education, 3*(1), 1–20.

Friend, M. (2014). *Co-teach! Building and sustaining effective classroom partnership in inclusive schools* (2nd ed.). Marilyn Friend, Inc.

Friend, M. (2021). *Interactions: Collaboration skills for school professionals* (9th ed.). Pearson.

Friend, M., & Cook, L. (2004). *Co-teaching: Principles, practices, and pragmatics.* New Mexico Public Education Department. https://files.eric.ed.gov/fulltext/ED486454.pdf

Friend, M., Cook, L., Hurley-Chamberlain, D. A., & Shamberger, C. (2010). Co-teaching: An illustration of the complexity of collaboration in special education. *Journal of Educational & Psychological Consultation, 20*(1), 9–27. doi:10.1080/10474410903535380

Grazino, K. J., & Navarrete, L. A. (2012). Co-teaching in a teacher education classroom: Collaboration, compromise, and creativity. *Issues in Teacher Education, 21*(1), 109–125.

Hentz, S. (2018). *Co-teaching essentials.* Association for Supervision and Curriculum Development.

Individuals with Disabilities Education Act, 20 U.S.C. § 1400. (1990). https://sites.ed.gov/idea/statute-chapter-33

Individuals with Disabilities Education Improvement Act, Pub. L. No. 108-446 (2004). https://www.govinfo.gov/content/pkg/PLAW-108publ446/pdf/PLAW-108publ446.pdf

Israel, M., Maynard, K., & Williamson, P. (2013). Promoting literacy-embedded, authentic STEM instruction for students with disabilities and other struggling learners. *Teaching Exceptional Children, 45*(4), 18–25. doi:10.1177/004005991304500402

Johnson, H. N., Wakeman, S. Y., & Clausen, A. (2021). *How to support students with significant cognitive disabilities during think-alouds* (TIPS Series: Tip #21). University of Minnesota. https://publications.ici.umn.edu/ties/foundations-of-inclusion-tips/how-to-support-students-with-significant-cognitive-disabilities-during-think-alouds

Joint Legislative Audit and Review Commission. (2020). *K–12 special education in Virginia.* JLARC. http://jlarc.virginia.gov/pdfs/reports/Rpt545-1.pdf

Klimaitis, C. C., & Mullen, C. A. (2021a). Access and barriers to science, technology, engineering, and mathematics (STEM) education for K–12 students with disabilities and females. In C. A. Mullen (Ed.), *Handbook of social justice interventions in education* (pp. 813–836). Springer. doi:10.1007/978-3-030-35858-7_125

Klimaitis, C. C., & Mullen, C. A. (2021b). Including K–12 students with disabilities in STEM education and planning for inclusion. *Educational Planning, 28*(2), 27–43.

Koh, M.-S., & Shin, S. (2017). Education of students with disabilities in the USA: Is inclusion the answer? *International Journal of Learning. Teaching and Educational Research, 16*(10), 1–17.

Krischler, M., Powell, J. J. W., & Ineke, M. P.-T. C. (2019). What is meant by inclusion? On the effects of different definitions on attitudes toward inclusive education. *European Journal of Special Needs Education, 34*(5), 632–648. doi:10.1080/08856257.2019.1580837

Lombardi, P. (2021). *Instructional methods, strategies, and technologies to meet the needs of all learners*. LibreTexts. https://socialsci.libretexts.org/Bookshelves/Early_Childhood _Education/Instructional_Methods_Strategies_and_Technologies _(Lombardi_2018)

Mason-Williams, L., Bettini, E., Peyton, D., Harvey, A., Rosenberg, M., & Sindelar, P. T. (2020). Rethinking shortages in special education: Making good on the promise of an equal opportunity for students with disabilities. *Teacher Education and Special Education, 43*(1), 45–62. doi:10.1177/0888406419880352

Miles, M. B., Huberman, A. M., & Saldaña, J. (2020). *Qualitative data analysis: A methods sourcebook* (4th ed.). Sage.

Mullen, C. A., & Hunt, T. K. (2022). Emotional disability and strategies for supporting student outcomes: Interviews with K–12 special education teachers. *Teacher Development, 26*(4), 453–471. doi:10.1080/ 13664530.2022.2108129

Murray, A. (2009). *Is inclusion effective?* [Unpublished master's thesis, St. John Fisher University]. https://fisherpub.sjf.edu/cgi/viewcontent.cgi?article=1083&context=education_ETD_masters

National Center for Education Statistics. (2022). *Students with disabilities*. NCES. https://nces.ed.gov/ programs/coe/indicator/cgg

Orr, A. C. (2009). New special educators reflect about inclusion: Preparation and K–12 current practice. *Journal of Ethnographic and Qualitative Research, 3*(4), 228–239.

Patrick, S. K. (2022). Organizing schools for collaborative learning: School leadership and teachers' engagement in collaboration. *Educational Administration Quarterly, 58*(4), 1–36. doi:10.1177/0013161X221107628

Scruggs, T. E., & Mastropieri, M. A. (2017). Making inclusion work with co-teaching. *Teaching Exceptional Children, 49*(4), 284–293. doi:10.1177/0040059916685065

Section 504 of the Rehabilitation Act of 1973, 34 C.F.R. § 300.101 (1973). https://www.dol.gov/agencies/oasam/centers-offices/civil-rights-center/statutes/section-504-rehabilitation-act-of-1973

Smith, V. M. (2012). *Co-teaching: A case study of teachers' perceptions* [Unpublished doctoral dissertation, Northeastern University]. https://www.proquest.com/docview/1039147424

Strogilos, V., Tragoulia, E., Avramidis, E., Voulagka, A., & Papanikolaou, V. (2017). Understanding the development of differentiated instruction for students with and without disabilities in co-taught classrooms. *Disability & Society, 32*(8), 1216–1238. doi:10.1080/09687599.2017.1352488

Sukhai, M. A., & Mohler, C. E. (2017). *Creating a culture of accessibility in the sciences*. Elsevier.

US Department of Education. (2010). *Twenty-five years of progress in educating children with disabilities through IDEA*. USDE. https://www2.ed.gov/print/policy/speced/leg/idea/history.html

KEY TERMS AND DEFINITIONS

BASICS strategy: A lesson development plan for cotaught inclusive settings serving diverse learners with individual needs.

Co-teaching: An instructional practice in which two or more general and special educators partner to educate diverse learners in the general education classroom.

Differentiated instruction: A teaching method that customizes instruction for all students by varying instruction based on learner abilities, strengths, interests, and needs.

Duet and Map and Navigate: Co-teaching models that include adding, transforming, and complementing as approaches; types of groupings are readiness and mixed readiness.

Inclusion: Including SWD in the general education classroom as fully engaged members of the learning community whose learning needs are addressed, and educational services provided.

Inclusive setting: A general education classroom in which SWD are taught along with their peers, where belonging matters and instruction supports learning and outcomes.

Least restrictive environment: Inclusive classrooms that provide greater opportunities for students in special education to be educated and in the same classroom as other children.

Universal Design for Learning: A pedagogical framework that is implemented to benefit different learners, and plan activities and tasks for meeting diverse learning needs.

Chapter 10
Exploring Ways to Design Mathematics Education Promoting Inclusion and Equity for Every Student

Helena Roos
Malmö University, Sweden

ABSTRACT

The aim of this chapter is to reflect on how inclusion and equity can be used when moving from defining them theoretically and identifying critical aspects, into using them practically in designing mathematics education. In this chapter inclusive and equitable education is understood as an education striving for every student's opportunity to take part in learning processes in mathematics. Theoretically Ainscows' framework for inclusion and equity is combined with Skovsmoses' notions regarding inclusive landscape of investigation. This combination is done to create a conceptual framework for promotion of inclusion and equity in mathematics education. The result of the meta-analysis displays seven interrelated critical aspects: see the students; develop and anchor inclusion and equity principles; supportive administration and organization; educational strategies; tasks; representations; collaborations and mathematical discussions. These aspects need to be considered in the implementation of inclusive and equitable mathematics.

INTRODUCTION

The notion of inclusion stems from the 1994 World Conference on Special Needs Education in Salamanca, Spain (Ainscow, 2020), where it was stated that inclusive education enables schools to serve all children, particularly those defined as having special educational needs (UNESCO, 1994). This led to an international declaration, the UNESCO Salamanca Statement, which was a strong political statement focusing on the special needs of children and their right to get access to education all over the world. In 2019, UNESCO reinforced and revised the definition of inclusion to serve as a principle strengthen-

DOI: 10.4018/978-1-6684-7370-2.ch010

Copyright © 2023, IGI Global. Copying or distributing in print or electronic forms without written permission of IGI Global is prohibited.

Designing Mathematics Education Promoting Equity for Every Student

ing equal access to qualitative learning opportunities for all (Ainscow, 2020). When placing this new revised definition of inclusion in the context of mathematics education a complexity of the use appears.

Mathematics education research often uses the notion of inclusion when discussing mathematics education for all students, for example, to describe how to give every student a *possibility to access* mathematics learning (e.g., Roos, 2019b). Here, issues of equity and inclusion are seen as central for *every* student learning mathematics (Atweh, 2011). Nevertheless, both research and practice in mathematics education often struggle to include aspects of equity and inclusion (Roos, 2019a) due to the complexity and multiplicity of issues to consider regarding equity and inclusion in this context (Kollosche et al., 2019). Moreover, when striving for equity and inclusion in mathematics, sometimes we end up producing exclusion (Valero, 2017): some sort of in(ex)clusion. This process of in(ex)clusion is generated by "the effects of defining the norms of inclusion" (Valero, 2017, p. 2). Although it is a struggle to work with inclusion and equity and although there is a risk of producing exclusion, we need to find ways of working inclusively and equitably in mathematics education. We need to move from identifying critical aspects for inclusion and equity towards finding ways to work with these aspects in both research and practice in mathematics education (Roos, 2019a).

One way to move towards working with inclusion and equity is to think of diversity as a point of departure (Sullivan, 2015). From this perspective, inclusive and equitable school practices can be defined as different ways of meeting the diversity of students in the classroom to create opportunities for every student to participate in learning (Barton, 1997). Here, the wording "every student" is of importance. "Every student" implies, in the spirit of Popkewitz (2004), not departing from the differences of the students and trying to accommodate all students into what is understood as "normal" for similarly aged students regarding learning mathematics but departing from the opportunities of *every student* (Roos, 2019b). To be able to depart from the opportunities of every student, teachers must identify the needs in the education to empower every student and create ideal learning opportunities. One way of doing this is to identify special educational needs in mathematics (SEM). Bagger and Roos (2015) suggest the term "students *in* special educational needs in mathematics" instead of *with* because it invites a social, relational, and pedagogical perspective on mathematics learning and participation. In such a perspective, the focus lies on the teaching and learning activities and how they influence students' learning in mathematics. Deriving from this, SEM is a notion unfolding a specific need in the mathematics education to meet diversity. However, the interpretation of what is needed depends on the institutional environment in which it is situated. This suggests that SEM should be understood differently depending on national and school environments.

The aim of this chapter is to reflect on how to promote inclusion and equity when moving from defining them theoretically and identifying critical aspects into using them practically in designing mathematics education. Here, the mathematics education considers SEM and is based on experience from both research and practice. In the following sections, this chapter discusses and reflects on the research question, What important aspects do we have to consider in designing an inclusive and equitable mathematics education based on experience from both research and practice and from both a teacher and a student perspective?

INCLUSION AND EQUITY IN MATHEMATICS EDUCATION

In this section, I define inclusion and equity and discuss how they relate to each other in a mathematics educational context.

Most often, inclusion and equity are used in a pair in research (e.g., Ainscow, 2020). Research often does not actually define these notions or explain their relation when using them. It is somewhat taken for granted. But are these notions and their relation so easily understood that they can be taken for granted in research? And are these notions easily put into practice in school by mathematics teachers? My answer to these questions is no, we cannot take equity and inclusion and their relation for granted in research, and they are not easily put into practice in school by mathematics teachers. There is always a need to be explicit and define these notions and how they relate to each other. In doing so, research can help practice with the first step in understanding how they can put inclusion and equity into practice.

Inclusion in Mathematics Education

Inclusion in mathematics education research, specifically, is most often discussed either as an ideology or as a way of working in the classroom (Roos, 2019a). This makes issues of inclusion in mathematics education somewhat one eyed, and it creates a risk of research and practice developing in different directions regarding inclusion. However, since inclusion is a notion used in many different research paradigms, there might not be one single definition; instead, there might be a need for a spectrum of definitions (Roos, 2019a). The existence of different interpretations and discourses requires researchers to be vigilant and ask the question, inclusion into what and of whom (Skovsmose, 2019)? Nonetheless, to promote a sustainable development and understanding of inclusion and equity, the definitions of these notions need to originate "from the same core, but with variations expressing its various aspects and connecting and interrelating the ideological and operational aspects" (Roos, 2019a, p. 37).

An interpretation of inclusion found in mathematics education research is something that welcomes diversity (Askew, 2015). This way of looking upon inclusion is evident when research discusses inclusion in relation to differences, namely, that all people are not the same and different approaches are needed to include all (e.g., Aragón et al., 2016). Diaz (2013) has a slightly different way of describing inclusion; she describes it as equal mathematics for all, but she also questions this by stating that "embedded in the relationship between math education and questions of inclusion a particular logic of equality paradoxically reinserts notions of inequality as differences between children" (p. 36). Another way of defining inclusion in research is to discuss stories about participation (e.g., Kleve & Penne, 2016), possibilities to participate (Secher Schmidt, 2016), or processes of participation (Roos, 2019b).

Skovsmose (2019) suggests that we consider inclusion as an "inclusive landscape of investigation," where the landscape is not predetermined but instead dependent on the participants in the classroom and the mathematics to be explored. This inclusive landscape is at its core inviting and accessible to everybody, and it facilitates collaborations (Skovsmose, 2019). Although it sounds inviting to define and use inclusion in mathematics as an inclusive landscape of investigation, it is important to understand that "one needs to struggle for the formation and implementation of inclusive landscapes of investigation" (Skovsmose, 2019, p. 82). In this struggle, it is important to take the students, the institutional context, and the specific mathematical content into consideration and look upon inclusion as processes of participation of every student (Roos, 2019b).

Equity in Mathematics Education

In mathematics education research, the notion of equity is often used without clarification, implying a natural understanding despite the diverse use in research (Pais & Valero, 2011). This diversity is evident

Designing Mathematics Education Promoting Equity for Every Student

in how equity is used in relation to many different aspects of inequalities in mathematics education, for instance, power and politics (e.g., Pais & Valero, 2011), socioeconomics (e.g., Thien, 2016), gender (e.g., Leder & Forgasz, 2008), ethnicity (e.g., Martin, 2019), cultural background (e.g., Meaney et al., 2016), language (e.g., Planas et al., 2018), disability (e.g., Tan et al., 2019), curriculum (e.g., Askew, 2015), educational approaches (e.g., Kolloshe et al., 2019), and assessment (e.g., Bagger, 2017).

Since equity in mathematics education is used diversly, there are many different interpretations and usages (just as for inclusion). Nasir and Cobb (2007) state that they "view equity as situated and relational and as being informed both by local schooling practices and by practices and ideologies that transcend school" (p. 5). In relation to ideologies that transcend school, Pais and Valero (2011) highlight the fact that research on equity requires a gaze towards "social and political approaches that situate the problem in a broader context than the classroom or schools" (p. 38). Pais (2014) develops these thoughts on equity by writing, "achieving equity means to fight different battles (for groups of people considered to be in disadvantage, inequity of resources, teacher formation, mathematical content for social justice, etc.)" (p. 1088). Another interpretation is made by Bishop and Forgasz (2007), who strongly connect equity with access, stating that "without *access* to mathematics education there can be no *equity*; thus, in this view *equity* is referring to an outcome whereas *access* is a means of getting there" (p. 1146). In common in these four ways of interpreting equity is that they do not actually define it explicitly but talk about what is important to consider in relation to it. They beat around the bush concerning what they explicitly mean by equity. This is not at all strange, since it is very hard to get to the core of what equity can be. Cobb and Hodge (2007) come somewhat closer to the core in their interpretation of equity as something that "encompasses students' development of a sense of efficacy (empowerment) in mathematics together with the desire and capability to learn more about mathematics when the opportunity arises" (p. 181). In line with this, Gates and Zevenbergen (2009) summarize existing research regarding what makes the foundation for equity: "What might we all agree on then as fundamentals of a socially just mathematics education? Perhaps we can list: access to the curriculum; access to resources and good teachers; conditions to learn; and feeling valued" (p. 165).

The Intersection of Inclusion and Equity

Inclusion and equity intersect regarding what they aim to achieve. In this chapter, they are interpreted in the context of designing a mathematics education. Inclusion is here defined as processes of participation in and access to learning and teaching in mathematics (Roos, 2019). Participation is here a variable and concerns taking part in the mathematics education and relating to other peers and teachers in learning situations in mathematics, and access is about the available opportunities to gain entry to and take part in the mathematics presented. Equity in this chapter is understood as something that "contributes to student empowerment, development, and in turn, their ability and agency to learn" (p. 71; Bagger, 2017).

In the intersection of inclusion and equity, issues of *agency and participation in learning* are central. Hence, inclusive and equitable education is understood in this chapter as an education striving to give every student an opportunity to take part in learning processes in mathematics. It is an education that considers equity and, at the same time, develops learning in mathematics (Roos & Bagger, 2021).

A FRAMEWORK FOR INCLUSION AND EQUITY IN MATHEMATICS EDUCATION

In this section, I firstly present a framework for inclusion and equity in educational systems (Ainsworth, 2020). Secondly, I present Skovmose's (2019) landscape of investigation. Thirdly, I argue for a combination of the two different frameworks to create a framework for inclusion and equity in mathematics education.

A Framework for Promoting Inclusion and Equity

Ainscow (2020) presents a framework for promoting inclusion and equity in educational systems. The framework places school development at its core, and it focuses on whole-school approaches developed by teachers. Around this core, there are contextual influences that bear on the way schools carry out their work (Figure 1). These influences can work as both encouragement for and hindrance to inclusive education, depending on the direction of views upon inclusion and equity.

Figure 1. Ainscow's (2020, p.9) framework for inclusion and equity

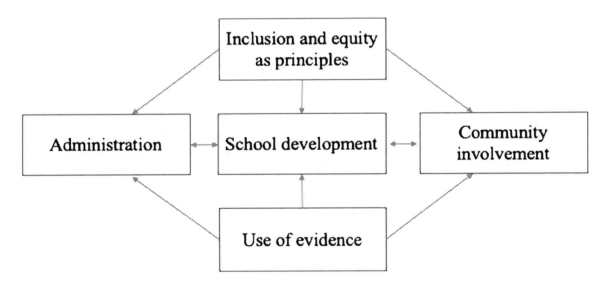

Regarding *inclusion and equity as principles*, Ainscow (2020) suggests a definition of inclusive education as a process that focuses on the removal of barriers to promote the presence, participation, and achievement of all students. At the same time, this education or process emphasizes groups of students at risk of marginalization, exclusion, and underachievement. Inclusion and equity as principles needs to be put in context and discussed by every stakeholder involved in an ongoing process to find a wider understanding.

Use of evidence in inclusion development concerns the importance of collecting evidence with care and being vigilant since "what gets measured gets done" (Ainscow, 2020, p. 10). Educational strategies should be informed by evidence regarding the impact of current practices on the presence, participation, and achievement of all students.

Designing Mathematics Education Promoting Equity for Every Student

Regarding *administration*, the supporting administrative educational system(s) need to offer the teachers guidance in how to lead and promote inclusion and equity in their work. This can be done through constant dialogue within and between different educational systems to share resources, expertise, and ideas.

Community involvement is relevant for inclusion development since there are lessons to be learned from the experience and expertise of everybody involved with the students, not least the students themselves.

Inclusive Landscapes of Investigation in Mathematics Education

Skovsmose (2019) presents inclusive landscapes of investigation as a way of facilitating "meetings amongst differences" to promote inclusion in mathematics. These inclusive landscapes have three major elements: they facilitate investigations, provide an environment that is accessible to everybody, and facilitate collaborations (p. 81).

Regarding *facilitating investigations*, Skovsmose (2019) emphasizes that an inclusive mathematics education provides "invitations for students to engage in inquiry processes." That is, it creates spaces for students to ask questions, formulate their hypothesis, try out their arguments, and listen to arguments from peers. Engagement in a dialogic process creates engagement in investigations.

Further, inclusive landscapes of investigation provide an environment *accessible to everybody*. Here the differences amongst students are acknowledged when meeting challenges in the landscapes.

Regarding *facilitating collaborations*, the possibilities for shared engagement are key. In inclusive landscapes, these possibilities are not demarcated by students' differences since such landscapes invite dialogues. In these kind of dialogues, "the very notions of normal, not-normal, ability and disability lose significance" (Skovsmose, 2019, p. 81).

A Combined Conceptual Framework

In this section, Ainscow's (2020) framework is combined with Skovsmose's (2019) notions regarding inclusive landscapes of investigation to create a conceptual framework for promoting inclusion and equity in mathematics education. Combining is a networking strategy suggested by Prediger et al. (2008) to deal with the diversity of theories in mathematics education research. It offers a way to add different theoretical approaches together in order to get "a multi-faced insight" into an empirical phenomenon (Prediger et al., 2008). Therefore, it was used here not to create a new coherent theory but to get a multi-faced way of looking at inclusion and equity in mathematics education. Ainscow's (2020) framework for promoting inclusion and equity enables a coverage of overarching issues of school development in relation to equity and inclusion, and Skovsmose's (2019) notions enables a coverage at the classroom level, focusing on teaching and learning. Thus, combining the two creates possibilities to reflect on how inclusion and equity can be a fundament when designing mathematics education for every student.

INCLUSION IN MATHEMATICS EDUCATION FROM A TEACHER AND STUDENT PERSPECTIVE

In this section, the results from two previous research studies on inclusion from both a teacher (Roos, 2015) and a student perspective (Roos, 2019b) are presented and meta-analyzed using the combined conceptual framework for inclusion and equity in mathematics education. Hence, the methodological

Designing Mathematics Education Promoting Equity for Every Student

and theoretical approaches from the two prior projects are only briefly described in this chapter. Instead, this chapter focuses on their results, addressing them from a perspective of designing for inclusion and equity in mathematics education. Here, the overarching aim of this chapter—to reflect on how inclusion and equity can be promoted by moving from defining them theoretically and identifying critical aspects into using them practically—serves as a guide.

The Study of Inclusion from a Teacher Perspective

The first study (Roos, 2015) aimed to understand how all students can be included in mathematics teaching from a teacher perspective. The study asked the following research questions: What can inclusion in mathematics be in primary school and what influences the process of inclusion in mathematics? What, from an inclusive perspective, appears to be important in the learning and teaching of mathematics?

The study employed a didactic perspective to understand what inclusion in mathematics education can be in primary school. It also used a participatory perspective, where learning was seen as participation. Part of a learning theory that focuses on communities of practice (Wenger, 1998) was used together with a conceptual framework dealing with inclusion from three aspects—spatial, didactic, and social (Asp-Onsjö, 2006)—to analyze how teachers talk about inclusion in mathematics. Ethnography was used as a guide for the case study, where a large primary and middle school was followed for two years. A special education teacher in mathematics was followed over two years, and she was interviewed 28 times. The mathematics teachers she collaborated with was interviewed 10 times, whereof three were focus group interviews. The principal was interviewed one time. The data included observations of the mathematics education made on 31 occasions, both in the regular classroom and in a small group where the special education teacher taught. The data also included written documentary sources, such as the school's "local plan for systematic quality," the plan "Results in Focus," and the school's "student health teams' cycle." The data revealed three cases (the special education teacher, the mathematics teachers, and the principal) and four interrelated communities. The cases' participation in these communities of practice in the form of inclusion in mathematics was analyzed by content analysis.

Results

The results showed that the process of inclusion in mathematics at the investigated school could be described with three forms that interacted with each other: dynamic inclusion, content inclusion, and participating inclusion.

Dynamic inclusion was practiced to fulfill a need for flexible solutions in the school to promote inclusion. One way to contribute to flexible solutions at the investigated school was to work with courses in mathematics. Here students who had a similar specific need in relation to the mathematical content were grouped into a smaller group for a few times to work intensely with a specific issue with the special education teacher in mathematics. Working intensely with some students during the mathematics class was another flexible solution. Teaching SEM-students both in the regular math classroom and sometimes alone was another way to be flexible. All this put demands on the organization to provide opportunities for teachers and special education teachers in mathematics to collaborate and discuss their different roles.

In content inclusion, the focus was on how to give the SEM-students access to the mathematical content and to reach and challenge them. Here, the teachers talked about knowledge of different representations and tasks that invite the students to be part of the mathematics class. They perceived that if the tasks

172

Designing Mathematics Education Promoting Equity for Every Student

were inviting to the students, their achievement in the classroom could be enhanced. Further, flexibility in teaching was required to have an effective teaching. This flexibility in the teaching of mathematics required knowledge of differences in mathematical representations. There was also a need to help the SEM-students to recognize mathematical similarities between different situations, to help them make the mathematics content generic. Accordingly, representations and strategies used in a specific situation needed to be used in another situation to help the student recognize the similarities.

The participating inclusion involved focusing on listening to the students' voice in order to reach all of them. The teachers talked about being responsive, listening to students, and encouraging students' participation. Notably, students' self-esteem and self-confidence indicate the need for letting the students be a natural participating part of the education. The results indicated that a teacher in mathematics needed to be responsive to the SEM-students and listen to what they want and how they feel regarding mathematics. The teacher needed to let the students take part in the mathematics content and decisions regarding the teaching. This would enable the teacher to organize and represent mathematics in different ways and to choose tasks that help the students recognize similarities and strategies.

In sum, the results revealed several important aspects of inclusion in mathematics from a teacher perspective: organizational actions to support collaboration and discussions between teachers; well-functioning teams that work with preventive actions in mathematics teaching; knowledge of and in mathematics education and the ability to listen to the students' voices.

The Study of Inclusion from a Student Perspective

The second study (Roos, 2019b) aimed to understand students' meaning(s) of inclusion in mathematics education. Three research questions guided the study: What meaning(s) is/are ascribed and how is inclusion used in mathematics education research? What meaning(s) do the students ascribe to inclusion in mathematics learning and teaching? And what frames students' meaning(s) of inclusion in mathematics learning and teaching?

The study involved a case study of three students in Grade 7 (14 years old) and Grade 8 (15 years old) and their meaning(s) of inclusion in mathematics education. Two of the students were perceived as being in SEM by the teachers due to their struggle to get access to the mathematics presented in the classroom, and hence in struggle to access learning. One of the students was perceived by the teachers as a being in SEM since, even though he was in access to the mathematics presented, he was not in access to learning since he already knew the presented mathematical content. The school selected for the study was a lower secondary school in an urban area of Sweden. The school had set out to be inclusive, meaning their aims were to include all students in the regular classroom teaching in every subject and to incorporate special education into the regular teaching with no fixed special education groups. The collected data consisted of both observations and repeated interviews (Roos, 2021) conducted during one semester. Discourse analysis, as described by Gee (2014), was used both as a theoretical frame and as an analytical tool because of its explanatory view on discourse, with description foregrounded. Gee (2014) uses the theoretical notions *Discourse* and *discourse*: Discourse (with an uppercase "D") represents a wider context, both social and political, and is constructed upon ways of saying, doing, and being, whereas discourse (with a lowercase "d") focuses on language in use, meaning the relations between words and sentences and how these relations visualize themes within the conversations.

Results

The results showed three interrelated overarching Discourses: assessment, accessibility in mathematics education, and mathematics education setting. Within these Discourses, smaller discourses make visible the issues concerning the meanings of inclusion for the students. The relation between the D(d)iscorses is displayed in Table 1 below.

Table 1. The relation between D(d)iscourses in the study

Discourse(s)	discourse(s)
Discourse of assessment	Tests Grades
Discourse of accessibility in mathematics education	Tasks The importance of the teacher (Not) being valued Dislike
Discourse of mathematics education setting	Classroom organization Being in a small group

In the *Discourse of assessment*, all the students somehow talked about assessment and how it influenced inclusion in mathematics negatively in terms of tests and grades. Regardless of whether the students were struggling to access the mathematics presented in the classroom or not, their inclusion in mathematics was limited by assessments. Further, regarding the *Discourse of accessibility*, the students highlighted the importance of getting access to the mathematics education by doing tasks to help their mathematical development. They also highlighted the importance of being valued in the classroom as a SEM student and the importance of having variation in the teaching and learning to avoid making them dislike mathematics. In the *Discourse of mathematics education setting*, the students struggling to access mathematics highlighted the importance of sometimes being able to be in a small group and getting instructions from the special education teacher. In addition, variation in the teaching approaches was something the students talked about as a positive factor for inclusion, in relation to this, they all emphasized the importance of the teachers' reflection on what and how to present information on the white board as well as students' discussions with peers.

META-ANALYSIS OF INCLUSION IN MATHEMATICS

Below, the results from the two prior projects are meta-analyzed to pinpoint critical aspects to consider when designing for inclusion and equity in mathematics education. Here, the prior results serve as a pathway to finding critical issues related to designing an inclusive and equitable mathematics education. A two-step content-analysis (Patton, 2002) was carried out on the results in relation to the combined conceptual framework described above. In the first step, the analysis identified issues related to the different parts of the framework. In the second step, the issues were categorized into the different parts of the conceptual framework. The second step also involved making thematic summaries of the categorizations. Below, these summaries are presented as narratives.

Designing Mathematics Education Promoting Equity for Every Student

Inclusion and Equity as Principles

From a teacher perspective, the results showed a lack of principles for inclusion and equity on the level of the state, municipality, region, and school as an organization. Though, there were a lot of thoughts and discussions about this amongst teachers at the investigated school. They discussed the issue in terms of how they can develop their own knowledge and make use of the competences at the school to be able to support and challenge the SEM students. At a school organizational level, there are regular and regulated meetings of mathematics and special education teachers; however, at the investigated school, their meetings were often cancelled due to other school matters. This left the investigated school without any forum to discuss these matters.

From a student perspective, it was evident that there were principles of inclusion at the investigated school. These principles concerned the school organization focusing on not having any static groupings of students; instead, the focus was on creating inclusive environments in the classrooms and trying to support all students within the classrooms with as much co-teaching as possible. Nonetheless, it seemed that these principles were not anchored in the students' views and that there was a need to be more dynamic in relation to the initial spatial principle of inclusion.

Use of Evidence

From a teacher perspective, knowledge of the importance of preventive actions in mathematics teaching was a key issue for inclusion, as well as teacher knowledge of and in mathematics education. Here, the teachers struggled to find educational strategies to increase participation and achievement of all students.

It was evident in the student perspective that although the school set out to promote evidence-based inclusion, there were organizational, group, and individual aspects to consider. Namely, it is important to implement not only evidence-based practice but also a constant revision. That is, inclusion must be seen as a dynamic process situated in time and space.

Administration

From a teacher perspective, teachers evidently needed organizational actions to support their collaboration and discussions. There was an intention from the organization to provide support, but it became clear that what was planned looked differently in practice. Hence, the school needed to strengthen its administration to be able to guide teachers in promoting inclusion and equity. The teachers also believed they need to discuss the sharing of resources, expertise, and ideas.

From a student perspective, the results indicated that the administration needed to support the teachers regarding assessments in relation to participation. The students seemed to be hindered in their participation due to tests. Further, the students perceived a need for teachers to organize discussions amongst themselves on how to work with the classroom organization to be able to cater for participation, inclusion, and equity.

Community Involvement

From a teacher perspective, the results did not directly point towards community involvement. However, they indicated the need for teachers to listen to the students' voices. The students are a part of the community, which in turn signals for a need to look beyond the school organization in order to promote equity and inclusion.

Results from the student perspective stressed the importance of the teacher. The teachers' education and knowledge about the students helped the students get a feeling of being valued. Hence, the teachers need to have a more holistic view of the student and a connection to the community in which the student is involved. Moreover, the students have evidently fostered a dislike for mathematics. How this dislike is related to the community and society might be an important factor to investigate. This dislike may be connected to how assessment seemed to frame and restrain students' inclusion. Thus, how the community views assessment in mathematics is of importance.

Facilitating Investigations

Being careful choosing tasks to facilitate investigation seemed to be an important inclusion factor. From a teacher perspective, mathematics education needs to reach and challenge the students. This can be done by working with tasks that facilitate investigations and invite students to engage and be part of the subject.

Tasks are also important from a student perspective. To engage the students, the tasks need to be inviting and the theme of the tasks relevant. In addition, problem-solving tasks sometimes need to be unfolded for students and adjusted according to the students' specific needs.

Accessibility to Everybody

From a teacher perspective, flexible solutions both on an organization and classroom level are of importance for making the education accessible. Teachers also have to be responsive to the students to find out what they need to access learning. This requires teacher knowledge of different representations and of ways to help students recognize similarities in mathematics between different situations.

Meanwhile, students emphasized the importance of tasks that help their mathematical development and give them access to learning. Being valued in the classroom as a SEM student and having variation in the teaching and learning were other important aspects to make the mathematics education accessible. The students also highlighted appreciating the opportunity to sometimes be able to join a small group to get a calmer learning space and access to more representations.

Facilitating Collaborations

Teachers indicated a need to collaborate with each other to facilitate student collaborations. Further, they need to know their students to be able to support them in collaborations and mathematical discussions.

From a student perspective, there is a need to have fruitful discussions amongst peers. This can be seen as a way to facilitate collaboration if combined with carefully chosen tasks and well-planned discussions. Students also need teachers to reflect on how the classroom is organized to facilitate collaboration in terms of ways of working.

DESIGNING FOR INCLUSION AND EQUITY IN MATHEMATICS EDUCATION

Using the developed conceptual framework in relation to the data revealed critical aspects in teacher and student perspectives on equity and inclusion in mathematics. These critical aspects can be seen as challenges, or even barriers, for designing an inclusive and equitable mathematics education. At the core of all these aspects is *seeing the students*. Namely, there is a need to have a holistic view of the student, both as a human being and a learner and to see the student as having agency to be a part of the mathematics education. To do so and to give the students the right support (Roos, 2015), the teachers need to know their students.

A critical aspect around *seeing the students* is the need to *develop and anchor inclusion and equity principles* not only in the organization and for the teachers but also for the students, considering school specific issues. Here, there is a need to see inclusion as a dynamic process situated in time and space (Roos, 2019b) and to have a constant revision of the work. As a result, hidden processes of exclusion (Valero, 2017) might be avoided.

Another critical aspect is having a *supportive administration and organization* that can guide teachers in promoting inclusion and equity. Here, the teachers need time and space to discuss the sharing of resources, how to use the expertise at the school, and share didactical ideas (Roos & Gadler, 2018).

Yet another critical aspect is finding *educational strategies* to increase the participation and achievement of every student. Here, evidence-based research needs to be anchored in the mathematics education in relation to the students and the setting (Ainscow, 2020). A variation in the teaching and learning of mathematics is also needed. An important issue to consider in relation to educational strategies and inclusion and equity is how assessments are constructed and what demands they put on the students in relation to how the content has been dealt with in the regular education.

Educational strategies are relevant for two other critical aspects. *Tasks* are central from both a teacher and a student perspective when discussing inclusion and equity. This aspect concerns how the task invites the students to engage and how the education can help unfold the task for the student, for example, by using supportive representations and explanations of words that might hinder understanding. The other critical aspect in relation to educational strategies is *representations*. Here, teachers must have both knowledge of different representations in mathematics and knowledge of how to help students recognize similarities between representations and situations.

The last critical aspect seen in the data is *collaborations and mathematical discussions*. That is, an inclusive education needs to be able to cater for students' shared engagement (Skovsmose, 2019). The teachers need to know their students to be able to adjust their teaching, organize the classroom, and make fruitful peer-group formations.

The aim of this chapter has been to reflect on how inclusion and equity can be promoted when moving from defining them theoretically and identifying critical aspects into using them practically in a mathematics education setting. Taking inclusion and equity as a point of departure for designing mathematics education for every student, this chapter has identified and discussed critical aspects to consider in the design process. The results of the meta-analysis contain seven interrelated critical aspects: *seeing the students; developing and anchoring inclusion and equity principles; having supportive administration and organization; employing educational strategies; utilizing tasks; recognizing representations; and having collaborations and mathematical discussions*. These aspects need to be considered in the implementation of an inclusive and equitable mathematics education as they can easily become barriers in the development of such an education. This is not at all an easy task since there are multiple aspects to consider in schools constantly and simultaneously. Furthermore, since inclusive and equitable education needs to be in a constant process of development, there is no end to the task at hand. It cannot be static; it needs to be seen as a living organism relative to the educational environment in which it resides.

REFERENCES

Ainscow, M. (2020). Promoting inclusion and equity in education: Lessons from international experiences. *Nordic Journal of Studies in Educational Policy, 6*(1), 7–16. doi:10.1080/20020317.2020.1729587

Aragón, O. R., Dovidio, J. F., & Graham, M. J. (2016). Colorblind and multicultural ideologies are associated with faculty adoption inclusive teaching practices. *Journal of Diversity in Higher Education, 3*(10), 1–15.

Askew, M. (2015). Diversity, inclusion and equity in mathematics classrooms: From individual problems to collective possibility. In A. J., Bishop, H. Tan, & T. N. Barkatsas (Eds), Diversity in mathematics education: Towards inclusive practices (pp. 129–145). Cham: Springer International Publishing.

Atweh, B. (2011). Quality and equity in mathematics education as ethical issues. In B. Atweh, M. Graven, W. Secada, & P. Valero (Eds.), *Mapping equity and quality in mathematics education* (pp. 63–75). Springer. doi:10.1007/978-90-481-9803-0

Atweh, B., Graven, M., Secada, W., & Valero, P. (Eds.). (2011). *Mapping equity and quality in mathematics education*. Springer. doi:10.1007/978-90-481-9803-0

Bagger, A. (2017). Quality and Equity in the Era of National Testing. The case of Sweden. In J. Allan & A. Artiles (Eds.), *The Routledge Yearbook of Education 2017, Assessment Inequalities* (pp. 68–88). Routledge.

Barton, L. (1997). Inclusive education: Romantic, subversive or realistic? *International Journal of Inclusive Education, 1*(3), 231–242. doi:10.1080/1360311970010301

Bernard Martin, D. (2019). Equity, inclusion, and antiblackness in mathematics education. *Race, Ethnicity and Education, 22*(4), 459–478. doi:10.1080/13613324.2019.1592833

Bishop, A. J., & Forgasz, H. J. (2007). Issues in access and equity in mathematics education. In F. K. Lester Jr., (Ed.), *Second handbook of research on mathematics teaching and learning* (pp. 1145–1167). Information Age Publishing.

Bishop, A. J., Tan, P., & Barkatsas, T. N. (2015). *Diversity in mathematics education: Towards inclusive practices*. Springer International Publishing. doi:10.1007/978-3-319-05978-5

Cobb, P., & Hodge, L. L. (2007). Culture, identity, and equity in the mathematics classroom. In S. N. Nasir & P. Cobb (Eds.), *Improving access to mathematics: Diversity and equity in the classroom* (pp. 159–164). Teachers College Press.

Diaz, J. D. (2013). Governing equality: Mathematics for all? *European Education, 45*(3), 35–50. doi:10.2753/EUE1056-4934450303

Gates, P., & Zevenbergen, R. (2009). Foregrounding social justice in mathematics teacher education. *Journal of Mathematics Teacher Education, 12*, 161–170. doi:10.100710857-009-9105-4

Gee, J. P. (2014). *How to do Discourse Analysis: A toolkit* (2nd ed.). Routledge. doi:10.4324/9781315819662

Kleve, B., & Penne, S. (2016). Learning subjects in school: Being outsiders or insiders in the disciplinary discourses of mathematics and Language 1. *International Journal of Educational Research, 78*, 41–49. doi:10.1016/j.ijer.2016.05.014

Kolloshe, D., Marcone, R., Knigge, M., Gody Penteado, M., & Skovsmose, O. (2019). *Inclusive mathematics education. State-of-the-art research from Brazil and Germany.* Springer. doi:10.1007/978-3-030-11518-0

Leder, G., & Forgasz, H. (2008). Mathematics education: New perspectives on gender. *ZDM Mathematics Education, 40*(4), 513–518. doi:10.100711858-008-0137-5

Martin, D. B. (2019). Equity, inclusion, and antiblackness in mathematics education. *Race, Ethnicity and Education, 22*(4), 459–478. doi:10.1080/13613324.2019.1592833

Meaney, T., Edmonds-Wathen, C., McMurchy-Pilkington, C., & Trinick, T. (2016). Distribution, Recognition and Representation: Mathematics Education and Indigenous Students. In K. Makar, S. Dole, J. Visnovska, M. Goos, A. Bennison, & K. Fry (Eds.), *Research in Mathematics Education in Australasia.* Springer. (Original work published 2012) doi:10.1007/978-981-10-1419-2_8

Nasir, N., & Cobb, P. (2007). Introduction. In N. Nasir & P. Cobb (Eds.), *Improving access to mathematics: Diversity and equity in the classroom* (pp. 1–9). Teachers College, Columbia University.

Pais, A., & Valero, P. (2011). Beyond disavowing the politics of equity and quality in mathematics education. In B. Atweh, M. Graven, W. Secada, & P. Valero (Eds.), *Mapping equity and quality in mathematics education.* Springer.

Patton, M. Q. (2002). *Qualitative research & evaluation methods* (3rd ed.). SAGE.

Planas, N., Morgan, C., & Schütte, M. (2018). Mathematics education and language: Lessons and directions from two decades of research. In T. Dreyfus, M. Artigue, D. Potari, S. Prediger, & K. Ruthven (Eds.), *Developing research in mathematics education. Twenty years of communication, cooperation and collaboration in Europe* (pp. 196–210). Routledge. doi:10.4324/9781315113562-15

Popkewitz, T. (2004). The alchemy of the mathematics curriculum: Inscriptions and the fabrication of the child. *American Educational Research Journal, 41*(1), 3–34. doi:10.3102/00028312041001003

Prediger, S., Bikner-Ahsbahs, A., & Arzarello, F. (2008). Networking strategies and methods for connecting theoretical approaches – First steps towards a conceptual framework. *ZDM - The International Journal on Mathematics Education, 40*(2), 165–178.

Roos, H. (2015). *Inclusion in mathematics in primary school: What can it be?* [Thesis, Växjö: Linnaeus University].

Roos, H. (2019a). Inclusion in mathematics education: An ideology, a way of teaching, or both? *Educational Studies in Mathematics, 100*(1), 25–41. doi:10.100710649-018-9854-z

Roos, H. (2019b). *The meaning of inclusion in student talk: Inclusion as a topic when students talk about learning and teaching in mathematics.* [Ph. D. Thesis. Linnaeus University: Växjö].

Roos, H. (2021). Repeated interviews with students – critical methodological points for research quality. *International Journal of Research & Method in Education.* doi: 10.1080/1743727X.2021.1966622

Roos, H., & Bagger, A. (2021). Developing mathematics education promoting equity and inclusion: Is it possible? In D. Kollosche (Ed.), *Exploring new ways to connect: Proceedings of the Eleventh International Mathematics Education and Society Conference* (Vol. 1, pp. 223–226). Tredition.

Roos, H., & Gadler, U. (2018). Kompetensens betydelse i det didaktiska mötet – en modell för analys av möjligheter att erbjuda varje elev likvärdig utbildning enligt skolans uppdrag. *Pedagogisk forskning i Sverige, 23,* 290–307.

Secher Schmidt, M. C. (2016). Dyscalculia ≠ maths difficulties: An analysis of conflicting positions at a time that calls for inclusive practices. *European Journal of Special Needs Education, 31*(3), 407–421. doi:10.1080/08856257.2016.1163016

Skovsmose, O. (2019). Inclusions, Meetings, and Landscapes. In D. Kollosche, R. Marcone, M. Knigge, M. Godoy Penteado, & O. Skovsmose (Eds.), *Inclusive Mathematics Education. State-of-the-Art Research from Brazil and Germany* (pp. 71–84). Springer. doi:10.1007/978-3-030-11518-0_7

Sullivan, P. (2015). Maximising opportunities in mathematics for all students: Addressing within-school and within-class differences. In: A. J., Bishop, H. Tan & T. N. Barkatsas (Eds.), Diversity in Mathematics Education – Towards Inclusive Practices (pp. 239–253). Cham: Springer publishing.

Tan, P., Lambert, R., Padilla, A., & Wieman, R. (2019). A disability studies in mathematics education review of intellectual disabilities: Directions for future inquiry and practice. *The Journal of Mathematical Behavior, 54*(June), 100672. doi:10.1016/j.jmathb.2018.09.001

Thien, L. M. (2016). Malaysian students' performance in mathematics literacy in PISA from gender and socioeconomic status perspectives. *The Asia-Pacific Education Researcher, 25*(4), 657–666. doi:10.100740299-016-0295-0

UNESCO. (1994). *Final report: World conference on special needs education: Access and quality.* UNESCO.

KEY TERMS AND DEFINITIONS

Access to mathematics education: An opportunity to take part in the teaching and learning of mathematics.

Diversity: A range of people with various racial, ethnic, socioeconomic, and cultural backgrounds with various experiences and interests.

In(ex)clusion: A theoretical term describing when the effects of defining the norms of inclusion creates exclusion.

Inclusive and Equitable Mathematics Education: An education striving to provide every student access to learning processes in mathematics.

Designing Mathematics Education Promoting Equity for Every Student

Inclusive Landscapes of Investigation: A theoretical notion by Skovsmose (2019) describing an approach in inclusive and equitable mathematics education.

Students *in* special educational needs in mathematics: A social, relational, and pedagogical perspective on mathematics learning and participation for students in the mathematics education.

UNESCO Salamanca Statement: A report from the United Nations education agency that calls on the endorsement of inclusive schools by implementing practical and strategic changes.

Chapter 11
Critical Whiteness as a Professional Approach to Inclusive Teaching in Teacher Education

Anne Schröter
Leibniz University, Hannover, Germany

Britta Konz
Johannes Gutenberg University, Mainz, Germany

ABSTRACT

Teachers are in a powerful position in the context of education in schools. They produce and reproduce norms and expectations of normality in relation to their students and their diversity. This does not mean intentional exclusion, but processes that are subtle. However, these processes can have an immense impact on students' educational careers, achievement, well-being, and participation. Therefore, inclusive education in schools requires a professionalisation of teacher education at universities, where future teachers are sensitised in dealing with inequality dimensions. While dimensions such as gender and disability have received attention for a long time, the dimension race and the significance of racist structures and dynamics in education have only recently come into focus in the German discourse. In this chapter, Critical Whiteness will be discussed as a professional approach to inclusive teaching in higher education.

INTRODUCTION

Teachers are in a powerful position in the context of education in schools. They produce and reproduce norms and expectations of normality in relation to their students and their diversity (Schröter & Zimenkova, 2019). Their actions are not intentional exclusion, but rather, processes that are subtle and without reflection. However, as Schwab (2014) showed, these processes can have an immense impact on young

DOI: 10.4018/978-1-6684-7370-2.ch011

Copyright © 2023, IGI Global. Copying or distributing in print or electronic forms without written permission of IGI Global is prohibited.

Critical Whiteness as a Professional Approach to Inclusive Teaching

people's educational careers, achievement, well-being, and participation. Therefore, inclusive education in schools requires professionalization of teacher education at universities, where future teachers are sensitized in dealing with dimensions of inequality. This professionalization involves the perception of diversity as an "opportunity for taking up new perspectives, for the further development of persons and institutions" (Kiper, 2008, p. 91), but at the same time also of heterogeneity as a "product of social inequalities" in the sense of unequal "social positioning, access to resources, educational opportunities, contexts of origin, socialisation conditions, social experiences and educational prerequisites" (Walgenbach, 2019, p. 29). (In this paper, we have translated direct quotations in German into English.)

Therefore, in the sense of "informed heterogeneity," differentiating between "difference" (e.g., with regard to lifestyles, culture, or religion) and "inequality" (such as social inequality or cognitive differences) (Grümme, 2017) and taking into account the intersectionality of the different dimensions of inequality are necessary. However, heterogeneity does not "automatically transform into productive learning processes" because "social heterogeneity dimensions hierarchically structure society as a whole and thus also shape educational processes and educational institutions" (Walgenbach, 2017, p. 29). Both students and teachers can hold "simplified views" that "also go along with exclusion processes" (Walgenbach, 2017, p. 28). Social inequality is not only brought to the school from the outside but also produced within the institution (Walgenbach, 2017). Therefore, strategies for dealing with exclusion must be practiced in teacher education. At the same time, future teachers should be sensitized to the perception of "normative paternalism and claims to validity" (Walgenbach, 2017, p. 28).

Although dimensions of inequality such as gender and disability have received attention for some time, the dimension of race and the significance of racist structures and dynamics in educational processes have only recently come into focus in German discourse. For a long time, the assumption prevailed that Germany was not a significant colonial nation and therefore did not need to come to terms with its colonial history. However, the Black Lives Matter and Me Two movements, as well as the debates about the restitution of stolen art or the renaming of colonialist street names, led to an awareness that Germany also has a colonial past and is shaped by colonial patterns and interpretations. Although many schools in Germany now carry the label schule ohne rassimus (school without racism), students of color usually attend a school where no (or few) teachers have their skin color and where most teachers have not yet addressed the still existing middle-class bias, racism, and the factor of whiteness as an "unmarked marker" (Ogette, 2017). Academic spaces are also still predominantly white spaces (Röggla 2012, p. 35). Thus, the "critical whiteness" debate is not new, but has not yet reached the depths of higher education.

This chapter therefore aims to contribute to the awareness of faculty in teacher education and to the decolonization of higher education by encouraging a critical engagement with the category of whiteness. The authors of this chapter identify as white, which might carry the potential danger of a problematic re-centering on whiteness insofar as whiteness is given special attention (Röggla, 2012, p. 33). At the same time, only by making whiteness visible can the category white can lose its claim of normality and become visible in the first place as a characteristic embedded politically and in social power structures. We therefore want our contribution to be read as a possibility of power sharing or allyship (Tißberger, 2020), which uses the powerful position of the speaker to draw attention to racist structures in educational contexts and to contribute to their dismantling.

We first briefly discuss German colonial history and in particular the epistemic violence that served to legitimize colonial dominance and is still inscribed in social and academic discourses today. We then outline the discourse on critical whiteness and, building on this discussion, address universities as white

183

spaces in a third step. Finally, we suggest how critical whiteness can be made useful as a resource for reflection on inclusive teaching in higher education.

COLONIALISM: A GERMAN REALITY

The fact that Germany has a colonial history and was a colonial nation has long been toned down in the discussion of German history (Castro Varela & Dhawan, 2005). However, for addressing whiteness in the German context, the discussion of European colonial history and the transatlantic slave trade is crucial (Röggla, 2012, p. 31). Postcolonial theory pays attention to the power and supremacy that emerged in colonialism and have been constantly reproduced in neocolonial relations ever since. The prefix "post" does not mark the formal end of European colonial domination, but refers to the dimensions of inequality that work beyond it. Postcolonial theory is intended as a critical category of analysis that makes its social aftereffects visible (Röggla, 2012, p. 31).

Colonization was a relationship of domination that was "enforced with physical, military, epistemological and ideological violence and legitimized, for instance, through discourses of race and culture ..." (Castro Varela & Dhawan, 2005, p. 12). Modern colonization began in 1492 with the so-called discovery or invasion of the North American continent. The main driving force was the search for rare natural resources, which established the ruthless, violent plundering and, last but not least, human trafficking (Castro Varela & Dhawan, 2005). To legitimize the violence and resolve the opposition to the ideals of the enlightenment and the civil revolutions in Europe, colonization was legitimized as a "civilizing ... mission" (Arndt, 2006, p. 17). Ideologies were developed that asserted a fundamental difference between the colonizers and the colonized and assigned dichotomous attributions to people, such as white-black or civilized-uncivilized. The colonized were infantilized and described as primitive peoples (Arndt, 2006) who were not yet capable of deciding for themselves and managing their resources. Therefore, the white man had to educate and save them. Here, the concept of the white man's "burden" became central, with which a kind of perpetrator-victim turn was carried out, as impressively illustrated in the poem "The White Man's Burden" by the British-Indian author Rudyard Kipling:

Take up the White Man's burden—

Send forth the best ye breed—

Go, bind your sons to exile

To serve your captives' need

To wait, in heavy harness

On fluttered folk and wild—

Your new-caught, sullen peoples,

Half devil and half child (Arndt 2006, p. 52).

Critical Whiteness as a Professional Approach to Inclusive Teaching

By placing black people at the limits of humanity and demonizing them (Arndt, 2006), Europeans were able to construct themselves as rational, civilized, superior, and enlightened compared with black people, regardless of the fact that the violence exercised by the colonizers was diametrically opposed to such ideals. Demonization served to justify the violence of colonial domination, which stood in sharp contrast to the ideals of the Enlightenment and the civil revolutions in Europe, and to legitimize it under the pretext of a "civilizing mission" (Arndt, 2006, p. 17). In addition, metaphors from the field of biology were used to justify the actions. Colonial neologisms (Arndt, 2006) such as *Naturvölker* appeared. (Naturvölker is derived from natur [nature or wilderness] and völker [peoples]. It originally meant a group of people living in a natural, primitive form in unity with nature. Nowadays, it is considered outdated and pejorative.) In the process, a dichotomization of nature and culture was established. The concept of race served to maintain the system of order since the Enlightenment (Hirsbrunner, 2012). There was a fear that the mixing of races would lead to the decline of the superior—white—race. Kant's and Hegel's reflections were also fed by this idea. Kant stated: "So essential is the difference between these two human races, and it seems to be as great in regard to the faculty of mind as in regard to colour" (Kant, 1839, p. 436). Hegel even denies that people of color are human: "The [N.] represents ... the natural man in all his wildness and unrestraint: one must abstract from all reverence and morality, from what is called feeling, if one wants to understand him correctly; there is nothing in this character that echoes the human" (Hegel, 1858, p. 115). (Note: The N-word is a white construct that carries power, violence, and humiliation. It is deeply racist and is used by whites, whenever they utter it, to ensure their own domination. Because the word in the given context does not have a deconstructive but a constituent character, it will be referred to only by the commonly used abbreviation [Kilomba, 2009]).

Race is produced as a social reality. In fact, there are no purely hereditary sub-populations that are genetically homogeneous (Arndt, 2006)—in other words, there are no separable human races. The paradox here is that despite the assumption that race is a construct that does not actually exist, the concept and its underlying thought structures persist (Arndt, 2006). "Race does not exist. But it does kill people" (Guillaumin 1995, p. 107). Racism serves as an instrument to guarantee the dominance of a group that considers itself superior to a group of dominated people. This protection takes the form of various forms of discrimination, segregation, persecution, and even extermination (Renschler & Preiswerk, 1981).

Two types of behavior are identified with regard to racism. One is open and violent racism, which manifests itself not only in direct but also in structural violence. The other, more subtle form of racism recognizes equal rights for all people, but still retains paternalism and cultural arrogance, revealing itself in the form of epistemic violence in a knowledge hegemony of those who consider themselves superior.

The historical determination of separating humankind into races, which was made by whites in Europe, is still the ideological ground for today's racialism. The structures formed in colonialism are reproduced (largely unconsciously) in socialization and are found in all areas of our everyday lives. Recognizing and exposing these thought structures and seeing racism not only in right-wing extremist acts of violence means thinking critically of racism. At the same time, however, we must note that belonging to a group can be identity building. This belonging must be recognized and strengthened. However, the discrimination of people on this basis and their classification in terms of value must be resolutely opposed.

Regarding this issue, racism is often subtle, but nonetheless powerful because of its influence on practices of subjectification and the associated allocations of resources. Besides overt violence, more subtle practices can negatively affect persons of color (Renschler & Preiswerk, 1981). Education mirrors the value system of a society and is designed to maintain it (Renschler & Preiswerk, 1981). Images in school textbooks that show the white conqueror as the savior over the savages reproduce stereotypes and

185

the hierarchizing division of people (Renschler & Preiswerk, 1981). The same stereotyping applies to the subtle normalization of a purely white and westernized reading list in classes and lectures in higher education, which gives students the impression that western assumptions can be applied to contexts all over the world. For example, in pedagogical terms, there is not just one childhood, but different ones that are "lived and co-created" by children around the world under different social, political, religious, and cultural frameworks (Kaul, Schmidt, & Thole, 2018, p. 2). Nevertheless, the Western ideal of a long "sheltered childhood" in the sense of a "westernization of childhood" (Andresen & Neumann, 2018, p. 53) has also gained global impact (Joos, Betz, Bollig, & Neumann, 2018). Accordingly, children from countries of Africa, Asia, and Latin America are still often perceived sweepingly as "helpless and vulnerable victims in extreme circumstances" (Liebel, 2017, p. 11) or "children without childhood" and become the object of paternalistic pedagogy.

CRITICAL WHITENESS AS AN ANALYTICAL FRAMEWORK IN TEACHER EDUCATION

As explained above, colonial interpretation is reproduced in all social institutions and structures. Educational institutions, such as universities, are challenged to critically examine the extent to which curricula and teaching materials "help to produce postcolonial subjects" and join "unquestioned or little questioned positions in society" (Bliemetsrieder & Beinzger, 2022, p. 116). The analysis of the position of the teaching faculty must be the subject of a reflected, racism-critical attitude of a university. In this paper, we show to what extent critical whiteness can be made useful as a category of analysis in teacher education. In addition to pointing out the concerns of critical whiteness, we also address the concerns of critical reflections of critical whiteness to finally formulate suggestions for higher education.

After research on racism had long been concerned only with the construction of the *other*, a change took place in the 1990s, with Toni Morrison as one of its most popular representatives. She called for an examination of the effects of racism on those in power:

A good deal of time and intelligence has been invested in the exposure of racism and the horrific results on its objects. … But had well-established study should be joined with another, equally important one: the impact of racism on those who perpetuate it … to see what racial ideology does to the mind, imagination, and behavior of masters (Morrison, 1992, S. 11).

A concept that started in the United States, critical whiteness, is now being practiced in Europe in various approaches (Arndt, 2006). Here, the category of whiteness serves as a starting point for critically reflecting on the construction of the norm that is given by whiteness and from which the others as the deviation—namely people of color—are produced. At the same time, it becomes clear that whiteness itself is not a neutral or universal category and must always be understood as interdependent (Butler, 1993).

Just like postcolonial criticism, critical whiteness calls for a change of perspective, away from the images of the so-called others and toward those who produce these images. Together, they pursue the goal of radically questioning the construction of a "coherent, stable white Western subject" that constructs itself in opposition to the colonial other and of exposing "homogeneously imagined collectives such as 'people' or 'nation' as imaginary constructions" (Wollrad, 2005, p. 124). The aim of critical whiteness is to question the construction of normality and of whiteness as an "unmarked marker" (Frankenberg,

Critical Whiteness as a Professional Approach to Inclusive Teaching

1997, p. 1) and to mark it as racialized (Röggla 2012, 30): "As long as race is something only applied to non-white peoples, as long as white people are not racially seen and named, they/we function as a human norm. Other people are raced, we are just people" (Dyer, 2011, p. 9). In this context, whiteness as a nonvisible norm is examined in terms of its power and structural anchoring to find out how power is produced and access to resources is linked to it (Hirsbrunner, 2012, p. 30). At the same time, the unconsciously racist structures are to be uncovered.

When we are white, we learn to accept whiteness as such granted that we can't even notice that being white in a racist society is an incredible privilege. The position protects us from so many painful experiences: being excluded; being rudely questioned and interrogated; being afraid in spaces that others would describe as neutral; being shamed and ridiculed; not being waited on ... (do Castro Varela, 2017, n. pag.).

"Critical whiteness" focuses on the idea that whiteness is not an immutable "component of body and identity" (Wollrad, 2005, p. 82), but a "relational category" (Wollrad, 2005, p. 127). It is produced in opposition to homogenized constructions of so-called non-whites, e.g. by describing them as backward, misogynistic, and unsophisticated (Frankenberg, 1997; Wollrad, 2005). Race gets its meaning through multiple coded attributions (Nghi Ha, 2011). Whiteness is produced in an ambivalent, quite violent, and painful process of internalizing norms, curtailing sensibilities, sanctioning relationships, and practicing "distancing oneself from those who are not supposed to belong" (Rommelspacher, 2002, p. 84).

Whiteness is "not a fixed and unloseable element of body and identity" but can be "imposed, lost or fought for" (Wollrad, 2005, p. 127). Wollrad describes whiteness as an ambivalent process: Even if it is perceived as a seemingly natural state, it requires explicit efforts to guarantee the permanent whiteness of the offspring (Wollrad, 2005). This is a thoroughly violent and painful process of internalizing norms, practicing "distancing oneself from those who are not supposed to belong" (Rommelspacher, 2002, p. 19). In the 1950s, for example, white German women who had children with black men were forced to give their children to foster care (Wollrad, 2005). For Wollrad, this results in a "violation of integrity" (Wollrad, 2005, p. 82). She refers to "the wages for whiteness" (Wollrad, 2005, p. 82) because, in her view, whiteness must be analyzed "also in terms of damage," linked to an analysis of the "feelings of horror, pain, loss, anger and rage" about the loss of "richer and more inclusive dimensions of one's own sentience" (Wollrad, 2005, p. 84).

Whiteness thus functions as a trait, a master signifier (Seshadri-Crooks, 2000) that selects by including and excluding individuals through certain visually visible physical characteristics (Arndt, 2006). Insofar as whiteness is entangled with other dimensions of inequality such as gender and class, the subtle effect of exclusionary processes based on skin color is intensified (Wollrad, 2005). Because society is constituted through multilayered forms of exclusion and discrimination and because one can also lose belonging to the normal group, whiteness promises a belonging that one apparently obtains without one's own explicit efforts and apparently cannot be lost. It is the "reward of whiteness" (Wollrad, 2005, p. 84) that belonging to the white group promises to be unquestioningly valid, as do the privileges that come with it: to simply feel normal, to belong to a group of people to whom a certain superiority is inherent (Wollrad, 2005).

In fact, however, even belonging to the white group is not an untouchable privilege and must be defended (even if often unconsciously). Kerner cites the different starting points of the engagement with whiteness in Europe, especially in Germany, and the United States and their different histories of racism (Kerner, 2013). In addition to the history of colonial racism, Germany is marked by a history of "antisemitism, antiziganism and, more recently, anti-muslimism," and has developed forms of racism that were formed in "recourse to national, cultural, or religious differences" (Kerner, 2013, p. 283). According to Kerner, these are "forms of racism that take place between whites, as measured by the U.S. state classification system, and not between whites and non-whites" (Kerner, 2013, p. 283). Whiteness is not nonhierarchical, but contested, and belonging to the group of the superior is contested.

White people are often subject to "color blindness" (Amesberger & Halbmayr, 2008, p. 124). This refers to the denial and defense of white people regarding their socio-political role within racial ideology. This is an expression of the invisibility of whiteness (Hirsbrunner, 2012). Because one's own identity is not be seen in racialized terms, the socialization teaches people to overlook whiteness in the so-called majority society and to focus on the othering of non-white people. Because society does not want to be perceived as racist (anymore), noticing otherness in this context is marked by the fact that it is understood as a "tactful, generous gesture" to ignore the perception of race. In fact, according to Amesberger and Halbmayr (2008), the opposite is true: to claim that everyone is equal is not to acknowledge and even deny an experience of discrimination. To recognize race is to "acknowledge an already discredited difference" (Morrison, 1992, p. 30).

Ha (2014) points out that those who, by virtue of a carefully cultivated self-image, already consider themselves "enlightened and free of prejudice" are reluctant to be irritated by perspectives and insights that challenge supposed self-evident truths," such as the freedom to name minoritized others to one's own liking or the [supposed] right to polemic, as white privilege debunks" (Ha, 2014, n. pag.).

In the more recent debate on critical whiteness, criticism of dogmatically hardened interpretations of the critique of privilege also emerges. In the German-language reception of critical whiteness studies, this is understood programmatically (Kerner, 2013). Nevertheless, critical whiteness should challenge a reflection on whiteness that is not misunderstood as a form of intellectual confession. Contrary to a "dogmatically ossified whiteness approach" (Ha, 2014, p. 53), neither critical whiteness nor people of color politics should be interpreted schematically. In the discussion about privilege, it is therefore important to consider the intersectionality of inequality dimensions and to note that it is not possible to "shed White socialization and White privilege on the basis of an individual decision alone" (Wollrad, 2005, p. 87). This "trivialises ... the institutional character of whiteness as a social power factor" (Wollrad, 2005, p. 87). Just as individuals cannot become white independently of the structures of white supremacy, individuals cannot shed their whiteness like a "worn-out coat" (Wollrad, 2005, p. 87).

If we adopt this less individualized, and unfortunately more pessimistic notion of racism and white privilege, it becomes clear that these forms of injustice cannot be undone by mere acts of making them visible and by personal endeavors of sharing that might follow from such acts. Instead, larger scale societal change is needed to undo these wrongs, change that affects institutions, societal patterns of thought and representation as well as individual mindsets (Kerner, 2007, n. pag.).

Bee (2013) states that at an individual level, it should therefore not be about a listing of privileges, but about building real relationships and political movements with the intention of really making a difference; for example, by working together with your neighbors against gentrification.

Therefore, I hold that white self-reflection attempting the change of white self-perceptions can never be the final or sufficient political goal of Critical Whiteness Studies. Rather, it should be considered as one possible starting point within broadly defined antiracist efforts that address and attack the other dimensions as well. Surely this is a very demanding task. But as long as there is racism, quick and easy solutions don't seem to be on offer (Kerner, 2007, n. pag.).

Whiteness is also a performative act. There are three forms:

1. Participation in the denial of whiteness and the refusal to locate oneself and others in a racial construct
2. The overemphasis and exaggeration of whiteness as the epitome of purity and superiority
3. The white gaze on blacks, which functions as "taxing and marking" (Wollrad 2003, p. 132) the "othered" body

It is important to say that through the pigmentation of the skin, differences between people are constructed out of white power of definition (Hirsbrunner, 2012). Overcoming difference is not done by ignoring or denying it.

HIGHER EDUCATION AS WHITE SPACE

Unfortunately, it is not sufficient to structurally embed topics that address discrimination dynamics, such as the compulsory implementation of courses on heterogeneity or diversity. If students and faculty are forced to complete those courses, this can lead to a de-politicization of the topics by faculty and a rather indifferent and dismissive and ultimately unreflective attitude of students toward racism and the critique of racism (Boger & Simon, 2022).

Nevertheless, the nature of education in higher education is political, and must be, because every social order is a product of powerful mechanisms (Grabau, 2022). Following Hannah Arendt's reflections on the political in education, that the claim of a common world excludes the experiences and voices of those who do not feel belonging in it (Grabau, 2022), educational institutions such as higher education are places of narration of what the common world is in detail. This refers to traditions, institutions, rules, and narratives. Where these shared narratives, which are always expressions of domination, are at stake because they are challenged, the function and authority of the teachers are also at stake (Grabau, 2022). Therefore, maintaining traditional teaching practices such as presuppositions and certain formats also always has a privilege-preserving function.

Thus, starting from an epistemological moment, higher education that is aware of diversity is able to overcome social power relations or reduce them more and more (Mecheril & Melter, 2010). At the same time, on a didactic level, it must be questioned which experiences are heard and are not being heard (Grabau, 2022).

SOLUTIONS AND RECOMMENDATIONS: CRITICAL WHITENESS AS A FRAMEWORK FOR INCLUSIVE TEACHING IN HIGHER EDUCATION

In higher education, the defensive mechanisms against critical reflection on racism must be taken into account. Insofar as racist practices are mostly unconsciously adopted, students often react in a frightened and defensive way when confronted with the ideas of critical whiteness. Ogette (2017) refers to the state in which white people live before they actively and consciously engage with racism "Happyland." Here, there is a consensus that racists are the Other, that racism is something morally bad and has to do with intention: "The only person who can be accused of racism, then, is someone who deliberately decides that the action or what follows should be racist" (Ogette 2017, p. 22). As a result of equating racism with being a "bad person," white Germans react "defensively and angrily to even the slightest suggestion that anything in their behaviour or utterances indicates racism" (Ogette 2017, p. 22).

In addition, as a result of multiple dimensions of inequality in society, there is often a confused debate in which different dimensions of inequality are played off against each other. However, the debate on white privilege does not deny that there are also white people who are affected by other dimensions of inequality (such as disability), who have had negative experiences, and who do not benefit from various privileges. However, it shows that being of color is a meaningful dimension of inequality that cuts off access to resources, while whiteness is the norm. The challenge is therefore not to narrow the multilayered discourse on privilege and inequality dimensions, but to focus on the inequality dimension of race and to stimulate a reflection on whiteness that has hardly been done so far.

Because debates about privilege often end up in justifications and confusing debates about dimensions of inequality, the method of zooming helps to make people aware of which dimension of inequality should be focused on in the discussion without ignoring that there are others as well. The method of zooming uses the image of a camera that has a lens. With the help of the zoom, the photographer can zoom in on a detail of the whole to be seen, sharpen it, and thus enable a detailed view. Transferred to the complex intersectional field of inequality dimensions, the method also pursues the intention of creating a sharpness of detail by zooming in on a dimension of the complex set of circumstances: Against the background of the complex diversity of students at universities, a certain structural category (e.g., race or gender) is zoomed in and brought into focus. The focus is "with sensitivity for the fact that this is never independent from its further structural influences" (Wischer & Spiering-Schomborg, 2020, p. 370). This is therefore a focus on detail, but does not claim to grasp diversity in all its complexity (Wischer & Spiering-Schomborg, 2020).

The list of characteristics in which people can differ is long and accentuated differently depending on the point of view. In this chapter, we consider the following bipolar differences as characteristics of a person relevant in educational settings: gender, sexuality, race, ethnicity, nationality/state, class/social status, religion, language, culture, disability, age, North-South/West-East, and level of social development (Krüger-Potratz & Lutz, 2002). Race is only one aspect among many that is sometimes given little weight. However, it is important to implicitly address the many possible backgrounds of students to make their personal learning meaningful (Riemeier, 2007). Making race a permanent topic is unnecessary; it is rather the basic attitude and the communicated openness to give space, from the learners' own positions, to make the aspects relevant to them a topic and here also to acknowledge their personal life realities and experiences as a kind of expertise. The Center for Teaching and Learning at Columbia University has published a highly regarded Guide for Inclusive Teaching at Columbia. This guide aims to provide a supportive learning environment for all students by explicitly taking into account their social, cultural, health, and educational backgrounds. The guide includes five teaching principles:

1. Create and support a classroom climate that promotes belonging for all students
2. Set explicit expectations towards students
3. Select course content that acknowledges diversity and recognises barriers towards inclusion
4. Design all course elements to be accessible

Critical Whiteness as a Professional Approach to Inclusive Teaching

5. Reflect on own beliefs about teaching to maximise awareness and commitment to inclusion (CLT, 2020, p. 8)

Especially relevant for teaching in higher education from a reflective, critically white perspective are principles 1 (belonging), 2 (diversity/course content), and 5 (own beliefs).

These teaching principles stem from the approach of universal design for learning, a teaching concept designed to provide instruction that is relevant and accessible to all students and that serves here as a lens for aspects that should be considered in preparing courses. Based on current learning research, universal design for learning offers suggestions for designing flexible conducive learning environments for all learners so that barriers to learning can be removed and actual learning can become the focus.

Columbia University takes an approach that focuses more on teaching in higher with a focus on social justice. A far more technical approach that focuses on school-based teaching is taken by CAST, who distribute didactic decisions on a framework that is divided at the top level into engagement, representation, action, and expression (CAST, 2018). Under the aspect of engagement, the teaching person should give space to the students' personal interests and take their life realities into account. This includes reflecting on the fact that their lives can be completely different from their own (white) reality. Under the aspect of representation, the teacher can take a look at the participants' preconditions and ask him or herself whether he or she is compatible with the contents of the seminar and the tasks. A key aspect at this point is the selection of materials and content.

In summary, it can be quite rewarding to embrace race as a relevant category in teaching. Consciously reflecting on critical whiteness has the potential to be a big step towards inclusive teaching in higher education, which we hope to encourage through our contribution.

REFERENCES

Amesberger, H., & Halbmayr, B. (2008). *Das privileg der unsichtbarkeit: Rassismus unter dem blickwinkel von weißsein und dominanzkultur*. Braumüller.

Arndt, S. (2006). The racial turn: Kolonialismus, weiße mythen und critical whiteness studies. In M. Bechhaus-Gerst & S. Gieseke (Eds.), *Koloniale und postkoloniale Kontruktionen von Afrika und Menschen afrikanischer Herkunft in der deutschen Alltagskultur* (pp. 11–26). Peter Lang.

Bechhaus-Gerst, M., & Gieseke, S. (Eds.). (2006). *Koloniale und postkoloniale kontruktionen von Afrika und menschen Afrikanischer herkunft in der Deutschen alltagskultur*. Peter Lang.

Bee, M. (2018). *Das problem mit critical whiteness*. Migrazine. http://migrazine.at/artikel/das-problem-mit-critical-whiteness

Betz, T., Bollig, S., Joos, M., & Neumann, S. (Eds.). (2018). *Gute Kindheit: Wohlbefinden, Kindeswohl und Ungleichheit*. Juventa.

Bliemetsrieder, S., & Beinzger, D. (2022). Das Ethische und das Politische als Kritik an und in der Lehrer*innenbildung: Verantwortung und gerechtigkeitsambitionierte Einmischungen als normative Orientierungen. In O. Ivanova-Chessex, S. Shure, & A. Steinbach (Eds.), *Lehrer*innenbildung: (Re-) Visionen für die Migrationsgesellschaft* (pp. 116–131). Beltz.

Boger, M.-A., & Simon, N. (2022). Kritik im Pflichtmodul Heterogenität: Paradoxien der (Ent-) Politisierung in der Lehrer*innenbildung. In O. Ivanova-Chessex, S. Shure, & A. Steinbach (Eds.), *Lehrer*innenbildung: (Re-)Visionen für die Migrationsgesellschaft* (pp. 20–35). Beltz.

Butler, J. (1993). *Bodies that matter: On the discursive limits of "sex."*. Routledge.

Center for Teaching and Learning. (2020). *Guide for inclusive teaching at Columbia.* Columbia CTL. https://ctl.columbia.edu/resources-and-technology/resources/inclusive-teaching-guide/download/

do Mar Castro Varela, M. (2017). *(Un-)Wissen: Verlernen als komplexer lernprozess.* Migrazine. https://www.migrazine.at/artikel/un-wissen-verlernen-als-komplexer-lernprozess

do Mar Castro Varela, M. (2022). Schule, nationalstaat und die vermittlung von herrschaftswissen: Postkoloniale betrachtungen. In O. Ivanova-Chessex, S. Shure, & A. Steinbach (Eds.), *Lehrer*innenbildung: (Re-)visionen für die migrationsgesellschaft* (pp. 36–49). Beltz.

do Mar Castro Varela, M., & Dhawan, N. (2005). *Postkoloniale Theorie: Eine kritische Einführung* (Transcript). Center for Applied Special Technology.

Dyer, R. (2011). The matter of whiteness. In P. S. Rothenberg (Ed.), *White privilege: Essential readings on the other side of racism* (pp. 9–14). Worth Publishing.

Essed, P., & Goldberg, D. T. (Eds.). (2001). *Race critical theories: Text and context.* Wiley-Blackwell.

Foucault, M. (1977). *Dispositive der macht: Über sexualität, wissen und wahrheit.* Merve.

Frankenberg, R. (Ed.). (1997). *Local whitenesses, localizing whiteness, displacing whiteness: Essays in social and cultural criticism.* Duke University Press.

Frankenberg, R. (1997). Introduction. In R. Frankenberg (Ed.), *Local whitenesses, localizing whiteness, displacing whiteness: Essays in social and cultural criticism* (pp. 1–34). Duke University Press.

Gewöhnliche Unterscheidungen. (2010). Wege aus dem rassismus. In P. Mecheril, M. do Mar Castro Varela, İ. Dirim, A. Kalpaka, & C. Melter (Eds.), *Bachelor | master migrationspädagogik* (pp. 150–178). Beltz GmbH, Julius.

Grabau, C. (2022). Wessen welt ist die welt? Hannah Arendt, Little Rock und die "autorität des lehrers.". In O. Ivanova-Chessex, S. Shure, & A. Steinbach (Eds.), *Lehrer*innenbildung: (Re-)visionen für die migrationsgesellschaft* (pp. 55–60). Beltz.

Grümme, B. (2017). *Heterogenität in der religionspädagogik: Grundlagen und konkrete bausteine.* Herder.

Guillaumin, C. (1995). *Racism, sexism, power and ideology.* Routledge.

Ha, K. N. (2010). *Unrein und vermischt: Postkoloniale grenzgänge durch die kulturgeschichte der hybridität und der kolonialen rassenbastarde.* Transcript.

Ha, K. N. (2014). *Mittelweg: Zur kritik am people of color—und critical whiteness—ansatz.* Heimatkunde. https://heimatkunde.boell.de/de/2014/01/29/mittelweg-zur-kritik-am-people-color-und-critical-whiteness-ansatz

Critical Whiteness as a Professional Approach to Inclusive Teaching

Hegel, G. W. F. (1848). *Vorlesung über die philosophie der geschichte.* Suhrkamp.

Hirsbrunner, S. (2012). *Sorry about colonialism: Weiße helden in kontemporären hollywoodfilmen.* Tectum Wissenschaftsverlag.

hooks, b. (1992). *Black looks: Race and representation.* South End Press.

Ivanova-Chessex, O., Shure, S., & Steinbach, A. (Eds.). (2022). *Lehrer*innenbildung: (Re-)visionen für die migrationsgesellschaft.* Beltz.

Joos, M., Betz, T., Bollig, S., & Neumann, S. (2018). Gute kindheit als gegenstand der forschung: Wohl-befinden, kindeswohl und ungleiche kindheiten. In T. Betz, S. Bollig, M. Joos, & S. Neumann (Eds.), *Gute kindheit: Wohlbefinden, kindeswohl und ungleichheit* (pp. 7–27). Beltz Juventa.

Kant, I. (1983). Kritik der urteilskraft: Beobachtungen über das gefühl des schönen und erhabenen. In W. Weischedel (Ed.), *Immanuel Kants werke: Gesamtausgabe in zehn bänden* (Vol. 7). Wissenschaftliche Buchgesellschaft.

Kaul, I., Schmidt, D., & Thole, W. (Eds.). (2018). *Kinder und kindheiten. Studien zur empirie der kind-heit: Unsicherheiten, herausforderungen und zumutungen.* Springer. doi:10.1007/978-3-658-19484-0

Kaul, I., Schmidt, D., & Thole, W. (2018). Blick auf kinder und kindheiten unsicherheiten, herausfor-derungen und zumutungen. In I. Kaul, D. Schmidt, & W. Thole (Eds.), Kinder und kindheiten. Studien zur empirie der kindheit: Unsicherheiten, herausforderungen und zumutungen (pp. 1–11). Springer.

Kerner, I. (2013). Critical whiteness studies: Potentiale und grenzen eines wissenspolitischen projekts. *Feministische Studien: Zeitschrift Für Interdisziplinäre Frauen- Und Geschlechterforschung, 31*(2), 278–293. doi:10.1515/fs-2013-0209

Kerner, I. (2017). *Challenges of critical whiteness studies.* EIPCP. https://translate.eipcp.net/strands/03/kerner-strands01en.html

Kilomba, G. (2009). *Das N-wort.* BPB. https://www.bpb.de/gesellschaft/migration/afrikanischediaspora/

Kiper, H. (2008). Zur diskussion um heterogenität in gesellschaft, pädagogik und unterrichtstheorie. In H. Kiper & S. Miller (Eds.), *Lernprozesse professionell gestalten* (pp. 78–105).

Kiper, H., & Miller, S. (Eds.). (2008). *Lernprozesse professionell gestalten.* Klinkhardt.

Knauth, T., Möller, R., & Pithan, A. (Eds.). (2020). *Inklusive religionspädagogik der vielfalt: Konzep-tionelle grundlagen und didaktische konkretionen.* Waxmann.

Krüger, D., & Vogt, H. (Eds.). (2007). *Theorien in der biologiedidaktischen forschung: Springer-Lehrbuch.* Springer. doi:10.1007/978-3-540-68166-3

Krüger-Potratz, M., & Lutz, H. (2002). Sitting at a crossroads: Rekonstruktive und systematische überlegungen zum wissenschaftlichen umgang mit differenzen. *Tertium Comparationis, 8*(2), 81–92. doi:10.25656/01:2922

McIntosh, P. (Ed.). (2019). *On privilege, fraudulence, and teaching as learning: Selected essays 1981–2019.* Routledge. doi:10.4324/9781351133791

McIntosh, P. (2019). White privilege: Unpacking the invisible knapsack. In P. McIntosh (Ed.), *On privilege, fraudulence, and teaching as learning: Selected essays 1981–2019*. Routledge., doi:10.4324/9781351133791

Mecheril, P., do Mar Castro Varela, M., Dirim, İ., Kalpaka, A., & Melter, C. (Eds.). (2010). *Bachelor | master migrationspädagogik*. Beltz.

Mecheril, P., & Melter, C. (2010). Gewöhnliche unterscheidungen: Wege aus dem rassismus. In P. Mecheril, İ. Dirim, M. do Mar Castro Varela, A. Kalpaka, & C. Melter (Eds.), *Migrationspädagogik* (pp. 150–178). Beltz.

Morrison, T. (1992). *Playing in the dark: Whiteness and the literary imagination*. Vintage Books (A Division of Random House, Inc.).

Morrison, T. (2001). Black matters. In P. Essed & D. T. Goldberg (Eds.), *Race critical theories*. Wiley-Blackwell.

Ogette, T. (2017). *Exit racism: Rassismuskritisch denken lernen*. Unrast.

Renschler, R., & Preiswerk, R. (Eds.). (1981). *Das gift der frühen jahre: Rassismus in der jugendliteratur*. Basel Lenos.

Riemeier, T. (2007). Moderater konstruktivismus. In D. Krüger & H. Vogt (Eds.), Theorien in der biologiedidaktischen forschung: Springer-Lehrbuch (pp. 69–79). Springer. doi:10.1007/978-3-540-68166-3_7

Röggla, K. (2012). *Critical whiteness studies und ihre politischen handlungsmöglichkeiten für weiße antirassistinnen*. Mandelbaum.

Rommelspacher, B. (2002). *Anerkennung und ausgrenzung: Deutschland als multikulturelle gesellschaft*. Campus.

Rothenberg, P. S. (Ed.). (2011). *White privilege: Essential readings on the other side of racism*. Worth Publishers.

SchröterA.ZimenkovaT. (2019). Norm und normalität: Reflexion der eigenen positionen von angehenden lehrkräften innerhalb des machtfeldes schule und schaffung nicht-normativer räume in der lehre. *Herausforderung Lehrer_innenbildung, Zeitschrift Zur Konzeption, Gestaltung Und Diskussion, 2*(3), 47–62. doi:10.4119/hlz-2455

Schwab, S. (2014). *Schulische integration, soziale partizipation und emotionales wohlbefinden in der schule. Ergebnisse einer empirischen Längsschnittstudie*. Lit. Verlag.

Tißberger, M. (2009). Die psyche der macht, der rassismus der psychologie und die psychologie des rassimus. In M. Tißberger, G. Dietze, D. Hrzán, & J. Husmann-Kastein (Eds.), *Weiß—Weißsein—Whiteness: Kritische studien zu gender und rassismus—Critical studies on gender and racism* (pp. 13–29). Peter Lang.

Tißberger, M., Dietze, G., Hrzán, D., & Husmann-Kastein, J. (Eds.). (2009). *Weiß—Weißsein—Whiteness: Kritische studien zu gender und rassismus—Critical studies on gender and racism*. Peter Lang.

Walgenbach, K. (2017). *Heterogenität—intersektionalität–diversity in der erziehungswissenschaft*. UTB. doi:10.36198/9783838586700

Weischedel, W. (Ed.). (1983). *Immanuel Kants werke: Gesamtausgabe in zehn bänden* (Vol. 7). Wissenschaftliche Buchgesellschaft.

Wischer, M., & Spiering-Schomborg, N. (2020). Zooming: Ein werkzeug zum produktiv-verändernden umgang mit intersektionalität in religiösen lernprozessen. In T. Knauth, R. Möller, & A. Pithan (Eds.), *Inklusive religionspädagogik der vielfalt: Konzeptionelle grundlagen und didaktische konkretionen* (pp. 363–374). Waxmann.

Wollrad, E. (2003). *Zur dekonstruktion von weißsein*. PolyLog. https://them.polylog.org/4/cwe-de.htm

Wollrad, E. (2005). *Weißsein im widerspruch: Feministische perspektiven auf rassismus, kultur und religion*. Ulrike Helmer Verlag.

KEY TERMS AND DEFINITIONS

Critical Whiteness: A theoretical approach that addresses the power of whiteness within racism. Whiteness is critically looked at as a category that plays a role within racism and is not invisible.

Higher Education: Higher Education is teaching at universities. It is curricularly organised. Students should acquire certain competences. These include professional competences (knowledge and methods) and personal competences (social and personal abilities, and skills).

Inclusive Teaching in Higher Education: Inclusive Teaching in Higher Education focuses on the diversity of its students. Teaching is designed on the basis of the different prerequisites for learning. For example, through different ways of taking exams or learning according to one's own strengths and interests.

Inclusive Teaching: Inclusive teaching aims to ensure that every pupil, with their talents, challenges and backgrounds, can follow the mainstream curriculum with the individual support they need.

Postcolonialismus: Postcolonialism is a school of thought that deals with the history of European colonialism and imperialism. It aims at decolonisation and political sovereignty of the former colonies. It also raises awareness of the persistence of imperialist structures in various areas of life, such as politics and economics.

Racism: Racism is an ideology that stereotypes people based on external characteristics or negative ascriptions. They are categorised as a "race" or "ethnicity" and excluded. This is done primarily on the basis of biological characteristics (skin colour, shape of face and body, etc.). Racism is used to justify slavery, exploitation and even genocide.

Universal Design for Learning: A framework based on current learning research, which offers suggestions for designing flexible conducive learning environments for all learners so that barriers to learning can be removed and actual learning can become the focus.

Chapter 12

Special Education Policy in the United States and Ireland:
Comparisons and Analysis Through the Lens of Universal Design for Learning

Andrea R. Harkins-Brown
School of Education, Johns Hopkins University, USA

Margaret Flood
Maynooth University, Ireland

ABSTRACT

A global human rights and social justice agenda has influenced governments to recognize their responsibility to achieve a system of inclusive education for students with disabilities. Inclusive education in the United States is defined by the premise that all eligible students be provided with a free appropriate public education, as outlined by the Individuals with Disabilities Education Act. In Ireland, though now in a period of review, the Education of Persons with Special Educational Needs Act is considered a coherent framework for inclusive education for students with special educational needs. Internationally, universal design for learning is recognized as an approach that supports the development of inclusivity in schools. This chapter outlines the national policies governing special education in American and Irish schools. Using a UDL lens, this chapter provides a synthesis of key principles of the IDEA and EPSEN; highlights alignments between these acts and the principles of UDL; and compares the policies to provide a critical analysis within an international context.

INTRODUCTION

The purpose of this chapter is to examine two national policies that were enacted in 2004: The Individuals with Disabilities Education Act (IDEA) in the United States and The Education for Persons with Special Educational Needs Act (EPSEN) in Ireland. A detailed description of the key principles of each policy will be outlined, accompanied by an analysis of each through the lens of Universal Design for

DOI: 10.4018/978-1-6684-7370-2.ch012

Copyright © 2023, IGI Global. Copying or distributing in print or electronic forms without written permission of IGI Global is prohibited.

Special Education Policy in the United States and Ireland

Learning (UDL). These comparisons and analysis will support the justification of UDL as a vehicle for enhancing inclusive education for all children, including those with disabilities. This cross-national comparison is designed to advance scholarly and policy-oriented advocacy discussions related to the reauthorization of both acts and emphasize the ways that these countries can learn from one another's legislation. Finally, the relationship of these acts in the United States and Ireland will be more broadly situated within an international agenda for inclusive education as a means of promoting greater equity for students with disabilities (SWDs) across the world.

BACKGROUND

Inclusion and the International Context

This chapter focuses on inclusive policy in the United States and Ireland. These examples of national legislation have been influenced by the international community and a global context. Inclusive education for children with disabilities has been a pervasive, worldwide challenge (Entrich, 2021). One of the most widely recognized efforts at achieving international inclusive education is exemplified by the *Salamanca Statement and Framework for Action on Special Needs Education* (commonly referred to as the Salamanca Agreement), developed by the United Nations Educational, Scientific and Cultural Organization (UNESCO) in 1994 (UNESCO, 1994). The Salamanca Agreement was a groundbreaking effort culminating in a written statement designed to create international prioritization of inclusive education for children with disabilities around the world, receiving support from 92 governments and 25 international organizations (Shyman, 2015). The Agreement emphasized nations' obligations to act by developing policies that supported the infrastructure of inclusive education, later leading to the United Nations Convention on the Rights of Persons with Disabilities. The Convention ultimately led to the development of an international policy framework known as *Education for All* in 2000, which established six main priorities for providing comprehensive services, including early childhood education, to vulnerable children (Shyman, 2015). Despite these actions, including a myriad of other related initiatives at the international level by UNESCO and the Organization for Economic Co-operation and Development (OCED), there are disproportionate opportunities and cross-national differences in inclusive education afforded to children worldwide (Entrich, 2021; Hardy & Woodcock, 2015).

Current data on the implementation of inclusive policy and how it impacts children across countries is problematic and wrought with cross-national discrepancies that make reporting and analysis challenging (Entrich, 2021). Overall, national policies vary, with little consistency in countries' interpretations of the existing UNESCO guidance (Hardy & Woodcock, 2015). Hardy and Woodcock (2015) conducted an analysis of inclusive education policies in the United States, Canada, England, and Australia, using a critical lens. While all the examined countries had drafted national policies that addressed the right to inclusive education for SWDs, countries varied in their implementation of stated expectations, exemplified by the key barriers commonly discussed in the literature and situated within specific national contexts (Hardy & Woodcock, 2015). For instance, due to the decentralization of education to provinces and conditions related to economic competitiveness in education, Canadian schools were identified as being in the early stages of inclusion. Similarly, in England, inclusive education revealed sporadic patterns of inclusion, exemplified by policies that "lack coherence and consistency over time" (Hardy & Woodcock,

2015, p. 159). At the national level, Australia showed signs of progress toward inclusive education, but with variations in how inclusion was implemented within various states (Hardy & Woodcock, 2015).

Because countries differ significantly in their cultural contexts, some have hypothesized that economics plays a role in a country's ability to include children with disabilities in public education. However, in a study of cross-national differences of over 50 societies, Entrich (2021) found that factors such as economic resources and political conviction "were found to exert no effect on the provision of inclusive education" and that additional financial resources were not necessarily required to achieve the aim of inclusive education (p. 36). International experts concur that the gap between policy intent and implementation of inclusive schooling may not be the result of economic resources. In a study examining the perspectives of international inclusion experts, participants shared that while fiscal resources could ease the strain of costs associated with inclusion and special education, it was more often conflicting beliefs that prevented the inclusive education of SWDs (Kurth et al., 2018). In fact, an overabundance of resources can hinder inclusive education, such as in wealthier countries where money can be used to create separate schools and programs (Kurth et al., 2018). Internationally, cultural context is critical in inclusive education, particularly when governments are forced to make decisions based on exigent priorities, such as natural disasters, disease, or political unrest (Kurth et al., 2018). For these reasons, the implementation of a country's policy is not always straightforward and can result in a series of unintended consequences (Hardy & Woodcock, 2015). The comparisons here between the IDEA and EPSEN are meant to serve as examples of two inclusive acts existing in different cultural contexts, with an emphasis on the ways that UDL can be used as a bridge to support inclusive education.

UNIVERSAL DESIGN FOR LEARNING

UDL is a pedagogical approach to inclusive education informed by research in the neurosciences. With a focus on neuro-variability (CAST, 2018; Meyer at al., 2014), UDL's three key principles align to how the brain recognizes, processes, organizes, evaluates, engages with, and responds to information in a variety of ways. These principles include:

- Multiple Means of Engagement: the 'why' of learning which aligns to recruiting learner interest, sustaining learner effort and persistence, and learner regulation.
- Multiple Means of Representation: the 'what' of learning which aligns to learner perception, clarifying and understanding of language and symbols, and comprehension.
- Multiple Means of Action and Expression: the 'how' of learning which aligns to physical action with learning, expression and communication of learning while learning, and learner executive functioning to plan and organize their own learning.

The UDL principles and guidelines provide a way of designing learning experiences that proactively meet the needs of all learners, regardless of whether students are identified as having a disability. Universally designed classrooms are paramount to inclusive education because these learning environments embrace learner variability as the norm, allowing every student the opportunity to access instruction. The framework provides practical ways that educators can proactively reduce barriers to learning for all students, making UDL a foundational element for inclusive education.

Special Education Policy in the United States and Ireland

Federal Legislation in the United States

In the United States, introduction of federal legislation through passage of the IDEA has significantly influenced the services, supports, and educational opportunities available to SWDs. In the law, the United States Congress concluded that:

Disability is a natural part of the human experience and in no way diminishes the rights of individuals to participate in or contribute to society. Improving educational results for children with disabilities is an essential component of our national policy of ensuring quality of opportunity, full participation, independent living, and economic self-sufficiency for individuals with disabilities (IDEA, 2004, § 682).

The purpose of the IDEA is to provide all eligible children with disabilities access to a free and appropriate public education (FAPE) and to make certain that the rights afforded to these children and their parents are upheld as outlined in the law. The IDEA provides funding and implementation support to federal, state, and local education agencies for school-age children and establishes interagency systems of early intervention services for children ages birth to three. The IDEA is made up of six key principles: (1) the provision of FAPE; (2) nondiscriminatory evaluation procedures; (3) development, and implementation of an IEP for eligible students; (4) educational services provided in the least restrictive environment (LRE); (5) parent and student participation in decision-making; and (6) procedural due process or procedural safeguards. While the law is commonly referred to as having six principles, some argue that the law's concept of zero reject be considered a standalone principle (i.e., Lengyel et al., 2021). In this chapter, the principle of zero reject is discussed within the context of FAPE. In addition to outlining these six principles, we will also analyze each, wherever appropriate, through a UDL lens.

Figure 1. Six key principles of the individuals with disabilities education act

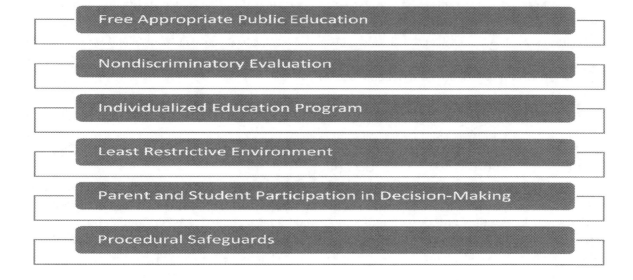

THE INDIVIDUALS WITH DISABILITIES EDUCATION ACT

IDEA Principle 1: Free Appropriate Public Education

Prior to the passage of the IDEA, children with disabilities were excluded from school and denied the opportunity to access instruction in the United States. The law outlines comprehensive coverage for all eligible children to receive special education and related services as defined by the zero reject principle. This principle is designed to prevent disability-based exclusion, discipline-based exclusion, and other forms of exclusion due to insufficient resources (Turnbull et al., 2007). The IDEA provides comprehensive coverage to all eligible children, including those who are not of traditional school age. Part C of the IDEA outlines the provision of services to eligible children from birth through age two with early intervention services, and Part B addresses eligibility and service provision for children between the ages of three and 21. Presently, implementation of the law affects more than seven million children and families in the United States. In 2019, more than 425,000 infants and toddlers were served under Part C and over 7.2 million children were served under Part B (USDE, 2022).

To provide all eligible children with FAPE, children who qualify must be located and identified. Each state and local jurisdiction has an obligation to identify and assess children who may be eligible for special education and related services. Through Child Find, the IDEA requires that each state and district identify, locate, and evaluate children suspected of having a disability or developmental delay in their respective jurisdictions, including children who are homeless, are wards of the state, or attend private schools (20 U.S.C. §1412(a)(3)). Once a child is identified, assessed, and deemed eligible, this child has a right to FAPE according to the IDEA. To understand the meaning of FAPE, it is helpful to break down each word in the acronym. *Free* means that the educational entity must provide the student with services at public expense and at no cost to the parent. *Appropriate* means that each child with a disability is entitled to an education, including special education and related services that meet his or her unique, individualized needs. *Public* refers to the rights of a child with a disability to access services in the public school system as outlined by the zero reject principle. All SWDs have a right to attend school, regardless of the severity of their disability. Finally, the term *education* guarantees that eligible children with disabilities receive a public education that includes access to general education and special education and related services as directed by the child's IEP. This education should prepare the child for the future, including employment and independent living.

Implementing FAPE

Response to Intervention, Multi-Tiered Systems of Support, and Universal Design for Learning

The IDEA recognizes that the basic tenets of high-quality instruction must be in place for all students, regardless of whether they are found eligible for special education. Response to Intervention, or RTI, involves a data-driven set of procedures using a tiered approach that analyzes a learner's needs and administers appropriate levels of support to that student (Parrish et al., 2021). Multi-Tiered Systems of Support (MTSS) is a related framework that systematically provides increasing levels of academic and behavior support and intensity. These frameworks are designed to prevent the overidentification of SWDs and ensure that all students receive timely evidence-based interventions that are designed to meet their unique needs.

As outlined previously, UDL recognizes the variability of all learners and is not specific to SWDs or special education. The framework is essential for ensuring that all students' academic and social emotional needs are met regardless of whether a child is eligible for special education. UDL emphasizes ways that educators can address and minimize barriers by maximizing accessibility in the instructional planning and implementation process, a mainstay of inclusive education (Parrish et al., 2021). For all students, including those with disabilities, the UDL principles should be integrated across all tiers of instruction and in all environments. Figure 2 outlines the tiered approach of RTI and MTSS, emphasizing the integration of UDL at all levels.

Figure 2. Application of universal design for learning to response to intervention and multi-tiered systems of support
(Source: Parrish et al., 2021)

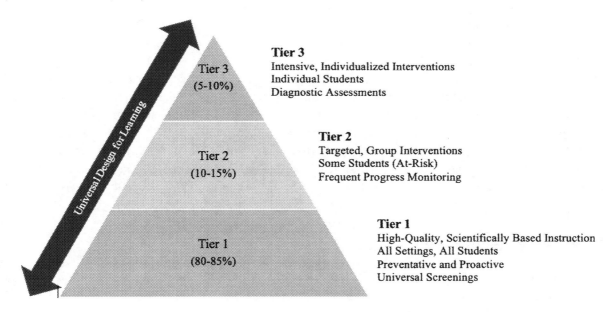

Specially Designed Instruction

In the United States, each student's IEP outlines the specific services and supports they need to receive FAPE. A primary element of FAPE is specially designed instruction, or the unique services and supports that the child with a disability needs to access and make progress in the general education curriculum. The IDEA (2004) defines specially designed instruction as:

Adapting, as appropriate to the needs of an eligible child under this part, the content, methodology or delivery of instruction (i) to address the unique needs of the child that result from the child's disability; and (ii) ensure access of the child to the general curriculum, so that the child can meet the educational standards within the jurisdiction of the public agency that apply to all children." (34 CFR § 300.39(b)(3))

Specially designed instruction looks different for each child with a disability, but for most children with disabilities, this involves more than differentiating instruction or integrating UDL. It may involve delivery of services from a special educator and/or other related service provider(s); intensive instruction delivered in an explicit and systematic manner; and/or remedial instruction that addresses achievement gaps as outlined in the child's IEP. Specially designed instruction must be delivered in a manner that is consistent with a student's IEP, accompanied by progress monitoring, and delivered by a qualified service provider.

IDEA Principle 2: Nondiscriminatory Evaluation

In the United States, a child is found eligible for special education and related services following a comprehensive, non-discriminatory evaluation. An evaluation is the process for determining whether a child has a disability and needs special education and related services. The term evaluation is not synonymous with *assessment* or *test*, as it refers to a *process*. The IDEA requires that a child suspected of having a disability receive a comprehensive evaluation prior to the initiation of services (20 U.S.C. 1414 § 614).

To conduct a comprehensive evaluation, the IDEA outlines that professionals must use a variety of assessment tools and strategies to gain information about a child's functional, development, and academic needs, rather than relying on a single test (20 U.S.C. 1414 § 614). This involves assessing a child in all areas of the suspected disability using technically sound instruments. Professionals select valid and reliable assessments which are not racially or culturally discriminatory and are administered in accordance with standardization protocols (20 U.S.C. 1414 § 614). When standardized assessments are used for eligibility purposes, there are less options for incorporating UDL, such as offering choice or flexibility in responding. Tests are provided in the student's native language or in a form most likely to yield accurate information unless it is not feasible to do so. Finally, the IDEA outlines that assessments be administered by personnel who have the requisite training and knowledge to serve as qualified examiners (20 U.S.C. 1414 § 614).

Disability Classification

The IDEA defines a child with a disability as one who (a) has an educational disability within a named classification area within the law, (b) experiences adverse educational impact due to that disability, and (c) needs specially designed instruction to address the effects of the disability on the child's educational performance. Appendix 1 outlines the IDEA disability categories and definitions for special education and related service eligibility (34 CFR § 300.8 (c)).

IDEA Principle 3: Individualized Education Program

In the United States, an IEP is a written statement for each child with a disability that is developed, reviewed, and revised by a child's IEP Team (34 CFR § 614 (d)(1)(a)(i)). The primary purpose of an IEP is to outline what constitutes FAPE for the child and the document is meant to ensure that a student with a disability receives FAPE. While the IEP is as a compliance and monitoring tool, it also serves other important functions. It is a communication vehicle between professionals, the family, and the child; a commitment of resources by the school and district; and a management tool and evaluation device for a student's annual progress (Pierangelo & Giuliani, 2007). A school or district is obligated to implement the support and services on a child's IEP with fidelity to provide the child with FAPE (Pierangelo & Giuliani, 2007). Figure 3 outlines the multiple purposes of the IEP, as described by Pierangelo and Giuliani (2007).

Figure 3. Purposes of an individualized education program

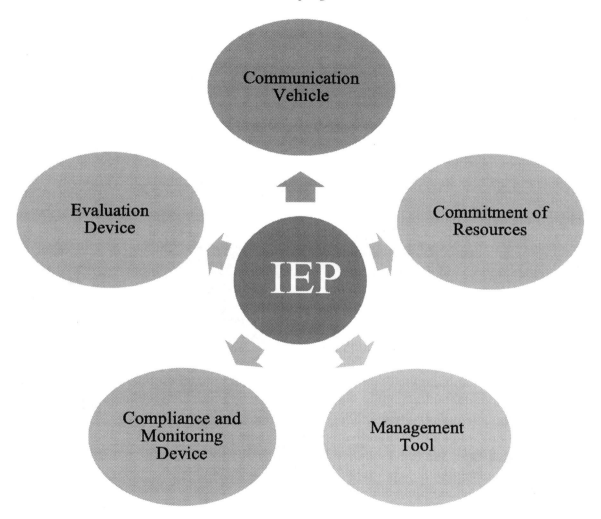

While states are entitled to develop their own formats for an IEP, there are key components that the IDEA specifies must be present. IEP Team members use current and relevant student-specific assessment information to develop a child's IEP. Each portion of the IEP is developed by answering a series of fundamental questions. While not an exhaustive list, Table 1 provides an overview of the key questions the IEP Team answers when developing a child's IEP as well as relevant applications for incorporating the principles of UDL.

Table 1. Fundamental questions to ask when developing the IEP and applications of UDL

IEP Component	Fundamental Questions, per the IDEA	Possible Applications of UDL
Present Levels of Academic Achievement and Functional Performance	• What are the child's present levels of academic achievement and functional performance, as indicated by current, relevant data and input from the child's parents? • How does the child's disability affect his or her involvement and progress in the general education curriculum? Or, for preschool students, how does the child's disability affect his or her participation in age-appropriate activities?	• Incorporate multiple means of action and expression when collecting informal classroom data for a student's present levels of academic achievement and functional performance.
Annual Goals and Short-Term Objectives	• What measurable annual goals, including academic and functional goals, are necessary to meet the student's needs that result from the disability, to allow the student access to the general education curriculum, and to address other educational needs resulting from the disability?	• Provide options for sustaining effort and persistence by heightening the salience of a student's IEP goals and objectives. • Provide options for perception; options for language and symbols; and options for comprehension in the condition statements within student IEP goals and objectives. • Provide multiple means of action and expression within statements of an expected observable, measurable student behavior.
Program Modifications, Accommodations, Supplementary Aids, and Services	• What special education and related services; supplementary aids and services; program modifications; or supports for school personnel will be provided to the child to (a) advance in attaining annual goals, (b) to be involved and make progress in the general education curriculum, and (c) to be educated with other children with disabilities and nondisabled children?	• Identify supplementary aids and program modifications that recruit a student's interest; provide options for sustaining effort and persistence; and provide options for self-regulation. • Outline the possible options for perception, language and symbols, and comprehension that are the best match for the student, based on the characteristics of his or her disability. • Based on assessment data, identify the multiple means of action and expression that align best with the student's disability characteristics, including those which the student has been most responsive to during previous assessment and instruction.
Student Participation in State and District Assessments	• Will the student participate in state and district-wide assessments aligned with the grade level achievement standards in the assigned grade or content area, and will the student require accommodations to participate?	• Consider and incorporate the UDL principles when selecting available accommodations. • Identify the allowable and applicable accommodations that a student needs to participate in state and district-wide assessments, based on relevant student data.
Extended School Year (ESY) Services	• Does the student qualify for ESY services based on the emergence of new skills; potential regression or recoupment of skills; or due to a lack of self-sufficiency? • If eligible, which services delineated in the IEP will be provided during the ESY timeframe and which critical skills will be addressed?	• Address UDL-infused IEP goals and objectives during extended school year services if the student is eligible for these services.
Least Restrictive Environment (LRE)	• To what extent, if any, will the student *not* be able to participate in the general education classroom? • How and to what extent will the student participate with nondisabled peers in nonacademic and extracurricular activities?	• In LRE decision-making, emphasize how the student can be successful in the general education classroom, when the UDL principles are present there. For example, a student should not have to exit the general education classroom to receive choice and flexibility in instruction. If elements of UDL are not present in the classroom, thoughtfully consider and create an action plan for how these principles can be incorporated to support the student's success in the general education classroom. • Address how the principles of UDL can be integrated across all learning environments, including specialized programs.
Secondary Transition Needs	• What coordinated, individualized activities are necessary to promote the student's successful transition from school to adulthood and to meet intended post-secondary outcomes?	• When designing a student's secondary transition goals, provide options for recruiting interest, sustaining effort and persistence in achieving goals, and options for self-regulation. • Provide opportunities for a student to practice and apply secondary transition-related skills in authentic environments.

Collaboration in the IEP Process

The IDEA mandates that the development of an IEP be a collaborative process involving professionals; the child's family; and, whenever appropriate, the child. This provides avenues for resolving disputes that arise between parents and the public agency and requires that the process engages both parents

Special Education Policy in the United States and Ireland

and professionals to participate in meaningful discussions (Pierangelo & Giuliani, 2007). The required members of the IEP Team include the parent and at least one general education teacher of the child if the child is or may be participating in the general education classroom. The team must also include at least one special educator, a representative of the public agency, and an individual qualified to interpret evaluation results. At the discretion of the parent or district, the team may also include other individuals who have knowledge or specific expertise regarding the child (34 CFR § 300.321). The IEP Team process is meant to exemplify partnership between professionals and families of SWDs. The most productive and effective team meetings are used as communication vehicles rather than formalities. IEP meetings provide an opportunity to discuss and brainstorm, share data, problem solve, share successes, and communicate challenges.

IEP Implementation and Progress Monitoring

Effective implementation of a child's IEP begins with service providers who are knowledgeable about the IEP's contents. Providers often need to collaborate to implement a child's IEP with fidelity. While collaboration among providers is important, so is the confidentiality of students. The IEP is a legal, confidential document. The Federal Educational Rights and Privacy Act (or FERPA) allows schools to disclose personally identifiable information only to school personnel who have a legitimate educational interest in this information (FERPA, 1974).

The IDEA requires that a child's special education program, as outlined, be in effect (20 U.S.C. 1414 (d)(2)). Determining whether a student's IEP is being implemented with fidelity is a critical factor in determining whether the student is being provided FAPE and for explaining how and to what extent a student is meeting expected outcomes. Fidelity in implementing a student's IEP is critical for maximizing the effectiveness of the interventions outlined (Jung et al., 2008). Assessing the fidelity of IEP implementation means determining whether school personnel are implementing the IEP services and supports in the way they are described and with the correct frequency and duration in the appropriate setting (IRIS Center, 2019). Reporting a student's progress toward annual goals is a requirement of the IDEA (34 CFR § 614(b)). Schools conduct IEP progress monitoring to determine if a child is progressing toward meeting his or her stated annual goals. The law requires that each IEP indicates how parents will be informed of their child's progress. Progress reports should include how the goal is being measured, the level of student progress, and an indication of whether the child is expected to meet each goal within the established timeframe (34 CFR § 614(b)).

IDEA Principle 4: Least Restrictive Environment

The concept of LRE, often referred to as inclusion, requires that SWDs be educated with nondisabled students to the greatest extent possible (20 U.S.C. 1412 (a) (5)). The IDEA is clear about the foundational research that supports its principle of educating SWDs in the LRE:

Almost 30 years of research and experience has demonstrated that the education of children with disabilities can be made more effective by having high expectations for such children and ensuring their access to the general education curriculum in the regular classroom to the maximum extent possible. (20 U.S.C. 1400 (c)(5))

The LRE principle is characterized by its emphasis on three key components: (a) access to peers without disabilities, (b) access to the general education curriculum, and (c) affordance of a continuum of service delivery options. Figure 4 shows these prevailing ideas of the LRE principle.

Figure 4. Key Components in the Least Restrictive Environment Principle

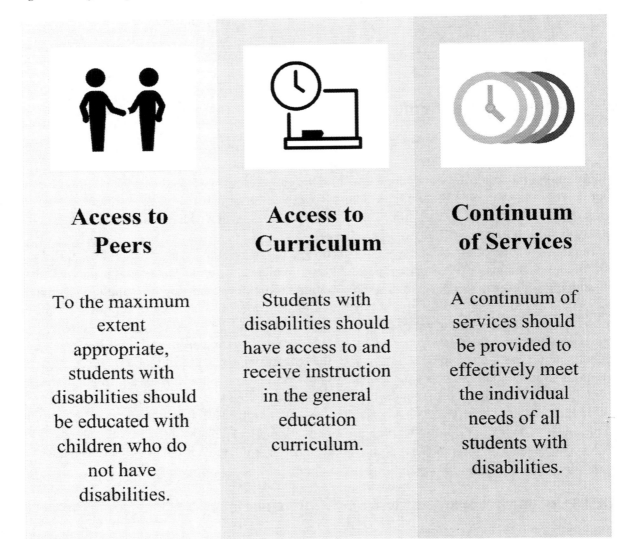

Research-Based Benefits of Inclusion

Literature provides empirical evidence of the benefits of inclusion for SWDs. In a synthesis of 280 studies examining the effects of inclusive education in 25 countries, Hehir et al. (2016) found strong evidence that SWDs academically outperformed students who were excluded from general education and positive trends in the social and emotional development of SWDs who were included. Studies have shown that inclusion in the general education classroom has positive effects on the academic achievement of students (Cole et al. 2020) and on the postsecondary outcomes of SWDs (Cole et al., 2022). Taylor et al. (2020) found that in studies examining the impact of the inclusion of students with intellectual and developmental disabilities, eight out of nine studies "reported a positive relationship between at least one inclusive education predictor and at least one postsecondary outcome in either employment or postsecondary education" (p. 306).

Research indicates that excluded students who were not provided access to the general education classroom experience poorer academic and post-secondary outcomes (Schiller et al., 2008). Specifically, students with severe disabilities receiving instruction in self-contained environments were found to show significantly lower levels of social interaction and engagement than those with similar disabilities educated in general education (Hunt et al., 1994). While some worry that the inclusion of SWDs negatively affects students who do not have disabilities, syntheses of research show either positive or neutral effects on the academic and social outcomes of general education students (i.e., Hehir et al., 2016; Kart & Kart, 2021). A report published by the National Council on Disability (2018) indicates ". . . research demonstrates that inclusive education results in the best learning outcomes; there is no research that supports the value of a segregated special education class and school" (p. 9).

Continuum of Services

While the IDEA emphasizes that a student's IEP Team consider education in the general education classroom to the maximum extent possible, the law also acknowledges that the removal of SWDs to separate classes or separate schools may be necessary if the nature or severity of a child's disability is such that the child's needs cannot be met satisfactorily in the regular classroom with supplementary aids and services (20 U.S.C. 1412 (a)(5)). This requires schools to provide a range of placement options, referred to as a continuum of services. The placement of a student with a disability within the continuum is determined by the child's individualized needs. Figure 5 provides an overview of the service delivery models within this continuum. As a best practice, the UDL principles should be integrated within all services and environments along this continuum.

Figure 5. Continuum of Services for Students with Disabilities

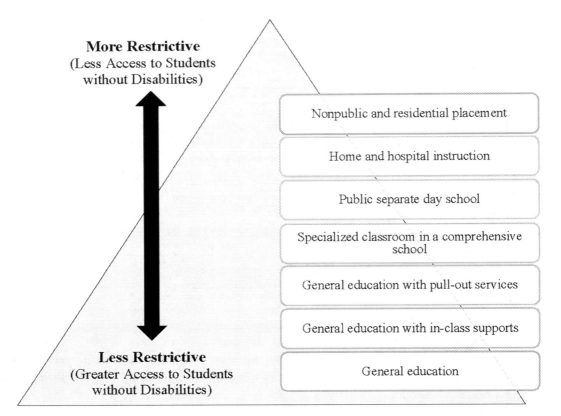

Student-Centered Decision-Making

Determining a student's placement is a decision made by the IEP Team and must be based on the needs of the student. Information from a student's Present Levels of Academic Achievement and Functional Performance, as well as the goals and objectives, supplementary aids, and services, are used to determine a student's LRE. Simply stated, "The IEP is written to fit the student. [Then], the placement is chosen to fit the IEP" (Pierangelo & Giuliani, 2007, p. 9). However, barriers to successfully including SWDs can permeate placement decisions. One such barrier is the attitudes and beliefs of professionals involved in this high-stakes decision. Research shows that teachers who view inclusion less favorably are less apt to provide learning opportunities that satisfactorily meet the diverse needs of students and these educators may be hesitant to accept SWDs in their classrooms (Grant & Jones-Goods, 2016). Strong teacher self-efficacy and positive attitudes toward inclusion increases teachers' willingness to apply inclusive practices (Grant & Jones-Goods, 2016; Park et al., 2016; Werner et al., 2021); and, thus, can support members of the IEP Team to take a more objective view.

Special Education Policy in the United States and Ireland

IDEA Principle 5: Parent and Student Participation in Decision-Making

The IDEA values parents as equal partners in decision-making. The law stipulates that schools take steps to ensure the full participation of parents in a child's IEP Team (34 CFR § 300.300; 34 CFR § 300.322) and outlines procedural safeguards to ensure that the rights of children and families are protected. Over time as the field of early intervention and early childhood education has evolved, the focus has shifted from a lens on *parents* to *families*. With this holistic view, a family systems approach leads to balanced decisions for children (Turnbull et al., 2015). Deep, meaningful partnerships between professionals and families of children with disabilities are at the heart of the IDEA and are central to creating positive outcomes. While the roles and responsibilities of each member varies, partnership occurs through a common vision between families and professionals. When enacted, true partnership goes beyond allowing family members to participate, as is outlined in the law. Meaningful partnerships are grounded in honest forms of mutual respect and a commitment to what each partner brings to the decisions involved in raising and educating a child with a disability. Turnbull et al. (2015) present seven principles for partnering with families of SWDs: communication, professional competence, respect, commitment, equality, advocacy, and trust. Figure 6 displays these principles and their relationship to one another. While each principle plays a critical role, the foundation of all meaningful partnerships is *trust*.

Figure 6. Seven principles of partnerships with families of students with disabilities

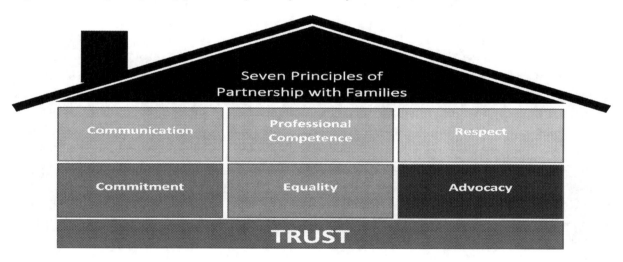

Student Participation and Self-Advocacy

In addition to parental participation the IDEA indicates that, whenever appropriate, the child with a disability be involved in his or her IEP Team process (20 U.S.C. 1414 (d)). When a student with an IEP reaches the age of 16; and in some states, age 14, the IEP Team begins developing and implementing transition planning to prepare the student to be successful in their life after high school. Transition planning for a student with a disability is personally defined—with postsecondary goals developed around a student's strengths, needs, and interests, so it is advantageous to involve the student in this process.

IDEA Principle 6: Procedural Due Process

The IDEA outlines procedural safeguards for parents of SWDs. These safeguards are intended to protect the rights of children and families and to support partnerships. The primary procedural safeguards outlined in the law include parents' right to a complete explanation of all the safeguards and a right to inspect and review materials that are part of their child's educational record (20 U.S.C. 1415 (a)(b)). Parents have a right to participate in the IEP Team meeting, to request an independent educational evaluation, and to receive prior written notice of all matters related to their child's identification, evaluation, placement, or details regarding FAPE (20 U.S.C. 1415 (c)). Parents also have a right to give or deny consent prior to certain actions, such as the initiation of special education services. The law provides mechanisms for resolving disputes, including the right to an appeal. There are formal processes outlined by the IDEA for resolving disputes, including mediation, a state complaint, or due process (20 U.S.C. 1415(a)).

LEGISLATION IN IRELAND

In Ireland, the Report of the Special Education Review Committee (SERC) (Department of Education, DE; 1993) reviewed the state of special education provision and made recommendations for the progression of special education provision in the country. The SERC Report served as an impetus for the promotion of inclusion in mainstream schools for students with special education needs (SEN) and its main implications were the obligation for schools to cater to all learners and student-focused decision making and legislation (Banks et al., 2011).

The influence of the SERC Report (DE, 1993) was evident in the *White Paper on Education: Charting our Future* (Government of Ireland, 1998), which stated that "all students regardless of their personal circumstances have a right of access to and participation in the education system according to their potential and ability" (p. 26). The white paper identified the lack of substantive legislation for education in Ireland and set the focus of future legislation. Subsequently, a succession of legislation followed that impacted the provision of support for students with SEN. This legislation has been significant in facilitating policy change toward inclusive education. The Education Act (1998) addressed the lack of legislation for children with SEN. It gives practical effect to Article 42 of the Irish Constitution with respect to the rights of the child to a minimum education, for children with SEN (Government of Ireland, 1998) and legislated supports to meet students' needs. It also provided the first definition of disability in the context of Irish education legislation.

The EPSEN Act (2004) built on the foundations of the SERC Report (DE, 1993) and Education Act (1998). EPSEN was significant in that it marked the shift from general education legislation that included mandates for children with SEN to the Irish government, creating education legislation specific to students with SEN. EPSEN re-defined SEN to include any condition that impacts a person's learning. EPSEN uses the term inclusive education and states that children with SEN must be educated in an inclusive environment with mainstream peers unless to do so would be inconsistent with the best interests of the child or their typically developing peers (Government of Ireland, 2004). EPSEN is considered a coherent framework for legislation and policy on inclusive education (National Council for Special Education, NCE, 2011). Though not fully enacted, the NCSE found that EPSEN is still "the most effective blueprint for delivering resources" (NCSE, 2014, p. 3). EPSEN extended the remit of the NCSE which was established as an independent statutory body in 2003 to improve the delivery of education

Special Education Policy in the United States and Ireland

services to persons with SEN with particular emphasis on children. As School-Self-Evaluation (SSE) was adopted as a practice in schools, one focus of NCSE has been to provide a resource to enable schools to reflect on their inclusive practices within their SSE. *The Inclusive Education Framework* (NCSE, 2011) provides guidance on what constitutes good practice for including students with SEN through a process of reflection on inclusive practices, a collaborative approach to inclusion, and a coordinated response to challenges. Nineteen years after the publication of EPSEN, the Act is currently under review to provide assurance that the law governs the provision of education for children with SEN and to ensure its adequacy in the context of Irish society today.

EDUCATION FOR PERSONS WITH SPECIAL EDUCATIONAL NEEDS ACT

In its current form, EPSEN is made up of several principles for persons with SEN. This chapter focuses on four key principles due to their alignment with IDEA and UDL as a pedagogy for inclusion: (1) the provision of appropriate education in an inclusive environment; (2) the right to the same educational benefits as their peers; (3) parental involvement; (4) and the right to educational plans and assessments of need. While these four principles are commonly referred to, it is argued that under Section 13 of EPSEN, it is the duty of the Ministers for Education and Health and Children to make resources available for the preparation and implementation of education plans for students with SEN. This goes to the core of what the government of Ireland seeks to achieve in the Act (O'Toole, 2006).

EPSEN PRINCIPLE 1: APPROPRIATE EDUCATION IN AN INCLUSIVE ENVIRONMENT

EPSEN outlines the provision of appropriate education in an inclusive environment. Section 2 of EPSEN sets out the legislative provision in Ireland, requiring that:

A child with special educational needs shall be educated in an inclusive environment with children who do not have such needs unless the nature or degree of those needs of the child is such that to do so would be inconsistent with:

- The best interests of the child in accordance with any assessment carried out under this Act.
- The effective provision of education for children with whom the child is educated. (Government of Ireland, 2004, p. 7)

To achieve this, Circular 02/05 (DE, 2005) outlines the entitlements of students with SEN to support. The circular introduces the General Allocation Model (GAM) to meet students' needs immediately. The model allocates 'high incidence' teaching hours to schools based on student numbers in addition to hours allocated to individual students based on their diagnosis or category of need. However, arguments have been made that diagnostic categorizations are heterogeneous with respect to SEN (i.e., Desforges & Lindsay, 2010; Norwich & Lewis, 2005; NCSE, 2014) and create inequitable resource allocations (NCSE, 2014). Thus, the new special education teacher allocation model (Department of Education,

2017) replaces GAM to facilitate a more equitable, rights-based approach to education provision for students with SEN with and without a psychological assessment or diagnosis of disability (Kenny et al., 2020). Under this model, provision is allocated to the school, not individual students, to best meet the needs of students in their care. One of the guiding principles of the new model of allocation is that every student, irrespective of SEN, is welcomed and supported to enroll in their local school. Schools provide support using the Continuum of Support (DE, 2007) which draws on the principles that underpin RTI (NCSE, 2014), where a whole-school approach to education of students, including program planning is adopted by schools. The Continuum of Support provides a framework for schools to identify and respond to students' needs using evidence-based interventions in a flexible manner.

UDL aligns with the practices of a Continuum of Support available to all students to promote meaningful access, participation, and achievement for every student regardless of their abilities. Introducing UDL principles into the school's mainstream teaching, learning and assessment practice means most students can have a successful learning experience without additional support. In addition to this support for all, selective measures must also be available to those students who require them, such as the provision of reasonable accommodations. UDL can be found at the system, school, and classroom levels. However, due to its student-centered nature, UDL is most often realized at the *classroom support for all level* (International Disability Alliance, 2021). This facilitates planning according to UDL principles to be contextualized and to account for the variability and characteristics of classroom communities. Thus, UDL can be a successful bottom-up, whole-school approach within the Continuum of Support to provide appropriate education to all students. EPSEN's defines a "special educational need" as:

A restriction in the capacity of the person to participate in and benefit from education on account of an enduring physical, sensory, mental health or learning disability, or any condition which results in a person learning differently from a person without this condition (Government of Ireland, 2004, p.6)

This definition creates a barrier to enacting a UDL approach, because it takes a deficit model or medical perspective of disability that places the barrier within the learner. This centers failure within the student, citing the need for remediation rather than identifying barriers to learning as a problem for educators to resolve (Mac Ruairc, 2016).

EPSEN PRINCIPLE 2: THE RIGHT TO THE SAME EDUCATIONAL BENEFIT AS PEERS

At the outset, EPSEN establishes that "people with special educational needs have the same right to an appropriate education as do their peers who do not have such needs (Government of Ireland, 2004, p. 5), giving practical effect to Article 42 of the Irish constitution regarding the rights of the child to a minimum education and the promotion of equality and access to participate in education. To address this, government bodies have provided guidelines and directives to educators teaching and supporting students with SEN. This work commenced prior to EPSEN with the National Council for Curriculum and Assessment's (NCCA) paper *Special Educational Needs: Curriculum Issues,* which acknowledged that students with SEN "are entitled to access to a full educational experience, but the pathways they need to take and the time they need to achieve this may be different from many of their mainstream peers" (NCCA, 1999, p. 18). It emphasized the necessity to balance the common curriculum, developmental

Special Education Policy in the United States and Ireland

curriculum, and additional curricula to meet the needs and abilities of individual students, and that content and strategies used to achieve this "should minimize rather than emphasize difference" (NCCA, 1999, p.25). NCCA proposed key development and life skills for learning and teaching which could be linked to the common curriculum.

Initially, this proposal resulted in the development of guidelines to support teaching and learning for students with various disabilities. In the absence of a curriculum that included all students, schools looked to such guidelines and international programs as an alternative curriculum for their students with SEN. However, as the global rights and universal education agenda influenced governments internationally, curriculum development in Ireland has moved towards more inclusive and relevant education to meet the needs of all students. This process has included three stages: (1) the new framework for junior cycle in 2015; (2) the primary curriculum framework in 2023; and (3) the senior cycle redevelopment, which is in progress. Each of these processes address diversity, equity, and inclusion through the design of one national curriculum for all students. The curriculum is designed to provide schools with autonomy and flexibility that account for the best interests of students and parents as well as school and community contexts (DE, 2015; NCCA, 2023). Such developments signal a strong commitment to inclusion and UDL in Ireland (Howe & Griffin, 2020). There are arguments (i.e., Westwood, 2001) that a singular curricular design purports a utopian vision that fails to account for the practical and individual needs of SWDs. However, the transition toward universal curriculum and UDL is evident in the structure of the new Irish curricular frameworks. Each framework has common principles and key competencies that make up its foundation. From there, flexible options and pathways provide multiple means of engagement, representation, and action and expression for students and teachers. This is achieved through curriculum areas and subjects, progression milestones through choices of subjects, short courses and programs that offer access and participation at varying levels to suit learning needs and preferences.

EPSEN PRINCIPLE 3: PARENTAL INVOLVEMENT

Sections 3 and 8 of EPSEN outline the role of parents of children with SEN in educational decision-making. While EPSEN establishes safeguards to ensure parental rights, the Act does not guarantee collaborative relationships (Griffin & Shevlin, 2007). There is concern that the system of due process through mandatory mediation restricts the rights of parents in decision-making which may compromise the appropriate and inclusive education of children when litigation is not a practical route (Carey, 2005; Thomson & Svaerd, 2019). Parents should feel confident to apply knowledge of their child's learning and social needs (NCSE, 2019). In accordance with EPSEN, parents must consent to an assessment, be involved with the preparation of an educational plan, and may appeal decisions, with the above-mentioned restrictions. According to NCSE (2006) there is no one defined process relating to parental involvement. The main objective is to make finding a school, assessment, and educational planning a positive experience for parents and maximize their involvement in decision-making.

Turnbull et al.'s (2015) seven principles for partnering with families of SWDs support a UDL approach to ensuring that parents can meaningfully contribute to their child's education. Novak (2017) offers practical examples of using the three principles of UDL to support parents' engagement in their child's education. These examples can also be applied to collaborating with parents of children with SEN regarding sections 3 and 8 of EPSEN. To provide multiple means of engagement schools must evaluate traditional expectations of parents that create barriers to engagement. Schools need to identify the barriers parents may experience and how these affect their participation. Firstly, schools must consider the access point for parents. Thus, schools should begin by providing flexible options for engagement. Some may prefer a one-to-one meeting before a planning meeting, giving parents time to express their views in advance. Parents may also choose not to attend an education planning meeting. In these instances, their views can be sought in advance and shared later. To provide multiple means of representation schools must connect with parents to share information. Taking a UDL approach ensures parents access to information. While NCSE (2006) recommends sharing information in writing, consideration must be given to parents who require information in alternative forms, such as parents with low reading ability or English as an Additional Language (EAL). Thus, it is important to apply various modes of communication. To provide multiple means of action and expression, schools must consider the modes used to gather information and feedback. This requires consideration of parents' commitments and the potential barriers to attending meetings during school hours. Here, offering the opportunity to meet before or after school, help of the Home School Community Liaison Officer, or offering an online meeting provides parents with opportunities to communicate their knowledge of, and wishes for, their child.

EPSEN PRINCIPLE 4: RIGHT TO EDUCATIONAL PLANS AND ASSESSMENT OF NEEDS

An essential component of EPSEN (Sections 3, 8, 9 11 and 15) is the assessment of special needs to ensure appropriate education plan and supports. Under EPSEN, these plans are referred to as IEPs. The language has since changed to Student Support Files (SSF). In the Iris context, the primary purpose of the IEP is to facilitate monitoring of a student's progress through the Continuum of Support, documenting progress and needs over time. The IEP addresses the priority learning needs of students with SEN through necessary teaching strategies, resources, and supports (NCSE, 2006; Ní Bhroin et al., 2016). Student goals within the IEP are to be achieved over a period not exceeding 12 months (Section 9.2) and each IEP must be reviewed at least once a year (Section, 11.1). EPSEN is clear about the significant role of parents in the IEP process and establishes requirements for consultation with parents. Schools should support and encourage students to participate in the IEP process, including attending meetings (NCSE, 2006). EPSEN clearly outlines the roles of stakeholders in the IEP process including the principal, teachers, psychologists, the Special Educational Needs Organizer, parents, the Health Service Executive, IEP Coordinator, the student, Special Needs Assistants and Visiting Teachers. Unfortunately, the sections of EPSEN still not commenced are those that would have conferred statutory entitlements to educational assessments for all children with SEN, a statutory IEP, and delivery of educational services as part of the IEP. It has been argued that the requirement to have a diagnosis of SEN without available access to professionals to make the assessment was "inequitable at best and potentially confirmed social advantage and reinforced social disadvantage" (NCSE, 2014, p.3). This has resulted in the introduction of a new model of allocation (DE, 2017). The guidelines for this model clearly indicate a transition towards UDL as stresses the primacy of the classroom teacher in the care and education of all students, offering suggestions and strategies for teaching within the mainstream classroom.

CRITIQUES AND COMPARISONS OF IDEA AND ESPEN

Prevalence of Inclusive Education

While American and Irish policies are discussed favorably in the international discourse on inclusive education, questions have emerged as to whether the IDEA and EPSEN have achieved their ideals. Both Acts share common goals for inclusive education and the system requirements to achieve these goals, but implementation data contraindicate intended results. Both Acts clarify that SWDs must be educated with typical peers to the maximum extent possible and that the removal of SWDs to separate settings is only warranted based on the nature and severity of a child's disability. However, only 65% of all school-aged children with IEPs in the United States received services in the general education classroom for 80% or more of the school day in 2019 (USDE, 2022). Likewise, 17% of SWDs in the United States spent 40-79% of their school day in general education and 18% of SWDs spent less than 40% of their day in general education or were educated in other more restrictive settings (USDE, 2022). This means that more than two million children in America were removed from general education for more than 20% of the school day. In Ireland, statistics are less available. Using EPSEN's definition of SEN, Banks et al. (2011) found a prevalence rate of 25% of children in Ireland having some form of SEN which impacts their learning. Education indicators (Government of Ireland, 2023) recorded 946,486 students were enrolled in primary and post-primary mainstream schools. Based on the prevalence rates cited by Banks et al., 27,859 of those children had SEN as defined in EPSEN. Education indicators also recorded 11,918 students were enrolled in special classes in primary and post-primary mainstream schools. In Ireland, the number of special classes is expected to rise from 2150 in 2022 to 2,200 because of the 2023 budget which allocated €12 million for additional teachers supporting students with SEN. An additional 8,683 students were enrolled in NCSE-supported special schools. These data indicate that while inclusive education remains a goal in both countries and progress has been made since their inception, a great deal remains to be done in achieving full implementation of the Acts' intended goals.

The basic tenets of equitable access to education are outlined in each Act, though different terminology is used to describe them. Additionally, America's MTSS model aligns with Ireland's Continuum of Support. MTSS and the Continuum of Support frameworks are applied to assist teachers to identify and respond to students' needs and these frameworks each utilize tiered models of support, with an emphasis on early intervention. IEPs are often used within these frameworks, particularly when students need higher tiers of intervention. IEPs are common practice in America and Ireland, though they are applied in different variations. However, unlike Ireland where sections of EPSEN are still not commenced to require IEPs as a legal obligation, IEPs are federally mandated under IDEA in the United States. IDEA and EPSEN both outline what an IEP should include, but to varying degrees. Overall, the IDEA provides greater specificity throughout its legislation as compared to EPSEN. EPSEN provides a description of the IEP process, content, and roles of responsibility. However, the NSCE is responsible for delivering guidelines for the process to schools. Further, while the IDEA emphasizes the use of research-based interventions arising from IEPS for SWDs, it is the NCSE guidelines (not EPSEN) that make this emphasis. These differences make clear that there are expressly different educational systems and contexts at play within the United States and Ireland. While each country has federal legislation designed to serve SWDs, the mechanisms by which each country implements its legislation are vastly different.

Family Collaboration and Student Participation

The importance of collaboration and involvement of families in educational decision-making is a key principle in both Acts. Each Act highlights parents' role as well as their rights to procedural due process. Parental involvement is required and emphasized in IDEA. EPSEN is clear in its intention that parents play a central role; however, it is argued that this role is curtailed, particularly in their options to dispute decisions (Thomson & Svaerd, 2019). The involvement of families extends to collaboration with students in the IDEA. While student participation is indicated in the IDEA, research indicates that the level of student participation in the American IEP progress could be improved. Because transition planning is personally defined, it is advantageous to involve the student in this process. According to the IRIS Center (2017), students invited to participate in the IEP Team are often only minimally involved. Too often the adults in charge of coordination may not plan and facilitate these meetings with the student's participation in mind. Based on a large-scale study of more than 11,000 students, although 94% of students attended their IEP meetings, only 12.2% offered significant input (IRIS Center, 2017). Ideally, as students' progress toward planning for their future, they should be actively involved in the transition process and serve as self-advocates. Conversely, student participation and decision-making are not emphasized in EPSEN, though it does form part of the IEP guidelines (NCSE, 2006) that followed EPSEN.

FUTURE DIRECTIONS

While inclusion remains an ideal in the IDEA and EPSEN, a critique of the Acts and consideration of a UDL approach to achieving inclusion shows that the realization of these ideals has remained a challenge in both countries. Experts have posited new directions and opportunities for improvements in special education in the United States, including a greater alignment among research and the law, with recommendations for future reauthorization. This is also the case in Ireland, as EPSEN is currently undergoing a review to ensure that Irish law governing the provision of education to children with SEN is sufficient. These reauthorizations require parameters, informed by research and practice. As members of the European Union (EU), the Irish government must abide by EU laws which take precedence over conflicting Irish law (European Union, 2008), including those on inclusion. Additionally, Ireland's ratification of the United Nations' Convention on the Rights of Persons with Disabilities (UNCRPD) in 2018 means that Ireland has an obligation to do so in accordance with the aims and purpose of that treaty. In 2019, NCSE noted that Ireland is currently in contravention of Article 24 of the Convention to uphold and provide for the rights of people with disabilities to have the opportunity to attend mainstream schools as part of an inclusive education system. Ireland's obligations under Article 24 are cited by the Government of Ireland as one reason for the review of Convention. Though inspired by the Americans with Disabilities Act (ADA), the UNCRPD goes further than ADA in many aspects (Kanter, 2019). The UNCRPD has yet to be ratified by the United States, removing international oversight on any reauthorization of the IDEA.

In addition to the long overdue reauthorization of the IDEA and EPSEN, scholarly discourse has focused on how the international community increases effective implementation of inclusive education worldwide. Shyman (2015) advocates the development of a more globally sensitive definition of inclusive education, citing "that the supposed international efforts toward inclusion have merely attempted to reproduce the model of education practiced in the West, mainly by the United States and the United Kingdom" (p. 357). In Ireland, definitions of inclusive education are still evolving and there is increased

Special Education Policy in the United States and Ireland

recognition that education should be based on equity of access and participation. Therefore, since there are opportunities for improving Western policies in special education, these Acts cannot be expected to serve as exemplars without additional consideration. While there are steps needed to improve the IDEA and EPSEN in future reauthorizations, Turnbull and Turnbull (2003) emphasize that the main dilemma we face is not in reforming the law itself, but in addressing the systemic issues that contribute to poor implementation of any law. Future Acts must include both a structure and resources necessary to ensure that schools have the capacity to meet requirements. Additionally, both Acts need a greater emphasis on a person-centered approach. UDL provides a structure to support this within various systems, such as the model adopted in New Brunswick, Canada, where UDL has been embedded and applauded by the United Nations (UNESCO, 2014).

Research is needed in both the United States and Ireland regarding the implementation and outcome of UDL as an inclusive pedagogy (Capp, 2017; Flood & Banks, 2021) as well as the involvement of SWDs in the IEP process. Trends have shown that few American special education studies discuss relevant implications of their findings to the IDEA. In a systematic review of every published article within a 10-year period in three top American special education journals, Lewis et al. (2021) found that only 23% of articles discussed specific implications for the IDEA. The small portion of studies that did address the IDEA defaulted to discussions of procedural, compliance-based implications, rather than discussions of how the IDEA could be reformed (Lewis et al., 2021). This is critical, particularly because further research is needed to understand how the IDEA and EPSEN should be revised. To achieve maximum effectiveness, existing federal law should be grounded in diverse methodological approaches (Lewis et al., 2021). Overall, the United States legal system have been criticized for its overly complicated nature toward implementing inclusive education through adherence to procedural compliance, rather than measures of high-quality instruction to SWDs (Turnbull & Turnbull, 2003; Wolf, 2006). The special education community can contribute to an increased focus on quality by helping the United States Congress to refine the definition of FAPE in future reauthorizations (Lewis et al., 2021). This could, in turn, inform international policy language that addresses implementation barriers to inclusion and the provision of special education services. While the IDEA has contributed to great strides in providing rights to children with disabilities and their families, the LRE principal of the law is inconsistently implemented in states, regions, and local school districts (Lim, 2020). Alternative frameworks for re-envisioning the LRE principle, such as moving away from an outcomes-based judgment that requires students to earn their way in and instead focusing on a capabilities approach, is one potential way to create more equitable inclusive opportunities (Lim, 2020).

CONCLUSION

The purpose of this chapter has been to examine American and Irish policies governing special education services and inclusive education through the lens of UDL. Both Acts have significantly influenced the services, supports, and inclusive educational opportunities afforded to SWDs. Each Act aims to achieve the same goal, but they operate within different educational systems. While the processes in each country are different, the intended outcome remains the same: inclusive education with access to typically developing peers for the maximum extent appropriate as well as access to and participation in general education. To achieve this goal, interpretative guidance needs to be provided at the commencement of the Act, not after the fact. This guidance must be developed by government bodies, not fragmented attempts or acts of good will. The Acts, exemplified by key principles, were designed to shift the educational paradigm toward inclusive education. Both IDEA and EPSEN are critical in the international discourse on inclusive education because place high ideals for inclusion and are aligned with other international inclusion statements. While the Acts remain influential in addressing the inclusion, scholars have suggested new opportunities and future directions for reauthorizations of both Acts that would help them reach to reach their high ideals. Such coordinated efforts at the international level would support the advancement of inclusion around the globe and could be used to improve national policies, including the IDEA and EPSEN.

ACKNOWLEDGMENT

This manuscript received no specific grant from any funding agency in the public, commercial, or not-for-profit sectors.

REFERENCES

Banks, J., McCoy, S., & Shevlin, M. (2011). Inclusive education research: Evidence from growing up in Ireland. *Trinity Education Paper, 2*(2), 24-35. https://www.researchgate.net/profile/Joanne_Banks2/publication/259146535

Brown v. Board of Education, 347 U.S. 483 (1954). https://www.oyez.org/cases/1940-1955/347us483

Capp, M. Y. (2017). The effectiveness of universal design for learning: A meta-analysis of literature between 2013 and 2016. *International Journal of Inclusive Education, 21*(8), 791–807. doi:10.1080/13603116.2017.1325074

Carey, D. (2005). *The essential guide to special education in Ireland.* CJ Fallon.

CAST. (2018). *UDL and the learning brain.* CAST. https://www.cast.org/binaries/content/assets/common/publications/articles/cast-udlandthebrain-20220228-a11y.pdf

Cole, S. M., Murphy, H. R., Frisby, M. B., Grossi, T. A., & Bolte, H. R. (2020). The relationship of special education placement and student academic outcomes. *The Journal of Special Education, 54*(4), 1–11. doi:10.1177/0022466920925033

Cole, S. M., Murphy, H. R., Frisby, M. B., & Robinson, J. (2022). *The relationship between special education placement and high school outcomes. The Journal of Special Education.* Online First., doi:10.1177/00224669221097945

Department of Education, Ireland. (1993) Report of the special education review committee (SERC). Stationary Office.

Department of Education. (2005). *White paper on education: Charting our future.* DoE. https://assets.gov.ie/24448/0f3bff53633440d99c32541f7f45cfeb.pdf

Special Education Policy in the United States and Ireland

Department of Education. Ireland. (2015). *Framework for junior cycle.* Department of Education, Ireland. https://www.gov.ie/en /publication/aed00b-framework-for-junior-cycle/

Department of Education. Ireland. (2017). *Special education teaching allocation.* Department of Education, Ireland. https://www.gov.ie/en /circular/b1ee7005c95747cea9e6406b8a5b 3c67/

Desforges, M. (2010). *Procedures used to diagnose disability and to assess special educational needs.* National Council for Special Education. https://ncse.ie/wp-content/uploads/2014/10/5_NCSE_Diag_Ass.p df

Entrich, S. R. (2021). Understanding cross-national differences in inclusive education coverage: An empirical analysis. *Journal of Education: Inclusive Education*, *9*(1), 21–40. https://iafor.org/journal/ iafor-journal-of-education/volume-9-issue-1/article-2/

European Union. (2008). Primacy of EU law (precedence, supremacy). *European Journal.* https://eur-lex.europa.eu/legal-content/EN/ALL/?uri=LEGISSUM :primacy_of_eu_law

Family Educational Rights and Privacy Act of 1974, 20 U.S.C. § 1232g (1974).

Flood, M., & Banks, J. (2021). Universal Design for Learning: Is it gaining momentum in Irish education? *Education Sciences*, *11*(7), 341. doi:10.3390/educsci11070341

Government of Ireland. (1998). *Education Act.* Government of Ireland. *https://www.oireachtas.ie/en/ bills/bill/2003/34/*

Government of Ireland. (2004). *Education for Persons with Special Educational Needs Act (EPSEN).* https://www.oireachtas.ie/en/bills/bill/2003/34/

Government of Ireland. (2023). *Education indicators for Ireland.* Government of Ireland. *file:///C:/Users/mflood/Downloads /246552_96fc2eb5-b7c9-4a17-afbc-de288a471b3f.pdf.*

Grant, M. C., & Jones-Goods, K. M. (2016). Identifying and correcting barriers to successful inclusive practices: A literature review. *Journal of the American Academy of Special Education Professionals*, 64–71. https://eric.ed.gov/?id=EJ1129815

Griffin, S., & Shevlin, M. (2007). *Responding to special educational needs: An Irish perspective.* Gill & MacMillan.

Hardy, I., & Woodcock, S. (2015). Inclusive education policies: Discourses of difference, diversity, and deficit. *International Journal of Inclusive Education*, *19*(2), 141–164. doi:10.1080/13603116.2014.908965

Hehir, T., Grindal, T., Freeman, B., Lamoreau, R., Borquaye, Y., & Burke, S. (2016). *A summary of the evidence on inclusive education.* Abt Associates. https://www.abtassociates.com/sites/default/files/2019-03/A _Summary_of_the_evidence_on_inclusive_education.pdf

Howe, C., & Griffin, C. (2020). Is Ireland at a crossroads of inclusive education? *REACH Journal of Special Needs Education in Ireland, 33*(1), 44–56. https://reachjournal.ie/index.php/reach/article/view/8

Hunt, P., Farron-Davis, F., Beckstead, S., Curtis, D., & Goetz, L. (1994). Evaluating the effects of placement of students with severe disabilities in general education versus special classes. *The Journal of the Association for Persons with Severe Handicaps, 19*(3), 200–214. doi:10.1177/154079699401900308

Individuals With Disabilities Education Act, 20 U.S.C. § 1400 (2004).

International Disability Alliance. (2021). *Universal Design for Learning and its role in ensuring access to inclusive education for all.* https://www.internationaldisabilityalliance.org/sites/defaul t /files/universal_design_for_learning_final_8.09.2021.pdf

IRIS Center. (2017). *Secondary transition: Student-centered planning.* IRIS. https://iris.peabody.vanderbilt.edu/module/tran-scp/

IRIS Center. (2019). *IEPs: How administrators can support the development and implementation of high-quality IEPs.* IRIS. https://iris.peabody.vanderbilt.edu/module/iep02/

Jung, L. A., Gomez, C., Baird, S. M., & Galyon Keramides, C. L. (2008). Designing intervention plans: Bridging the gap between individualized education programs and implementation. *Teaching Exceptional Children, 41*(1), 26–33. doi:10.1177/004005990804100103

Kanter, S. (2019). Let's try again: Why the United States should ratify the United Nations Convention on the Rights of People with Disabilities (2019). *Touro Law Review, 35.* https://ssrn.com/abstract=3373259

Kart, A., & Kart, M. (2021). Academic and social effects of inclusion on students without disabilities: A review of the literature. *Education Sciences, 11*(16), 16. doi:10.3390/educsci11010016

Kenny, N., McCoy, S., & Mihut, G. (2020). Special education reforms in Ireland: Changing systems, changing schools. *International Journal of Inclusive Education*, 1–20. doi:10.1080/13603116.2020.1 821447

Kurth, J. A., Miller, A. L., Gross Toews, S., Thompson, J. R., Cortes, M., Dahal, M. H., de Escallon, I. E., Hunt, P. F., Porter, G., Richler, D., Fonseca, I., Singh, R., Siska, J., Villamero, R., & Wangare, F. (2018). Inclusive education: Perspectives on implementation and practice for international experts. *Intellectual and Developmental Disabilities, 56*(6), 471–485. doi:10.1352/1934-9556-56.6.471

Lengyel, L. S., & Vanbergeijk, E. (2021). A brief history of special education: Milestones in the first 50 years. *Exceptional Parents Magazine.* https://reader.mediawiremobile.com/epmagazine/issues /207207 /viewer doi:10.1086/713825

Lewis, M. M., Burke, M. M., & Decker, J. R. (2021). The relation between the Individuals with Disabilities Education Act and special education research: A systematic review. *American Journal of Education, 127*, 345–368. doi:10.1086/713825

Lim, S. (2020). The capabilities approach to inclusive education: Re-envisioning the Individuals with Disabilities Education Act's least restrictive environment. *Disability & Society, 35*(4), 570–588. doi:1 0.1080/09687599.2019.1649119

Mac Ruairc, G. (2016, May 18). Leadership for inclusive schools [webinar]. In *Teaching Council Research Webinars*. https://www.teachingcouncil.ie/en/research-croi-/research-we binars-/past-webinars/leadership-for-inclusive-schools-webin ar-slides.pdf

Meyer, A., Rose, D. H., & Gordon, D. T. (2014). *Universal design for learning: Theory and practice.* CAST Professional Publishing.

National Council for Curriculum and Assessment. (1999). *Special educational needs: Curriculum issues.* https://ncca.ie/en/resources/special_educational_needs_curriculum_issues_-_discussion_paper/

National Council for Curriculum and Assessment. (2023). *Primary curriculum framework.* https://www.gov.ie/en/publication/0db24-primary-curriculum-framework/

National Council for Special Education. (2006). *Guidelines on the Individual Education Plan process.* https://ncse.ie/wp-content/uploads/2014/10/final_report.pdf

National Council for Special Education. (2011). *Inclusive education framework: A guide for schools on the inclusion of pupils with special education needs.* https://ncse.ie/wp-content/uploads/2014/10/InclusiveEducatio nFramework_InteractiveVersion.pdf

National Council for Special Education. (2014). *Delivery for students with special educational needs: A better and more equitable way.* https://ncse.ie/wp-content/uploads/2014/09 /Allocating_resou rces_1_5_14_Web_accessible_version_FINAL.pdf

National Council for Special Education. (2019). *Policy Advice on Special Schools and Classes An Inclusive Education for an Inclusive Society?* https://ncse.ie/wp-content/uploads/2019/11 /Progress-Report-Policy-Advice-on-Special-Schools-Classes-website-upload.pdf

National Council on Disability. (2018). *IDEA Series: The segregation of students with disabilities.* https://ncd.gov/sites/default/files/NCD_Segregation-SWD_508.pdf

Ní Bhrion, O., King, F., & Prunty, A. (2016). Teachers' knowledge and practice relating to the individual education plan and learning outcomes for pupils with special educational needs. *REACH Journal of Special Needs Education in Ireland, 29*(2), 78-90. Irish Association of Teachers in Special Education. https://reachjournal.ie/index.php/reach/article/view/45

Norwich, B., & Lewis, A. (2005). How specialised is teaching pupils with disabilities and difficulties? *Pedagogies for Inclusion, 20*(1), 31–55. doi:10.1080/00220270601161667

Novak, K. (2017). *Engaging parents in UDL implementation.* https://www.learningdesigned.org/sites/default/files/Novak_2017.pdf

O'Toole, J. (2006). *Education for persons with special educational needs: An interpretation for teachers.* https://www.oireachtas.ie/en/bills/bill/2003/34/

Park, M. H., Dimitrov, D. M., Das, A., & Gichuru, M. (2016). The teacher efficacy for inclusive practices (TEIP) scale: Dimensionality and factor structure. *Journal of Research in Special Educational Needs, 16*(1), 2–12. doi:10.1111/1471-3802.12047

Parrish, A. H., Kouo, J., Carey, L., & Swanson, R. C. (2021). Using Universal Design for Learning in meeting the diverse needs of students in virtual learning environments. In M. Neiss & H. Gillow-Wiles (Eds.), *Transforming teachers' online pedagogical reasoning for teaching K-12 students in virtual learning environments*. IGI Global., https://www.igi-global.com/chapter/implementing-universal-design-for-learning-in-the-virtual-learning-environment/284517, doi:10.4018/978-1-7998-7222-1.ch003

Pierangelo, R., & Giuliano, G. (2007). *Understanding, developing, and writing effective IEPs: A step-by-step guide for educators*. Corwin Press.

Schiller, E., Sanford, C., & Blackorby, S. (2008). *A national profile of the classroom experiences and academic performance of students with learning disabilities: A special topic report from the special education elementary longitudinal study*. https://www.seels.net/info_reports/SEELS_LearnDisability_%20SPEC_TOPIC_REPORT.12.19.08ww_FINAL.pdf

Shyman, E. (2015). Toward a globally sensitive definition of inclusive education based on social justice. *International Journal of Disability Development and Education*, *62*(4), 351–362. doi:10.1080/1034912X.2015.1025715

Taylor, J. P., Rooney-Kron, M., Whittenburg, H. N., Thoma, C. A., Avellone, L., & Seward, H. (2020). Inclusion of students with intellectual and developmental disabilities and postsecondary outcomes: A systematic literature review. *Inclusion (Washington, D.C.)*, *8*(4), 303–319. doi:10.1352/2326-6988-8.4.303

Thomson, M., & Svaerd, A. K. (2019). Unintended consequences of special-needs law in Ireland and Sweden. *Kybernetes*, *48*(2), 333–247. doi:10.1108/K-06-2018-0307

Turnbull, A. P., Turnbull, H. R., Erwin, E. J., Soodak, L. C., & Shogren, K. A. (2015). *Families, professionals, and exceptionality: Positive outcomes through partnership and trust* (7th ed.). Pearson.

Turnbull, H. R., Stowe, M. J., & Huerta, N. E. (2007). *Free appropriate public education: The law and children with disabilities* (7th ed.). Love.

Turnbull, H. R., & Turnbull, A. P. (2003). Reaching the ideal. *Education Next*, *3*(1), 32–37. https://www.educationnext.org/reachingtheideal/

United Nations, Department of Economic and Social Affairs. (2018). *Convention on the Rights of Persons with Disabilities*. https://www.un.org/development/desa/disabilities/convention-on-the-rights-of-persons-with-disabilities/convention-on-the-rights-of-persons-with-disabilities-2.html

United Nations Educational, Scientific and Cultural Organization (UNESCO). (1994). *The UNESCO Salamanca Statement*. Adopted by the World Conference on Special Needs Education: Access and Quality. Salamanca, Spain. http://www.csie.org.uk/inclusion/unesco-salamanca.shtml

United Nations Educational, Scientific and Cultural Organization (UNESCO). (2014). UNESCO/Emir Jaber al-Ahmad al-Jaber al-Sabah prize to promote quality education for persons with intellectual disabilities. https://en.unesco.org/prizes/digitalempowerment/previous-winners#2013

United States Department of Education. (2022). *43rd annual report to Congress on the implementation of the Individuals with Disabilities Education Act, 2021.* Office of Special Education and Rehabilitative Services. https://sites.ed.gov/idea/2021-individuals-with-disabilities-education-act-annual-report-to-congress/

Werner, S., Gumpel, T. P., Koller, J., Wiesenthal, V., & Weintraub, N. (2021). Can self-efficacy mediate between knowledge of policy, school support and teacher attitudes towards inclusive education? *PLoS One, 16*(9), e0257657. doi:10.1371/journal.pone.0257657 PMID:34543328

Westwood, P. (2001). Differentiation as a strategy for inclusive classroom practice: Some difficulties identified. *Australian Journal of Learning Disabilities, 6*(1), 5–11. doi:10.1080/19404150109546651

Wolf, P. J. (2006). Sisyphean tasks. *Education Next, 3*(1), 24–32. https://www.educationnext.org/sisypheantasks/

KEY TERMS AND DEFINITIONS

Education for Persons with Special Education Needs Act (EPSEN): Act providing for the education of children with special educational needs aged under 18 years of age in Ireland.

Free Appropriate Public Education (FAPE): The principle of the Individuals with Disabilities Education Act that indicates (a) educational entities must provide eligible children with disabilities with services at public expense; (b) each child with a disability is entitled to an education, including special education and related services that meet his or her unique, individualized needs; (c) a child with a disability has a right to access services in the public school system as outlined by the zero reject principle; and (d) eligible children with disabilities receive a public education that includes special education and related services as directed by the child's Individualized Education Program and access to general education.

Individualized Education Plan (IEP): A written document, as outlined by the Education for Persons with Special Education Needs Act, prepared for a named student which specifies the learning goals that are to be achieved by the student over a set period as well as the teaching strategies, resources and supports necessary to achieve those goals.

Individualized Education Program (IEP): A written statement for each child with a disability that is developed, reviewed, and revised in accordance with the Individuals with Disabilities Education Act.

Individuals with Disabilities Education Act (IDEA): A federal United States law that makes a free appropriate public education available to all eligible children with disabilities throughout the nation and ensures special education and related services are provided to those children. The IDEA governs how states and public agencies provide early intervention, special education, and related services to eligible infants, toddlers, children, and youth with disabilities in the United States.

Least Restrictive Environment (LRE): The principle of the Individuals with Disabilities Education Act that indicates that children with disabilities, to the maximum extent appropriate, should be educated with children who are not disabled. Special classes, separate schooling, or other removal of children with disabilities from the regular educational environment should occur only when the nature or severity of the disability of a child is such that education in regular classes with the use of supplementary aids and services cannot be achieved satisfactorily.

National Council for Special Education (NCSE): An independent statutory body established under the Education for Persons with Special Education Needs Act. The primary aim of NCSE is to improve the delivery of education services to persons with special educational needs arising from disabilities with particular emphasis on children.

Specially Designed Instruction: Adapting, as appropriate to the needs of an eligible child the content, methodology or delivery of instruction to address the unique needs that result from the child's disability and to ensure access to the general curriculum.

Universal Design for Learning (UDL): A pedagogical approach to inclusive education informed by research in the neurosciences. UDL offers multiple means of educational access, participation, and engagement by reducing barriers in the learning environment.

Special Education Policy in the United States and Ireland

APPENDIX 1

Table 2. Disability eligibility categories under the Individuals with Disabilities Education Act

Eligibility Category	Definition
Autism	A developmental disability significantly affecting verbal and nonverbal communication and social interaction, generally evident before age three that adversely affects a child's educational performance. Other characteristics often associated with autism are engagement in repetitive activities and stereotyped movements, resistance to environmental change or change in daily routines, and unusual responses to sensory experiences. Autism does not apply if a child's educational performance is adversely affected primarily because the child has an emotional disturbance. A child who manifests the characteristics of autism after age three could be identified as having autism if the criteria in the first paragraph above are satisfied.
Deaf blindness	Concomitant hearing and visual impairments, the combination of which causes such severe communication and other developmental and educational needs that they cannot be accommodated in special education programs solely for children with deafness or children with blindness. Deafness means a hearing impairment that is so severe that the child is impaired in processing linguistic information through hearing, with or without amplification, that adversely affects a child's educational performance.
Hearing impairment	An impairment in hearing, whether permanent or fluctuating, that adversely affects a child's educational performance but that is not included under the definition of deafness in this section.
Intellectual disability	Significantly subaverage general intellectual functioning, existing concurrently with deficits in adaptive behavior and manifested during the developmental period, that adversely affects a child's educational performance.
Multiple disabilities	Concomitant impairments (such as intellectual disability-blindness or intellectual disability-orthopedic impairment), the combination of which causes such severe educational needs that they cannot be accommodated in special education programs solely for one of the impairments. Multiple disabilities does not include deaf-blindness.
Orthopedic impairment	A severe orthopedic impairment that adversely affects a child's educational performance. The term includes impairments caused by a congenital anomaly, impairments caused by disease (e.g., poliomyelitis, bone tuberculosis), and impairments from other causes (e.g., cerebral palsy, amputations, and fractures or burns that cause contractures).
Other health impairment	Having limited strength, vitality, or alertness, including a heightened alertness to environmental stimuli, that results in limited alertness with respect to the educational environment, that: • Is due to chronic or acute health problems such as asthma, attention deficit hyperactivity disorder, diabetes, epilepsy, a heart condition, hemophilia, lead poisoning, leukemia, nephritis, rheumatic fever, sickle cell anemia, and Tourette syndrome; and • Adversely affects a child's educational performance.
Serious emotional disturbance	A condition exhibiting one or more of the following characteristics over a long period of time and to a marked degree that adversely affects a child's educational performance: • An inability to learn that cannot be explained by intellectual, sensory, or health factors. • An inability to build or maintain satisfactory interpersonal relationships with peers and teachers. • Inappropriate types of behavior or feelings under normal circumstances. • A general pervasive mood of unhappiness or depression. A tendency to develop physical symptoms or fears associated with personal or school problems. Emotional disturbance includes schizophrenia. The term does not apply to children who are socially maladjusted, unless it is determined that they have an emotional disturbance under the conditions outlined above.
Specific learning disability	A disorder in one or more of the basic psychological processes involved in understanding or in using language, spoken, or written, that may manifest itself in the imperfect ability to listen, think, speak, read, write, spell, or to do mathematical calculations, including conditions such as perceptual disabilities, brain injury, minimal brain dysfunction, dyslexia, and developmental aphasia. Specific learning disability does not include learning problems that are primarily the result of visual, hearing, or motor disabilities, of intellectual disability, of emotional disturbance, or of environmental, cultural, or economic disadvantage.
Speech or language impairment	A communication disorder, such as stuttering, impaired articulation, a language impairment, or a voice impairment, that adversely affects a child's educational performance.
Traumatic brain injury	An acquired injury to the brain caused by an external physical force, resulting in total or partial functional disability or psychosocial impairment, or both, that adversely affects a child's educational performance. Traumatic brain injury applies to open or closed head injuries resulting in impairments in one or more areas, such as cognition; language; memory; attention; reasoning; abstract thinking; judgment; problem-solving; sensory, perceptual, and motor abilities; psychosocial behavior; physical functions; information processing; and speech. Traumatic brain injury does not apply to brain injuries that are congenital or degenerative, or to brain injuries induced by birth trauma.
Visual impairment, including blindness	An impairment in vision that, even with correction, adversely affects a child's educational performance. The term includes both partial sight and blindness.

Chapter 13

The Universal Design for Learning in the Context of Brazilian Education:
Challenges and Possibilities for Inclusive Education

Elizabete Cristina Costa-Renders
University of São Caetano do Sul, Brazil

ABSTRACT

The topic discussed in this chapter is teacher professional development committed to inclusive education. The text presents partial results of a research on the application of the principles of universal design for learning in school inclusion processes in Brazilian schools. It aims to present and reflect on the reports of the participating teachers about the challenges and possibilities of building inclusive education based on UDL. On the one hand, the challenges consist of difficulties in designing activities to include all students considering the class heterogeneity, the institutional bureaucratization that compromises the time to plan teaching, and the scarce means to overcome such difficulties. On the other hand, advances demand the democratic management of school, the ethical leap arising from inclusive education, and the epistemological supports of universal design for learning and pedagogy of seasons. The results of the introduction of UDL are promising and show improvements, but structures and skills need a more permanent pedagogical companionship.

INTRODUCTION

The 2030 Agenda for Sustainable Development (United Nations, 2015) points – in goal 4 – to inclusive and equitable education as a goal to be achieved in school systems worldwide. In Brazil, the challenges to achieve this goal have been great. However, there are regulatory frameworks – such as the Federal Constitution of 1988 and the National Education Guidelines and Framework Law (Law No. 9394/96) –

DOI: 10.4018/978-1-6684-7370-2.ch013

Copyright © 2023, IGI Global. Copying or distributing in print or electronic forms without written permission of IGI Global is prohibited.

that sets forth the State's duty to guarantee equitable access and permanence for all people in the school system.

Inclusive Education in the Brazilian Context

The Brazilian educational policy is in line with international documents, especially the World Conference on Special Needs Education (Salamanca, 1994), the Convention on the Rights of Persons with Disabilities (United Nations, 2006) and the Education 2030 – Incheon Declaration (Incheon, 2015).

Designed from the Federal Constitution (1988) to the National Education Guidelines and Framework Law (LDB, 1996), the new policy prioritized the "equality of conditions for access and permanence in school" (LDB/9394, art.3, item I) and proposed a significant change in the educational system. In its conception, the inclusion paradigm brought a technical and social impact on the Brazilian educational system. The need for changes in management processes, teacher training, educational methodologies with shared actions and collaborative practices that respond to the necessities of all students (Brazil, 2008) became evident.

Specifically, special education is one of the goals of the National Education Plan 2014-2024 (Brazil, 2014) to ensure the universal access of people with disabilities to the education system in the country, without segregating them in special schools. Special education ceased to take place in separate schools and began to be offered at all levels of the education system, by providing accessibility conditions and specialized services in schools. However, different researchers (Carvalho, 2005; Mantoan, 2015; Costa-Renders, 2018) point to some contradictions in this process, such as limited resources for inclusive education, the tendency to discriminate against students with disabilities within the school system, and the need for teacher training to build an accessible curriculum approach.

Recent data related to inclusion and equity in Brazilian elementary education indicate that students with disabilities are directed to schools with more resources. "However, the negative association between teachers' expectations in relation to students and the proportion of this group of students in school stands out. That is, the higher the number of students with disabilities enrolled, the more the teaching expectations are modest" (UNESCO/Brazil, 2021, p.6).

In terms of access to the education system, Brazil has made great progress in enrolling students with disabilities. *The National Institute of Educational Studies and Research Anísio Teixeira* (Brazil, 2019) pointed out the significant growth in enrollment of these students in schools, totaling 87.2%. Consequently, there is a gradual reduction in enrollments in exclusive classes and schools, totaling 12.8%. However, there are still important challenges in this process.

The development of new special education practices is fundamental for an inclusive school. Therefore, it is important to broaden the understanding of special education, by creating communities of knowledge that promote the discussion on inclusive teaching practice. This scenario shows that the Universal Design for Learning (UDL) can support the construction of special education from an inclusive perspective in Brazilian schools, by proposing a curricular approach accessible to everyone.

In Brazil, the *National Education Plan 2014-2024* recommends "fostering the continuing education of male and female teachers for specialized educational services" (Brazil, 2014). Directly related to the necessary changes for inclusive education is the professional development in this new school. However, this document does not consider this training perspective. Thus, it is relevant to formulate technical pedagogical propositions for special education from an inclusive perspective.

RESEARCH IN THE BRAZILIAN CONTEXT: METHODOLOGICAL PROCEDURES

Based on this background, this chapter aims to introduce and analyze some results from the research entitled *School for All: Inclusive Special Education in Connection with Universal Design for Learning*. This study counted on the collaboration of ten (10) Brazilian teachers interested in building inclusive education based on the principles of the UDL.

This research was conducted between 2019 and 2021, within the ACESSI (School Accessibility and Inclusive Society) study group. ACESSI is linked to the Graduate Program of the Municipal University of São Caetano do Sul (USCS/Brazil) that offers the Master's in Education, where teacher education is one of the lines of research. Therefore, by interfacing basic and higher education, this research aimed to contribute to the professional development of teachers through research applied to teachers who work in schools in the ABC Region of São Paulo. We collected reports of inclusive education in basic education and, at the same time, reflected on such experiences within the scope of master's degree studies in education. Teachers' narratives pervade this text. The names presented herein are not real because we sought to preserve the privacy of research participants.

The underlying concepts of the research were democratic education (Freire, 2005), inclusive education (Mantoan, 2015), UDL (CAST, 2018), ecologies of knowledge (Santos, 2008), and pedagogy of seasons (Costa-Renders, 2019). The assumption was a teaching that recognizes and appreciates variability in and among students (Meyer et al., 2014), and extends the degree to which learners can influence the curricular approach. However, this is something that is deemed very difficult to accomplish at school by the teachers who participated in the research. According to teachers, this difficulty is due to the bureaucratization of teaching profession and the consequent lack of time for planning inclusive education. Therefore, this chapter promotes a discussion on the challenges to the application of UDL in different school contexts, especially considering the direct relationship between inclusive education and democratic education.

The methodological procedure was qualitative research using narrative research combined with developmental research. The narrative research enabled the collection of teachers' experiences with inclusive education, as well as allowed the consideration of their challenges in educational inclusion processes involving people with disabilities. This was performed via pedagogical letters, narrative interviews, and round-table discussions. The developmental research, in turn, allowed the construction of learning objects that support teachers in the process of educational inclusion, engaging both people with and without disabilities. However, in this chapter the focus is not on development but narrative research.

The narrative research was based on studies by Connelly and Clandinin (1990), especially because the interest was on teachers' experiences with school inclusion were of interest. A triple understanding of the research participants' narratives were considered in three aspects: enunciation, everyday practices, and what is implicit in the unspoken words.

The narrative research made it possible to consider the complexity of the investigation on teaching and learning processes. This methodology can also account for the educator's professional development process in a humanistic and participatory way. The starting point was the understanding of teacher professional development as:

(…) a construction of the professional self, which evolves throughout their careers. Which can be influenced by school, reforms and political contexts, and which integrates personal commitment, willingness to learn to teach, beliefs, values, knowledge about the subjects they teach and how they teach them, past experiences, as well as professional vulnerability itself (Marcelo, 2009, p. 7).

The Universal Design for Learning in the Context of Brazilian Education

Then, we sought to provide opportunities for narrating by writing pedagogical letters, and for training in conversation circles.

Chart 1 presents all the field research phases, and the results presented in this chapter refer to phases 1, 2 and 3.

Table 1. Steps of the field research

Steps	Activity	Instrument
1	Become aware of problem situations	Training Meeting 1
2	Survey on the inclusive process in the classroom (advances and challenges)	Pedagogical letters written by teachers
3	Thematization of the pedagogical letters with the research participants	Training Meeting 2 and 3
4	Reflection on how lesson plans considered variability in the classroom	Training Meeting 4
5	Monitoring inclusive education planning based on the UDL Guidelines	Training Meeting 5

As mentioned above, this text discuss the results of the first three phases with emphasis on the thematization of the pedagogical letters. The other steps would require further analysis, which would not fit in the limit of the paper.

Among the results achieved, the creation of a space for sharing experiences and challenges with inclusive education stands out. The epistemological interests focused on the reflection on inclusive education and its challenges. In this sense, UDL has contributed to re-signifying special education from an inclusive perspective.

RESULTS AND DISCUSSION

Based on the results achieved in this investigative process, this chapter highlights three central themes that arose from the reflection on the challenges and possibilities of inclusive education. After collecting the pedagogical letters written by the research participants, the reflective process on the narrated experiences began. This took place in conversation circles with teachers and the researcher.

In the first round of conversation, we carried out a study on the principles of UDL. To consider the differences in teaching and learning processes requires more effort than to recognize differences as a human condition. This demands the transformation of the school towards the practice of inclusive education. Therefore, studies on UDL were fundamental, starting from the recognition of the variability of neural learning networks.

UDL proposal is based on three guiding principles of barrier-free teaching. Teachers should plan a teaching that provides multiple means of representing content, as well as of action and expression, and supports multiple forms of self-involvement of learners in the proposed curricular approach (CAST, 2018). This happens based on the recognition of the variability of learning neural networks, which must be respected in the planning and development of a lesson. According to Rose et al. (2014), these are: recognition networks (what), strategic networks (how) and affective networks (why).

In the studies on inclusive education in Brazil, it is common to read about respect for diversity and differences in the school context. However, one hardly sees the consideration of the variability of learning neural networks when reflecting on the uniqueness of learners. In this sense, the researcher considered that this would be a central discussion in the first round of conversation with the participants of this narrative research.

On planning their lessons, it is important that teachers have a clear picture about the variability in the classroom, and direct their attention to both the variability in the group (interpersonal) and the internal variability (intrapersonal) relevant to each learner.

The concept of neuro-variability is important for educators, because it reminds us that learners do not have an isolated learning "style", but instead rely on many parts of the brain working together to function within a given context. There is no single way a brain will perceive, engage with, or execute a task. Variability is not just an important consideration for thinking about differences between students, but also within students in different contexts (CAST, 2018, p. 2).

Evidently, the respect for variability demands a flexible curriculum that is open to the influence of learners. Hence, inclusive education is only possible in schools that are open to the influence of learners in the curricular approach, by ensuring the participation of students, and welcoming the variability of each one in learning.

What is even more detrimental to learning is that fixed, one-size-fits-all curricula are designed and developed to address the needs of mainstream learners and, consequently, disregard the diversity in skills, needs, and interest that individuals bring to learning. In contrast, a UDL curriculum is designed and developed to take full advantage of the inherent variability in individual learners (Strangman et al., 2014, p. 16).

Following the conversation circles, we reflected on the experiences narrated in the letters, highlighting the challenges pointed out by the research participants. We could perceive that these challenges were in line with what had already been reported by other researchers (Carvalho, 2005; Mantoan, 2015; Costa-Renders, 2018). Then, the research participants defined three topics for discussion.

The first theme was the ethical leap inherent to inclusive education, as inclusive education is only possible in the context of democratic school management intertwined with lovingness in the act of teaching (Freire, 2002). This provides an accessible and participatory curricular approach. The second topic of discussion was the need to face the bureaucratization of teaching work, as teachers have been pressured by the monoculture of time/space (Santos, 2008) of teaching/learning at school. In this axis, the UDL provided elements for overcoming monoculture by proposing multiplicity and variability as teaching guidelines. The third theme concerns the epistemological supports for inclusive education. This demanded the approximation of UDL to the metaphor of pedagogy of seasons (Costa-Renders, 2019). Following this chapter, excerpts from the pedagogical letters as a starting point for the epistemological discussion proposed by the research.

The Ethical Leap Demanded by Inclusive Education

`You are sure that your room is inadequate, the furniture is inadequate, and that's not going to change anytime soon.´ (Experience Report, Teacher Marina, 2020)

The epigraph above is one of the teachers' narratives included in the research and portrays one of the most challenging moments of the round-table discussions about inclusive education approached to the principles of UDL. However, this report indicates the ethical debate that permeated the research *School for all.*

The inclusion paradigm arises from the principle that every human being has the right to access the common good produced by humanity throughout history, among which school education stands out. In contemporary society, education is considered a fundamental human right, given the complexity of our way of life. However, as reported by Teacher Marina and referenced by UNESCO, "school systems reflect the highly unequal societies in which they are situated" (2020, p. ix), so it is necessary to ensure equal opportunities for access to the common good by all citizens. Therefore, the democratic ethical principle of the right to education precedes inclusive education.

Inclusive education is only possible in democratic systems, where the rights of all citizens are recognized and respected. In another perspective, the common good provided, cutting across school systems, leads us to ensure the ethical leap in education, by means of social technologies that promote: making common, communicating, forming commitments, and operating changes with a view to inclusive and equitable education. Therefore, democratizing access to school is not enough. The democratic school management is mandatory, aiming to emancipate the individuals (Freire, 2005) inside and outside the educational institution.

Based on this background, Rios (2001) highlights the importance of the critical perspective in professional teacher development. The teacher must "continuously assume a critical attitude that question about the basis and meaning of setting the content, methods, and goals, taking into account the advocacy of rights, and the common good" (Rios, 2001, p. 89).

This supports the ideas of Freire (2002), because, for him, educating is a political act, a critical and conscious process. Thus, the practice of thinking, as a liberating and emancipatory consciousness movement, demands political engagement and ethical commitment, factors that provide the recognition of why and how to teach. In the case of inclusive education, this issue also matters. If educating is a political and critical act, how can we ensure the ethics of inclusion in the act of teaching?

First of all, we need to investigate the misconceptions of the concept 'inclusion'. The *Global Monitoring Report on Education 2020 in Latin America and the Caribbean* (UNESCO, 2020) showed reductionist understandings of inclusion.

About 60% of the countries in the region have a definition of inclusive education, but only 64% of these definitions cover multiple marginalized groups, suggesting that most countries have not yet adopted a broad concept of inclusion. Compared to the rest of the world, more ministries of education have created laws targeting individual groups, for example, addressing disability (95%), gender (66%), and ethnic minorities and indigenous peoples (64%). But in the case of students with disabilities, the laws provide for education in separate settings in 42% of the countries and for inclusive education in only 16%; the rest opt for combinations of segregation and integration. (UNESCO, 2020, p. ix)

The persistence on segregating special schools, for example, suggests the so-called inclusive educational policies could be on the verge of exclusion when they do not overcome the classifying, selective, and excluding mindset supported by old dichotomies, fed by the horror of differences. Thus, it is important to have a discussion about how children and young people inhabit the school and under what conditions this has been happening. "Inclusion policies require making explicit the values that are implicit in the idea of inclusion" (UNESCO, 2022, p.15) such as the pursuit of equity and sustainability, respect for human rights.

Inclusion is not a catchall for an education system set apart by marking differences. This is called segregation. Inclusion demands equal conditions of access to all equipment, technology, and language that promotes the right to learn, while being different, in the school community. It must also be stated that the movement of "integrating with the environment as it is" is not an inclusive movement. Inclusion demands that the school space, by means of democratic management, constantly transform itself to ensure accessibility in its various dimensions (attitudinal, communicational, physical, curricular etc.).

Chief among these expectations is that our learning environments be designed with a deep understanding and appreciation for individual variability. That is a fundamental premise of universal design for learning and the educational systems made with UDL principles in mind. (Meyer et al., 2014, p.46)

There are arguments, experiences, and testimonies that can leverage the ethical leap proposed by the inclusive education paradigm. UNESCO advocates a broad view of inclusive education, where inclusion reflects equity. Thus, it is considered that "inclusion is both a process – the actions and practices aimed at diversity and respect for the value and potential of each person – and a situation or outcome, which has a multifaceted nature." (UNESCO, 2022, p. 18). This understanding of inclusive education also finds support in Freire's ideas.

Freire's perspective brings aspects that condition not only teaching practice, but also inclusive education.

[...] Teaching requires risk, acceptance of the new, and rejection of any form of discrimination [...] Teaching requires critical reflection on practice [...] Teaching requires the recognition and assumption of cultural identity [...] Teaching requires the recognition of being conditioned [...] Teaching requires the conviction that change is possible [...] Teaching requires readiness for dialog [...] Teaching requires loving the students [...] (Freire, 2002, p. 6)

In this research, 'loving the students' was approximated to the principle of engagement proposed by UDL. The teachers understood that every effort to offer learning support systems can be linked to the loving teaching proposed by Freire.

Discrimination, inequality, and violation of rights need to be tackled on different fronts. On the one hand, the rejection of any form of discrimination puts into perspective the ethical leap towards overcoming the individual merit continually affirmed through performance evaluations, based on the school's prescriptive curriculum. The inequality among individuals is the social starting point offered to them since they are born, as – vulnerable at this moment – the individual is already conditioned by his cultural and social environment.

One step ahead, in the school community, critical reflection demands consideration of the mode of educational management and the supporting educational policies, because there is also a social dimension to inequality. It is necessary to consider the equalization of structural conditions among schools, considering the inequalities among them in a territory – thus, in the case of Brazil, this assumes continental dimensions. The ethical leap demanded by inclusive education therefore also involves "positive discrimination in the allocation of resources to schools, states and municipalities" (UNESCO, 2022) and, from this author's perspective, also to countries.

On the other hand, when affirming the ethics of inclusive education, it is certainly important to provide opportunities for the professional development of teachers based on the conviction that change is possible. This perspective was considered by one of the teachers participating in the research in the

The Universal Design for Learning in the Context of Brazilian Education

following terms: `We are moving forward. I would say that we are on a fine line of transformation on the ways of teaching; I have no doubt that universal design for learning contributes to this aim´ (Experience Report, Teacher Carolina). In this sense, UDL can support us as an educational technology committed to changing the way we teach, respecting each and every one. Compared to Freirian ideas, would not this be lovingness?

The change needed is collectively and collaboratively constructed, based on the lovingness of those who educate. Therefore, the ethical leap towards inclusive education also demands collective and dialogic spaces that seek to signify what it means to care for the students. This demonstrates the relevance of narrative research in the field of inclusive education, as it opens space for teachers to reflect on their own teaching practice, which is something fundamental for the teaching professional development, according to Freire (2002).

UDL and the Necessary Confrontation With Bureaucratization of Teaching Work

Teachers are very overloaded with numerous documents that the Department of Education has been demanding. If only we could have other types of records that did not commit so much time to planning! If this time were extended, teachers could have a more qualified planning, being able to think about each and every one, in each proposal to be delivered. (Experience Report, Teacher Elisa, 2020)

This teacher's statement introduces a central problem of working with UDL in Brazilian schools – the hijacking of the time and space allocated for planning instruction. This investigation has come across the persistent tension between monoculture and ecologies (Santos, 2008) in teaching practice. On the one hand, there was the institutionalization of time/space for teaching and learning by the institution. On the other hand, the work with UDL demanded the ecologies of differently wise knowledges in schools. The clashes were especially between the prescriptive curriculum and the new teaching approaches proposed by UDL, which should be more flexible and open to the influence of the learners. Therefore, as educational design, UDL demands change in the restricted educational system, because, as pointed out by Teacher Gabriela, "institutional bureaucratization compromises the time to plan".

Schools that choose to work with the principles of UDL need to face the problem of the bureaucratization of school work and rethink their physical and organizational structure, and opening up the curriculum is paramount. To have contexts tied to prescriptive and inflexible curricula is to inevitably have numerous barriers in teaching and learning process. This needs to be overcome. A prescriptive curriculum will hardly provide an opening for a re-signification of the teaching and learning process, since it already determines what, when, and how to learn. Changing these rigid spaces and times requires another curricular conception, such as the one proposed by UDL.

There is an understanding that in Brazil, since the Federal Constitution of 1988, following the assurance of educational rights for all, the prescriptive curriculum would be doomed and replaced by a new organization of a more flexible and dynamic teaching and learning process. This is consistent with the accessible curriculum proposed by UDL.

The process of planning and building an accessible curricular approach demands greater narrativity, openness, and curricular flexibility in the sense of extending students' degree of students on the learning journey. This is relevant for learner engagement in school education as it respects the variability of

233

learning neural networks (recognition networks, strategic networks, and affective networks) as guided by UDL (CAST, 2018).

UDL brings the demand for designing a flexible, accessible curriculum approach. But flexibility does not mean improvisation, it is necessary to plan inclusive education and understand that, in school, the teaching professional has a central role in the planning of education and needs the necessary conditions for such an endeavor. There are foundations for inclusive education and they are non-negotiable, among them are time and space to think about inclusive education. Therefore, inclusive education requires stopping the bureaucratic time of the school, demanding leisure and empty space, because new pedagogical practices can only happen where there is empty space for reflection. If all the time is taken up with hegemonic (Freire, 2005) and monocultural (Santos, 2008) school practices, there will be no way to develop inclusive education in such school.

But what has led to the increasing bureaucratization of school work in Brazilian schools? There are several possible causes for this, from the implementation of managerialism in the school (Jeffrey, 2012) to curriculum prescription (Silva, 2010) that demand monitoring and control of teaching work and its performativity.

In this text, this author proposes an approximation with Biesta's ideas, who considers that, in contemporary society, the language of education has been replaced by the language of learning. This has been termed *learnification* by the author (Biesta, 2013). There is an imposition of what should be learned, and the school, most of the times, continues to work with a hegemonic pedagogy guided by extreme rationality, monitoring, and control, disregarding that educating involves affectation, sensibility, and risk. Thus, in the process of building the inclusive school, more questions are important: how to question the `learning society´? How can we take back the issue of inclusive education and give it the centrality it deserves?

Biesta (2013) warns us that educational action is difficult and there are risks in it, so it is necessary to trust teachers and students, who are central actors in education. Even if there is, in the educational market, an insane race to guarantee a hegemonic type of learning to the student, it is necessary to affirm that the educator has the function of teaching. Reducing education to a commodity distorts the role of both the teacher and the student in the dynamic process of school education.

The act of learning is unique for each student, and they alone are the author of this process, because learning is a response, not an acquisition. No school or teacher makes a learner learn. It is the individual who learns, and every individual learns differently. In this scenario, it is important to understand UDL guidelines as a support for every teacher who intends to teach guided by the inclusion paradigm.

In this investigative process, two movements were noticed. On the one hand, the curricular opening proposed by UDL impacted the organization of teaching and learning times and spaces, pointing to the impossibility of its application without affecting the school's pedagogical project. On the other hand, the persistent bureaucratization of teaching work and the consequent lack of time for planning teaching made it impossible to work with the principles of UDL and discouraged teachers interested in inclusive education.

The main challenges pointed out by the teachers participating in this research were: the difficulty in developing activities that include all students considering the heterogeneity of the class, the institutional bureaucratization that compromises the time to plan the teaching, and the scarce means to overcome the difficulties encountered.

These challenges, however, will only be overcome in the school collective, because it is necessary that the educators have guaranteed conditions to perform their teaching role. The school must systematically be a space for teaching and learning, providing the foundations for this, not ignoring the fact that all individuals learn, including the teachers. Thus, UDL proposal also demands time for teachers to learn new practices. This leads us to teacher professional development in the field of inclusive education.

Given this background, this research, by opting for the narrative approach combined with developmental research, provided an opportunity for on-the-job training, stemming from reflection on one's own practice and the search for the necessary conditions for making inclusive education effective at school. During this process, it was necessary to recognize and value differences as learning opportunities, working towards appreciation for variability (CAST, 2018).

UDL was a support in this investigative process together with the teachers, by being both a new epistemological basis for teaching and a method to reach the inclusive curriculum approach. After the research conclusion, UDL continued to impact teaching in schools, with challenges and advances. For example, one of the education networks involved in the research has included UDL into its educational policy as follows: "UDL is a tool that should be part of the lesson plan, contributing to the transformation of the pedagogical environment, prioritizing the elimination of barriers" (São Caetano do Sul, 2022, p.8) in teaching.

Also, when the research *School for all* was completed by 2022, participants of the ACESSI research group were asked to write a pedagogical letter telling beginning teachers what inclusive education would look like. The results were very interesting, indicating both demands and guiding principles of inclusive education.

The demands included planning as a priority practice, partnership among peers at school, the deconstruction of the established standard for teaching and learning, accessibility resources, and the need for teachers to always learn. As for the principles of inclusive education, the following is the final excerpt of one of the pedagogical letters, by teacher Ana Carolina. The teacher listed four principles of inclusive education. Namely:

- Universality, equality and equity in the access and permanence in school;
- Recognition that every person is capable of learning;
- Providing different learning journeys,
- Coexistence in the common school environment that benefits everyone. (Pedagogical Letter, Teacher Ana Carolina, 2022)

If considered in a circular and interdependent relationship as imbricated dimensions in the understanding of what inclusive education is, these principles meet the inclusion paradigm. However, if deemed in a Cartesian fashion, i.e., in insolation, they can lead to reductionist pitfalls. For example, the principle of "providing different learning journeys" can lead to segregation of differently abled students, as already mentioned in the previous axis of discussion. Thus, it is important to reflect on the epistemological supports for inclusive education.

Epistemological Supports for Inclusive Education: Approaches Between UDL and the Pedagogy of Seasons

In Brazil, the inclusion in school of students eligible for special education services has been emblematic when considering the epistemological foundations of inclusive education. The poem in the epigraph that opens this axis of discussion was written by a teacher who works in the specialized educational service offered to students with disabilities in Brazilian schools.

Brazilian researchers such as Prais (2017), Zerbato and Mendes (2018), Bock, Gesser and Nuernberg (2018), Sebastian-Heredero (2020) and Costa-Renders (2019, 2020) have pointed to the relevance of studies on the application of UDL within the Brazilian school. The studies on UDL have indicated that, still, there are important conceptual tensions when analyzing the transversality of special education in the school system. This is demonstrated especially with regard to the paradox inherent in inclusive practices: attending to the universal (everyone) and the particular (each one). Such a problem also emerges when putting into perspective the changes needed in the school environment to support *expert learners*, because "UDL aims to change the environment design rather than the learner. When environments are intentionally designed to reduce barriers, all learners can engage in rigorous and meaningful learning" (CAST, 2018). Thus, it has been a challenge to account for the variability of strategies required by learners without losing sight of the global scale.

In facing this paradox, this author has proposed the metaphor of the Pedagogy of Seasons (Costa-Renders, 2019) which considers the seasons as a metaphor for inclusive education. There is a conceptual tripod that underpins the Pedagogy of Seasons, namely: the paradigmatic transition in education, simultaneous plurality, and narrative learning (Goodson, 2010). Therefore, it is necessary to

[...] consider that knowledge reaches everyone in different times and spaces, respecting the ecology of knowledge and temporalities.

[...] ask about the temporalities and spaces of human learning that are not fixed in a pedagogical time marked by curricular rigidity, but are continuously differentiated.

[...] consider the variations and work to broaden the degree of influence learners has on curricular dynamics [...] (Costa-Renders, 2019, p. 164-165)

The Pedagogy of Seasons is close to the principles of UDL, especially regarding the dynamics of variation in the act of learning and works to increase the degree of student influence on the curricular approach. This metaphor has been important in helping to overcome the tension between institutionalized time (monoculture) and the experiential temporalities (ecologies) of different learners.

As the concept of variability is little known among Brazilian teachers, the approximation of the metaphor of seasons to UDL has provided the opportunity to reflect on the simultaneous plurality required by inclusive education. The pedagogy of the seasons allows us to put – in the same equation – the universal and particular aspects of learning, as it is in this exact movement from the multiple to the singular that the dynamics of learning temporalities/spatiality take place.

As the pedagogy of seasons enables the experience of cyclical time, in spiral, it is also possible to use multi-purpose spaces and differentiated resources for building knowledge based on simultaneous plurality. Thus, in addition to recognizing differences, all teaching and learning spaces must also consider the interpersonal variability that makes up the group.

If, as a human condition, differences are not fixed, it is important to respect variability when planning inclusive education. Our starting point is to rely on a plan that provides multiple means for learners, and not on a standard merely deemed necessary. Thus, based on the concept of variability, it is mandatory to counteract any monocultural conception of teaching.

Teaching while respecting variability also demands constantly considering that the learning object used needs to ensure possibilities of access and to vary according to the specificities shown by the

The Universal Design for Learning in the Context of Brazilian Education

learner during the educational process. In this sense, UDL proposes that, instead of adapting a proposal for a single learner, multiple and variable proposals should be presented for all learners, achieving the engagement of a greater number of individuals in the teaching and learning process.

Thus, among the learning objects developed in this research, the _Learning Stations Workshop_ is highlighted. Based on the theoretical basis of the variability of learning neural networks, this learning object seeks to support teachers in their teaching processes, aiming to contribute to inclusive education. This is a digital learning object – available on the _Sway_ platform – that proposes the application of the principles of UDL in a didactic sequence in math teaching.

In light of the Pedagogy of Seasons, the idea is to organize learning seasons in a classroom, so that the students can choose the way they would like to appropriate the curricular content presented by the teacher. The workshop took place in a space of the school premises, outside the classroom, where the learners were organized in learning seasons in rounds. There was always a mediator at each learning season, represented by a more experienced learner. This contributed both to develop new learning strategies and to value the exchange of knowledge among peers.

The _Learning Stations Workshop_ brought teachers closer to working with simultaneous plurality as proposed by the Pedagogy of Seasons. In other words, they provided an opportunity for students to work simultaneously on the same topic, but using different means and possibilities for action and expression in the classroom. The outcome of this curriculum approach pointed to the greater participation of learners in curriculum decisions, as well as the better assimilation of the curriculum content by learners.

The Pedagogy of Seasons demands a flexible curriculum, open to the influence of learners. Therefore, it is a curricular approach that must consider differences in their multiple dimensions, proposing pedagogical strategies to prevent marking differences for classification, segregation, or exclusion.

When the curriculum is not open to change and teachers are not willing to modify their plans according to the variability of learners, the prescription prevails and excludes. Therefore, it is necessary to ensure the conditions of physical, communicational, and attitudinal accessibility in schools (Costa-Renders, 2019, p.16).

Thus, it is important to understand how pedagogical intentions of greater complexity come up against models of school management and teaching practice fixed in the prescriptive curriculum. It is also important to reflect on what kind of school management would be able to contribute to a creative movement towards the recognition of human differences and the valuing of variability in and among learners in school communities. Such a perspective refers, consequently, to the required democratic management of the school, which must be based on joint decisions of the school staff in accordance with the curriculum implemented in the school.

FINAL CONSIDERATIONS

At the end of this research, it is important to highlight both the results that point to challenges inherent in the Brazilian context and the necessary epistemological revision for all teaching systems that are based on the paradigm of inclusive education.

The pedagogical letters written by the Brazilian teachers, as well as the discussions that took place in the conversation circles, pointed out that the narrative research methodology meets the principles of

UDL. This methodology made it possible to listen and record the main challenges faced by Brazilian teachers in the construction of inclusive education. As a result of this reflective process on inclusive teaching based on UDL, the daily reality of Brazilian schools pointed to the difficulty in developing activities that include all students considering the heterogeneity of the class, the institutional bureaucratization that compromises the time to plan teaching, and the scarce means to overcome the difficulties encountered. This scenario demands the continuity of Brazilian research that brings the principles of UDL closer to inclusive education. Within the scope of the ACESSI study group, new research questions are posed, among which the following stands out: From the UDL perspective, is it possible to work on the epistemological review proposed by the epistemologies of the South (decolonial), considering the relationship 'knowledge and power' in the micro and macro social dimension?

For the final theoretical construct of this research, globally, it is pointed out the indispensable discussion of the semantic scope of the concept "universal design". If it is interpreted as curriculum planning based on a universalizing standard, the concept contradicts inclusive education. But if it is considered as a curriculum planning that aims at "extending the learners' degree of influence on the learning journeys", "universal design" contributes significantly to the realization of inclusive education. Here, understanding the variability of learning neural networks becomes more important, because only by respecting variability can learners participate in curriculum decisions in the school context.

Recognizing variability meets the challenge of perceiving heterogeneity in the school for all, in the sense that teachers build teaching based on the recognition of differences as a value and inspiration for building new pedagogical strategies in the classroom. Planning based on the principles of UDL becomes relevant in this situation, as it supports teachers in the process of anticipating learning situations, ensuring multiple means of representation, action, expression, and engagement to meet the needs of each and every person in inclusive education.

REFERENCES

Biesta, G. (2013). *Para além da aprendizagem: educação democrática para um futuro humano*. Autêntica.

Brazil. (1996). Casa Civil. *Lei n° 9.394, de 20 de dezembro de 1996*. Estabelece as Diretrizes e Bases da Educação Nacional. Casa Civil. http://www.planalto.gov.br/ccivil_03/leis/l9394.htm

Brazil. (2008). Ministério da Educação. *Política Nacional de Educação Especial na Perspectiva da Educação Inclusiva*. Ministério da Educação. http://portal.mec.gov.br/seesp/arquivos/pdf/politica.pdf

Brazil. (2014). Ministério da Educação. *Plano Nacional de Educação 2014-2014*. Ministério da Educação. https://pne.mec.gov.br/

Brazil (2015). Instituto Nacional de Estudos e Pesquisa Educacionais. *Censo Escolar 2015*. http://portal.inepp.gov.br/web/guest/sinopses-estatisticas-da-educacao-basica

CAST. (2018). *UDL and the learning brain*. Wakefield, MA: Author. Retrieved from https://www.cast.org/our-work/publications/2018/udl-learning-brainneuroscience.html

Clandinin, D. J., & Connelly, F. M. (2004). *Narrative Inquiry: Experience and Story in Qualitative Research*. Jossey-Bass.

Costa-Renders, E. C. (2019). Pedagogy of Seasons and UDL: the multiple temporalities of learning involving the university as a whole. In *Bracken, S. & Novak, K. (org) Transforming Higher Education Through Universal Design for Learning an International Perspective* (pp. 159–178). Routledge. doi:10.4324/9781351132077-10

Freire, P. (2002). *Pedagogia da autonomia: saberes necessários à prática educativa* (25th ed.). Paz e Terra.

Freire, P. (2005). Pedagogy of the oppressed. *Continuum.*

Goodson, I. (2010). *Narrative Learning.* Routledge. doi:10.4324/9780203856888

Jeffrey, D. C. (2012). A constituição do gerencialismo na educação brasileira: Implicações na valorização dos profissionais da educação. *Revista Exitus, 2,* 51–60.

Mantoan, M. T. E. (2015). *Inclusão Escolar: o que é? Por quê? Como fazer?* Summus.

Marcelo, C. G. (2009) Desenvolvimento profissional docente: passado e futuro. *Sísifo – Revista de Ciências da Educação,* [S.I.], n. 8, p. 7-22.

Meyer, A., Rose, D. H., & Gordon, D. (2014). *Universal design for learning: Theory and practice.* Cast Professional Publishing.

Rios, T. A. (2001). *Compreender e ensinar: por uma docência de melhor qualidade.* Cortez.

Santos, B. S. (2008). *B.S. A gramática do tempo.* Cortez.

SCS. (2022). *Política municipal de educação especial a serviços da educação inclusive.* SCS..

Silva, T. T. (2010). *Documentos de identidade: uma introdução às teorias do currículo.* Autêntica Editora.

Strangman, N., Vue, G., Hall, T., & Meyer, A. (2004). *Graphic Organizers and Implications for Universal Design for Learning: Curriculum Enhancement Report.* National Center on Accessing the General Curriculum.

UNESCO. (2020). *Relatório de monitoramento global da educação, 2020, América Latina e Caribe: Inclusão e educação: todos sem exceção, principais mensagens e recomendações.* UNESCO. https://unesdoc.unesco.org/ark:/48223/pf0000374790_por

UNESCO/BRAZIL. (2022). *Inclusão, equidade e desigualdades entre estudantes das escolas públicas de ensino fundamental no Brasil.* UNESCO. https://unesdoc.unesco.org/ark:/48223/pf0000382175

United Nations. (2006). *Convention on the rights of persons with disabilities.* UN. https://www.un.org/disabilities/documents/convention/Convoptprot-e.pdf

United Nations. (2015). *The Sustainable Development Goals (SDG) 2030 Agenda.* UN. https://www.undpp.org/sustainable-development-goals

KEY TERMS AND DEFINITIONS

Accessible Curriculum: A learning journey that offers the conditions of accessibility, in its multiple dimensions (attitudinal, physical, communicational, pedagogical etc.), to all students.

Democratic Education: Open educational process, based on the guarantee of collective representation, with freedom of expression and participation of all individuals in decision making.

Inclusive Education: Ethical principle committed to human rights and an open educational process that recognizes the right of all people to school education, striving to ensure conditions of accessibility, equal opportunities, and academic success for all.

Inclusive Teaching: Teaching ethically committed to an accessible curriculum approach, which balances equality and difference in the classroom, by means of pedagogical strategies based on the conditions of accessibility and academic success for all students.

Pedagogy of Seasons: A metaphor applicable to open teaching and learning processes, based on providing different learning seasons simultaneously, while respecting the different temporalities and spatiality of each student's learning.

Teacher Professional Development: The process by which the identity and professional character of teachers are built, involving their initial and continuing education, on-the-job training, development of their repertoire of knowledge, and their professional careers.

Universal Design for Learning: Curriculum approach that supports teachers in the process of breaking down barriers in education by delivering curriculum content in multiple media, in different kinds of action and expression, and respecting engagement.

Chapter 14
The Professional Development Needs of Special Education Teachers Teaching Students With Autism Spectrum Disorder in Western China

Chen Han
https://orcid.org/0000-0001-5122-0087
University of New South Wales, Australia

Therese M. Cumming
https://orcid.org/0000-0003-4113-6046
University of New South Wales, Australia

Geraldine Townend
University of New South Wales, Australia

ABSTRACT

Students with autism spectrum disorder (ASD) often require specialised support. This highlights the need for the provision of high-quality professional development to improve teachers' skills to support these students. There is a dearth of literature investigating the types, duration, and quality of professional development that influence teacher practices with students with ASD in the Chinese context. This chapter aims to fill the gap and explore the professional development needs of special education teachers teaching students with ASD in Western China. The results of the study conducted by the authors indicated that teachers in Western China had a strong desire to participate in autism-specific professional development, but it was rarely available and/or did not meet their needs. The chapter concludes with implications and directions for future teacher professional development in special education.

DOI: 10.4018/978-1-6684-7370-2.ch014

Copyright © 2023, IGI Global. Copying or distributing in print or electronic forms without written permission of IGI Global is prohibited.

INTRODUCTION

Autism spectrum disorder (ASD) is a complex and lifelong neurodevelopmental disability, characterised by persistent impairments in social communication and interaction and restricted or/and repetitive patterns of behaviours, interests, or activities, according to the *Diagnostic and Statistical Manual of Mental Disorders, Fifth Edition, Text Revision (DSM-5-TR™)* (American Psychological Association [APA], 2022). Because of these unique characteristics, individuals with ASD often have difficulties in social interactions and engagement and engage in challenging behaviours (APA, 2022; Hattier et al., 2011; Newcomb & Hagopian, 2018). Hattier et al. (2011) indicated that approximately 94% of children with ASD demonstrated at least one type of challenging behaviours.

Challenging Behaviours

Challenging behaviours are socially inappropriate behaviours that may negatively influence individuals with ASD and other people's health, well-being, and safety (Esteves et al., 2021). Externalising behaviours (e.g., aggressive behaviours, non-compliance, and disruptions) and internalising behaviours (e.g., self-injurious behaviours) are two main categories of challenging behaviours (Kaat & Lecavalier, 2013; Newcomb & Hagopian, 2018). Esteves et al. (2021) stressed that students with ASD with challenging behaviours are less likely to be engaged in education. This highlights the need for teachers to implement effective teaching strategies to ensure that all students, including students with ASD with behavioural problems, can receive an appropriate education.

In recent years, under the government initiatives of inclusive education, more and more children with ASD, including those with low-functioning ASD, worldwide have engaged in school education (Gargiulo & Metcalf, 2017). Also, according to the *United Nations Conventions on the Rights of Persons with Disabilities* (UNCRPD), individuals with disabilities must have equal opportunities to receive an appropriate and quality education (United Nations Division for Social Policy and Development Disability [UNDSPDD], 2006). Thus, providing reasonable accommodations and adjustments for all students are the leading educational practices to promote inclusion. However, although improving student access to inclusive education has been emphasised in international and national policies, many schools still experience difficulties providing quality education for students with disabilities, especially students with ASD (Cooc, 2019; Han & Cumming, 2022).

A shortage of special education teachers and mainstream teachers who lack sufficient knowledge in special and inclusive education are two significant issues that lead to low-quality educational provisions for students with disabilities, especially students with ASD. Rae et al. (2010) stressed that teachers' beliefs about the education of students with disabilities were attributed to the types and severities of disabilities; thus, teachers often had unfavourable beliefs toward students with severe developmental or behavioural disorders, such as ASD. Indeed, many studies showed that teachers often felt ill-prepared to teach students with ASD due to a lack of knowledge and training about autism (Bellini et al., 2016; Hyman & Levy, 2013; Low et al., 2020; Morrier et al., 2011).

Evidence-Based Practices

Evidence-based practices (EBPs) refer to effective instructional or intervention strategies supported by high-quality research to promote students' academic learning, social participation, and behavioural out-

Needs of Special Education Teachers of ASD Students in West China

comes (Boutot, 2016; Cook et al., 2015). Lubas et al. (2015) and Wong et al. (2015) stressed that implementing EBPs was essential to decrease the incidence of challenging behaviours by students with ASD. Thus, teachers are encouraged to use EBPs in classrooms to support students in learning and modifying their problematic behaviours and meet students' academic and social needs (Marder & deBettencourt, 2015). However, although many empirical studies have explored the effectiveness of EBPs for students with ASD, a gap exists between research and practice (Cook & Schirmer, 2003; Eldevik et al., 2009).

On the one hand, some EBPs focus on intensive child-centred interventions, so those EBPs are often implemented in highly controlled settings instead of the school environment (Pas et al., 2016; Stahmer et al., 2015). There is little evidence to show how teachers translate those EBPs into classrooms (Pas et al., 2016). On the other hand, teachers typically receive insufficient training in EBPs to limit their use of EBPs during practice (Stahmer et al., 2015). For instance, Odom et al. (2013) found that special education teachers were less likely to implement EBPs during teaching practice, and their implementation was often inconsistent with fidelity. Although teachers can learn EBPs from textbooks or research studies, Stahmer et al. (2014) emphasised that teachers must receive supervised practicum training for several hours or even over the years to master those intervention strategies. Therefore, after the initial teacher preparation, professional development is the primary method to develop teachers' skills and knowledge to teach students with ASD (Billingsley & Bettini, 2017), especially in implementing effective EBPs to support the behaviours of students with ASD.

Professional Development

Local governments and schools often respond to this lack of knowledge by providing professional development opportunities and redesigning the training for teachers in special education, especially in autism and EBPs, to improve teachers' skills in teaching these students (Chao et al., 2016; Garrad et al., 2019; Robinson, 2017). Professional development is recognised as an essential component of the profession that aims to support teachers to learn specific and advanced knowledge in teaching and build on their skills to meet student needs and support the attainment of positive student outcomes (Britton & Anderson, 2010; Johnson, 2020). According to international surveys, teachers in many places are required to engage in professional development at least 10.5 days per year (Sellen, 2016). Because teachers' income and job titles are often associated with their engagement in professional development (Chetty et al., 2014), a lack of professional support can lead to job dissatisfaction and burnout (Bettini et al., 2017). Coman et al. (2013) and Corona et al. (2017) indicated that professional development could prevent special education teacher burnout.

Self-efficacy refers to how people feel about their capabilities to meet challenges in a specific context. For example, if people believe they can solve problems in particular situations, they may have positive attitudes and perform well (Bandura, 1977). Research shows that teachers who engaged in professional development in autism were often more confident and had high self-efficacy when teaching students with ASD; hence, they were more likely to hold positive attitudes toward students with ASD and inclusive education (Corona et al., 2017).

Teachers' professional development has various formats, such as formal and informal learning, workshops, mentoring, coaching, etc. (Jemsem & Rasmussen, 2018). Thacker (2017) stated that formal professional development differed from informal professional learning. Informal professional development refers to some voluntary and incidental experiences that teachers participate in, such as discussing with colleagues, and it is not formally organised by schools (Thacker, 2017; Tonga et al., 2022). Conversely,

243

formal professional development is defined as systematically structured training to prepare teachers with sufficient knowledge for their teaching practices (Thacker, 2017; Tonga et al., 2022). There is a positive correlation between teachers' professional development and students' educational outcomes (Glackin, 2016). This, alongside other educational experiences, can determine teacher quality, as teachers with sufficient knowledge of course content and classroom management can efficiently implement their expertise into teaching practice (Tonga et al., 2022).

Numerous professional development approaches exist to support teachers working with students with ASD. However, Brock et al. (2014) indicated that some common forms of professional development, such as stand-alone workshops, might limit teachers' capacity to implement appropriate strategies for students with ASD. Other studies also showed that the stand-alone training or workshops had little or no impact on teachers' daily practice, as teachers faced challenges when generalising content learned from the training without any follow-up support (Barnes et al., 2011; Hall et al., 2010). In contrast, some other types of professional development have been deemed effective in supporting teacher practice; these include ongoing consultation, one-to-one coaching or supervision, modelling, and performance feedback (Bertuccio et al., 2019; Brock & Carter, 2015). Nevertheless, some effective professional development models have rarely been used in schools. In addition, whether teachers participate in professional development depends on how they perceive their needs for professional development (Cooc, 2019). Therefore, some issues that influence the quality of professional development must be explored.

The first issue that influences the quality of professional development is highlighted by Brock et al. (2014), who stated that teachers' professional development needs were highly variable. There is a lack of evidence identifying the exact professional development needs of teachers teaching students with ASD (Brock et al., 2014; Cooc, 2019). Secondly, since school administrators and local governments often determine which teaching strategies should be generalised within professional development, it is unclear whether each teacher who works with students with ASD has similar or diverse preferences about training topics (Brock et al., 2014). Thirdly, a review of the pertinent international literature revealed that very few studies identified the types, duration, and quality of professional development that influence teachers' practice in teaching students with ASD (Billingsley & Bettini, 2019). Lastly, no studies have been conducted in this field in the Chinese context. Therefore, this chapter aims to fill the gap and investigate the professional development requirements and the needs of special education teachers teaching students with ASD in Western China. This is accomplished by examining the results of a study conducted by the authors (Han et al., 2022).

WESTERN CHINA AND PROFESSIONAL DEVELOPMENT FORMATS IN CHINA

Western China refers to the western part of China, including six provinces (Gansu, Guizhou, Qinghai, Shaanxi, Sichuan, and Yunnan), five autonomous regions (Guangxi, Inner Mongolia, Ningxia, Tibet, and Xinjiang), and one municipality (Chongqing). In 2000, the Chinese Central Government launched the *Western Development Plan* [西部大开发战略 Xibu dakaifa zhanlue], which divided China into eastern, central, and western regions based on economic development (Wang & Zhao, 2014). Western China covers approximately 71% of the land area of China, with 28% of the total population (Ren & Li, 2019). However, its social and economic development has been relatively slower than in central and eastern regions, due to challenging natural conditions and undeveloped transportation networks (Lee et al., 2016). In addition, 44 out of 56 ethnic minority groups in Western China have diverse cultures and languages.

Needs of Special Education Teachers of ASD Students in West China

People's educational levels in this area are also comparatively lower than in other regions. Thus, Western China is often known as a remote, barren, vast, and beautiful place (Deng & Poon-McBrayer, 2016).

Since 1999, the Chinese government has proposed the *Regulation of Continuing Education for Primary and Secondary School Teachers* [中小学教师继续教育规定 Zhongxiaoxue jiaoshi jixu jiaoyu guiding] and has encouraged school-based training (Ministry of Education of the People's Republic of China [MOE PRC], 1999). Since then, school-based training has become the main in-service professional development approach for primary and secondary teachers in China (Jiang et al., 2017). There are various formats of school-based training, such as mentorship, teaching modelling, staff workshops or seminars, and teaching and research activities (Yang & Rao, 2021). Hiebert et al. (2002) highlighted that school-based training was essential in developing teachers' instructional and research skills during teaching. However, some factors, such as unique teacher characteristics and experiences, resource provisions, school leadership and culture, and teacher teaching schedules, influence the quality of school-based training (Xia, 2006). Because teachers in remote or rural areas have a relatively lower educational background than teachers in developed regions, Zhang et al. (2012) found that most teachers in rural schools lacked the motivation to engage in school-based training due to low-quality professional development provisions.

Because of the issues of school-based training, the Chinese government in 2010 launched the *National Teacher Training Plan Program* (NTTP) (国培计划 Guopei jihua). It aims to provide standard and high-quality training opportunities for teachers in remote and rural areas, especially those teachers in Western China (Ministry of Education of the People's Republic of China [MOE PRC], 2010). The three main approaches of the NTTP include short-term and intensive face-to-face workshops, long-distance online learning, and full-time study in teacher education tertiary institutions for three to six months. In addition, this national professional development program provides teachers with knowledge of teaching ethics, subject-specific content, and pedagogical practices (Ministry of Education of the People's Republic of China [MOE PRC], 2012). The NTTP aims to improve the overall quality of teachers, especially teachers in remote or rural areas in Western China, and to promote the balanced development of compulsory education between urban and rural regions (Han, 2012; MOE PRC, 2010). According to the recent national statistics in 2020, more than 16,800,000 teachers participated in the NTTP in the past ten years, from 2010 to 2019, and 94% (approximately 15,740,000 teachers) were from Central and Western China (China Education Online, 2020). Indeed, the NTTP has become the most crucial government initiative to improve education equity between urban and rural areas in Western China (Lu et al., 2019).

Because local governments in each province are responsible for organising and implementing the NTTP, the quality and effectiveness of professional development vary across areas (Yang & Rao, 2021). Due to urban-rural disparities, teachers' characteristics (e.g., knowledge, qualifications, and experiences) in remote or rural areas are much more complex than in urban areas (Hong et al., 2015). Thus, teachers in remote or rural areas often lack professional development opportunities or receive low-quality training (Glover et al., 2016; Lin & Zhang, 2012). Moreover, very few studies have explored the effectiveness of professional development on student academic outcomes in China (Lu et al., 2019). Only one study in China conducted by Zhang et al. (2013) concluded no impact on teacher performance and students' English examination results in mainstream education after teachers received short-term professional development. No research has evaluated the effects and quality of professional development in special education in China. This emphasises the significance of a study conducted by Han et al. (2022) in exploring special education teachers' professional development needs when working with students with ASD in Western China.

The researchers employed a qualitative research design, using semi-structured interviews, under the interpretive or constructivist paradigm to explore teachers' beliefs in professional development when teaching students with ASD. This study was essential to identify special education teachers' experiences and professional development needs in Western China. Ethics approval was obtained for this study from the university with which the researchers were affiliated. Then, purposeful sampling was used in the study to recruit relevant participants. A total of 23 teachers currently teaching students with ASD from six special education schools or services in Western China were recruited for the study. The following sections contain recommendations for teachers, schools, training providers, and policymakers grounded in the results of the researchers' study to inform the provision of teacher professional development.

TEACHERS' BELIEFS AND NEEDS ABOUT PROFESSIONAL DEVELOPMENT IN WESTERN CHINA

Teachers' Beliefs About Current Professional Development Opportunities

Professional development is essential in supporting teachers' competence in teaching students with disabilities (Hirsch et al., 2020). In the current study, most teacher participants held positive beliefs about the professional development they had participated in previously. In addition, they acknowledged that some in-service and outside-service formal training could build on their knowledge in special education, especially in autism and behavioural management. Previous studies indicated that teachers who participated in the appropriate and effective professional development in special education could not only develop their knowledge, hands-on experience, and confidence levels during teaching practice, but also promote students' academic outcomes and social and emotional well-being (Hu et al., 2017; Feng & Sass, 2013; Segall & Campbell, 2012). This finding is consistent with previous literature that suggests professional development can improve teachers' teaching skills and construct positive beliefs towards the education of students with ASD (Hu et al., 2017; Feng & Sass, 2013).

However, many participants in the current study believed that short-term or traditional professional development was not helpful to their practice. Most participants indicated that they felt challenged to translate knowledge learned from lecture-style training into actual teaching practices, which reflects the majority of existing literature. For instance, Bethune and Wood (2013) and Wei (2010) emphasised that short-term training and single-event workshops or lectures were ineffective in supporting teachers' daily practice. Also, Wei (2010) indicated that inadequate professional development might negatively affect teachers' teaching practice, because teachers often felt frustrated when not learning the requisite skills or knowledge to teach. Thus, it is critical to provide follow-up training, such as ongoing constructive feedback, to increase teachers' skills to be flexible to implement knowledge into teaching practices.

In the current study, most participants complained that much professional development that they participated in was too general and theoretical, so they felt unsatisfied with those training sessions. Darling-Hammond et al. (2017) proposed a framework for effective professional development: (a) focus on specific teaching skills, (b) design activities to motivate teachers during training sessions, (c) provide sufficient practical examples, and (d) provide teachers time and opportunities to learn and implement knowledge. Woulfin and Jones (2021) also constructed three tenets of effective professional development, including extended duration, collaborative and contextualised learning, and specialised content. There are similarities between the two frameworks, as they emphasise that professional development must focus on specific knowledge or instructional skills that can meet teachers' training needs. Also, training should combine both theoretical knowledge and practical examples or opportunities to build on teachers' skills in real-day practice. Therefore, professional development should integrate specific content, pedagogical knowledge, and practical examples or opportunities. Woulfin and Jones's (2021) framework also emphasised the importance of collaboration among teachers and other school personnel. This highlighted that teachers and school personnel should work together to design and organise professional development to meet teachers' needs in teaching (Woulfin & Jones, 2021).

In addition, the current study showed that most participants felt that professional development within a more extended period would efficiently help their understanding and practical implementation. Indeed, an extended duration of professional development has been emphasised in Darling-Hammond et al.'s (2017) and Woulfin and Jones' (2021) frameworks. More time spent in professional development could provide teachers with sufficient time and opportunities to learn new ideas, implement new knowledge during practice, and support reflection and evaluation (Darling-Hammond et al., 2017). Therefore, based on the research results and the two frameworks described above, future professional development for special education teachers should be extended, with multiple and sufficient practical examples and opportunities, to prepare teachers with relevant theoretical and practical knowledge to teach students with ASD.

Nevertheless, this study showed a negative correlation between teachers' educational backgrounds and professional development beliefs (or needs). For instance, some participants with low-level educational backgrounds believed that it was unnecessary to learn advanced instructional or intervention strategies or the most recent research findings in autism when teaching students with ASD. Instead, they thought having basic special education knowledge was enough to handle their teaching practices. Also, some participants working in country towns believed they were not responsible for implementing additional support for students with ASD, as very few students were diagnosed with ASD in the classrooms. Thus, these teachers were less likely to participate in autism-related professional development. Indeed, this finding from the current study is surprising, as most past studies found that teachers were motivated to be engaged in professional development, and most teachers showed a high level of desire to gain more knowledge and skills through professional development (Cooc, 2019; Hagaman & Casey, 2018). This finding highlights that teachers should be consulted when designing professional development to meet their professional development needs, rather than only designing sessions based on the providers' knowledge or expertise. Professional development should be practical, and teachers' teaching practices can inform and support the design of future training sessions.

Teachers' Needs for Future Professional Development

All participants in the current study intended to engage in autism-related training, as they thought that teaching students with ASD differed from teaching students with other disabilities. However, most participants expressed their interest in learning more about speech and language therapy, because they believed that supporting student speech and language skills was their priority as special education teachers working with students with ASD. They also thought that the main reason for challenging behaviours shown by students with ASD was language and communication impairments. Very few participants in the study wanted to learn about positive behaviour support, even though they struggled with managing student behavioural problems. This is inconsistent with recommendations provided in previous literature that teachers must have a solid knowledge of behavioural management strategies, such as Applied Behaviour Analysis (ABA), to teach students with ASD (Han & Cumming, 2022). This reveals that special education teachers in remote or rural areas have some misconceptions about the functions of misbehaviours demonstrated by these students. This also provides some implications for training providers to design and organise appropriate and effective professional development for teachers, especially in positive behaviour support.

External Factors Influencing Teachers' Professional Development Needs

According to Bettini et al. (2016), Chao et al. (2016), and others, external factors, such as teachers' characteristics and beliefs, levels of cooperation with other professionals or experts, and school conditions and context, may influence teacher beliefs and needs in professional development.

Teachers' professional development needs may be influenced by their characteristics (e.g., educational background and qualifications) (Chao et al., 2016). For example, most participants in Western China had a lower level of education and qualifications than teachers in developed provinces in East China, so some participants who received diplomas or technical training certificates were less likely to value the benefits of professional development. Furthermore, participants with negative beliefs towards the education provision of students with ASD had low motivation to engage in professional development. This finding is consistent with some international studies, such as Feng (2012), who found that teachers in China had more negative perceptions of inclusive education and professional development if they had lower competencies and knowledge in special education. Conversely, teachers in the United States who possessed advanced degrees and were certified in special education lacked the motivation to be engaged in professional development (Sharma et al., 2013). These two previous studies had controversial findings regarding special education teachers' professional development needs. However, the results highlight that teachers are more likely to feel confident teaching students with ASD if they obtain sufficient knowledge and intervention skills (e.g., EBPs) via preservice and in-service training. As such, appropriate training is the most crucial component for teachers teaching students with ASD.

Teachers' beliefs also influence their professional development needs (Darling-Hammond et al., 2009). In the current study, all participants wanted to participate in professional development and were willing to be engaged in autism-specific training in the future. This finding is aligned with Opfer (2016), who found that teachers had strong intentions to seek professional development opportunities if they felt responsible for providing accommodations and adjustments for all students in the classrooms, including those with ASD. This suggests that teachers should frequently reflect on their beliefs about teaching students with ASD. It also emphasises that teachers should actively support and meet the needs of students with ASD to participate in their classrooms rather than just having them physically attend. For example, teachers can address students' challenging behaviours quickly by implementing EBPs instead of ignoring their behaviours. Also, training sessions in the future should focus more on practical aspects and provide teachers with the relevant skills to create a more tolerant and autism-friendly environment for students with ASD.

Moreover, teachers' levels of cooperation with other teachers or experts is another factor influencing their professional development needs (Loxley et al., 2007). For example, teacher participants in Western China, especially those working in country towns, had little contact with other teachers and were not interested in engaging in professional development. Also, because schools and local governments in country towns often provided few professional development opportunities in special education, teachers lacked opportunities to communicate with experts outside schools. The research findings are similar to

Arndt and Liles (2010), who mentioned that teachers who did not collaborate with colleagues were less likely to participate in professional development, even though they had high training needs.

Further, school conditions, including resource provisions, administrative support, and training opportunities, influence special education teachers' professional development needs (Bettini et al., 2016). The current study showed that teachers in provincial capital cities had more professional development opportunities than teachers working in country towns. Although rural teachers had the chance to participate in the NTTP, they felt that much professional development training was related to mainstream education than special education. Indeed, a lack of school support can reduce teachers' interest in engaging in professional development, which was evident in the current study. Some teacher participants complained that they could only engage in professional development during school holidays due to their heavy workloads. This finding is consistent with Yang and Rao (2021), who found that rural teachers in Shaanxi province, China, had demanding teaching responsibilities during the workdays, making it difficult to engage in professional development. This highlights the need for schools and local governments to provide teachers with support that lessens their workloads or provides them with teaching relief so that they have the time to attend professional learning. Reforming professional development is also essential to ensure that all special education teachers who participate in professional development can be benefits from training. In addition, professional development provisions should not be restricted to intensive workshops or seminars. Ongoing mentoring and coaching should be provided on workdays to help teachers learn appropriate knowledge during teaching practices; then, teachers can be beneficial in balancing their time between work and life.

IMPLICATIONS FOR PRACTICE

The findings discussed above provide a snapshot of how special education teachers' beliefs affect their professional development needs in Western China. This study also has practical implications for the provision of future professional development.

Firstly, providing autism-related professional development is essential to support teachers with less substantial educational backgrounds and qualifications to gain theoretical and practical knowledge about autism. Although this statement should be made to cover students with other disabilities in special education, teachers showed more challenges and insufficient understanding and confidence in teaching students with ASD, especially applying EBPs to address students' behaviours. Moreover, training providers should provide more training related to speech and language therapy to meet teachers' training needs. Indeed, language and communication impairments are one of the factors that lead to behavioural problems exhibited by students with ASD (Han & Cumming, 2022), but teachers should also understand that student misbehaviour can serve different functions. Teachers must analyse the causes of students' behaviours during practice. In order to design and implement appropriate interventions, teachers must first determine the functions/causes of the behaviours. This emphasises the need for more training related to positive behaviour support and EBPs, especially in functional behaviour assessment (FBA) and ABA. Professional development around positive behaviour support can also help teachers form more positive beliefs toward students and their behaviours and guide them in supporting students with ASD to learn appropriate behaviours rather than just passively managing or stopping misbehaviours.

Secondly, professional development should be provided based on teachers' priorities and needs across different contexts. School administrators must consider teachers' education and skill levels and what knowledge and intervention strategies can best support their teaching practice. For instance, the current study showed that most teachers in non-government services did not have degrees or qualifications in special education. Thus, these teachers may require more training related to fundamental knowledge in autism and behaviour management, and more practical demonstrations and opportunities should be offered during professional development. In contrast, in government special education schools, most teachers majored in special and inclusive education but still felt ill-prepared to teach students with ASD during practice. This suggests that training providers need to focus more on positive behaviour support and EBPs, so teachers can better understand behavioural support strategies and implement knowledge into practice. In addition, research results suggest that professional development should provide sufficient practical examples and opportunities to guide teachers to be flexible and confident in implementing what they learned from professional development into actual teaching practices.

Thirdly, the duration of professional development should be extended to give teachers time to get familiar with the required knowledge and implement knowledge into practice. Many previous studies, such as Bethune and Wood (2013) and Stewart (2014), alongside the findings from the current study, indicated that traditional professional development (e.g., short-term lectures and handouts) was ineffective in building on teachers' skills, as teachers only could receive knowledge passively but lacked opportunities to try knowledge in practice. Therefore, more follow-up training, such as ongoing feedback, mentoring, or coaching, should be provided to increase teachers' skills to implement new instructional or intervention strategies with fidelity. Further, research results indicated that teachers had difficulties participating in professional development during workdays due to heavy workloads. Therefore, school administrators should provide ongoing mentoring and coaching for teachers working with students with ASD, and then, teachers can receive progressive guidance and feedback during practice.

Fourthly, mentoring and coaching should be provided to meet teachers' teaching levels, subjects, and training needs. In the current study, although some participants stated they had mentors when they started working at schools, some mentors often were ineffective in providing guidance and support, as mentors' teaching levels and subjects often did not match early-career teachers' needs. According to previous literature, one-to-one coaching or mentoring has often been recognised as the most effective professional development type for special education teachers to promote teaching and learning outcomes. This notion supports the use of Darling-Hammond et al.'s (2017) characteristics of effective professional development to guide the design of mentoring and coaching. In addition, mentoring needs to be sustained over time, and such ongoing mentoring should involve relevant subject knowledge and general pedagogical knowledge.

Fifthly, school administrators and local governments, especially in rural areas, should provide more professional development opportunities in special and inclusive education for rural teachers to improve their knowledge and skills. For example, in Western China, most rural special education teachers are recognised as transferred teachers (转岗教师 Zhuangang Jiaoshi). This means that those rural teachers move their teaching positions from mainstream schools to special education schools, due to government initiatives to increase the number of teachers in special education in country towns. Because transferred teachers often have little knowledge of special education, transferred teacher training is essential to prepare these teachers to teach students with disabilities before they enter special education schools. Thus, transferred teacher training programs can combine mainstream and special education knowledge. It will be beneficial for rural teachers to integrate their practical experiences in mainstream education into teaching students with disabilities. Also, rural schools can provide these teachers with more opportunities to learn the most advanced intervention strategies, such as EBPs, through the NTTP.

Finally, the study results demonstrated that teachers in Western China had a high demand for participation in professional development. Therefore, high-quality professional development should be provided to meet teachers' training needs. Regarding school-based training, it will be significant to involve outside expertise in professional development, as experts from outside often can provide fresh input to challenge teachers' thinking and knowledge (Dunst et al., 2015). Moreover, Darling-Hammond et al.'s (2017) and Woulfin and Jones's (2021) frameworks about effective professional development may be followed when designing or organising autism-specific professional development. Training providers and trainers are recommended to ensure professional development focuses on specific instructional or intervention skills, such as positive behaviour support and EBPs. Providing more activities and practical examples is crucial to motivate teachers to get involved in training. More importantly, sufficient time and opportunities should be offered during training sessions to encourage teachers first to learn knowledge in autism and then implement knowledge into actual practices. Training providers are also encouraged to frequently reflect and evaluate their professional development design to ensure that professional development training is high-quality and appropriate for teachers working with students with ASD.

CONCLUSION

This chapter has examined special education teachers' beliefs and needs regarding professional development when teaching students with ASD in Western China. The findings showed that many participating teachers valued professional development and believed that professional development could improve their knowledge and skills in teaching students with ASD and support them in constructing positive beliefs towards these students and behavioural management. However, there was a negative correlation between teachers' educational levels and their beliefs and needs about professional development. Researchers found that teachers with low-level educational backgrounds, such as diplomas or technical training certificates, were less likely to participate in professional development.

On the other hand, this study found that all teachers working in Western China wanted and expected to participate in autism-specific professional development and learn more knowledge and intervention strategies when teaching students with ASD. Nevertheless, teachers' characteristics, beliefs, levels of cooperation, and school contexts were four external factors influencing teachers' professional development needs when teaching students with ASD in Western China. Because teachers' professional development needs are affected by multiple components, it highlights the need for teachers, schools, training providers, and local governments to reform the current training provisions to provide high-quality professional development and to meet teachers' training needs.

ACKNOWLEDGMENT

We would like to thank principals and leaders who gave the researchers access to their schools or services and all participating teachers who generously shared their beliefs and values.

The research reported in this article was supported by 2020 HDR Faculty Supported Research Funding Scheme, University of New South Wales.

REFERENCES

American Psychiatric Association. (2022). *Diagnostic and statistical manual of mental disorders* (fifth Edition, text revision). American Psychiatric Association.

Arndt, K., & Liles, J. (2010). Preservice teachers' perceptions of co-teaching: A qualitative study. *Action in Teacher Education, 32*(1), 15–25. doi:10.1080/01626620.2010.10463539

Bandura, A. (1977). Self-efficacy: Toward a unifying theory of behavioural change. *Psychological Review, 84*(2), 191–215. doi:10.1037/0033-295X.84.2.191 PMID:847061

Barnes, C. S., Dunning, J. L., & Rehfeldt, R. A. (2011). An evaluation of strategies for training staff to implement the picture exchange communication system. *Research in Autism Spectrum Disorders, 5*(4), 1574–1583. doi:10.1016/j.rasd.2011.03.003

Bertuccio, R. F., Runion, M. C., Culler, E. D., Moeller, J. D., & Hall, C. M. (2019). A comparison of autism-specific training outcomes for teachers and paraeducators. *Teacher Education and Special Education, 42*(4), 338–354. doi:10.1177/0888406419839771

Bethune, K. S., & Wood, C. L. (2013). Effects of coaching on teachers' use of function-based interventions for students with severe disabilities. *Teacher Education and Special Education, 36*(2), 97–114. doi:10.1177/0888406413478637

Bettini, E. A., Crockett, J. B., Brownell, M. T., & Merrill, K. L. (2016). Relationships between working conditions and special educators' instructions. *The Journal of Special Education, 50*(3), 178–190. doi:10.1177/0022466916644425

Bettini, E. A., Jones, N., Brownell, M., Conroy, M., Park, Y., Leite, W., Crockett, J., & Benedict, A. (2017). Workload manageability among novice special and general educators: Relationships with emotional exhaustion and career intentions. *Remedial and Special Education, 38*(4), 246–256. doi:10.1177/0741932517708327

Billingsley, B., & Bettini, E. (2017). Improving special education teacher quality and effectiveness. In J. M. Kauffman, D. P. Hallahan, & P. C. Pullen (Eds.), *Handbook of special education* (2nd ed., pp. 501–520). Routledge. doi:10.4324/9781315517698-39

Billingsley, B., & Bettini, E. (2019). Special education teacher attrition and retention: A review of the literature. *Review of Educational Research, 89*(5), 697–744. doi:10.3102/0034654319862495

Boutot, E. A. (2016). *Autism spectrum disorders: Foundations, characteristics, and effective strategies* (2nd ed.). Pearson Education.

Britton, L. R., & Anderson, K. A. (2010). Peer coaching and preservice teachers: Examining an underutilised concept. *Teaching and Teacher Education, 26*(2), 306–314. doi:10.1016/j.tate.2009.03.008

Brock, M. E., & Carter, E. W. (2015). Effects of a professional development package to prepare special education paraprofessionals to implement evidence-based practice. *The Journal of Special Education, 49*(1), 39–51. doi:10.1177/0022466913501882

Brock, M. E., Huber, H. B., Carter, E. W., Juarez, A. P., & Warren, Z. E. (2014). Statewide assessment of professional development needs related to educating students with autism spectrum disorder. *Focus on Autism and Other Developmental Disabilities*, *29*(20), 67–79. doi:10.1177/1088357614522290

Chao, C. N. G., Forlin, C., & Ho, F. C. (2016). Improving teaching self-efficacy for teachers in inclusive classrooms in Hong Kong. *International Journal of Inclusive Education*, *20*(11), 1142–1154. doi:10.1080/13603116.2016.1155663

Chetty, R., Friedman, J. N., & Rockoff, J. E. (2014). Measuring the impacts of teachers I: Evaluating bias in teacher value-added estimates. *The American Economic Review*, *104*(9), 2593–2632. doi:10.1257/aer.104.9.2593

China Education Online. (2020). *Shinian yue 1,680wan renci de jiaoshi canyu 'guopei jihua'* (十年约1680万人次的教师参与"国培计划") [More than 1.68 million teachers have participated in national teacher training plan program in the past ten years]. China Education Online. https://baijiahao.baidu.com/s?id=1676875761328745757&wfr=spider&for=pc

Coman, D., Alessandri, M., Novotny, S., Gutierrez, A., Boyd, B., & Hume, K. (2013). Commitment to classroom model philosophy and burnout symptoms among high fidelity teachers implementing preschool programs for children with autism spectrum disorders. *Journal of Autism and Developmental Disorders*, *43*(2), 345–360. doi:10.100710803-012-1573-1 PMID:22706583

Cooc, N. (2019). Teaching students with special needs: International trends in school capacity and the need for teacher professional development. *Teaching and Teacher Education*, *83*, 27–41. doi:10.1016/j.tate.2019.03.021

Cook, B. G., & Schirmer, B. R. (2003). What is special about special education? Overview and analysis. *The Journal of Special Education*, *37*(3), 200–205. doi:10.1177/00224669030370031001

Cook, B. G., Tankersley, M., Cook, L., & Landrum, T. J. (2015). Republication of "evidence-based practices in special education: Some practical considerations". *Intervention in School and Clinic*, *50*(5), 310–315. doi:10.1177/1053451214532071

Corona, L. L., Christodulu, K. V., & Rinaldi, M. L. (2017). Investigation of school professionals' self-efficacy for working with students with ASD: Impact of prior experience, knowledge, and training. *Journal of Positive Behavior Interventions*, *19*(2), 90–101. doi:10.1177/1098300716667604

Darling-Hammond, L., Hyler, M. E., & Gardner, M. (2017). *Effective teacher professional development*. Learning Policy Institute. doi:10.54300/122.311

Darling-Hammond, L., Wei, R. C., Andree, A., Richardson, N., & Orphanos, S. (2009). *Professional learning in the learning profession: A status report on teacher development in the U.S. and abroad*. National Staff Development Council.

Deng, M., & Poon-McBrayer, K. F. (2016). Development of special and inclusive education in Western China. In J. C.-K. Lee, Z. Yu, X. Huang, & E. H.-F. Law (Eds.), *Educational developmental in Western China: Towards quality and equity* (pp. 301–309). Sense Publishers. doi:10.1007/978-94-6300-232-5_16

Dunst, C. J., Bruder, M. B., & Hamby, D. W. (2015). Meta-synthesis of in-service professional development research: Features associated with positive educator and student outcomes. *Educational Research Review*, *10*(12), 1731–1744. doi:10.5897/ERR2015.2306

Eldevik, S., Hasting, R. P., Hughes, J. C., Jahr, E., Eikeseth, S., & Cross, S. (2009). Meta-analysis of early intensive behavioural intervention for children with autism. *Journal of Clinical Child and Adolescent Psychology*, *38*(3), 439–450. doi:10.1080/15374410902851739 PMID:19437303

Esteves, J., Perry, A., Spiegel, R., & Weiss, J. A. (2021). Occurrence and predictors of challenging behaviour in youth with intellectual disability with or without autism. *Journal of Mental Health Research in Intellectual Disabilities*, *14*(2), 189–201. doi:10.1080/19315864.2021.1874577

Feng, L., & Sass, T. R. (2013). What makes special-education special? Teacher training and achievement of students with disabilities. *Economics of Education Review*, *36*, 122–134. doi:10.1016/j.econedurev.2013.06.006

Feng, Y. (2012). Teacher career motivation and professional development in special and inclusive education: Perspectives from Chinese teachers. *International Journal of Inclusive Education*, *16*(3), 331–351. doi:10.1080/13603116.2010.489123

Gargiulo, R. M., & Metcalf, D. (2017). *Teaching in today's inclusive classrooms: A universal design for learning approach* (3rd ed.). Cengage Learning.

Garrad, T.-A., Rayner, C., & Pedersen, S. (2019). Attitudes of Australian primary school teachers towards the inclusion of students with autism spectrum disorders. *Journal of Research in Special Educational Needs*, *19*(1), 58–67. doi:10.1111/1471-3802.12424

Glackin, M. (2016). 'Risky fun' or 'Authentic science'? How teachers' beliefs influence their practice during a professional development programme on outdoor learning. *International Journal of Science Education*, *38*(3), 409–433. doi:10.1080/09500693.2016.1145368

Glover, T. A., Nugent, G. C., Chumney, F. L., Ihlo, T., Shapiro, E. S., Guard, K., Koziol, N., & Bovaird, J. (2016). Investigating rural teachers' professional development, instructional knowledge, and classroom practice. *Journal of Research in Rural Education*, *31*(3), 1–16.

Hagaman, J. L., & Casey, K. J. (2018). Teacher attrition in special education: Perspectives from the field. *Teacher Education and Special Education*, *41*(4), 277–291. doi:10.1177/0888406417725797

Hall, L. J., Grundon, G. S., Pope, C., & Romero, A. B. (2010). Training paraprofessionals to use behavioural strategies when educating learners with autism spectrum disorders across environments. *Behavioral Interventions*, *25*(1), 37–51. doi:10.1002/bin.294

Han, C., & Cumming, T. M. (2022). Behavioural supports for students with autism spectrum disorders: Practice, policy, and implications for special education reform in China. *International Journal of Inclusive Education*, *26*(1), 41–60. doi:10.1080/13603116.2019.1629120

Han, C., Cumming, T. M., & Townend, G. (2022). *Behavioural supports for students with autism spectrum disorder receiving special education services in Western China: An analysis of teacher characteristics, beliefs, and implantation of evidence-based practices* [PhD thesis, The University of New South Wales (UNSW), Australia].

Han, X. (2012). Big moves to improve the quality of teacher education in China. *On the Horizon, 20*(4), 324–335. doi:10.1108/10748121211272461

Hattier, M. A., Matson, J. L., Belva, B. C., & Horovitz, M. (2011). The occurrence of challenging behaviours in children with autism spectrum disorders and atypical development. *Developmental Neurorehabilitation, 14*(4), 221–229. doi:10.3109/17518423.2011.573836 PMID:21732806

Hiebert, J., Gallimore, R., & Stigler, J. W. (2002). A knowledge base for the teaching profession: What would it look like and how can we get one? *Educational Researcher, 31*(5), 3–15. doi:10.3102/0013189X031005003

Hirsch, S. E., Randall, K. N., Common, E. A., & Lane, K. L. (2020). Results of practice-based professional development for supporting special educators in learning how to design functional assessment-based interventions. *Teacher Education and Special Education, 43*(4), 281–295. doi:10.1177/0888406419876926

Hong, X., Luo, L., & Cui, F. (2015). Investigating regional disparities of preschool education development with cluster analysis in Mainland China. *International Journal of Child Care and Education Policy, 7*(1), 67–80. doi:10.1007/2288-6729-7-1-67

Hu, B. Y., Wu, H. P., Su, X. Y., & Roberts, S. K. (2017). An examination of Chinese preservice and in-service early childhood teaches' perspectives on the importance and feasibility of the implementation of key characteristics of quality inclusion. *International Journal of Inclusive Education, 21*(2), 187–204. doi:10.1080/13603116.2016.1193563

Hyman, S. L., & Levy, S. E. (2013). Autism spectrum disorders. In M. L. Batshaw, N. J. Roizen, & G. R. Lotrecchiano (Eds.), *Children with disabilities* (7th ed., pp. 345–368). Brookes.

Jiang, Y., Pang, L. J., & Sun, J. (2017). Early childhood teacher education in China. In N. Rao, J. Zhou, & J. Sun (Eds.), *Early childhood education in Chinese societies* (pp. 85–100). Springer Netherlands. doi:10.1007/978-94-024-1004-4_6

Johnson, S. M. (2020). *Where teachers thrive: Organising schools for success*. Harvard Education Press.

Kaat, A. J., & Lecavalier, L. (2013). Disruptive behaviour disorders in children and adolescents with autism spectrum disorders: A review of the prevalence, presentation, and treatment. *Research in Autism Spectrum Disorders, 7*(12), 1579–1594. doi:10.1016/j.rasd.2013.08.012

Lee, J. C.-K., Yu, Z., Huang, X., & Law, E. H.-F. (2016). Educational development in Western China: Towards quality and equity. In J. C.-K. Lee, Z. Yu, X. Huang, & E. H.-F. Law (Eds.), *Educational developmental in Western China: Towards quality and equity* (pp. 1–20). Sense Publishers. doi:10.1007/978-94-6300-232-5_1

Lin, Y., & Zhang, K. (2012). Pingkun diqu youer jiaoshi peixun zhuangkuang yu fazhan jianyi (贫困地区幼儿教师培训状况与发展建议) [On the preschool teachers training in the poor areas]. *Studies in Preschool Education, 205*(1), 28–32.

Low, H. M., Lee, L. W., & Ahmad, A. C. (2020). Knowledge and attitudes of special education teachers towards the inclusion of students with autism spectrum disorder. *International Journal of Disability Development and Education, 67*(5), 497–514. doi:10.1080/1034912X.2019.1626005

Loxley, A., Johnston, K., Murchan, D., Fitzgerald, H., & Quinn, M. (2007). The role of whole-school contexts in shaping the experiences and outcomes associated with professional development. *Journal of In-service Education, 33*(3), 265–285. doi:10.1080/13674580701487034

Lu, M., Loyalka, P., Shi, Y., Chang, F., Liu, C., & Rozelle, S. (2019). The impact of teacher professional development programs on student achievement in rural China: Evidence from Shaanxi Province. *Journal of Development Effectiveness, 11*(2), 105–131. doi:10.1080/19439342.2019.1624594

Lubas, M., Mitchell, J., & De Leo, G. (2015). Evidence-based practice for teachers of children with autism: A dynamic approach. *Intervention in School and Clinic, 51*(3), 188–193. doi:10.1177/1053451215585801

Marder, T., & deBettencourt, L. U. (2015). Teaching students with ASD using evidence-based practices: Why is training critical now? *Teacher Education and Special Education, 38*(1), 5–12. doi:10.1177/0888406414565838

Ministry of Education of People's Republic of China [MOE PRC]. (2010). *Jiaoyubu caizhengbu guanyu shishi "zhongxiaoxue jiaoshi guojia peixun jihua de tongzhi"* 教育部财政部关于实施"中小学教师国家培训计划的通知[Circular of National Primary and Secondary School Teacher Training Plan by the Ministry of Education and Ministry of Finance]. MOE PRC. https://www.gov.cn/gzdt/2010-06/23/content_1634944.htm

Ministry of Education of the People's Republic of China [MOE PRC]. (1999). *Zhongxiaoxue jiaoshi jixujiaoyu guidin* (中小学教师继续教育规定) [The regulation of teacher continuing education]. Beijing, China: Government Printing Office. http://www.moe.gov.cn/srcsite/A02/s5911/moe_621/199909/t19990913_180474.html

Ministry of Education of the People's Republic of China [MOE PRC]. (2012). Guopei jihua (国培计划) [National teacher training plan program]. MOE PRC. http://www.moe.gov.cn/jyb_xwfb/moe_2082/s6236/s6811/201209/t20120903_141516.html

Morrier, M. J., Hess, K. L., & Heflin, L. J. (2011). Teacher training for implementation of teaching strategies for students with autism spectrum disorders. *Teacher Education and Special Education, 34*(2), 119–132. doi:10.1177/0888406410376660

Newcomb, E. T., & Hagopian, L. P. (2018). Treatment of severe problem behaviour in children with autism spectrum disorder and intellectual disabilities. *International Review of Psychiatry (Abingdon, England), 30*(1), 96–109. doi:10.1080/09540261.2018.1435513 PMID:29537889

Odom, S. L., Cox, A. W., & Brock, M. E. (2013). Implementation science, professional development, and autism spectrum disorders. *Exceptional Children, 79*(3), 233–251. doi:10.1177/001440291307900207

Opfer, D. (2016). *Conditions and practices associated with teacher professional development and its impact on instruction in TALIS 2013.* OECD Working Paper.

Pas, E. T., Johnson, S. R., Larson, K. E., Brandenburg, L., Church, R., & Bradshaw, C. P. (2016). Reducing behaviour problems among students with autism spectrum disorder: Coaching teachers in a mixed-reality setting. *Journal of Autism and Developmental Disorders*, *46*(12), 3640–3652. doi:10.100710803-016-2898-y PMID:27590663

Rae, H., Murray, G., & McKenzie, K. (2010). Teachers' attitudes to mainstream schooling. *Learning Disability Practice*, *13*(10), 12–17. doi:10.7748/ldp2010.12.13.10.12.c8138

Ren, B., & Li, M. (2019). Xinshidai xibu diqu xindongneng peiyu de kuangjia, neirong yu lujing (新时代西部地区新动能培育的框架、内容与路径) [The framework, content and path of the new kinetic energy cultivation in the Western region under the background of the new era]. In B. Ren, L. Yue, A. He, H. Guo (Eds.), Xibu lanpishu: Zhongguo xibu fazhan baokao (西部蓝皮书:中国西部发展报告) [Blue book of the western region: Annual report on development in the western region of China (2019)] (pp. 1-27). Social Sciences Academic Press (China).

Robinson, D. (2017). Effective inclusive teacher education for special educational needs and disabilities. *Teaching and Teacher Education*, *61*, 164–178. doi:10.1016/j.tate.2016.09.007

Segall, M. J., & Campbell, J. M. (2012). Factors relating to education professionals' classroom practices for the inclusion of students with autism spectrum disorders. *Research in Autism Spectrum Disorders*, *6*(3), 1156–1167. doi:10.1016/j.rasd.2012.02.007

Sellen, P. (2016). *Teacher workload and professional development in England's secondary schools: Insights from TALIS*. Education Policy Institute.

Sharma, U., Forlinb, C., Deppelera, J., & Yang, G.-X. (2013). Reforming teacher education for inclusion in developing countries in the Asia-Pacific region. *Asian Journal of Inclusive Education*, *1*(1), 3–16. doi:10.59595/ajie.01.1.2

Stahmer, A. C., Rieth, S., Lee, E., Reisinger, E. M., Mandell, D. S., & Connell, J. S. (2015). Training teachers to use evidence-based practices for autism: Examining procedural implementation fidelity. *Psychology in the Schools*, *52*(2), 181–195. doi:10.1002/pits.21815 PMID:25593374

Stewart, C. (2014). Transforming professional development to professional learning. *Journal of Adult Education*, *43*(1), 28–33.

Thacker, E. S. (2017). "PD is where teachers are learning!" High school social studies teachers 'formal and informal professional learning. *Journal of Social Studies Research*, *41*(1), 37–52. doi:10.1016/j.jssr.2015.10.001

Tonga, F. E., Eryiğit, S., Yalçın, F. A., & Erden, F. T. (2022). Professional development of teachers in PISA achiever countries: Finland, Estonia, Japan, Singapore and China. *Professional Development in Education*, *48*(1), 88–104. doi:10.1080/19415257.2019.1689521

United Nations Division for Social Policy and Development Disability [UNDSPDD]. (2006). *United Nations convention on the rights of persons with disabilities*. UN. https://www.un.org/disabilities/documents/convention/convoptprot-e.pdf

Wang, W., & Zhao, Z. J. (2014). (Forthcoming). Spatial decomposition of funding inequality in China's basic education: A four-level Theil Index analysis. *Public Finance and Management, 14*(4), 416–436.

Wei, R. C., Darling-Hammond, L., & Adamson, F. (2010). *Professional development in the United States: Trends and challenges*. National Staff Development Council.

Wong, C., Odom, S. L., Hume, K. A., Cox, A. W., Fettig, A., Kucharczyk, S., Brock, M. E., Plavnick, J. B., Fleury, V. P., & Schultz, T. R. (2015). Evidence-based practices for children, youth, and young adults with autism spectrum disorder: A comprehensive review. *Journal of Autism and Developmental Disorders, 45*(7), 1951–1966. doi:10.100710803-014-2351-z PMID:25578338

Woulfin, S. L., & Jones, B. (2021). Special development: The nature, content, and structure of special education teachers' professional learning opportunities. *Teaching and Teacher Education, 100*, 103277. doi:10.1016/j.tate.2021.103277

Xia, Y. (2006). Lixing kandai yuanben peixun de liyubi (理性看待园本培训的利与弊) [Dialectical view on the preschool-based training for teachers]. *Studies in Early Childhood Education, 2006*(7), 45–47.

Yang, Y., & Rao, N. (2021). Teacher professional development among preschool teachers in rural China. *Journal of Early Childhood Teacher Education, 42*(3), 219–244. doi:10.1080/10901027.2020.1726844

Zhang, L., Lai, F., Pang, X., Yi, H., & Rozelle, S. (2013). The impact of teacher training on teacher and student outcomes: Evidence from a randomised experiment in Beijing migrant schools. *Journal of Development Effectiveness, 5*(3), 339–358. doi:10.1080/19439342.2013.807862

Zhang, Y., Wang, D., Shi, L., Song, Y., & Jiang, Y. (2012). Nongcun youer jiaoshi peixun de xianzhuang, pingjia jiqi xuqiu (农村幼儿教师培训的现状、评价及其需求) [On the rural preschool training]. *Studies in Preschool Education, 2012*(1), 33–38.

KEY TERMS AND DEFINITIONS

Autism Spectrum Disorder (ASD): A complex neurodevelopmental disability characterised by persistent impairments in social communication and interaction and restricted or/and repetitive patterns of behaviours, interests, or activities.

Challenging Behaviours: Socially inappropriate behaviours that may negatively influence individuals with ASD and other people's health, well-being, and safety.

Evidence-based Practices (EBPs): Refer to effective instructional or intervention strategies supported by high-quality research to promote students' academic learning, social participation, and behavioural outcomes.

Low-functioning Autism Spectrum Disorder: Refers to the severity of autism, especially in difficulties in social communication and interaction and showing challenging behaviours.

National Teacher Training Plan Program (NTTP): Refers to a series of national teacher training programs organised by the Chinese Government. NTTP aims to provide in-depth training of teachers, principals and trainers in rural primary and secondary schools and kindergartens in the less developed areas in Central and Western China.

Professional Development: Refers to the training given to managers and people working in professions to increase their knowledge and skills.

Western China: Refers to the west part of China, including six provinces (Gansu, Guizhou, Qinghai, Shaanxi, Sichuan, and Yunnan), five autonomous regions (Guangxi, Inner Mongolia, Ningxia, Tibet, and Xinjiang), and one municipality (Chongqing).

Chapter 15

Engaging on Common Ground:
Inclusion of the Gifted Student in the Classroom

Kimberely Fletcher Nettleton
Morehead State University, USA

Michael W. Kessinger
Morehead State University, USA

Lesia Lennex
Morehead State University, USA

ABSTRACT

Educational programs for gifted students are varied, with many schools in the United States using a pullout program to address the needs of students. In spite of these programs, unless gifted students are educated in a school dedicated to their educational needs, gifted students will spend the majority of their time in a mainstream classroom. In this environment, gifted students often languish, becoming bored or losing interest in learning. Classroom teachers and teacher preparation programs can address this waste by purposely creating a program to include gifted student.

INTRODUCTION

Little Anne was so excited. After a great day in her third-grade class, she ran to the bus and was gleaming the whole trip home. Jumping out of the bus, she ran home and exploded into the house.

"Mom, mom – I did it, I did it. I'm gifted!"

"What Anne? What do you mean? Slow down baby." A big hug was given with the hopes to slow Anne down. She was so excited.

DOI: 10.4018/978-1-6684-7370-2.ch015

Copyright © 2023, IGI Global. Copying or distributing in print or electronic forms without written permission of IGI Global is prohibited.

Engaging on Common Ground

"Mrs. Stanley saw me in the hallway, and she told me I passed the test. I'm going to be getting special instruction because I'm gifted. Mom, I'm smart."

"Anne, we always knew you were smart. I'm so happy for you."

A few days later, Anne's mom was meeting with Mrs. Stanley and Anne's regular teacher, Ms. Peterson.

"So tell me, what services will Anne be getting because of her test scores?"

Mrs. Stanley smiled and said, "What we will be doing is providing Anne with some enrichment activities during her regular class. We don't take our gifted students out of their regular class, but instead, we provide them with extra work or work that is designed to meet their academic needs. We know how important it is for Anne to be around her friends and to share time with them. Also, we just can't afford to have a separate class for the gifted students all the time. But we do have some special events that we hold a couple of times during the year so all our gifted students can get together and learn new stuff. I will be working with Anne's teacher to lay out some extra materials for her to help her to continue to grow in her special areas."

Anne's mom was happy to hear that Anne will be staying with her friends and with Ms. Peterson. Anne really likes Ms. Peterson and is very comfortable around her. Also, being in the inclusive classroom will enable Anne to continue to be around and develop stronger relationships with her friends, help other students who might not understand a particular concept, and will help her not to be excluded because she has been identified as gifted.

The challenges for the regular classroom teacher to help meet the needs of gifted students is no different for students with disabilities. Students must have a plan in place to address their academic needs. Having the necessary resources, a plan, and even adjusting the instructional delivery for the gifted child are tasks many teachers will find as being difficult.

How Does a Gifted Label Impact Classroom Inclusion?

Students with gifts and talents are those students who learn or perform above the level of other students in the classroom. Whether formally identified or acknowledged, they exist in schools around the world. How they progress throughout their educational years, both intellectually, socially, and emotionally depends a great deal on the support they receive each day in school. While many schools support a pullout program for gifted students, the majority of students' time is spent with the classroom teacher (Mondale & Patton, 2001). Educating students with gifts and talents should not end when they enter a mainstream classroom. This chapter presents a brief historical background of gifted education, followed by a discussion of ways in which inclusive education can benefit gifted students in school. Instructional and assessment strategies are examined, providing a model for an inclusive classroom that can be implemented into any K-12 classroom.

BACKGROUND

Historical Events

From the beginning of public education in the United States, the purpose of schools was to provide basic skills and knowledge to the children of the community (U.S. Department of Education, 2021). In the early 19th century, the school was a single building, sometimes located in the center of the township, where children would gather to be taught four days a week (Cuban, 1993). These one-room schoolhouses had children from early ages, typically 6 years old, until mid-teens, around 16 years old, and would typically be in the first through the eighth grade (Davis, 2001). To add to the challenge, there was one teacher, typically a young, single woman whose task was to instruct the students. In some cases, the teacher would only have an eighth-grade education (Perlman & Margo, 2001). Typically, she would arrange the classroom in order to have some help teaching the younger children. The older students would not only learn their lessons, but helped the younger students learn their lessons (Cuban).

Figure 1. Interior of "little red schoolhouse," in Crossville, Tennessee, USA. Taken in 1935.
The Miriam and Ira D. Wallach Division of Art, Prints and Photographs: Photography Collection, The New York Public Library.

The teacher was there to not only maintain order but also to provide lessons structured to the concepts being covered. Because all the students were in the same room, lessons for each student were based

Engaging on Common Ground

on their ability, not their age. While there were a wide range of abilities in that one-room schoolhouse, it was the teacher whose role was to help plan lessons for each child. Four basic subjects were taught in each of the eight grades – reading, writing, spelling, and arithmetic, along with history, geography, grammar, and physiology for the older students.

Having a single teacher responsible for all students and for all subjects seemed to be a challenge. Regardless of the ability of the student, all were included in the single room school. The classroom could have as little as 6 or as many as 50 students packed into the single classroom. "The teacher was like a conductor of an orchestra leading all the different types of musical instruments, but the members of the orchestra, the students, were all playing different pieces of music at the same time" (Westerville Public Library, 2023, para 3).

Many one-room schoolhouses were located in rural areas within three to five miles of students (Davis, 2001). There were schools in major cities that had the same goal of providing education to the youth of the community. But rather than having a single school, with a single teacher, many of the city schools would have multiple teachers and would have students grouped by age (Cuban, 1993). Ability grouping was not a wide concern until 1868. In that year, William Torrey Harris, who was the superintendent of the St. Louis public schools, implemented efforts to provide enrichment education for gifted students (Jolly, 2009). At that time, gifted students were those who were able to demonstrate advanced academic abilities and were then allowed to progress based on those academic achievements.

Intelligence Testing

During the 1800's, there was no formal way of identifying the intellectual ability of an individual. Identification was solely based on the child's outstanding academic ability in a content area. No scientific method was used to identify giftedness. That is not until early 1900s, when two French researchers, Binet and Simon, developed a series of tests with the purpose of assessing the mental abilities of an individual (National Association for Gifted Children, 2023a). Their thought was the mental abilities of an individual was a better indicator of one's cognitive abilities and thus, the results could be used to identify those students needing additional academic support. Today, the Stanford-Binet Intelligence Scales is used to obtain an individual's intelligence quotient (IQ). Considered one of the best IQ measure for gifted students, it is used not only to identify students with academic disabilities, but also students who possess academic giftedness (Silverman, 2002).

Gifted Professional Organization

The organization of the National Association of Gifted Children (NAGC) in 1954 provided a foundation to support the needs of gifted children. The original mission of the association was to "support educators and others to enhance the growth and development of gifted children not only through education" (History of Gifted Education, n.d., para. 1). The association was not only concerned with the education of gifted children, but also supporting the teachers, parents, and research to better understand the gifted population as well as possible. Over the years, the organization has expanded their mission statement and now "supports and engages in research and development, staff development, advocacy, communication, and collaboration with other organizations and agencies who strive to improve the education for all students" (NAGC, 2023b, para 1). Through this organization many changes have taken place at the national level which has impacted gifted education.

Eye Opening Event

In 1957 an eye-opening event occurred that caused the leadership of the United States and the education system of America to take a look at the quality of schooling, specifically in the mathematics and science areas, being offered in schools. The launching of Sputnik 1 by the Soviet Union initiated a change in the teaching of quantitative subjects (Roberts, 1999). There was also a significant amount of funding used to identify students with extra-ordinary abilities and skills in the mathematics, sciences, and industrial technologies (NAGC, 2023a).

Following the reaction to Sputnik 1 in 1957, the National Defense Education Act (NDEA) of 1958 was passed (Roberts, 1999). This Act provided the first major focus by the federal government on gifted education. For many gifted students, the NDEA provided the resources needed to further their knowledge and skills in their specific areas. Many students were able to receive scholarships, loans, and graduate fellowships to further their education. Also noted by Jolly (2009), "NDEA also provided matching funds to states, allowing for improvements in elementary and secondary mathematics, science, and foreign language curriculum and instruction" (p. 41). The ultimate impact of these funds was an increase in the number of "rigorous classes for gifted and talented students" (Jolly, p. 41).

Various National Reports

In 1972, a report titled *Education of the Gifted and Talented*, known as the Marland Report was released by the U.S. Department of Education. This report did a couple of things. First, it led to the establishment of the Office of Gifted and Talented Education within the U.S. Department of Education. Second, the Marland Report established six categories of giftedness. "These areas were (1) general intellectual ability, (2) specific academic abilities, (3) creative or productive thinking, (4) leadership ability, (5) visual and performing arts, and (6) psychomotor ability" (Marland, 1971, Section 1, p. 4)

Twenty-five years after the enactment of the National Defense Education Act, the report, *A Nation at Risk* (1983) was published. This landmark report of the United States National Commission on Education Excellence, published by the Reagan administration, pointed out the failure of the American educational system to prepare students for life. It also pointed out the average performance of students in the United States was below students in other countries. The report recommended higher standards for teacher-preparation programs, better salaries for teachers, establishment of a rigorous set of standards of the content being taught, and a new set of high school graduation criteria. The new curriculum criteria required four courses in English, three in mathematics, three in science, three in social studies, and one-half credit in computer science. For individuals planning on attending college, two credits in a foreign language were recommended.

Two reports that followed the *Nation at Risk* report specifically address the shortcomings with respect to educating gifted and talented (G/T) students. In 1993, the *National Excellence: The Case for Developing America's Talent* report, followed 11 years later by *A Nation Deceived: How Schools Hold Back America's Brightest Students* discussed how talent and gifted students were being neglected. Both reports provided recommendations and strategies for addressing the needs of gifted students.

The *National Excellence* recommendations are very clear and well-defined. "School and parents need to encourage hard work, hold high expectations for students, and push students to the outer limits of their potential" (Ross, 1993, p. 27). Excellence gaps occur when G/T students are not provided opportunities to learn at high levels (Plucker & Peters, 2016). Students must not be allowed to just sit back and coast.

Engaging on Common Ground

When a student has an outstanding talent, opportunities must be provided for them to excel and to rise to the top. Curriculum should be enriched and challenging for all students, not just those identified as gifted. The report also "stresses that 'outstanding talents are present in children and youth from all cultural groups, across all economic strata, and in all areas of human endeavor'" (Roberts, 1999, p. 55).

In the *A Nation Deceived* report, Colangelo et al. (2004) pointed out the benefits of academic acceleration as an intervention to help students to learn at the rate they, the students, are comfortable. Too many times, the teachers hold students back to keep everyone on the same level in order to move through the required curriculum schedule. This report discusses the benefits of some types of accelerations, such as early admission to school (starting school at age 4 rather than age 6), skipping a grade (being in third-grade one year, then fifth-grade the next year), taking a class earlier than the typical student (taking high school Algebra 2 as a 7th grader), or taking dual-credit or advanced placement (AP) courses (College Level English Composition instead of high school English). Students who are ready for more challenging work must be provided the opportunity to move ahead (Plucker & Peters, 2016).

At the same time NAGC was advocating for G/T students to have an enriched education, students with disabilities were being removed from their regular classroom and put into a self-contained classroom with other disabled students. The idea was to provide an instructional program that fits the intellectual level of the students. In addition, the special education teacher, along with the assistants, could better meet the needs of students. With the enactment of the Education for All Handicapped Children Act (EHA) in 1975, and the authorization in 1990 of what we know of today as the Individuals with Disabilities Education Act (IDEA), students with disabilities are to be placed in the least restrictive environment (LRE) to best address the educational needs of the students. Students might be pulled from the regular classroom for a particular subject, for the whole day and all subjects, or might be served in an inclusive classroom with regular students and have the services of an instructional assistant as needed. The LRE means a student with a disability can be educated within the same classroom as non-disabled peers to the fullest extent possible. Prior to IDEA, many children with disabilities were segregated and kept separate from the typical classroom environment.

Understanding Gifted and Talented Students

When talking with G/T students, their educational experiences typically involved being pulled out of the regular classroom and provided services in a type of resource room, similar to what is done for students with special needs. There is support for programming decisions that provide gifted students within special classrooms for curriculum acceleration purposes. The costs are prohibitive, especially in rural schools or those with high poverty rates (Lewis & Bosell, 2020). Pull out programming is an option that provides students with the opportunity to explore advanced topics and to address learning at the appropriate intellection level (NAGC, 2019). The NAGC provides programming standards which provide direction in identification, education, curriculum delivery, instructional strategies, and educator training (NAGC, 2019). All programming standards are focused on meeting the individual needs of gifted students.

Because the gifted students have been identified in various areas –mathematics, science, language arts, or performing arts – the pullout setting provided a wide range of experiences. There are some disadvantages to pullout programs. The cost is often prohibitive to many school districts (Lewis & Boswell, 2020). In some cases, all gifted students, regardless of their identified area, are provided with the same lessons and activities to complete. Unlike the one-room schoolhouse where lessons were geared to the individual child (Davis, 2001), the pullout program typically provides the same enriched lessons to every child, despite their individual are or level of giftedness. In this type of program, the gifted child is segregated from those not identified as gifted, although many have expressed their opinion that this type of program provides a stimulating environment when students can interact with others who think as they do (Lennex, Nettleton, & Kessinger, 2015).

It is difficult for counselors or the school's G/T teacher to schedule all students with the same gifted area together. There are not that many hours in the school day. In many schools, the decision was made to just group all the students together for the gifted teacher to figure out the best way to service the students. Doing so assumes the gifted student will not experience any academic problems, will not need any additional guidance or support, will not have any socio-emotional issues, and will just succeed on their own (Peterson, 2009a).

Much can be learned about the path gifted education has taken over the past 150 years. There have been many events that have impacted gifted education not discussed previously which can be reviewed on NAGC's website (NAGC, 2023a). Today, there is still a challenge with respect to the equitable delivery of services to student with gifts and talents (Horn, 2015). While there are states that provide funding for services, many states just do not provide the level of support needed (Hafenstein et al., 2022). In addition, the challenges related to the delivery of services either by the regular classroom teacher or the gifted education teacher still need to be addressed either locally or at the state level.

The role of scheduling GT students should not fall on the shoulders of the regular classroom teacher, the gifted education teacher, or a flip of the coin. The school counselor has a significant role in scheduling all students: regular, special needs, and gifted students (Lewis & Boswell, 2020). However, the challenge for the counselor is to be prepared to address the various needs of GT students. Counselors need to have an understanding of the potential challenges that could be faced when trying to come up with scheduling strategies to meet specific G/T student needs. In addition, "it is prudent school counselors first develop knowledge about giftedness, GT learners' characteristics, school district policies, and specific needs of the GT students" (Boulden et al., 2021, p. 227).

The seamless inclusion of G/T children into the P-12 schools has presented both delights and issues to educators. Gifted and talented learners are inquisitive, fearless, and out-of-the box thinkers who approach learning in many different ways. It can be quite the feat for teachers to provide integrated learning for G/T learners within a heterogeneous classroom (Lewis & Boswell, 2020).

At the secondary school level, not unlike earlier grade levels, a common curriculum approach has been to engage learners in accelerated coursework (Colangelo et al., 2004). Offering advanced placement (AP) and dual credit courses are now two ways many high schools are addressing G/T student's academic needs. Other recent curriculum approaches have taken into account holistic learning in a Parallel Curriculum Model (Tomlinson, 2002), and Problem-Based Learning (Fukuzawa & Cahn, 2019).

MAIN FOCUS OF THE CHAPTER

After a discussion of a series of models, which will include examples of implementation and success (or failure) from classrooms, the final section of the chapter will include a discussion of the best practices for inclusion of gifted students in school.

Engaging on Common Ground

Issues, Controversies, Problems

In most classrooms across the United State, there is a group of students who are generally ignored in the classroom. In informal discussions with G/T teachers from around the US, they the practices of many classroom teachers. They have observed classroom teachers who, after handing out assignments, believe that their GT students do not need their expertise, and consequently do not spend much time supporting understanding or growth in their GT students. This is especially true with children of color (Hemmler et al., 2022; Novak et al., 2020). The dispositions of both classroom and GT teachers must include skills in collaboration, empathy, flexibility, commitment, and accountability (Stephens, 2019). Xiang et al. (2011) discovered that across the United States, these students have the lowest achievement gain each year.

Who is this overlooked, neglected, underserved, and ignored collection of exceptional students in US classrooms? They are:

The high achievers.

The gifted students.

Identifying and defining giftedness in students is difficult. Each G/T research study helps to refine the understanding of this category of exceptional students. The federal Elementary and Secondary Education Act used this definition of giftedness in its Title IX documents:

Students, children, or youth who give evidence of high achievement capability in areas such as intellectual, creative, artistic, or leadership capacity, or in specific academic fields, and who need services and activities not ordinarily provided by the school in order to fully develop those capabilities. (Title IX, Part A, Definition 22, 2011, p. 1539)

Additionally, the National Association of Gifted Children (NAGC) has updated their definition of gifted students, in part, to: "Students with gifts and talents perform - or have the capability to perform - at higher levels compared to others of the same age, experience, and environment in one or more domains" (National Association of Gifted Children, 2019, para 2).

These definitions and many others shape the understanding of gifted students and their needs. At the heart of all of them, however, is the concept that gifted students can perform at higher levels than their age peers and need special services to develop their abilities. As an exceptional child, it essential that their educational requirements be addressed.

In the United States, although almost all states report having gifted services in schools, only 24 states have a state law mandating gifted education (Rinn et al., 2020). Less than half of the 50 states have standards or provide funding to school districts in support of gifted education (Rinn et al.). Only nine states (18%) require universal identification screening and 40% of states do not require any training for teachers of gifted students (Hafenstein et al., 2022; Rinn et al.).

According to Reis et al. (1993), gifted students make the least progress in school than any other group. They learn less, per year, than their classmates. Sadly, in the 30 years since this study, there are still gaps in GT student learning each year (Plucker & Peters, 2016). Gifted students should be making the most gain each year or at least as much as the special needs students. This leads to an important question for teachers and administrators to consider: *Why are GT students behind everyone else in achievement growth?*

Plucker and Peters (2016) claim that over fifty years of educational policies in the United States have focused on students reaching minimal competency, thus creating a system that promotes low expectations of students. The emphasis on students who are struggling does not encourage learning beyond the proficiency level. From the Elementary and Secondary Education Act (ESEA) to the No Child Left Behind (NCBL), education in the United States has a stated goal of assuring that all students meet a level of minimum proficiency. In a minimal competency environment, children who are gifted have no opportunity to grow (Tomlinson, 2002).

As a result, of the expectation of students reaching proficiency, GT students, who are often already at the proficiency level, have not been supported (Al-Fadhli & Singh, 2010). Teachers, expecting their gifted students to quickly complete assignments with negligible oversight or support, are attentive to the needs of struggling students. The learning needs of students who have gifts and talents are largely ignored in, as without effort, they have already met the desired level (Roberts & Inman, 2023).

In many classrooms, the GT student completes their classwork before everyone else, is often used as a mini-teacher to assist slower students. Instructors may plan assignments so that their gifted students can assist students who express the need for help. Often, gifted students are assigned to partner with a student with a learning disability or low IQ. G/T students have expressed their frustration over always being expected to help peers (Lennex et al, 2015). Instead of providing instruction or assignments that have been differentiated to meet the needs of the students with disabilities, teachers claim it helps the gifted student to learn material by teaching others. (Roberts & Inman, 2023).Why students who have demonstrated that they understand the curriculum need this reinforcement is never clearly explained by these teachers. However, this frees the teacher's time so that more students can be helped.

Unintended problems arise when gifted students are set up by teachers to be experts. Socially, gifted students, expected by their classmates and teachers to always know the answer, are often teased when they answer incorrectly in class.

"Ooooh, Joey got it wrong," a student will pounce.

In fact, gifted students are often used by others as an excuse:

"If Anna didn't get it right, how did you expect me to get it right?"

This often effects students to the extent where they are afraid to try something if they cannot master it immediately. The push for perfectionism can be crippling to a gifted student's willingness to explore new learning. When everything comes easy, gifted students begin to believe that they are invincible. When they run into a class or area of study challenges or requires extra effort, these students often will give up right away. Not used to having to work at learning, they perceive themselves as not capable of learning the new material. The farther along they are in their progress through school, the more likely it is that the gifted students will be devastated when they run into difficulties. (Grugen et al, 2021). The perception that they must be perfect causes many gifted students to demean an area of study or to become anxious, depressed, or suicidal. Teachers must make gifted students understand that their "self-worth is not dependent on being perfect." (Hyatt, 2010, p. 531). Because of their mask of perfectionism, counselors often are not aware of the GT student's anxiety over problems. Some GT students will leave college, drop out of high school, or turn to substance abuse as a way to cope (Peterson, 2009b).

Engaging on Common Ground

What gifted students need is a sustained curriculum that encourages them to learn curriculum at high levels (Reis & Boeve, 2009). GT students who are not taught at high levels or in classrooms with low teacher expectations, the outcome will be "underachievement, student boredom, and virtual stagnation" (Roberts & Inman, 2023, p. 22). GT students must be fully engaged in learning.

As much of students' time is spent in a regular classroom, our gifted students must be treated like students, not teacher aides. They must be provided with an education at their learning level. This means that teachers need to look for ways in meet their brightest students' needs as well as those that are struggling. Teachers of gifted students need training in order to meet students' needs (Aulls & Ibrahim, 2012; Roberts & Inman, 2023); but classroom teachers should also undergo ongoing training. In higher education, every pre-service teacher should be taught how to help their gifted students (Robinson & Dietz, 2022). Currently in the US, only 8% of the states require pre-service teacher training in gifted education (Rinn et al., 2022). Van Tassel-Baska (2022) points out that in order for gifted students to progress, teachers must not only be trained to use appropriate resources but how to differentiate for students when using resources. Learning at a high level requires synthetization, evaluation, and analysis (Agarwal, 2019; Forehand, 2005). Higher level learning is under-utilized by teachers, in part because many feel they do not have the time to develop appropriate rubrics to grade students at a higher level (Roberts & Inman, 2023).

Inclusion Through Cluster Grouping

Effective instructional methods are needed to teach GT students effectively in an inclusive classroom. Cluster grouping is a popular strategy. Due to its extensive use, Johnson et al. (2020) examined cluster grouping and how it is used in classrooms across the United States. Students are taken from classes across all grade levels for a specific area of study and grouped in small clusters. Teachers work with students who share the same learning level (Matthews et al., 2013). This allows all students to learn together with a teacher who is focused on teaching at an appropriate level. Cluster group instruction continues throughout the year, not once or twice a week or month. Working together, classroom teachers use cluster grouping to make sure that the curriculum is at the intensity that all students need. Gifted students learn at a more enriched level and move through the curriculum much faster and a deeper degree. Students who need more time are taught at a slower pace in their cluster group. The wide range of students' learning level is minimized in cluster grouping. All students learn at their educative level. Gifted students show significant growth when cluster grouping is used as an instructional model (Brulles, 2010).

By its very nature, cluster grouping supports inclusion of all students. Built in flexibility allows for reformation of groups as curriculum subjects change throughout the day. Students can be grouped in a variety of ways throughout the day thus providing a malleable learning experience tailored to every child's learning needs.

Inclusion Through Assessment

First and foremost, teachers must begin units of study with pre-assessment. Pre-assessment allows teachers to assess student understanding. The pre-assessment must include curriculum questions at several of the higher thinking skill levels: analyzing, evaluating, and creating. In this way, teachers can accurately determine students' understanding and learning level by subject and topics (Roberts & Bogges, 2011).

Pre-assessment can be completed in a variety of ways (Roberts & Inman, 2023). Performance assessment or real world products can provide as much information to a teacher as a paper and pencil test (Mueller, 2003). These assessments use higher level thinking skills to complete. Pre-assessment may also be completed via multiple choice, essays, or by oral questioning. Anything that allows a teacher to analyze student understanding and prior knowledge can provide the data needed to address student learning needs.

One of the most overlooked ways of including G/T students in the classroom is through focused assessment. Focused assessment is a tool used by instructors when students are provided with challenging assignments that involve more than low level repetition of facts. Whatever the assignment: from summarizing a book chapter, creating a PowerPoint, sharing information, or engaging in a presentation, the instructor creates assessments that meet the learning levels of students (Roberts & Inman, 2023). Through differentiated assessments, students are assessed at their instructional level, over the content they have learned, rather than being assessed with a one-size-fits-all approach.

Roberts and Inman (2023) call the process of creating different levels of assessments, *Developing and Assessing Products (DAP)*. Teachers devise rubrics at different levels. For example, a short story rubric would focus assessment on different skills when it is provided to a student with a learning disability, a gifted student, or a student who does not have any exceptional needs. Each student uses the appropriate level of rubric to guide their written assignment and the teacher uses the most suitable rubric to assess the submitted writing project. By assessing at the appropriate learning level and content learned, the coursework automatically challenges all students, providing teachers the opportunity to engage students with feedback at appropriate learning levels (Roberts & Inman, 2023).

Once a teacher has created a series of rubrics at different levels for a project, presentation, or research, these can easily be adapted to many assignments. This makes the rubrics very flexible and easy to use. Every student can be assigned the same task, but their final product will most closely match their level of understanding.

Inclusion Through Acceleration

Gifted and talented learners tend to appear as more significantly advanced than the average learner in a given classroom. One would be remiss in not asking, "*Is this student at the right level?*" If it is possible to move a child, accelerate to the point they are in an acceptably academically challenging environment, several questions may arise. The social and emotional needs of a child must be considered in making a decision about acceleration. One cannot blindly move a first grader into a fourth-grade setting. While gifted students may progress cognitively, other areas of their development may not be as advanced. Physical and emotional, asynchronous development occurs and while gifted students may be advanced cognitively, they can be at or below their peers in these developmental areas. Skipping grades or starting school at an earlier age may be appropriate for some G/T learners but prove disastrous for others. The Iowa Acceleration Scale (IAS) was developed (Assouline et al, 2009), to support appropriate whole grade acceleration decisions.

The IAS provides a framework to evaluate a student's readiness for acceleration by examining developmental factors, interpersonal skills, attitude and support, school/academic factors, student ability, achievement, and aptitude. The total of subscale scores in these areas provides a rationale for acceleration placements as teachers and parents work together on educational decisions.

Engaging on Common Ground

Although there are over 20 types of acceleration such as early admission to first grade, self-paced instruction, and curriculum compacting (Assouline et al., 2015), most US schools do not use whole grade acceleration as a means to address the needs of the gifted student, in spite of research that overwhelmingly points out its positive impact on gifted students (Lupkowski-Shoplik et al., 2022). By far, the most utilized form of acceleration in the United States is subject acceleration (Riegle & Behrens, 2022).In this manner, students remain in their age-peer classroom, but are accelerated for specific subjects. When it is time for math, a student would move from their regular classroom to one that is at a higher grade level within the school. School districts may work together to allow students from an elementary school to travel to middle (typically 6-8th grade) or secondary school (9th through 12th grade) for appropriate level of subject instruction.

Acceleration (Colangelo et al., 2004) is "really about letting students soar. Acceleration is a strategy that respects individual differences and acknowledges the fact that some of these differences merit educational flexibility. It provides cumulative educational advantage." (p. 5). Riegel and Behrens (2022), found that positive outcomes of acceleration occur when administrators and GT leaders have training and communicate. In spite of research in support of acceleration practices (Colangelo et al., 2004, Howley, 2002, Horne & Dupay,1981) there many teachers and administrators still resist providing accelerated learning (Howley, 2002; Boyle, et al, 2010; Assouline, et al, 2015).

In considering the needs of an elementary child with less inclination to advance to a higher-grade level altogether, a teacher may choose to utilize enrichment strategies such as field trips or ability grouping with specific higher-grade level content.

Inclusion in Higher Education

Colleges and Universities can provide additional options for gifted learners. These inclusive options include alternative schooling and dual-credit college enrollment. Alternative schooling can provide students with the opportunity to undertake some college coursework, if available (Hargrove, 2012). These courses may be taught online or the student may travel to a nearby university for a course and then return to the local high school for the remainder of their courses. The course is considered a dual credit because it fulfills both university and secondary school requirement. Dual credit courses are a preferred method of inclusion and acceleration for many secondary students during their final two years of high school.

In the state of Kentucky, a unique option for advanced high school juniors and seniors was developed. Students, having fulfilled specific requirements to enter a dual credit program, may apply for a fully-immersed collegiate experience such as either the Gatton Academy of Mathematics and Science (https://www.wku.edu/academy/about/index.php) or the Craft Academy for Excellence in Science and Mathematics (https://moreheadstate.edu/academics/colleges/craft-academy/#:~:text=The%20Craft%20Academy%20for%20Excellence,by%20enrolling%20in%20college%20courses). Applicants must have successfully completed Algebra I, Algebra II, and Geometry, as well as United States History. These students finish their final two years of high school education by living on a college campus while taking a full load of undergraduate courses.

Students begin this journey in sixth or seventh grade by taking advanced public school courses. The successful applicant to the program is considered a dual credit student at the university. While they are registered as special status students, in the classroom, there is no difference in expectations, assignments, or assessments. These students are fully included in higher education courses and are expected to learn alongside their older peers. While these students are at college, they must be sure to meet complete the rest of the required courses necessary for a high school diploma. With two years of college completed by the time they graduate high school, these students are poised to pursue their dreams.

Across three years, Lennex, Nettleton, and Kessinger (2015) interviewed students admitted to one of Kentucky's residential secondary academies. Students who were selected to the Craft Academy for Excellence in Science and Mathematics cited their reasons for applying. By far, the most common response was the lack of challenging academics in their home school districts. Several commented that they were acting as teachers or teacher aides in their high schools' lower-level courses because there was no other avenue for coursework in specific mathematics and sciences. More than half the students who were interviewed expressed a need for more advanced coursework, challenging instructors, and comparable peers. Many commented they were "bored" with their home high school and needed to be challenged.

Higher education can provide an inclusive environment for gifted students. With this program, students are in a position to complete a bachelor's degree by the age of 20 and pursue advanced fields of study. To have held these learners in place because of their age would have been an injustice. Further research regarding the challenges of dual credit programs is currently in progress by the authors.

Constructing Curriculum

Curriculum, as it is classically defined, are the courses within an area of study. Creating a P-12 curriculum conducive to bringing educational enlightenment to large groups of heterogeneous learners, therefore, is a prodigious task. The gifted and talented population presents unique circumstances in which many educators find themselves either supplementing or substituting a district-wide curriculum Gifted and talented learners, like all learners, can neither be quantified nor processed according to formula (Tomlinson, 2005). Each learner is an individual who deserves to learn in a multitude of pathways each leading to its own intrinsic destination as a lifelong pursuit.

Well, one can dream that that occurs.

In reality, as many teachers instruct to the proficiency level, they will also employ many diverse and individualized strategies as are practicably possible. They will develop targeted remediation to bring lagging learners to baseline performance levels. Differentiated education provides a wide variety of strategies that can be utilized to reach all students (Van Tassel-Baska, 2021). In the interest of mainstreaming G/T students within the heterogeneous classroom, overviews of several inclusive curricula are described: The Parallel Curriculum Model (PCM) and the Problem-Based Learning (PBL) model with two examples from a high school biology classroom.

Parallel Curriculum

A highly adaptable and well-received P-12 curriculum is the Parallel Curriculum Model developed by Tomlinson et al. (2001). This model promotes the use of four independent, parallel, curriculum elements to comprise a challenging and progressive methodology toward critical thinking. The elements of core, connections, practice, and identity coalesce to bring greater depth and complexity to any unit of study. As Purcell et al. (2002) describes, the core derives largely from the discipline area standards and identifying the thread of measurable knowledge for any unit will translate to the overall *understanding* goal of the unit. The connections provide tangible real-life attainable and knowable cultural or scientific links to student lives. The practice element supports student learning and achievement with creative problem solving and allows for many varied learning activities. Teachers would necessarily provide many learning activities

Engaging on Common Ground

incorporating challenging and open-ended tasks and products. Lastly, the identity component brings this curriculum a very highly prized intrinsic motivation: self-actualization. According to Maslow (1954), self-actualization is a higher order thinking which empowers individuals to seek their inner potential. With this in mind, the identity component of the parallel curriculum is the key to intrinsic motivation. Creating a parallel curriculum classroom requires flexible management and confidence in the academic discipline (Tomlinson, 2015; Tomlinson & Imbeau, 2010).

In further discussing this model, one must separate the concepts of ability grouping and differentiation. Often, teachers will be encouraged to ability group students with G/T individuals ostensibly leading a group within a cooperative learning scenario. Differentiation is quite another thing. In discussing her work in the PCM with Carol Ann Tomlinson (Wu, 2013), Tomlinson (2015) states,

Encouraging learners to bring their own style and envision individual outcomes which incorporate the desired unit and module-level learning objectives, will increase the learner's potential to internalize the learning process and engender lifelong learning. (p.127)

Elementary school teachers often create learning centers for students. Throughout the morning, small groups of students rotate to a variety of tables where instructional activities are provided. At one table, the teacher may work on sight word recognition. In another, students may write a simple story. In another, students may grapple with alphabetical order. It is very easy to differentiate by learning level or activity. The difference with the parallel curriculum is that while all students may be learning the same lesson, they learn it at their own learning level. Consider a study on the pyramids of Egypt. In a parallel classroom, students may be reading a variety of books, magazine articles, or completing research into the topic at their own learning level. Students can come together to share what they have learned or go on to engage in activities that match their level of understanding. In this way, a parallel curriculum can address all learners in the classroom.

Problem-Based Learning

Problem-based learning, PBL, presents a problem to be solved. Students identify the issue(s), the tools or skills necessary to solve the issue, and collaboratively forge a path to its solution(s) by applying those tools, skills, and collaboration. Successful traditional learners, those who best receive information passively, memorize, and selectively apply discrete skills or knowledge, may be resistant to PBL (Fukuzawa & Cahn, 2019). Inasmuch as PBL creates a different mindset among a classroom, it flings wide the door to informed learning. Bruce and Hughes (2010) state,

Informed learning is about simultaneous attention to information use and learning, where both information and learning are considered to be relational; and is built upon a series of key concepts such as second-order perspective, simultaneity, awareness, and relationality. Informed learning also relies heavily on reflection as a strategy for bringing about learning. As a pedagogical construct, informed learning supports inclusive curriculum design and implementation. (A2)

PBL affords many opportunities to bring real-world issues to the classroom. In one example, a school principal and fifth grade teacher worked together to turn a controversial decision into a lesson on the democratic process. The class was inclusive, with both gifted and special needs students in the popula-

Engaging on Common Ground

tion. An unpopular decision had been made and students were no longer allowed to bring or drink pop (highly sweet, carbonated beverages) during the lunch hour. As the students were learning about the Revolutionary War period in US history, with a little subtle encouragement by their teacher, the fifth graders were soon posting signs that mimicked the Stamp Act slogans:

No "No pop" without representation!

Give us pop or give us death? (A little dramatic perhaps, but they were fired up).

To make sure that this real-life problem became part of the learning process, the principal and teacher worked together to make sure that the students activities mirrored the historical events. Students wrote their own draft the declaration of independence and sent it to the principal, explaining their position, and requesting that their voices be heard. They called the local newspaper and requested that a reporter visit the school.

In this naturally occurring PBL, all of the students worked together. Using their skills on a real world problem, all students were able to contribute. Unlike in a typical classroom setting where the gifted students were often working apart from their peers, in the fight for their right to pop, the students were worked together. The students who were gifted in leadership developed their skills as they organized their battle. The artistic students led brainstorming sessions on banners while those who were gifted in writing, drafted letters in committee with class members.

Before the historical parallel became too great and a war broke out, the principal called the local county judge executive and requested that he come and arbitrate the issue. In the United States, a judge executive is an elected official in a county, whose executive branch responsibilities include managing the daily operations of the agencies and departments within the county government.

At a meeting with this official, the students presented their argument and the school presented theirs. After careful deliberation and a plateful of cookies, the judge executive ruled that pop could be served one day a week with lunch. This met with the approval of all sides and the students learned several lessons through this PBL.

In a personal example from the former high school biology classroom of one of the authors, she encouraged students to view ecological issues through a PBL lens. The educational setting was nestled in a rural, mountainous area chock-full of lesser seen vegetation, birds, and trees. A special area of interest for the author's students were the commonly seen, for them, *Cypripedium parviflorum and Cypripedium acaule*, or yellow lady's slipper and pink lady's slipper. There are several North American varieties of lady's slipper, but the yellow and pink slippers are perhaps most commonly noticed from walking trails.

Lady's slippers depend on mycorrhizal fungi to propagate and thrive. This fungus reduces abiotic stressors and improves the flow of nutrients and water to trees (Usman et al., 2021; Mycorrhizal Applications How It Works, 2017; Mosse et al., 1981). Predation and selective germination also decrease the number of flowering plants produced each year. Through several years' study, the students observed and developed counter measures for the effects of deforestation, selective tree harvesting, poaching, and wildlife predation. The geographic area in which this author formerly taught remains primarily protected forests and large tracts of undisturbed lands. PBL created a group of informed citizens that used scientific reasoning to solve real-world issues.

Another lab based PBL activity used in a secondary biology classroom was the examination of sex-linked eye color in *Drosophila melanogaster*. Based on Thomas Morgan's work establishing chromosomal

Engaging on Common Ground

heredity theories (Genome News Network, 2004), this experiment seeks to determine the sex-linked inheritance of white eyes. The author initially established a cross between red-eyed females and white-eyed males. Generation one, F_0, was sex sorted and eye color noted, breeding newly-hatched red-eyed females to white-eyed males. The resulting eggs were introduced as generation one to students. This second generation, F_1, will produce 100% red-eyed females and males. With a newly-hatched population of at least ten males and ten females in each breeding vial, generation two, F_2, was produced. The resulting generation was then sex-sorted, and eye color noted. Half of the male flies should have white eyes, 50% red eyes, and 100% of the females will have red eyes. Students, having established proficiency with Punnett squares up to four characteristics, were familiar with Mendelian genetics models. Students had maintained lab logs of their examinations and generational notes. Using those notes, students created Punnett squares demonstrating their theories of sex-linked inheritance. By working in small, inclusive groups, every student contributes to the solving of a problem. For gifted students, investigations and problem solving turns a typical lab experience into one of exploration and enrichment.

The science examples in this section may be supported with mathematical growth models for the *Cypripedia* population projections, and mathematical probability models to explain any variance among second-generation *Drosophila*. Problem Based Learning may be integrated into a Parallel Curriculum model or used as an instructional method on its own.

Other Models

Models which operate more broadly as individualized education appear to generate greater success among G/T students. Models based on historical study, such as role-play, case study, and musicals, are highly complex pedagogical constructs that combine ethnography, archaeology, historiography, and cultural studies. Gonzalez-Gonzalez et al. (2022) states,

Thinking historically is one way to achieve quality education in history instruction, especially in secondary school. As a key competence in our subject, a priority objective is for pupils to develop critical, contextualized, source- and perspective-based, empathetic, and informed thinking. (p. 3)

One such example is a middle school classroom role-playing activity based on the United States (U.S.) historical Constitutional Convention. Students randomly drew the name of a specific real-life political character from the Convention and were provided with a brief, one paragraph biography of each character. The role-play could have begun the learning activity at this point, but the teacher encouraged further research into each character so that students had a more robust representation of their role in the forming of the United States. After this research, students compiled character sheets and drafted dialogue which was reviewed and coordinated prior to the whole group activity. The classroom was transformed into the Constitutional Convention setting and the students, in their own words, were able to enact the historical events.

Pull Out Programs or Exceptional Schools

Many schools rely on a pull out program or magnet schools to provide an enriched curriculum to gifted students. A pull out program involves gathering the gifted students within a school or district and providing instruction on a specialized topic. The pull out is scheduled anywhere from one hour once a week to a full day, but gifted students eventually return to their classrooms. Many students love the pull-out program because for a brief time, they are challenged. Bui et al. (2012) questioned whether magnet schools for gifted students are effective. Pull-out supports growth in social skills and enrichment, but very few programs provide more than a Band-Aid to the needs of gifted students. The importance of determining the learning level of gifted students and making sure that they are in the correct, inclusive learning environment, allows students to be part of a learning environment that meets their unique learning needs.

SOLUTIONS AND RECOMMENDATIONS

There is a not a universal curriculum suitable for gifted and talented learners in the mainstreamed classroom. While it is true that G/T learners should be equally challenged by any content or discrete learning skills acquisition, it is also true that these learners tend to quickly absorb instructional materials and methodology (Roberts & Inman, 2023). Parallel Curriculum Models may prove to be a greater learning tool for G/T students. With this curriculum, teachers are integrating several disciplines' concepts and learning goals in seeking critical thinking demonstrations of conceptual understanding. Similar to presentations of the Next Generation Science Standards (2017), the discipline-area concept and associated cross-cutting themes within and external to the discipline are displayed alongside content target goals.

FUTURE RESEARCH DIRECTIONS

Inclusion of gifted students into classrooms depends a great deal on school policies and the creativity of classroom teachers. Innovative inclusive programs, whose strength is strong collaboration between classroom teachers, administration, and specially trained teachers of gifted students, have been found to be successful (Horn, 2015; Lupart & Webber, 2012). Further examination of strong collaborative models and long term effects on gifted students compared to the efficacy of pull out programs should be a priority.

In spite of overwhelming research into the success of whole grade acceleration for gifted students, it is an under-utilized method of inclusion (Lupkowski-Shoplik et al., 2022). While research based teaching practices are encouraged, school policies limit many methods of inclusion available to gifted students. Further research into successful instructional models that can be implemented by classroom teachers needs to be explored.

As a result of the worldwide COVID pandemic, online teaching became widely practiced and as a result, there was a vast improvement in delivery. New learning platforms supported student and teacher interaction. Many gifted students found distance learning to be inclusive in a way that the face to face classroom had not been (Gelen & Kaçan, 2022). The use of online platforms and distance learning as an effective instructional model, while researched in the past, should be looked at more closely as teachers and students are more comfortable with the improved technology.

Based on the funding of gifted services, it is clear that the intellectual growth of gifted students is not a current educational priority in the United States (Hafenstein et al., 2022). Research should not only address the ways in which funding is most effective in gifted services, but also in determining why a strong bias exists against providing adequate education to students.

In the United States, teacher preparation programs provide minimal to no education for pre-service teachers in gifted education (Berman et al., 2012). Teachers currently learn through experience or by self-study. Research on the impact of teacher preparation in understanding and instructional strategies should be undertaken. What differences in development and growth will occur when professionals are trained to identify and understand the unique needs of gifted students?

CONCLUSION

As previously stated, constructing a singular curriculum for inclusion of the gifted and talented learner to a heterogeneous classroom is simply impossible. Carol Tomlinson, as interviewed by Wu (2013), stated,

Good teaching is not following a syllabus or "covering" curriculum. It's certainly not managing behavior. It's inspiring young people to discover their strengths and to invest fully in cultivating them. That requires having a dynamic vision of a classroom and a desire to collaborate with the people who share classroom space and time with you. (p. 132)

One hopes that all educators have an extensive content discipline knowledge as well as a thorough compendium of pedagogical strategies with which to encourage and inspire all learners to seek knowledge. A good resource to start building Parallel Curriculum is Tomlinson and Strickland (2005). This is a compiled a resource guide that includes fully developed lessons in secondary grades mathematics, social studies, language arts, and art.

REFERENCES

Agarwal, P. K. (2019). Retrieval practice & Bloom's taxonomy: Do students need fact knowledge before higher order learning? *Journal of Educational Psychology, 111*(2), 189–209. doi:10.1037/edu0000282

Al-Fadhli, H. M., & Singh, M. (2010). Unequal moving to being equal: Impact of No Child Left Behind in the Mississippi Delta. *The Journal of Negro Education, 79*(1), 18–32.

Assouline, S., Colangelo, N., Lupkowski-Shoplik, A., Libscomb, J., & Forstadt, L. (2009). *Iowa Acceleration Scale* (3rd ed.). Great Potential Press, Inc.

Assouline, S. G., Colangelo, N., Van Tassel-Baska, J., & Lupkowski-Shoplik, A. (2015). A nation empowered, Vol 2. University of Iowa.

Aulls, M. W., & Ibrahim, A. (2012). Preservice teachers' perceptions of effective inquiry instruction: Are effective instruction and effective inquiry instruction essentially the same? *Instructional Science, 40*(1), 119–139. doi:10.100711251-010-9164-z

Berman, K. M., Schultz, R. A., & Weber, C. L. (2012). A lack of awareness and emphasis in preservice teacher training: Preconceived beliefs about the gifted and talented. *Gifted Child Today, 35*(1), 18–26. doi:10.1177/1076217511428307

Boulden, R., Stone, J., & Raisa, S. A. (2021). Supporting the college and career needs of gifted and talented learners in rural elementary schools: Strategies for school counselors. *The Clearing House: A Journal of Educational Strategies, Issues and Ideas, 94*(5), 223–235. doi:10.1080/00098655.2021.1939248

Boyle, C., McDonald, J., Komar, G., Rakow, S., Amidon, S., & Sheldon, A. (2010). Acceleration in Ohio: An analysis of statewide survey data. Ohio Association for Gifted Children, 1(1), 19-27.

Bruce, C., & Hughes, H. (2010). Informed learning: A pedagogical construct attending simultaneously to information use and learning. *Library & Information Science Research*, *32*(4), A2–A8. doi:10.1016/j.lisr.2010.07.013

Brulles, D., Saunders, R., & Cohn, S. J. (2010). Improving performance for gifted students in a cluster grouping model. *Journal for the Education of the Gifted*, *34*(2), 327–350.

Bui, S., Craig, S., & Imberman, S. (2012). Poor results for high achievers. *Education Next*, *12*(1), 70–76.

Colangelo, N., Assouline, S. G., & Gross, M. U. M. (2004). *A nation deceived: How schools hold back America's brightest students, (Vol. 1)*. The Templeton National Report on Acceleration. Belin-Blank Center at the University of Iowa.

Cross, T. L. (2014). Social emotional needs: Can the obsessions of gifted students be positive drivers in their development? *Gifted Child Today*, *37*(2), 123–125. doi:10.1177/1076217514520632

Cuban, L. (1993). *How teachers taught*. Teachers College Press.

Davis, C. (2001). *Forty years in the one-room schools of Eastern Kentucky, A memoir*. The Jesse Stuart Foundation.

Forehand, M. (2005). Bloom's taxonomy: Original and revised. In M. Orey (Ed.), *Emerging perspectives on learning, teaching, and technology*. https://www.d41.org/cms/lib/il01904672/centricity/domain/422/bloomstaxonomy.pdf

Fukuzawa, S., & Cahn, J. (2019). Technology in problem-based learning: Helpful or hindrance? *International Journal of Information and Learning Technology*, *36*(1), 66–76. doi:10.1108/IJILT-12-2017-0123

Gelen, I., & Kaçan, A. (2022). Teaching practices and evaluation with distance education of gifted students. *Journal for the Education of Gifted Young Scientists*, *10*(3), 411–433. doi:10.17478/jegys.1140286

Genome News Network. (2004). *Genetics and genomics timeline, 1910*. Thomas Hunt Morgan. http://www.genomenewsnetwork.org/resources/timeline/1910_Morgan.php

Gonzalez-Gonzalez, J., Franko-Calvo, J., & Espanol-Solana, D. (2022, June 10). Educating in history: Thinking historically through historical re-enactment. *Social Sciences (Basel, Switzerland)*, *11*(256), 1–18. doi:10.3390ocsci11060256

Grugan, M. C., Hill, A. P., Madigan, D. J., Donachie, T. C., Olsson, L. F., & Etherson, M. E. (2021). Perfectionism in academically gifted students: A systematic review. *Educational Psychology Review*, *33*(4), 1631–1673. doi:10.100710648-021-09597-7

Hafenstein, N. L., Boley, V., & Lin, J. (2022). State policy and funding in gifted education. *Gifted Child Today*, *45*(4), 226–234. doi:10.1177/10762175221110938

Hargrove, K. (2012, January). From the classroom: Advocating acceleration. *Gifted Child Today*, *72-73*. doi:10/1177/1076217511428309

Engaging on Common Ground

Hemmler, V. L., Azano, A. P., Dmitrieva, S., & Callahan, C. M. (2022). Representation of Black Students in rural gifted education: Taking steps toward equity. *Journal of Research in Rural Education, 38*(2), 1–25. doi:10.26209/jrre3802

History of Gifted Education. (n.d.). *History of gifted education.* Sutori. https://www.sutori.com/en/item/1954-national-association-of-gifted-children-is-founded-by-ann-isaacs-1954-i

Horn, C. V. (2015). Young scholars. *Gifted Child Today, 38*(1), 19–31. doi:10.1177/1076217514556532

Horne, D. L., & Dupuy, P. J. (1981). In favor of acceleration for gifted students. *The Personnel and Guidance Journal, 60*(2), 103–106. doi:10.1002/j.2164-4918.1981.tb00652.x

Howley, A. (2002). The progress of gifted students in a rural district that emphasized acceleration strategies. *Roeper Review, 24*(3), 158–160. doi:10.1080/02783190209554168

Hyatt, L. (2010). A case study of the suicide of a gifted female adolescent: Implications for prediction and prevention. *Journal for the Education of the Gifted, 33*(4), 514–535. doi:10.1177/016235321003300404

Johnsen, S. K., Fearon-Drake, D., & Wisely, L. W. (2020). A formative evaluation of differentiation practices in elementary cluster classrooms. *Roeper Review, 42*(3), 206–218. doi:10.1080/02783193.2020.1765921

Jolly, J. L. (2009). A resuscitation of gifted education. *American Educational History Journal, 36*(1), 37–52.

Lennex, L., Nettleton, K., & Kessinger, M. W. (2015*). Interviews with incoming freshman dual credit students to a gifted and talented academy.* Manuscript in preparation.

Lewis, K. D., & Boswell, C. (2020). Perceived challenges for rural gifted education. *Gifted Child Today, 43*(3), 184–198. doi:10.1177/1076217520915742

Lupart, J., & Webber, C. (2012). Canadian schools in transition: Moving from dual education systems to inclusive schools. *Exceptionality Education International, 22*(2), 8–37. doi:10.5206/eei.v22i2.7692

Lupkowski-Shoplik, A., Assouline, S. G., & Lane, R. (2022). Whole-grade acceleration: From student to policy. *Gifted Child Today, 45*(3), 143–149. doi:10.1177/10762175221091856

Marland, S. P., Jr. (1971). *Education of the gifted and talented – Volume 1: Report to the Congress of the United States* (ED056243). ERIC. https://files.eric.ed.gov/fulltexxt/ED056243.pdf

Maslow, A. H. (1954). *Motivation and personality.* Harper and Row.

Matthews, M. S., Ritchotte, J. A., & McBee, M. T. (2013). Effects of schoolwide cluster grouping and within-class ability grouping on elementary school students' academic achievement growth. *High Ability Studies, 24*(2), 81–97. doi:10.1080/13598139.2013.846251

Mondale, S., & Patton, S. B. (2001). *School: The story of American public education.* Beacon Press.

Mosse, B., Stribley, D. P., & LeTacon, F. (1981). Ecology of mycorrhizae and mycorrhizal fungi. In M. Alexander (Ed.), *Advances in microbial ecology* (Vol. 5). Springer., doi:10.1007/978-1-4615-8306-6_4

Mueller, J. (2003). *Authentic assessment toolbox: Enhancing student learning through online faculty development*. JOLT. https://jolt.merlot.org/documents/VOL1No1mueller.pdf

National Association for Gifted Children. (2019). *2019 Pre-K-Grade 12 gifted programming standards*. NAGC. https://nagc.org/page/National-Standards-in-Gifted-and-Talented-Education

National Association for Gifted Children (NAGC). (2023a). *A brief history of gifted and talented education*. NAGC. https://dev.nagc.org/resources-publications/resources/gifted-education-us/brief-history-gifted-and-talented-education

National Association for Gifted Children (NAGC). (2023b). *About NAGC*. NAGC. https://www.nagc.org/about-nagc

National Association of Gifted Children (NAGC). (2019). *Position statement: A definition of giftedness that guides best practice*. NAGC. https://www.nagc.org/sites/default/files/Position%20Statement/Definition%20of%20Giftedness%20%282019%29.pdf

Next Generation Science Standards. (2017). *About*. NGSS. https://ngss.nsta.org/AccessStandardsBy-Topic.aspx

Novak, A. M., Lewis, K. D., & Weber, C. L. (2020). Guiding principles in developing equity-driven professional learning for educators of gifted children. *Gifted Child Today, 43*(3), 169–183. doi:10.1177/1076217520915743

Perlman, J., & Margo, R. A. (2001). *Women's work? American schoolteachers, 1650-1920*. University of Chicago Press. doi:10.7208/chicago/9780226660417.001.0001

Peterson, J. S. (2009a). Myth 17: Gifted and talented individuals do not have unique social and emotional needs. *Gifted Child Quarterly, 53*(4), 280–282. doi:10.1177/0016986209346946

Peterson, J. S. (2009b). *Gifted and at risk: Poetic portraits*. Great Potential Press.

Plucker, J. A., & Peters, S. J. (2016). *Excellence gaps in education: Expanding opportunities for talented students*. Harvard Education Press.

Purcell, J., Burns, D., & Leppin, J. (2002, April). The parallel curriculum model (PCM): The whole story. *National Association for Gifted Children, 4*(1), 1–4.

Reis, S. M., & Boeve, H. (2009). How academically gifted elementary, urban students respond to challenge in an enriched, differentiated reading program. *Journal for the Education of the Gifted, 33*(2), 203–240. doi:10.1177/016235320903300204

Reis, S. M., Westberg, K. L., Kulikowich, J. K., Caillard, F., Hébert, T. P., Plucker, J., Purcell, J. H., Smist, J. M. (1993). *Why not let high ability students start school in January? The curriculum compacting study* (Research Monograph No. 93106). University of Connecticut, The National Research Center on the Gifted and Talented.

Riegel, B. D., & Behrens, W. A. (2022). Subject-based acceleration. *Gifted Child Today, 45*(4), 192–200. doi:10.1177/10762175221110937

Rinn, A. N., Mun, R. U., & Hodges, J. (2020). *2018-2019 State of the states in gifted education.* National Association for Gifted Children and the Council of State Directors for Programs for the Gifted. https://www.nagc.org/2018-2019-state-states-gifted-education

Rinn, A. N., Mun, R. U., & Hodges, J. (2022). *2020-2021 State of the states in gifted education.* National Association for Gifted Children and the Council of State Directors of Programs for the Gifted. https://cdn.ymaws.com/nagc.org/resource/resmgr/2020-21_state_of_the_states_.pdf

Roberts, J. L. (1999). The top 10 events creating gifted education for the new century. *Gifted Child Today, 22*(6), 53–55. doi:10.1177/107621759902200615

Roberts, J. L., & Boggess, J. R. (2011). *Teacher's survival guide: Gifted Education.* Prufrock Press.

Roberts, J. L., & Inman, T. F. (2023). *Strategies for differentiating instruction: Best practices for the classroom* (4th ed.). Routledge.

Robinson, A., & Deitz, C. (2022). Teachers count in the classroom and in policy: Legislation, rules, and regulations as pathways in gifted education. *Gifted Child Today, 45*(4), 220–225. doi:10.1177/10762175221110940

Ross, P. O. (1993). National excellence: A case for developing America's talent. U.S. Department of Education. ISBN-0-16-042928-5

Silverman, L. K. (2002). *Upside down brilliance: The visual-spatial learner.* DeLeon Publishing, Inc.

Stephens, K. R. (2019). Teacher dispositions and their impact on implementation practices for the gifted. *Gifted Child Today, 42*(4), 187–195. doi:10.1177/1076217519862330

The Miriam and Ira D. Wallach Division of Art. Prints and Photographs: Photography Collection, The New York Public Library. (1935). *Interior of "little red schoolhouse." Crossville, Tennessee.* https://digitalcollections.nypl.org/items/f33f13f0-da35-0132-3212-58d385a7bbd0

Title, I. X. (2011). U.S. Code 2011, Part A, Definition 22. https://www.govinfo.gov/content/pkg/USCODE-2011-title20/pdf/USCODE-2011-title20-chap70-subchapIX-partA-sec7801.pdf

Tomlinson, C. A. (2002, November 6). Proficiency is not enough. *Education Week.*

Tomlinson, C. A. (2005, Spring). Quality curriculum and instruction for highly able students. *Theory into Practice, 44*(2), 160–166. doi:10.120715430421tip4402_10

Tomlinson, C. A. (14 April 2015). Teaching for excellence in academically diverse classrooms. *Symposium: 21st Century Excellence in education,* 203-209. 10.100712115-015-9888-0

Tomlinson, C. A., & Imbeau, M. (2010). *Leading and managing a differentiated classroom.* Association for Supervision and Curriculum Development.

Tomlinson, C. A., Kaplan, S., Renzulli, J., Purcell, J., Leppien, J., & Burns, D. (2001). *The parallel curriculum: A design to develop high potential and challenge high-ability learners.* Corwin Press.

Tomlinson, C. A., & Strickland, C. (2005). *Differentiation in practice: A resource guide for differentiating curriculum, Grades 9-12*. Association for Supervision and Curriculum Development.

U.S. Department of Education. (2021). *The federal role in education*. USDE. https://www2.ed.gov/about/overview/fed/role.html

Usman, M., Plágero, T., Frank, H., Calvo-Palanco, M., Gaillard, I., Garcia, K., & Zimmerman, S. (2021, September 20). Mycorrhizal symbiosis for better adaptation of trees to abiotic stress caused by climate change in temperate and boreal forests. *Frontiers in Forests and Global Change, 4*, 742392. Advance online publication. doi:10.3389/ffgc.2021.742392

VanTassel-Baska, J. (2022). Assumptions about schooling: The myths of advanced learning. *Gifted Child Today, 45*(4), 235–237. doi:10.1177/10762175221110939

VanTassel-Baska, J., & Brown, E. (2022). An analysis of stakeholder perceptions of gifted programs: A report card on gifted program performance. *Gifted Child Today, 45*(3), 160–175. doi:10.1177/10762175221091859

Westerville Public Library. (2023). *Teaching in a one-room schoolhouse: The early days of education in Westerville*. Westerville Public Library. https://westervillelibrary.org/education-teaching/

Wu, E. H. (2013). The path leading to differentiation: An interview with Carol Tomlinson. *Journal of Advanced Academics, 24*(2), 125–133. doi:10.1177/1932202X13483472

Xiang, Y., Dahlin, M., Cronin, J., Thacker, R., & Durant, S. (2011). Do highfliers maintain their altitude? Performance trends of top performers. Thomas B. Fordham Institute.

ADDITIONAL READING

Almukhambetova, A., & Hernández-Torrano, D. (2021). On being gifted at university: Academic, social, emotional, and institutional adjustment in Kazakhstan. *Journal of Advanced Academics, 32*(1), 70–91. doi:10.1177/1932202X20951825

Arundel, K. (2021). Gifted education's future requires more diversity, inclusion and access. *K-12Dive*. https://www.k12dive.com/news/the-struggles-and-success-of-diversifying-gifted-education/609200/

Delisle, J. R. (1999). For gifted students, full inclusion is a partial solution. *Educational Leadership, 57*(3), 80–83.

Ford, D. Y., Davis, J. L., Whiting, G. W., & Moore, J. L. III. (2021). Going beyond lip service when it comes to equity: Characteristics of equity-minded, culturally responsive allies in gifted and talented education. *Gifted Child Today, 44*(3), 174–178. doi:10.1177/10762175211011210

Gallagher, S., & Smith, S. R. (2013). Acceleration for talent development: Parents' and teachers' attitudes towards supporting the social and emotional needs for gifted children. *International Journal for Talent Development and Creativity, 1*(2), 97–112.

Grigorenko, E. L. (2020). Twice exceptional students: Gifts and talents, the performing arts, and juvenile delinquency. In E. L. Greigorenko (Ed.), *Research with underrepresented population of children and adolescents: Ideas, samples, and methods. New Directions for Child and Adolescent Development, 169,* 59-74., doi:10.1002/cad.20326

Joyce, B. R. (1991). Common misconceptions about cooperative learning and gifted students. *Educational Leadership, 48*(6), 72–74.

Sapon-Shevin, M. (1994/1995). Why gifted students belong in inclusive schools. *Educational Leadership, 52*(4), 64–68, 70.

Savitch, J., & Serling, L. (1994/1995). Paving a path through untracked territory. *Educational Leadership, 52*(4), 72–74.

Tomlinson, C. A. (1994/1995). Gifted learners too: A possible dream? *Educational Leadership, 52*(4), 68–69.

Van Tassel-Baska, J. (2010). The history of urban gifted education. *Gifted Child Today, 33*(4), 18-27.

Van Tassel-Baska, J. (2021). Curriculum in gifted education: The core of the enterprise. *Gifted Child Today, 44*(1), 44–47. doi:10.1177/1076217520940747

Wiley, K. R. (2020). The social and emotional world of gifted students: Moving beyond the label. *Psychology in the Schools, 57*(10), 1528–1541. doi:10.1002/pits.22340

Zakreski, M. J. (2018). When emotional intensity and cognitive rigidity collide: What can counselors and teachers do? *Gifted Child Today, 41*(4), 208–216. doi:10.1177/1076217518786984

KEY TERMS AND DEFINITIONS

Acceleration: In education, acceleration refers to moving through curriculum at a faster pace than one's age-peers. Acceleration can range from moving through discipline specific subject matter to whole-grade skipping.

Assessment: Assessment can be either be pre-assessment, formative, or summative. It is used to provide data on student learning or achievement. Pre-assessment delivers information on what is already known, while formative assessment provides the educator with information on how students are learning new content. Summative assessment gives a comprehensive understanding of what has been learned.

Gifted Education: Curriculum designed to meet the educational needs of gifted students.

Instructional Strategies: Strategies used by an educator to present curriculum to learners. They are used for introduction or practice of discipline specific content.

Parallel Curriculum: An instructional strategy that provides the same curriculum to all classroom students but is stratified to reflect the learning level of students.

Problem Based Learning: An instructional strategy that typically provides students with real-world problems to solve. Learning takes place through the research and activities that solve the problem.

Social-Emotional Needs: A phrase that addresses both the social needs of students (inclusion, friendship), and the emotional needs (well-being, acceptance).

Compilation of References

Aabi, M., & Bracken, S. (2023). Drawing from the global to act local: How Universal Design for Learning lends itself to facilitating inclusion in Moroccan higher education. In, Kelly, A., Padden, L., Fleming, B (Eds) (2023) Making Inclusive Higher Education a Reality: Creating a University for All. London: Routledge. doi:10.4324/9781003253631-17

Afsharnejad, B., Falkmer, M., Picen, T., Black, M. H., Alach, T., Fridell, A., Coco, C., Milne, K., Perry, J., Bölte, S., & Girdler, S. (2022). "I met someone like me!": Autistic adolescents and their parents' experience of the KONTAKT social skills group training. *Journal of Autism and Developmental Disorders*, *52*(4), 1458–1477. doi:10.100710803-021-05045-1 PMID:33942186

Agarwal, P. K. (2019). Retrieval practice & Bloom's taxonomy: Do students need fact knowledge before higher order learning? *Journal of Educational Psychology*, *111*(2), 189–209. doi:10.1037/edu0000282

Ainscow, M., Booth, T., & Dyson, A. (2006). Improving schools, developing inclusion. Routledge.

Ainscow, M. (2019). *Ensuring inclusive education for all*. Routledge.

Ainscow, M. (2020). Inclusion and equity in education: Making sense of global challenges. *Prospects*, *49*(3-4), 123–134. doi:10.100711125-020-09506-w

Ainscow, M. (2020). Promoting inclusion and equity in education: Lessons from international experiences. *Nordic Journal of Studies in Educational Policy*, *6*(1), 7–16. doi:10.1080/20020317.2020.1729587

Al-Fadhli, H. M., & Singh, M. (2010). Unequal moving to being equal: Impact of No Child Left Behind in the Mississippi Delta. *The Journal of Negro Education*, *79*(1), 18–32.

Al-Hendawi, M., Keller, C., & Muhammad, S. K. (2023). Special education in the Arab Gulf countries: An analysis of ideals and realities. *International Journal of Educational Research Open*, *4*, 100217. doi:10.1016/j.ijedro.2022.100217

Alsalamah, A. (2020). Assessing students in higher education in light of UDL principles. *American Research Journal of Humanities & Social Science*, *3*(1), 24–27.

American Psychiatric Association (APA). (2013). *Diagnostic and Statistical Manual of Mental Disorders: DSM-5* (5th ed.). American Psychiatric Publishing.

American Psychiatric Association. (2022). *Diagnostic and statistical manual of mental disorders* (fifth Edition, text revision). American Psychiatric Association.

Amesberger, H., & Halbmayr, B. (2008). *Das privileg der unsichtbarkeit: Rassismus unter dem blickwinkel von weißsein und dominanzkultur*. Braumüller.

Anastasiou, D., & Kauffman, J. M. (2011). A social constructionist approach to disability: Implications for special education. *Exceptional Children*, *77*(3), 367–384. doi:10.1177/001440291107700307

Compilation of References

Andriana, E. (2018). *Engaging with student voice through arts-informed methods: Exploring inclusion in three schools Providing Inclusive Education in Yogyakarta, Indonesia*. [Doctoral Thesis, University of Sydney].

Aragón, O. R., Dovidio, J. F., & Graham, M. J. (2016). Colorblind and multicultural ideologies are associated with faculty adoption inclusive teaching practices. *Journal of Diversity in Higher Education, 3*(10), 1–15.

Arndt, K., & Liles, J. (2010). Preservice teachers' perceptions of co-teaching: A qualitative study. *Action in Teacher Education, 32*(1), 15–25. doi:10.1080/01626620.2010.10463539

Arndt, S. (2006). The racial turn: Kolonialismus, weiße mythen und critical whiteness studies. In M. Bechhaus-Gerst & S. Gieseke (Eds.), *Koloniale und postkoloniale Kontruktionen von Afrika und Menschen afrikanischer Herkunft in der deutschen Alltagskultur* (pp. 11–26). Peter Lang.

Askew, M. (2015). Diversity, inclusion and equity in mathematics classrooms: From individual problems to collective possibility. In A. J., Bishop, H. Tan, & T. N. Barkatsas (Eds), Diversity in mathematics education: Towards inclusive practices (pp. 129–145). Cham: Springer International Publishing.

Asmussen, B., Harridge-March, S., Occhiocupo, N., & Farquhar, J. (2013). The multi-layered nature of the internet-based democratization of brand management. *Journal of Business Research, 66*(9), 1473–1483. doi:10.1016/j.jbusres.2012.09.010

Assouline, S. G., Colangelo, N., Van Tassel-Baska, J., & Lupkowski-Shoplik, A. (2015). A nation empowered, Vol 2. University of Iowa.

Assouline, S., Colangelo, N., Lupkowski-Shoplik, A., Libscomb, J., & Forstadt, L. (2009). *Iowa Acceleration Scale* (3rd ed.). Great Potential Press, Inc.

Atweh, B. (2011). Quality and equity in mathematics education as ethical issues. In B. Atweh, M. Graven, W. Secada, & P. Valero (Eds.), *Mapping equity and quality in mathematics education* (pp. 63–75). Springer. doi:10.1007/978-90-481-9803-0

Aulls, M. W., & Ibrahim, A. (2012). Preservice teachers' perceptions of effective inquiry instruction: Are effective instruction and effective inquiry instruction essentially the same? *Instructional Science, 40*(1), 119–139. doi:10.100711251-010-9164-z

Austin, V. L. (2001). Teachers' beliefs about co-teaching. *Remedial and Special Education, 22*(4), 245–255. doi:10.1177/074193250102200408

Austin, V. L. (2016). Introduction to the special issue pedagogies and behaviors that benefit students with exceptional learning needs. *Insights into Learning Disabilities, 13*(1), 1–6.

Australia Government. (2022). Quality initial teacher education report. Australian Government.

Australian Curriculum, Assessment, Reporting Authority. (2023). *Australian curriculum* (9th version). Australian Curriculum. https://v9.australiancurriculum.edu.au

Australian Disability Clearinghouse on Education and Training (ADCET). (n.d.). ADCET. https://www.adcet.edu.au/

Australian Disability Clearinghouse on Education and Training. (n.d.). *Communities of practice*. ADCET. https://www.adcet.edu.au/resources/communities-of-practice

Australian Government. (2014). *Review of the Australian Curriculum: Final report*. Australian Government. https://www.education.gov.au/australian-curriculum/resources/review-australian-curriculum-final-report-2014

Australian Government. (2020, November 27). *National Disability Coordination Officer Program*. Department of Education. https://www.education.gov.au/access-and-participation/ndco

Australian Government. (2022, October 10). *Higher Education Statistics*. Department of Education. https://www.education.gov.au/higher-education-statistics

Australian Institute of Housing and Welfare. (2017). *Disability in Australia: changes over time in inclusion and participation in education*. AIHW. https://www.aihw.gov.au/getmedia/34f09557-0acf-4adf-837d-eada7b74d466/Education-20905.pdf.aspx

Avramidis, E., Bayliss, P., & Burden, R. (2000). Student teachers' attitudes towards the inclusion of children with special educational needs in the ordinary school. *Teaching and Teacher Education, 16*(3), 277–293. doi:10.1016/S0742-051X(99)00062-1

Avramidis, E., & Norwich, B. (2010). Teachers' attitudes towards integration/inclusion: A review of the literature. *European Journal of Special Needs Education, 17*(2), 129–147. doi:10.1080/08856250210129056

Avramidis, E., Toulia, A., Tsihouridis, C., & Strogilos, V. (2019). Teacher's attitudes towards inclusion and their self-efficacy for inclusive practices as predictors of willingness to implement peer tutoring. *Journal of Research in Special Educational Needs, 19*(S1, s1), 49–59. doi:10.1111/1471-3802.12477

Bagger, A. (2017). Quality and Equity in the Era of National Testing. The case of Sweden. In J. Allan & A. Artiles (Eds.), *The Routledge Yearbook of Education 2017, Assessment Inequalities* (pp. 68–88). Routledge.

Baglieri, S., Bejoian, L. M., Broderick, A. A., Connor, D. J., & Valle, J. (2011). [Re]claiming "inclusive education" towards cohesion in educational reform: Disability studies unravels the myth of the normal child. *Teachers College Record, 113*(10), 2122–2154. doi:10.1177/016146811111301001

Bahou, L. (2011, January). Rethinking the challenges and possibilities of student voice and agency. *Educate*, (Special Issue), 2–14.

Balli, D. (2016). Importance of Parental Involvement to Meet the Special Needs of their Children with Disabilities in Regular Schools. *Academic Journal of Interdisciplinary Studies, 5*(1), 147–152. doi:10.5901/ajis.2016.v5n1p147

Bandura, A. (1977). Self-efficacy: Toward a unifying theory of behavioural change. *Psychological Review, 84*(2), 191–215. doi:10.1037/0033-295X.84.2.191 PMID:847061

Bandura, A. (1997). Self-efficacy. The exercise of control. *The Freeman*.

Banks, J., McCoy, S., & Shevlin, M. (2011). Inclusive education research: Evidence from growing up in Ireland. *Trinity Education Paper, 2*(2), 24-35. https://www.researchgate.net/profile /Joanne_Banks2/publication/259146535

Barnes, C. S., Dunning, J. L., & Rehfeldt, R. A. (2011). An evaluation of strategies for training staff to implement the picture exchange communication system. *Research in Autism Spectrum Disorders, 5*(4), 1574–1583. doi:10.1016/j.rasd.2011.03.003

Barton, L. (1997). Inclusive education: Romantic, subversive or realistic? *International Journal of Inclusive Education, 1*(3), 231–242. doi:10.1080/1360311970010301

Basham, J. D., Gardner, J. E., & Smith, S. J. (2020). Measuring the implementation of UDL in classrooms and schools: Initial field test results. *Remedial and Special Education, 41*(4), 231–243. doi:10.1177/0741932520908015

Basit, A., & Evans, D. (n.d.). Including all students in education: students with cerebral palsy in Pakistan.

Bateman, D. F., & Yell, M. L. (2019). *Current trends and legal issues in special education*. Corwin. doi:10.4135/9781071800539

Compilation of References

Beach, P., & Willows, D. (2014). Investigating teachers' exploration of a professional development website: An innovative approach to understanding the factors that motivate teachers to use Internet-based resources. *Canadian Journal of Learning and Technology / La revue canadienne de l'apprentissage et de la technologie, 40*(3), Canadian Network for Innovation in Education. https://www.learntechlib.org/p/148504/

Beaumont, C., O'Doherty, M., & Shannon, L. (2011). Reconceptualising assessment feedback: A key to improving student learning? *Studies in Higher Education, 36*(6), 671–687. doi:10.1080/03075071003731135

Bechhaus-Gerst, M., & Gieseke, S. (Eds.). (2006). *Koloniale und postkoloniale kontruktionen von Afrika und menschen Afrikanischer herkunft in der Deutschen alltagskultur*. Peter Lang.

Beck Wells, M. (2022). Student perspectives on the use of universal design for learning in virtual formats in higher education. *Smart Learning Environments, 9*(1), 1–12. doi:10.118640561-022-00218-6

Bee, M. (2018). *Das problem mit critical whiteness*. Migrazine. http://migrazine.at/artikel/das-problem-mit-critical-whiteness

Bell, D. (2021). South Africa has advanced the use of sign language. But there are still gaps. *The Conversation*. https://theconversation.com/south-africa-has-advanced-the-use-of-sign-language-but-there-are-still-gaps-168424https://theconversation.com/south-africa-has-advanced-the-use-of-sign-language-but-there-are-still-gaps-168424

Bell, D., & Swart, E. (2018). Learning experiences of students who are hard of hearing in higher education: Case study of a South African university. *Social Inclusion (Lisboa), 6*(4), 137–148. doi:10.17645i.v6i4.1643

Bell, J. (2010). Clearing the AIR. *Communication World, 27*(1), 27–30.

Beninghof, A. M. (2020). *Co-teaching that works structures and strategies for maximizing student learning* (2nd ed.). Jossey-Bass.

Bennett, S., Dawson, P., Bearman, M., Molloy, E., & Boud, D. (2017). How technology shapes assessment design: Findings from a study of university teachers. *British Journal of Educational Technology, 48*(2), 672–682. doi:10.1111/bjet.12439

Berghs, M., Atkin, K., Hatton, C., & Thomas, C. (2019). Do disabled people need a stronger social model: A social model of human rights? *Disability & Society, 34*(7-8), 1034–1039. doi:10.1080/09687599.2019.1619239

Berman, K. M., Schultz, R. A., & Weber, C. L. (2012). A lack of awareness and emphasis in preservice teacher training: Preconceived beliefs about the gifted and talented. *Gifted Child Today, 35*(1), 18–26. doi:10.1177/1076217511428307

Bernard Martin, D. (2019). Equity, inclusion, and antiblackness in mathematics education. *Race, Ethnicity and Education, 22*(4), 459–478. doi:10.1080/13613324.2019.1592833

Bertuccio, R. F., Runion, M. C., Culler, E. D., Moeller, J. D., & Hall, C. M. (2019). A comparison of autism-specific training outcomes for teachers and paraeducators. *Teacher Education and Special Education, 42*(4), 338–354. doi:10.1177/0888406419839771

Bethune, K. S., & Wood, C. L. (2013). Effects of coaching on teachers' use of function-based interventions for students with severe disabilities. *Teacher Education and Special Education, 36*(2), 97–114. doi:10.1177/0888406413478637

Bettini, E. A., Crockett, J. B., Brownell, M. T., & Merrill, K. L. (2016). Relationships between working conditions and special educators' instructions. *The Journal of Special Education, 50*(3), 178–190. doi:10.1177/0022466916644425

Bettini, E. A., Jones, N., Brownell, M., Conroy, M., Park, Y., Leite, W., Crockett, J., & Benedict, A. (2017). Workload manageability among novice special and general educators: Relationships with emotional exhaustion and career intentions. *Remedial and Special Education, 38*(4), 246–256. doi:10.1177/0741932517708327

Betz, T., Bollig, S., Joos, M., & Neumann, S. (Eds.). (2018). *Gute Kindheit: Wohlbefinden, Kindeswohl und Ungleichheit*. Juventa.

Biesta, G. (2013). *Para além da aprendizagem: educação democrática para um futuro humano*. Autêntica.

Biggs, J. (1996). Enhancing teaching through constructive alignment. *Higher Education, 32*(3), 347–364. doi:10.1007/BF00138871

Billingsley, B., & Bettini, E. (2017). Improving special education teacher quality and effectiveness. In J. M. Kauffman, D. P. Hallahan, & P. C. Pullen (Eds.), *Handbook of special education* (2nd ed., pp. 501–520). Routledge. doi:10.4324/9781315517698-39

Billingsley, B., & Bettini, E. (2019). Special education teacher attrition and retention: A review of the literature. *Review of Educational Research, 89*(5), 697–744. doi:10.3102/0034654319862495

Bishop, A. J., & Forgasz, H. J. (2007). Issues in access and equity in mathematics education. In F. K. Lester Jr., (Ed.), *Second handbook of research on mathematics teaching and learning* (pp. 1145–1167). Information Age Publishing.

Bishop, A. J., Tan, P., & Barkatsas, T. N. (2015). *Diversity in mathematics education: Towards inclusive practices*. Springer International Publishing. doi:10.1007/978-3-319-05978-5

Black, R. D., Weinberg, L. A., & Brodwin, M. G. (2014). Universal Design for instruction and learning: A pilot study of faculty instructional methods and attitudes related to students with disabilities in higher education. *Exceptionality Education International, 24*(1). doi:10.5206/eei.v24i1.7710

Bliemetsrieder, S., & Beinzger, D. (2022). Das Ethische und das Politische als Kritik an und in der Lehrer*innenbildung: Verantwortung und gerechtigkeitsambitionierte Einmischungen als normative Orientierungen. In O. Ivanova-Chessex, S. Shure, & A. Steinbach (Eds.), *Lehrer*innenbildung: (Re-)Visionen für die Migrationsgesellschaft* (pp. 116–131). Beltz.

Boger, M.-A., & Simon, N. (2022). Kritik im Pflichtmodul Heterogenität: Paradoxien der (Ent-)Politisierung in der Lehrer*innenbildung. In O. Ivanova-Chessex, S. Shure, & A. Steinbach (Eds.), *Lehrer*innenbildung: (Re-)Visionen für die Migrationsgesellschaft* (pp. 20–35). Beltz.

Bölte, S. (2014). Is autism curable? *Developmental Medicine and Child Neurology, 56*(10), 927–931. doi:10.1111/dmcn.12495 PMID:24840630

Bölte, S., Leifler, E., Berggren, S., & Borg, A. (2021). Inclusive practice for students with neurodevelopmental disorders in Sweden. *Scandinavian Journal of Child and Adolescent Psychiatry and Psychology, 9*(1), 9–15. doi:10.21307jcapp-2021-002 PMID:33928049

Bond, C., Symes, W., Hebron, J., Humphrey, N., & Morewood, G. (2016). Educating persons with autistic spectrum disorder – A systematic literature review. NCSE Research Reports No: 20. University of Manchester.

Boulden, R., Stone, J., & Raisa, S. A. (2021). Supporting the college and career needs of gifted and talented learners in rural elementary schools: Strategies for school counselors. *The Clearing House: A Journal of Educational Strategies, Issues and Ideas, 94*(5), 223–235. doi:10.1080/00098655.2021.1939248

Boutot, E. A. (2016). *Autism spectrum disorders: Foundations, characteristics, and effective strategies* (2nd ed.). Pearson Education.

Boyle, C., McDonald, J., Komar, G., Rakow, S., Amidon, S., & Sheldon, A. (2010). Acceleration in Ohio: An analysis of statewide survey data. Ohio Association for Gifted Children, 1(1), 19-27.

Compilation of References

Boyle, C., & Anderson, J. (2020). The justification for inclusive education in Australia. *Prospects, 49*(3-4), 203–217. doi:10.100711125-020-09494-x

Bracken, S., & Novak, K. (Eds.). (2019). *Transforming higher education through universal design for learning: An international perspective*. Routledge. doi:10.4324/9781351132077

Brame, C. J. (2016). Effective Educational Videos: Principles and Guidelines for Maximizing Student Learning from Video Content. *CBE Life Sciences Education, 15*(4), es6. doi:10.1187/cbe.16-03-0125 PMID:27789532

Brand, S., Favazza, A. E., & Dalton, E. M. (2012). Universal design for learning: A blueprint for success for all learners. *Kappa Delta Pi Record, 48*(3), 134–113. doi:10.1080/00228958.2012.707506

Braun, V., & Clarke, V. (2006). Using thematic analysis in psychology. *Qualitative Research in Psychology, 3*(2), 77–101. doi:10.1191/1478088706qp063oa

Brazil (2015). Instituto Nacional de Estudos e Pesquisa Educacionais. *Censo Escolar 2015*. http://portal.inepp.gov.br/web/guest/sinopses-estatisticas-da-educacao-basica

Brazil. (1996). Casa Civil. *Lei n° 9.394, de 20 de dezembro de 1996*. Estabelece as Diretrizes e Bases da Educação Nacional. Casa Civil. http://www.planalto.gov.br/ccivil_03/leis/l9394.htm

Brazil. (2008). Ministério da Educação. *Política Nacional de Educação Especial na Perspectiva da Educação Inclusiva*. Ministério da Educação. http://portal.mec.gov.br/seesp/arquivos/pdf/politica.pdf

Brazil. (2014). Ministério da Educação. *Plano Nacional de Educação 2014-2014*. Ministério da Educação. https://pne.mec.gov.br/

Britton, L. R., & Anderson, K. A. (2010). Peer coaching and preservice teachers: Examining an underutilised concept. *Teaching and Teacher Education, 26*(2), 306–314. doi:10.1016/j.tate.2009.03.008

Brock, M. E., & Carter, E. W. (2015). Effects of a professional development package to prepare special education paraprofessionals to implement evidence-based practice. *The Journal of Special Education, 49*(1), 39–51. doi:10.1177/0022466913501882

Brock, M. E., Huber, H. B., Carter, E. W., Juarez, A. P., & Warren, Z. E. (2014). Statewide assessment of professional development needs related to educating students with autism spectrum disorder. *Focus on Autism and Other Developmental Disabilities, 29*(20), 67–79. doi:10.1177/1088357614522290

Brookfield, S. (2017). *Becoming a critically reflective teacher*. Jossey-Bass, A Wiley Brand.

Brown v. Board of Education, 347 U.S. 483 (1954). https://www.oyez.org/cases/1940-1955/347us483

Brown, N. (2021). Deafness and hearing loss in higher education. In N. Brown (Ed.), *Lived experiences of ableism in academia. Strategies for inclusion in higher education* (pp. 141–158). Bristol University Press. doi:10.2307/j.ctv1nh3m5m.17

Bruce, C., & Hughes, H. (2010). Informed learning: A pedagogical construct attending simultaneously to information use and learning. *Library & Information Science Research, 32*(4), A2–A8. doi:10.1016/j.lisr.2010.07.013

Brulles, D., Saunders, R., & Cohn, S. J. (2010). Improving performance for gifted students in a cluster grouping model. *Journal for the Education of the Gifted, 34*(2), 327–350.

Bui, S., Craig, S., & Imberman, S. (2012). Poor results for high achievers. *Education Next, 12*(1), 70–76.

Butler, J. (1993). *Bodies that matter: On the discursive limits of "sex."*. Routledge.

Capp, M. Y. (2017). The effectiveness of universal design for learning: A meta-analysis of literature between 2013 and 2016. *International Journal of Inclusive Education, 21*(8), 791–807. doi:10.1080/13603116.2017.1325074

Carballo, R., Morgado, B., & Cortés-Vega, M. D. (2019). Transforming faculty conceptions of disability and inclusive education through a training programme. *International Journal of Inclusive Education*, 1–17. doi:10.1080/13603116. 2019.1579874

Carey, D. (2005). *The essential guide to special education in Ireland.* CJ Fallon.

Carpenter, J. P., Krutka, D. G., & Trust, T. (2022). Continuity and change in educators' professional learning networks. *Journal of Educational Change, 23*(1), 85–113. doi:10.100710833-020-09411-1

Carrington, S. (1999). Inclusion needs a different school culture. *International Journal of Inclusive Education, 3*(3), 257–268. doi:10.1080/136031199285039

Carrington, S., Lassig, C., Maia-Pike, L., Mann, G., Mavropoulou, S., & Saggers, B. (2022). Societal, systemic, school and family drivers for and barriers to inclusive education. *Australian Journal of Education, 66*(3), 251–264. doi:10.1177/00049441221125282

Casale-Giannola, D. (2012). Comparing inclusion in the secondary vocational and academic classrooms: Strengths, needs, and recommendations. *American Secondary Education, 40*(2), 26–42.

CAST. (2018). *UDL and the learning brain.* CAST. https://www.cast.org/binaries/content/assets/common /publications/ articles/cast-udlandthebrain-20220228-a11y.pdf

CAST. (2018). *UDL and the learning brain.* Wakefield, MA: Author. Retrieved from https://www.cast.org/our-work/ publications/2018/udl-learning-brainneuroscience.html

CAST. (2018). *Universal Design for Learning Guidelines version 2.2.* CAST. http://udlguidelines.cast.org

CAST. (2022). *About Universal Design for Learning.* CAST. https://www.cast.org/impact/universal-design-for-learning-udl

CAST. (2022, May 16). *Timeline of innovation.* CAST. https://www.cast.org/impact/timeline-innovation

Center for Teaching and Learning. (2020). *Guide for inclusive teaching at Columbia.* Columbia CTL. https://ctl.columbia. edu/resources-and-technology/resources/inclusive-teaching-guide/download/

Chang, Bey-Lih (2009) Inclusive Education in Taiwan. *National Taiwan Normal University Division of Educational Practicum and Professional Development Secondary Education, 60*(4), 8-18.

Chao, C. N. G., Forlin, C., & Ho, F. C. (2016). Improving teaching self-efficacy for teachers in inclusive classrooms in Hong Kong. *International Journal of Inclusive Education, 20*(11), 1142–1154. doi:10.1080/13603116.2016.1155663

Chen, H., & Evans, D. (2023). Moving towards inclusive education: Secondary school teacher attitudes towards universal design for learning in Australia. *Australasian Journal of Special and Inclusive Education.*

Chen, H.-C. (2019) *Implementation of Inclusive Education of the Convention on the Rights of Persons with Disabilities in the Taiwanese Laws* [Unpublished master's thesis, National Cheng-chi University, Taipei, Taiwan].

Cheng, C.-F. (2012). The Growth out of Nothing in Special Education: Discussion on the Phenomenon of Marginalization of Students with Disabilities in Regular Class. *Special Education Quarterly, 122*, 45–52.

Chetty, R., Friedman, J. N., & Rockoff, J. E. (2014). Measuring the impacts of teachers I: Evaluating bias in teacher value-added estimates. *The American Economic Review, 104*(9), 2593–2632. doi:10.1257/aer.104.9.2593

Compilation of References

China Education Online. (2020). *Shinian yue 1,680wan renci de jiaoshi canyu 'guopei jihua'* (十年约1680万人次的教师参与"国培计划") [More than 1.68 million teachers have participated in national teacher training plan program in the past ten years]. China Education Online. https://baijiahao.baidu.com/s?id=1676875761328745757&wfr=spider&for=pc

Chiu, Y.-C. (2021). Inclusive Education and The Promotion Program of Special Education. *Student Affairs and Guidance Counseling, 59*(4), 63–67.

Chiwandire, D., & Vincent, L. (2019). Funding Mechanisms to Foster Inclusion in Higher Education Institutions for Students with Disabilities. *African Journal of Disability, 8*, 1–12. doi:10.4102/ajod.v8i0.503 PMID:30899686

Chu, Y.-C., & Chang, S.-H. (2019). Service-Learning Program to Improve Elementary School Students' Peer Acceptance Attitude towards Students with Disabilities. *Special Education Forum, 27*, 17-34.

Chu, S.-M., & Chen, S.-Y. (2019). Study on the Process of Implementing Inclusion Activities in Class-Field Courses-A Special Education Class of a Taipei Municipal Elementary School as a Case. *The Development of Special Education, 68*, 43–56.

Clandinin, D. J., & Connelly, F. M. (2004). *Narrative Inquiry: Experience and Story in Qualitative Research.* Jossey-Bass.

Clark, C., Dyson, A., Milward, A., & Skidmore, D. (1995). Dialectical analysis, special needs and schools as organisations. In C. Clark, A. Dyson, & A. Milward (Eds.), *Towards inclusive schools.* Fulton.

Clarke, P. (2020, June 17). What Is Strategic Communications? *Medium.* https://medium.com/@Peter_Clarke/what-is-strategic-communications-8738b713e77

Cobb, P., & Hodge, L. L. (2007). Culture, identity, and equity in the mathematics classroom. In S. N. Nasir & P. Cobb (Eds.), *Improving access to mathematics: Diversity and equity in the classroom* (pp. 159–164). Teachers College Press.

Coco, C., Fridell, A., Borg, A., & Bölte, S. (2023). *SKOLKONTAKT®, Manual. Social färdighetsträning i grupp* [Social skills group training, the manual]. Hogrefe.

Colangelo, N., Assouline, S. G., & Gross, M. U. M. (2004). *A nation deceived: How schools hold back America's brightest students, (Vol. 1).* The Templeton National Report on Acceleration. Belin-Blank Center at the University of Iowa.

Cole, S. M., Murphy, H. R., Frisby, M. B., Grossi, T. A., & Bolte, H. R. (2020). The relationship of special education placement and student academic outcomes. *The Journal of Special Education, 54*(4), 1–11. doi:10.1177/0022466920925033

Cole, S. M., Murphy, H. R., Frisby, M. B., & Robinson, J. (2022). *The relationship between special education placement and high school outcomes. The Journal of Special Education.* Online First., doi:10.1177/00224669221097945

Cologon, K. (2019) *Towards inclusive education: A necessary process of transformation.* Report for Children and Young People with Disability Australia (CYDA).

Coman, D., Alessandri, M., Novotny, S., Gutierrez, A., Boyd, B., & Hume, K. (2013). Commitment to classroom model philosophy and burnout symptoms among high fidelity teachers implementing preschool programs for children with autism spectrum disorders. *Journal of Autism and Developmental Disorders, 43*(2), 345–360. doi:10.100710803-012-1573-1 PMID:22706583

Cooc, N. (2019). Teaching students with special needs: International trends in school capacity and the need for teacher professional development. *Teaching and Teacher Education, 83*, 27–41. doi:10.1016/j.tate.2019.03.021

Cook, B. G., & Schirmer, B. R. (2003). What is special about special education? Overview and analysis. *The Journal of Special Education, 37*(3), 200–205. doi:10.1177/00224669030370031001

Cook, B. G., Tankersley, M., Cook, L., & Landrum, T. J. (2015). Republication of "evidence-based practices in special education: Some practical considerations". *Intervention in School and Clinic, 50*(5), 310–315. doi:10.1177/1053451214532071

Cook, L., & Friend, M. (1995). Co-teaching: Guidelines for creating effective practices. *Focus on Exceptional Children, 28*(3), 1–16.

Cook-Sather, A. (2018). Tracing the Evolution of Student Voice in Educational Research. In R. Bourke & J. Loveridge (Eds.), *Radical Collegiality through Student Voice.* Springer. doi:10.1007/978-981-13-1858-0_2

Corona, L. L., Christodulu, K. V., & Rinaldi, M. L. (2017). Investigation of school professionals' self-efficacy for working with students with ASD: Impact of prior experience, knowledge, and training. *Journal of Positive Behavior Interventions, 19*(2), 90–101. doi:10.1177/1098300716667604

Costa-Renders, E. C. (2019). Pedagogy of Seasons and UDL: the multiple temporalities of learning involving the university as a whole. In *Bracken, S. & Novak, K. (org) Transforming Higher Education Through Universal Design for Learning an International Perspective* (pp. 159–178). Routledge. doi:10.4324/9781351132077-10

Council of Australian Governments - Education Council. (2019). *Alice Springs (Mparntwe) education declaration.* Council of Australian Governments. https://uploadstorage.blob.core.windows.net/public-assets/education-au/melbdec/ED19-0230%20-%20SCH%20-%20Alice%20Springs %20(Mparntwe)%20Education%20Declaration_ACC.pdf

Crenshaw, K. W. (2017). *On intersectionality: Essential writings.* The New Press.

Cross, T. L. (2014). Social emotional needs: Can the obsessions of gifted students be positive drivers in their development? *Gifted Child Today, 37*(2), 123–125. doi:10.1177/1076217514520632

Cuban, L. (1993). *How teachers taught.* Teachers College Press.

Cumming, T. M., & Rose, M. C. (2022). Exploring universal design for learning as an accessibility tool in higher education: A review of the current literature. *Australian Educational Researcher, 49*(5), 1025–1043. doi:10.100713384-021-00471-7

Da Fonte, M. A., & Baron-Arwood, S. M. (2017). Collaboration of general and special education teachers: Perspectives and strategies. *Intervention in School and Clinic, 53*(2), 99–106. doi:10.1177/1053451217693370

Dalton, E., Lyner-Cleophas, M. M., Ferguson, B., & Mckenzie, J. (2019). Inclusion, universal design and universal design for learning in higher education: South Africa and the United States. *African Journal on Disability.* https://journals.co.za/doi/abs/10.4102/ajod.v8i0.519

Dalton, E. M., Mckenzie, J. A., & Kahonde, C. (2012). The implementation of inclusive education in South Africa: Reflections arising from a workshop for teachers and therapists to introduce universal design for learning. *African Journal of Disability, 1*(1), 1–7. http://dx.doi.rg/10.4102/ajod.v1i1.13. doi:10.4102/ajod.v1i1.13 PMID:28729974

Darling-Hammond, L., Hyler, M. E., & Gardner, M. (2017). *Effective teacher professional development.* Learning Policy Institute. doi:10.54300/122.311

Darling-Hammond, L., Wei, R. C., Andree, A., Richardson, N., & Orphanos, S. (2009). *Professional learning in the learning profession: A status report on teacher development in the U.S. and abroad.* National Staff Development Council.

Davis, C. (2001). *Forty years in the one-room schools of Eastern Kentucky, A memoir.* The Jesse Stuart Foundation.

De Boer, A., Pijl, S. J., & Minnaert, A. (2011). Regular primary schoolteachers' attitudes towards inclusive education: A review of the literature. *International Journal of Inclusive Education, 15*(3), 331–353. doi:10.1080/13603110903030089

Compilation of References

Deaf Federation of South Africa. (2018). *Report on performance of deaf learners in schools for the deaf in South Africa in 2017.* DFSA. http://www.included.org.za/wp-content/uploads/2017/03/Grade1 2Report_2016_DeafSA_final.2.pdf

Deng, M., & Poon-McBrayer, K. F. (2016). Development of special and inclusive education in Western China. In J. C.-K. Lee, Z. Yu, X. Huang, & E. H.-F. Law (Eds.), *Educational developmental in Western China: Towards quality and equity* (pp. 301–309). Sense Publishers. doi:10.1007/978-94-6300-232-5_16

Department of Education, Employment, and Workplace Relations (DEEWR). (2009). *The early years learning framework for Australia, belonging, being, becoming.* Department of Education, Employment and Workplace Relations (DEEWR). https://www.education.gov.au/child-care-package/national-qua lity-framework/approved-learning-frameworks

Department of Education, Ireland. (1993) Report of the special education review committee (SERC). Stationary Office.

Department of Education. (2005). *White paper on education: Charting our future.* DoE. https://assets.gov.ie/24448/0f 3bff53633440d99c32541f7f45cfeb.pdf

Department of Education. Ireland. (2015). *Framework for junior cycle.* Department of Education, Ireland. https://www. gov.ie/en /publication/aed00b-framework-for-junior-cycle/

Department of Education. Ireland. (2017). *Special education teaching allocation.* Department of Education, Ireland. https://www.gov.ie/en /circular/b1ee7005c95747cea9e6406b8a5b 3c67/

Department of Inclusive Education. (2020). *Students with complex learning profile: statistics 2020.* Department of Inclusive Education.

Department of Inclusive Education. (2021). *Annual Report 2021.* Department of Education.

Department of Inclusive Education. (2022a). *Annual Report 2022.* Department of Inclusive Education.

Department of Inclusive Education. (2022b). *Shaamiluveshi project activity report on ICT, monitoring and PD (unpublished report).* Department of Inclusive Education.

Department of Inclusive Education. (2022c). *Transforming inclusive pedagogy: inclusive teachers for inclusive schools (unpublished report).* Department of Inclusive Education.

Department of Inclusive Education. (2022d). *Transforming inclusive pedagogy: training of in-service teachers (unpublished report).* Department of Inclusive Education.

Desforges, M. (2010). *Procedures used to diagnose disability and to assess special educational needs.* National Council for Special Education. https://ncse.ie/wp-content/uploads/2014/10/5_NCSE_Diag_Ass.p df

di Biase, R., & Maniku, A. A. (2021). Transforming Education in the Maldives. In P. M. Sarangapani & R. Pappu (Eds.), *Handbook of Education Systems in South Asia. Global Education Systems* (pp. 545–573). Springer. doi:10.1007/978-981-15-0032-9_14

Diaz, J. D. (2013). Governing equality: Mathematics for all? *European Education, 45*(3), 35–50. doi:10.2753/EUE1056-4934450303

Diliberti, M. K., & Schwartz, H. L. (2023). *Educator turnover has markedly increased, but districts have taken actions to boost teacher ranks.* Rand Corporation. https://www.rand.org/pubs/research_reports/RRA956-14.html

Disability Awareness. (2020, March 10). Disability Awareness. https://disabilityawareness.com.au/elearning/disability-awareness/

do Mar Castro Varela, M. (2017). *(Un-)Wissen: Verlernen als komplexer lernprozess.* Migrazine. https://www.migrazine.at/artikel/un-wissen-verlernen-als-komplexer-lernprozess

do Mar Castro Varela, M., & Dhawan, N. (2005). *Postkoloniale Theorie: Eine kritische Einführung* (Transcript). Center for Applied Special Technology.

do Mar Castro Varela, M. (2022). Schule, nationalstaat und die vermittlung von herrschaftswissen: Postkoloniale betrachtungen. In O. Ivanova-Chessex, S. Shure, & A. Steinbach (Eds.), *Lehrer*innenbildung: (Re-)visionen für die migrationsgesellschaft* (pp. 36–49). Beltz.

Donohue, D., & Bornman, J. (2014). The challenges of realising inclusive education in South Africa. *South African Journal of Education, 34*(2), 1–14. https://www.sajournalofeducation.co.za/index.php/saje/article/view/806/415. doi:10.15700/201412071114

Draffan, E. A., James, A., & Martin, N. (2017). Inclusive teaching and learning: What's next? *The Journal of Inclusive Practice in Further and Higher Education, 9*(1). https://eprints.soton.ac.uk/415140/

Dudley-Marling, C., & Burns, M. B. (2014). Two perspectives on inclusion in the United States. *Global Education Review, 1*(1), 14–31.

Dunst, C. J., Bruder, M. B., & Hamby, D. W. (2015). Meta-synthesis of in-service professional development research: Features associated with positive educator and student outcomes. *Educational Research Review, 10*(12), 1731–1744. doi:10.5897/ERR2015.2306

Dutta, İ. (2016). Open educational resources (OER): Opportunities and challenges for Indian higher education. *Turkish Online Journal of Distance Education, 17*(2), 0-0. doi:10.17718/tojde.34669

Dyer, R. (2011). The matter of whiteness. In P. S. Rothenberg (Ed.), *White privilege: Essential readings on the other side of racism* (pp. 9–14). Worth Publishing.

Education act, Maldives (Law no. 24/2020), (2020).

Education for All Handicapped Children Act. Pub. L. No. 94-142 (1975). https://www.govinfo.gov/content/pkg/STATUTE-89/pdf/STATUTE-89-Pg773.pdf

Eldevik, S., Hasting, R. P., Hughes, J. C., Jahr, E., Eikeseth, S., & Cross, S. (2009). Meta-analysis of early intensive behavioural intervention for children with autism. *Journal of Clinical Child and Adolescent Psychology, 38*(3), 439–450. doi:10.1080/15374410902851739 PMID:19437303

Elementary and Secondary Education Act, Pub. L. No. 89-10 (1965). https://www2.ed.gov/documents/essa-act-of-1965.pdf

Ensig, T. T., & Johnstone, C. J. (2014). Is there something rotten in the state of Denmark? The paradoxical policies of inclusive education – Lesson from Denmark. *International Journal of Inclusive Education, 19*(5), 469–486. doi:10.1080/13603116.2014.940068

Entrich, S. R. (2021). Understanding cross-national differences in inclusive education coverage: An empirical analysis. *Journal of Education: Inclusive Education, 9*(1), 21–40. https://iafor.org/journal/iafor-journal-of-education/volume-9-issue-1/article-2/

Essed, P., & Goldberg, D. T. (Eds.). (2001). *Race critical theories: Text and context.* Wiley-Blackwell.

Compilation of References

Esteves, J., Perry, A., Spiegel, R., & Weiss, J. A. (2021). Occurrence and predictors of challenging behaviour in youth with intellectual disability with or without autism. *Journal of Mental Health Research in Intellectual Disabilities, 14*(2), 189–201. doi:10.1080/19315864.2021.1874577

European Union. (2008). Primacy of EU law (precedence, supremacy). *European Journal.* https://eur-lex.europa.eu/legal-content/EN/ALL/?uri=LEGISSUM:primacy_of_eu_law

Evans, D., Andriana, E., Setiani, P., & Kumara, A. (2018). Building teachers' capacity to support all children in Pesisir Gunung Kidul. In M. Best, T. Corcoran, & R. Slee (Eds.), *Who's in? Who's out? What to do about inclusive education.* Sense.

Ewe, L. P. (2019). ADHD symptoms and the teacher-student relationship: A systematic literature review. *Emotional & Behavioural Difficulties, 24*(2), 136–155. doi:10.1080/13632752.2019.1597562

Family Educational Rights and Privacy Act of 1974, 20 U.S.C. § 1232g (1974).

Feng, L., & Sass, T. R. (2013). What makes special-education special? Teacher training and achievement of students with disabilities. *Economics of Education Review, 36,* 122–134. doi:10.1016/j.econedurev.2013.06.006

Feng, Y. (2012). Teacher career motivation and professional development in special and inclusive education: Perspectives from Chinese teachers. *International Journal of Inclusive Education, 16*(3), 331–351. doi:10.1080/13603116.2010.489123

Ferguson, B. T., McKenzie, J., Dalton, E. M., & Lyner-Cleophas, M. (2019). Inclusion, universal design and universal design for learning in higher education: South Africa and the United States. *African Journal of Disability, 8*(1), 1–7. PMID:31392169

Fidelak, D., & van Tol, K. (2021). Reducing accommodation requests in post-secondary education by implementing practical UDL strategies. In *Handbook of Research on Applying Universal Design for Learning Across Disciplines* (pp. 48–71). IGI Global. doi:10.4018/978-1-7998-7106-4.ch003

Fletcher-Watson, S., Adams, J., Brook, K., Charman, T., Crane, L., Cusack, J., Leekam, S., Milton, D., Parr, J. R., & Pellicano, E. (2019). Making the future together: Shaping autism research through meaningful participation. *Autism, 23*(4), 943–953. doi:10.1177/1362361318786721 PMID:30095277

Flood, M., & Banks, J. (2021). Universal Design for Learning: Is it gaining momentum in Irish education? *Education Sciences, 11*(7), 341. doi:10.3390/educsci11070341

Florian, L., Black-Hawkins, K., & Rouse, M. (2017). *Achievement and Inclusion in Schools.* Routledge.

Florian, L., & Linklater, H. (2010). Preparing teachers for inclusive education: Using inclusive pedagogy to enhance teaching and learning for all. *Cambridge Journal of Education, 40*(4), 369–386. doi:10.1080/0305764X.2010.526588

Florian, L., & Spratt, J. (2013). Enacting inclusion: A framework for interrogating inclusive practice. *European Journal of Special Needs Education, 28*(2), 119–135. doi:10.1080/08856257.2013.778111

Fong, J., & Burton, S. (2008). A cross-cultural comparison of electronic word-of-mouth and country-of-origin effects. *Journal of Business Research, 61*(3), 233–242. doi:10.1016/j.jbusres.2007.06.015

Ford, J. (2013). Educating students with learning disabilities in inclusive classrooms. *Electronic Journal for Inclusive Education, 3*(1), 1–20.

Forehand, M. (2005). Bloom's taxonomy: Original and revised. In M. Orey (Ed.), *Emerging perspectives on learning, teaching, and technology.* https://www.d41.org/cms/lib/il01904672/centricity/domain/422/bloomstaxonomy.pdf

Forlin, C. (2010). *Teacher education for inclusion. Changing paradigms and innovative approaches.* Routledge. doi:10.4324/9780203850879

Foucault, M. (1977). *Dispositive der macht: Über sexualität, wissen und wahrheit.* Merve.

Foundation of Tertiary Institutes of the Northern Metropolis. (2011). *Disability in higher education project report.* UCT. www.uct.ac.za/usr/ disability/reports/annual_report_10_11.pdf

Fovet, F. (2020b). Beyond novelty: "Innovative" accessible teaching as a return to fundamental questions around social justice and reflective pedagogy. In Enhancing Learning Design for Innovative Teaching in Higher Education (pp. 22-42). IGI Global.

Fovet, F. (2020a). Universal design for learning as a tool for inclusion in the higher education classroom: Tips for the next decade of implementation. *Education Journal, 9*(6), 163–172. doi:10.11648/j.edu.20200906.13

Fovet, F. (2021). *Reshaping graduate education through innovation and experiential learning. Using universal design for learning as a lens to rethink graduate education pedagogical practices.* Royal Roads University.

Fovet, F. (2021). UDL in higher education: A global overview of the landscape and its changes. In F. Fovet (Ed.), *Applying Universal Design for Learning Across Disciplines.* IGI Global. doi:10.4018/978-1-7998-7106-4.ch001

Francis, G. L., Duke, J. M., Fukita, M., & Sutton, J. C. (2019). "It's a constant fight:" Experiences of college students with disabilities. *Journal of Postsecondary Education and Disability, 32*(2), 247–261. https://files.eric.ed.gov/fulltext/EJ1236871.pdf

Frankenberg, R. (1997). Introduction. In R. Frankenberg (Ed.), *Local whitenesses, localizing whiteness, displacing whiteness: Essays in social and cultural criticism* (pp. 1–34). Duke University Press.

Frankenberg, R. (Ed.). (1997). *Local whitenesses, localizing whiteness, displacing whiteness: Essays in social and cultural criticism.* Duke University Press.

Freire, P. (2002). *Pedagogia da autonomia: saberes necessários à prática educativa* (25th ed.). Paz e Terra.

Freire, P. (2005). Pedagogy of the oppressed. *Continuum.*

Friend, M., & Cook, L. (2004). *Co-teaching: Principles, practices, and pragmatics.* New Mexico Public Education Department. https://files.eric.ed.gov/fulltext/ED486454.pdf

Friend, M. (2014). *Co-teach! Building and sustaining effective classroom partnership in inclusive schools* (2nd ed.). Marilyn Friend, Inc.

Friend, M. (2021). *Interactions: Collaboration skills for school professionals* (9th ed.). Pearson.

Friend, M., Cook, L., Hurley-Chamberlain, D. A., & Shamberger, C. (2010). Co-teaching: An illustration of the complexity of collaboration in special education. *Journal of Educational & Psychological Consultation, 20*(1), 9–27. doi:10.1080/10474410903535380

Fritzgerald, A. (2020). *Antiracism and universal design for learning: Building expressways to success.* CAST Professional Publishing.

Fukuzawa, S., & Cahn, J. (2019). Technology in problem-based learning: Helpful or hindrance? *International Journal of Information and Learning Technology, 36*(1), 66–76. doi:10.1108/IJILT-12-2017-0123

Compilation of References

Gaible, E., & Burns, M. (2007). *Using Technology to Train Teachers: Appropriate Uses of ICT for Teacher Professional Development in Developing Countries.* World Bank. https://documents.worldbank.org/en/publication/documents-reports/documentdetail/900291468324835987/using-technology-to-train-teachers-appropriate-uses-of-ict-for-teacher-professional-development-in-developing-countires

Gargiulo, R. M., & Metcalf, D. (2017). *Teaching in today's inclusive classrooms: A universal design for learning approach* (3rd ed.). Cengage Learning.

Garrad, T.-A., & Nolan, H. (2022). Rethinking higher education unit design: Embedding Universal Design for learning in online studies. *Student Success*, *13*(2). doi:10.5204sj.2300

Garrad, T.-A., Rayner, C., & Pedersen, S. (2019). Attitudes of Australian primary school teachers towards the inclusion of students with autism spectrum disorders. *Journal of Research in Special Educational Needs*, *19*(1), 58–67. doi:10.1111/1471-3802.12424

Gates, P., & Zevenbergen, R. (2009). Foregrounding social justice in mathematics teacher education. *Journal of Mathematics Teacher Education*, *12*, 161–170. doi:10.100710857-009-9105-4

Gebauer, J., Füller, J., & Pezzei, R. (2013). The dark and the bright side of co-creation: Triggers of member behavior in online innovation communities. *Journal of Business Research*, *66*(9), 1516–1527. doi:10.1016/j.jbusres.2012.09.013

Gee, J. P. (2014). *How to do Discourse Analysis: A toolkit* (2nd ed.). Routledge. doi:10.4324/9781315819662

Gelen, I., & Kaçan, A. (2022). Teaching practices and evaluation with distance education of gifted students. *Journal for the Education of Gifted Young Scientists*, *10*(3), 411–433. doi:10.17478/jegys.1140286

Genome News Network. (2004). *Genetics and genomics timeline, 1910.* Thomas Hunt Morgan. http://www.genomenewsnetwork.org/resources/timeline/1910_Morgan.php

Gewöhnliche Unterscheidungen. (2010). Wege aus dem rassismus. In P. Mecheril, M. do Mar Castro Varela, İ. Dirim, A. Kalpaka, & C. Melter (Eds.), *Bachelor | master migrationspädagogik* (pp. 150–178). Beltz GmbH, Julius.

Glackin, M. (2016). 'Risky fun' or 'Authentic science'? How teachers' beliefs influence their practice during a professional development programme on outdoor learning. *International Journal of Science Education*, *38*(3), 409–433. doi:10.1080/09500693.2016.1145368

Glover, T. A., Nugent, G. C., Chumney, F. L., Ihlo, T., Shapiro, E. S., Guard, K., Koziol, N., & Bovaird, J. (2016). Investigating rural teachers' professional development, instructional knowledge, and classroom practice. *Journal of Research in Rural Education*, *31*(3), 1–16.

Gonzalez-Gonzalez, J., Franko-Calvo, J., & Espanol-Solana, D. (2022, June 10). Educating in history: Thinking historically through historical re-enactment. *Social Sciences (Basel, Switzerland)*, *11*(256), 1–18. doi:10.3390ocsci11060256

Goodson, I. (2010). *Narrative Learning.* Routledge. doi:10.4324/9780203856888

Göransson, K., & Nilholm, C. (2014). Conceptual diversities and empirical shortcomings – A critical analysis of research on inclusive education. *European Journal of Special Needs Education*, *29*(3), 265–280. doi:10.1080/08856257.2014.933545

Government of Ireland. (1998). *Education Act.* Government of Ireland. *https://www.oireachtas.ie/en/bills/bill/2003/34/*

Government of Ireland. (2004). *Education for Persons with Special Educational Needs Act (EPSEN).* https://www.oireachtas.ie/en/bills/bill/2003/34/

Government of Ireland. (2023). *Education indicators for Ireland.* Government of Ireland. *file:///C:/Users/mflood/Downloads/246552_96fc2eb5-b7c9-4a17-afbc-de288a471b3f.pdf.*

Grabau, C. (2022). Wessen welt ist die welt? Hannah Arendt, Little Rock und die "autorität des lehrers.". In O. Ivanova-Chessex, S. Shure, & A. Steinbach (Eds.), *Lehrer*innenbildung: (Re-)visionen für die migrationsgesellschaft* (pp. 55–60). Beltz.

Grant, M. C., & Jones-Goods, K. M. (2016). Identifying and correcting barriers to successful inclusive practices: A literature review. *Journal of the American Academy of Special Education Professionals*, 64–71. https://eric.ed.gov/?id=EJ1129815

Grazino, K. J., & Navarrete, L. A. (2012). Co-teaching in a teacher education classroom: Collaboration, compromise, and creativity. *Issues in Teacher Education*, *21*(1), 109–125.

Griffin, S., & Shevlin, M. (2007). *Responding to special educational needs: An Irish perspective*. Gill & MacMillan.

Gronseth, S. L., & Dalton, E. M. (Eds.). (2019). *Universal access through inclusive instructional design: International perspectives on UDL*. Routledge. doi:10.4324/9780429435515

Grugan, M. C., Hill, A. P., Madigan, D. J., Donachie, T. C., Olsson, L. F., & Etherson, M. E. (2021). Perfectionism in academically gifted students: A systematic review. *Educational Psychology Review*, *33*(4), 1631–1673. doi:10.100710648-021-09597-7

Grümme, B. (2017). *Heterogenität in der religionspädagogik: Grundlagen und konkrete bausteine*. Herder.

Guillaumin, C. (1995). *Racism, sexism, power and ideology*. Routledge.

Ha, K. N. (2014). *Mittelweg: Zur kritik am people of color—und critical whiteness—ansatz*. Heimatkunde. https://hei-matkunde.boell.de/de/2014/01/29/mittelweg-zur-kritik-am-people-color-und-critical-whiteness-ansatz

Hafenstein, N. L., Boley, V., & Lin, J. (2022). State policy and funding in gifted education. *Gifted Child Today*, *45*(4), 226–234. doi:10.1177/10762175221110938

Hagaman, J. L., & Casey, K. J. (2018). Teacher attrition in special education: Perspectives from the field. *Teacher Education and Special Education*, *41*(4), 277–291. doi:10.1177/0888406417725797

Ha, K. N. (2010). *Unrein und vermischt: Postkoloniale grenzgänge durch die kulturgeschichte der hybridität und der kolonialen rassenbastarde*. Transcript.

Hall, L. J., Grundon, G. S., Pope, C., & Romero, A. B. (2010). Training paraprofessionals to use behavioural strategies when educating learners with autism spectrum disorders across environments. *Behavioral Interventions*, *25*(1), 37–51. doi:10.1002/bin.294

Hameed, A., & Manzoor, A. (2019). Similar Agenda, Diverse Strategies: A Review of Inclusive Education Reforms in the Subcontinent. *Bulletin of Education and Research*, *41*(2), 53–66.

Han, C., Cumming, T. M., & Townend, G. (2022). *Behavioural supports for students with autism spectrum disorder receiving special education services in Western China: An analysis of teacher characteristics, beliefs, and implantation of evidence-based practices* [PhD thesis, The University of New South Wales (UNSW), Australia].

Han, C., & Cumming, T. M. (2022). Behavioural supports for students with autism spectrum disorders: Practice, policy, and implications for special education reform in China. *International Journal of Inclusive Education*, *26*(1), 41–60. doi:10.1080/13603116.2019.1629120

Hanesworth, P., Bracken, S., & Elkington, S. (2019). A typology for a social justice approach to assessment: Learning from universal design and culturally sustaining pedagogy. *Teaching in Higher Education*, *24*(1), 98–114. doi:10.1080/13562517.2018.1465405

Compilation of References

Han, X. (2012). Big moves to improve the quality of teacher education in China. *On the Horizon, 20*(4), 324–335. doi:10.1108/10748121211272461

Hardy, I., & Woodcock, S. (2015). Inclusive education policies: Discourses of difference, diversity, and deficit. *International Journal of Inclusive Education, 19*(2), 141–164. doi:10.1080/13603116.2014.908965

Hargreaves, A., & Braun, H. (2012). *Leading for all: Final report of the review of the development of essential for some, good for all: Ontario's strategy for special education reform devised by the Council of Directors of Education.* Council of Directors of Education.

Hargrove, K. (2012, January). From the classroom: Advocating acceleration. *Gifted Child Today, 72-73.* doi:10/1177/1076217511428309

Hattier, M. A., Matson, J. L., Belva, B. C., & Horovitz, M. (2011). The occurrence of challenging behaviours in children with autism spectrum disorders and atypical development. *Developmental Neurorehabilitation, 14*(4), 221–229. doi:10.3109/17518423.2011.573836 PMID:21732806

Hedegaard-Sørensen, L. (2021). *Inklusion og eksklusion i undervisningen [Inclusion and exclusion in teaching].* Pædagogisk Indblik, Aarhus Universitet. https://dpu.au.dk/fileadmin/edu/Paedagogisk_Indblik/Inklusio n_og_eksklusion/14_-_Inklusion_og_eksklusion_i_undervisninge n_-_15-12-2021.pdf

Hedegaard-Sørensen, L. (2022). *Inklusion og fag [Inclusion and subjects].* Pædagogisk Indblik, Aarhus Universitet. https://dpu.au.dk/viden/paedagogiskindblik/inklusion-og-eksk lusion-i-skolen

Hedegaard-Sorensen, L., & Grumløse, S. P. (2018). Exclusion: The downside of neoliberal education policy. *International Journal of Inclusive Education, 24*(6), 631–644. doi:10.1080/13603116.2018.1478002

Hedegaard-Sørensen, L., & Penthin Grumloese, S. (2020). Student-teacher-dialogue for lesson planning: Inclusion in the context of national policy and local culture. *Nordic Journal of Studies in Educational Policy., 6*(1), 25–36. doi:10.1080/20020317.2020.1747376

Hedegaard-Sørensen, L., Riis-Jensen, C., & Tofteng, D. (2018). Interdisciplinary collaboration as a prerequisite for inclusive education. *European Journal of Special Needs Education, 33*(2), 382–395. doi:10.1080/08856257.2017.1314113

Hegel, G. W. F. (1848). *Vorlesung über die philosophie der geschichte.* Suhrkamp.

Hehir, T., Grindal, T., Freeman, B., Lamoreau, R., Borquaye, Y., & Burke, S. (2016). *A summary of the evidence on inclusive education.* Abt Associates. https://www.abtassociates.com/sites/default/files/2019-03/A_Summary_of_the_evi dence_on_inclusive_education.pdf

Hemmler, V. L., Azano, A. P., Dmitrieva, S., & Callahan, C. M. (2022). Representation of Black Students in rural gifted education: Taking steps toward equity. *Journal of Research in Rural Education, 38*(2), 1–25. doi:10.26209/jrre3802

Hentz, S. (2018). *Co-teaching essentials.* Association for Supervision and Curriculum Development.

Hibbert, M., Kerr, K. R., Garber, A. A., & Marquart, M. (2016). The human element. In *Creating Teacher Immediacy in Online Learning Environments* (pp. 91–112). IGI Global. doi:10.4018/978-1-4666-9995-3.ch006

Hiebert, J., Gallimore, R., & Stigler, J. W. (2002). A knowledge base for the teaching profession: What would it look like and how can we get one? *Educational Researcher, 31*(5), 3–15. doi:10.3102/0013189X031005003

Hills, M., Overend, A., & Hildebrandt, S. (2022). Faculty perspectives on UDL: Exploring bridges and barriers for broader adoption in higher education. *The Canadian Journal for the Scholarship of Teaching and Learning, 13*(1). doi:10.5206/cjsotlrcacea.2022.1.13588

Hirsbrunner, S. (2012). *Sorry about colonialism: Weiße helden in kontemporären hollywoodfilmen.* Tectum Wissenschaftsverlag.

Hirsch, S. E., Randall, K. N., Common, E. A., & Lane, K. L. (2020). Results of practice-based professional development for supporting special educators in learning how to design functional assessment-based interventions. *Teacher Education and Special Education, 43*(4), 281–295. doi:10.1177/0888406419876926

History of Gifted Education. (n.d.). *History of gifted education.* Sutori. https://www.sutori.com/en/item/1954-national-association-of-gifted-children-is-founded-by-ann-isaacs-1954-i

Hitchcock, C., Meyer, A., Rose, D., & Jackson, R. (2002). Providing New Access to the General Curriculum: Universal Design for Learning. *Teaching Exceptional Children, 35*(2), 8–17. doi:10.1177/004005990203500201

Hitch, D., Brown, P., Macfarlane, S., & Watson, J. (2019). The transition to higher education: Applying Universal Design for Learning to support student success. In *Transforming Higher Education Through Universal Design for Learning.* Routledge., doi:10.4324/9781351132077-6

Hockings, C. (2010). *Inclusive learning and teaching in higher education: A synthesis of research.* Higher Education Academy.

Hodges, A., Cordier, R., Joosten, A., & Bourke-Taylor, H. (2021). Closing the gap between theory and practice: Conceptualisation of a school-based intervention to improve the school participation of primary school students on the autism spectrum and their typically developing peers. *Journal of Autism and Developmental Disorders, 52*(7), 3230–3245. doi:10.100710803-021-05362-5 PMID:34862953

Holmqvist, M., & Lelinge, B. (2021). Teachers' collaborative professional development for inclusive education. *European Journal of Special Needs Education, 36*(5), 819–833. doi:10.1080/08856257.2020.1842974

Hong, X., Luo, L., & Cui, F. (2015). Investigating regional disparities of preschool education development with cluster analysis in Mainland China. *International Journal of Child Care and Education Policy, 7*(1), 67–80. doi:10.1007/2288-6729-7-1-67

hooks, b. (1992). *Black looks: Race and representation.* South End Press.

Hoppey, D., & McLeaskey, J. (2014). What are qualities of effective inclusive schools? In J. McLeskey, N. Waldron, F. Spooner, & B. Algozzine (Eds.), *Handbook of effective inclusive schools: Research and practice* (pp. 17–29). Routledge. doi:10.4324/9780203102930.ch2

Hornby, G. (2015). Inclusive Special Education: Development of a new theory for the education of children with special educational needs and disabilities. *British Journal of Special Education, 42*(3), 234–256. doi:10.1111/1467-8578.12101

Hornby, G. (2021). Are inclusive education or special education programs more likely to result in inclusion post-school? *Education Sciences, 11*(304), 304. doi:10.3390/educsci11060304

Horn, C. V. (2015). Young scholars. *Gifted Child Today, 38*(1), 19–31. doi:10.1177/1076217514556532

Horne, D. L., & Dupuy, P. J. (1981). In favor of acceleration for gifted students. *The Personnel and Guidance Journal, 60*(2), 103–106. doi:10.1002/j.2164-4918.1981.tb00652.x

Compilation of References

Howe, C., & Griffin, C. (2020). Is Ireland at a crossroads of inclusive education? *REACH Journal of Special Needs Education in Ireland, 33*(1), 44–56. https://reachjournal.ie/index.php/reach/article/view/8

Howell, C. (2006). Disabled students and higher education in South Africa. In B. Watermeyer, L. Swartz, T. Lorenzo, M. Schneider, & M. Priestley (Eds.), *Disability and social change: A South African agenda* (pp. 164–178). HSRC Press.

Howley, A. (2002). The progress of gifted students in a rural district that emphasized acceleration strategies. *Roeper Review, 24*(3), 158–160. doi:10.1080/02783190209554168

Hsiu-li, K. (2008). *A study on peer acceptance towards mentally and physically challenged students in elementary school* [Unpublished master's thesis, National Pingtung University of Education, Pingtung, Taiwan].

Huang, H.-Y. (2017). *The Study of Special-Education Propaganda Executed by the Primary Schools in Taitung County* [Unpublished master's thesis, National Taitung University, Taitung, Taiwan].

Huang, Y.-F. (2010). A cooperative relationship and model between general teachers and special education teachers under integrated education. *Tung Wah Special Education, 44*, 14–19.

Hu, B. Y., Wu, H. P., Su, X. Y., & Roberts, S. K. (2017). An examination of Chinese preservice and in-service early childhood teaches' perspectives on the importance and feasibility of the implementation of key characteristics of quality inclusion. *International Journal of Inclusive Education, 21*(2), 187–204. doi:10.1080/13603116.2016.1193563

Humphreys, S., & Jimenez, B. (2018). The evolution of personalised learning: From different, to differentiated and now to universally designed. *Global Journal of Intellectual & Developmental Disabilities, 5*(4), 1–2. doi:10.19080/GJDD.2018.05.555666

Hunt, P., Farron-Davis, F., Beckstead, S., Curtis, D., & Goetz, L. (1994). Evaluating the effects of placement of students with severe disabilities in general education versus special classes. *The Journal of the Association for Persons with Severe Handicaps, 19*(3), 200–214. doi:10.1177/154079699401900308

Hyatt, L. (2010). A case study of the suicide of a gifted female adolescent: Implications for prediction and prevention. *Journal for the Education of the Gifted, 33*(4), 514–535. doi:10.1177/016235321003300404

Hyman, S. L., & Levy, S. E. (2013). Autism spectrum disorders. In M. L. Batshaw, N. J. Roizen, & G. R. Lotrecchiano (Eds.), *Children with disabilities* (7th ed., pp. 345–368). Brookes.

IBE-UNESCO. (2017). *Training tools for curriculum development: Developing and implementing curriculum frameworks*. IBE-UNESCO.

INCLUDE. (2020). *Action Oriented Values*. INCLUDE. https://include.wp.worc.ac.uk/action-oriented-values/

INCLUDE. (2022). *INCLUDE Webinars*. INCLUDE. https://include.wp.worc.ac.uk/webinars/

Individuals With Disabilities Education Act, 20 U.S.C. § 1400 (2004).

Individuals with Disabilities Education Act, 20 U.S.C. § 1400. (1990). https://sites.ed.gov/idea/statute-chapter-33

Individuals with Disabilities Education Improvement Act, Pub. L. No. 108-446 (2004). https://www.govinfo.gov/content/pkg/PLAW-108publ446/pdf/PLAW-108publ446.pdf

International Disability Alliance. (2020). *What an inclusive, equitable, quality education means to us: report of the international disability alliance*. International Disability Alliance.

International Disability Alliance. (2021). *Universal Design for Learning and its role in ensuring access to inclusive education for all.* https://www.internationaldisabilityalliance.org/sites/defaul t /files/universal_design_for_learning_final_8.09.2021.pdf

IRIS Center. (2017). *Secondary transition: Student-centered planning.* IRIS. https://iris.peabody.vanderbilt.edu/module/tran-scp/

IRIS Center. (2019). *IEPs: How administrators can support the development and implementation of high-quality IEPs.* IRIS. https://iris.peabody.vanderbilt.edu/module/iep02/

Israel, M., Maynard, K., & Williamson, P. (2013). Promoting literacy-embedded, authentic STEM instruction for students with disabilities and other struggling learners. *Teaching Exceptional Children, 45*(4), 18–25. doi:10.1177/004005991304500402

Ito, T. (2011). An examination of motives for voluntary activities. Gakushuin University, The annual collection of essays and studies. *Faculty of Letters, 27,* 35–55.

Ivanova-Chessex, O., Shure, S., & Steinbach, A. (Eds.). (2022). *Lehrer*innenbildung: (Re-)visionen für die migrationsgesellschaft.* Beltz.

Jeffrey, D. C. (2012). A constituição do gerencialismo na educação brasileira: Implicações na valorização dos profissionais da educação. *Revista Exitus, 2,* 51–60.

Jian, X.-H. (2014). *A study of peer acceptance program to improve peer acceptance of students with intellectual disabilities in elementary school* [Unpublished master's thesis, National Kaohsiung Normal University, Kaohsiung, Taiwan].

Jiang, Y., Pang, L. J., & Sun, J. (2017). Early childhood teacher education in China. In N. Rao, J. Zhou, & J. Sun (Eds.), *Early childhood education in Chinese societies* (pp. 85–100). Springer Netherlands. doi:10.1007/978-94-024-1004-4_6

Jimenez, B., & Hudson, M. (2019). Including students with severe disabilities in general education and the potential of universal design for learning for all children. In M. Schuelka, C. Johnstone, G. Thomas, & A. Artiles (Eds.), *SAGE Handbook of inclusion and diversity in education.* SAGE. doi:10.4135/9781526470430.n25

Johnsen, S. K., Fearon-Drake, D., & Wisely, L. W. (2020). A formative evaluation of differentiation practices in elementary cluster classrooms. *Roeper Review, 42*(3), 206–218. doi:10.1080/02783193.2020.1765921

Johnson, H. N., Wakeman, S. Y., & Clausen, A. (2021). *How to support students with significant cognitive disabilities during think-alouds* (TIPS Series: Tip #21). University of Minnesota. https://publications.ici.umn.edu/ties/foundations-of-inclusi on-tips/how-to-support-students-with-significant-cognitive-d isabilities-during-think-alouds

Johnson, S. M. (2020). *Where teachers thrive: Organising schools for success.* Harvard Education Press.

Joint Legislative Audit and Review Commission. (2020). *K–12 special education in Virginia.* JLARC. http://jlarc.virginia.gov/pdfs/reports/Rpt545-1.pdf

Jolly, J. L. (2009). A resuscitation of gifted education. *American Educational History Journal, 36*(1), 37–52.

Jonsson, U., Choque Olsson, N., Coco, C., Görling, A., Flygare, O., Råde, A., & Bölte, S. (2019). Long-term social skills group training for children and adolescents with autism spectrum disorder: A randomized controlled trial. *European Child & Adolescent Psychiatry, 28*(2), 189–201. doi:10.100700787-018-1161-9 PMID:29748736

Joos, M., Betz, T., Bollig, S., & Neumann, S. (2018). Gute kindheit als gegenstand der forschung: Wohlbefinden, kindeswohl und ungleiche kindheiten. In T. Betz, S. Bollig, M. Joos, & S. Neumann (Eds.), *Gute kindheit: Wohlbefinden, kindeswohl und ungleichheit* (pp. 7–27). Beltz Juventa.

Compilation of References

Jung, L. A., Gomez, C., Baird, S. M., & Galyon Keramides, C. L. (2008). Designing intervention plans: Bridging the gap between individualized education programs and implementation. *Teaching Exceptional Children, 41*(1), 26–33. doi:10.1177/004005990804100103

Jwad, N., O'Donovan, M.-A., Leif, E., Knight, E., Ford, E., & Buhne, J. (2022). *Universal Design for Learning in Tertiary Education: A Scoping Review and Recommendations for Implementation in Australia.* Monash. https://research.monash.edu/en/publications/universal-design-for-learning-in-tertiary-education-a-scoping-rev

Kaat, A. J., & Lecavalier, L. (2013). Disruptive behaviour disorders in children and adolescents with autism spectrum disorders: A review of the prevalence, presentation, and treatment. *Research in Autism Spectrum Disorders, 7*(12), 1579–1594. doi:10.1016/j.rasd.2013.08.012

Kanter, A. (2019). The right to inclusive education for students with disabilities under international human rights law. In G. De Beco, S. Quinlivan, & J. Lord (Eds.), *The right to inclusive education under international human rights law* (pp. 15–57). Cambridge University Press. doi:10.1017/9781316392881.003

Kanter, S. (2019). Let's try again: Why the United States should ratify the United Nations Convention on the Rights of People with Disabilities (2019). *Touro Law Review, 35.* https://ssrn.com/abstract=3373259

Kant, I. (1983). Kritik der urteilskraft: Beobachtungen über das gefühl des schönen und erhabenen. In W. Weischedel (Ed.), *Immanuel Kants werke: Gesamtausgabe in zehn bänden* (Vol. 7). Wissenschaftliche Buchgesellschaft.

Kart, A., & Kart, M. (2021). Academic and social effects of inclusion on students without disabilities: A review of the literature. *Education Sciences, 11*(16), 16. doi:10.3390/educsci11010016

Kaul, I., Schmidt, D., & Thole, W. (2018). Blick auf kinder und kindheiten unsicherheiten, herausforderungen und zumutungen. In I. Kaul, D. Schmidt, & W. Thole (Eds.), Kinder und kindheiten. Studien zur empirie der kindheit: Unsicherheiten, herausforderungen und zumutungen (pp. 1–11). Springer.

Kaul, I., Schmidt, D., & Thole, W. (Eds.). (2018). *Kinder und kindheiten. Studien zur empirie der kindheit: Unsicherheiten, herausforderungen und zumutungen.* Springer. doi:10.1007/978-3-658-19484-0

Kelly, J. F., McKinney, E. L., & Swift, O. (2020). Strengthening teacher education to support deaf learners. *International Journal of Inclusive Education, 26*(13), 2289–1307. doi:10.1080/13603116.2020.1806366

Kenny, N., McCoy, S., & Mihut, G. (2020). Special education reforms in Ireland: Changing systems, changing schools. *International Journal of Inclusive Education,* 1–20. doi:10.1080/13603116.2020.1821447

Kerner, I. (2013). Critical whiteness studies: Potentiale und grenzen eines wissenspolitischen projekts. *Feministische Studien: Zeitschrift Für Interdisziplinäre Frauen- Und Geschlechterforschung, 31*(2), 278–293. doi:10.1515/fs-2013-0209

Kerner, I. (2017). *Challenges of critical whiteness studies.* EIPCP. https://translate.eipcp.net/strands/03/kerner-strands01en.html

Kett, M., Deluca, M., & Carew, M. (2019). How prepared are teachers to deliver inclusive education: Evidence from Kenya, Zimbabwe and Sierra Leone. In N. Singal, P. Lynch, & S. Johansson (Eds.), *Education and disability in the global south: New perspectives from Africa and Asia* (pp. 203–222). Bloomsbury Academic. doi:10.5040/9781474291231.ch-011

Kilomba, G. (2009). *Das N-wort.* BPB. https://www.bpb.de/gesellschaft/migration/afrikanischediaspora/

Kilpatrick, S., Johns, S., Barnes, R., Fischer, S., McLennan, D., & Magnussen, K. (2017). Exploring the retention and success of students with disability in Australian higher education. *International Journal of Inclusive Education, 21*(7), 747–762. doi:10.1080/13603116.2016.1251980

Kiper, H. (2008). Zur diskussion um heterogenität in gesellschaft, pädagogik und unterrichtstheorie. In H. Kiper & S. Miller (Eds.), *Lernprozesse professionell gestalten* (pp. 78–105).

Kiper, H., & Miller, S. (Eds.). (2008). *Lernprozesse professionell gestalten*. Klinkhardt.

Klefbeck, K. (2021). Lesson Study as a Way of Improving School-Day Navigation for Pupils with Severe Intellectual Disability and Autism. *International Journal for Lesson and Learning Studies, 10*(4), 348–361. doi:10.1108/IJLLS-03-2021-0024

Kleve, B., & Penne, S. (2016). Learning subjects in school: Being outsiders or insiders in the disciplinary discourses of mathematics and Language 1. *International Journal of Educational Research, 78,* 41–49. doi:10.1016/j.ijer.2016.05.014

Klimaitis, C. C., & Mullen, C. A. (2021a). Access and barriers to science, technology, engineering, and mathematics (STEM) education for K–12 students with disabilities and females. In C. A. Mullen (Ed.), *Handbook of social justice interventions in education* (pp. 813–836). Springer. doi:10.1007/978-3-030-35858-7_125

Klimaitis, C. C., & Mullen, C. A. (2021b). Including K–12 students with disabilities in STEM education and planning for inclusion. *Educational Planning, 28*(2), 27–43.

Knauth, T., Möller, R., & Pithan, A. (Eds.). (2020). *Inklusive religionspädagogik der vielfalt: Konzeptionelle grundlagen und didaktische konkretionen*. Waxmann.

Knight, C., Clegg, Z., Conn, C., Hutt, M., & Crick, T. (2022). 'Aspiring to include versus implicit "othering": Teachers' perceptions of inclusive education in Wales'. *British Journal of Special Education, 49*(1), 6–23. doi:10.1111/1467-8578.12394

Koh, M.-S., & Shin, S. (2017). Education of students with disabilities in the USA: Is inclusion the answer? *International Journal of Learning. Teaching and Educational Research, 16*(10), 1–17.

Kolloshe, D., Marcone, R., Knigge, M., Gody Penteado, M., & Skovsmose, O. (2019). *Inclusive mathematics education. State-of-the-art research from Brazil and Germany*. Springer. doi:10.1007/978-3-030-11518-0

Ko, M. W., & Chen, M. H. (2009). Finding a stage for students with special needs - Promoting integrated education in Dunhua Junior High School. *National Taiwan Normal University Division of Educational Practicum and Professional Development Secondary Education, 60*(4), 168–179.

Kooiman, J. (Ed.). (2007). *Governing as governance*. Sage.

Köpfer, A., & Óskarsdóttir, E. (2019). Analysing support in inclusive education systems – A comparison of inclusive school development in Iceland and Canada since the 1980s focusing on policy and in-school support. *International Journal of Inclusive Education, 23*(7–8), 876–890. doi:10.1080/13603116.2019.1624844

Kortering, L. J., McClannon, T. W., & Braziel, P. M. (2008). Universal Design for Learning: A Look at What Algebra and Biology Students With and Without High Incidence Conditions Are Saying. *Remedial and Special Education, 29*(6), 352–363. doi:10.1177/0741932507314020

Koshy, P. (2020). *Equity student participation in Australian higher education: 2014--2019*. National Centre for Student Equity in Higher Education. https://www.voced.edu.au/content/ngv:88552

Krischler, M., Powell, J. J. W., & Ineke, M. P.-T. C. (2019). What is meant by inclusion? On the effects of different definitions on attitudes toward inclusive education. *European Journal of Special Needs Education, 34*(5), 632–648. doi:10.1080/08856257.2019.1580837

Krüger, D., & Vogt, H. (Eds.). (2007). *Theorien in der biologiedidaktischen forschung: Springer-Lehrbuch*. Springer. doi:10.1007/978-3-540-68166-3

Compilation of References

Krüger-Potratz, M., & Lutz, H. (2002). Sitting at a crossroads: Rekonstruktive und systematische überlegungen zum wissenschaftlichen umgang mit differenzen. *Tertium Comparationis, 8*(2), 81–92. doi:10.25656/01:2922

Küller, R. (1991). Environmental assessment from a neuropsychological perspective. In T. Gärling & G. W. Evans (Eds.), *Environment; Cognition and Action: An integrated approach*. Oxford University Press.

Kumar, A., Bezawada, R., Rishika, R., Janakiraman, R., & Kannan, P. K. (2016). From social to sale: The effects of firm-generated content in social media on customer behavior. *Journal of Marketing, 80*(1), 7–25. doi:10.1509/jm.14.0249

Kurniawati, F., de Boer, A., Minnaert, A., & Mangunsong, F. (2014). Characteristics of primary teacher programmes on inclusion: A literature focus. *Educational Research, 56*(3), 310–326. doi:10.1080/00131881.2014.934555

Kurth, J. A., Miller, A. L., Gross Toews, S., Thompson, J. R., Cortes, M., Dahal, M. H., de Escallon, I. E., Hunt, P. F., Porter, G., Richler, D., Fonseca, I., Singh, R., Siska, J., Villamero, R., & Wangare, F. (2018). Inclusive education: Perspectives on implementation and practice for international experts. *Intellectual and Developmental Disabilities, 56*(6), 471–485. doi:10.1352/1934-9556-56.6.471

Lai, M. J. (2012). *A study of the political effects of integrated education policies* [Unpublished master's thesis, National Taiwan Normal University, Taipei, Taiwan].

Lamprecht, S. (2022). *Commitment and resilience enable deaf teacher to realise his dream*. Stellenbosch University. https://www.sun.ac.za/english/Lists/news/DispForm.aspx? ID=9651

Laurillard, D. (2013). *Teaching as a design science: Building pedagogical patterns for learning and technology*. Routledge. doi:10.4324/9780203125083

Lave, J. (1991). Situating learning in communities of practice. In L. B. Resnick, J. M. Levine, & S. D. Teasley (Eds.), *Perspectives on socially shared cognition* (pp. 63–82). American Psychological Association. doi:10.1037/10096-003

Layer, G. (2017). *Disabled students sector leadership group (DSSLG) inclusive teaching and learning in higher education as a route to excellence*. Department for Education.

Leder, G., & Forgasz, H. (2008). Mathematics education: New perspectives on gender. *ZDM Mathematics Education, 40*(4), 513–518. doi:10.100711858-008-0137-5

Lee, S.-Y., & Lee, H.-S. (2014). Analysis of the Influence of Factors Related to Student Satisfaction with Web-based University Courses: Comparison between 2005 and 2014. In Advanced Science and Technology Letters. doi:10.14257/astl.2014.59.17

Lee, J. C.-K., Yu, Z., Huang, X., & Law, E. H.-F. (2016). Educational development in Western China: Towards quality and equity. In J. C.-K. Lee, Z. Yu, X. Huang, & E. H.-F. Law (Eds.), *Educational developmental in Western China: Towards quality and equity* (pp. 1–20). Sense Publishers. doi:10.1007/978-94-6300-232-5_1

Leifler, E. (2022). *Educational inclusion for students with neurodevelopmental conditions*. [PhD Thesis. Dep. of Women's and Children's Health. Karolinska Institute].

Leifler, E. (2020). Teachers' capacity to create inclusive learning environments. *International Journal for Lesson and Learning Studies, 9*(3), 221–244. doi:10.1108/IJLLS-01-2020-0003

Leifler, E., Borg, A., & Bölte, S. (2022b). A multi-perspective study of perceived inclusive education for students with neurodevelopmental disorders. *Journal of Autism and Developmental Disorders, 2022*(Jul), 4. doi:10.100710803-022-05643-7 PMID:35781856

305

Leifler, E., Carpelan, G., Zakrevska, A., Bölte, S., & Jonsson, U. (2020). Does the learning environment make the grade? A systematic literature review of accommodations for children on the autism spectrum in mainstream school. *Scandinavian Journal of Occupational Therapy, 28*(8), 582–597. doi:10.1080/11038128.2020.1832145 PMID:33078981

Leifler, E., Coco, C., Fridell, A., Borg, A., & Bölte, S. (2022a). Social skills group training for students with neurodevelopmental disorders in senior high school: A qualitative multi-perspective study of social validity. *International Journal of Environmental Research and Public Health, 19*(1487). PMID:35162512

Lengyel, L. S., & Vanbergeijk, E. (2021). A brief history of special education: Milestones in the first 50 years. *Exceptional Parents Magazine.* https://reader.mediawiremobile.com/epmagazine/issues /207207 /viewer doi:10.1086/713825

Lennex, L., Nettleton, K., & Kessinger, M. W. (2015). *Interviews with incoming freshman dual credit students to a gifted and talented academy.* Manuscript in preparation.

Leung, C. H., & Mak, K. Y. (2010). Training, understanding, and the attitudes of primary school teachers regarding inclusive education in Hong Kong. *International Journal of Inclusive Education, 14*(8), 829–842. doi:10.1080/13603110902748947

Lewis, K. D., & Boswell, C. (2020). Perceived challenges for rural gifted education. *Gifted Child Today, 43*(3), 184–198. doi:10.1177/1076217520915742

Lieberman, A., & Pointer Mace, D. (2009). Making Practice Public: Teacher Learning in the 21st Century. *Journal of Teacher Education, 61*(1-2), 77–88. doi:10.1177/0022487109347319

Lim, S. (2020). The capabilities approach to inclusive education: Re-envisioning the Individuals with Disabilities Education Act's least restrictive environment. *Disability & Society, 35*(4), 570–588. doi:10.1080/09687599.2019.1649119

Lin, H.-C. (2021). *Identifying the Special Needs of Students: A Study of Board Game Design for Special Education Advocacy Activities* [Unpublished master's thesis, National Taipei University of Education, Taipei, Taiwan].

Lin, J. J. (2008). *A study of the integration of curriculum programs on the acceptance of special education students' attitudes by students in elementary school regular classes* [Unpublished master's thesis, National Taiwan University, Taitung].

Lin, Y., & Zhang, K. (2012). Pingkun diqu youer jiaoshi peixun zhuangkuang yu fazhan jianyi (贫困地区幼儿教师培训状况与发展建议) [On the preschool teachers training in the poor areas]. *Studies in Preschool Education, 205*(1), 28–32.

Lombardi, P. (2021). *Instructional methods, strategies, and technologies to meet the needs of all learners.* LibreTexts. https://socialsci.libretexts.org/Bookshelves/Early_Childhood_Education/Instructional_Methods_Strategies_and_Technologies_(Lombardi_2018)

Lord, C., Charman, T., Havdahl, A., Carbone, P., Anagnostou, E., Boyd, B., Carr, T., de Vries, P. J., Dissanayake, C., Divan, G., Freitag, C. M., Gotelli, M. M., Kasari, C., Knapp, M., Mundy, P., Plank, A., Scahill, L., Servili, C., Shattuck, P., & McCauley, J. B. (2021). The Lancet Commission on the future of care and clinical research in autism. *Lancet, 399*(10321), 271–334. doi:10.1016/S0140-6736(21)01541-5 PMID:34883054

Low, H. M., Lee, L. W., & Ahmad, A. C. (2020). Knowledge and attitudes of special education teachers towards the inclusion of students with autism spectrum disorder. *International Journal of Disability Development and Education, 67*(5), 497–514. doi:10.1080/1034912X.2019.1626005

Loxley, A., Johnston, K., Murchan, D., Fitzgerald, H., & Quinn, M. (2007). The role of whole-school contexts in shaping the experiences and outcomes associated with professional development. *Journal of In-service Education, 33*(3), 265–285. doi:10.1080/13674580701487034

Compilation of References

Lubas, M., Mitchell, J., & De Leo, G. (2015). Evidence-based practice for teachers of children with autism: A dynamic approach. *Intervention in School and Clinic, 51*(3), 188–193. doi:10.1177/1053451215585801

Lu, M., Loyalka, P., Shi, Y., Chang, F., Liu, C., & Rozelle, S. (2019). The impact of teacher professional development programs on student achievement in rural China: Evidence from Shaanxi Province. *Journal of Development Effectiveness, 11*(2), 105–131. doi:10.1080/19439342.2019.1624594

Luo, T., Freeman, C., & Stefaniak, J. (2020). "Like, comment, and share"—professional development through social media in higher education: A systematic review. *Educational Technology Research and Development, 68*(4), 1659–1683. doi:10.100711423-020-09790-5

Lupart, J., & Webber, C. (2012). Canadian schools in transition: Moving from dual education systems to inclusive schools. *Exceptionality Education International, 22*(2), 8–37. doi:10.5206/eei.v22i2.7692

Lupkowski-Shoplik, A., Assouline, S. G., & Lane, R. (2022). Whole-grade acceleration: From student to policy. *Gifted Child Today, 45*(3), 143–149. doi:10.1177/10762175221091856

Lyner-Cleophas, M. (2019). Assistive technology enables inclusion in higher education: The role of Higher and Further Education Disability Services Association. *African Journal of Disability, 8*(6), 1–6. doi:10.4102/ajod.v8i0.558 PMID:31534917

Lyner-Cleophas, M. M. (2020). The prospects of universal design for learning in South Africa to facilitate the inclusion of all learners. In S. L. Gronseth & E. M. Dalton (Eds.), *Universal access through inclusive instructional design: International perspectives on UDL* (pp. 35–45). Routledge.

Lyner-Cleophas, M. M., Apollis, L., Erasmus, I., Willems, M., Poole, L., Minnaar, M., & Louw, P. (2021). Disability Unit practitioners at Stellenbosch University: COVID-19 pandemic reflections. *Journal of Student Affairs in Africa, 9*(1), 223–234. doi:10.24085/jsaa.v9i1.1440

Mac Ruairc, G. (2016, May 18). Leadership for inclusive schools [webinar]. In *Teaching Council Research Webinars.* https://www.teachingcouncil.ie/en/research-croi-/research-we binars-/past-webinars/leadership-for-inclusive-schools-webin ar-slides.pdf

Magnússon, G., Göransson, K., & Lindqvist, G. (2019). Contextualizing inclusive education in educational policy: The case of Sweden. *Nordic Journal of Studies in Educational Policies, 5*(2), 67–77. doi:10.1080/20020317.2019.1586512

Majeed, A. (2009). *Key reforms for quality improvement in education: New interventions in curricula and textbooks.* Ministry of Education, Government of Pakistan.

Maldives Bureau of Statistics. (2020). *Statistical Year Book 2020.* Ministry of Education.

Mangope, B., & Mukhopadhyay, S. (2015). Preparing teachers for inclusive education in Botswana: The role of professional development. *Journal of International Special Needs Education, 18*(2), 60–72. doi:10.9782/2159-4341-18.2.60

Mantoan, M. T. E. (2015). *Inclusão Escolar: o que é? Por quê? Como fazer?* Summus.

Marcelo, C. G. (2009) Desenvolvimento profissional docente: passado e futuro. *Sísifo – Revista de Ciências da Educação,* [S.I.], n. 8, p. 7-22.

Marder, T., & deBettencourt, L. U. (2015). Teaching students with ASD using evidence-based practices: Why is training critical now? *Teacher Education and Special Education, 38*(1), 5–12. doi:10.1177/0888406414565838

Marland, S. P., Jr. (1971). *Education of the gifted and talented – Volume 1: Report to the Congress of the United States* (ED056243). ERIC. https://files.eric.ed.gov/fulltexxt/ED056243.pdf

Maslow, A. H. (1954). *Motivation and personality.* Harper and Row.

Mason-Williams, L., Bettini, E., Peyton, D., Harvey, A., Rosenberg, M., & Sindelar, P. T. (2020). Rethinking shortages in special education: Making good on the promise of an equal opportunity for students with disabilities. *Teacher Education and Special Education, 43*(1), 45–62. doi:10.1177/0888406419880352

Matthews, K. E., & Dollinger, M. (2023). Student voice in higher education: The importance of distinguishing student representation and student partnership. *Higher Education, 85*(3), 555–570. doi:10.100710734-022-00851-7

Matthews, M. S., Ritchotte, J. A., & McBee, M. T. (2013). Effects of schoolwide cluster grouping and within-class ability grouping on elementary school students' academic achievement growth. *High Ability Studies, 24*(2), 81–97. doi:10.1080/13598139.2013.846251

Mayer, R. E. (2014). Incorporating motivation into multimedia learning. *Learning and Instruction, 29*, 171–173. doi:10.1016/j.learninstruc.2013.04.003

Mayhew, E., Davies, M., Millmore, A., Thompson, L., & Bizama, A. P. (2020). The impact of audience response platform Mentimeter on the student and staff learning experience. *Research in Learning Technology, 28*(0). doi:10.25304/rlt.v28.2397

McIntosh, P. (Ed.). (2019). *On privilege, fraudulence, and teaching as learning: Selected essays 1981–2019.* Routledge. doi:10.4324/9781351133791

McKenzie, J. A., & Dalton, E. M. (2020). Universal design for learning in inclusive education policy in South Africa. *African Journal of Disability, 9*, a776. doi:10.4102/ajod.v9i0.776 PMID:33392062

Meaney, T., Edmonds-Wathen, C., McMurchy-Pilkington, C., & Trinick, T. (2016). Distribution, Recognition and Representation: Mathematics Education and Indigenous Students. In K. Makar, S. Dole, J. Visnovska, M. Goos, A. Bennison, & K. Fry (Eds.), *Research in Mathematics Education in Australasia.* Springer. (Original work published 2012) doi:10.1007/978-981-10-1419-2_8

Mecheril, P., do Mar Castro Varela, M., Dirim, İ., Kalpaka, A., & Melter, C. (Eds.). (2010). *Bachelor | master migrationspädagogik.* Beltz.

Mecheril, P., & Melter, C. (2010). Gewöhnliche unterscheidungen: Wege aus dem rassismus. In P. Mecheril, İ. Dirim, M. do Mar Castro Varela, A. Kalpaka, & C. Melter (Eds.), *Migrationspädagogik* (pp. 150–178). Beltz.

Meer, N. M., & Chapman, A. (2014). Assessment for confidence: Exploring the impact that low-stakes assessment design has on student retention. *International Journal of Management Education, 12*(2), 186–192. doi:10.1016/j.ijme.2014.01.003

Melvin, S., Landsberg, E., & Kagan, S. (2020). International curriculum frameworks: Increasing equity and driving systemic change. *Young Children, 75*(1), 10–21. doi:10.2307/26906570

Messiou, K. (2017). Research in the field of inclusive education: Time for a rethink? *International Journal of Inclusive Education, 21*(2), 146–159. doi:10.1080/13603116.2016.1223184

Messiou, K., & Ainscow, M. (2020). Inclusive inquiry: Student-teacher dialogue as a means of promoting inclusion in schools. *British Educational Research Journal, 46*(3), 670–687. doi:10.1002/berj.3602

Compilation of References

Meyer, A., & Rose, D. H. (2005). The future is in the margins: The role of technology and disability in educational reform. In D. H. Rose & A. &. H. Meyer (Eds.), The universally designed classroom: Accessible curriculum and digital technologies (pp. 13–35). Harvard Education Press.

Meyer, A., Rose, D. H., & Gordon, D. (2014). *Universal design for learning: Theory and practice.* CAST Professional Publishing.

Meyer, A., Rose, D. H., & Gordon, D. (2014). *Universal Design for Learning: Theory and practice.* CAST.

Meyer, A., Rose, D., & Gordon, D. (2014). *Universal design for learning: Theory and Practice.* CAST Professional Publishing.

Miles, M. B., Huberman, A. M., & Saldaña, J. (2020). *Qualitative data analysis: A methods sourcebook* (4th ed.). Sage.

Ministry of Education & Ministry of higher education. (2019). *Maldives education sector plan 2019-2023.* Ministry of Education.

Ministry of Education of People's Republic of China [MOE PRC]. (2010). *Jiaoyubu caizhengbu guanyu shishi "zhongxiaoxue jiaoshi guojia peixun jihua de tongzhi"* 教育部财政部关于实施"中小学教师国家培训计划的通知 [Circular of National Primary and Secondary School Teacher Training Plan by the Ministry of Education and Ministry of Finance]. MOE PRC. https://www.gov.cn/gzdt/2010-06/23/content_1634944.htm

Ministry of Education of the People's Republic of China [MOE PRC]. (1999). *Zhongxiaoxue jiaoshi jixujiaoyu guidin* (中小学教师继续教育规定) [The regulation of teacher continuing education]. Beijing, China: Government Printing Office. http://www.moe.gov.cn/srcsite/A02/s5911/moe_621/199909/t19990913_180474.html

Ministry of Education of the People's Republic of China [MOE PRC]. (2012). Guopei jihua (国培计划) [National teacher training plan program]. MOE PRC. http://www.moe.gov.cn/jyb_xwfb/moe_2082/s6236/s6811/201209/t20120903_141516.html

Ministry of Education. (1995). Report on Education for the Physically and Mentally Handicapped in the Republic of China. Ministry of Education.

Ministry of Education. (1999). Report on Special Education Statistics in 1999. Ministry of Education.

Ministry of Education. (2002). *Making special arrangements in schools for people with special needs (Circular no 02/2002)* [Khaassa ehee ah beynunvaa dharivarunna, muvazzafunnai, beleniverinnah khiyaalufulhu bahattavaigen schoolthakuge inthizaamuthah kurevvun]. Ministry of Education.

Ministry of Education. (2009). Report on Special Education Statistics in 2009. Ministry of Education..

Ministry of Education. (2013). *Inclusive education policy (Circular no 02/2013).* Ministry of Education.

Ministry of Education. (2016). *School statistics.* Ministry of Education.

Ministry of Education. (2019). Report on Special Education Statistics in 2019. Ministry of Education.

Ministry of Education. (2019). *School Statistics 2019.* Ministry of Education.

Ministry of Education. (2020). *Inclusive education policy (Circular no 22-E/CIR/2020/ 58)* [Hurihaa dharivarun shaamilukoggen thau'leemu dhinumuge usoolu]. Ministry of Education.

Ministry of Education. (2021). Report on Special Education Statistics in 2021. Ministry of Education.

Ministry of Education. (2021a). Inclusive Educational Policy. Ministry of Education.

Ministry of Education. (2021b). *Inclusive education policy* [Hurihaa dharivarun shaamilukoggen thau'leemu dhinumuge siyaasathu]. Ministry of Education.

Ministry of Education. (2021c). *School statistics 2021/2022*. Ministry of Education.

Mitchell, D. (2010). *Education that fits: Review of international trends in the education of students with special educational needs. Final report*. University of Canterbury.

Miyauchi, H. (2020). A systematic review on inclusive education of students with visual impairment. *Education Sciences, 10*(11), 346. doi:10.3390/educsci10110346

Molbaek, M., & Hedegaard-Sørensen, L. (In press). *Universal Design for Learning – fleksible og tilgængelige læringsmiljøer for alle [Universal design for learning – flexible and accessible learning environments for all]*.

Molbaek, M. (2018). Inclusive teaching strategies – Dimensions and agendas. *International Journal of Inclusive Education, 22*(10), 1048–1061. doi:10.1080/13603116.2017.1414578

Mondale, S., & Patton, S. B. (2001). *School: The story of American public education*. Beacon Press.

Morrier, M. J., Hess, K. L., & Heflin, L. J. (2011). Teacher training for implementation of teaching strategies for students with autism spectrum disorders. *Teacher Education and Special Education, 34*(2), 119–132. doi:10.1177/0888406410376660

Morris, M. (2019). *Student Voice and Teacher Professional Development: Knowledge Exchange and Transformational Learning*. Palgrave Macmillan. doi:10.1007/978-3-030-23467-6

Morrison, T. (1992). *Playing in the dark: Whiteness and the literary imagination*. Vintage Books (A Division of Random House, Inc.).

Morrison, T. (2001). Black matters. In P. Essed & D. T. Goldberg (Eds.), *Race critical theories*. Wiley-Blackwell.

Mosse, B., Stribley, D. P., & LeTacon, F. (1981). Ecology of mycorrhizae and mycorrhizal fungi. In M. Alexander (Ed.), *Advances in microbial ecology* (Vol. 5). Springer., doi:10.1007/978-1-4615-8306-6_4

Muega, M. A. (2016). Inclusive education in the Philippines: Through the eyes of teachers, administrators, and parents of children with special needs. *Social Science Diliman, 12*(2), 5–28.

Mueller, J. (2003). *Authentic assessment toolbox: Enhancing student learning through online faculty development*. JOLT. https://jolt.merlot.org/documents/VOL1No1mueller.pdf

Muff, K. (Ed.). (2017). *The collaboratory: a co-creative stakeholder engagement process for solving complex problems*. Routledge. doi:10.4324/9781351285681

Mullen, C. A., & Hunt, T. K. (2022). Emotional disability and strategies for supporting student outcomes: Interviews with K–12 special education teachers. *Teacher Development, 26*(4), 453–471. doi:10.1080/13664530.2022.2108129

Murawski, W., & Scott, K. L. (Eds.). (2019). *What really works with universal design for learning*. Corwin Press.

Murray, A. (2009). *Is inclusion effective?* [Unpublished master's thesis, St. John Fisher University]. https://fisherpub.sjf.edu/cgi/viewcontent.cgi?article=1083&context=education_ETD_masters

Nasir, N., & Cobb, P. (2007). Introduction. In N. Nasir & P. Cobb (Eds.), *Improving access to mathematics: Diversity and equity in the classroom* (pp. 1–9). Teachers College, Columbia University.

National Association for Gifted Children (NAGC). (2023a). *A brief history of gifted and talented education*. NAGC. https://dev.nagc.org/resources-publications/resources/gifted-education-us/brief-history-gifted-and-talented-education

Compilation of References

National Association for Gifted Children (NAGC). (2023b). *About NAGC.* NAGC. https://www.nagc.org/about-nagc

National Association for Gifted Children. (2019). *2019 Pre-K-Grade 12 gifted programming standards.* NAGC. https://nagc.org/page/National-Standards-in-Gifted-and-Talented-Education

National Association of Gifted Children (NAGC). (2019). *Position statement: A definition of giftedness that guides best practice.* NAGC. https://www.nagc.org/sites/default/files/Position%20Statement/Definition%20of%20Giftedness%20%282019%29.pdf

National Center for Education Statistics. (2022). *Students with disabilities.* NCES. https://nces.ed.gov/programs/coe/indicator/cgg

National Center on Universal Design for Learning. (2012). *UDL Guidelines - Version 2.0.* NCUDL. http://www.udlcenter.org/aboutudl/udlguidelines/principle3

National Council for Curriculum and Assessment. (1999). *Special educational needs: Curriculum issues.* https://ncca.ie/en/resources/special_educational_needs_curriculum_issues_-_discussion_paper/

National Council for Curriculum and Assessment. (2023). *Primary curriculum framework.* https://www.gov.ie/en/publication/0db24-primary-curriculum-framework/

National Council for Special Education. (2006). *Guidelines on the Individual Education Plan process.* https://ncse.ie/wp-content/uploads/2014/10/final_report.pdf

National Council for Special Education. (2011). *Inclusive education framework: A guide for schools on the inclusion of pupils with special education needs.* https://ncse.ie/wp-content/uploads/2014/10/InclusiveEducationFramework_InteractiveVersion.pdf

National Council for Special Education. (2014). *Delivery for students with special educational needs: A better and more equitable way.* https://ncse.ie/wp-content/uploads/2014/09 /Allocating_resources_1_5_14_Web_accessible_version_FINAL.pdf

National Council for Special Education. (2019). *Policy Advice on Special Schools and Classes An Inclusive Education for an Inclusive Society?* https://ncse.ie/wp-content/uploads/2019/11 /Progress-Report-Policy-Advice-on-Special-Schools-Classes-website-upload.pdf

National Council on Disability. (2018). *IDEA Series: The segregation of students with disabilities.* https://ncd.gov/sites/default/files/NCD_Segregation-SWD_508.pdf

Ndlovu, S., & Walton, E. (2016). Preparation of students with disabilities to graduate into professions in the South African context of higher learning: Obstacles and opportunities. *African Journal of Disability, 5*(1), 1–8. doi:10.4102/ajod.v5i1.150 PMID:28730040

Nedellec, C. M. (2015). *Teachers' understanding of differentiated instruction in Swiss elementary schools. (Doctoral Dissertation). Available from ProQuest Dissertations & Theses. (Order No. 3718012).*

Nel, N., Kempen, M., & Ruscheinski, A. (2011). Differentiated pedagogy as inclusive practice: The "learn not to burn" curriculum for learners with severe intellectual disabilities. *Education as Change, 15*(2), 191–208. doi:10.1080/16823206.2011.619145

Nelson, A. (2014). *Design and deliver: Planning and teaching using universal design for learning.* Paul H Brookes.

Newcomb, E. T., & Hagopian, L. P. (2018). Treatment of severe problem behaviour in children with autism spectrum disorder and intellectual disabilities. *International Review of Psychiatry (Abingdon, England), 30*(1), 96–109. doi:10.1 080/09540261.2018.1435513 PMID:29537889

Next Generation Science Standards. (2017). *About.* NGSS. https://ngss.nsta.org/AccessStandardsByTopic.aspx

Ní Bhrion, O., King, F., & Prunty, A. (2016). Teachers' knowledge and practice relating to the individual education plan and learning outcomes for pupils with special educational needs. *REACH Journal of Special Needs Education in Ireland, 29*(2), 78-90. Irish Association of Teachers in Special Education. https://reachjournal.ie/index.php/reach/article/view/45

Nilholm, C. (2021). Research about inclusive education in 2020 – How can we improve our theories in order to change practice? *European Journal of Special Needs Education, 36*(3), 358–370. doi:10.1080/08856257.2020.1754547

Norwich, B. (2020). *Lesson study for special needs and inclusive education.* Lesson Study Send. https://www.lesson-studysend.co.uk/

Norwich, B., & Lewis, A. (2005). How specialised is teaching pupils with disabilities and difficulties? *Pedagogies for Inclusion, 20*(1), 31–55. doi:10.1080/00220270601161667

Novak, K. (2017). *Engaging parents in UDL implementation.* https://www.learningdesigned.org/sites/default/files/Novak_2 017.pdf

Novak, K. (2019). *UDL implementation rubric.* Novak Education. https://www.novakeducation.com/blog/udl-implementation-rubric

Novak, K., & Rodriguez, K (2018). *The UDL progression rubric.* CAST.

Novak, A. M., Lewis, K. D., & Weber, C. L. (2020). Guiding principles in developing equity-driven professional learning for educators of gifted children. *Gifted Child Today, 43*(3), 169–183. doi:10.1177/1076217520915743

O'Connor, A., & Shumate, M. (2018). A Multidimensional Network Approach to Strategic Communication. *International Journal of Strategic Communication, 12*(4), 399–416. doi:10.1080/1553118X.2018.1452242

O'Toole, J. (2006). *Education for persons with special educational needs: An interpretation for teachers.* https://www.oireachtas.ie/en/bills/bill/2003/34/

Odom, S., Cox, A., & Brock, M. (2013). Implementation science, professional development, and autism spectrum disorders. *Exceptional Children, 79*(2), 233–251. doi:10.1177/001440291307900208l

Ogette, T. (2017). *Exit racism: Rassismuskritisch denken lernen.* Unrast.

Opfer, D. (2016). *Conditions and practices associated with teacher professional development and its impact on instruction in TALIS 2013.* OECD Working Paper.

Orr, A. C. (2009). New special educators reflect about inclusion: Preparation and K–12 current practice. *Journal of Ethnographic and Qualitative Research, 3*(4), 228–239.

Page, A., Mavropoulou, S., & Harrington, I. (2020). Culturally responsive inclusive education: The value of the local context. *International Journal of Disability Development and Education,* 1–14. doi:10.1080/1034912X.2020.1757627

Pais, A., & Valero, P. (2011). Beyond disavowing the politics of equity and quality in mathematics education. In B. Atweh, M. Graven, W. Secada, & P. Valero (Eds.), *Mapping equity and quality in mathematics education.* Springer.

Parkin, I. (2010). Factors affecting deaf education in South Africa. *American Annals of the Deaf, 155*(4), 490-493. https://www.jstor.org/stable/26235088seq=1#metadata_info_tab_contents

Compilation of References

Park, M. H., Dimitrov, D. M., Das, A., & Gichuru, M. (2016). The teacher efficacy for inclusive practices (TEIP) scale: Dimensionality and factor structure. *Journal of Research in Special Educational Needs, 16*(1), 2–12. doi:10.1111/1471-3802.12047

Parrish, A. H., Kouo, J., Carey, L., & Swanson, R. C. (2021). Using Universal Design for Learning in meeting the diverse needs of students in virtual learning environments. In M. Neiss & H. Gillow-Wiles (Eds.), *Transforming teachers' online pedagogical reasoning for teaching K-12 students in virtual learning environments*. IGI Global., https://www.igi-global.com/chapter/implementing-universal-design-for-learning-in-the-virtual-learning-environment/284517, doi:10.4018/978-1-7998-7222-1.ch003

Parsons, S., Guldberg, A., MacLeod, A., Jones, G., Punty, A., & Balfe, T. (2011). International review of the evidence on best practice in educational provision for children on the autism spectrum. *European Journal of Special Needs Education, 26*(1), 47–63. doi:10.1080/08856257.2011.543532

Parveen, A., & Qounsar, T. (2018). Inclusive education and the challenges. *National Journal of Multidisciplinary Research and Development, 3*(2), 64–68.

Pas, E. T., Johnson, S. R., Larson, K. E., Brandenburg, L., Church, R., & Bradshaw, C. P. (2016). Reducing behaviour problems among students with autism spectrum disorder: Coaching teachers in a mixed-reality setting. *Journal of Autism and Developmental Disorders, 46*(12), 3640–3652. doi:10.100710803-016-2898-y PMID:27590663

Patrick, S. K. (2022). Organizing schools for collaborative learning: School leadership and teachers' engagement in collaboration. *Educational Administration Quarterly, 58*(4), 1–36. doi:10.1177/0013161X221107628

Pattison, P., Bridgeman, A., Bulmer, A., McCallum, P., & Miles, R. (2022). Renewing the Sydney undergraduate curriculum. *Higher Education*, 1–18. doi:10.100710734-022-00982-x PMID:36536882

Patton, M. Q. (2002). *Qualitative research & evaluation methods* (3rd ed.). SAGE.

Pawlowski, J., & Hoel, T. (2012). *Towards a Global Policy for Open Educational Resources: The Paris OER Declaration and its Implications*. White Paper, Version 0.2, Jyväskylä, Finland.

Pellicano, E., Bölte, S., & Stahmer, A. (2018). The current illusion of educational inclusion. *Autism, 22*(4), 386–387. doi:10.1177/1362361318766166 PMID:29600722

Perlman, J., & Margo, R. A. (2001). *Women's work? American schoolteachers, 1650-1920*. University of Chicago Press. doi:10.7208/chicago/9780226660417.001.0001

Peterson, J. S. (2009a). Myth 17: Gifted and talented individuals do not have unique social and emotional needs. *Gifted Child Quarterly, 53*(4), 280–282. doi:10.1177/0016986209346946

Peterson, J. S. (2009b). *Gifted and at risk: Poetic portraits*. Great Potential Press.

Petersson -Bloom. L. (2022). *Equity in education for autistic students. Professional learning to accommodate inclusive education.* [Doctoral Dissertation in Education, Malmö University].

Pierangelo, R., & Giuliano, G. (2007). *Understanding, developing, and writing effective IEPs: A step-by-step guide for educators*. Corwin Press.

Pinnock, H., & Athif, A. (2015). Using special educational needs as an entry point for inclusive education in the Maldives. *Enabling Education Review, 4*, 16–17.

Pitman, T. (2022). *Supporting persons with disabilities to succeed in higher education: Final Report*. Curtin University. https://www.ncsehe.edu.au/wp-content/uploads/2022/03/Pitman_Curtin_EquityFellowship_FINAL.pdf

Pitman, T., Brett, M., & Ellis, K. (2021). Three decades of misrecognition: Defining people with disability in Australian higher education policy. *Disability & Society, 38*(25), 1–19. doi:1 doi:0.1080/09687599.2021.1937061

Planas, N., Morgan, C., & Schütte, M. (2018). Mathematics education and language: Lessons and directions from two decades of research. In T. Dreyfus, M. Artigue, D. Potari, S. Prediger, & K. Ruthven (Eds.), *Developing research in mathematics education. Twenty years of communication, cooperation and collaboration in Europe* (pp. 196–210). Routledge. doi:10.4324/9781315113562-15

Plantin Ewe, L., & Aspelin, J. (2021). Relational competence regarding students with ADHD– An intervention study with in-service teachers. *European Journal of Special Needs Education, 37*(2), 293–308.

Plucker, J. A., & Peters, S. J. (2016). *Excellence gaps in education: Expanding opportunities for talented students.* Harvard Education Press.

Popkewitz, T. (2004). The alchemy of the mathematics curriculum: Inscriptions and the fabrication of the child. *American Educational Research Journal, 41*(1), 3–34. doi:10.3102/00028312041001003

Postman, J. (2009). *SocialCorp: Social media goes corporate.* New Riders.

Prediger, S., Bikner-Ahsbahs, A., & Arzarello, F. (2008). Networking strategies and methods for connecting theoretical approaches – First steps towards a conceptual framework. *ZDM - The International Journal on Mathematics Education, 40*(2), 165–178.

Price & Slee, R. (2021). An Australian Curriculum that includes diverse learners: The case of students with disability. *Curriculum Perspectives, 41*(1), 71–81 doi:10.1007/s41297-021-00134-8

Prochaska, J. O., & Diclemente, C. C. (1986). Toward a Comprehensive Model of Change. In W. R. Miller & N. Heather (Eds.), *Treating Addictive Behaviors: Processes of Change* (pp. 3–27). Springer US. doi:10.1007/978-1-4613-2191-0_1

Purcell, J., Burns, D., & Leppin, J. (2002, April). The parallel curriculum model (PCM): The whole story. *National Association for Gifted Children, 4*(1), 1–4.

Rae, H., Murray, G., & McKenzie, K. (2010). Teachers' attitudes to mainstream schooling. *Learning Disability Practice, 13*(10), 12–17. doi:10.7748/ldp2010.12.13.10.12.c8138

Rajotte, E., Grandisson, M., Hamel, C., Couture, M., Desmarais, C., Gravel, M., & Chrétien-Vincent, M. (2022). Inclusion of autistic students: Promising modalities for supporting a school team. *Disability and Rehabilitation.* doi:10.1080/09638288.2022.2057598 PMID:35389757

Ralabate, P. K. (2011). Universal Design for Learning: Meeting the Needs of All Students. *ASHA Leader, 16*(10), 14–17. Advance online publication. doi:10.1044/leader.FTR2.16102011.14

Rao, K., & Meo, G. (2016). Using Universal Design for Learning to Design Standards-Based Lessons. *SAGE Open, 6*(4), 2158244016680688. doi:10.1177/2158244016680688

Ravet, J. (2011). Inclusive/exclusive? Contradictory perspectives on autism and inclusion: The case for and integrative position. *International Journal of Inclusive Education, 15*(6), 667–682. doi:10.1080/13603110903294347

Regmi, N. P. (2017). *Inclusive Education in Nepal - From Theory to Practice.* [Dissertation, Ludwig-Maximilians-University].

Reindal, S. M. (1995). Some problems encountered by disabled students at the University of Oslo: Whose responsibility? *European Journal of Special Needs Education, 10*(3), 227–241. doi:10.1080/0885625950100304

Compilation of References

Reis, S. M., Westberg, K. L., Kulikowich, J. K., Caillard, F., Hébert, T. P., Plucker, J., Purcell, J. H., Smist, J. M. (1993). *Why not let high ability students start school in January? The curriculum compacting study* (Research Monograph No. 93106). University of Connecticut, The National Research Center on the Gifted and Talented.

Reis, S. M., & Boeve, H. (2009). How academically gifted elementary, urban students respond to challenge in an enriched, differentiated reading program. *Journal for the Education of the Gifted, 33*(2), 203–240. doi:10.1177/016235320903300204

Ren, B., & Li, M. (2019). Xinshidai xibu diqu xindongnéng peiyu de kuangjia, neirong yu lujing (新时代西部地区新动能培育的框架、内容与路径) [The framework, content and path of the new kinetic energy cultivation in the Western region under the background of the new era]. In B. Ren, L. Yue, A. He, H. Guo (Eds.), Xibu lanpishu: Zhongguo xibu fazhan baokao (西部蓝皮书:中国西部发展报告) [Blue book of the western region: Annual report on development in the western region of China (2019)] (pp. 1-27). Social Sciences Academic Press (China).

Renschler, R., & Preiswerk, R. (Eds.). (1981). *Das gift der frühen jahre: Rassismus in der jugendliteratur.* Basel Lenos.

Ren, Y., Harper, F. M., Drenner, S., Terveen, L., Kiesler, S., Riedl, J., & Kraut, R. E. (2012). Building member attachment in online communities: Applying theories of group identity and interpersonal bonds. *Management Information Systems Quarterly, 36*(3), 841–864. doi:10.2307/41703483

Republic of South Africa, Department of Education. (2001). *Education White Paper 6: Special Needs Education: Building an Inclusive Education and Training System.* Republic of South Africa DoE. https://www.education.gov.za/Portals/0/Documents/Legislation/White%20paper/Education%20%20White%20Paper%206.pdf?ver=2008-03-05-104651-000

Republic of South Africa. (1996). *Constitution of the Republic of South Africa, Act No. 2 of 1996.* Government Printer.

Republic of South Africa. (2018). *Strategic Policy Framework on Disability for the Post-School Education and Training System.* Republic of South Africa. https://www.dhet.gov.za/SiteAssets/Gazettes/Approved%20Strategic%20Disability%20Policy%20Framework%20Layout220518.pdf

Ricketts, M. A. (2014). *The lived experiences of teachers in implementing differentiated instruction in the inclusive classroom.* [Dissertation, Walden University]. *ProQuest Dissertations & Theses.* (Order No. 3645551).

Riegel, B. D., & Behrens, W. A. (2022). Subject-based acceleration. *Gifted Child Today, 45*(4), 192–200. doi:10.1177/10762175221110937

Riemeier, T. (2007). Moderater konstruktivismus. In D. Krüger & H. Vogt (Eds.), Theorien in der biologiedidaktischen forschung: Springer-Lehrbuch (pp. 69–79). Springer. doi:10.1007/978-3-540-68166-3_7

Rinn, A. N., Mun, R. U., & Hodges, J. (2020). *2018-2019 State of the states in gifted education.* National Association for Gifted Children and the Council of State Directors for Programs for the Gifted. https://www.nagc.org/2018-2019-state-states-gifted-education

Rinn, A. N., Mun, R. U., & Hodges, J. (2022). *2020-2021 State of the states in gifted education.* National Association for Gifted Children and the Council of State Directors of Programs for the Gifted. https://cdn.ymaws.com/nagc.org/resource/resmgr/2020-21_state_of_the_states_.pdf

Rios, T. A. (2001). *Compreender e ensinar: por uma docência de melhor qualidade.* Cortez.

Rizwan, S. (2017). Mainstreaming students with disabilities: a survey of teachers' attitudes towards inclusion. In *Proceedings of International Teachers' Conference 4, Curriculum, Pedagogy & Assessment: Innovative Visions to Foster Effective Learning.* National Institute of Education.

Roberts, J. L. (1999). The top 10 events creating gifted education for the new century. *Gifted Child Today, 22*(6), 53–55. doi:10.1177/107621759902200615

Roberts, J. L., & Boggess, J. R. (2011). *Teacher's survival guide: Gifted Education.* Prufrock Press.

Roberts, J. L., & Inman, T. F. (2023). *Strategies for differentiating instruction: Best practices for the classroom* (4th ed.). Routledge.

Robinson, A., & Deitz, C. (2022). Teachers count in the classroom and in policy: Legislation, rules, and regulations as pathways in gifted education. *Gifted Child Today, 45*(4), 220–225. doi:10.1177/10762175221110940

Robinson, D. (2017). Effective inclusive teacher education for special educational needs and disabilities. *Teaching and Teacher Education, 61,* 164–178. doi:10.1016/j.tate.2016.09.007

Rogers, M., Hodge, J., & Counts, J. (2020). Self-regulated strategy development in writing and mathematics for students with specific learning disabilities. *Teaching Exceptional Children, 53*(2), 104–112. doi:10.1177/0040059920946780

Röggla, K. (2012). *Critical whiteness studies und ihre politischen handlungsmöglichkeiten für weiße antirassistinnen.* Mandelbaum.

Rommelspacher, B. (2002). *Anerkennung und ausgrenzung: Deutschland als multikulturelle gesellschaft.* Campus.

Roos, H. (2015). *Inclusion in mathematics in primary school: What can it be?* [Thesis, Växjö: Linnaeus University].

Roos, H. (2019b). *The meaning of inclusion in student talk: Inclusion as a topic when students talk about learning and teaching in mathematics.* [Ph. D. Thesis. Linnaeus University: Växjö].

Roos, H., & Bagger, A. (2021). Developing mathematics education promoting equity and inclusion: Is it possible? In D. Kollosche (Ed.), *Exploring new ways to connect: Proceedings of the Eleventh International Mathematics Education and Society Conference* (Vol. 1, pp. 223–226). Tredition.

Roos, H., & Gadler, U. (2018). Kompetensens betydelse i det didaktiska mötet – en modell för analys av möjligheter att erbjuda varje elev likvärdig utbildning enligt skolans uppdrag. *Pedagogisk forskning i Sverige, 23,* 290–307.

Roos, H. (2019a). Inclusion in mathematics education: An ideology, a way of teaching, or both? *Educational Studies in Mathematics, 100*(1), 25–41. doi:10.100710649-018-9854-z

Roos, H. (2021). Repeated interviews with students – critical methodological points for research quality. *International Journal of Research & Method in Education.* doi: 10.1080/1743727X.2021.1966622

Rose, D. H., & Meyer, A. (2002). *Teaching every student in the digital age: Universal design for learning.* ASCD.

Rose, D. H., & Strangman, N. (2007). Universal design for learning: Meeting the challenge of individual learning differences through a neurocognitive perspective. *Universal Access in the Information Society, 5*(4), 381–391. doi:10.100710209-006-0062-8

Rose, D., Gravel, J., & Domings, Y. (2012). UDL unplugged: The role of technology in UDL. In T. Hall, A. Meyer, & D. Rose (Eds.), *Universal design for learning in the classroom: Practical applications* (pp. 120–134). Guilford Press.

Rose, D., & Meyer, A. (2002). *Teaching Every Student in the Digital Age: Universal Design for Learning.* ASCD.

Rose, D., Meyer, A., & Hitchcock, C. (2005). *The Universally Designed Classroom: Accessible Curriculum and Digital Technologies.* Harvard Education Press.

Rose, R., & Doveston, M. (2015). Collaboration across cultures: Planning and delivering professional development for inclusive education in India. *Support for Learning. Special Issue: Themes and Perspectives from India, 30*(3), 177–191.

Ross, P. O. (1993). National excellence: A case for developing America's talent. U.S. Department of Education. ISBN-0-16-042928-5

Compilation of References

Rothenberg, P. S. (Ed.). (2011). *White privilege: Essential readings on the other side of racism.* Worth Publishers.

Ruddock, P. (2005). *Disability standards for education 2005.* Commonwealth of Australia. Federal Register of Legislative Instruments F2005L007672006

Rushdhee, A. (2021). In-service teachers' perceptions on implementing universal design for learning in the republic of Maldives. *SAARC Journal of Educational Research, 14,* 1–34.

Rushdhee, A. (2022). In-service teachers' sentiments, attitudes, and concerns on implementing inclusive education in the Republic of Maldives. *International Research Symposium on Education, IRSE, 2022.*

Sanders, S., Rollins, L., Mason, L., Shaw, A., & Jolivette, K. (2021). Intensification and individualization of self-regulation components within self-regulated strategy development. *Intervention in School and Clinic, 56*(3), 131–140. doi:10.1177/1053451220941414

Santos, B. S. (2008). *B.S. A gramática do tempo.* Cortez.

Satar, A. A. (2019). Innovative Strategies for Creating Inclusive Spaces for Hearing-Impaired and Visually Impaired Students in an Open Distance And e-Learning (ODeL) Environment: A Case Study of the University of South Africa (Unisa). In Strategies for Facilitating Inclusive Campuses in Higher Education: International Perspectives on Equity and Inclusion (Vol. 17, pp. 253-267). Emerald Publishing Limited.

Schiller, E., Sanford, C., & Blackorby, S. (2008). *A national profile of the classroom experiences and academic performance of students with learning disabilities: A special topic report from the special education elementary longitudinal study.* https://www.seels.net/info_reports/SEELS_LearnDisability_%20SPEC_TOPIC_REPORT.12.19.08ww_FINAL.pdf

SchröterA.ZimenkovaT. (2019). Norm und normalität: Reflexion der eigenen positionen von angehenden lehrkräften innerhalb des machtfeldes schule und schaffung nicht-normativer räume in der lehre. *Herausforderung Lehrer_innenbildung, Zeitschrift Zur Konzeption, Gestaltung Und Diskussion, 2*(3), 47–62. doi:10.4119/hlz-2455

Schultz, D. E., & Peltier, J. J. (2013). Social media's slippery slope: Challenges, opportunities and future research directions. *Journal of Research in Interactive Marketing, 7*(2), 86–99. doi:10.1108/JRIM-12-2012-0054

Schwab, S. (2014). *Schulische integration, soziale partizipation und emotionales wohlbefinden in der schule. Ergebnisse einer empirischen Längsschnittstudie.* Lit. Verlag.

Scruggs, T. E., & Mastropieri, M. A. (2017). Making inclusion work with co-teaching. *Teaching Exceptional Children, 49*(4), 284–293. doi:10.1177/0040059916685065

SCS. (2022). *Política municipal de educação especial a serviços da educação inclusive.* SCS..

Secher Schmidt, M. C. (2016). Dyscalculia ≠ maths difficulties: An analysis of conflicting positions at a time that calls for inclusive practices. *European Journal of Special Needs Education, 31*(3), 407–421. doi:10.1080/08856257.2016.1163016

Section 504 of the Rehabilitation Act of 1973, 34 C.F.R. § 300.101 (1973). https://www.dol.gov/agencies/oasam/centers-offices/civil-rights-center/statutes/section-504-rehabilitation-act-of-1973

Segall, M. J., & Campbell, J. M. (2012). Factors relating to education professionals' classroom practices for the inclusion of students with autism spectrum disorders. *Research in Autism Spectrum Disorders, 6*(3), 1156–1167. doi:10.1016/j.rasd.2012.02.007

Segars, S. (2021). *Deaf student's accomplishment a first for SU.* Stellenbosch University. https://www.sun.ac.za/english/Lists/news/DispForm.aspx?ID=8824

Sellen, P. (2016). *Teacher workload and professional development in England's secondary schools: Insights from TALIS.* Education Policy Institute.

Sharma, U., Forlinb, C., Deppelera, J., & Yang, G.-X. (2013). Reforming teacher education for inclusion in developing countries in the Asia-Pacific region. *Asian Journal of Inclusive Education, 1*(1), 3–16. doi:10.59595/ajie.01.1.2

Sharma, U., Shaukat, S., & Furlonger, B. (2015). Attitudes and self-efficacy of pre-service teachers towards inclusion in Pakistan. *Journal of Research in Special Educational Needs, 15*(2), 97–105. doi:10.1111/1471-3802.12071

Shyman, E. (2015). Toward a globally sensitive definition of inclusive education based on social justice. *International Journal of Disability Development and Education, 62*(4), 351–362. doi:10.1080/1034912X.2015.1025715

Silva, T. T. (2010). *Documentos de identidade: uma introdução às teorias do currículo.* Autêntica Editora.

Silverman, L. K. (2002). *Upside down brilliance: The visual-spatial learner.* DeLeon Publishing, Inc.

Sivertzen, A. M., Nilsen, E. R., & Olafsen, A. H. (2013). Employer branding: Employer attractiveness and the use of social media. *Journal of Product and Brand Management, 22*(7), 473–483. doi:10.1108/JPBM-09-2013-0393

Skovsmose, O. (2019). Inclusions, Meetings, and Landscapes. In D. Kollosche, R. Marcone, M. Knigge, M. Godoy Penteado, & O. Skovsmose (Eds.), *Inclusive Mathematics Education. State-of-the-Art Research from Brazil and Germany* (pp. 71–84). Springer. doi:10.1007/978-3-030-11518-0_7

Slee, R. (2013). How do we make inclusive education happen when exclusion is a political predisposition? *International Journal of Inclusive Education, 17*(8), 895–907. doi:10.1080/13603116.2011.602534

Slee, R. (2019). *Inclusive education isn't dead, it just smells funny.* Routledge.

Slee, R., & Allen, J. (2001). Excluding the included: A reconsideration of inclusive education. *International Studies in Sociology of Education, 1*(2), 173–192. doi:10.1080/09620210100200073

Slee, R., Corcoran, T., & Best, M. (2021). Disability studies in education – Building platforms to reclaim disability and recognise disablement. *Journal of Disability Studies in Education, 1*(1-2), 3–13. doi:10.1163/25888803-00101002

Smith, V. M. (2012). *Co-teaching: A case study of teachers' perceptions* [Unpublished doctoral dissertation, Northeastern University]. https://www.proquest.com/docview/1039147424

Spandagou, I., Evans, D., & Little, C. (2008). *Primary education pre-service teachers' attitudes on inclusion and perceptions on preparedness to respond to classroom diversity.* Paper presented at the Australia Association for Research in Education National Conference, Brisbane.

Stahmer, A. C., Rieth, S., Lee, E., Reisinger, E. M., Mandell, D. S., & Connell, J. S. (2015). Training teachers to use evidence-based practices for autism: Examining procedural implementation fidelity. *Psychology in the Schools, 52*(2), 181–195. doi:10.1002/pits.21815 PMID:25593374

Stellenbosch University. (2018). *Disability Access Policy.* Stellenbosch University. http://www.sun.ac.za/english/policy

Stellenbosch University. (2021). *Assessment Policy.* Stellenbosch University. http://sunrecords.sun.ac.za/controlled/C4%20Policies%20and%20Regulations/SU%20Assessment%20Policy_FINAL.pdf

Stellenbosch University. (2021). *Language Policy.* Stellenbosch University. http://sunrecords.sun.ac.za/controlled/C4%20Policies%20and%20Regulations/English%20Language%20Policy_final_2Dec2021.pdf

Stellenbosch University. (2022). *Report: Centre for Student Counselling and Development (CSCD): Reasonable accommodation for exams and tests.* Stellenbosch University.

Compilation of References

Stellenbosch University. (2023). *Student Information System Support. Students with disabilities statistics.* Stellenbosch University.

Stepaniuk, I. (2019). Inclusive education in Eastern European countries: A current state and future directions. *International Journal of Inclusive Education, 23*(3), 328–352. doi:10.1080/13603116.2018.1430180

Stephens, K. R. (2019). Teacher dispositions and their impact on implementation practices for the gifted. *Gifted Child Today, 42*(4), 187–195. doi:10.1177/1076217519862330

Stewart, C. (2014). Transforming professional development to professional learning. *Journal of Adult Education, 43*(1), 28–33.

Strangman, N., Vue, G., Hall, T., & Meyer, A. (2004). *Graphic Organizers and Implications for Universal Design for Learning: Curriculum Enhancement Report.* National Center on Accessing the General Curriculum.

Strogilos, V., Tragoulia, E., Avramidis, E., Voulagka, A., & Papanikolaou, V. (2017). Understanding the development of differentiated instruction for students with and without disabilities in co-taught classrooms. *Disability & Society, 32*(8), 1216–1238. doi:10.1080/09687599.2017.1352488

Subba, A. B., Yangzom, C., Dorji, K., Choden, S., Namgay, U., Carrington, S., & Nickerson, J. (2019). Supporting students with disability in schools in Bhutan: Perspectives from school principals. *International Journal of Inclusive Education, 23*(1), 42–64. doi:10.1080/13603116.2018.1514744

Sukhai, M. A., & Mohler, C. E. (2017). *Creating a culture of accessibility in the sciences.* Elsevier.

Sullivan, P. (2015). Maximising opportunities in mathematics for all students: Addressing within-school and within-class differences. In: A. J., Bishop, H. Tan & T. N. Barkatsas (Eds.), Diversity in Mathematics Education – Towards Inclusive Practices (pp. 239–253). Cham: Springer publishing.

Sunny, X. (2017). *A Multicultural Curriculum Research of In-class Publicity Programs with Special Education Issue.* [Unpublished master's thesis, National Taiwan Normal University, Taipei, Taiwan].

Su, Y.-H., & Wang, T.-M. (2003). Ideals and challenges of integrated education: The experience of teachers in elementary school regular classes. *Journal of Special Education Research, 24*, 39–62.

Taipei City C Elementary School. (2010). *The authors are all good friends ~ Multi-Modal Area Curriculum Integration Activities in Zhongshan.* CIRN-Exemplar of Standards. https://cirn.moe.edu.tw/userfiles/file/benchmark/99/team/B39.pdf

Tangen, R. (2009). Conceptualising quality of school life from pupils' perspectives: A four-dimensional model. *International Journal of Inclusive Education, 13*(8), 829–844. doi:10.1080/13603110802155649

Tan, P., Lambert, R., Padilla, A., & Wieman, R. (2019). A disability studies in mathematics education review of intellectual disabilities: Directions for future inquiry and practice. *The Journal of Mathematical Behavior, 54*(June), 100672. doi:10.1016/j.jmathb.2018.09.001

Tavares, R., Vieira, R., & Pedro, L. (2021). Mobile app for science education: Designing the learning approach. *Education Sciences, 11*(2), 79. doi:10.3390/educsci11020079

Taylor, J. P., Rooney-Kron, M., Whittenburg, H. N., Thoma, C. A., Avellone, L., & Seward, H. (2020). Inclusion of students with intellectual and developmental disabilities and postsecondary outcomes: A systematic literature review. *Inclusion (Washington, D.C.), 8*(4), 303–319. doi:10.1352/2326-6988-8.4.303

Tench, R., Meng, J., & Moreno, A. (Eds.). (2022). *Strategic communication in a global crisis: National and international responses to the covid-19 pandemic* (1st ed.). Routledge. doi:10.4324/9781003184669

Thacker, E. S. (2017). "PD is where teachers are learning!" High school social studies teachers 'formal and informal professional learning. *Journal of Social Studies Research, 41*(1), 37–52. doi:10.1016/j.jssr.2015.10.001

The Miriam and Ira D. Wallach Division of Art. Prints and Photographs: Photography Collection, The New York Public Library. (1935). *Interior of "little red schoolhouse." Crossville, Tennessee.* https://digitalcollections.nypl.org/items/f33f13f0-da35-0132-3212-58d385a7bbd0

Thien, L. M. (2016). Malaysian students' performance in mathematics literacy in PISA from gender and socioeconomic status perspectives. *The Asia-Pacific Education Researcher, 25*(4), 657–666. doi:10.100740299-016-0295-0

Thomas, D. (2022). *South African Sign Language Approved as South Africa's 12th Official Language.* EWN. https://ewn.co.za/2022/05/28/south-african-sign-language-approved-as-sa-s-12th-official-language

Thomas, G., & Loxley, A. (2001). *Deconstructing Special Education and Constructing Inclusion.* Open University Press.

Thomson, M., & Svaerd, A. K. (2019). Unintended consequences of special-needs law in Ireland and Sweden. *Kybernetes, 48*(2), 333–247. doi:10.1108/K-06-2018-0307

Thorell, L. B. (2007). Do delay aversion and executive function deficits make distinct contributions to the functional impact of ADHD symptoms? A study of early academic skill deficits. *Journal of Child Psychology and Psychiatry, and Allied Disciplines, 48*(11), 1061–1070. doi:10.1111/j.1469-7610.2007.01777.x PMID:17995481

Timberlake, M. T. (2018). Nice, but we can't afford it: Challenging austerity and finding abundance in inclusive education. *International Journal of Inclusive Education, 22*(9), 954–968. doi:10.1080/13603116.2017.1412518

Tißberger, M. (2009). Die psyche der macht, der rassismus der psychologie und die psychologie des rassimus. In M. Tißberger, G. Dietze, D. Hrzán, & J. Husmann-Kastein (Eds.), *Weiß—Weißsein—Whiteness: Kritische studien zu gender und rassismus—Critical studies on gender and racism* (pp. 13–29). Peter Lang.

Tißberger, M., Dietze, G., Hrzán, D., & Husmann-Kastein, J. (Eds.). (2009). *Weiß—Weißsein—Whiteness: Kritische studien zu gender und rassismus—Critical studies on gender and racism.* Peter Lang.

Title, I. X. (2011). U.S. Code 2011, Part A, Definition 22. https://www.govinfo.gov/content/pkg/USCODE-2011-title20/pdf/USCODE-2011-title20-chap70-subchapIX-partA-sec7801.pdf

Tomlinson, C. A. (14 April 2015). Teaching for excellence in academically diverse classrooms. *Symposium: 21st Century Excellence in education,* 203-209. 10.100712115-015-9888-0

Tomlinson, C. A. (2002, November 6). Proficiency is not enough. *Education Week.*

Tomlinson, C. A. (2005, Spring). Quality curriculum and instruction for highly able students. *Theory into Practice, 44*(2), 160–166. doi:10.120715430421tip4402_10

Tomlinson, C. A., & Imbeau, M. (2010). *Leading and managing a differentiated classroom.* Association for Supervision and Curriculum Development.

Tomlinson, C. A., Kaplan, S., Renzulli, J., Purcell, J., Leppien, J., & Burns, D. (2001). *The parallel curriculum: A design to develop high potential and challenge high-ability learners.* Corwin Press.

Tomlinson, C. A., & Strickland, C. (2005). *Differentiation in practice: A resource guide for differentiating curriculum, Grades 9-12.* Association for Supervision and Curriculum Development.

Compilation of References

Tomlinson, S. (2012). The irresistible rise of the SEND industry. *Oxford Review of Education, 38*(3), 267–286. doi:10.1080/03054985.2012.692055

Tonga, F. E., Eryiğit, S., Yalçın, F. A., & Erden, F. T. (2022). Professional development of teachers in PISA achiever countries: Finland, Estonia, Japan, Singapore and China. *Professional Development in Education, 48*(1), 88–104. doi:10.1080/19415257.2019.1689521

Tracy, S. J. (2013). *Qualitative Research Methods: Collecting Evidence, Crafting Analysis, Communicating Impact.* Blacwell Publishing., doi:10.5613/rzs.43.1.6

Trainor, K. J., Andzulis, J. M., Rapp, A., & Agnihotri, R. (2014). Social media technology usage and customer relationship performance: A capabilities-based examination of social CRM. *Journal of Business Research, 67*(6), 1201–1208. doi:10.1016/j.jbusres.2013.05.002

Trust, T., Krutka, D. G., & Carpenter, J. P. (2016). "Together we are better": Professional learning networks for teachers. *Computers & Education, 102*, 15–34. doi:10.1016/j.compedu.2016.06.007

Tschannen-Moran, M., & Woolfolk Hoy, A. (2001). Teacher efficacy: Capturing an elusive construct. *Teaching and Teacher Education, 17*(7), 783–805. doi:10.1016/S0742-051X(01)00036-1

Turnbull, A. P., Turnbull, H. R., Erwin, E. J., Soodak, L. C., & Shogren, K. A. (2015). *Families, professionals, and exceptionality: Positive outcomes through partnership and trust* (7th ed.). Pearson.

Turnbull, H. R., Stowe, M. J., & Huerta, N. E. (2007). *Free appropriate public education: The law and children with disabilities* (7th ed.). Love.

Turnbull, H. R., & Turnbull, A. P. (2003). Reaching the ideal. *Education Next, 3*(1), 32–37. https://www.educationnext.org/reachingtheideal/

Turner, R. (2010). The dawn of a new approach to security. *Computer Fraud & Security, 15*(4), 15–17. doi:10.1016/S1361-3723(10)70040-3

U.S. Department of Education. (2021). *The federal role in education.* USDE. https://www2.ed.gov/about/overview/fed/role.html

Ulvseth, H., Jørgensen, C., & Tetler, S. (2017). *Elevers engagement i undervisningen – om metoder til inddragelse af alle elevers stemmer* [Pupils' involvement in teaching – About methods for including the voices of all pupils]. Dafolo.

UNDP. (2014). *Maldives human development report 2014.* UNDP.

UNESCO. (1990). World declaration on education for all and framework for action to meet basic learning needs. Adopted at *World Conference on Education for All: Meeting Basic Learning Needs.* UNESCO.

UNESCO. (1994). *Final report: World conference on special needs education: Access and quality.* UNESCO.

UNESCO. (1994). The Salamanca statement and framework for action on special education needs. Adopted at *World Conference on Special Education Needs: Access and Quality.* UNESCO.

UNESCO. (1994). *The Salamanca Statement and Framework for Action on Special Needs Education. World Conference on Special Needs Education: Access and Quality, Salamanca, Spain.* UNESCO. https://unesdoc.unesco.org/ark:/48223/pf0000098427

UNESCO. (2000). Dakar framework for action. Adopted at *World Education Forum*, Dakar, Senegal. UNESCO.

UNESCO. (2004). *Education for all: the quality imperative.* UNESCO.

UNESCO. (2005). *Guidelines for inclusion: ensuring access to education for all.* UNESCO.

UNESCO. (2009). *Policy guidelines on inclusion in education.* UNESCO.

UNESCO. (2018). *Inclusive education.* UNESCO.

UNESCO. (2020). *Global Education Monitoring Report 2020: Inclusion and education: All means all.* UNESCO.

UNESCO. (2020). *Global education monitoring report 2020: Inclusion and education: All means all.* UNESCO. https://unesdoc.unesco. org/ark:/48223/pf0000373718

UNESCO. (2020). *Relatório de monitoramento global da educação, 2020, América Latina e Caribe: Inclusão e educação: todos sem exceção, principais mensagens e recomendações.* UNESCO. https://unesdoc.unesco.org/ark:/48223/pf0000374790_por

UNESCO. (2020a). *Global education monitoring report 2020: inclusion and education: all means all.* UNESCO.

UNESCO. (2020b). *Towards inclusion in education: status, trends and challenges.* UnESCO.

UNESCO. (2021a). *Kiribati - inclusion.* UNESCO. https://education-profiles.org/oceania/kiribati/~inclusion

UNESCO. (2021b). *Sri Lanka - Inclusion.* UNESCO.

UNESCO/BRAZIL. (2022). *Inclusão, equidade e desigualdades entre estudantes das escolas públicas de ensino fundamental no Brasil.* UNESCO. https://unesdoc.unesco.org/ark:/48223/pf0000382175

UNICEF. (2021a). *Disability-inclusive education practices in Bangladesh.* UNICEF.

UNICEF. (2021b). *Disability-inclusive education practices in Bhutan.* UNICEF.

UNICEF. (2021c). *Disability-Inclusive Education Practices in Maldives.* UNICEF.

UNICEF. (2021d). *Disability-inclusive education practices in Nepal.* UNICEF.

UNICEF. (2021e). *Disability-inclusive education practices in Sri Lanka.* UNICEF.

UNICEF. (2021f). *Mapping of disability-inclusive education practices in South Asia.* UNICEF.

United Nations (UN). *Sustainable Development Goals. Agenda 2030.* UN. https://www.un.org/sustainabledevelopment/sustainable-development-goals/

United Nations Division for Social Policy and Development Disability [UNDSPDD]. (2006). *United Nations convention on the rights of persons with disabilities.* UN. https://www.un.org/disabilities/documents/convention/convoptprot-e.pdf

United Nations Educational, Scientific and Cultural Organization (UNESCO). (1994). *The Salamanca Statement and framework for action on special needs education.* UNESCO.

United Nations Educational, Scientific and Cultural Organization (UNESCO). (1994). *The UNESCO Salamanca Statement.* Adopted by the World Conference on Special Needs Education: Access and Quality. Salamanca, Spain. http://www.csie.org.uk/inclusion/unesco-salamanca.shtml

United Nations Educational, Scientific and Cultural Organization (UNESCO). (2005). *Guidelines for inclusion: Ensuring Access to Education for All.* UNESCO.

United Nations Educational, Scientific and Cultural Organization (UNESCO). (2014). UNESCO/Emir Jaber al-Ahmad al-Jaber al-Sabah prize to promote quality education for persons with intellectual disabilities. https://en.unesco.org/prizes/digitalempowerment/previous-winners#2013

Compilation of References

United Nations Educational, Scientific and Cultural Organization (UNESCO). (2015). *Sub-Education Policy Review Report: Inclusive Education*. UNESCO.

United Nations, Department of Economic and Social Affairs. (2018). *Convention on the Rights of Persons with Disabilities*. https://www.un.org/development/desa/disabilities/convention-on-the-rights-of-persons-with-disabilities/convention-on-the-rights-of-persons-with-disabilities-2.html

United Nations. (2006). Convention on the rights of persons with disabilities and optional protocol. UN. https://www.un.org/development/desa/disabilities/convention-on-the-rights-of-persons-with-disabilities.html

United Nations. (2006). *Convention on the rights of persons with disabilities*. UN.

United Nations. (2006). *Convention on the rights of persons with disabilities*. UN. https://www.un.org/disabilities/documents/convention/Convoptprot-e.pdf

United Nations. (2006). *Convention on the rights of persons with disabilities*. UN. www.un.org/disabilities/documents/convention/convoptprote.pdf

United Nations. (2015). *The 17 Sustainable Development Goals. UN Department of Economic and Social Affairs*. UN. https://sdgs.un.org/goals

United Nations. (2015). *The Sustainable Development Goals (SDG) 2030 Agenda*. UN. https://www.undpp.org/sustainable-development-goals

United Nations. (2015). Transforming our world: The 2030 agenda for sustainability development. UN. https://sdgs.un.org/2030agenda

United Nations. (2016). *Convention on the rights of persons with disability: General comment No. 4*. UN. https://www.refworld.org/docid/57c977e34.html

United Nations. (2016). *Disability and development report*. UN.

United Nations. (2016). *General comment No. 4 on the right to inclusive education. Committee on the Rights of Persons with Disabilities*. United Nations.

United Nations. (2022). *United Nations Sustainable Goals*. UN. https://www.un.org/sustainabledevelopment/sustainable-development-goals/

United States Department of Education. (2022). *43rd annual report to Congress on the implementation of the Individuals with Disabilities Education Act, 2021*. Office of Special Education and Rehabilitative Services. https://sites.ed.gov/idea/2021-individuals-with-disabilities-education-act-annual-report-to-congress/

US Department of Education. (2010). *Twenty-five years of progress in educating children with disabilities through IDEA*. USDE. https://www2.ed.gov/print/policy/speced/leg/idea/history.html

Usman, M., Plágero, T., Frank, H., Calvo-Palanco, M., Gaillard, I., Garcia, K., & Zimmerman, S. (2021, September 20). Mycorrhizal symbiosis for better adaptation of trees to abiotic stress caused by climate change in temperate and boreal forests. *Frontiers in Forests and Global Change, 4*, 742392. Advance online publication. doi:10.3389/ffgc.2021.742392

Valle, J. W., & Connor, D. J. (2019). *Rethinking disability: a disability studies approach to inclusive practices*. Routledge. doi:10.4324/9781315111209

Vallely, K. S. A., & Gibson, P. (2018). Engaging students on their devices with Mentimeter. *Compass (Eltham), 11*(2). doi:10.21100/compass.v11i2.843

VanTassel-Baska, J. (2022). Assumptions about schooling: The myths of advanced learning. *Gifted Child Today*, *45*(4), 235–237. doi:10.1177/10762175221110939

VanTassel-Baska, J., & Brown, E. (2022). An analysis of stakeholder perceptions of gifted programs: A report card on gifted program performance. *Gifted Child Today*, *45*(3), 160–175. doi:10.1177/10762175221091859

Walgenbach, K. (2017). *Heterogenität—intersektionalität–diversity in der erziehungswissenschaft*. UTB. doi:10.36198/9783838586700

Wang, W., & Zhao, Z. J. (2014). (Forthcoming). Spatial decomposition of funding inequality in China's basic education: A four-level Theil Index analysis. *Public Finance and Management*, *14*(4), 416–436.

Watkins, L., Ledbetter-Cho, K., O'Reilly, M., Barnard-Brak, L., & Garcia-Grau, P. (2019). Interventions for students with autism in inclusive settings: A best-evidence synthesis and meta-analysis. *Psychological Bulletin*, *145*(5), 490–507. doi:10.1037/bul0000190 PMID:30869925

Watkins, L., O'Reilly, M., Ledbetter-Cho, K., Lang, R., Sigafoos, J., Kuhn, M., Lim, N., Gevarter, C., & Caldwell, N. (2017). A meta-analysis of school-based social interaction interventions for adolescents with autism spectrum disorder. *Review Journal of Autism and Developmental Disorders*, *4*(4), 277–293. doi:10.100740489-017-0113-5

Wehmeyer, M. (2020). The importance of self-determination to the quality of life of people with intellectual disability: A perspective. *International Journal of Environmental Research and Public Health*, *17*(19), 7121. doi:10.3390/ijerph17197121 PMID:33003321

Wei, R. C., Darling-Hammond, L., & Adamson, F. (2010). *Professional development in the United States: Trends and challenges*. National Staff Development Council.

Weischedel, W. (Ed.). (1983). *Immanuel Kants werke: Gesamtausgabe in zehn bänden* (Vol. 7). Wissenschaftliche Buchgesellschaft.

Werner, S., Gumpel, T. P., Koller, J., Wiesenthal, V., & Weintraub, N. (2021). Can self-efficacy mediate between knowledge of policy, school support and teacher attitudes towards inclusive education? *PLoS One*, *16*(9), e0257657. doi:10.1371/journal.pone.0257657 PMID:34543328

Westerville Public Library. (2023). *Teaching in a one-room schoolhouse: The early days of education in Westerville*. Westerville Public Library. https://westervillelibrary.org/education-teaching/

Westwood, P. (2001). Differentiation as a strategy for inclusive classroom practice: Some difficulties identified. *Australian Journal of Learning Disabilities*, *6*(1), 5–11. doi:10.1080/19404150109546651

Wilcox, G., Fernandez, C. C., & Kowbel, A. (2021). Using evidence-based practice and data-based decision making in inclusive education. *Education Sciences*, *11*(129), 129. doi:10.3390/educsci11030129

Wischer, M., & Spiering-Schomborg, N. (2020). Zooming: Ein werkzeug zum produktiv-verändernden umgang mit intersektionalität in religiösen lernprozessen. In T. Knauth, R. Möller, & A. Pithan (Eds.), *Inklusive religionspädagogik der vielfalt: Konzeptionelle grundlagen und didaktische konkretionen* (pp. 363–374). Waxmann.

Wolf, M. M. (1978). Social validity: The case for subjective measurement or how applied behavior analysis is finding its heart1. *Journal of Applied Behavior Analysis*, *1978*(11), 203–214. doi:10.1901/jaba.1978.11-203 PMID:16795590

Wolf, P. J. (2006). Sisyphean tasks. *Education Next*, *3*(1), 24–32. https://www.educationnext.org/sisypheantasks/

Wollrad, E. (2003). *Zur dekonstruktion von weißsein*. PolyLog. https://them.polylog.org/4/cwe-de.htm

Compilation of References

Wollrad, E. (2005). *Weißsein im widerspruch: Feministische perspektiven auf rassismus, kultur und religion*. Ulrike Helmer Verlag.

Wong, C., Odom, S. L., Hume, K. A., Cox, A. W., Fettig, A., Kucharczyk, S., Brock, M. E., Plavnick, J. B., Fleury, V. P., & Schultz, T. R. (2015). Evidence-based practices for children, youth, and young adults with autism spectrum disorder: A comprehensive review. *Journal of Autism and Developmental Disorders, 45*(7), 1951–1966. doi:10.100710803-014-2351-z PMID:25578338

Wong, H.-B., & Lee, K.-C. (2021). Implementation of a regular classroom curriculum for students with intellectual disabilities in a centralized special education class in elementary schools. *Taiwan Education Review Monthly, 10*(5), 147–152.

World Bank. (2020). *Pivoting to inclusion: Leveraging lessons from the COVID-19 crisis for learners with disabilities*. World Bank. https://policycommons.net/artifacts/1248231/pivoting-to-inclusion/1805965/

Woulfin, S. L., & Jones, B. (2021). Special development: The nature, content, and structure of special education teachers' professional learning opportunities. *Teaching and Teacher Education, 100*, 103277. doi:10.1016/j.tate.2021.103277

Wright, D. K., & Hinson, M. (2009). Examining how public relations practitioners actually are using social media. *The Public Relations Journal, 3*(3). https://www.prsa.org/

Wu, E. H. (2013). The path leading to differentiation: An interview with Carol Tomlinson. *Journal of Advanced Academics, 24*(2), 125–133. doi:10.1177/1932202X13483472

Xiang, Y., Dahlin, M., Cronin, J., Thacker, R., & Durant, S. (2011). Do highfliers maintain their altitude? Performance trends of top performers. Thomas B. Fordham Institute.

Xia, Y. (2006). Lixing kandai yuanben peixun de liyubi(理性看待园本培训的利与弊)[Dialectical view on the preschool-based training for teachers]. *Studies in Early Childhood Education, 2006*(7), 45–47.

Xu, C.-F., & Wang, M.-C. (2014). Exploring the teaching of social skills for children with intellectual disabilities. *Yunjia Journal of Special Education, 20*, 28–36.

Yang, Y., & Rao, N. (2021). Teacher professional development among preschool teachers in rural China. *Journal of Early Childhood Teacher Education, 42*(3), 219–244. doi:10.1080/10901027.2020.1726844

Zhang, H., & Zhao, G. (2019). Universal design for learning in China. In S. Groseth & E. Dalton (Eds.), *Universal access through inclusive instructional design* (pp. 68–75). Routledge. https://www.taylorfrancis.com/chapters/edit/10.4324/9780429435515-8/universal-design-learning-china-haoyue-zhang-george-zhao doi:10.4324/9780429435515-8

Zhang, L., Lai, F., Pang, X., Yi, H., & Rozelle, S. (2013). The impact of teacher training on teacher and student outcomes: Evidence from a randomised experiment in Beijing migrant schools. *Journal of Development Effectiveness, 5*(3), 339–358. doi:10.1080/19439342.2013.807862

Zhang, Y., Wang, D., Shi, L., Song, Y., & Jiang, Y. (2012). Nongcun youer jiaoshi peixun de xianzhuang, pingjia jiqi xuqiu (农村幼儿教师培训的现状, 评价及其需求) [On the rural preschool training]. *Studies in Preschool Education, 2012*(1), 33–38.

Zhou, T., Lu, Y., & Wang, B. (2009). The Relative Importance of Website Design Quality and Service Quality in Determining Consumers' Online Repurchase Behavior. *Information Systems Management, 26*(4), 327–337. doi:10.1080/10580530903245663

About the Contributors

Kiyoji Koreeda is a professor at Toyo University in Japan. His work focuses on educational support for persons with various disabilities in Special Needs Education Schools and Social Welfare Facilities. Dr. Koreeda completed his doctoral course at the United Graduate School of Education, Tokyo Gakugei University, Japan. After seventeen years as a special needs education school teacher in Kanagawa Prefecture, he worked as a researcher at the National Institute of Special Needs Education for six years. He then moved to Toyo University, where he currently trains social workers.

Masayoshi Tsuge is a professor of humanities at the University of Tsukuba, Japan. He belongs to the research field of intellectual disabilities, developmental disabilities, and behavioral disorders. He is also the leader of the Disability Science doctoral degree program. He received a Ph.D. from the University of Tsukuba. During this time, he is the head of the Department of Education for Mild Intellectual Disabilities at the National Institute of Special Education in Japan, a visiting researcher at the Mental Retardation Research Center at the University of California, Los Angeles, USA, and a specialist in mildly developmental disabilities at the Special Needs Education Division of the Ministry of Education in Japan. And then, a professor at the Graduate School of Special Needs Education at Hyogo University of Education in Japan, and director of Educational Information Department at the National Institute for Special Needs Education. And now he is working at the University of Tsukuba. During this time, he served as an editorial committee member, director, and president of academic societies in Japan and overseas. etc. He also served as a member of the Cabinet Office's Policy Committee for Persons with Disabilities and a member of the Ministry of Education's Central Council for Education. Currently, he is working on pedagogical and psychological research on people with intellectual disabilities, developmental disabilities, and behavioral disorders at the University of Tsukuba with doctoral students from Japan and abroad.

Shigeru Ikuta is now a Senior Scholar at Institute of Human Culture Studies, Otsuma Women's University, Japan. He is an education technologist, teacher educator in Science, and special educator with a focus on student learning and development on the basis of communication aids. He completed his graduate work and earned a doctorate in science at Tohoku University in Sendai, Japan. He had been working as a Professor of Computation Chemistry at Tokyo Metropolitan University for twenty-nine years. He moved to University of Tsukuba and has started collaborative works with schoolteachers, affiliated with the University. He has been conducting many school activities in cooperation with the schoolteachers all over the world for more than 17 years using original handmade teaching materials with dot codes, e-books with Media Overlays, and Augmented Reality in supporting the students' learn-

About the Contributors

ing both at the special needs and general schools. He is honored to be an Emeritus Professor of Otsuma Women's University and Tokyo Metropolitan University.

Elizabeth Dalton is senior consultant for Dalton Education Services International (DESI), and Director Emeritus of Development and Research for TechACCESS of RI, regional assistive technology center in Rhode Island, USA. Dr. Dalton has worked 45+ years in education, focused on developing curricula, teaching students at many levels, and preparing teachers in special education and assistive technology for K-12 and higher education settings. Most recently, Dr. Dalton focuses on Universal Design for Learning, which she studied in a post-doctoral fellowship with CAST and Boston College. She develops and delivers training and curricula in UDL principles and strategies, both online and f2f. A widely published author, her work includes a co-edited book, Universal Access Through Inclusive Instructional Design: International Perspectives on UDL (Routledge 2020). Dr. Dalton served as president of the Inclusive Learning Network of the International Society for Technology in Education (ISTE), editor for JIASE, Journal of the International Association for Special Education (IASE), and co-chair of the UDL Special Interest Group of the Society for Information Technology and Teacher Education (SITE). Currently she serves on the Steering Committee of the International Collaboratory for Leadership in Universally Designed Education (INCLUDE), as well as co-leader for Professional Development and Training

Linda Plantin Ewe is a Doctor of Philosophy in Special Education at the Department of Special Education, Faculty of Education at Kristianstad University in Sweden. Linda works as a teacher trainer within the Special Education Teacher Programs. She is interested in inclusive education, accessibility, equity, and social justice. Her research focuses primarily on students with neurodevelopmental disorders. More specifically, it focuses on the relationship between teachers and students with neurodevelopmental disorders. Dr. Ewe is a co-leader in the Professional Development and Training Team in the International Collaboratory for Leadership in Universally Designed Education (INCLUDE).

***

Mustapha Aabi is a Professor at the University of Ibn Zohr, Agadir - Morocco. He has taught courses in Education and Linguistics in the UK, Middle East and Morocco. He has 30 years of experience as a lecturer and over 15 years as an education expert. He has served in several education leadership positions. His research interests lie in the areas of humanities and education. He has collaborated actively with researchers from different academic backgrounds on issues at the educational, linguistic and cultural intersections.

Ashiya Abdool Satar is an academic in the Department of Communication Science at the University of South Africa (Unisa). She has diverse research interests that mirror her educational pursuits in the areas of organizational communication, media studies, inclusive education, and Open Distance and e-Learning (ODeL) in the Higher Education sector. Ashiya is currently involved in projects focusing on active youth citizenship, social justice, media identity and representation, social media research, public sector communication, and inclusive education, with a particular focus on the universal design of learning (UDL) approach. She is currently part of the steering committees for the International Collaboratory for Leadership in Universally Designed Education (INCLUDE) and the International Conference on Education Quality (ICEQ).

About the Contributors

Lizelle Apollis is an Inclusivity & Access Support Officer at the Disability Unit at Stellenbosch University. She provides and facilitates wrap around support to students with disabilities. Her background is in occupational therapy. She has completed a Master's degree in Occupational Therapy and is currently working towards a PhD in the field of disability inclusion. Her work is systemic of nature, where it entails working with students, their faculties, their parents and specialists. She does both group and individual work on a preventative and curative level.

Abdul Basit is working in field of Special Education since twenty Years. He has worked in both public and private institutes of Inclusive Education and Special Education during his career. He is teaching in University of Education, Department of Special Education as visiting faculty. He has done double masters in Special Education (Hearing Impairment and Visual Impairment). He did MS/M.Phil. in Inclusive Education. He received his doctoral degree from Institute of Special Education, University of the Punjab, Lahore recently. His work focused on the Education and Development of Children with Cerebral Palsy. He did various diplomas and certificates (Audiology, Low Vision, Braille. Management of Autism, Management of Down Syndrome, Assessment and Interventions for mentally Challenge, Manual Research etc.) during his career. His seventeen research articles has published in national and International renowned journals. He presented his researches in international and national conferences.

Jessica Buhne is an Inclusion and Disability Services Officer at the University of Sydney and works with students to facilitate the implementation of reasonable adjustments and supports to meet their academic potential. Jessica has a background in Social Sciences, Counselling, and Business (Legal Services). For over 10 years Jessica has worked in the disability sector in the areas of education, employment and advocacy, including working with and supporting young people to navigate post-school pathways. Jessica has worked on an individual and systemic level to remove barriers to participation and inclusion of people with disability through advocacy and capacity building initiatives.

Therese M. Cumming is Professor of Special Education in the School of Education, the Academic Lead Education for the UNSW Disability Innovation Institute, and a Scientia Education Fellow at the University of New South Wales (UNSW), Sydney, Australia. Her research interests are centred around special education, focused on the following areas: students with emotional and behavioural disorders, social skills training, positive behavioural interventions, the use of technology in the classroom, and lifespan transitions for people with disabilities. Her research aims to improve the experiences of students with disabilities by working with schools to reduce the research-to-practice gap through the implementation of evidence-based practices in special and inclusive education. Prior to her university teaching and research work, Dr Cumming has many years' experience as a special educator and behaviour mentor in the United States.

David Evans is Professor of Special and Inclusive Education in the Sydney School of Education and Social Work at the University of Sydney. He teaches and researches in the area of inclusive curriculum and pedagogies. He is a community representative on the Students with Disabilities Advisory Committee, for the Australian Curriculum, Assessment, and Reporting Authority. Dr Evans is Adjunct Professor at Universiti Pendidikan Sultan Idris, Malaysia.

About the Contributors

Jennifer L. Fleming, EdD, is a veteran special education teacher and educational facilitator who teaches English (grades 8–12) at the Wise County Regional Learning Academy, an alternative education school, in Wise, Virginia, USA. She received her doctorate in Educational Leadership and Policy Studies from Virginia Tech. A public educator for two decades, she has worked with students with disabilities and taught English. Her research and pedagogical interests in public schools are collaboration and inclusive practices for students with disabilities.

Kimberely Fletcher Nettleton earned an Ed. D in Curriculum and Instruction, with an emphasis on Instructional Design and Technology, from the University of Kentucky. She holds a Masters in elementary education from Georgetown College, and another MA School Administration. She is currently an Associate Professor at Morehead State University. In addition to teaching at Morehead State, she is the Director of University Assessment. As both a former classroom teacher and principal, she is a firm believer in the healing power of chocolate.

Margaret Flood is an Assistant Professor in Inclusive Education and the MAP Academic Advisor for the Education Department. Her experience in inclusive and special education includes teaching, teacher professional learning design and delivery, policy development and curriculum design. Before joining Maynooth University in 2022, Margaret was the Education Officer with responsibility for Inclusive Education and Diversity at the National Council for Curriculum and Assessment (NCCA). She led and collaborated on inclusive curriculum review and design projects across primary and post-primary. Margaret also worked in the teacher professional development service, Junior Cycle for Teachers (JCT) where she designed and delivered continuous professional development training on specific curriculum programmes for students with intellectual disabilities, inclusive practices in the mainstream classroom, and Universal Design for Learning (UDL). As a Fulbright Scholar, in 2021 Margaret worked with Lynch School of Education and Humanities at Boston College and CAST to explore equity, diversity, inclusion, and social justice through the lens of UDL.

Oressa Power is Education Technology Coordinator at William James College, Office of Educational Development and Innovation in Massachusetts, USA. She earned her M.Ed. in Global Perspectives: Teaching, Curriculum, and Learning Environments at Boston College. Her research interests are in Universal Design for Learning (UDL), Internationalization of the Curriculum (IoC), culturally responsive learning design, and digital media applications in education.

Chen Han is Lecturer of Special Education in the Department of Special Education, School of Education, Central China Normal University, Wuhan, China. She graduated with her PhD from the University of New South Wales (UNSW), Sydney, Australia. Chen's field of study is in Special Education. Her research interests include positive behaviour support, teachers' beliefs and practices, and social skill training for students with autism spectrum disorder (ASD). Her research aims to support the inclusion of students with disabilities by collaborating with schools to reduce the gaps between research and practice and improve teachers' quality in implementing evidence-based practices in special and inclusive education.

Andrea Harkins-Brown is the Assistant Deputy Director of the IDEALS Institute and an Assistant Research Scientist in the School of Education at Johns Hopkins University. Prior to joining Johns Hopkins University, Dr. Harkins-Brown was the Graduate Program Director and Assistant Professor in Special

329

About the Contributors

Education at Towson University. She has served as a special educator and central office administrator, providing technical assistance in special education at the district-wide level. Dr. Harkins-Brown's research focuses on effective implementation of special education policies and procedures, school-based implementation of evidence-based practices, effective technology integration, online learning, and innovative teaching practices to support diverse populations of learners. Dr. Harkins-Brown holds a B.S. in Special Education from Towson University, an M.Ed. in Special Education from Johns Hopkins University, a post-baccalaureate certificate in Educational Administration from Goucher College, and an Ed.D. in Instructional Technology from Towson University.

Richard Jackson is internationally recognized as a pioneer in the nascent field of Universal Design for Learning (UDL). He first brought the UDL framework to Boston College in 1999 through a partnership with CAST and the Harvard Children's Initiative to form the National Center for Accessing the General Curriculum. This federally funded Center's role was to provide the nation with guidance on how best to include students with disabilities in a standards-based, public education. Jackson won a five-year leadership grant from the US Department of Education to train eight postdoctoral "UDL Fellows" whose efforts continue to advance this new field in improving results for students with disabilities. UDL's twenty-year presence at Boston College under Jackson's leadership has been instrumental in the design of accessible blended learning courses and in the development of inclusive instructional practices campus-wide.

Michael Kessinger is currently an associate professor of education leadership at Morehead State University (KY), Volgenau College of Education, Foundational and Graduate Studies in Education Department. He serves as program leader for the K-12 Instructional Leadership and P-12 Administrative Leadership Doctor of Education program. His research, publications, and presentations have included areas in professional development, education technology, gifted education, and school leadership. Dr. Kessinger's background includes 38 years in public education and has served as secondary math and computer science teacher, secondary assistant principal, gifted education coordinator, finance director, chief information officer, and assistant superintendent. He received his doctorate (EdD) from the University of Kentucky, Education Specialist (EdS) and Master of Education from Morehead State University, and Bachelor of Science from the University of Wisconsin-Eau Claire with a teaching emphasis in mathematics and psychology.

Aashna Khurana is a Ph.D. student in the Lynch School of Education and Human Development at Boston College. She is also a professional special educator and has worked as an Assessment Associate at ASER Centre, Pratham Education Foundation. She has worked on development of Assessment for All (AfA) Tool, focused on including children with special needs in large scale assessments in India, and ASER 2019 Early Years tool to assess numeracy, literacy, cognitive and socio-emotional skills of children aged 4-8 years. She has understanding of large-scale surveys, and in design, development, translation of assessment tools in various regional languages. She has also developed frameworks for assessments, translations and adaptations, textbooks analysis and adapted curriculum to address the needs of children with disabilities. Currently, she is one of the lead researchers on the Boston Public Schools Inclusion Initiative that aims to reform inclusive education service delivery system. Her research interests lie in the areas of inclusive education, Universal Design for Learning (UDL), inclusive assessments and leadership for school improvement.

About the Contributors

Dagmar Kminiak is a management professional with a Psychology and Rehabilitation Counselling background. Dagmar is currently employed as the Manager of Inclusion and Disability Services at the University of Sydney and has extensive experience in implementing diversity and inclusion initiatives, programs and policies. Adept at the design and implementation of training and support programs, relationship building, professional networking, team mentoring, and staff coaching for the benefit of both individuals and organisations. Success built upon the ability to rapidly identify strengths, opportunities, and priorities.

Britta Konz received her diploma in protestant theology as well as her doctors's degree at Ruprecht Karls University in Heidelberg/Germany and her Master of Education in art education and religious education. She is currently a full professor of religious education at Johannes Gutenberg-University in Mainz/Germany. She writes and presents widely on issues of interreligious learning, flight, migration and religion, heterogeneity-sensitive learning with art, postcolonial theology.

Emma Leifler, Med Dr. from the the Department of Women's and Children's Health, Karolinska Institutet (KI), teacher educator at the University of Gothenburg at the Department of Pedagogical, Curricular and Professional Studies. Her research area is inclusive education for students with neurodevelopmental conditions. She has worked as a special needs teacher and with school projects regarding inclusive education. In her current position, lecturer in special education, she investigates how schools can develop and improve educational inclusion.

Lesia Lennex is a Professor of Education at Morehead State University in the Department of Middle Grades and Secondary Education. She teaches P-12 curriculum, instruction, and technology. Research areas include P16 3D technologies, technology issues and integration for P16 schools, biology and social studies curriculum, and ethnobotany. Dr. Lennex has been quite active in Faculty Senate, having twice been elected as Chair and is currently the President of MSU's American Association of University Professors (AAUP). Dr. Lennex is an awardee of MSU's Distinguished Researcher, an Adron Doran Fellow, and is professionally committed to scholarly productions and leadership with the Society for Information Technology and Teacher Education (SITE). She has served as Chair of the special interest groups (SIG) Social Studies Education, Science Education, and Information Technology Education. Dr. Lennex took her Doctorate in Curriculum and Instruction, Social Studies education, with supporting areas in botany and American history from the University of Tennessee, Knoxville. She also holds a BA in Anthropology (zooarchaeology) and MS in Curriculum and Instruction, Social Studies education.

Cathy Little is Senior Lecturer in Special Education, and Chair of Initial Teacher Education in the Sydney School of Education and Social Work at the University of Sydney. Her teaching and research is in the area of students diagnosed with ASD, and preparedness of pre-service teacher educators to address the diversity of student needs in the classroom.

Marcia Lyner-Cleophas initiated and manages the Disability Unit at Stellenbosch University (SU) since 2007. Disability inclusion from a policy, practice, review and renewal perspective forms a core part of her work. She has a vested interest in contributing to the successful academic lives of students at SU by making an impact at multi-sectoral levels. She is involved in training and the mentoring of interns. Dr Marcia has published articles and book chapters on disabilityinclusion, universal design and universal

About the Contributors

design for learning, supervised and examined master's and Doctoral theses, with the main theme being disability inclusion in the post-school education phase. She is a HERS and Erasmus Mundus alumni and has presented several papers internationally and nationally. Currently, she is a member of the Higher and Further Education Disability Services Association (HEDSA) in South Africa, the African Network of Evidence to Action in Disability (AfriNEAD) based at Stellenbosch University and is on several other management committees.

Mette Molbæk is associate professor and PhD at the teacher training program, VIA University College, Denmark. Mette Molbæk is the program leader for the research program Childrens wellbeing in and across day care, school and home, where she, together with colleagues from various research fields, research in children's wellbeing with the aim of creating more nuanced understandings and practices in relation to children's wellbeing. Mette Molbæk's research focus primarily on inclusion and exclusion processes in schools, collaboration between professionals and the development of a more inclusive school. Most recently, and together with Lotte Hedegaard-Sørensen, she has published a book on 'Universal Design for Learning' in Denmark.

Isobelle Montague is an Inclusion and Disability Services Officer at the University of Sydney and works with students to facilitate the implementation of reasonable adjustments and supports to meet their academic potential. Isobelle has a Bachelor of Arts and Bachelor of Laws from the University of Wollongong. Isobelle has been working in the disability sector for the last 6 years. Various roles in the sector have included being a disability support worker to working with participants of the National Disability Insurance Scheme to develop their support packages.

Visal Moosa holds a PhD in Education from Universiti Brunei Darussalam. He completed his Master's degree in educational management and leadership from Universiti Malaya and Bachelors' degree in teaching from Maldives College of Higher Education. Beginning his professional career as a secondary Mathematics teacher in 2002, he has served in various positions in the education sector including leading teacher, principal and educational development officer at the Ministry of Education. Currently he is a senior lecturer at Islamic University of Maldives. Dr. Visal is a consultant in quantitative data analysis. He is also an active figure in research and publication and has contributed to a number of WOS/SCOPUS indexed journal articles.

Carol A. Mullen, PhD, is a tenured Professor of Educational Leadership and Policy Studies at Virginia Tech, Blacksburg, Virginia, USA. Dr. Mullen is a J. William Fulbright Senior Scholar alumnus and former editor of Mentoring & Tutoring. A pedagogical researcher in educational leadership, teacher development, and mentoring, she applies policy, justice, and equity lenses within international and national contexts. She has authored or edited 28 academic books, including the Handbook of Social Justice Interventions in Education (2021, edited, Springer) and The Risky Business of Education Policy (2022, coedited, Routledge). Her publishing record includes over 240 book chapters and articles in high-impact journals. The University of Toronto honored her with the 2020 Excellence Award, an OISE Leaders and Legends Award. Other prestigious accolades include the 2022 Master Professor Award and the 2016 Jay D. Scribner Mentoring Award from the University Council for Educational Administration (UCEA). Currently, she is President of the UCEA and Immediate Past-President of the Society of Professors of Education. Her PhD is from the University of Toronto, Canada.

About the Contributors

Luigia Nicholas is the marketing and training coordinator at the Disability Unit in the Centre for Student Counselling and Development at Stellenbosch University in the Western Cape, South Africa. She completed her Postgraduate Diploma in Disability and Rehabilitation studies in 2022 and her Bachelors of Commerce degree in Business Management at Stellenbosch University (SU) in 2019. She is a disability and inclusion advocate who is passionate about creating awareness on disability related issues. She is a Steering Group Member at the International Collaboratory for Leadership in Universally Designed Education as well as a management committee member of Changeability, an organisation that assist people with disabilities in the community. Luigia was the South African Representative for the Global Disability Youth Network and an advisory group member for the Leonard Cheshire, United Nations Girls Education Initiative and World Bank Joint Report on Gender, Disability and Education. She was a National Executive Committee member and the Chairperson of the Committee for the Rights of Persons with Disabilities in the South African Union of Students in 2022 and the previous Special Needs Manager on the Student Representatives Council for 2019 until 2021 at SU.

Elizabete Cristina Costa-Renders is Brazilian. She is trained in education and works as a university professor since 2001. She has a PhD in education from the State University of Campinas / UNICAMP (2012). Since 2016, she is a Professor at the [Post]Graduate Program in Education at the University of São Caetano do Sul (São Paulo, Brazil). She is the leader of the group of studies - ACESSI (school accessibility and inclusive society). In her research, she highlights the following topics: inclusive education, universal design for learning, teachers training and emerging epistemologies. Hear research is accessible at:

Shuhudha Rizwan works as a Senior Curriculum Development Analyst at the School of Research and Development at the National Institute of Education. She has 26 years of experience in the education sector, starting as a teacher. Since 2007, she has been an education development professional and currently plays a key role in conducting policy research related to the development of the education sector in the Maldives. She is also involved in developing national-level policies on curriculum implementation and teacher professional development. Ms. Shuhudha has led the development of the Maldives National Professional Standards for Teachers, the National Professional Development Framework for Teachers, and the School-Based Professional Development Policy.

Helena Roos is a distinguished scholar and educator in the field of inclusive mathematics education. Her research focuses on special educational needs in mathematics, inclusion, and equity in mathematics education. The notions participation, a school for all, and early interventions are central in her research. Helena's contributions to the field of mathematics education extend beyond the mathematics classroom. She has published numerous scholarly articles in prestigious journals, shedding light on the latest research and advancements in the field. Currently, she holds a faculty position at Malmö university, where she teaches and conducts groundbreaking research.

Adhila Rushdhee works at the Department of Inclusive Education / Ministry of Education as a Senior Inclusive Education Analyst. She has 20 years of experience in the education sector and worked as a primary teacher, middle school teacher, qualified teacher, teacher educator, and education development officer coordinator. In 2010 – 2018 she worked in the field of teacher professional development at NIE and joined DoIE in 2018. She presented papers in the 2nd, 4th, 5th and 6th International Teachers'

About the Contributors

Conference organised by the National Institute of Education and completed various short term training programmes related to teacher professional development. She has completed her thesis on 'In-service teachers' perceptions on implementing Universal Design for Learning, Co-Teaching Model and Inclusive Education in the Maldives'.

Rosmalily Binti Salleh is Principal Assistant Director of, the Curriculum Development Division, Ministry of Education Malaysia. She was an educator with almost 20 years of teaching experience, she taught the primary and secondary levels, then focused on Special Educational Needs (SEN), before coming to MOE. A National Trainer for the LINUS programme, and was given the recognition of Excellence Teacher of Special Education accolade in 2011. Dr Rosmalily received her doctorate from the University of Southampton, with a focus on continuous professional development and inclusive education. Her research interest includes inclusive education, inclusive curriculum, educational planning and teachers' continuous professional development.

Claudia Saunderson has a PhD in Educational Psychology from Stellenbosch University (SU). She holds multiple portfolios at SU. At the Faculty of Education, SU, she lectures on a part-time basis. Additionally, she works in the Disability Unit as a Diversity, Inclusion and Student Success Coach where she works integrally with students who need mentoring and coaching. Her final post is one of the psychometrist at the Centre for Student Counselling and Development. Her research focus areas are on approaches and perspectives that can inform the reduction of social exclusion and inequality. She works both at a group and individual level with students.

Anne Schröter received her Master of Education in Special Education and her Master of Arts in educational sciences at University of Oldenburg/Germany. Later she receives her doctor's degree in rehabilitation sciences at TU Dortmund University/Germany. She is currently research assistant at Leibniz University Hannover/Germany. She works on issues of social difference in classrooms, measuring attitudes towards disability, and the intersection of disability and religion.

Mariyam Shareefa is an Assistant Professor at the Centre for Research and Publication of the Islamic University of Maldives. She has obtained PhD in Education, Master of Education (by Research) and Bachelor of Teaching English as a Second Language. Beginning her career as a primary teacher in 1995, she has served at different positions in the education sector. Dr. Mariyam Shareefa has made contributions to several publications in WOS/SCOPUS journal articles. Her most frequent publication areas are on differentiated instruction, inclusive education, and multi-grade teaching.

Andy Smidt is a Speech Pathology Lecturer in the faculty of medicine and health at the University of Sydney. She is also the faculty disability liaison officer supporting implementations of academic plans containing reasonable adjustments for students with disability in the faculty.

Tonnette Stanford is an Education Designer / Manager at the University of Sydney and a writer/ director. Her films have won numerous awards and have screened at over 200 festivals internationally and nationally, including Oscar recognised festivals.

About the Contributors

Geraldine Townend is a published academic with over a decade of experience in the field of gifted education, having expertise in the area of twice exceptionality, in the School of Education at the University of New South Wales (UNSW), Sydney, Australia. Her research interests focus on supporting gifted and twice-exceptional students to aspire to their potential in education, which includes the development of positive academic self-concept. Geraldine's research findings indicate that there are several sociological and psychological influences on academic self-concept, including a social comparison theory, and she is particularly interested in the interaction between teachers and their students. She has also focused on outcomes for pre- and post-graduate teachers' understandings of diversity in education, including inclusive classroom practices and applications of the National Curriculum. Her university teaching was recognised with the award of Teaching Excellence Commendation.

Index

A

Academic Plan 43, 58

Acceleration 265, 270-271, 276-280, 282-283

Access to mathematics education 169, 180

Accessibility 2, 5, 7, 9, 11-12, 14, 19, 24, 42, 47, 56, 82, 86, 97, 122, 129, 160, 164, 174, 176, 201, 227-228, 232, 235, 237, 240

Accessible Curriculum 18, 57, 131, 133, 142, 227, 233-234, 240

Assessment 4, 9, 12, 16, 32, 43, 47, 52-53, 55, 57, 63, 69, 76, 80-83, 85-93, 96-97, 108, 116, 121, 130, 135-137, 142, 156, 159, 161, 169, 174, 176, 178, 202-203, 211-214, 221, 249, 253, 260-261, 269-270, 280, 283

Attitudes 9, 23, 36, 56, 64, 68, 73, 75, 79, 82, 86, 92, 101-103, 115-116, 122-123, 125, 127, 129, 132, 138, 140-142, 144, 156-157, 164, 208, 223, 243, 254, 256-257, 282

Australia 39-42, 57-58, 131, 133-135, 138, 140-144, 197-198, 241, 255

Autism Spectrum Disorder (ASD) 62, 241-242, 258

B

Barriers 2-5, 8, 12-13, 19-20, 25-26, 28, 34-35, 39, 41, 45-47, 63-64, 70, 72, 79, 81-82, 85-87, 91-92, 94, 100-101, 109-110, 114, 131-132, 134, 137-141, 150-151, 156, 158, 161, 163, 170, 177, 190-191, 195, 197-198, 201, 208, 212-214, 217, 219, 224, 233, 235-236, 240

BASICS strategy 152, 165

Beliefs 73, 83, 133, 135-136, 162, 191, 198, 208, 228, 241-242, 246-249, 251, 254-255, 277

C

CAST 2, 4-5, 15-17, 19, 22, 26-27, 36-37, 40, 45-47, 56, 89, 94-95, 138, 143, 191, 198, 218, 221, 228-230, 234-236, 238-239

Challenges 2, 4, 10, 14-15, 18, 23, 25, 35, 39, 42, 60, 62, 71-73, 84-85, 87-88, 90, 98, 100-102, 105, 109-112, 114, 116-117, 122, 126, 129, 132, 138-139, 141-142, 154, 156, 171, 177, 193, 195, 205, 211, 226-230, 234-235, 237-238, 243-244, 249, 258, 261, 266, 268, 270, 272, 279

Challenging Behaviours 242-243, 247-248, 255, 258

Collaboration 2, 5, 8, 12-13, 18, 24, 29, 31-36, 38, 46, 52, 64-65, 67, 71, 74, 79, 82-83, 87, 92, 110-111, 113, 122, 126-127, 147, 151, 153-154, 158, 161-164, 173, 175-176, 179, 204-205, 216, 228, 247, 263, 267, 273, 276

Collaboratory 1-6, 9-14, 17, 19

Co-teaching 32, 35, 111, 134, 147-165, 175, 252

Course Coordinator 50, 52-53, 58

Critical Whiteness 182-184, 186-189, 191-195

Cycle of Planning 45, 58

D

Deaf student teachers 80-81, 83, 89-91, 96

Democratic Education 226, 228, 240

Denmark 21-23, 35-36

Department of Basic Education 84-85, 96

Differentiated Instruction 19, 111, 116, 147, 150-151, 153, 164-165

Diversity 3, 9, 14, 19, 21, 24, 28-29, 34, 38, 41, 55, 59-66, 69, 73-74, 79-82, 86, 92-93, 97, 99-100, 102, 126, 133, 143-144, 167-168, 171, 178-180, 182-183, 189-191, 195, 213, 219, 230, 232, 282

Duet and Map and Navigate 165

E

Education for Persons with Special Education Needs Act (EPSEN) 223

Elective course 50, 58

Equity 4, 9, 13, 18-19, 36, 41, 55, 57, 59, 62, 64, 77,

Index

80, 82, 102-103, 114, 143, 166-167, 169-172,
174-180, 197, 213, 217, 227, 231-232, 235, 245,
253, 255, 279, 282
Evidence-based Practices (EBPs) 242, 258
Evidence-based Strategies 66-67, 147-148, 150-152,
154-155, 158, 161
Evolution 2, 15, 98, 100, 106-107, 117, 143

F

Flexible learning environments 21, 25, 34, 38
Foundation Phase 81, 87, 96
Free Appropriate Public Education (FAPE) 223

G

Gifted Education 260-261, 263-264, 266-267, 269,
276, 278-279, 281-283

H

Higher Education 1-3, 9, 11-13, 15-18, 40-41, 55-57,
81-87, 90-96, 101, 109, 112, 116, 178, 182-184,
186, 189, 191, 195, 228, 239, 269, 271-272

I

Implementation 2, 4, 9, 11, 13, 19, 22, 29, 33-34, 36-
37, 40-46, 54, 56-57, 59, 63, 67, 70, 72, 77, 82,
85, 91, 94, 98, 100-101, 103-105, 108-113, 117,
120, 123-125, 127-130, 136-137, 147-148, 152,
156, 158-159, 161, 166, 168, 177, 189, 197-201,
205, 211, 215-217, 220-221, 223, 234, 243, 247,
255-257, 266, 273, 281
Implementing Inclusion Activities in Class-Field
Courses 124, 129
In(ex)clusion 167, 180
Inclusion 1-6, 8-9, 11, 13-16, 18-19, 21-25, 29, 31, 34-
38, 42-44, 54-56, 58-68, 72-78, 80, 82-85, 91-95,
97-99, 101-103, 106, 108-114, 116-117, 119-122,
124-125, 127-129, 132-133, 138, 142-145, 147-
150, 156-158, 160-180, 190-191, 197-198, 205,
207-208, 210-211, 213, 216-218, 220-222, 226-
228, 231-232, 234-235, 242, 254-257, 260-261,
266, 269-271, 276-277, 282-283
Inclusion and Disability Services (IDS) 42, 58
Inclusive and Equitable Mathematics Education 167,
174, 177, 180-181
Inclusive Education 1-3, 5, 10-19, 21-23, 31-32, 36-
37, 42, 56-57, 59, 61-65, 72-78, 81-82, 85, 87,
91-95, 98-128, 131-134, 137-144, 157-158, 161-

164, 166, 170, 177-178, 182-183, 196-198, 201,
206-207, 210-211, 213, 215-224, 226-238, 240,
242-243, 248, 250, 253-255, 257, 261
Inclusive Landscapes of Investigation 168, 171, 181
inclusive pedagogy 59, 63, 72, 74-75, 108-112, 115, 217
Inclusive Practice 21, 25, 56, 75-76, 116, 141
Inclusive setting 150, 165
Inclusive Special Education 61, 76, 78, 115, 228
Inclusive Teaching 22, 24, 29, 37, 41, 54, 56-57, 68, 108,
178, 182, 184, 189-192, 195, 226-227, 238, 240
Inclusive Teaching in Higher Education 182, 184,
189, 191, 195
Incremental 39, 45-46
Individualized Education Plan (IEP) 129, 223
Individualized Education Program (IEP) 223
Individuals with Disabilities Education Act 148, 163,
196, 199-200, 220, 223, 225, 265
Individuals with Disabilities Education Act (IDEA)
148, 196, 223, 265
Institution-Specific Levels 39
Instructional Strategies 113, 147, 149, 155, 159, 260,
265, 277, 283
Interaction and Joint Learning by Subjects 120, 125, 129
Interventions 59-66, 71-74, 78-79, 143, 163, 201, 205,
212, 215, 243, 249, 252-255
IRL vs Digital Training 78

K

K–12 Classroom 147
Key Milestones 98, 100, 117

L

Leadership 1-2, 4-6, 8, 11, 41, 57, 113, 138, 147-148,
150-151, 156, 158, 161, 164, 221, 245, 264, 267,
274, 282-283
Learner Voice 1, 8-9, 11-13, 19
Learning Environment 3, 22, 24-26, 28, 45, 58-61, 63,
65-69, 72-74, 76, 78-79, 89, 91, 119, 138-140,
147, 151-152, 155, 161, 190, 224, 276
Learning Management System (LMS) 47, 58
Least restrictive environment 121, 148, 165, 199, 205-
206, 220, 223, 265
Least Restrictive Environment (LRE) 121, 148, 199,
223, 265
Lesson Study 64, 66, 76-77, 79
Low-functioning Autism Spectrum Disorder 258

M

Malaysia 131, 134-136, 140-141
mathematics education 166-181
Mental barrier-free 122, 129
milestones 98-100, 104, 106, 110-111, 117, 213, 220

N

National Council for Special Education (NCSE) 224
National Curriculum Guidelines 126, 130
National Teacher Training Plan Program (NTTP) 245, 258
Naturalistic Settings 60, 62, 71, 79
Needs 1-2, 4, 7-9, 13-14, 16-20, 23-26, 28-29, 31, 35-36, 38, 40-43, 46, 58-64, 67, 72-74, 76-77, 81-88, 91-92, 95, 100-103, 106, 108-110, 113-130, 132-135, 138-140, 142, 144, 148-152, 154-155, 157-160, 162, 164-168, 170, 176-178, 180-181, 196-198, 200-202, 207-215, 217, 219, 221-224, 227, 230, 233-234, 236, 238, 241, 243-251, 253-254, 257, 260-261, 263-271, 273, 276-278, 280, 282-283
Neurodevelopmental Conditions 59-60, 62, 76, 79

P

Pakistan 131, 133-134, 137-144
Parallel Curriculum 260, 266, 272-273, 275-277, 280-281, 283
participation 3, 5-6, 20, 22-23, 25, 28-30, 32, 34-35, 42, 57, 59-60, 62-63, 71, 74-76, 79, 86, 120, 126, 129, 131, 137-139, 141-142, 166-170, 172-173, 175, 177, 181-183, 189, 199, 209-210, 212-214, 216-217, 224, 230, 237, 240, 242, 251, 258
Pedagogy of Seasons 226, 228, 230, 235-237, 239-240
Policy 2, 8, 13, 17, 19, 21-23, 36-38, 41-42, 59, 61, 63-64, 72-73, 78, 80-83, 85, 91-93, 95-96, 98-105, 107-115, 121, 132-133, 136-137, 141, 149, 160, 165, 178, 196-199, 210, 217, 221, 223, 227, 235, 242, 253-255, 257, 278-279, 281
Post school education and training (PSET) 96
Postcolonialismus 195
Problem Based Learning 260, 275, 283
Professional Development 1, 3, 6-7, 10-19, 54, 59, 63-66, 68-69, 72-74, 77-79, 85, 93, 102, 113, 115, 128, 156, 226-228, 232-233, 235, 240-241, 243-259
Professional learning communities 6, 32, 38
Professional related organization personnel 127, 130

R

Racism 5, 183, 185-190, 192, 194-195
RCTs, Random Controlled Trials 79
recommendations 52, 57, 65, 73-74, 91, 98, 100, 103, 112, 114, 126, 147, 151, 153, 159, 162, 189, 210, 216, 246-247, 264, 276

S

School Culture 28, 31, 114
School development 21, 37-38, 170-171
Self-Assessment 39, 45, 49, 53, 159
Self-efficacy 60, 65-66, 68, 73-75, 131, 138, 141-142, 144, 208, 223, 243, 252-253
Social Media 3, 5-8, 17-20
Social Skills Group Training 60, 65, 69-72, 74-76, 79
Social-Emotional Needs 283
South African Sign Language (SASL) 80-81, 96
Special Didactics 63, 74, 79
Special Education 2, 4, 16, 18, 23, 36, 57, 59-61, 65, 73-74, 76-78, 101-102, 106, 110-112, 115, 119-131, 135, 137, 148-150, 153-154, 156-158, 160-165, 172-175, 196, 198, 200-202, 205, 207, 210-211, 216-224, 227-229, 235-236, 241-246, 248-256, 258, 265
Special education advocacy 120, 123, 126-127, 129-130
Special education advocacy activities 120, 123, 126-127, 129-130
Special education teachers 23, 112, 122, 128, 130, 135, 147, 158, 162, 164, 172, 175, 241-251, 256, 258
Specially Designed Instruction 151, 158, 201-202, 224
Stages-of-Change Model 39, 44
Stellenbosch University 1, 80-81, 84, 94-97
Student success 56, 80, 96, 150
student voice 8-9, 11, 15, 17, 142
Students in special educational needs in mathematics 167, 181
Students with disabilities 4, 40-41, 56, 60-62, 65, 80-82, 85-86, 91-97, 99, 102, 111-112, 116, 120-123, 126, 128, 130-141, 143, 147-148, 163-164, 196-197, 208-209, 221, 227, 231, 235, 242, 246, 250, 254, 261, 265, 268
Support Services for Students with Disabilities Measures 123, 130

T

Taiwan 119-124, 126-130
Teacher Development 98, 104, 118, 127, 164, 231, 253
Teacher Education 3, 17, 23, 71, 76-77, 94, 141-142,

Index

163-164, 179, 182-183, 186, 228, 245, 252-258

Teacher Professional Development 16-17, 226, 228, 235, 240-241, 246, 253, 256, 258

Teaching 8, 16, 18, 21, 23-43, 46-50, 54-57, 60, 63-64, 66, 68, 73, 75, 77, 79-83, 85-94, 97, 108-110, 112-113, 122-125, 129-130, 133-134, 139-140, 142-144, 147-149, 151-152, 154, 156-161, 163-165, 167, 169, 171-180, 182, 184, 186, 189-195, 211-214, 219-223, 226-238, 240-258, 262, 264, 268-269, 276-278, 281-282

Tertiary 39-42, 57-58, 85, 94, 101, 245

The Special Education Law 120-121, 130

U

UDL 2-5, 7, 9, 11, 13, 16, 20, 35-37, 39-47, 49-56, 80-83, 86-95, 97, 131, 144, 151, 197-199, 201-204, 207, 211-214, 216-218, 221, 224, 226-229, 231-236, 238-239

UNESCO Salamanca Statement 166, 181, 222

United States 4, 16, 94, 121, 133, 147-148, 150, 161-162, 186-187, 196-197, 199-202, 215-217, 220, 223, 248, 258, 260, 262, 264, 267-269, 271, 274-276, 279

Universal Access (UA) 97

Universal Design 2-5, 10-12, 14-29, 31-37, 40-41, 43-44, 47, 55-58, 79-82, 86-87, 89, 91, 93-97, 111, 116, 121, 131, 134, 138-145, 150-151, 165, 182, 191, 195-196, 198, 200-201, 218-222, 224, 226-228, 232-233, 238-240, 254

Universal Design for Learning 2-4, 11, 14-29, 31-37, 40-41, 43-44, 47, 55-58, 79-82, 86-87, 89, 91, 93-97, 111, 116, 131, 134, 138-145, 150-151, 165, 182, 191, 195-196, 198, 200-201, 218-222, 224, 226-228, 232-233, 239-240, 254

Universal Design for Learning (UDL) 2-3, 20, 44, 81, 97, 151, 196, 224, 227

W

Way Forward 98, 100, 112, 118

Western China 244-246, 248-251, 253, 255, 258-259

Recommended Reference Books

IGI Global's reference books are available in three unique pricing formats:
Print Only, E-Book Only, or Print + E-Book.

Order direct through IGI Global's Online Bookstore at
www.igi-global.com or through your preferred provider.

Online Distance Learning Course Design and Multimedia in E-Learning

ISBN: 9781799897064
EISBN: 9781799897088
© 2022; 302 pp.
List Price: US$ 215

Global and Transformative Approaches Toward Linguistic Diversity

ISBN: 9781799889854
EISBN: 9781799889878
© 2022; 383 pp.
List Price: US$ 215

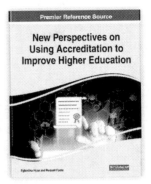

New Perspectives on Using Accreditation to Improve Higher Education

ISBN: 9781668451953
EISBN: 9781668451960
© 2022; 300 pp.
List Price: US$ 195

Impact of School Shootings on Classroom Culture, Curriculum, and Learning

ISBN: 9781799852001
EISBN: 9781799852018
© 2022; 355 pp.
List Price: US$ 215

Modern Reading Practices and Collaboration Between Schools, Family, and Community

ISBN: 9781799897507
EISBN: 9781799897521
© 2022; 304 pp.
List Price: US$ 215

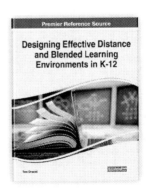

Designing Effective Distance and Blended Learning Environments in K-12

ISBN: 9781799868293
EISBN: 9781799868316
© 2022; 389 pp.
List Price: US$ 215

Do you want to stay current on the latest research trends, product announcements, news, and special offers?
Join IGI Global's mailing list to receive customized recommendations, exclusive discounts, and more.
Sign up at: **www.igi-global.com/newsletters**.

Publisher of Timely, Peer-Reviewed Inclusive Research Since 1988

Ensure Quality Research is Introduced to the Academic Community

Become an Evaluator for IGI Global Authored Book Projects

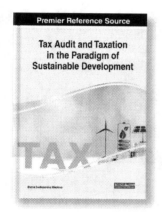  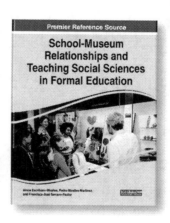 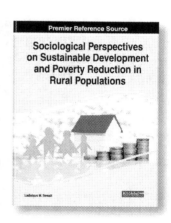

The overall success of an authored book project is dependent on quality and timely manuscript evaluations.

Applications and Inquiries may be sent to:
development@igi-global.com

Applicants must have a doctorate (or equivalent degree) as well as publishing, research, and reviewing experience. Authored Book Evaluators are appointed for one-year terms and are expected to complete at least three evaluations per term. Upon successful completion of this term, evaluators can be considered for an additional term.

If you have a colleague that may be interested in this opportunity, we encourage you to share this information with them.

Easily Identify, Acquire, and Utilize Published
Peer-Reviewed Findings in Support of Your Current Research

IGI Global OnDemand

Purchase Individual IGI Global OnDemand Book Chapters and Journal Articles

For More Information:
www.igi-global.com/e-resources/ondemand/

Browse through 150,000+ Articles and Chapters!

Find specific research related to your current studies and projects that have been contributed by international researchers from prestigious institutions, including:

- Accurate and Advanced Search
- Affordably Acquire Research
- Instantly Access Your Content
- Benefit from the InfoSci Platform Features

> *It really provides* an excellent entry into the research literature of the field. *It presents a manageable number of* highly relevant sources *on topics of interest to a wide range of researchers. The sources are* scholarly, but also accessible *to 'practitioners'.*

- Ms. Lisa Stimatz, MLS, University of North Carolina at Chapel Hill, USA

Interested in Additional Savings?

Subscribe to

IGI Global OnDemand *Plus*

Learn More

Acquire content from over 128,000+ research-focused book chapters and 33,000+ scholarly journal articles for as low as US$ 5 per article/chapter (original retail price for an article/chapter: US$ 37.50).

7,300+ E-BOOKS. ADVANCED RESEARCH. INCLUSIVE & AFFORDABLE.

IGI Global e-Book Collection

- Flexible Purchasing Options (Perpetual, Subscription, EBA, etc.)
- Multi-Year Agreements with No Price Increases Guaranteed
- No Additional Charge for Multi-User Licensing
- No Maintenance, Hosting, or Archiving Fees
- Continually Enhanced & Innovated Accessibility Compliance Features (WCAG)

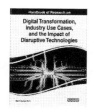

Handbook of Research on Digital Transformation, Industry Use Cases, and the Impact of Disruptive Technologies
ISBN: 9781799877127
EISBN: 9781799877141

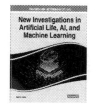

Handbook of Research on New Investigations in Artificial Life, AI, and Machine Learning
ISBN: 9781799886860
EISBN: 9781799886877

Handbook of Research on Future of Work and Education
ISBN: 9781799882756
EISBN: 9781799882770

Research Anthology on Physical and Intellectual Disabilities in an Inclusive Society (4 Vols.)
ISBN: 9781668435427
EISBN: 9781668435434

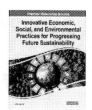

Innovative Economic, Social, and Environmental Practices for Progressing Future Sustainability
ISBN: 9781799895909
EISBN: 9781799895923

Applied Guide for Event Study Research in Supply Chain Management
ISBN: 9781799889694
EISBN: 9781799889717

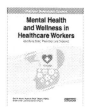

Mental Health and Wellness in Healthcare Workers
ISBN: 9781799888130
EISBN: 9781799888147

Clean Technologies and Sustainable Development in Civil Engineering
ISBN: 9781799898108
EISBN: 9781799898122

Request More Information, or Recommend the IGI Global e-Book Collection to Your Institution's Librarian

For More Information or to Request a Free Trial, Contact IGI Global's e-Collections Team: eresources@igi-global.com | 1-866-342-6657 ext. 100 | 717-533-8845 ext. 100